FOR REFERENCE

GEMSTONES OF NORTH AMERICA

In Two Volumes

Volume I

GEMSTONES OF NORTH AMERICA
In Two Volumes

Volume I

JOHN SINKANKAS

VNR VAN NOSTRAND REINHOLD COMPANY
New York Cincinnati Toronto London Melbourne

DEDICATED TO MY MOTHER

Printed in the United States of America

Published in 1959 by Van Nostrand Reinhold
Company
A Division of Litton Educational Publishing, Inc.
450 West 33rd Street, New York, NY 10001

Van Nostrand Reinhold Limited
1410 Birchmount Road
Scarborough, Ontario M1P 2E7, Canada

Van Nostrand Reinhold Australia Pty. Ltd.
17 Queen Street
Mitcham, Victoria 3132, Australia

Van Nostrand Reinhold Company Ltd.
Molly Millars Lane
Wokingham, Berkshire, England

16   15   14   13

PREFACE TO THE NEW EDITION

The quantity of new information accumulated since publication of this volume in 1959 is so large and so different in character that it was determined to retain the first volume intact and issue such new information in a second volume. Thus the present book becomes Volume I. while the new information is published separately in Volume II. Virtually no repetition of information takes place inasmuch as the first volume treats gemstones of North America up to 1959 while the second volume takes up events and developments from that data up to the end of 1974.

John Sinkankas

San Diego, California
July, 1975

Preface

THE countries of North America have busied themselves for so many years with digging vast quantities of coal, leveling mountains of iron ore, and tapping subterranean lakes of oil, that their considerable gemstone resources have often been ignored. This is nowhere so well shown as in the tremendous North American geological literature which numbers thousands of volumes and millions of words, yet has comparatively nothing to say about gemstones. All of this is understandable if regrettable, for even such scientific men as geologists and mineralogists must hew to the lines of greatest economic promise no matter how intrigued they may be by fascinating but unimportant minerals. However, as a result of this preoccupation with the raw materials of industry and commerce, there are presently few comprehensive works to which one can turn for information on North American gemstones. It is the purpose of this book to fill this gap.

Aside from personal satisfaction in writing about the world of gems, I have attempted to assemble mainly those facts which should be most useful to the student, the collector and connoisseur of gems, to museums, and of course, to the host of jewelers whose interest in native gemstones encourages the development of gemstone resources. Aspects of curious lore involving superstitions, alleged medicinal properties, and other exotic attributes of gems have been held to a minimum because they have been so thoroughly covered in many books, some of which devote themselves solely to these subjects. The principal emphasis has been laid upon what gemstones are to be found in North America, their properties and appearance, and where and in what quantity and quality they occur.

Like other sciences, the study of gemstones includes its share of technical terms used to describe certain features and properties. Without some explanation, the average reader is apt to be completely mystified unless he has had a formal course in some branch of Earth Science. Although as many technical terms have been avoided as possible, some are so descriptive or without reasonable substitute that avoiding their use would be a distinct disservice to the reader. Furthermore, if the greatest appreciation of gemstones is to be had, some understanding of their physical properties is necessary. For these reasons, Chapter I, dealing with the nature of gemstones, has been prepared to inform the reader of the essential properties and features which make gemstones objects of beauty and to acquaint him with the terminology used throughout the remainder of the book. The treatment is necessarily brief but if further reading is desired, a list of excellent books on the subject is furnished in the bibliography in Appendix I, while additional technical terms are explained in the glossary in Appendix II.

Succeeding chapters take up individual gemstones, singly if important, or if of lesser importance, several allied species are discussed together. Only the major scientific aspects of each are covered, especially in connection with varieties that yield gemstones; omitted are data that are of mineralogic interest only. Every species discussion begins with a brief explanation of the gemstone, its scientific name, varietal names, and other useful data. This is followed by a section dealing with the chemical, physical, and optical properties of the species concerned as well as a discussion of color, quality, and other features which add or detract from its value as a gemstone or affect its commercial importance. At the close, localities are described beginning with those in the northernmost lands and finishing with places in Central America and the West Indies. If known, information on features of mineralogy and geology of the gemstone deposit is also furnished. In this connection, a tabular review of the geology of gemstone deposits is provided in Appendix III and will prove useful in understanding how and under what circumstances gemstones are likely to occur.

The arrangement of species within the body of the book takes into account their commercial importance, abundance or rarity, their specific uses in jewelry or ornamentation, and, whenever possible, brings together those which are closely related in some important respect. The first of the gemstone chapters, entitled Principal Gemstones, embraces those minerals furnishing the most treasured gems of commerce. The next chapter is called Important Gemstones, and as its name implies, deals with well-known species customarily handled in the jewelry trade but not enjoying top rank. The enormous variety and wealth of locality information concerning quartz gemstones are recognized in a separate chapter while another is devoted to rare and unusual gemstones and discusses those species which are primarily cut as gemological curiosities with little or no regular place in commerce. Coarser gemstones, or those which are rock-like in character or abundance, are treated in still another chapter while the last chapter embraces substances such as pearl and amber which are of animal or vegetable origin.

The closing pages of the book include in addition to the previously mentioned bibliography, glossary, and tabular review of gemstone deposits, miscellaneous notes on collections and collecting furnished in Appendix IV, and a geographical index which provides a quick method of referring to any locality in the book.

J. S.

Arlington, Virginia.
June, 1959

Acknowledgments

THE successful conclusion of this book would not have been possible without the generous assistance of numerous friends and others sincerely interested in the literature dealing with the world of gems. Special acknowledgment is due the United States National Museum, in particular to Dr. George Switzer, for providing access to study collections of American minerals, and supplying many of the photographs which appear upon later pages. Dr. Joseph P. E. Morrison of this institution was also helpful in suggesting improvements in the section on Pearl and Shell. Many of the uniformly excellent publications of the United States Geological Survey were consulted in the preparation of this work and as the reader will note, a large number of photographs were supplied by this agency from its extensive files. Photographs and information on the Petrified Forest National Monument were supplied by Fred C. Fagergren, Superintendent, while similar services in respect to Isle Royale National Park were rendered by Superintendent John G. Lewis and Park Historian Lloyd Abelson in the case of Pipestone National Monument. Information on gems and gemstones in the American Museum of Natural History was supplied by David M. Seaman. Reference material on Canadian deposits was furnished by the Department of Mines and Technical Surveys of the Geological Survey of Canada, while specific Canadian locality information was supplied by Dr. Victor Ben Meen of the Royal Ontario Museum, Carl B. Gerber of Arlington, Virginia, and in the case of gemstone deposits in British Columbia, by Ivy Willis of Chilliwack.

Many state geological surveys have been helpful in providing information on gemstone occurrences or directing the author to useful references; among them may be mentioned: Vermont, Pennsylvania, North Carolina, Oregon, Kansas, Alabama, Ohio, Oklahoma, Arkansas, Wyoming, Montana and Illinois. Detailed information on the State of Georgia was supplied by Dr. A. S. Furcron, Chief Geologist of the Department of Mines, Mining and Geology; on the State of Michigan by Robert W. Kelley of the Department of Conservation; and on the Four Peaks amethyst deposit in Arizona by Dr. F. W. Galbraith of the University of Arizona. Robert O. Vernon of the Florida Geological Survey kindly arranged the loan of photographs of Tampa Bay silicified coral.

An outstanding compilation of Mexican gemstone information was furnished by Col. E. M. Barron of the Southern Gem and Mineral Company of El Paso, Texas. Information on the Virgin Valley opal deposits was given by G. Keith Hodson of Scottsdale, Arizona. A similar service in the case of the diamonds of Murfreesboro, Arkansas, was performed by Howard A. Millar. Fred M. Bahovec of Baranof, Alaska, provided data on gemstones found in that region; the Southern Onyx and Marble Company of San Diego, California, furnished information and a photograph on the calcite onyx deposits of Baja California. Owen H. Perry of Marine Minerals, Inc., formerly of Helena, Montana, supplied data on the production of Montana alluvial sapphires. Oregon chalcedonies were ably described by Chet and Marge Springer of Bend, as well as by Herbert W. Lawson of Terrebonne, Oregon. Information was also supplied by Dowse's Agate Shop, Salt Lake City, Utah, by William J. Bingham of St. Paul, Minnesota, by Guy Wilson of Stevens Point, Wisconsin, and by A. L. Mahaffey of Nevada, Missouri. The well-known Texas agate localities of the Alpine Region were described in detail by J. Frank Woodward while an especially complete account of the agates found in the Mississippi Valley was provided by Irving W. Hurlbut of Muscatine, Iowa. The fine photographs of pearling in Baja California waters are from the files of the well-known traveler and lecturer John D. Craig, while another traveler, Ross Hastie of Cleveland, Ohio, provided two excellent photographs of the Kobuk jade locality.

Descriptions of San Diego County, California, gemstones and the mines in which they occur are based largely on numerous personal observations made over a two-year period; however, the many visits made to these localities would have been impossible without the generous assistance of many residents of that county. My special thanks are extended to Elbert H. McMacken of Escondido, who guided, assisted, and encouraged me on virtually every field trip taken. Without his intimate knowledge of many mines and prospects— and, more important, how to get to them!—a most pleasant chapter in my life would not have been written. Splendid photographs illustrating scenes and gemstones of this region were generously provided by George Ashley and Roy M. Kepner while Louis B. Spaulding, owner and operator of the Little Three Mine at Ramona, and Ralph R. Potter of the Himalaya Mine at Mesa Grande provided every courtesy in respect to personal visits and observations of these fascinating and important gem deposits. Permission to visit other mines in the Pala area was kindly granted by Charles Reynolds of Lilac and Monta C. Moore of Pala. Many favors were also extended by William C. Woynar, who, with his wife, extended their unstinting hospitality on numerous occasions, while noisy but welcome companionship was provided during this period by my son John who accompanied me on virtually every field trip.

Many photographs which appear without special credit were prepared by Joseph M. Delaney of Arlington, Virginia, under the supervision of the author. The final manuscript was skillfully typed by Dorothy M. Krawiec of Arlington, Virginia. Lastly, I wish to express my gratitude to my wife Marjorie and her mother, for invaluable assistance throughout each phase of manuscript preparation.

Contents

Contents

List of Illustrations

The Project

CHAPTER I

The Properties of Gemstones

FROM the earliest times, man has turned to the soil and rock beneath his feet for much of his livelihood, whether it be for growing crops or for obtaining stones which could serve as tools or weapons. It is not difficult to imagine that in seeking these commonplace necessities, he soon discovered vividly colored pebbles or crystals whose beauty at once distinguished them from ordinary stone. How pleased and excited he must have been as he hurried back to show his discovery to others! Perhaps his fellow tribesmen promptly set off an ancient-day "gold rush" in their eagerness to get some of these pebbles for themselves. In any case, it is easy to imagine that the most appropriate place to show off his treasure was upon the person of the lucky finder. Perhaps in this way was born the use of gems for ornament.

Every continent records the use of gemstones for ornamental or ceremonial purposes well beyond written history. In North America, ancient graves from Panama to the Aleutians have yielded an amazing variety of minerals used for this purpose by aboriginal inhabitants. Sydney H. Ball compiled a list of minerals mined by American Indians, naming over twenty used as gemstones. Jade was used in various forms by the Pre-Columbian Mexicans and the Eskimos of the Far North. Turquois found wide esteem in the West. Another thirty rocks and minerals were used for such mundane purposes as household implements, hunting and fishing tools, for weapons, and when attractively colored or patterned, for ornamental and ceremonial purposes. The value placed on certain of these stones stemmed not only from their ornamental and practical uses but also from certain supposed magical powers or medicinal properties.

The fascination that our primitive ancestors felt for gems has been passed on to us and requires some explanation of those qualities and properties which make them so highly prized.

GEMSTONE QUALITIES

The first quality that a gemstone must have above all else is *beauty*. Without it and regardless of whatever other qualities it possesses it cannot be regarded as a gemstone. Unfortunately beauty is often not enough—a large number of minerals are entrancingly beautiful, but alas, far too soft to fit them for wear. Even some of our well-known gems such as opal and turquois, suffer greatly when worn in rings. A careless knock, immersion in hot water, or an accidental soaking in grease may ruin them. Nevertheless their beauty outweighs other defects of character and they remain highly prized.

It has been the custom in the past to consider hardness as one of the outstanding virtues of any gemstone, making exceptions for the softer ones like those mentioned above. However, with the increase in amateur interest in a wider range of minerals, many species which are far too soft to be considered seriously for jewelry, are being cut and polished for the sake of their beauty alone. Many collectors of such finished gems do not harbor illusions about their jewelry value but adopt the view that owning them, taking them out to look at them and thereby enjoying their beauty, are reward enough for the time and trouble taken to cut them.

The ability of a gemstone to resist wear is measured by two properties: *hardness* and *toughness*. The first is purely a measure of its resistance to abrasion or how easily it scratches if rubbed against another hard substance. The second property is structural and depends more upon the ability of the gemstone to resist chipping or shattering if given a blow. While diamond is the hardest substance known to man and therefore scratches everything else, its toughness is not great. As a matter of fact, a crystal of diamond can be shattered easily by a hammer tap, yet it is inconceivably harder than the steel of the hammer used to destroy it. The scale commonly used to designate the hardness of minerals and gemstones, is the Mohs Scale, named after the mineralogist who devised it:

MOHS SCALE OF HARDNESS
(In order of increasing hardness)

1 Talc
2 Gypsum
3 Calcite
4 Fluorite
5 Apatite
6 Feldspar
7 Quartz
8 Topaz
9 Corundum
10 Diamond

In the scale above, talc is scratched by every other mineral; gypsum can be scratched by the fingernail; calcite can be cut by a knife; fluorite is scratched readily by a knife but apatite only with difficulty; feldspar may be barely scratched by a knife but yields readily to the file (feldspar is just hard enough to scratch ordinary glass); quartz, and minerals harder than quartz, scratch glass easily. Diamond is many times harder than its closest competitor, corundum, scratching that mineral very readily. The Mohs Scale is not very accurate, in fact all that it is supposed to do is to tell in a convenient manner which minerals can scratch others.

Some minerals lack hardness to appreciable degree but more than make up for it by their great toughness. Jade, for example, is quite soft compared to many other gemstones but its tight-woven texture of millions of inter-locked crystals make it so tough that it can be reduced to extremely thin sections without fear of breaking. The Chinese prize it highly for this reason among others, and are able to execute their fantastically delicate carvings solely on account of this property. Thus hardness and toughness are not necessarily related, both are desirable of course but only a few gemstones combine them to outstanding degree.

Another quality which a mineral must have before it can be seriously considered for use as a gem, is that of *rarity*. This may seem like a negative quality and indeed it is, but so many common substances are both beautiful and reasonably durable that if these were the only requirements, we would find ourselves surrounded by "gems" on every hand. The introduction of synthetic sapphire about fifty years ago was viewed with much alarm by members of the jewelry trade. Here was a man-made gemstone, chemically and physically the same as the genuine material. It was just as hard, and, as manufacturing processes improved, it was made equally beautiful. Fears proved groundless. The widely-heralded advent of synthetic gems merely attracted more attention to natural stones which promptly showed a gratifying increase in sales and value. The rare and beautiful gem crystals—the "flowers of the Mineral Kingdom"—will always be prized above similar creations from the chemist's laboratory.

Perhaps it is a peculiarity of human nature to prize the genuine over the false, even when both are so alike that only an expert can tell them apart. Nevertheless, judging gems by this standard does not differ from judging clothing where the label of an exclusive London shop or a Parisian salon is prized above all else. Fashion exercises a very real influence upon gems, determining the esteem in which they are held and therefore regulating demand and the prices received for them. The rise and fall of entire gem-mining ventures has often been traced to the dictates of fashion. Were it not for the firmly entrenched esteem which people all over the world hold for diamonds, it is doubtful that the huge mining industry for this mineral would survive on the "bread and potatoes" sale of industrial diamonds alone.

The factors governing suitability of a mineral for gemstone purposes are very flexible. As has been mentioned before in the case of opal, allowances are made for qualities which are unique or superior. No other gemstone, real or synthetic, can ever rival the opal in respect to color although many exceed it in terms of hardness and toughness. Value is also greatly influenced by *size* since some gem minerals occur in large masses but others are never found except in small pieces. Among expensive gems, rubies and emeralds over several carats in weight, rapidly overtake diamonds in respect to value per carat until a point is reached where each costs more than a diamond of equal weight! On the other hand, the pale blue variety of beryl known popularly as aquamarine, is mineralogically identical to emerald but costs far less principally because it occurs in such large quantities. At the present time it is mined by hundreds of pounds in Brazil and one year's production probably exceeds in quantity all of the emeralds mined in the last fifty.

ORGANIC GEMSTONES

Because of their beauty and rarity, pearls and amber have been customarily considered as gems in spite of the fact that they are of organic origin. Pearls are formed inside the shells of various nacreous mollusks and owe their existence to the ability of these animals to secrete nacre upon small particles of irritating material which accidentally enter the shell. Amber is likewise a product of living creation, being a fossilized gum or resin exuded from the bark of long-extinct trees of the Pine Family. It is always found in sedimentary formations of no great age, usually as loose lumps in clay or soil. So recent has been its formation that it is scarcely distinguishable from some resins of modern trees. Another organic material, coral, is also ordinarily considered to be a gemstone although its creation is due to the efforts of small animals which obtain lime from the sea and deposit it as beautiful scaffoldings to hold themselves aloft in their briny world. Lastly, one other substance of organic origin should be mentioned: jet, a variety of lignite coal. This material differs from ordinary coal in that it still preserves the cellular structure of the wood from which it formed. It too is called a gemstone although like amber, the borderline between classing it as a true mineral or merely as organic matter buried in the earth is not at all sharp.

ROCKS, MINERALS, AND GEMSTONES

With the exception of pearl and coral, and perhaps the borderline organic substances amber and jet, all gemstones can be classed as simple minerals or as mixtures of minerals, or rocks. Strictly speaking, each mineral is a well-defined chemical compound which has its own characteristic properties which enable it to be distinguished from all others. On the other hand, the mineral mixtures known as rocks vary widely in composition, texture, and in appearance. They rarely have a set composition in terms of "so much of *this* and so much of *that*," and their classification is far less exact accordingly. It is least confusing to think of *rocks* as the large masses of the earth's crust and *minerals* as the ingredients.

Each mineral—or *species*—has not only a specific chemical composition but more importantly, a definite arrangement of the various kinds of atoms of which it is composed. The chemistry is expressed by a combination of letters and numbers which tell what elements are present and in what proportions. In common quartz, for example, only two are present: silicon and oxygen. The latter always outnumbers silicon two to one. Accordingly the formula is written to show both elements and how many atoms of each are present thus: SiO_2. Other mineral formulas are often more complex but in every case always express the kinds of atoms and the proportions in which they occur. Minerals (and gemstones) are classified according to their chemical composition as follows:

ELEMENTS: These are the primitive forms of matter, nothing else is found in them except one element, e.g.: gold, lead, silver, etc. The only elemental gemstone is *diamond*, or pure carbon (C).

SULFIDES: Combinations of metals with sulfur as in *pyrite* (FeS_2), *marcasite* (FeS_2), and *sphalerite* (ZnS).

OXIDES: Combinations of metals with oxygen as in *corundum* (Al_2O_3) and *quartz* (SiO_2).

HALIDES: Only one gemstone is here represented, *fluorite* (CaF_2). In this class, occur those minerals which consist of halogen elements such as fluorine, chlorine, etc., combined with metals.

CARBONATES: Combinations of metals with special groupings of carbon and oxygen atoms (CO_3) as in *calcite* ($CaCo_3$) and *rhodochrosite* ($MnCO_3$), etc.

SULFATES: Combinations of metals with special groupings of sulfur and oxygen atoms (SO_4) as in *gypsum* ($CaSO_4 \cdot H_2O$). Water is also present in gypsum and is indicated by the formula: H_2O.

PHOSPHATES AND BORATES: Combinations of metals with special groupings of phosphorus or boron atoms, e.g.: *variscite* ($AlPO_4 \cdot 2H_2O$), an aluminum phosphate with water.

SILICATES: This class contains by far the largest number of gemstones and includes those minerals which contain silicon and oxygen groupings, plus one or more metals or other elements, e.g.: *topaz* ($Al(F,OH)_2SiO_4$), *beryl* ($Be_3Al_2(SiO_3)_6$), etc.

Later, when individual gemstones are described, the chemical composition of each species will be expressed by its word name and by chemical formula. Some formulas become very complex, especially among the silicates.

A good example, the tourmaline, moved the noted essayist and mineralogist, John Ruskin, to remark: "—on the whole, the chemistry of it is more like a medieval doctor's prescription, than the making of a respectable mineral—." The physical properties of gemstones are of course greatly influenced by the chemistry but merely stating what atoms are present and in what proportions is not enough. The *way* in which these atoms combine is the most important factor and is one of the miracles of nature.

If it were possible for us to shrink like Alice in her Adventures in Wonderland, we might take a most instructive journey through a chemical compound to see what atoms look like and how they are arranged. Our first impression is sure to be the wondrous regularity of their spacing, for this is the heart and soul of all matter. Each atom takes its place according to size and its degree of attraction or repulsion for its neighbors. Small atoms snuggle between large atoms, providing they *attract* each other, while large atoms rub shoulders. And this arrangement is not accidental by any means, it pervades all solid substances and gives them their characteristic properties. Furthermore, for any given gemstone species, a trip inside one specimen will show exactly the same pattern employed as in any other, even if we should select specimens from opposite points of the globe. The arrangements are many and varied since over ninety elements are involved—all different both in respect to size and in degree of attraction. That is why over 1600 species of minerals are known at the present time and the list is steadily growing. In this book, well over a hundred species are treated as gemstones.

CRYSTALS

When minerals which possess the regular arrangement of atoms remarked upon above are given an opportunity to grow without interference, they develop beautiful geometric forms called *crystals*. Each household has millions in every saltbox and only a magnifying glass is needed to see that each salt crystal grain is bounded by flat faces like those of a cube. Granular sugar, although not a mineral, also shows crystals, however, these appear as tablets with roof-like terminations on opposite ends. One glance is enough to show that in both substances, every grain crystallizes in the same fashion. In the science of mineralogy, this tendency to grow in the same form is called the *habit*, and is one of the distinguishing features of many minerals. At times, it is so distinctive that experts are able to tell one species from another merely by seeing the habit displayed by the several faces on the crystals. Sometimes crystals develop so perfectly that an uninitiated person thinks the flat and brilliant planes have been polished by a gem cutter. This wonderful geometric perfection is not an accident of nature but the outward expression of the way in which the constituent atoms are arranged. It is even more astonishing to know that through a careful study of the way in which crystal faces are arranged, mineralogists years ago were able to arrive at sound conclusions as to how the internal atoms had also to be arranged in order to make this possible. More about this will be said later.

The most perfect crystals are found in open cavities. Others, crowded by their neighbors, frequently show no outside faces whatsoever and appear only as formless grains. This can be seen clearly in granite where three minerals, quartz, feldspar, and mica, are sprinkled in salt-and-pepper fashion throughout the rock. In some cases, as in diamond and sapphire, crystals of good form are found solidly encased by other minerals. This merely shows that these gemstones crystallized first and grew to perfection before the surrounding minerals could solidify. In the case of jade, which is almost wholly found in massive form, the failure to grow large perfect crystals is a distinct advantage for it is the numerous minute interlocked individuals which lend the great strength so highly prized in this gemstone.

Crystals grow to all sizes, from minute slivers too small to see with the naked eye to monsters dozens of feet in length and many tons in weight. The Etta Mine in the Black Hills of South Dakota, once yielded a single spodumene crystal over forty feet long! Flawless blue beryl crystals tipping the scales at 100 pounds or better have come from Brazil, while just recently, a splendid red tourmaline of twenty pounds weight was brought here from Mozambique and purchased by the U.S. National Museum in Washington, D.C. However, these overgrown crystals are very unusual and the majority are far smaller.

The lowest extreme of crystallization is found in *chalcedony*, a variety of quartz which is widespread and abundant, and much used for cutting into inexpensive gems. In its colored forms it is familiar to readers as *bloodstone*, *jasper*, *agate*, *carnelian*, etc. Deposited from solution along seams, cracks, or in cavities, it forms layers of crystals so exceedingly small that ordinary microscopes cannot bring them into focus. Minerals of this type are known as *cryptocrystalline* in reference to their lack of an easily detected crystal structure. Turquois and variscite, to name a few other gemstones, also occur in similar form.

Some minerals are neither crystalline nor cryptocrystalline, in fact, they have no orderly atomic structure whatsoever. Ordinary glass is an excellent example for it is made by melting a hodge-podge of ingredients which are cooled so quickly that none of them have time to get together in a systematic fashion. Solids of this kind, including minerals, are called *amorphous* from the Greek words meaning "no form" in allusion to their lack of orderly atomic structure. Amorphous minerals tend to be weak and break easily in typical shining shell-like or *conchoidal* fractures exactly like those noted in ordinary glass. They are also very sensitive to changes in temperature and scratch easily on account of their softness. Scientists regard amorphous substances as mid-way between the liquid and solid states of matter and point out that even something as stable as glass, actually "flows" over a long period of time as shown by measurements of plate glass windows which gradually thicken at the bottom with the passage of time. Obsidian, or glassy lava, belongs to this class of minerals as do opal, and, among organic substances, amber and jet. As a rule, gems cut from amorphous minerals and substances require special protection against hard knocks and sudden temperature changes.

THE GEOMETRY OF CRYSTALS

As was mentioned earlier, one of the most astonishing features of any well-formed crystal is the wondrous flatness of its *faces* and the way in which they are disposed over the surface. It seems surprising that early men of science were so slow in recognizing that these faces were not haphazardly sprinkled about but actually followed a systematic arrangement, nevertheless, it was not until several centuries ago after mankind had handled and cut thousands upon thousands of crystals, that anyone took the trouble to look further into the matter. A startling truth immediately emerged—it was found that if the angles between adjoining faces on crystal were measured, they proved to be the same all around the crystal! For example, in quartz which tends to grow in long narrow prisms, the long rectangular faces around the prism join each other in 120° angles and cause the cross section to be a hex-agon. At the top, where six more faces are found tapering to a sharp point, the same constancy in angle between these faces is noted also although the value is not the same as for the prism faces. In any case, this interesting discovery set off an intensive examination of as many crystals as these early mineralo-gists could lay their hands on and gave rise to the science of crystal geometry now known as *crystallography*. As more and more knowledge was developed it became clear that all crystalline substances owed every feature to an orderly internal arrangement of atoms although the actual proof that such existed had to wait until several decades ago when the methods of using x-rays to diagram atomic structures were developed. Furthermore, as the mathematics of crystals were worked out, it was discovered that only a few atomic arrangements could possibly exist and that all crystals could be related to one of these pat-terns. To make matters simple, it was decided to place each crystalline mineral in one of six geometrical groups or *systems*. Still in use today, these systems are as follows: Isometric (Cubic), Tetragonal, Hexagonal, Orthorhombic, Monoclinic, and Triclinic. In each, it is easiest to think of crystal faces as grouped about imaginary *axes* which pass through certain directions in the crystal. The six systems and their axes are diagrammed in Fig. 1.

In the Isometric System, there are three axes at right angles to each other

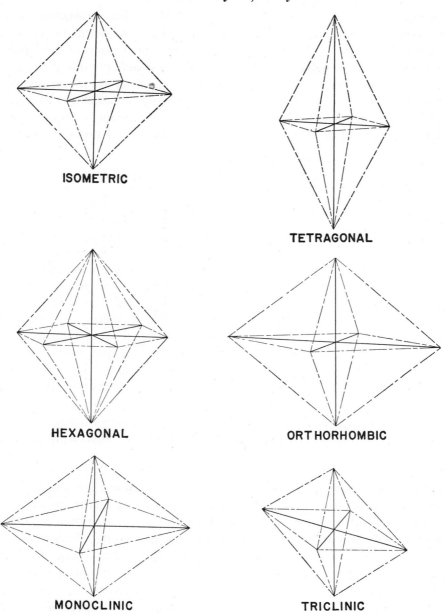

ISOMETRIC

TETRAGONAL

HEXAGONAL

ORTHORHOMBIC

MONOCLINIC

TRICLINIC

FIGURE 1. The six crystal systems showing the several axes and their relationships.

and its simplest geometric solid is a cube. The internal atomic structure which gives rise to such geometry is also cubic, that is, atoms are stacked in nice square rows, up, down, and sideways. For this reason the distance between neighboring atoms is the same in any direction and therefore the crystal axes must also be of the same length. Figure 2 which shows a geometric scheme of sphalerite (ZnS), indicates the square arrangement of the large zinc atoms and the balanced position which the sulfur atoms take within their network. One crystal axis can be passed through this structure cell vertically, another through the side, and the last at right angles to each. Thus, when describing the basic geometry of the Isometric System, it can be seen why it is stated as: three axes of *equal* length all at right angles to each other. Examples of gemstones belonging to the Isometric System are sphalerite, used for the illustra-

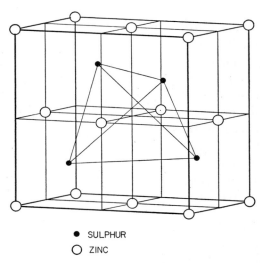

● SULPHUR
○ ZINC

FIGURE 2. The remarkable regularity of atom spacing is shown in this drawing of sphalerite crystal structure. This same pattern is repeated throughout the entire mass of the crystal.

tion above, diamond, and garnet. One would expect after this explanation that both minerals would crystallize as cubes; unfortunately this is seldom the case, sphalerite most often forming wedge-shaped crystals while diamond is found in octahedrons and other forms little resembling a cube! However, the important point to remember is that if one carefully measures the angles between the faces, it would be found that the crystals could only be related to the Isometric System.

When the atoms of several elements combine to form crystals, it is frequently necessary for them to make allowances for each other's size and for the degree of attraction they hold for each other. These adjustments seldom lead to square arrangements and consequently only a small fraction of all minerals belong to the Isometric System. All the rest belong to the remaining five systems and represent increasingly greater complexity in atomic arrangement. In the Tetragonal System, three axes are again used to describe the geometry and again are at right angles to each other but one is now either shorter or longer than the other two. Zircon belongs to this system and typically forms crystals with square cross sections capped by pyramids at the ends. In the Hexagonal System, there are *three* axes of equal length plus a *fourth* of different length but poised at right angles to the plane made by the others. The three equal axes also cross each other at 60°-120° angles. Typical Hexagonal gemstones are quartz which has already been mentioned, and beryl. The Orthorhombic System again returns to a total of three axes which are at right angles to each other and differ from Isometric and Tetragonal in that *none* of the axes are of equal length. The simplest geometric solid of this system would resemble an ordinary shoe box. Topaz is an example of a gemstone belonging to this system. In the Monoclinic System, the axes are the same as in the Orthorhombic except for one small but significant difference, one of the axes is now tilted and is no longer at right angles to the other two. Squarish blocky crystals of feldspar are good examples of Monoclinic symmetry in a gem mineral. The last system, the Triclinic, differs again only slightly from its predecessor because now all three axes are neither of the same length nor fixed at right angles to each other. This tipping of all axes frequently results in odd-shaped crystals with sharp edges, a good gemstone example being axinite, so-called because its crystals resemble ax-heads. Perfect axinite crystals are often so sharp that it is possible to cut a finger on the edges.

This brief review of the six crystal systems points out the relationship between the geometry of crystals and the internal atomic structure. Later on it will be shown that many important properties of crystals are also derived from their internal atomic arrangement and lead to the wondrous display of optical phenomena which delight our eyes and cause us to admire gems.

CRYSTAL GROWTH

Crystals are seldom perfect in geometry—all sorts of changes in their environment during growth can cause drastic changes in appearance, color, purity, and clarity. Modern crystal-growing experiments show how delicately-balanced are such factors as temperature, pressure, vibration, or even the slightest trace of impurity in the nourishing solutions. In nature, changes in conditions are beautifully shown in "phantom" or "ghost" crystals, especially in quartz which provides excellent examples. Suspended in the centers of such crystals can be seen what appears to be nothing more than a series of other crystals, one inside the other, and mimicking the form of the parent crystal. Actually there is nothing mysterious about this phenomenon, all it represents is the sprinkling of the growing crystal with another mineral at various stages of its growth. In any case, when the crystal resumes growth, these impurities are trapped within and preserved forever, a faithful reproduction of what the parent crystal looked like in its younger days. Other minerals such as rutile and tourmaline may be trapped in quartz also, providing two very popular and beautiful gemstones, rutilated quartz and tourmalinated quartz.

If the nourishing solution changes chemical composition at any time during growth, radical changes in color may result, often producing banded zones in strongly contrasted hues within the crystal. This is strikingly apparent in gem tourmaline which as a matter of fact, is more often color-zoned than not. Careful analyses of the various colored portions of tourmaline crystals show decided changes in chemical composition which account for the changes in color. Sometimes changing conditions also cause altered crystal habits as shown in fluorite from Illinois and Kentucky. If one of the crystals is broken open, it can be seen that the color banding in the center follows a different geometrical pattern than that noted closer to the exterior. Color bands often pose a problem to lapidaries because some skill is needed to be sure that they do not appear on top of the finished gem; this is particularly a problem in amethyst which is almost always color-zoned.

Crystals may grow singly or in groups, some are seldom found except in groups while others prefer a solitary life. The mode of growth often depends upon the type of wall-lining which a cavity contains, for example, amethyst frequently grows in solid sheets of crystals with nothing but a forest of points exposed to view. Examination of the wall-lining shows that it is all quartz and therefore the nourishing solution containing this mineral in solution had many places to begin growing crystals. On the other hand, as in the small cavities in limestone in Herkimer County, New York, only one quartz crystal may be found in each opening, showing that only one place was finally selected upon which the quartz began to grow. Crystals grown together in solid sheets with numerous points exposed are known as *druses*. On the other hand, if many individual crystals grow without chance of developing faces, the resulting mass is known as a *crystalline aggregate*. A good example of a crystalline aggregate is jadeite which consists of millions of small crystal grains showing no trace of external form.

A special type of crystal growth is known as *twinning* and means that two or more individuals have developed in contact with each other in accordance with some established rule or *law*. Twinning laws merely state that there must be some relationship between the atomic structures of both crystals; in other words, just because two crystals happened to grow together is not sufficient reason to say that they are *twinned*. It is necessary to prove that the angles between them are related to the geometry of each crystal. Quartz is often twinned, the joint between twins being shown by zigzag lines which run across faces and down the length of the prism. Twinning is very common in a large number of minerals and is of course also seen in gemstones. Sometimes the changes across the twinning line make polishing a little more difficult but by and large twinning is not of great significance in gemstones.

CLEAVAGE

The atomic structure of some crystals often makes it easy for them to break along certain well-defined planes. These are called *cleavage planes* and are observed to some degree in the majority of minerals, including gemstones. Cleavage planes cannot be present in amorphous minerals since these lack orderly internal structure, therefore minerals of this class will often break with a characteristic scooped-out *conchoidal* fracture but never with the geometrically flat surface of a true *cleavage*. Some crystalline minerals show not the slightest tendency to cleave, a good example being garnet which prefers to break in a fashion almost like that of an amorphous mineral. Cleavages may be amazingly flat and glistening from the perfection of the surfaces left behind; at other times they may be interrupted or so indistinct that one cannot be too sure that a cleavage plane exists in the first place. The ease with which a cleavage can be started also varies considerably, some gemstones like kyanite needing only the touch of a sharp-pointed knife to start and others like topaz requiring a good sharp blow. The quality of the surface upon a cleavage plane is said to vary from *perfect* to *poor* while the ease with which it is started may be described as *very easy* to *very difficult*. There are all variations of course, but when a very perfect cleavage is very easily developed in a gemstone, one can be sure that the lapidary will have a great deal of trouble in cutting whatever mineral it happens to be. Spodumene is notorious among cutters in this respect, it being exceedingly difficult to even finish a gem no less do it well.

SPECIFIC GRAVITY

An important property of gemstones is their weight relative to the weight of an equal volume of water, a measurement which is expressed by a numerical value called the *specific gravity*, or *density*. The comparison is made by weighing a gem in air and then suspended in water, the difference between the two readings being equal to the volume of water displaced. A simple calculation then gives *how many times the gem is heavier than an equal volume of water*. Water is assigned a standard value of 1.0 and naturally all gemstones are heavier by a comfortable margin except amber which is only slightly more dense. As an example, opal is about 2.0 on the scale of specific gravity and means that if an ice cube and a cube of opal of exactly the same size were weighed, the opal would prove to be twice as heavy. Each gemstone has its own specific gravity which varies between narrow limits depending upon purity and composition. This provides a valuable identification feature and is much used in the science of gemology. In the entire range of gemstones, wide variations occur, the lightest gemstone being amber with S. G. = 1.05, or only a little heavier than water, opal is about 2.0, diamond about 3.5, and zircon, the heaviest of the common gemstones, about 4.0. It is easy to see that if one buys a zircon of 4 carats, it will have only half the volume of an opal of the same weight.

All of the physical properties discussed so far will be mentioned, where appropriate, in each gemstone discussion which follows later in this book.

LIGHT UPON GEMS

In their rough state, gemstones are often disappointingly plain in appearance. Even the peculiar silvery luster of diamond is not so distinctive that mistakes in identity cannot be made. It has been said that when Edward VII saw the Cullinan Diamond prior to cutting, he held it up to the light and remarked, "I should have kicked it aside as a lump of glass if I had seen it in the road!" His reaction was typical and not unexpected of anyone unfamiliar with the great change wrought in gemstones by the act of cutting and polishing. This transformation is due entirely to the clever employment of well-established principles of optics as they pertain to gems.

In general, two modes of cutting are employed for gemstones: a rounded form or *cabochon* cut, and a geometric form or *facet* cut in which all of the surface of the gem is covered with polished flat planes. The first is used most frequently for non-transparent gemstones or for those which display some special optical effect or *phenomenon*, i.e., star sapphire, moonstone, cat's eye, etc. The second is seldom used except for perfectly transparent material. It permits light to enter the gem, pass from facet to facet, and finally emerge to give the familiar sparkling effect of brilliancy.

When light rays enter a transparent gemstone they immediately lose speed and are bent from their original path. The degree of bending depends upon the nature of the gemstone and the angle made by the rays. Bending, or *refraction*, is illustrated in Figure 3 where rays at various angles are shown falling upon the surface of the gem. Vertical rays are not changed in direction but all others are bent an increasing amount as the angle lessens.

Once inside, an interesting occurrence takes place as the rays meet the back facets. Instead of passing through, each ray is *totally reflected* from the opposite facets until it emerges to meet the eye. Figure 3 illustrates the path followed by a single ray in a typical faceted gem. It is this process, multiplied many times, which makes faceted gems sparkle.

The strength of refraction in any gemstone is given a numerical value called the *refractive index*. Air is almost zero, water is 1.33, while diamond

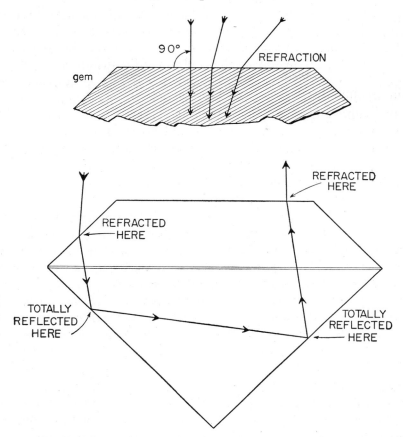

FIGURE 3. In the upper drawing, a series of light rays are drawn to show how they are bent as they enter a gem. In the lower drawing, a single ray of light is followed through a cut stone to show how both refraction and total reflection bring the ray back up through the top of the gem to give brilliance.

which possesses the highest index among common gemstones is about 2.42. Strong refraction is accompanied by superior reflecting capabilities and permits gemstones of high index to be cut somewhat more thinly without loss of brilliance than those of low values. In contrast, gemstones of very low refractive power never appear lively because poor reflection from back facets causes serious leakage of light.

As mentioned earlier, crystal structure has everything to do with the properties of solid matter, and in this case, it has its effects upon optical behavior. In minerals showing no well-defined structure at all—the amorphous kind—and in minerals belonging to the Isometric System, light passes through transparent specimens just as we would expect it to do, that is, it enters the gem, is bent a certain amount as shown in Figure 3, and then leaves to lose itself in the surrounding atmosphere. But what happens in transparent crystals belonging to the other five systems? In these it is found that a most curious event takes place at the instant the light ray enters the gem. Now instead of being merely bent, the ray splits into *two parts*, with each being bent a certain amount depending on the nature of the gemstone itself. This is shown in Figure 4 where a piece of clear calcite, a mineral noted for its

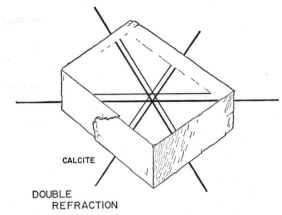

CALCITE

DOUBLE
REFRACTION

FIGURE 4. The property of double refraction illustrated by a piece of calcite. Lines ruled upon paper appear doubled when the calcite is placed over them.

remarkable display of this property, is placed over several lines ruled upon a piece of paper. The light rays reflected from each line split into two parts as they enter the specimen, and emerging from the top to meet the eye, give the impression that each line is *doubled*. This peculiar behavior of crystals belonging to the Tetragonal, Hexagonal, Orthorhombic, Monoclinic, and Triclinic Systems, is called *double refraction*. In some gemstones, this property is so pronounced that back facets viewed through the top of a cut stone appear blurred.

The measurement of refraction is accomplished on a *refractometer*, an instrument much used by gemologists, jewelers and many amateurs. This is a small optical device upon which may be placed a polished gem and its refractive index quickly determined visually. Inside is a small viewing scale which is numbered from 1.30 to 1.85, upon which appears a line corresponding to the index of the stone being tested. In the case of amorphous and Isometric minerals, only one line will appear because they are *singly refractive*, but in all other cases, two lines will be seen corresponding to *double refraction*. The maximum spread between the two readings noted when measuring doubly refractive gemstones is called the *birefringence*. It may vary from as little as 0.004 in apatite to as much as 0.280 in rutile; in Fig. 4 the large amount of image doubling is due to the large birefringence of calcite: 0.172.

In earlier days, when the curious optical behavior of doubly-refractive crystals was looked into further, it was found that Tetragonal and Hexagonal crystals showed one direction in which light rays did not split at all. This direction is the same as the vertical crystal axis, and, in Fig. 5, corresponds to the arrow labeled "pure blue" in the sapphire crystal, and the arrow labeled "olive green" in the tourmaline crystal; both of these gemstones, incidentally, are Hexagonal in crystallization. If vertical sections of each crystal are cut and polished and placed upon the refractometer, one can observe the single refrac-

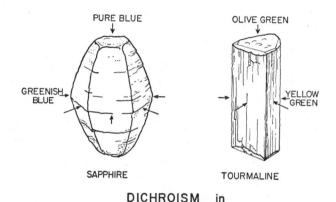

DICHROISM in
GEMSTONES

FIGURE 5. Strong dichroism as displayed by colored crystals of sapphire and tourmaline. Arrows indicate directions along which differing colors may be observed.

tion by carefully turning the specimen until only one line is seen on the viewing scale. Conversely, by turning the polished section 90°, the single line will split into two, one line moving away from the other as the 90° position is approached. The maximum spread at the 90° position corresponds to the birefringence of the gemstone, or the difference in value between the line which remained immovable and the line which moved away. The direction along which no separation of light rays occurs is called the *optical axis*, and as said before, is the same as the vertical axis in all crystals belonging to the Tetragonal or Hexagonal Systems.

In order to label the two light rays seen in crystals of these systems, it was decided to call the one which remained fixed in value the *ordinary ray*, and the other which did move, the *extraordinary ray*. The ordinary ray is given the Greek identifying letter ω which corresponds to our "o," and the other ray labeled ϵ, which in Greek corresponds to our "e." Throughout this book, values of refractive index for gemstones belonging to the Tetragonal and Hexagonal Systems will be preceded by these letters.

All of this appears very complicated to the uninitiated reader and indeed it is, but complexity is not finished by any means until the curious behavior of minerals crystallizing in the Orthorhombic, Monoclinic, and Triclinic Systems is reviewed. In these minerals it was found that instead of one optical axis, there were *two*, or in other words, two directions in each crystal along which single refraction could be observed, and it was also found that three refractive indices could be measured instead of only two. Again Greek letters were adopted to label each light ray, the least in value as measured on a refractometer being called α, the Greek equivalent for our letter "a," the intermediate value labeled β for our "b," and the largest value labeled γ for our "c." As before, each of these letters will be used to designate refractive indices throughout this book.

Since only one optical axis is found in Tetragonal and Hexagonal minerals, they are called *uniaxial*, while those belonging to the Orthorhombic, Monoclinic, and Triclinic Systems are called *biaxial*. Although in the first group it was found that the optical axis coincides with the vertical crystal axis, this is no longer the case in the others; in them, the optical axes occupy a position somewhere between the three crystal axes. All of these quirks of optical behavior are extremely useful in identifying minerals, including gemstones, and find much application in gemology and in the study of rocks and minerals by geologists and mineralogists, who by the use of petrographic microscopes, are able to identify minerals even when minute fragments are the largest samples available.

Another aid in identification is the distinction between *optically positive* and *optically negative* minerals. In the Tetragonal and Hexagonal Systems, the following rule is observed:

> If the value of the ordinary ray ω is less than ε, the mineral is said to be *positive*.
> If the value of ε is less than ω, the mineral is *negative*.

In the Orthorhombic, Monoclinic, and Triclinic Systems, the following rule applies:

> When the intermediate value β is nearer α, the mineral is *positive*.
> When the intermediate value β is nearer γ, the mineral is *negative*.

It is not always practical to determine the *optical signs*, as the above are called, using ordinary refractometers, but anyone equipped with a petrographic microscope finds determination easy to accomplish and a valuable aid in identifying minerals. In the description of gemstones which follow later, all of the optical characters discussed above will be mentioned in the proper places as applicable.

DISPERSION

The many sparkles of color which flash from a cut diamond while it is turned about under strong light arise from an optical property which this gemstone possesses in outstanding degree. This property is called *dispersion* and as the name implies, is the scattering or dispersion of light into its spectral colors occurring at the moment a ray of light enters a gemstone. Figure 6

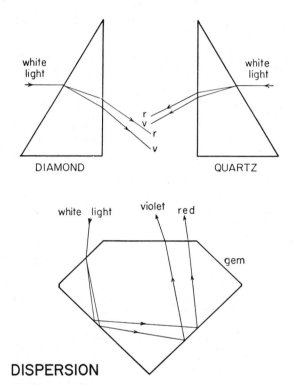

FIGURE 6. The upper illustration shows the greater strength of dispersion in diamond as compared to quartz. The lower drawing shows a single ray of light traced through a gem cut from dispersive material. This is the property which causes flashes of color to appear in a colorless gem.

shows dispersion at work in prisms of quartz and diamond, and illustrates how this property is more pronounced in the latter gemstone. Actually if it were not for its great dispersive powers, colorless diamond would have little to commend it as a gemstone. In the lower illustration of Fig. 6, a beam of light is shown passing through a faceted gem and spreading apart to display all the colors of the spectrum between violet and red. Since the display is proportionate to the distance traveled by the light ray, dispersive effects are more pronounced in larger gems. In addition to diamond, high dispersion is well shown by sphalerite, zircon, andradite garnet and sphene. Dispersive coloration is often called "fire" but this term is misleading since it is also applied to precious opal, especially a rich red kind from Mexico. Dispersion in many gemstones is often masked by their body coloration and is therefore seen in greatest perfection only in colorless stones.

Since each ray of light entering a dispersive gem is split up into a band of colored components, measurement of refractive indices is made more difficult because a miniature spectrum is seen on the viewing scale of the refractometer instead of a single sharp line. In unusually dispersive species, the observer is posed with the problem of exactly where the index should be read. Mineralogists have agreed that the standard reading should take place in the *yellow* part of the spectral band so that when values of refraction are given in any textbook it will be understood that measurement took place in the yellow. This book follows this rule and every refractive index given is understood to be for yellow light. Some gemologists and jewelers solve this problem by using a source of yellow light for testing gems, either a dark yellow filter which fits over the eyepiece of the refractometer, or a special incandescent sodium lamp which emits vivid yellow light of exactly the right hue.

COLOR IN GEMS

The vast majority of gems owe their beauty largely to color; except in the case of colorless gems displaying marked dispersion, all others depend heavily upon their native hues to render them pleasing to the eye. As yet, however, the cause of color is imperfectly understood. At one time it was thought that impurities sprinkled throughout the gemstone in the form of invisible particles screened the light and permitted only a colored portion to pass through. Now it is believed that the electrical field surrounding each atom interferes with the passage of light and causes part of it to be destroyed in the process. Recent experiments in inducing color in gemstones by means of atomic pile radiations seem to confirm this theory. Apparently certain elements are more effective than others in this respect, for when present in a gemstone, resulting colors are apt to be dingy and dull. The presence or absence of such color-inducing elements accounts for the wide variety of shades displayed in a single crystal. Actually, almost all gemstones would be quite colorless if absolutely pure except for a few like turquois, malachite, and azurite, whose colors are inherent and unchangeable.

Color often varies within a single piece of material, sometimes because of changing amounts of impurities or because the nature of the crystal itself causes light to be affected more strongly in one direction than in another. Patchy coloration is a common defect of amethyst and sapphire, requiring special treatment during cutting to overcome. In other gemstones, varying chemical composition in different parts of a single crystal may give rise to several distinct and unrelated hues. This has been pointed out in the case of tourmaline which often shows as many as five or six distinct colors in a single crystal.

In certain gemstones, variations in color are not due simply to impurities and their unequal distribution but arise from peculiar features of the crystal structure. In such crystals, striking changes in color are noted depending on the direction of view. Two examples are shown in Fig. 5 where the effect, known as *dichroism*, is so obvious that it can be seen with the naked eye. In most other gemstones, however, the difference in color is not so pronounced and one must use a small optical instrument called a *dichroscope* to assist the eye in distinguishing the colors. The dichroscope employs a small piece of clear calcite which by virtue of its very large double refraction causes the light image from the gemstone to be split into two parts each of different color and allowing each to be viewed separately. As will be explained below, some minerals show two colors, or dichroism, but others show three colors in which case the effect is known as *trichroism*. The differences in color in some crystals, depending on direction, is so intense that special pains must be taken by the gem cutter to be sure that the finest one appears "face up" in the finished gem. Referring again to Fig. 5, the best color in sapphire is pure blue; to be sure that this color appears to best advantage in the cut stone, the crystal must be cut in such a way that the large top facet of the finished gem lies across the vertical axis. In tourmaline, it is exactly opposite; in order to *avoid* the dingy olive green color which is seen along the crystal axis, it is necessary to place the top facet of the finished gem parallel to the side of the crystal prism.

Dichroism and trichroism occur only in doubly refractive gemstones and result from each of the several rays absorbing its own distinctive color as it passes through the crystal. In uniaxial minerals, that is, those included in the Tetragonal and Hexagonal Systems, only two colors can be observed because there are only two rays, the ordinary ray (ω), and the extraordinary ray (ϵ). Furthermore, in the direction of single refraction in these crystals, which, if it is recalled passes through the crystal parallel to the principal crystal axis, only one color can be observed. Thus, if a cross-section were cut through such a crystal, an examination through the top can only show one color in the dichroscope, on the other hand, an examination through the side will show the colors carried by both ω and ϵ. In similar fashion it is possible to examine clear specimens of minerals belonging to the Orthorhombic, Monoclinic, and Triclinic Systems, and observe three shades of color or changes of hue corresponding to the rays α, β, and γ. Because these minerals are biaxial, it is necessary to rotate the specimen to several positions to be sure to test all directions along which colors appear. Before passing on, it is worthwhile remarking that minerals which are not doubly refractive cannot show the effects just discussed. Thus, in garnet, a singly-refractive gemstone, there can be only one light ray and therefore only one color. This is of course also true for transparent amorphous minerals. Even in gemstones which can show dichroism or trichroism, the effect is most pronounced when colors are darkest and conversely, least apparent when colors lighten; when there is no color at all, no change is possible of course. Not all colored gemstones respond the same way as shown in the case of peridot as compared to tourmaline. Peridot is often found in rich green color, yet, when tested before the dichroscope, the change noted is so weak that it is almost imperceptible. On the other hand, green tourmaline responds very strongly, even faintly-colored varieties showing distinct dichroism.

SPECIAL OPTICAL EFFECTS

So far, the optical effects discussed in this chapter are those which result from the behavior of light in ordinary gem material. Occasionally special effects are noted which are caused by peculiarities in structure or arise from reflections of light from countless inclusions in the gemstone. One of the most common and most beautiful effects is that known as *chatoyancy*. It appears in gemstones which contain numerous hair-like fibers of another mineral, light reflected from polished specimens possessing a fibrous sheen reminding one of satin or silk. The same effect is also noted when the inclusions are thin hollow tubes as is the case in certain gemstones which have grown under unusual conditions. This type of chatoyancy is frequently seen in beryl and tourmaline. In still other cases, notably in the variety of gypsum known as satin spar, in ulexite, and in fibrous serpentine, the reflections come from the surfaces of numerous individual crystals which grow in parallel bundles.

A special type of chatoyancy known as *asterism* results when several sets of inclusions are present in one crystal. It is found that each set gives rise to its own streak of reflected light, with several streaks crossing to form the star in such well-known star stones such as sapphire, ruby, and garnet. In the first two gemstones, there are three sets of inclusions visible at the same time and hence a six-legged star appears in polished stones, while in garnet there are usually only two sets to be seen and the resulting star will be four-legged. In each of these minerals, the fine fibrous inclusions which give rise to asterism grow only in certain directions within the host crystal and require cutting in a certain way if the star effect is to appear on top of the finished gem.

Reflections of light from numerous small wafer-like inclusions of foreign minerals within a host gemstone which act like tiny mirrors give rise to the effect known as *aventurescence* and such stones are called *aventurines*. The minute brilliant spangles are usually exceedingly thin crystals of hematite, goethite, or mica. The first two are bright orange or orange-red in color and impart a corresponding hue in whatever gemstone they happen to be in. Flakes of mica may either be silvery in luster and without color, or deep green in hue as in the variety known as *fuchsite*. In either case, the host gemstone may be quite drab without these inclusions but transformed into an object of beauty when they are present. Hematite and goethite inclusions are very common in feldspar species and when especially brilliant, cause them to be called *sunstones*. Similar to aventurescence is the effect known as *schiller*, but its cause is not due to inclusions but to numerous flat separations along cleavage planes which reflect a silvery light when the gemstone is held in certain positions. Schiller is often observed in feldspars.

Another effect known as *adularescence* is common in several species of feldspar and is familiar to readers as the bluish or silvery gleam seen in moonstones. Although specimens showing this effect appear to be entirely flawless, microscopic examination shows development of grid-like structures within the gemstones. X-ray analyses indicate that this grid structure is due to another species of feldspar growing as exceedingly thin inclusions within the host crystal and causing ordinary light to be broken into its component colors, one or more of which are then reflected back to the eye of the observer. The beautiful and intense multi-colored reflections of labradorite feldspar, an effect sometimes called *labradorescence*, is also ascribed to this cause as well as *peristerism*, a lovely pearly reflection mottled by various pastel shades of color observed in certain Canadian feldspars. A very similar reason is stated to be the cause of the gorgeous colors noted in precious opal, but in this instance, the grid structure is formed by certain types of quartz which have partially crystallized within the opal. The special effect seen in this gemstone is called *play of color*.

An interesting *iridescence* is noted in certain translucent chalcedonies which contain layers of microscopic goethite crystals. By judicious cutting, beautiful reflections of red, brown, and green, appear as the chalcedony covering the goethite is made thinner and thinner. If care is used, only enough material will be left to protect the goethite without offering more than the minimum obstruction to light. Still another handsome effect is seen in some grayish chalcedonies in which closely-banded growth layers act like a diffraction grating and cause white light to be broken up into all the colors of the rainbow. This astonishing effect is best seen when the chalcedony is sliced as thinly as possible across the layers and polished. The colors are observed only when light is viewed through the specimen, the best results being obtained by holding the section at arm's length several feet away from a pinpoint light such as a single electric bulb or a candle. Chalcedonies of this kind are known as *iris agates* and are found in a number of places in the western United States and in Mexico.

With the exception of opal, almost every special optical effect bears a definite relationship to the crystal structure of the host mineral. Thus, as a moonstone is turned on edge, the silvery sheen promptly diminishes and then disappears. In labradorite, the effect is even more pronounced, only a slight tilting being needed to cause an abrupt eclipse of the wondrous colors displayed a moment before. Needless to say, the gem cutter must exercise considerable skill to be sure that the effect wanted appears squarely atop the finished stone. In this connection, the author was once asked to examine a star sapphire which the proud owner had brought from Ceylon. It was immediately apparent that the stone had been cut for weight and weight alone, for the star appeared far to one side of the apex. The owner stated that his hesitancy to buy the stone because of this defect was removed by the positive assurance, "Sir, a lopsided star is the mark of a *genuine* stone!" It was difficult to convince him that every star sapphire, genuine or otherwise, could be cut to place the star at the top where it belongs.

CHAPTER II

Principal Gemstones

GEMSTONES of crystalline or massive form which are traditionally accorded first rank in commerce and generally provide gems of greatest value.

FROM ALLUVIAL DEPOSITS AND FROM IGNEOUS ROCKS:
Diamond
Corundum (Ruby and Sapphire)
FROM PEGMATITES:
Beryl
Topaz
FROM VOLCANIC ROCKS:
Opal

DIAMOND

First place among gemstones is generally accorded to diamond; it is easily the best known gemstone, having a long and colorful history in virtually every civilized society and constantly in the news even today. The qualities which place diamond in the forefront are its supreme hardness, no other mineral even approaching it in this respect, its exceptional brilliance in cut form, and its "fire" or dispersion, a property which lifts it from the commonplace among colorless gems. In North America diamond has been found in many places but never in the quantities noted in African, Brazilian, and Indian occurrences; nevertheless the widespread distribution of loose crystals found in alluvium arouses hope that someday important in-place deposits will be found.

The name of diamond is directly derived from its superior hardness and comes to us from the Latin *adamantem*, or *adiamentem*, in turn, derived from the Greek *adamas,* meaning "invincible." In mineralogy, the peculiar silvery sub-metallic luster of diamond is called "adamantine."

There are two principal varieties of diamond: single or twinned crystals varying from those unfit for cutting to dazzlingly clear crystals, and *bort* or *carbonado* which are peculiar masses of diamond composed of numerous minute crystals fused together in exceedingly tough aggregates. The latter are often dead black in color (carbonado) or dark to light gray (bort). The use of diamond in ornamentation is well known but the value of this mineral in industry is sometimes not fully appreciated. Crushed diamond in all sizes is used in many abrasive operations. Virtually all faceted gems, including itself, are cut by diamond abrasive powders. In industry, powders are rubbed or fused into metal disks and wheels to provide abrasive wheels for grinding exceedingly hard substances or sawing them in two while single crystals are set into drill points or bored to provide wire-drawing dies through which many miles of wire can be reduced to correct size before wear forces the use of another diamond die.

In view of the enormous pressures and temperatures now known to be needed to form diamond, it is not surprising that it is relatively rare in nature despite the fact that millions of tons of carbon, the element which comprises it, are present in the earth's crust in the form of carbonates, while upon the surface, every living organism, animal or vegetable, contains much carbon in its makeup. Carbon (C) is found in three distinct forms: amorphous as in coke, charcoal, etc., crystallized in the Hexagonal System as in graphite, and crystallized in the Isometric System as diamond. Diamond crystal forms are mostly dodecahedrons, trisoctahedrons, hexoctahedrons, and more rarely, octahedrons, however, as shown in Figure 7, few are of perfect form. A large

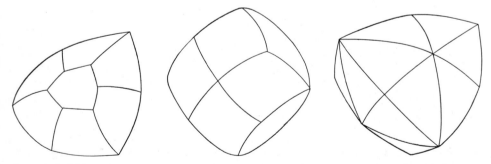

FIGURE 7. Three diamond crystals showing the rounded forms characteristic of many American specimens.

number have been unearthed which bear little trace of crystal faces and seem more like ordinary pebbles except for the unmistakable brilliant luster. Flat, bean-shaped crystals are also common. The rounded or irregular profile of

FIGURE 8. Murfreesboro diamond crystals in the U.S. National Museum. Unfortunately the photograph gives little idea of the wide range of color represented in these fascinating shiny crystals. Although most are colorless or nearly so, a few are pink, several are rich canary yellow, and others pale to dark coffee brown. The diamond which looks the largest is extremely flat and actually does not weigh as much as the distorted octahedral crystal above it to the right. The latter is magnificent yellow and weighs 17.85 carats. Courtesy Smithsonian Institution.

American crystals does not appear to be due to stream wear however, most crystals showing few signs of abrasion, and it is assumed that irregularities resulted from growth conditions at the time of formation. The majority of North American diamond crystals are of transparent gem quality varying in the degree of internal perfection. Some bort has been produced from the diamond mines of Arkansas but exact descriptions are lacking and the term may merely refer to material too cloudy or flawed for cutting rather than the compact type described previously. As has been found true elsewhere, predominant diamond colors are most often tints of yellow or brown, or colorless. Shades of green, blue, and pink have also been reported as well as vivid "fancy" yellows and browns. The distribution of color in crystals is usually uniform but grayish-green stones carry their color only skin-deep because the greenish cast disappears entirely after cutting. The typical part-silvery, part-greasy adamantine luster of diamond is just as distinctive in North American specimens as elsewhere and perhaps more than any other characteristic, has done most to attract attention to crystals wherever found. Figure 8 illustrates a typical group of crystals from the mines at Murfreesboro, Arkansas.

Diamond is 10 in hardness and occupies the highest place on the Mohs Scale. Perfect cleavages occur in planes parallel to octahedral crystal faces. Cleavages are rather easily developed, a property used to advantage in the splitting of diamond crystals preparatory to cutting, but in borts and carbonados, they are interrupted and consequently do not spread through the stone, a fact which imparts the toughness so desired in industrial applications. The specific gravity of diamond varies from 3.50 to 3.53; gem material averages 3.520. Refractive indices are single and vary only very slightly from the mean value of 2.4175.

The occurrence of diamond in North America is confined almost entirely to the United States. None has been found in Mexico or Central America while Canada records several doubtful occurrences. At Murfreesboro, Arkansas, diamond is found in-place but every other occurrence represents merely the area where crystals happened to be deposited by weathering, erosion, or glacial action. As can be seen in Figure 9 alluvial localities are both numerous and widespread although the actual quantity of crystals found to date could probably fit into a coffee cup with room left over. Only the Arkansas mines are commercially significant but even there the past history of production has been discouraging. The great interest in alluvial diamond crystals centers about the mystery of their origin. Stones have been picked up over wide areas and suggest that many more must still remain in the soil. Original sources must have been rich indeed to provide for such wholesale sprinkling! However, in spite of increasing familiarity with the regions in which these stones have been found, no sources have been discovered to date and the mystery remains unsolved.

Diamond finds in North America are concentrated in three principal areas of the United States: the Appalachians, Great Lakes, and the Western United States. In the Great Lakes region it was soon discovered that many crystals occur on the borders of the terminal moraines marking the southernmost expansion of the Great Glacier. The connection seems obvious; the glacier had taken up the stones somewhere in the northern reaches of Canada where perhaps they occurred originally, and had borne them to their final resting places along the moraine. This coincidence of finds with the southern limits of the glacier is also shown on the map in Figure 9. Studies of the

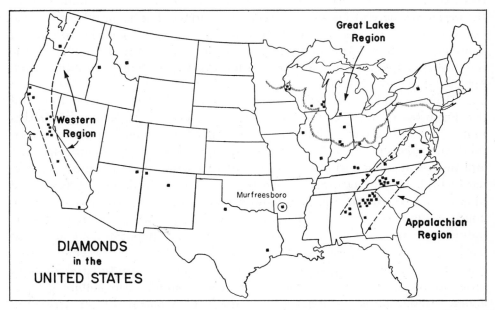

FIGURE 9. Map of the United States showing principal localities from which diamond has been reported in each of the three great regions. The single dot in Arkansas is the Murfreesboro locality. Hatched lines below the Great Lakes Region indicate the line of terminal moraines marking the southernmost expansion of the Great Glacier.

drift and the direction of the scratches left on exposed rocks pointed to a source near Hudson Bay or Ungava in Labrador. Up to date, however, no diamond-bearing rocks have been found in these regions.

The problem of origin in the Appalachian and Western regions is even more puzzling since no single agent of transportation existed which could have carried the diamond crystals and sprinkled them about so widely. Peridotite, the special kind of rock yielding diamond elsewhere, outcrops in both regions but each occurrence has proved to be barren, however, it is entirely possible that fruitful ones merely remain undiscovered. Speculation also centers about the possibility that peridotite outcrops may contain diamonds only in their upper parts; should these parts be worn away by weathering, only the barren sections would remain, thus accounting for the presence of diamonds in regions containing unproductive peridotite.

Some alluvial diamond crystals have been found through sheer chance but the majority owe their discovery to placer gold mining in which washing of sands and gravels is done to get rid of lighter materials and concentrate only the heaviest, including gold. Since the specific gravity of diamond is comparatively high, it frequently appears with gold in the "clean up." For this reason the discoveries of alluvial crystals have been most numerous in those places where placer mining has been conducted. The gaps between discoveries shown on the map in Figure 9, may not represent the absence of diamond as much as the absence of gold mining operations. There is little doubt that many crystals are still left in the soil if only someone did the necessary digging and washing.

When found in the rock of origin, diamond occurs in a special kind of peridotite known as *kimberlite*, receiving its name from the famous Kimberley mines in South Africa where it is the matrix of diamond. A number of minerals make up kimberlite but the principal species are olivine, enstatite, and mica, with much of the olivine altered to serpentine. The rock is ordinarily broken or brecciated and weathers easily into yellowish, greenish, or bluish material, the so-called "yellow ground" and "blue ground." Natural concentration makes surface deposits exceptionally rich since much of the lighter and more easily decomposed material has disappeared. Tough and hard unaltered rock of bluish, grayish, greenish, or black color is encountered with depth. Where time is no object, unaltered rock can be spread out to weather, becoming soft in a matter of months. In South African mining operations, weathering is no longer used to soften rock and it is now crushed in mills and then washed to concentrate the heavy minerals.

Because of the cylindrical shape of diamond-bearing bodies in South Africa—the so-called "pipes"—it was thought that kimberlite was volcanic in origin. This theory is now discredited since little evidence has been advanced to bear out its claims. It is now believed that kimberlite, like other peridotites, is a deep-seated rock allied to granite and not a product of eruption.

Diamond crystals are sufficiently rare in North America to warrant preserving each find in its natural form rather than cutting it up into gems. Once cut, identity is lost and the gem sinks into the sea of obscurity which characterizes all commercial stones. Unfortunately, far too many of poor color or perfection have been consigned to this fate in the misguided hope of monetary gain. For each crystal which turned out well, several times as many turned out poorly, very often costing more to cut than could be realized from their sale as finished gems. Anyone finding a diamond crystal in the United States is well advised to get expert opinion before incurring the expense of cutting. In any case, the crystals should be offered first to public or private museums and institutions where they can be preserved for the enjoyment and study of future generations.

In the United States, only five diamond crystals exceeding 20 carats weight each have been found as follows:

WEIGHT	PLACE	DATE	NAME
40.23 carats	Murfreesboro, Ark.	1924	the "Uncle Sam"
34.46	Peterstown, W. Va.	1928	the "Punch Jones"
27.21	Searcy, Ark.	1925	in possession of Tiffany and Co.
23.75	Manchester, Va.	1855	the "Dewey" (see Figure 10)
20.25	Murfreesboro, Ark.	1921	

The above will be more fully described under appropriate localities.

LOCALITIES

Diamond in Canada. Despite its vast size and the attractive theory that alluvial diamond crystals found along the fringes of the terminal moraines of the Great Glacier must be of Canadian origin, no authenticated occurrences of damond in place have been recorded. In the publication "Prospecting In Canada," Economic Geology Series No 7, Geological Survey of Canada (1956), it is flatly stated that no in-place deposits are known and furthermore, the supposed diamond crystals from the Bridge River and Tulameen regions of British Columbia were in reality, synthetic periclase formed by heat treatment of the samples of rock from which they

FIGURE 10. A replica of the Dewey Diamond, weight 23.75 carats, found at Manchester, Virginia in 1854. Courtesy Smithsonian Institution.

were obtained. By failure to mention other localities, it is assumed that these too are not authentic, however, as a matter of historical interest, the claimed finds are given below.

Quebec. Microscopic "diamonds" were separated from chromite from the Montreal Chrome Pit, one mile southeast of the south end of Little Lake St. Francis, Coleraine Township, Megantic County. Microscopic crystals were also reported from chromite found upon Olivine Mountain, Tulameen

River region, British Columbia; also from Scottie Creek, Bonaparte River, near Ashcroft, Cariboo District.

Appalachian Diamond—Virginia. The earliest mention of diamond in this state concerns a stone of the "first water" found in 1847 at the Vaucluse Gold Mine in Orange County. Details of color, quality, and size are lacking. In 1885 the famous Dewey diamond, shown in replica in Figure 10, was found in Manchester, Henrico County, by a laborer digging an excavation. The crystal, a rounded trigonal trisoctahedron, was originally valued in Richmond at $4,000 but the purchaser, Captain Samuel W. Dewey of Philadelphia, did not state what he actually paid for it. The crystal originally weighed 23.75 carats but was reduced to 11.69 carats after cutting by the firm of H. D. Morse who are said to have charged a fee of $1500 for the task. When cut, the gem proved off-color and imperfect, and was worth considerably less than the cost of cutting alone. The last diamond discovery in the state occurred in 1913 when a stone of fine color and excellent quality was found on the farm of Mr. Gillespie near Pounding Mill, Tazewell County. A gem cut from this crystal weighed .83 carat.

West Virginia. Only one diamond crystal, but a large one, has been found in this state. This was discovered by Grover C. Jones and his eldest son, William P. "Punch" Jones, while playing horseshoes in a vacant lot in Peterstown, Monroe County, in April 1928. Since it was "Punch" who found the crystal lying on the ground where it had been kicked loose by a horseshoe, it was named in his honor. Although found in 1928, verification of its identity waited until May 5, 1943 when it was submitted to Prof. Roy J. Holden of Virginia Polytechnic Institute. The crystal is well-formed, slightly greenish-gray in color, and weighs 34.46 carats. It is presently on loan to the U.S. National Museum where it appears on exhibit along with other American diamond crystals.

North Carolina. Diamond was first discovered in this state in 1843 by Dr. F. M. Stephenson who found a crystal valued at $100 in Brindletown Creek, Burke County. Since this date, crystals were reported at frequent intervals up to 1893 when the last discovery of record took place. The lack of more recent finds may be due to the exhaustion of gold-bearing gravels and the sharp reduction in placer mining. In 1845 a flawless crystal in the form of a distorted octahedron with curved faces of 1.33 carats was found at the J. D. Twitty placer mine in Rutherford County. At about the same time, another was reported from the same locality as well as still another from Burke County. In 1852 a half-carat crystal was found near Cottage Home, Lincoln County. This was also an octahedron, transparent, and of greenish hue. In the same year, a white crystal of about one carat was found in Todd's Branch, Mecklenburg County. An unusual "black" crystal of good size was reported from the same place at a later date, again incident to washing for gold. It is said that this valuable specimen was shattered by hammer blows in the mistaken belief that genuine diamond is indestructible. Sometime after 1852, two crystals, one a beautiful octahedron, were reported from the Portis Mine in Franklin County. In 1877, a lustrous white flawed crystal of 2.38 carats was found in McDowell County. At about the same time, another McDowell County locality was recorded when several small crystals were found in the headwaters of Muddy Creek. However, the most notable find occurred in the vicinity of Dysortville when an excellent stone of 4.33 carats was discovered on the A. Bright farm. Although its luster aroused much interest nothing was done about identification until it was sent to New York City. Shortly thereafter it came into the possession of Tiffany and Company and through them into the J. Pierpont Morgan gem collection. It is now in the American Museum of Natural History. The state museum at Raleigh possesses a .31 carat crystal found in some undetermined year in Burke County. The last find to be reported was discovered near King's Mountain, Cleveland County, and is described as a bright canary yellow crystal measuring 5/16 by 3/16 inches and weighing .75 carat.

Tennessee. In 1899 a diamond crystal of 3 carats was reported from Roane County where it had been found near an Indian mound on the south bank of the Clinch River. The stone is said to have yielded a cut gem of 1.25 carats. Another crystal of 1.81 carats, colorless and flawless, was found in Flat Creek, near Luttrell, Union County. A vague report states that three crystals have been found in Koko Creek, at the headwaters of the Tellico River in eastern Tennessee.

South Carolina. Unsubstantiated reports mention small diamond crystals from gold placers in various northern counties.

Georgia. The earliest mention of diamond in this state is in connection with gold mining in Hall and White Counties where small crystals were found in 1843 and for some years later. Those of Hall County were found mostly around Gainesville and in Glade Creek. In 1866 two small opaque crystals of less than one-eighth carat each were picked up at the Horshaw Mine in Racoochee Valley, White County. In April 1887, a 4.5 carat stone, slightly yellowish in color, was found ¾ mile northwest of Morrow Station, Clayton County, some 13 miles south of Atlanta. This crystal measured 3/8 by 3/8 by 5/16 inches and is the largest diamond on record from Georgia. More recently, a flattened hexoctahedron was found in Lee County in 1901. The color was stated to be greenish-white, the weight 3.5 carats, and the size 3/8 by 5/16 by 1/4 inches. The crystal was sent to Tiffany's in New York City and purchased by them for $80. Unconfirmed reports state that diamond has been found in Stockeneter Branch, 13 miles northeast of Gainesville in Hall County; also at a place 11 miles northeast of Macon in Twiggs County. The possibility of diamond occurring in any county in the northern half of the state is more than good. There can be little doubt that many crystals have been overlooked and thrown away in the course of the extensive gold mining which took place in northern Georgia, especially around Dahlonega in Lumpkin County.

Alabama. Several diamond crystals have been reported from this state, the latest in 1905 when a 2.41 carat crystal was found near Prescott Siding in St. Clair County about 1 ¼ miles east of Brompton. This stone measured about 5/16 by 3/16 inches and was said to be greenish in color. In 1900 a 4.25 carat stone, now in the American Museum of Natural History, was found near Birmingham in Shelby County. This is an octahedron of faint yellow color. A distorted octahedron of 4.50 carats from an unspecified point in Lee County is also in the same museum.

Arkansas. Before discussing the important in-place deposit at Murfreesboro, one alluvial find should be mentioned. This is a splendid crystal of perfect hexoctahedral form and virtually flawless, found by Mrs. Pellie Howell in 1925 or 1926. Now in the possession of Tiffany and Company, New York City, it was picked up in a newly-cleared field on her farm at Searcy, White County. This example, one of the finest from North America, weighs 27.31 carats. It has not been cut so far as is known.

The only true diamond mines in North America are located near Murfreesboro, Pike County. Two areas of diamond-bearing kimberlite have been recognized and mapped. The first, and most important, is called the Prairie Creek Area and is located 2 ½ miles south-southeast of Murfreesboro. It is a single outcrop, roughly triangular in outline, and situated atop hilly terrain of low elevation near the junction of Prairie Creek and the Little Missouri River. The second area encloses three distinct outcrops called the Kimberlite, American, and Black Lick prospects. The first two have been thoroughly tested but yielded only small returns while the Black Lick prospect has so far not produced any diamond at all.

The existence of peridotite in Arkansas was known as early as 1842, but the first detailed investigation of the geology did not take place until shortly before 1889. The striking similarity of the Pike County peridotites to those known to yield diamond in South Africa led one geologist to spend countless hours on his hands and knees looking for crystals. He was unsuccessful in his efforts but his suspicions proved well-founded later when a farmer owning property on the Prairie Creek outcrop discovered two stones on August 8, 1906. The farmer in question, John Wesley Huddleston, had heard about the possibility of diamonds occurring in the rocks of the neighborhood and it is to his credit that the shining pebbles he discovered were not kicked aside as unimportant. Taking his finds to persons experienced in such matters, he soon verified their genuineness and set off the remarkable and colorful chain of events which led to the rise and fall of the diamond mining industry in Arkansas. It is recorded that Huddleston's stones, the first to be found in their place of origin in North America, weighed about 2.375 and 1.375 carats.

The peridotite in each of the four outcrops is similar; each has been intruded into Carboniferous rocks and the Trinity formation of Cretaceous age. Although some writers have described the intrusions as "pipes" the Murfreesboro outcrops do not display the circular outlines typical of many South African pipes, however, they consist of rocks essentially identical to the kimberlites of that great diamond mining region. It is interesting to note that peridotite has been found in another part of the state in the vicinity of Blue Ball, Scott County, but although tested thoroughly by means of pits and crosscuts no diamond has been found.

In the Prairie Creek locality, the outcrop covers about 75 acres but only 12 acres are unweathered rock. The majority of the deposit is covered with topsoil darkened by decomposed organic matter and contains deteriorated peridotite colored various shades of green, blue, and yellow. Much of the unaltered rock is dull black, greenish-black, or brownish-black in color, very hard and tough, and consists mostly of serpentine and phlogopite mica with lesser amounts of olivine, augite, magnetite, and perovskite. Associated minerals recovered during mining have been hematite, quartz, pyrite, diopside, and epidote. Occasionally, specimens of facet grade amethyst, peridot, and garnet are found in small pieces. Weathered material is derived from peridotite which occurs in cemented aggregates of angular fragments or *breccias*. Both fine and coarse breccias cover extensive areas of the outcrop. It is this material which supplied the principal input for washing and concentrating plants.

Mining has been confined entirely to shallow surface workings, taking advantage of the richness of weathered material and the ease with which it is excavated. Initial efforts to wash the dirt and decomposed rock were very crude and reasonably efficient processes were not introduced until much later. The treatment eventually used followed the pattern developed so successfully in South Africa, i.e., crushing to size, washing to concentrate heavy minerals, and passing concentrates over greased tables to separate the diamonds. Excavated material was also spread and harrowed on the surface to hasten the decay brought about by exposure to the elements. This material was later fed to the mills where it passed through the processes noted above. Photographs of mining operations conducted in 1923 are reproduced in Figure 11. The record of production from the several mines on the Prairie Creek outcrop is not impressive either in terms of quantity of diamond produced or in financial gain. It is estimated that several million dollars have been invested in the mines but only a fraction of that sum has been realized from sales of stones. More than 10,000 crystals of about

Figure 11. Two views of the diamond mine near Murfreesboro, Arkansas in October, 1923. The upper view shows a portion of the kimberlite outcrop cleared of vegetation and partially excavated by means of a dragline scraper. The bottom view shows one of the workmen washing some of the ground to separate the diamond crystals. Courtesy U.S. Geological Survey.

3,000 carats weight have been recorded with the Arkansas Department of Revenue but probably many more have been taken through unlawful operations.

The latest sustained attempt at mining was conducted by the late Glenn L. Martin, the noted aircraft manufacturer, who is reported to have expended

$700,000 in the purchase and lease of several Prairie Creek properties, the erection of a processing plant, and the operation of the mine for one year beginning in October 1948. The "take" reported to the authorities of Arkansas amounted to 246.15 carats valued at only $984.60! The company obtained about 840 crystals, the largest a 4.5 carat stone. Ninety percent of the stones recovered were small industrials from .10 to 1.0 carat in size. The yield appeared to be about .16 carat per 100 loads, each load being equal to 16 cubic feet. This compares to 24 carats average per 100 loads realized in the Premier Mine of South Africa. Production consisted of 10% very imperfect distorted pieces of various colors, 5% seconds of dark brown tint, 20% small size mixed industrials, and 65% crushing bort. It is believed that one segment of the outcrop is still owned by the Martin interests but the major portion, originally belonging to the Arkansas Diamond Corporation, passed through many turns of fate into the hands of the Diamond Corporation of America, and thence into the control of Ethel P. Wilkinson of Logansport, Indiana. In 1950, a portion of the Prairie Creek area was set aside by several owners as the "Diamond Preserve of the United States, Inc.," and thrown open to visiting by the general public. After payment of a modest fee, searching for diamond is permitted with the understanding that "any diamond up to 5 carats absolutely free, over 5 carats royalty of 25% rough value paid by finder." This enterprise is now called the "Crater of Diamonds" and the information about rules under which visits are allowed has been extracted from advertisements appearing lately in popular lapidary and mineral magazines (1958).

The dismal results of the Martin testing operations of the Prairie Creek deposit compare unfavorably with testing operations carried on in 1912 by Howard A. Millar and Austin Q. Millar, who, in response to a request by the author for more information, supplied the following:

"In testing operations more than 100,000 diamonds were recovered by Howard A. Millar and Austin Q. Millar. 70% classed as industrials and 30% gem quality. 40% whites, 40% browns and 20% yellows. Less than 1% classed as crushing bort. The 30% gems were highest quality cutting material. No quantitative test has been made for microscopic diamonds. We have made qualitative tests which proved they are present in large quantity, both on fine grained breccia and coarse grained breccia.

"The average recovery in test operation was 11 carats to 100 tons of material processed. Average size was .26 cts. Hardness test was made by Henry Ford, Sr. He proved in actual test of 3 mo. using our diamonds in wheel dressers along side of diamonds from all other sources, that our diamonds gave 28% greater efficiency than any others."

The opening of the "Crater of Diamonds" has been attended with interesting and successful results as shown in the case of the finding of the crystal which was eventually cut into the "Star of Arkansas," a fine marquise gem of 8.27 carats. The finder, Mrs. Arthur L. Parker of Dallas, Texas, discovered the rough diamond lying upon the ground on March 4, 1956, less than an hour after she had begun to search. It proved to be a narrow and rather thin crystal, unlike any recognizable diamond crystal form, measuring 1½ inches long, about 7/16 inch wide, and ¼ inch thick. When it was cleaned it weighed 15.33 carats. Examinations showed it to be flawless and pure white. The stone was cut by the firm of Schenk & Van Haelen of New York City who stated that it was exceptionally difficult to cut. The "Star of Arkansas" measures about 1½ inches long and 7/16 inch wide, preserving much of the original size of the rough if not the weight. This gem is estimated as being worth about $11,000 to $15,000 but Mr. Millar feels that its value is higher stating: "The value of this stone has been established by several leading gemologists and jewelers at $100,000.00. The extra hardness and the fine color, along with the brilliance which is six times that of any diamond ever cut, as well as the publicity, etc., has made it of much higher value than first established." Schenck & Van Haelen also cut the "Uncle Sam" diamond which weighed 40.23 carats in the rough and finished into an emerald-cut pinkish gem of 14.24 carats, and an octahedral crystal weighing 20.25 carats found in 1921 which cut into two fine brilliants. Many of the gem quality stones from Murfreesboro have been cut by this company who are reputed to have handled several thousand in all. Mr. Howard A. Millar has informed the author that since Mrs. Parker's discovery, more than 200 diamond crystals have been found by visitors. Among the finds may be mentioned single crystals of 1.50, 1.45, 1.97, and 1.30 carats, and a beautiful rose colored crystal weighing .40 carat. One finder was rewarded by 9 crystals found in one day, weighing together 2.19 carats.

Diamond in the Great Lakes Region—Wisconsin. The earliest find of record occurred in 1876 when a faint yellow dodecahedral crystal with rounded edges weighing 15.37 carats was found in the Kettle Moraine near Eagle, Waukesha County. This stone appeared in hard yellowish ground at a depth greater than 40 feet during digging of a well. The crystal was not recognized immediately and was inadvertently sold for $1.00 to a Colonel Boynton who bought it as a "topaz." It was later sold by him to Tiffany and Company. In turn, Tiffany's sold the stone to J. Pierpont Morgan who later presented the collection containing the Eagle diamond to the American Museum of Natural History where it is now on exhibit.

In 1887 several crystals of less than a carat each were found in the gold-bearing gravels of Plum Creek, Rock Elm Township, Pierce County. Next year, four more were found on the surface and several feet below. In 1889, three stones from the west branch of Plum Creek were submitted for examination to G. F. Kunz of Tiffany's who described them as greenish-gray in color and weighing .8, .44, and .03 carats respectively. The crystal forms were rudely hexoctahedral.

In 1893 a grayish-green distorted and rounded dodecahedron weighing 3.87 carats was found in the Kettle Moraine, 2½ miles southwest of Oregon, Dane County. This crystal is now in the American Museum of Natural History. A few years later in 1896, a stone of good size was found at Saukville, Ozaukee County, 26 miles north of Milwaukee and only a mile or so from the shore of Lake Michigan. The crystal, a flattened trisoctahedron of white color, was variously reported as weighing 6.57 or 6.375 carats. A recent account states that this stone was actually found in 1881 but was not reported until 1896.

In 1903 another Wisconsin locality was recorded when a flattened crystal of 2.11 carats was found near Burlington, Racine County. The crystal form was said to be tetrahedral and twinned, the color faintly greenish gray.

The largest stone ever found in Wisconsin—the famous Kohlsville or "Theresa" diamond—has been reserved for last. This stone was found in 1886 by Louis Endlich on his farm in Washington County near Kohlsville. The crystal was a loaf-shaped specimen measuring ¾ inch by ½ inch by ⅜ inch with little trace of crystal faces and weighed 21.25 carats. A peculiar separation plane occurred midway through the stone marking the boundary between differently-colored sections, one half yellowish in tint and the other almost colorless. After being kept in the family for a number of years, the crystal was sent to New York City for cutting in 1918 and produced a total of 9.27 carats of finished gems. The largest gem weighed 1.48 carats.

Michigan. The sole diamond crystal to Michigan's credit was found in 1894 or 1895 in gravel near Dowagiac, Cass County. The stone weighed 10.875 carats and measured ½ inch by ⅜ inch by 7/16 inch; the form was that of a rounded hexoctahedron.

Illinois. In 1911 a report was circulated that 22 diamond crystals said to have come from the vicinity of Macomb, McDonough County had been submitted to a jewelry firm in St. Louis. A 7.75 carat crystal was also reported from Jefferson County about 3½ miles east of Ashley. Both finds are unconfirmed.

Indiana. Reports of the U.S. Geological Survey indicate that a 3-carat stone was found in 1878 in Little Indian Creek in Morgan County by miners panning for gold. From this year up to 1900 when authentic records of diamond discoveries in Indiana begin, no mention is made of further finds, however, it is reasonable to assume that a considerable number must have been found but were not considered important enough to report. In 1900, the 4.875 carat "Stanley" diamond was found in a small tributary of Gold Creek in Morgan County. The crystal took the form of a rounded octahedron of a peculiar greenish-yellow cast, and, when cut, produced two gems weighing

1.125 and 1.062 carats respectively. Vague reports indicate that a number of other smaller stones blue-white, brownish, yellowish, and colorless, were found in both Brown and Morgan counties at about the same time or perhaps somewhat earlier.

Morgan County again produced two or three small stones in 1904 when diamond crystals were found in heavy mineral concentrates incident to gold panning associated with waterworn crystals and fragments of ruby, sapphire and zircon; one piece of the latter yielded a clear gem of 4.62 carats. Most of the ruby and sapphire proved unfit for cutting but occasionally small clear pieces were found which could produce gems of one carat or less. From time to time massive forms of sapphire showing decided chatoyancy were found and afforded cat's eyes when suitably cut. In 1908, a one carat diamond was found in Morgan County followed by the discovery in 1911 of a .135 carat crystal at the junction of Gold Creek and Sycamore Creek. Next year, the same locality produced a colorless stone of 2.28 carats. In 1913 five crystals were washed from Gold Creek and Highland Creek in Morgan County and included a small greenish specimen of .20 carat, a colorless crystal of .73 carat, and a twinned crystal of yellowish hue weighing .69 carat. In 1916 a 1.48 carat crystal of yellowish color was panned from Lick Creek in Brown County, about 15 miles southeast of Martinsville. The stone measured 3/16 by ¼ by ⅜ inches and took the form of a rounded dodecahedron.

The latest reported discovery, in 1949, is a 3.93 carat crystal, apparently a flattened and distorted octahedron, which was brought to the late Dr. Frank B. Wade of Indianapolis for identification. The crystal measured about 9/16 by ⅜ by ⅛ inches and was triangular in outline. It was much too flat to cut a large stone but could possibly be cut into a shallow gem of perhaps 1.25 carats in weight. The crystal was discovered by a farmer near Peru in Miami County, which, it is to be noted, is considerably further north than either Brown or Morgan county. Dr. Wade has also reported other diamond finds personally examined by him including a crystal of 3.06 carats from Salt Creek in northeast Brown County and a minute specimen found in Gold Creek, Morgan County. In all, he examined ten authentic diamond crystals from various localities within the state.

Ohio. A single discovery only is reported for Ohio. In 1897, a 6 carat crystal was found at Milford, Clermont County, not far from Cincinnati. The stone was later cut and its ownership is now unknown.

Kentucky. The presence of alluvial diamond in Kentucky has long been a controversial question. Only two references mention diamond in this state but appear to be contradictory if one and the same stone is being discussed. For example, the Catalogue of the U.S. National Museum lists a yellowish crystal of .766 carat, measuring ⅜ by ⅛ by ⅛ inches and coming from a stream near Montpelier in Adair County. On the other hand, an earlier reference states that a stone of .44 carat was found in 1888 in the same stream but in Russell County.

Perhaps the chief claim to fame for Kentucky in respect to the King of Gemstones is the fact that diamond has *not* been found where every indication pointed to its probable presence. This interesting state of affairs happened shortly after the peridotites of Murfreesboro were found to be diamantiferous and attention was drawn to the fact that very similar rocks occurred along Ison's Creek in Elliot County. For several years the exciting prospect of diamond in Kentucky kept interest at a fever pitch but the most thorough explorations involving actual mining, milling, and concentration, all at considerable expense, failed to turn up a single stone. Aside from the lamentable absence of diamond, the Elliot County peridotites are essentially the same as those noted in South Africa as well as in Arkansas. The rock is composed principally of serpentine, olivine, enstatite, garnet, ilmenite, and small amounts of mica. Some of the enstatite is of good color and clear enough to facet, while the same is true of the pyrope garnet. It is interesting to note that both of these minerals not only occur in the famous Kimberley pipes, but also in facet quality.

New York. The existence of peridotite outcrops in the City of Syracuse has been known for some time. In many respects these rocks bear a strong resemblance to diamond-bearing kimberlite, but aside from unverified reports, the latest carried by newspapers in 1920 or 1921, no diamond crystals have ever been found in them. The earliest account of a "diamond find" related that a crystal had been found in a gravel pit south of Syracuse. In 1909, an unconfirmed find was made in Grass River near Massena, St. Lawrence County.

Diamond in the Western Region—California. The presence of diamond in the gold-bearing gravels of California was known as early as 1849 when the Reverend Mr. Lyman of New England, saw a light straw color crystal of about the size of a pea in the hands of a miner at an unnamed digging in this state. Several years later, diamond crystals were observed in the gravels near Cherokee, Butte County, as well as at other localities.

Diamond crystals in California have only been found in gravels and sands. Considerable interest was aroused in 1906 when a "diamond pipe" was discovered by M. J. Cooney about a mile north of Oroville in Butte County along the west bank of the Feather River. The rock outcrop bore a superficial resemblance to kimberlite, however, specimens sent to the U.S. Geological Survey only proved to be serpentinized amphibolite schist similar to that found in many areas of this part of the state and barren of diamond.

California diamond crystals are uniformly small, seldom exceeding 2 carats in weight. Although of excellent quality in respect to flawlessness, the majority are decidedly yellowish in tinge and therefore of little value. The largest example on record is a crystal of 7.25 carats from French Corral in Nevada County, while at the other extreme, microscopic diamonds have been reported from the black sands of the Trinity River near its junction with the Klamath in Trinity County. Very small crystals have also been reported from the Smith River in Del Norte County as well as an indefinite reference to specimens in the lower Trinity River in Humboldt County. It is likely that these too are microscopic in size.

The most productive localities were in Amador, Butte, and El Dorado counties, with lesser numbers of crystals found in Plumas County. A single find made along the banks of Alpine Creek in Tulare County in 1895 has never been authenticated as well as another near the Mexican border of Imperial County. Prominent discovery sites in Amador County are: Jackass Gulch and Rancheria near Volcano, Indian Gulch near Fiddletown, Loafer Hill near Oleta, more recently, near Plymouth. Figure 12 illustrates an old woodcut of a diamond crystal found in Amador County. In Butte County, Cherokee Flat is estimated to have produced more than 300 stones from 1853 to 1918. Lesser numbers have been found near Oroville, particularly from Thompson's Flat and Yankee Hill. In El Dorado County, Forest Hill, Webber Hill, White Rock Canyon, and Cedar Ravine near Placerville, as well as Smith's Flat, have all produced diamond. In Plumas County, finds have been recorded from Nelson Point, Sawpit Flat, Gopher Hill, and upper Spanish Creek.

FIGURE 12. An early woodcut of a diamond crystal found in Amador County, California. Courtesy California Division of Mines.

The most recent find occurred in 1934 near Plymouth, Amador County, when a crystal weighing 2.65 carats was picked up from gravel. This specimen measured ⅜ inch by ¼ inch in size and is an irregular octahedron with several of its points terminated by flat planes.

Diamond crystals have also been reported from near Ramona in San Diego County. It is stated that in the early 1900's, A. W. Pray found three crystals in the riffles of a sluice box during placering for gold on Hatfield Creek, in the flats below the Little Three Mine. It is said that the stones were ⅛ inch in diameter, with curved faces, and were identified by competent authority; they were not waterworn.

Miscellaneous Diamond Discoveries—Idaho. In 1882, Dr. G. F. Kunz stated that several crystals were found in this state but mentioned no details. In 1913, three small specimens were found in the Rock Flat placers at the head of Little Goose Creek Canyon, 5 miles east of New Meadows, Adams County. The largest was an octahedral crystal of grayish color and .33 carat in weight. The Rock Flat gravels are best known for their production of sapphires of various colors as well as garnet, ruby, and some zircon. In 1947 an unconfirmed report stated that a 19.5 carat diamond had been found at Rock Flat, 4 miles west of McCall, however, nothing further has been heard of this "diamond." Microscopic crystals have been found in the black sands of the Snake River.

Montana. Some authorities flatly state that diamond has not been found in Montana but some reports, in considerable detail, seem to indicate otherwise. In 1883 a colorless dodecahedral crystal with triangular markings upon its faces, was reported from Nelson Hill, near Blackfoot, Deer Lodge County. In 1894, a .22 carat flawed white crystal was again reported from this county. In 1896 or 1897, A. F. White of Butte was said to have sent three crystals of diamond to New York City. These were from an unstated locality and weighed .19, .06, and .03 carats respectively. Diamond crystals have also been reported from Greenhorn Gulch in Madison County and Grasshopper Creek in Beaverhead County. A crystal from Deer Lodge County was said to have been found by a Chinaman who "delivered it to the owner of the claim, a Mr. Mason, who repeatedly refused large sums for it."

Texas. Several stones were reported in 1911 from Montgomery County but confirmation is lacking. The stones were said to weigh 2.5 and 3.5 carats. An authentic find in June 1911 was reported from Sec. 64, Block 44, Foard County. The diamond collection of the U.S. National Museum includes a crystal from Texas.

CORUNDUM

Better known to the public as *sapphire* and *ruby*, the mineral species corundum is a widely-distributed oxide of aluminum which ranks next to diamond in hardness and sometimes occurs so abundantly that it is mined for abrasive purposes. However, clear gemstone varieties are far less common than the coarse abrasive types, one of which, *emery*, a dark gray to black massive kind, is familiar to craftsmen as the coating on emery paper and as the substance of emery wheels. In North America, much abrasive corundum has been mined from deposits in Canada and the Eastern United States, while clear gem quality material has been obtained in large quantity only from Montana. Some specimens exhibit beautifully the effect known as *asterism*, forming the ever-popular *star sapphire* and *star ruby*, however, these are very rare in North American deposits.

By custom, the varietal name ruby is applied only to gem material of pure intense red, all other colors—including pink—being called sapphire. Thus it is proper to speak of green, yellow, orange, purple, blue, pink, and even colorless sapphire, but not red sapphire. Another variety much less translucent than gem grades, is known as *adamantine spar*, and is noted chiefly for its bronzy brown chatoyancy. Emery is merely an extremely impure massive corundum in which considerable magnetite, or black magnetic oxide of iron, is admixed. It is far less brittle than gem types and is therefore valued in industrial applications for this property as well as its hardness. *Common corundum* is generally cloudy, minutely seamed and cracked, and otherwise completely unsuited for any ornamental application although in some cases vividly-colored specimens are suitable for cabochon work.

The name corundum is a modified form of the Sanskrit word *korund* of unknown original significance except for its application to this mineral species, while sapphire is derived from the ancient Greek word for "blue." It appears that the latter term may have been applied originally to other blue gemstones, most likely lapis-lazuli, and was later attached to the blue variety of corundum. Ruby receives its name from the Latin *ruber*, meaning "red." Like sapphire, this term was also applied indiscriminately to any hard transparent red gemstone and was only affixed to red corundum within the last several hundred years. When corundum gems were introduced into Europe and England during Medieval times, their exact identity was unknown and they were frequently confused with the mineral species spinel which occurs in a similar gamut of colors in the gem deposits of the Far East.

In composition, corundum is aluminum oxide with the formula Al_2O_3 and if entirely pure would be colorless. To the delight of mankind it is seldom so, the slight traces of iron, chromium, titanium, and other metallic elements imparting splendid colors which make clear specimens prized as gems. The presence of chromium imparts the beautiful red of ruby while the blue of sapphire is caused by titanium and iron together. Chromium combined with oxygen as chromic oxide fits neatly into the crystal structure of corundum and tends therefore to impart uniform coloration to ruby. On the other hand, titanium, iron, and oxygen combine to form the mineral ilmenite which is not capable of fitting itself so nicely into the crystal lattice, tending to collect in clouds, patches or zones and imparting corresponding irregularities in coloration. In similar manner, other impurities give rise to uneven color distribution, sometimes causing several bands or patches of contrasting hue to appear within the same crystal.

Corundum crystallizes in the Hexagonal System and ordinarily appears in prismatic crystals of hexagonal outline, some shaped like small stubby barrels, others very much flattened and wafer-like, and still others which form long bipyramidal crystals tapering toward each extremity. There is a marked tendency for ruby to form flattened crystals with large basal planes ruled with triangular markings whereas sapphire prefers to crystallize in more elongated forms. Brilliantly smooth faces are largely absent on crystals and edges tend to be rounded while all surfaces are more or less deeply etched. Prism faces are often highly irregular or missing altogether, causing indefinite outlines as in the sapphire crystals from Yogo Gulch, Montana. River crystals from the same state often show recognizable hexagonal outlines although many stones are simply rounded masses.

Crystal forms are illustrated in Figure 13. In size, corundum crystals range from scarcely larger than a pinhead to some enormous coarse specimens which may reach several hundred pounds in weight; however, like so many other gemstones, large crystals very rarely contain much gem material.

The hardness of corundum on the Mohs Scale is 9 but decided variations are noted according to crystal directions, sometimes causing difficulties in cutting and polishing. Gem grade material of compact structure shows no

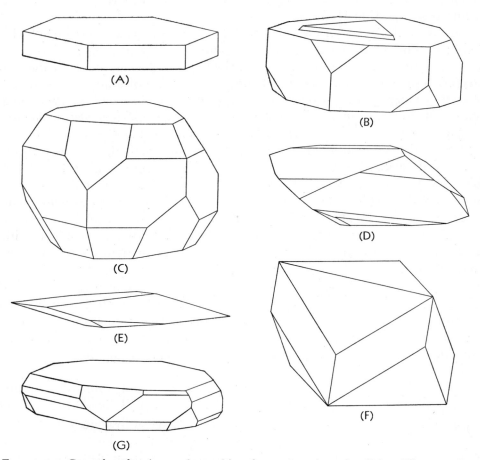

FIGURE 13. Crystals of ruby and sapphire from American localities. The common tabular habits of sapphire from Missouri River gravel and Ruby from Cowee Creek are shown in *a* and *b*; some ruby crystals from Cowee Creek also take the form noted in *c* but this form is most common in the sapphire crystals of the Missouri River. The thin, almost formless crystals from Yogo Gulch, would, if perfectly developed, look like drawings *d* and *e*. Another Missouri River crystal is shown in *f*, while *g* represents a form common in Rock Creek.

trace of cleavage, breaking with difficulty into glassy fracture fragments. In many types, however, parting planes almost as perfect as cleavages appear parallel to rhombohedral crystal faces or sometimes parallel to basal planes due to repeated twinning upon these planes. Material of this sort shatters readily into numerous angular fragments resembling cubes; much of the corundum from the Eastern United States is of this kind.

The specific gravity of gem varieties varies from 3.96 to 4.01 although if all varieties are included, the values would range from 3.91 to 4.10. The average value of gem material is very close to 4.0. Refractive indices range from $\omega = 1.770$-1.779 to $\epsilon = 1.759$-1.767; the birefringence is low, 0.008, while the dispersion is also low, only 0.018. The lack of dispersion causes colorless or nearly colorless gems to be less valued than strongly colored varieties. The optical character of corundum is uniaxial, negative.

Corundum occurs in many colors, the best known, of course, being the deep rich somewhat purplish-red of ruby and the blue of sapphire which can vary from dark inky purplish-blue to lovely rich pure blue to numerous shades of greenish-blue. Other colors occur in many tints of green, purple, yellow, orange, etc. Many ruby and sapphire crystals include several coloring agents in the same specimen since distinct banding, zoning, and clouds or patches of varying color are often seen. Combinations of blue and colorless, blue and yellow, and blue and red are also found. When several colors are present, a third color may result from their fusion, e.g., purple results from extremely thin alternate bands of blue and red.

Dichroism is distinct to strong in all richly colored specimens but yellow examples seldom display more than a slight change of shade if any can be detected at all.

DICHROIC COLORS IN AMERICAN CORUNDUM

BASIC COLOR	DICHROIC COLORS	
Cowee Creek, N. C.		
Red	purplish-red	orange-red
Yogo Gulch, Mont.		
Blue	blue	pale grayish green-blue
Blue	deep blue	pale blue
Purple	purple	pale grayish-green
Missouri River, Mont.		
Gray blue	blue	yellowish-green
Pale gray blue	very pale grayish-blue	very pale yellow-green
Pale blue	very pale purplish-blue	almost colorless
Pale violet	pale reddish-violet	very pale yellowish-green
Yellow	yellow	yellow
Orange	orange	yellow
Pink	pale purplish-pink	very pale yellow

Asterism and chatoyancy are generally absent from North American corundum although exceptions are noted. Some of the Montana river crystals display a strong silvery sheen when cut in cabochon form, owing this effect to the presence of exceedingly thin inclusions or partings parallel to the basal plane. Under the microscope, these inclusions look like miniature snowflakes and are concentrated most thickly near the centers of crystals. Some specimens of this sort display a feeble star when cut. At one North Carolina locality, a peculiar color-zoned blue corundum was once obtained which showed white bands intersecting at 60° to form six-legged crosses against a dark blue background, somewhat reminiscent of true stars but lacking their silky sheen and movement. These so-called "stars" are due entirely to mechanical structure and not to inclusions of rutile "silk" in distinct needles as is the case in genuine star stones. Some of the adamantine spar found in this state and elsewhere displays a very strong bronzy luster which is said to be due to numerous platelets of hematite oriented parallel to the basal plane of the crystal.

LOCALITIES

Alaska. Star sapphire of grayish color and star ruby are said to occur on the Copper River in the Juneau Indian Reservation of Southeastern Alaska.

North West Territories. Deep blue sapphire crystals up to ½ inch in diameter occur with quartz, mica, and andalusite, in veins cutting schist at the Philmore Mine on the Fox Group of Islands near the east-central end of Great Slave Lake in the Mackenzie District. The color of the crystals is said to be good cobalt-blue but transparent areas are not large enough to afford faceted gems although cabochons may perhaps be practical.

British Columbia. Minute grains of ruby have been found in gravels of some of the creeks tributary to the Tulameen River. A fine light green gem quality sapphire pebble of ¼ inch diameter was found in gold gravel in the Pend Oreille River, a tributary of the Columbia in the West Kootenay District.

Ontario. Rose and blue corundum occurs in metamorphic limestone on Lot 2, Concession IX in northern Burgess Township, Hastings County. Small transparent portions provide minute gems. East of York River in Dungannon Township on Lot 12, Concession XIV, in the same county, deep blue crystals occur in syenite and provide small clear areas suitable for minute faceted gems. An excellent specimen from this locality was exhibited as a "true" sapphire at the Pan-American Exhibition held in Buffalo in 1901. A gray-blue cabochon showing a feeble star weighing 4.6 carats has been cut from this material by a Canadian collector. In Peterborough County near the boundary between Methuen and Burleigh townships, on Lot 7, Concession XII (of

Burleigh), red syenite contains an abundance of corundum crystals mainly greenish-gray in color but sometimes blue in the centers. This material approaches gem quality but so far has not been found clear enough to facet. The chatoyant variety of adamantine spar occurs here also and can be cut into gems of bronzy luster. At this locality, the corundum-bearing syenite outcrops as a ridge along the shore of Stoney Lake and extends further to the northeast. Similar material from the large commercial deposit at Craigmont, Raglan Township, Renfrew County, has occasionally been cut into cabochons.

New Jersey. Small clear areas in red and blue corundum crystals found in the metamorphic limestone quarries of Newton, Franklin, and Sparta, Sussex County, occasionally afford poor quality faceted gems. Many years ago a small pocket containing beautifully crystallized transparent sapphires was discovered in metamorphic limestone on the shore of the pond on the Wallkill River in Franklin, Sussex County incident to preparing a foundation for the old iron blast furnace. The colors of the crystals were said to be bluish-gray and red. Pockets containing similar crystals have been found from time to time along the contact between the metamorphic limestone and its enclosing rocks from Franklin southward to Sterling Hill at Ogdensburg.

Pennsylvania. A corundum pit on a farm about ¼ mile south of Morgan Station in Aston Township, Delaware County, once yielded large brown crystals which could be cut into chatoyant cabochon gems; similar crystals were found in albite and loose in the soil in and around old corundum pits about ¼ mile south of Black Horse in a field on the west side of the road leading to Elwyn, Middletown Township. In Lehigh County, asteriated corundum crystals were found as large barrel-shaped individuals up to 6 inches in length at a locality ¾ mile north of Shimersville in Upper Milford Township.

North Carolina. The principal deposits of corundum in the Eastern United States occur in peridotitic rocks which outcrop in many places along a belt which extends from the Gaspe Peninsula in Canada to Tallapoosa County in Alabama. These rocks cut ancient crystalline rocks of the eastern part of the continent and although much altered, appear originally to be of igneous origin. In North Carolina, commercial corundum has been mined from deposits in several counties but gem material has come only from Jackson, Macon, and Clay counties in the southwestern section.

In Jackson County, small bits of gem quality corundum have been found in the gravels of streams near Sapphire almost on the border of Transylvania County. Several corundum mines once operated in the vicinity and from the Sapphire and Whitewater mines, some small clear blue pieces were obtained. At Montvale, the gravels of a small local stream yielded some gem quality ruby and blue and yellow sapphire crystals, which, when traced to their origin, were found to come from a narrow vein in decomposed peridotite.

In Macon County, commercial corundum, occasionally yielding facet material, was mined extensively at Corundum Hill located 4½ miles east-southeast of Franklin on the south slope of Higdon Mountain, ½ mile north of Highway 64, just west of Crows Branch, a small creek which enters the Cullasaja River at this point (see Figure 14). Culsagee Mine on this hill ex-

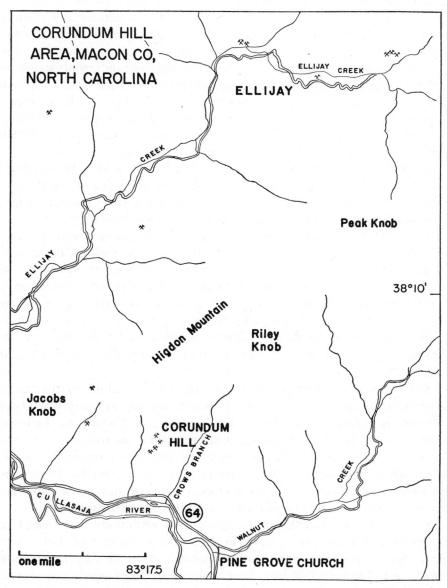

FIGURE 14. The Corundum Hill-Ellijay Area of Macon County, North Carolina, showing the principal mines and access roads.

ploited lenses and rounded masses of coarsely crystallized common corundum enclosed in dunite. The dunite body outcrops over an area of about 10 acres and has been opened in several places in search of corundum concentrations. In this locality as in others in this state and further south, corundum occurs as doubly-terminated barrel-shaped crystals or as nodules or masses of irregular form. Gem material was found in small crystals or as clear areas in large crystals or masses. One of the crystals from this locality weighed 312 pounds and contained several small clear areas of deep blue color. Many of the small crystals showed various shades of pink deepening to the red of ruby along the exteriors or at the ends. Good blue sapphire was found also as well as yellow and green material, sometimes with several colors combined in one specimen. A fine deep blue crystal measuring 4 by 2½ inches is in the Bement Collection in the American Museum of Natural History. None of the cut gems from this locality were much over one carat in weight although often of good color.

At the Mincey Mine near the small community of Ellijay on a branch of the North Prong of Ellijay Creek, 6½ miles east of Franklin, some facet grade ruby was produced in early mining days but this locality was principally noted for its bronzy corundum which could be cut into chatoyant gems or even into star gems (see Figure 14). Locally this material was known as "pearl corundum," a not unsuitable name in view of its decided luster. Most of this material occurred in rough prismatic crystals often so richly contaminated by hematite inclusions as to appear black. Cabochons up to ⅔ inch diameter and of fine luster have been cut from this variety as for example one of 10.69 carats in the U.S. National Museum.

The most important Macon County locality by far is that of Cowee Creek, noted for its production of ruby crystals from alluvial gravels filling the valley floor. The ruby area is shown in Figure 15 and lies in a broad basin through which flow Cowee Creek and Caler Fork of Cowee Creek. Cowee Creek empties into the Little Tennessee River at Wests Mill on Highway 28 about 6 miles north of Franklin. Testing operations have shown the presence of ruby for about 3 miles upstream from the mouth. The ruby tract lies at average elevations of slightly over 2000 feet above sea level with surrounding peaks and knobs reaching heights of 500 to 1000 feet above the valley floor. The gravels in which the gemstones occur are covered by topsoil and loam averaging 2 feet in depth but varying from as little as one foot to a maximum of 5 feet. Gravel consists primarily of waterworn masses of quartz and small pieces of gneiss, or gneiss and quartz derived from adjacent country rocks of the same type. Excavations to bedrock show the latter to be hornblende gneiss. No ruby has been found in this rock but upon a small ridge called In Situ Hill, about 3 miles upstream from the mouth of Cowee Creek, cloudy crystals have been found in some quantity but there is much doubt

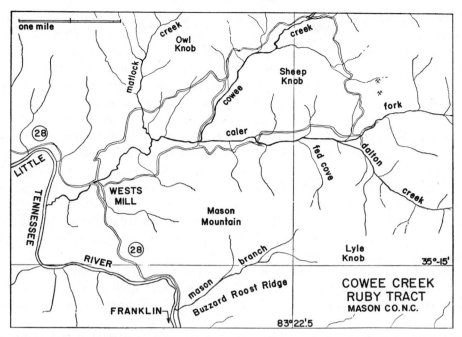

FIGURE 15. The Cowee Creek Ruby Tract in Macon County, North Carolina, showing the principal roads and streams. Mason Branch was formerly noted for its abundance of fine rhodolite garnet, however, ruby was found only in the gravels of Cowee Creek valley.

that the rock from which they were mined is the same which released gem quality specimens to the stream gravels. In the gravels, ruby crystals are found associated with rhodolite garnet crystals of irregular form and sand-blasted surface finish but also sometimes as small dodecahedral crystals, quartz, corundum of pale blue, amethystine and pink shades, black spinel (pleonaste), zinc spinel (gahnite) in octahedral crystals, chromite, rutile, ilmenite, bronzite, tremolite, hornblende, colorless iolite, kyanite, fibrolite, small fragments of perfectly transparent staurolite, monazite in small crystals, zircon in minute brilliant crystals, pyrite, and even some gold. Ruby crystals show various forms, first as flat waferlike individuals of hexagonal outline with edges beveled by rhombohedral faces, and second, as distinct hexagonal prisms terminated by simple basal planes (see Fig. 13). The latter vary from flattened tabular crystals to some which are twice as long as they are thick. Many crystals show typical triangular ruby markings and hillocks developed upon basal planes. Inclusions of rutile "silk" are frequently seen in some but others contain coarse black spots of rutile and ilmenite. Crystals containing fine inclusions of rutile sometimes can be cut into respectable star stones. The vast majority of crystals are small, perhaps averaging several stones per carat, but large specimens up to 30 carats have been found although seldom in gem grade. In 1955, it was reported that a crystal of 25 carats weight of good quality was found and estimated to be worth at least $3000; in 1954 a ruby crystal of $250 value was found. During active commercial mining many years ago, crystals large enough to cut gems of from 3 to 4 carats, absolutely clean and of fine color, were found but as a general rule, cut gems did not exceed one or two carats. The best color was stated to be equal to that of Burmese ruby, generally conceded to be the finest in the world.

Systematic mining of the Cowee Creek gravels commenced in 1895 under the direction of the American Prospecting and Mining Company of New York City. Hydraulic methods were used to wash the gravels, topsoil and small gravel being diverted into a series of sluice boxes which led to a sieve box, and thence into a rocker where further concentration was obtained. Concentrated gravels were then picked over by hand to separate the gemstones, including rhodolite garnet which occurred in some abundance. One of the early plants for washing gravel is shown in Figure 16. Placering operations continued for a number of years past the turn of the century and confined themselves mainly to the stretch of Cowee Creek between a point about

FIGURE 16. An old photograph (1897) of the ruby and rhodolite garnet diggings along Cowee Creek, North Carolina during the period when the mines were under the management of W. E. Hidden. Miners are digging gravel in the background which is then delivered to the washing rig at the left where crystals were separated from the worthless pebbles. The man in the foreground is seated at the sorting table. Courtesy U.S. Geological Survey.

1½ miles upstream from Wests Mill to about 3½ miles upstream close to In Situ Hill where the stream branches. When red corundum was found upon In Situ Hill in 1907, an exploratory shaft was sunk upon the corundum-bearing rock by the United States Ruby Mining Company and from this working a considerable quantity of material was removed. However, the best proved to be only translucent and bore little resemblance to the stones found in the stream. Work was stopped in this same year but resumed in 1913 by the Consolidated Ruby Company of New York City who undertook the extension of underground workings and a program of core drilling in an attempt to explore the underground ore body. Since results were discouraging, work ceased in 1914. In 1949, Sherman McMillen of New York City carried on systematic placering at the junction of Dalton Branch and Caler Fork but results were not announced. No formal mining has taken place since that year but today a considerable number of vacationers and visitors try their hand at panning the gravels as at the Gibson Ruby Mine about 2 miles upstream from Wests Mill and upon the Will Holbrook property nearby. A small fee for the privilege is obtained at both places.

In Clay County, much commercial abrasive corundum has been mined from the Cullakanee Mine in the Buck Creek area located in the eastern part of the county about 6 miles north of the Georgia line and about 20 miles southwest of Franklin. The Cat Eye Cut, about 600 feet southwest of Chestnut Knob was once famous for its production of a peculiar white corundum in which streaks of dark blue radiating outward from the centers of crystals formed six-legged "stars." These stars are not to be confused with the true asterias which owe their effect to numerous silky inclusions in transparent material. Locally, this mechanical pattern of color distribution caused such stones to be known as *cat eye corundum*. At the Cullakanee Mine and also at Elf on Shooting Creek, bright red corundum nodules distributed throughout emerald green amphibolite provided a handsome ornamental stone which is described elsewhere in this book.

Georgia. Corundum has been found in almost every northern county of this state but rarely in gem quality. Very small transparent areas within much larger crystals and masses of common corundum have provided minute faceted gems. The Laurel Creek Mine in Rabun County has produced some fine red material which is only semi-transparent at best and therefore fitted only for cabochons.

Alabama. Near Bradford, Coosa County, dark brown chatoyant corundum crystals have been found which were sometimes cut to show a six-rayed star.

Indiana. Bronzy chatoyant corundum, sometimes cuttable into handsome gems, has been found as waterworn pebbles in the glacial gravels of Morgan County. One productive locality is the bed of Highland Creek about 7 miles north-northwest of Martinsville where the gravels also contain magnetite, hematite, pyrite, ilmenite, garnet, zircon, and gold. Many basic igneous rock boulders are present in the bed of this stream and it is apparently from similar rocks that the corundum and some of the other minerals are derived (see p. 40).

Iowa. A curious but scarcely significant discovery of sapphire took place in 1912 when a stone resembling a piece of blue bottle glass was found along the shore of Lake Okoboji in Dickinson County. Examination showed this "glass" to be fine sapphire and from the pebble was cut a splendid gem of 1 3/8 carats.

Colorado. Transparent deep blue sapphire crystals up to 1/4 inch in diameter sometimes occur in schist adjacent to the iron ore body in the old Calumet Iron Mine located about 1/4 mile south of the former town site of Calumet City and about 3 miles west of the ghost town of Turret in Chaffee County.

Montana. The tremendous importance of the sapphire deposits of this state can only be realized from the statistics of production. Some authorities place the total value of industrial and gem sapphire produced to date between $3 and $5,000,000, with the Yogo Gulch mines accounting for about $2,500,-000 of the total in gemstones mostly up until the time they were shut down in 1929. Cut gems from the latter mines probably have a present day value of close to $25,000,000. During the period from 1936 to 1943, it has been estimated that alluvial deposits produced annually from $20 to $50,000 worth of industrial grade stones. The possibility that such production will be resumed in the future is very slim inasmuch as synthetic sapphire has taken over many of the tasks which natural stones once fulfilled, i.e., watch-bearings, instrument bearings, drawing dies, etc., nevertheless reserves of productive ground both in the dike at Yogo Gulch and in the gravels of the Missouri River and other streams in Montana are high.

Sapphire crystals were first discovered in Montana in the gravels of the Missouri River in 1865 in the deposits northeast of Helena, Lewis & Clark County. The beds, typical of others along the Missouri River, are layers of gravel lying upon terraces rising as much as 200 feet above river level. Although not actually within the confines of the river they are locally called "bars" and will be referred to as such. Because of their importance in the production of gold, each was given a name of its own. Crystals were most abundant in the Eldorado Bar located about 12 miles northeast of Helena but stones were found as far upstream as Emerald Bar and at the lower end of Magpie Gulch; in the opposite direction, sapphire was recovered from no further downstream than the American Bar. The gem-bearing gravels rest upon argillaceous rocks of the Belt series, containing debris ranging from sand to boulders several feet in diameter. Thickness varies but reaches as much as

40 feet in places. Below the city of Helena is situated a tremendous "flat" or bar which has been systematically dredged for gold, producing large quantities of sapphire crystals at the same time. Usual methods of dredging employ an enormous floating dredge which digs away gravel ahead of itself, passing the material inside where it is concentrated and the gold and sapphire extracted, and the rubbish disposed of to the rear in semi-circular piles of geometrical neatness. These huge "windrows" of gravel are still easily visible in many gold-mining regions of the West as well as in Montana. The origin of Missouri River sapphire is puzzling since no in place deposits have been found whose size would account for the enormous quantities of gemstones found in the river beds, however, it is now believed that the gravels represent remnants of local rocks stranded by erosion as the present river cut down its channel in the course of geologic time. The gravels have therefore traveled only a short distance. In 1889, a sapphire-bearing dike was discovered penetrating argillaceous rocks near French Bar about 6 miles southeast of Eldorado Bar. This dike is only 2 to 2 ½ feet in thickness and consists of an extremely fine-grained rock composed primarily of feldspar, biotite, augite, and an unidentified glassy material; it may be called a mica-augite andesite in which sapphire occurs only sparingly and it may be assumed that its erosion accounted only for a minute fraction of all stones found in the river.

Associated with sapphire in the river gravels are: gold, generally fine, garnet, topaz, kyanite, cassiterite (stream tin), chalcedony, and limonite replacing pyrite. The garnet is bright red, orange-red, or reddish-pink and frequently of gem quality though small in size; this material was identified incorrectly in earlier days as spinel. Sapphire crystals rarely exceed ¼ to ½ inch in diameter and are largely some shade of pale blue or blue green. Much of the blue is grayish in cast and results in gems which are not particularly attractive. Strong decided blue shades of pure hue are very rare but light blue, light pink, light green, pale red, purplish-blue, purple, decided green, yellow, orange, and other colors are known. Pink and reddish-purple crystals sometimes show peculiar brownish tints when observed through the sides. A dark blue-green stone is on record which showed the properties of alexandrite chrysoberyl, appearing distinctly reddish-purple in artificial light and normal color in daylight. Colors are frequently zoned with the faintest shade being in the crystal center; others are reversed and show the deepest color in the middle. Many show a silky sheen or pearly luster upon basal planes due to numerous minute platelets of hexagonal "snowflake" pattern or sometimes rods or openings. These inclusions are believed to be *negative* crystals. Most cavities are very small, no more than .055 mm, and being flat rather than long and narrow, cause only a silvery gleam in cut gems rather than asterism.

Missouri River crystals are rough and pitted, showing well-defined faces

only rarely (Fig. 13). This rough exterior is believed to be due to partial dissolution or etching within host rocks and not the result of stream abrasion.
However, many crystals have been found which are beautifully rounded and
smooth-surfaced and undoubtedly did suffer some degree of wear.

The use of Missouri River sapphire crystals for gems began shortly after
their discovery in 1865 when a stone was sent for cutting to Tiffany & Company of New York City. An English company was organized to mine sapphire and gold from the Eldorado Bar and adjacent bars in 1889, but after a
short period of operation, suspended work because so few of the pale colored
stones met public approval. During 1889 the gravels of the Metropolitan Bar
were worked for gold and some sapphire was produced as a byproduct. About
1890, several smaller companies worked the Spokane and Emerald bars and
the ground at the mouth of Prickly Pear Creek but in each case mining was
not long sustained. After these early years of generally unprofitable mining,
a long period of inactivity ensued until dams were built upon the river to
raise the water level and permit dredging operations. Large-scale continuous
operation afforded by dredges now made it economical to mine gold and of
course to recover large numbers of sapphire crystals in the process. During
1940 to 1944, the Perry-Schroeder Company of Helena operated a gold
dredge at the Eldorado Bar and recovered about 50,000 ounces of sapphire,
the majority of which was sold for industrial purposes. Upon occasion, the
yield dropped to as low as 0.4 ounces per 100 cubic yards. Larger stones
weighing from 4 to 7 carats were saved for gem purposes, selling from $.25 to
$1.00 per carat. Colors were mostly pale greenish-blue. Prices received for
industrial stones during this period were from $1 to $2 per ounce but declined
sharply after 1943 when synthetic manufacturing processes in the United
States were perfected and production of this substitute greatly increased.
Although no formal records of production from Missouri River bars have
been kept over the years, it seems reasonable to estimate that a total of over
100,000 ounces of sapphire has been recovered.

The famous Yogo Gulch "cornflower" blue sapphire was discovered
quite by accident. As the story goes, a gold placer mining company organized
to work the gravels lying east of the Yogo Fork of the Judith River spent
the entire summer of 1895 accumulating a miserly return of only $700 in gold
but also a large number of small, heavy, blue stones which appeared in every
"clean up." A cigar-box full collected at the time was dispatched to Tiffany
& Company in New York City who recognized them immediately as fine sapphire and reportedly paid $3750 for the lot. Actually, Yogo Gulch and Yogo
Creek had been prospected as early as 1879 when gold was discovered in the
gravels and its presence setting off a miniature "gold rush" which resulted in
several hectic years of mining and even caused the establishment of the town
of Yogo which at one time numbered from 1200 to 1500 souls. However,

the gravels were quickly depleted and by 1883 the district was all but deserted. Whether or not sapphire crystals were found during this time is a matter of conjecture but it seems scarcely possible that they could have been avoided. The discovery of the actual source of sapphire, an igneous dike intruded into limestone, is credited to a settler in the neighboring Judith River Valley, John Ettien, who in 1896 found crystals in the decomposed dike outcropping on top of the hills above the gulch. This put an end to speculation about their source, especially the theory advanced that the gravels in which they were found by the company mentioned above represented the debris of an old and elevated channel of Yogo Creek.

Yogo Gulch is located in Judith Basin County about 45 miles southwest of Lewiston or about 15 miles southwest of Utica from which town it is reached by road. The sapphire-bearing dike outcrops at an elevation 5000 feet above sea level and has been traced along the surface for almost five miles. Its strike is west-southwest to east-northeast and its dip nearly vertical. The average width as exposed in underground workings is 8 feet with some sections expanding to as much as 20 feet. At its eastern end, the dike crosses gently rolling grasslands while on the west, it is intersected by steep-walled Yogo and Kelly Gulches. The dike is intruded into Madison limestones of Mississippian age and in one place, into shales of the Amsden formation. A view of Yogo Gulch showing the limestone cliffs and an early mine working is shown in Figure 17. In the early days, the outcrop of the easily-weathered dike was marked by a shallow depression pockmarked by gopher holes and mounds of debris brought by these animals to the surface. A very similar dike occurs about 600 feet north but despite intensive testing has failed to show signs of any sapphire. At the surface and for some distance below, the dike rock is altered to a soft yellow or gray clay which fills the spaces between boulders of iron-stained limestone. Alteration extends to as much as 250 to 300 feet below the surface where the dike rock consists of easily-crumbled greenish-gray material and blue clay containing masses of unaltered rock and bits of limestone caught up by the intrusion of the igneous mass. The dike rock proper is fine textured and from its composition and other features, most closely approximates a type of igneous rock known as *ouachitite*. The principal constituents are pyroxene and biotite but many other accessory minerals are present, i.e., analcite, apatite, magnetite, zircon, hematite, feldspar, spinel, aegerite-diopside, zeolites, and calcite with dolomite present as vein fillings.

Sapphire crystals appear to be uniformly distributed throughout the dike and mining merely consisted of removing all dike rock encountered in the most systematic and efficient manner possible. In earlier days, outcrop material which was already severely decomposed was washed by hydraulic methods into a series of sluice boxes in which the heavy sapphire crystals were

FIGURE 17. The American Sapphire Mine in Yogo Gulch, Montana in 1912; view look-ing northeast across the gulch. The steep cliffs are limestone and is the rock in which the sapphire-bearing dike is intruded. At the extreme right as marked by the arrow, the narrow defile created by removal of the dike rock is still to be seen. Courtesy U.S. Geological Survey.

trapped. Later, underground tunnelling and drifting were adopted, mined material of firmer consistency being spread out upon the ground to weather and disintegrate prior to washing. Still later, it was found best to crush all material to a size best suited to recover the maximum yield of stones without being too fine to cause destruction of larger crystals. One authority who visited these mines during operation stated that from 1200 to 1500 carats of cuttable sapphire were recovered from every 20 cubic yards of material. Another authority stated that several thousand carats were won from every 100 loads although the size of each load was not specified; still another au-thority estimates the yield was probably from 20 to 50 carats per ton of rock.

The overwhelming majority of Yogo crystals are merely flattened wafers of approximately circular outline, often with tapered edges and like miniature pancakes in form. Crystal faces are virtually absent but sometimes are observed in larger specimens (Fig. 13). When removed from the rock each crystal is found to be coated with a layer of black material a fraction of a millimeter in thickness and apparently a granular aggregate of spinel, probably derived from alteration of the sapphire. Crystals or pieces over 2 carats are rare and the majority of gems cut from them do not exceed one carat in weight. In 1910, the largest stone ever found in the deposit proved to be a flattened specimen of 19 carats but because of its unfavorable form, the largest gem which could be cut from it was only 8½ carats. In 1919, a 10 carat crystal of superb color yielded a faceted gem of 5 carats which sold for approximately $1600 in Hatton Garden, London. The small size of the stones was often said to be the reason why the mines closed, sometimes a whole year of mining going by without a crystal over 3 or 4 carats being found. Of the total yield, about 75% was classed as industrial material because of small size.

Yogo sapphire crystals are exceptionally clear, flawless, and free of any inclusions, their suitability for gems being merely a question of size. This internal perfection is reflected in their toughness and fracture, the latter being conchoidal and glassy in luster. Specific gravity varies according to color, bright blue stones showing values of 4.001 to 4.003, nearly colorless giving 4.000, while reddish-purple specimens give 3.980. Colors vary from light to rather dark blue of the true cornflower tint so highly prized in sapphire, and resembling not at all similar hues noted in the river stones found elsewhere in this state. Some crystals are amethystine in hue while others of great rarity are true ruby red. However, the vast majority are simple blue showing no color zoning and remarkably perfect internally. An analysis of colors found in these crystals shows that 60 per cent are blue, 22 per cent carry some tint of purple or violet, 16 per cent are very pale blue or almost colorless, and only 2 per cent are decidedly purple. The former caretaker of the mine stated that in 30 years of mining, only 4 true rubies were produced. In earlier days, Yogo sapphire crystals brought from $5 to $25 per carat depending on size, later on in 1901, they brought from $30 to $75, while in relatively recent years, a 10 carat crystal brought $400. Poorer grades and stones too small to be cut were classed as industrials and sold from $2 to $6 per ounce and were highly regarded in the watchmaking industry because their form required less work to prepare them into finished jewels.

Historically, the Yogo Gulch mines received little attention until a considerable number of years after the discovery of sapphire. About 1896 or shortly after the dike deposit was discovered, an American company organized under the name of the New Mine Sapphire Syndicate attempted to obtain commitments from a domestic jewelry firm to handle the output of the mine; failing to arouse interest they sent an agent to London where a much warmer reception was found. As a result, a British firm was organized in 1898 to accept and market the output and later, after acquiring the shares of the original American organizers, came into full control of the mine. From 1902 to 1905, under British control and capital, mining was pressed vigorously, resulting in the production of about one million carats of crystals whose sale returned about $40,000 each year. In 1910, about 70,000 carats of gem material were mined along with 2000 ounces of industrials. The largest gem, the 19 carat crystal mentioned previously, was mined in this year along with a 12 carat stone from which a fine gem of 4⅜ carats was cut. During 1911 and 1912, production increased to 440,000 carats of industrials and 90,000 carats of gem grade crystals per year. By the summer of 1914, the entire deposit was in the hands of the British syndicate when American interests mining the western end of the dike failed to make a success of it. However, the intervention of war at this time curtailed mining operations and the only significant production came from reworking the tailings of the American mine from which a considerable number of crystals was obtained. Up to 1920, mining was fated to be interrupted by a variety of causes but in that year the highest production of any year except 1913 was recorded. In 1921 the value of gems mined reached almost $500,000, almost twice as much as any previous year. In 1923 disaster in the form of a cloudburst struck the workings causing considerable damage from which recovery was slow. Production gradually tapered for the next several years to a value of only $4860 in 1927, and, as increased taxes, higher labor costs, and the declining markets for small gems imposed further troubles, the mine was shut down in 1929. I have been informed by Hugh Leiper that the Yogo mine has resumed production. Information received by him from Thomas Sitwell of Billings, Montana and Beverly Hills, California, indicates that production reached 20,000 carats in 1958 of which 20 percent was gem quality. Production is expected to increase to 100,000 carats in 1959 as cleaning out of old workings and weathering of sapphire-bearing rock proceeds. The larger stones are being cut in the United States while the smaller are being sent to Germany and Siam for cutting.

Good Yogo Gulch sapphire gems are not common in private or public collections since most were not marketed in the United States, however, the American Museum of Natural History owns a series of splendid examples up to ½ inch in diameter of typical fine blue color.

Large quantities of sapphire destined primarily for industrial uses have been mined in the vicinity of Rock Creek, located about 16 miles southwest of Phillipsburg, Granite County. Some of these crystals proved to be suitable for faceted gems and a number were diverted to this purpose. Sapphire-bearing gravels at the Rock Creek locality underlie two small tributaries of Rock Creek which enter from the north side of its west fork. The westernmost

FIGURE 18. American Gem Syndicate sapphire mine on the west fork of Rock Creek, 20 miles southwest of Phillipsburg, Montana. Photo taken about 1914. The process of hydraulic mining for sapphire in the creek bed gravels is illustrated and involves the use of a head of water taken from the dam in the background and directed by a hose against the sapphire-bearing soil and gravel. Courtesy U.S. Geological Survey.

gulch is known as Anaconda Gulch while the other is called Sapphire Gulch, formerly known as Meyer Gulch. Figure 18 shows hydraulic operations conducted some years ago in the area. Bedrocks consist of argillites overlaid by volcanic rocks but the exact geology is obscured by the heavy covering of soil and vegetation. Gravels vary in thickness from 8 to 10 feet and form beds of from 30 to 100 feet wide. As yet, Rock Creek sapphire crystals have not been found in rocks of origin and from their waterworn condition, it may be safely assumed that they have been carried some distance by streams although their limited distribution suggests local origin.

Older accounts of Rock Creek crystals described their colors in glowing terms and spoke of "rich" hues or otherwise employed superlatives leading one to believe that here lay a deposit of magnificent gemstones. However, though occurring in perhaps greater variety of color than at Helena and other places where stream crystals have been found, there is actually very little difference in both quality and intensity of color; the majority are pale and some are merely dull or only translucent. Irregular distribution of color is common, many stones showing faded exteriors with bright spots of color confined to their centers. Locally, crystals of two colors are called "pintos." One investigator, privileged to examine a large parcel of small gems discarded from screenings, found that dull translucent bluish-gray stones comprised 33% of the lot, colorless to faintly tinted 16%, pale yellow to greenish-yellow 13%, pale bluish-green to pale yellowish-green 22%, pale blue to greenish-blue only 8%, and pink, orange, and purple gems comprised only 5%. An additional 3% were dark gray, brown, and greenish-brown, commonly showing chatoyancy or even faint asterism. The chatoyancy of Rock Creek sapphire is due to the same causes noted under crystals found in the Missouri River gravels but sometimes darker stones contain sufficient inclusions properly arranged to form small star gems. In these crystals, rutile needles have been determined as the cause of asterism as well as being the cause of the brown color. Crystals range in size from ¼ to ½ inch but larger specimens are common. Some crystals show sharp faces but the majority are well rounded and etched; unlike the barrel-shaped crystals common in the Missouri River, Rock Creek crystals are mainly thick crude tablets of hexagonal outline about as tall as they are wide.

Sapphire was discovered during placer gold mining in the Rock Creek area about 1892. Early acounts mention the richness of the deposits, stating that every pan of concentrated gravel contained numbers of crystals, however, recent experience indicates a much lesser concentration. About 1894, a production of 75 pounds was reported while from 1899 to 1900, 400,000 carats were recovered of which 25,000 were stated as suitable for cutting. Of the total Montana sapphire production of 86,000 ounces in 1911, of which 384,000 carats were gem material, most came from Rock Creek. During the late 1920's, production averaged about 20,000 ounces per year while from 1939 to 1943, the average was 10,000 ounces. In 1942, most of the 50,000 ounces produced in that year was diverted into the government stockpile as a hedge against loss of supplies of synthetic sapphire from abroad. Mining employs hydraulic methods principally, similar in many respects to the techniques used in gold mining. The water is brought from higher elevations by flume and directed against the gravel beds by hoses and nozzles. The finer material is directed into a series of riffled troughs where the heavier minerals are concentrated and the crystals picked out by hand (see Figure 18).

In Deer Lodge County, numerous sapphire crystals similar to Rock Creek and Missouri River stones have been found in the gravels of Dry Cottonwood Creek. This stream originates near the Continental Divide about 12 miles northwest of Butte, flowing westward to join Clark Fork about 11 miles south of the town of Deer Lodge. Most mining has taken place in the upper 4 miles of the south fork of Dry Cottonwood Creek. Sample pans taken from the gravels as high as 6500 feet altitude and almost at the head-waters show the presence of sapphire. Although a ledge supposedly containing sapphire in place has been reported, there is no confirmation.

Sapphire from Dry Cottonwood Creek occurs in rough crystals showing rounded faces, also as irregular masses and much waterworn pebbles. Those which show little water wear are etched and corroded and the low proportion of waterworn crystals indicates that most originated from rocks not too far distant. The proportion of gem quality crystals is low as it is elsewhere in similar Montana deposits. Predominant colors are deep and light greenish-blue and pale yellowish-green; others are light blue, light and dark yellow, straw yellow, yellowish-green somewhat like peridot, light and dark pink, rarely ruby red, lilac, and pale amethyst. A few stones are virtually colorless. Dichroism in bluish stones is markedly green and blue. A number of interesting crystals from this locality showed pink spots in the center of pale blue material and furnished very attractive faceted gems. Deep pinks from this deposit keep their color well under artificial light. A few red and brownish garnet crystals have been found associated with the sapphire.

Sapphire crystals are said to have been found in Dry Cottonwood Creek in 1889 but no important recovery work was done until 1907. About 1893 some 25 pounds of crystals were recovered during a few day's work about 5 miles east of the mining camp of Champion. Stones were apparently abundant in earlier days because as many as 30 were said to appear in one pan. The most active mining took place during the period 1907-1908, and from 1910 to 1911. It has been estimated that several thousand ounces of stones have been recovered from the gravels along with the gold which was originally the object of mining.

Small quantities of sapphire have been recovered with gold from Quartz Gulch and adjacent gulches in Granite County. These defiles enter Rock Creek about 5 miles south of the sapphire workings described previously. It is reported that crystals occurred in a variety of colors, including colorless to greenish-blue, light green, yellow, orange, pink, and some almost ruby red. The proportion of colored stones was said to be large.

A little sapphire has been recovered with gold from the gravels of Pole Creek which drains northwestward into Madison River in the northern part of Madison County. Although "considerable" gem material was reported from this locality, little has been heard from it in recent years and it must be presumed that production was never important. A large piece of "ruby corundum" weighing 588½ carats was reported from this locality while gem quality garnet is said to occur with the sapphire and gold.

Brown's Gulch in Silver Bow County was once briefly mentioned in connection with alluvial sapphires and is drained by a stream flowing through the first large valley northwest of Butte. An indefinite reference for sapphire has also been given to the northeastern part of Chouteau County but it may be possible that the downstream extension of the Missouri River is being referred to.

Idaho. Fine chatoyant bronze-colored tabular corundum crystals have been found in the gold placers near Resort in Idaho County. In Washington County, placer mines of Rock Flat near the town of Meadows once produced a quantity of small sapphire crystals, corundum, and even a few ruby crystals. The dominant country rock in this area is gneiss which is cut in one place by a wide dike of decomposed basalt from which the stones are said to be derived. Almost all gem quality crystals were quite small, seldom capable of being cut into gems over one carat in weight. Predominant colors found were gray to amethystine but some fine cornflower blue specimens were recovered as well as pink stones and a very few true ruby crystals. Pink crystals yielded gems up to one carat in weight while a few of the blues cut into gems of from ½ to 1 carat. Ordinary corundum of bronzy chatoyancy also occurred here, some of the crystals showing ends colored bright blue. Much of the sapphire was filled with "silk," affording, when cut, small but good star stones. In 1906, gem crystals worth from $300 to $500 were recovered including a pink specimen, the largest of the lot, weighing 1½ carats and valued at $20.

Washington. Good blue and pink corundum crystals containing small translucent to transparent areas are found near the thulite (zoisite) deposit on Tunk Creek, Okanogan County.

BERYL

Few gemstones are so universally favored as the several varieties of beryl. Who has not paused before a jeweler's window to admire the rich green of an *emerald*—or to observe with appreciation the unsurpassed clear sparkling blue of a well-cut *aquamarine?* Occurring in a bewildering range of colors, beryl can be found in forms suitable for the tastes and purses of prince and pauper alike. The use of beryl for gems antedates history, even the meaning of the species name being lost in the mists of time. It is obvious that our modern spelling is derived from the Greek *beryllus* but whence came this word and what it meant to the Ancients of that civilization appears nowhere in history.

Though once regarded as a separate species and consequently accorded its own name, emerald is derived from an old Persian word which was translated into Greek as *smaragdus*, and thence by several changes into the modern spelling. It is interesting to note that in German, the old spelling has

been largely retained since it is currently given as *smaragd*. The variety
aquamarine owes its name to the resemblance of its color to that of sea water
—*aqua* meaning water, and *marine* referring to the sea. Less well known
but lovely nevertheless and deserving of as much favor are the varieties
morganite, and *golden beryl*; a subvariety of the latter has been called
heliodor. Morganite was applied only since the early years of the Twentieth
Century, to a pinkish or pinkish-lilac variety found in the gem mines of
Southern California and named by Dr. G. F. Kunz in honor of John Pierpont
Morgan, the famous banker of New York City who acquired an outstand-

FIGURE 19. Aquamarine from various localities. The two transparent crystal sections
are pale blue in color and are parts of the same crystal taken from a pegmatite near
Centerville, Idaho. When placed together, the whole crystal measures 4 inches in
length and 1 inch in diameter. The faceted heart at the upper right is a lovely clear
blue-green beryl from the Roebling Mine in Connecticut; it is 7⁄8 inch long and weighs
40.44 carats. The center gem is pale yellow-green, approximately 1 inch in length, and
has been cut from material found in Yancey County, North Carolina. The lower left-
hand specimen is a fine blue gem from Maine, measuring 1 3⁄16 inches in length and
weighing 66 carats. Courtesy Smithsonian Institution.

ing gem collection heavily favoring American gemstones. The descriptive name heliodor, derived from the Greek words meaning in combination, "gift of the sun" was once applied to a beautiful golden yellow variety from Southwest Africa. Still another distinguishing varietal name is *goshenite*, originally applied by the early American mineralogist, C. U. Shepard, to a colorless beryl found at Goshen, Massachusetts. Aside from the well-established names emerald and aquamarine, the tendency in the jewelry trade is to call other color phases simply pink beryl, green beryl, yellow beryl, etc.

Beryl is beryllium aluminum silicate with the formula: $Be_3Al_2Si_6O_{18}$. The element beryllium, incidentally, is named after this species as a result of its isolation from this mineral. Dull yellowish-green beryl, usually only translucent at best, appears to be richest in beryllium and causes this kind to be prized as ore. On the other hand, in gem varieties, considerable replacement of beryllium by sodium, lithium, and cesium takes place, especially in colorless to pink and purplish types. In emerald, traces of chromic oxide cause the typical bright green color. The color of aquamarine is believed to be due to the presence of ferric oxide. The color of yellow varieties is ascribed to the same cause except that additionally a small amount of uranium oxide has been detected in the heliodor variety from Southwest Africa. The color of morganite may be due to the presence of lithium but dikes in which this element is present also give rise to other colored beryls, which through want of better name, are lumped under "morganite" although they may be peach, orange, or even pinkish-yellow in tint. In this connection, much of the so-called morganite can be reverted to pink or purplish colors by the application of high heat. This treatment is also effective in changing some yellowish-green material into fine blue, or removing traces of green from specimens which would be pure blue otherwise. The presence of various impurities in beryl causes marked changes in crystal habit, perhaps best noted in morganite which appears mostly in squat tabular crystals. In contrast, aquamarine crystals are frequently several times to many times as long as they are thick (see Figure 19). Emerald falls somewhere between these extremes, most often appearing as simple hexagonal prisms of no great length (see Figure 20). The system of crystallization to which beryl belongs is Hexagonal, and as remarked above, results in the majority of examples forming prismatic crystals of

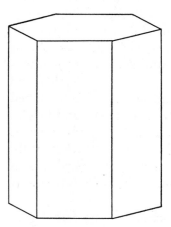

FIGURE 20. The simplest habit of beryl crystals, characteristic of many specimens removed from pegmatites and also of emerald.

hexagonal outline. These may be very simple but at times become complex due to the appearance of additional faces along the sides beveling the edges of larger faces or cutting corners upon the terminations. Large crystals wholly embedded in quartz and feldspar as is frequently the case in pegmatites, are usually poorly developed as compared to those which grow in cavities. The latter frequently show splendid shining surfaces, perfectly smooth, and in the case of small crystals which tend to be highly developed, sometimes give the appearance of having been artificially faceted, so great is the number and complexity of faces.

Beryl is almost exclusively a mineral of pegmatites, even emerald being found in or adjacent to small pegmatites in the North Carolina localities. By far the greatest quantity of beryl occurs as faulty crystals embedded in quartz or feldspar near the cores of pegmatites. Large numbers occur in many of the pegmatites of New England where they have been mined as beryllium ore. In occurrences of this type, crystals formed prior to their envelopment by quartz or feldspar and were, in many cases, originally transparent and of good gem quality. Unfortunately, during the process of dike formation, the enclosing minerals "froze" and exerted enormous pressures upon the crystals which consequently shattered into numerous angular fragments frequently too small for cutting purposes. However, where all or part of the crystal protruded into a cavity, such shattering did not take place and excellent gem quality material can be obtained from such specimens. Although many tons of crude beryl have been removed from numerous pegmatites in New England, only the smallest fraction has ever proved useful for gems for the reasons just stated. Morganite and goshenite on the other hand, are almost always found as crystals in pockets in lithia pegmatites. Important quantities are found in the pegmatites of the Southern California gem fields and also in similar deposits in New England. Most specimens are severely etched except for the basal faces which characteristically remain smooth and bright. At times, as at the Esmeralda Mine in Mesa Grande in California, crystals are seen that began growth as aquamarines embedded in the pocket walls, gradually changing from greenish-blue to the peach color of morganite as solutions nourishing them became rich in sodium, cesium or lithium. A morganite crystal is illustrated in Figure 24.

Beryl is a favorite gemstone of the lapidary because of its fair degree of hardness which varies from about $7\frac{1}{2}$ to 8 on the Mohs Scale, and its toughness which assures freedom from any tendency to split or cleave. It can be worked and polished in any direction with equal ease. There is sometimes a tendency to cleave along the basal plane but this is only observed when inclusions facilitate splitting. The ordinary fracture varies from irregular to conchoidal with glassy luster. Beryl crystals are resistant to shock and to heat as proved by the frequency with which cut stones of undesirable color are improved by subjecting them successfully to high temperatures. The specific gravity varies from 2.65 to 2.85 in gem material, depending upon the degree of impurity or replacement of beryllium by other elements. Values of 2.69 to 2.70 are observed in golden beryl and goshenite. Emerald varies from 2.65 to 2.76. Morganite shows a wide variation from 2.75 to 2.85, while aquamarines range from 2.68 to 2.73. Beryl is uniaxial, negative. Refractive indices vary with variety as follows: emerald from Hiddenite, North Carolina, $\omega = 1.578$, $\epsilon = 1.586$, birefringence 0.008; golden beryl from Maine, $\omega = 1.574$, $\epsilon = 1.579$, birefringence 0.005; deep blue aquamarine from Portland, Connecticut, $\omega = 1.580$, $\epsilon = 1.587$, birefringence 0.007. An absolutely colorless goshenite from Maine shows: $\omega = 1.579$, $\epsilon = 1.586$, birefringence 0.007. Dichroism is pronounced in almost every variety except in golden beryl where it is difficult to detect any color change. Blue most often shows dark blue in one window of the dichroscope and very pale blue or colorless in the other. Greenish-blue shows deep greenish-blue and pale yellowish-green. Pink or lilac morganite shows the basic color plus colorless to faint pink or lilac. Peach colored morganite exhibits a decided yellowish tinge and purplish-pink. Emerald shows bluish-green and yellowish-green. Color distribution in beryl is generally uniform but variations are sometimes noted in emerald, golden beryl, and in morganite. Emerald is often completely colorless to only faintly green in the core while the most intense coloration seems confined to a thin concentric layer near the outside. In golden beryl crystals, some sections show decided changes in tint from one end to the other, usually involving some shade of green or merely a paling or darkening of the basic hue. Morganite often shows typical aquamarine colors near the base of crystals, gradually changing to almost colorless and then to pink or peach at the terminations. Pronounced zoning in aquamarine is rare as a rule but is observed in crystals from Mount Antero, Colorado, which frequently show sharp bands of color arranged in layers across the long axes of prisms.

LOCALITIES

North West Territories. Green, light blue, yellow, and colorless beryl is widespread in pegmatites of the McKenzie District but up to now only small clear sections of much larger crystals have furnished faceting material.

Ontario. Good blue aquamarine occurs as clear portions in large shattered crystals in a pegmatite dike on Lot 23, Concession XV, Lyndoch Township, in Renfrew County. The locality is near the center of the northern boundary of the township not far from the community of Quadville. Crystals range up to 5 inches in diameter and the color, often very rich, matches the best from Brazil. Local cutters have produced gems up to 3.1 carats. Some of the massive beryl is deep enough to coloration to warrant use in cheaper grades of jewelry, possibly as tumbled gems or as cabochons.

Gems up to 2.1 carats of fine blue color have also been cut from aquamarine obtained from a pegmatite near Kearney, Butt Township, Nipissing District.

Maine. The largest flawless aquamarine ever cut from North American material came from a crystal section found near Sugar Hill in Stoneham Township, Oxford County. As the story goes, three pieces of beryl were found lying on the surface in a cultivated field, one of which was a doubly-terminated crystal measuring 1 3/5 inches in length and 3/5 inch in diameter, faint bluish-green in color and partly transparent, while the other two pieces fitted together as parts of a single crystal which originally was about 5 inches long and 3 inches wide. One of the latter pieces cut a fine greenish-blue gem measuring 1 2/5 by 1 2/5 by 3/4 inches and weighing 133.8 carats, now in the Chicago Natural History Museum. The crystal fragments from which this gem was cut showed a fine sea-green color when viewed through the end and a greenish-blue when viewed through the side. Stoneham Township has produced a considerable quantity of beryl from several localities besides the purely accidental discovery just related. Pegmatites on the south side of Sugar Hill, 3 miles northwest of North Lovell were opened in 1912 and 1913 yielding a variety of minerals including the exceedingly rare gemstone beryllonite. About 1/3 mile northeast of these prospects are other openings which show beryl crystals also. In another area of Stoneham Township, similar material has been obtained from a pegmatite which outcrops on the east side of Durgin Mountain, 4 miles north 30° west of North Lovell. The pegmatite is hard and shows a large quartz core in which are frozen dark golden yellow, yellowish-green, bluish-green and colorless beryl crystals. Not far away on Chapman Hill, about 3 miles due north of North Lovell, are other pegmatite workings. Two prospects are on the summit near the east side, one in a field and the other in woods about 1/4 mile south of the first. Both are reported to have produced fine blue beryl. About 5 miles north of North Lovell on Speckled Mountain, fine yellow beryl has been found on the old Andrews property.

A number of places in Buckfield Township, Oxford County, yielded gem quality beryl from pegmatites worked principally for feldspar. Some fine aquamarine and morganite has been obtained from the Bennett Quarry which lies about 3 miles west of the village of Buckfield and about 1/2 mile north of the Bennett Farmhouse. One aquamarine found here was 6 inches in diameter and about the same in length, much of it clear but not altogether flawless. The Lewis Mine, located about 2 miles southwest of Buckfield village, furnished some colorless cesium beryl from a quarry sunk upon the south slope of a small but steep hill just north of Highway 117. Some gem quality tourmaline was found here also. The J. H. Fletcher Mine just over 2 miles southwest of Buckfield village and about ¼ mile west of the Lewis Mine and almost the same distance north of Highway 117, produced some very fine cesium beryl and aquamarine from pockets in the pegmatite. The largest gem crystal, an aquamarine, was nearly 4 inches in diameter with one end clear gem material. About ½ mile south of the last locality are several pits comprising the Robinson Dudley Mine located on the north slope of a small hill about 2½ miles southwest of Buckfield village. At least one of the pits shows interesting mineralogy, having produced in addition to cesium beryl and aquamarine, the rare gem mineral, pollucite.

In the early mining days at Mt. Mica, the famous tourmaline mine located 1½ miles east of the village of Paris, Paris Township, Oxford County, some beautiful morganite crystals were obtained along with the gem tourmaline in pockets in pegmatite. One crystal measured 6 inches in diameter but only 1 inch thick; another irregular crystal was 6 inches tall but showed only four of the usual six prismatic faces. Despite their large size, these crystals contained only small flawless areas suitable for gems. The most recent excavations at this locality in June 1949 to the north of the main pit, resulted in opening a large pocket in which were found a number of colorless cesium beryl crystals of complex habit. Individuals ranged from ½ inch to 8 inches in length and showed development of faces over most of the exterior. All had milky cores with colorless and largely flawless outer zones.

In another part of Oxford County, fine gem quality aquamarine and rose quartz have been found in a prospect pit opened on a pegmatite near the crest of French Mountain in the eastern part of Albany Township. Small gem quality crystals of greenish and golden beryl also occur at the Scribner Mine located ½ mile northeast of Flints Mountain and 8.8 miles south 70° west of West Paris, Albany Township. The largest pit at this mine is Pit No. 2 and contains gem beryl embedded in quartz. Similar beryl is found in Pit No. 3, immediately to the north. In Newry Township, beautiful crystals of aquamarine sometimes occur in pockets in the pegmatites near the summit of the east spur of Plumbago Mountain, 3.9 miles north 40° west of the village of Rumford Point. At this locality, in the lowest of a series of pits known as the United Feldspar and Minerals Company Quarry, the small, greenish crystals are said to be of very fine quality. In Greenwood Township, pockets in Tamminen's Quarry at the base of Noyes Mountain, have yielded variously colored beryl including morganite. Fine gems of aquamarine and golden beryl have been cut from fragments of larger crystals occurring in a pegmatite on the steep south slope of Hedgehog Hill about 2 miles southeast of Dickvale, Peru Township. All of the preceding localities are in Oxford County.

In Sagadahoc County, fine gem-quality aquamarine has been taken from a number of pegmatites under much the same mineralogical circumstances. Some golden beryl has been recovered from a series of small pegmatites near the Thomas Feldspar Quarry in Phippsburg Township. This locality is 1.3 miles south 17° west of the tide mill in the village of Parker Head. In the township of Topsham a short distance north of Brunswick, are located a series of feldspar quarries atop low hills overlooking the Cathance River. Good aquamarine occurs from time to time in many of these quarries, especially from the northernmost workings on the hill immediately north of the village of Topsham. The Willes Quarries located about 1½ to 2 miles northwest of Cathance Station and north of Topsham have frequently provided fine, gem-quality crystals from pegmatite cavities up to one foot in diameter; also smoky quartz crystals and tourmaline. A beautiful faceted brilliant of yellow-green color and weighing 23.01 carats was cut from rough provided by one of the quarries in the Topsham area and is now in the U.S. National Museum in Washington, D.C.

The Mt. Apatite workings located on a low broad hill in the southwest corner of Auburn Township, 1½ miles east of Minot in Androscoggin County are noted more for gem pockets which produced beautiful gem-quality apatite and tourmaline than for beryl, but some morganite was also recovered from time to time. In 1914 a large light pink crystal 12 inches in diameter and fully 22 inches long was found. Despite its great mineralogical value and the presence of few flawless areas of gem material, it was, unfortunately, cut into a series of comparatively valueless gems of several carats each.

New Hampshire. Considerable gem-quality beryl has been obtained from numerous pegmatites outcropping in a belt running in a northerly direction from Cheshire County through Sullivan and Merrimack counties and into Grafton County. The heaviest and most worked concentrations are in the north central portion of Cheshire County north of Keene, and in the south central portion of Grafton County extending southward into Sullivan and Merrimack counties. Quantities of fine blue aquamarine were once obtained from a number of mines and prospects immediately to the southwest of Grafton Center in the southern part of Grafton County and in the adjoining northeastern part of Sullivan County. The most productive mines were the Columbia, Reynolds, and several others. Much of the mining in this area was done by the Passmore Gem Company of Boston, Massachusetts.

The occurrences of beryl are typical of New England as a whole, crystals being found partly in feldspar and partly in quartz at the margin of the pegmatite core. The best beryl is found where core quartz begins to achieve some measure of clarity. The great brittleness of quartz demands minimum use of explosives lest beryl crystals be unnecessarily shattered and in early days of mining, prybars were used extensively to wedge off blocks which could later be broken up carefully with hammers. Beryl crystals from the area mentioned above were found in sizes ranging from less than ¼ inch across to one on record of 12 inches in length and 3 inches in diameter. This magnificent crystal was found loose upon the ground where it had eroded from its pegmatite and was sold to a European collector for $1000. Even larger crystals were found, as for example, one of 10 by 4 inches in which the upper half was clear gem stock. The majority of crystals were shattered and as a rule no large gems could be obtained.

In Grafton County, gem beryl has been mined from the Charles Davis Mine located ¾ mile west-northwest of the village of North Groton in Groton Township. A famous producer of aquamarine was the Valencia Mine located high on the west flank of Fletcher Mountain, 2 miles northeast of North Groton in the same township. This mine was opened in 1880 and worked extensively for some years afterward. The quartz core of the pegmatite produced many beryl crystals from 1 to 6 inches in diameter with numerous clear spots of gem grade. Few of the cut gems were large, records show that in 1885 over 100 gems were cut but none were more than 4 carats.

In Sullivan County, much good gem beryl has been taken from the Reynolds and Columbia mines, located almost at the summit of the northeast prong of Pillsbury Ridge in Springfield Township. The Reynolds Mine consists of five small cuts made in pegmatites and is located 2¾ miles south-southwest of the village of Grafton, or about ¾ mile in the same direction from Robinson Corner. Beryl was rather plentiful here, some crystals reaching several inches across with clear spots of fine gem quality. The golden colors from this mine are especially fine; other colors are light to dark yellow, the latter in only very small sizes, yellowish-green, light to dark bluish-green, and greenish-blue. Several hundred yards northwest is the Columbia Gem Mine consisting of four small opencuts which produced small quantities of bluish aquamarine.

Several mines in Merrimack County have provided modest quantities of gem beryl. Crystals up to 4 inches in diameter and containing gemmy spots occur in a pegmatite which outcrops on the north slope of Severance Hill (Stuart Hill) in Wilmot Township, about 3¼ miles southeast of Grafton. Most of the beryl is opaque to translucent but some is clear and good gem material. Colors range from greenish-blue to yellowish-green to yellow. In this same township, a prospect opened in 1913 on the P. K. Filbert Farm, 1½ miles west-southwest of South Danbury, yielded beryls up to 2 inches in diameter of yellowish- to bluish-green color and sometimes containing clear areas. The deposit is on the west end of an elongated hill about 200 feet higher than the road along its west side.

In Cheshire County, gem beryl has been obtained from the Island Mica

Mine, so named because the workings are situated on a small knoll in a swamp 2¼ miles north-northwest of Gilsum and about ½ mile northwest of Mica Mine School. Three opencuts and a tunnel are driven into the pegmatite. Beryl crystals up to 12 inches in diameter occurred here, sometimes showing several colors in one specimen. Light to dark golden material of exceptional quality was found at this mine as well as the usual bluish to greenish hues. Considerable beryl was thrown over the dumps during early working of this mine and digging may unearth some. Further north, about 3½ miles north-northwest of Gilsum is located the Britton Mine which in its early days produced some clear material. This working is located about ¼ mile northeast of Crane Pond across the road from Gilsum to East Alstead. In Roxbury Township, two ledges on Bassett Hill located 5 miles east-northeast of Keene, have provided colorless or slightly colored beryl of cutting quality. Aquamarine large enough to cut gems up to 10 carats is reported from three prospects on the south side of Horse Hill situated 4½ miles east of Keene.

Massachusetts. Especially fine gem grade beryl was obtained in years past from the famous Beryl Hill locality (Reynolds Mine), 2½ miles north 68° east of Royalston, Worcester County. Beryl Hill is a low flat topped hill partly cleared for pasture on its summit and along its western side. Two parallel pegmatites along which five openings have been made, cross the hill. Four of the openings are on the top and the fifth is a short distance below the summit on the western side. The country rock is mica gneiss cut by biotite granite; the pegmatites show coarse texture but are simple in mineralization. Beryl occurs in the smoky quartz cores of the dikes, in light to dark blue, bluish-green, yellowish-green, and yellow crystals ranging up to 2 inches in diameter and 11 inches in length. In 1910 some fine blue material was uncovered, the best specimen being a splendid, almost flawless crystal about 3 inches long and 2¼ inches by ¾ inch across the base. A cut stone of 12 carats sold for $100. In 1911 especially fine crystals were removed, ranging in thickness from 1 to 2 inches. Most were pale to dark-green but some were pure blue. In 1914, additional work again produced much excellent material from which the following gems were cut: 16 carats, 15.7 carats and very fine blue, 14.2 carats, 10 carats, and 12.6 carats.

The locality which gave its name to goshenite, the colorless variety of beryl is somewhat obscured by the mists of time since the initial report of discovery was made in 1844. However, reliable accounts place the original occurrence in a pegmatite dike situated about 300 yards north of the north end of Lily Pond, 1½ miles north 80° west of Goshen, Hampshire County. Beryl of the usual bluish and greenish kinds was reported as "abundant" in this dike. This may be the same locality often referred to as the "Barrus Farm" after the name of the owner of the property.

Connecticut. The feldspar quarries around Middletown, Middlesex

County, have sometimes provided aquamarine from large crystals found in the quartz cores of pegmatites. Crystals range in color from pale greenish-blue to blue in various shades including an exceedingly rich blue as dark as any from Brazil or Madagascar. The National Museum, for example, has in its collections a very beautiful faceted gem weighing 14.26 carats, of deep blue-green color from this area. The Strickland Quarry on the west flank of Collins Hill, about 2½ miles northeast of Portland, Portland Township, has sometimes produced both aquamarine and morganite, the latter coming from the gem pockets along the eastern border of a large pegmatite dike. The morganite is salmon pink in color and usually much etched, and only small portions of such crystals are suitable for cutting. The Riverside Quarry in Middletown Township on the south bank of the Connecticut River and about ½ mile west of Benvenue has also furnished some clear fragments of aquamarine. The Slocum Quarry located 3½ miles southeast of East Hampton village in East Hampton Township, is famous for its golden beryl, part of which is exceptional in quality. Crystals occur next to quartz in the border zone of a pegmatite and range in size from 1/32 to 1/2 inch in diameter and from ½ to 2½ inches long. A beautiful doubly-terminated crystal measuring 1½ by 1 inches is in the collection of the American Museum of Natural History.

One of the most productive and commercially important gem mines in North America is the George Roebling or Merryall Mine, as it is commonly called, noted for its production of fine golden beryl and equally fine aquamarine. This pegmatite working is located in New Milford Township, Litchfield County, 5½ miles north 13° west of the village of New Milford. It is accessible by road but is difficult to find without local directions. This mine was opened in 1880 for feldspar and mica by S. L. Wilson and G. Roebling of Northville, Connecticut, and worked steadily up to 1900. Soon after work commenced, Roebling acquired all rights and the mine came to be named after him. In 1886 and 1887, some 4000 gems were cut costing $3000 for cutting charges but realizing $15,000 when sold. The colors include yellow of very fine shades, blue, green, and even some which were almost colorless. A beautiful blue-green faceted heart weighing 40.44 carats is in the U.S. National Museum (see Figure 19), while a bright yellow gem cut in oval form and weighing 14.9 carats is in the American Museum of Natural History. In four years after the opening of this mine a reported total of $17,000 worth of gems had been sold. After 1900, operations lapsed but resumed when the son of Jacob Orzech, the owner at the time, mined about one ton of beryl sometime after 1936. In 1944 the Roebling Mine was operated for a brief period by Cyril Ulman of Guilford, Connecticut. In the summer of 1955 a fine crystal of golden beryl, doubly-terminated, and mostly transparent, was found and offered for sale at the optimistic price of $2000. This crystal measures about 3 inches in length and 1 inch in width and weighs 220 carats; the exterior is smooth but shows many triangular etch marks.

The Roebling Mine is situated on the east slope of a steep, partly wooded hill upon which several pegmatites outcrop but only the largest provides gems. Beryl crystals occur in grayish to smoky granular quartz streaks and lenses near the central portion of the dike while masses of silvery muscovite in fine flakes are commonly associated with the beryl and frequently enclose it to an extent which prevents a view of the interior. The workings consist of two open cuts, the main one running northeast to southwest about 150 yards in length and about 20 feet in width. Good material has been obtained only from the southwest end of the main cut. The dike is simple in composition, consisting mainly of feldspar and quartz with accessory muscovite, biotite, black tourmaline, beryl, and red garnet, some crystals of the last being of gem quality. Although golden beryl crystals are generally small, those of aquamarine have been reported as large as 12 inches in diameter and perhaps 18 inches to 24 inches in length but the average seems to be from 2 inches to 3 inches in diameter and from 4 inches to 6 inches in length. All crystals are more or less cracked and pocket beryl is unknown. The prospects for finding additional gem material here are very promising.

Pennsylvania. Years ago, unusual and fine mineral specimens were found in a number of localities in Southeastern Pennsylvania, particularly in Delaware County. Beautiful aquamarine and golden beryl crystals were found in pegmatite at Deshong's Quarry on the east side of Ridley Creek about ½ mile west of Leiperville in Ridley Township. Though frequently large in size, only the smallest crystals proved to be of gem quality. Small but fine cutting grade crystals occurred at Leiper's Quarry at Avondale on the east side of Crum Creek in Springfield Township. In 1890 a superb golden beryl specimen from this quarry was cut into a gem of 35.7 carats; another of 20 carats is also on record. The beryl from this locality is generally yellow or yellowish-green but some colorless material was found also. Good gem stock came from time to time from the Shaw & Ezrey Quarry near Chester in Upper Providence Township; also from near White Horse, 3 to 4 miles below Darby. Small transparent crystals of greenish color occur in a pegmatite atop a small knoll near Linwood Mill Dam, about ½ mile north of Trainer Station, Lower Chichester Township.

North Carolina. It is only in this state that significant quantities of emerald have been produced. Deposits occur in three widely separated areas as follows: near Hiddenite in Alexander County; near Shelby in Cleveland County; and on Big Crabtree Mountain in Mitchell County. The most noted mine is that located upon the old Warren Farm, 1 mile north of Hiddenite, near Salem Church, Sharps Township, Alexander County. This locality drew attention when six emerald crystals, locally called "green bolts," were found in a cultivated field. Prior to this time, J. A. D. Stephenson of Statesville, had obtained an emerald from here as early as 1875 but the in place deposit was not found. However, the discovery of more crystals set off a series of intensive explorations by W. E. Hidden, including the digging of a series of trenches beneath the exact spot where the crystals were picked up. About five weeks of fruitless effort were spent in July and August of 1880 before a vein was found containing small prisms of emerald and an unusual emerald-green mineral. This strange species was soon identified as spodumene and named hiddenite in honor of its discoverer. The details of mineralogy and geology of this occurrence are given under SPODUMENE.

In 1881 the Emerald & Hiddenite Mining Company was organized to work the property. The next several years saw work upon the deposit pushed vigorously and gradually the mine was placed in a position where a swarm of small pegmatites in which beryls and spodumenes occurred in pockets, could be excavated systematically. The greatest number of emerald crystals were found in 1882, including one 8½ inches long and about 9 ounces in weight, the best of nine fine quality specimens taken from a single pocket and the largest ever found at this locality. Both color and transparency in this lot were good but larger crystals were too filled with flaws to merit cutting. In the Spring of 1882, a pocket was found from which 74 crystals were removed, ranging in size from 2 to 5 inches in length and all of good color. Emeralds from Mr. Hidden's mine sold readily as cabinet specimens, realizing from $25 to $1000 per crystal. Because of flaws in larger specimens, cuttable emerald only occurred in smaller crystals and realized up to about $32 per carat in finished form. From 1885, work ceased due to legal squabbles. After many years of inactivity, this mine was cleaned out and reopened by W. B. Colburn of Statesville in 1926 and 1927 and again produced some fine emerald and hiddenite.

In the Hiddenite emerald, coloration is confined mainly to an outer zone, the centers of crystals tending to be much paler in hue, or even colorless. Simple crystal forms prevail, being essentially six-sided hexagonal prisms with simple flat terminations upon the ends; small crystals, however, are far more complex and show numerous lustrous faces upon the ends. Some large crystals are fairly smooth but many are characteristically etched along the sides. At times, crevices within crystals may be filled with silvery muscovite mica; other crystals show overgrowths of calcite, muscovite, chlorite, and pyrite.

A magnificent crystal from this mine is now in the U.S. National Museum (see Figure 21); it measures 2¾ inches tall and 1⅝ inches in diameter, and weighs 9 ounces. As mentioned previously, the largest crystal recovered found its way into the American Museum of Natural History but was stolen. This 8½ inch prism is figured in color in Kunz' book "Gems and Precious Stones of North America."

In his early work at the mine, Hidden prospected intensively in the neighborhood and determined that his mine was situated upon a broad network of pegmatites as evidenced by the finding of loose crystals of beryl and rutile in the topsoil along a belt 3 miles in length. An outgrowth of this early prospecting led to the discovery of additional emerald deposits. Emerald crystals have been found upon the Osborne-Lackey place about 1/5 mile northwest of the original deposit and from this mine were removed about 50 ranging from ¾ to 2¾ inches in length and from ⅛ to ⅓ inches thick. All were transparent but pale in color and only one was large and dark enough in color to be worth faceting. Some hiddenite crystals of poor quality were also recovered from this deposit. About ½ mile west of Hiddenite, another prospect which produced both emerald and hiddenite was developed by the American Gem Mining Syndicate in 1907. The main workings produced both emerald and aquamarine, a crystal of the latter being 2 inches long by 1½ inches in diameter and weighing over 750 carats. Many other aquamarine crystals were found ranging from 10 to 20 carats in weight. A short distance away at the Ellis Prospect,

FIGURE 21. One of the largest emerald crystals found at the emerald and hiddenite mine near Hiddenite, North Carolina. This simple hexagonal prism measures 2¾ inches tall and is 1⅝ inches in diameter; its weight is 9 ounces. Courtesy Smithsonian Institution.

located ¼ mile east of Hiddenite, the syndicate obtained a dark green emerald of 276 carats, also about 200 carats of hiddenite crystals.

The Shelby emerald locality, the second important North Carolina occurrence, was discovered in 1908 on the land of W. B. Turner, 4¾ miles south 30° west of Shelby in Cleveland County, close to the east bank of the First Broad River, about ½ mile northeast of the dam. The discovery was brought about by finding loose emerald fragments in the topsoil. The mine was placed in operation shortly after 1909 under the direction of George English, a prominent mineral dealer of New York City. Occasionally known as the "Turner Mine" or the "English Prospect," the Shelby deposit was acquired sometime prior to 1912 by the Emerald Company of New York City and renamed the "Old Plantation Mine." In 1912 emerald of varying quality was produced totaling 2969 carats valued at $12,875 including an estimated 800 carats of cuttable material. Better grades in cut form realized about $200 per carat while a fine gem of slightly over 2 carats was sold wholesale for $200. By 1913 it was estimated that about 3000 carats of rough valued at $15,000 or more had been mined. The U.S. National Museum has in its collection a 7.05 carat faceted emerald from this deposit.

At the Shelby locality emerald occurs in a beryl-rich pegmatite enclosed by olivine gabbro and hornblende gabbro. Local exploration disclosed three other pegmatites containing beryl but only of the aquamarine variety. The emerald-bearing pegmatite varies in thickness from as little as a few inches to as much as 6 feet and consists of medium to coarse granular feldspar and quartz with small amounts of tourmaline, beryl, muscovite, and biotite. Figure 22 shows the pegmatite exposed in the opencut during the days of active mining. Pockets in the core provide crystals of smoky quartz, sometimes enclosing rutile needles, feldspar, tourmaline, and beryl. As at other localities emerald crystallizes in simple six-sided prisms terminated by a basal plane, however, a characteristic feature is the presence of numerous small tubes, sometimes imparting silky luster, which run down the length of prisms parallel to the principal crystal axis. Emerald is found not only in the pockets but also in the adjacent massive quartz and feldspar but these crystals are

FIGURE 22. The Turner Emerald Mine near Shelby, North Carolina, September 27, 1912. The emerald-bearing pegmatite dike is to the right and appears as a whitish crumbly feldspar streak passing from the top of the excavation to the bottom past the sledge hammer. The decomposed nature of the country rock is apparent in this photograph.
Courtesy U.S. Geological Survey.

never as fine as those found within the cavities themselves. Of the dikes mentioned, one 90 feet to the southeast of the emerald mine and another 200 feet to the east have produced gem quality aquamarine. In 1910, an emerald crystal 2¼ inches long and ⅝ inch in diameter was recovered weighing 131 carats. The color throughout was pale except at the termination where a deeper green prevailed. The crystal was striated along the sides. Many crystals from this locality show transparent material only in an exterior zone, the centers being milky white and almost opaque.

The last important emerald deposit in this state was discovered by J. L. Rorison and D. A. Bowman in July 1894 on Big Crabtree Mountain, fourteen miles from Bakersville, Mitchell County. The mine is located on the divide between Rush Creek and Crabtree Creek at an elevation of about 5000 feet above sea level. It has since been called the "Crabtree locality" after the name of the mountain. Emerald occurs in a pegmatite consisting of coarse-grained quartz and albite feldspar with accessory garnet and tourmaline, the latter reddish-black and translucent in thin sections. Enclosing rocks are biotite schists and gneisses. The pegmatite averages 5 feet in thickness showing very sharp wall contacts with the enclosing rocks. It is at these contacts that emerald is most likely to occur, the crystals gradually paling as they approach the center of the pegmatite and becoming aquamarine, white, or yellow beryl at their ends. The true emerald crystals themselves are mostly small, from hairlike crystals to those up to $\frac{5}{16}$ inch in diameter and 1 inch long. Occasionally some up to ¾ inch diameter and over an inch in length are noted. Crystals habitually form simple hexagonal prisms with flat terminations; some are clear but most are flawed.

The American Gem & Pearl Company of New York City worked this property extensively in 1906 and produced a number of perfectly transparent crystals which cut gems up to ¾ carat in weight. Also produced was massive material containing scattered emerald, known as "emerald matrix," and consisting of compact mixtures of white albite, with or without black tourmaline, and narrow prisms of bright green translucent emerald. Taking a fine polish, many attractive cabochons were cut from this matrix and sold readily although not for as high prices as pure emerald.

In July 1957 it was announced that the Little Switzerland Emerald Mines, Inc., had sub-leased the emerald property from the estates of E. Fortner and J. P. Grindstaff with the intent of resuming mining. Since the early period, the Crabtree mines have been worked for brief periods of time in 1919, 1935 and 1942. As of 1958 no news has been forthcoming as to the success of the latest venture.

Ordinary beryl, exclusive of emerald, occurs in North Carolina in pegmatites which traverse highly metamorphosed rocks of Archean age which outcrop in a belt running parallel to the Appalachian Mountains. The occurrences begin in Ashe County to the north and then swing southwest to the counties just north of the Georgia border. These pegmatites have been extensively worked for feldspar, quartz, and mica, and only incidentally for gemstones.

Good golden beryl and aquamarine have been obtained from the South Hardin Mica Mine in Ashe County. The workings are near the top of a small hill about 1½ miles southwest of Beaver Creek and produced crystals ranging in size from less than an inch to as much as 6 to 8 inches in diameter. The beryl proved translucent only but provided good cabochon gems. The Walnut Knob Mine also produced cabochon grade aquamarine from a working 2 miles northwest of Elk Cross Roads and ¾ mile south of Black Mountain.

In Mitchell County, the principal production of golden beryl and aquamarine has come from mines in the Wiseman Tract located ¼ mile southwest of English Knob, or 1.8 miles north slightly east of Spruce Pine. The Wiseman property was worked many years ago by the American Gem & Pearl Company and enough raw material was obtained to cut thousands of faceted gems ranging in size from 1 to 20 carats. Fine blues occurred only sparingly. The McChone mines located 1½ miles south-southwest of Spruce Pine and ½ mile east-southeast of Chalk Mountain have also produced quantities of clear material from large crystals. Some gem material was also obtained from the Hungerford Mine near Mica.

In Yancey County, the Ray Mica Mine located 1.7 miles northeast of Vixen or 2.3 miles south-southeast of Burnsville on Hurricane Mountain, has been the principal producer of gem beryl and probably produced the crystal from which the faceted gem shown in Figure 19 was cut. In Alexander County, a number of mines and prospects near Hiddenite and in the Taylorsville district have yielded small quantities of gem beryl. Aquamarine and golden beryl of gem quality have been mined from a pegmatite 8 feet thick on the Warren Place about 1½ miles southeast of Hiddenite, the largest crystal found was 1 by 1½ inches. Several prospects for beryl are located 1½ miles east of Hiddenite on the ridge between Davis Creek and the Little Yadkin River where quartz and rutile crystals as well as beryl were found loose in the soil. In the Taylorsville area, near All Healing Springs, are a number of prospects worthy of note. Especially fine beryl was obtained from a dike which was exposed by trenching on the farm of Eli Barnes, 1½ miles north-northwest of the Springs. The dike, about 4 feet thick, is located on the west slope of a small hill about 200 yards northwest of the farmhouse. The finest beryl, golden yellow in color, very clear, and weighing 352.5 carats was found in 1912 in the quartz core of the dike. Although fractured at the ends the crystal measured almost 2 inches long and about 1 inch in diameter. Golden, yellow, and green beryl has also come from a pegmatite on the Thomas Barnes place about 2 miles north-northwest of All Healing Springs. On the James Chapman place, 1¾ miles north-northeast of All Healing Springs, good yellow and golden beryl was recovered from the quartz core of an outcropping pegmatite. On the John Webster place, about 1¼ mile east-northeast of the Springs, gem quality crystals were found in pegmatites exposed by a series of three small pits.

In Buncombe County, gem beryl has been reported from the Balsam Gap Mine and from a prospect located 1½ miles southeast of Black Mountain Station.

The South Mountains of Burke County contain pegmatite bodies which have been mined for mica and feldspar; at times, some of the beryl associated with these minerals is of gem quality. In these mountains, the Joel Walker beryl prospect located on a hill ½ mile southwest of Walker Knob, 8 miles west-southwest of Morganton, has provided aquamarine and golden beryl. Another prospect is 1 mile east. In another area of the county, similar beryl has been obtained from the Burkmont prospect located 1¼ miles south-southwest of Burkmont Mountain, providing crystals up to 1 inch in diameter.

In Macon County, the Littlefield Beryl Mine has produced a few fine blue and yellow beryl crystals from a pegmatite 3½ to 5 feet in thickness outcropping on the headwaters of Tessentee Creek, one mile south of Whiterock Mountain. The crystals range from needle-like prisms to some ¾ inch in diameter and 2 inches long.

Several localities in Jackson County have also contributed fair to good gem beryl, notably the Grimshawe Mine, 1¾ miles due east of the top of Whiteside Mountain, and ½ mile northeast of Whiteside Cove. Large crystals were found here but as usual, gem material came only from small clear spots. Another locality is an unnamed prospect on a ridge 1¼ miles south-southeast of the junction of Johns Creek and Caney Fork where crystals up to 1 inch in diameter and several inches long were removed from a pegmatite. The Rice Mica Mine and the Beryl Mine located on a spur of Sassafras Mountain about ½ mile north of its summit and 2 miles south-southwest of Sapphire, have produced some gemmy fragments of beryl from large crystals.

In Cleveland County, a pegmatite opened to a depth of 30 feet on the Whisnant place on the west side of Broad River near Hollybush, produced yellow gem beryl.

South Carolina. A prospect on the old J. N. S. McConnell place, 3¼ miles north-northeast of Anderson, Anderson County, once produced very deep green aquamarine, almost emerald in hue. The prospect consists of a trench about 45 feet long sunk upon a mica-bearing pegmatite. In Cherokee County, emerald is said to come from near Earles Station, Blacksburg, and a faceted keystone-shaped gem from this locality is in the American Museum of Natural History. It is to be noted that Earles Station is about 10 miles directly south of the Shelby, North Carolina emerald locality.

Georgia. In Rabun County, large beryl crystals from the Beck Beryl Mine, 7 miles due east of Clayton, provide clear facet grade fragments. This locality is several miles south of War Woman Creek, and exploits a 6 to 12 feet thick pegmatite by means of several opencuts.

In Pickens County, some excellent facet-grade beryl has been found along the outcropping quartz core of a pegmatite on the Cook farm about 4 miles west of Tate. This flat-lying body is embedded in biotite granulite and is well-exposed for 40 feet of its length along the southeast side of Rock Creek. The beryl crystals occur at the margins of the quartz core, larger ones reaching 3 by 6 inches in size. Some are blue but most are yellow; other types are clear deep golden, almost honey yellow. This pegmatite was prospected in 1953 but is unworked at present.

In Cherokee County, the Cochran Mine produced small fragments of aquamarine from large crystals of beryl taken from a pegmatite mined extensively for mica. The deposit is located 2½ miles north 78° east of Ball Ground.

Perfectly clear fragments of beryl were discovered in 1910 in the topsoil of the T. J. Allen farm about 2 miles east of Vaughn in Spalding County. Attempts to locate the pegmatite by digging pits proved unsuccessful. Surface material provided the only gems, some of which were fine light blue color weighing 1½ to 2 carats.

Aquamarine has been found in various places in Elbert County, as close to Antioch Hill near Deweyrose; also on the ground near the Yellow Hill Mine on the north side of the Little Broad River, 3 miles from Ogleby. In Upson County, the Herron Mine located about ¼ mile east of the center of Yatesville has produced beryl crystals up to 7 inches in diameter with clear facet-grade portions. This mine is several hundred feet south of the Culloden Highway.

The most impressive production of gem beryl from any Georgia locality came from the large mine of the Minerals Processing Company located 8 miles north of La Grange and one mile south of Smith's Crossroads on the west side of Highway 219 in Troup County. This mine was operated as an opencut to exploit commercial beryl and scrap mica in a lens-shaped pegmatite some 400 feet in length and about 125 feet in maximum width. Beryls occurred as well-formed crystals along the edges of a large quartz core, much of which was fine rose quartz of gem grade (see QUARTZ). This core was about 320 feet in length and averaged 50 feet in width. All along its margin beryl crystals were found in all degrees of transparency from opaque to perfectly clean. The color graded from aquamarine of deep blue color to some which was smoky in hue. The largest crystal was 18 inches in diameter but those containing gem material were much smaller. It has been reported that 1300 pounds of aquamarine were shipped to California and smaller consignments to Ohio during the course of mining in the early 1950's. Clear fragments were rather large at times, flawless gems up to 15 carats having been cut from selected pieces. Mineralogically this pegmatite is very simple, consisting only of feldspar, largely decomposed to kaolin, muscovite, black tourmaline, and quartz. In another section of Troup County, clear fragments of beryl have been found on the ground near the Chromite Prospect near Louise; similar material has been found just north of the Calloway Airport.

Alabama. Fine golden beryl has come from near Hissop, Coosa County, an old locality of record being the Eliza Coggins place, ¾ mile southwest of the town; also on the J. H. Thomas place 1 mile northeast. In Randolph County, gem quality greenish aquamarine in small pieces has been found at the Pat Ayers Prospect No. 2 Mica Mine, 2¼ miles northeast of Pinetucky in the northern part of the county.

Colorado. Perhaps the highest gemstone locality in the entire North American Continent is atop Mount Antero in Chaffee County, where much fine aquamarine, quartz, phenakite, and other desirable minerals occur in pegmatite pockets. The pegmatites occur within a granite stock at altitudes ranging between 12,000 and 14,000 feet above sea level, encompassing a roughly elliptical area about 3 miles across. The summits of Mount Antero (14,245 feet) and White Mountain (13,900 feet) lie within the stock near the southern end of the Sawatch Range and are about 15 miles northwest of Salida or about 12 miles southwest of Nathrop. The pegmatites and veins are uniformly small, seldom over 3 feet thick and extend laterally only a few feet. All are well above timberline in barren desolate terrain littered with disintegrated rock which covers the underlying formations and thus prevents easy examination and prospecting. The method of locating a gem-bearing pegmatite calls for carefully examining this debris and attempting to trace such pocket minerals as may be found to their source. All of the gem minerals occur in disk-like or lenticular pockets which show from the outside graphic granite several inches thick followed by fine well-formed crystals of microcline, beryl, smoky to clear quartz, albite, and fluorite within the pockets. The latter may be filled with soil and debris which has infiltrated through cracks or crevices. The microcline crystals range up to 4 inches across while the smoky quartz forms fine sharp crystals of deep color up to 4 inches in length. Beryl occurs as pale greenish-blue to deep pure blue hexagonal prisms, simply crystallized, but often etched lightly on prism faces. Some are extensively etched and appear to be mere skeletons or masses of slender fibers. The largest beryl crystals found here were uncovered by Arthur Montgomery and Edwin Over in 1932 and are now in the Mineralogical Museum

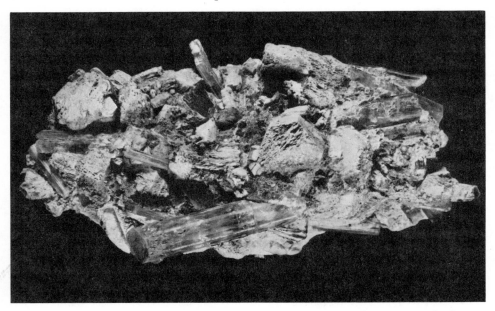

FIGURE 23. Bright blue aquamarine crystals of slender habit in feldspar matrix from a gem pocket found on White Mountain in the famed Mount Antero Region of Colorado. Associated minerals are cookeite, mica, and smoky quartz; size of specimen: 6¾ inches by 3 inches; largest crystal (bottom) measures 2½ inches by ½ inch. The jumbled appearance shown here is typical of the type of material found upon the floor of gem pockets. Courtesy Smithsonian Institution.

of Harvard University. The best was 1½ inches in diameter and not quite 8 inches in length, in part gemmy. The pocket from which this specimen came also yielded several others almost as large. Though some beryl is seen in the walls of pockets, only crystals from the interior are of gem quality. Recent finds of beryl have uncovered crystals of up to 3½ inches in length. Other accessory minerals noted from pockets are phenakite, bertrandite, muscovite, sericite, limonite, and albite. A typical pocket specimen of feldspar and blue aquamarine crystals from White Mountain is illustrated in Figure 23.

In years past, some good aquamarine was found half way up the south slopes of Mount Princeton about 5 miles north of Mount Antero. Not too far away from the first locality described is another series of beryl-bearing veins which occur on the south side of Carbonate Mountain (12,280 feet), almost exactly two miles southwest of Mount Antero. The beryl occurs in a quartz vein which has been mined for molybdenite, the workings being known as the California Mine. In places, pockets contained quartz crystals up to 12 inches in length and gem quality light bluish-green aquamarine, or, more rarely, beryl of light straw yellow color or even colorless. Some were markedly zoned with a clear termination running into a milky base. Crystals rarely exceeded an inch in length and were of interest mainly to mineral collectors.

In Jefferson County, some pale bluish-green aquamarine has been found in a pegmatite on the northwest flank of Centennial Cone, associated with smoky quartz in which it is sometimes embedded. Centennial Cone is a mountain lying about 15 miles west of Golden. In Fremont County, some beryl crystals showing small clear spots suitable for cutting have been obtained from a pegmatite on the Amazon Claim located 6½ miles north of Texas Creek in East Gulch.

South Dakota. Fragments of facet-grade golden beryl are sometimes obtained from large crystals found in a number of pegmatites near Keystone, Pennington County.

Wyoming. Aquamarine is infrequently found in the pegmatite dikes of the Bridger Mountains of Fremont County. The dikes occur in the northeast part of the county east of the Wind River Canyon and about 15 miles northeast of Shoshone, or about 20 miles southeast of Thermopolis and have been mined for mica, beryl and feldspar since 1906. Beryl occurs as crystals up to 8 inches in diameter of light blue to greenish-blue color.

Idaho. Gem quality aquamarine is rarely found in the numerous pegmatites which outcrop in Boise County in the region extending from Centerville north to Garden Valley. An exceptional transparent blue crystal in the U.S. National Museum comes from an unspecified locality near Centerville (see Figure 19).

Nevada. In 1939, emerald was reported from Rye Patch, Pershing County, occurring in a pegmatite penetrating limestone. The emerald color was confined to the exterior zones of the small crystals. No commercial importance was attached to the discovery.

New Mexico. Gem quality pale to deep green aquamarine has been found in some quantity in pegmatite at the Sunnyside Mine located just west of Globe Road above Alamos Canyon, 3½ miles southwest of South Petaca in Rio Arriba County. The pegmatite yielded more than 2500 pounds of common ore grade beryl in 1943, but all of the gem material occurred in peculiar cigar-shaped crystals embedded in schists next to the pegmatite. The crystals ranged from ½ inch to 6 feet in length and from 1/16 to 7 inches in diameter, and contained numerous clear areas of facet-grade material.

California. The famous gem mines of Riverside and San Diego counties in Southern California have produced considerable quantities of morganite and, more rarely, some fine aquamarine from pegmatite pockets. Almost all beryl in Riverside County has been produced from a few mines on Coahuila Mountain in the southern part of the county, principally from the Fano-Simmons Mine on the southeast slope, a locality which is now named the Williamson Mine. Aquamarine and a yellowish morganite were said to occur in the pockets and 250 pounds was obtained over a period of several years but only 5 per cent was suitable for gem purposes. A vague locality for aquamarine is given as 2 miles east of Riverside on the Mears property at the base of Box Springs Mountain. It is said that considerable blue green beryl, some suitable for gems, was mined here.

In San Diego County, beryl is found in virtually every gem-bearing pegmatite whether opened for beryl, for tourmaline, or for lepidolite. The first noteworthy occurrence is in the northern part of the county at the Pearson Mine, a series of cuts and short drifts in a long thick pegmatite crossing the shallow eastern slope of Chihuahua Valley and forming a conspicuous feature of the landscape. This mine is presently owned by Fleischer of Poway who accomplished some work in the middle 1950's recovering intensely dark indigo blue to black tourmaline crystals, sometimes transparent, as well as handsome smoky quartz groups and small prismatic aquamarine crystals of simple habit. Proceeding southward, the next mine is the Mountain Lily Mine, Emeralite No. 2, or Ware Mine, known by all three names, which once produced modest quantities of morganite from pockets within a much-crushed horizontal pegmatite outcropping on the eastern rim of Aguanga Mountain at an elevation of 4920 feet above sea level. This mine is near the Palomar Truck Trail which traverses the crest of the ridge connecting Aguanga Mountain and Palomar Mountain. Kunz mentions a crystal of morganite which came from this mine measuring $4\frac{3}{8}$ by 3 by $2\frac{1}{2}$ inches in size.

In the Mesa Grande District of San Diego County, several places have produced fine morganite beryl, a limited amount of aquamarine, and some colorless beryl. The most noted is the Esmeralda Mine whose workings are on top of a narrow steep-sided ridge between the Mesa Grande Truck Trail and the Lusardi Truck Trail, about ¾ mile south-southeast of their junction. The mine consists of several opencuts and a shaft on the northern edge of the ridge at an elevation of about 3,000 feet above sea level. The shaft exploited a steep-dipping pocket zone consisting of a much shattered quartz core in which pockets occurred containing large quartz crystals, some tourmaline, and peach to pink morganites in flat tabular crystals of simple habit. Kunz records a large crystal of quartz from this mine sprinkled with nine morganite crystals averaging $1\frac{1}{2}$ inches across. This specimen is said to now be in a European collection. Considerable massive beryl, colorless to pale yellowish-green, is found in a coarse feldspar-quartz wall unit, some being clear but not in sizes large enough to cut gems. A crystal of almost 5 inches in diameter, aquamarine at the base and gradually darkening into deep peach color at the termination, has come from this mine in recent years. Approximately $1\frac{1}{2}$ miles east-southeast from the Esmeralda is Gem Hill upon which are located the Himalaya and Mesa Grande mines, the former now producing gem tourmaline. Gem Hill is a rounded wooded dome rising to an altitude of

4058 feet above sea level, 2 miles northwest of Mesa Grande Schoolhouse in a direct line but about 4 by a tortuous, sometimes impassable dirt road. The northern spur of Gem Hill is underlain by the workings of the famous Himalaya Mine, noted for the enormous quantities of gem tourmaline ex-tracted from pockets in a pegmatite which seldom exceeds several feet in thickness. In the pockets are occasion-ally found fine morganite and very pale pink to colorless beryl crystals, some-times beautifully formed but at other times, so completely etched and dis-solved that no trace of faces remain. A morganite crystal from Mesa Grande is shown in Figure 24. In general, the crystals are small, seldom over an inch or so in diameter. A notable exception is the large richly-hued reddish orange crystal in the Warner Collection in the California Institute of Technology

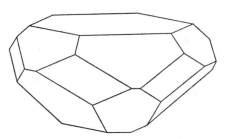

FIGURE 24. Morganite crystal from Mesa Grande, California. The basic form is a much compressed hexagonal prism whose edges have been deeply beveled by pyramidal faces. Larger morganite crystals are seldom this perfectly formed.

at Pasadena. This magnificent specimen is part of a tabular crystal showing prominent prism and pyramid faces along the edges and parts of basal planes on each end. It is approximately 6 inches in diameter and 3½ to 2¼ inches thick with 12 well developed faces and weighs 40 ounces. Implanted on one side are several dark green tourmaline prisms of small size. This particular color of morganite has not been noted before from the Himalaya and rumor has it that it actually came from one of the openings along the Cota pegmatite which outcrops below the Himalaya Mine road, low on the west slope of Gem Hill. The San Diego Mine is adjacent to the Himalaya on the east slope of Gem Hill and consists of numerous slumped workings as well as one adit in which some exploratory work has been done from time to time by its owner, Fred Rynerson of Lilac, California. Since the workings are on the same dike, the mineralization is similar.

Much morganite has been obtained further west in the Pala District from a group of gem mines tapping several outcropping pegmatites on Hiriart Hill, Pala Chief Mountain, and Tourmaline Queen Mountain. These three emi-nences rise from several hundred to over one thousand feet above the valley floor of the San Luis Rey River and ring the village of Pala to the north and northeast. Beginning with the easternmost hill, Hiriart Hill, magnificent crystals of morganite have been obtained from the Vanderburg Mine on its northeast shoulder, from the Katerina Mine, low on the southwest slope, and especially from the Senpe Mine which is located on the northwest slope about halfway up. The Senpe dike begins at the base of the hill and is traceable to the crest and over the other side. A number of tunnels and opencuts mark places where mining has been carried on in years past. Of all the mines in this region, this alone seemed to produce morganite crystals of exceptional clarity, pale peach to pink color, often with areas large enough to cut gems of 20 carats or so. An unusually good piece provided a gem of 48 carats. The dike varies considerably in thickness but probably averages about 8 feet and in places, as much as 12. The tunneled section was mined out during World War II for quartz crystals to be used in piezoelectric applications. During this period a large pocket was struck from which were obtained a considerable number of pinkish morganite crystals. Most of these were very sharp and regular with polished faces and a high degree of transparency. Further north from the Senpe Mine, and occupying a prominent rib of whitish feldspar which plunges down the steep slope of Hiriart Hill, is the San Pedro spodumene mine. This working has yielded some fine crystals of aquamarine of specimen grade but beryl is rare as a rule. A magnificent group of two large blue aquamarine crystals weighing 6 pounds was taken from this mine some years ago and is now in the Warner Collection of the California Institute of Technology.

Fine morganite has been obtained from the Pala Chief Mine near the top of Pala Chief Mountain immediately northwest of the summit. Many tunnels and drifts have honeycombed a thick flat-lying pegmatite noted for its production of magnificent spodumene and tourmaline. In the gem pockets, morganite occurred in tabular crystals of perhaps an inch to several inches in diameter, often embedded in a network of cleavelandite blades.

Tourmaline Queen Mountain, the westernmost of the three gem hills at Pala, is a steep brush-covered mountain which bears the famous Stewart Lithia Mine low on its southeast flank, the Tourmaline Queen Mine near the summit and ¼ mile below on the eastern slope, and the Tourmaline King Mine about ¼ mile northwest of the summit. All three have provided fine morganite from pockets in pegmatite. The pegmatite at the Stewart Lithia Mine reaches a thickness of 70 feet but the others average from 8 feet to 15 feet only. Morganite crystals are all peach color and vary in size from small brilliantly glassy perfect crystals of ½ inch to large tabular individuals as much as 3 inches or more across. Larger crystals are usually severely etched and contain numerous irregular gas- and liquid-filled inclusions. Those from the Tourmaline King are rich in faces as are those from the Stewart Lithia Mine. A splendid tabular crystal in the American Museum of Natural History measuring 6 by 6 by 3 inches exhibits an aquamarine core and is probably from the Tourmaline King although the locality on the label reads simply "Pala." Crystals from the Tourmaline Queen on the other hand, are relatively simple in form, showing prominent prism and basal planes, but medium size pyramidal faces. Because of internal imperfections the majority of morganite crystals from the localities mentioned above seldom afford cut gems over several carats in weight but a notable and unusual exception is a 122 carat gem from Pala in the U.S. National Museum.

In the Rincon District, small but perfectly-formed beryl crystals have been obtained from a number of mines which are on the slopes of a low mountain rising immediately to the east of the Rincon Indian Reservation in the upper part of Pauma Valley. Two of the mines, the Clark and the Victor are on the southwest spur of this mountain overlooking the junction of Paradise Creek and San Luis Rey River and immediately to the north of the latter. About ½ mile north-northwest of this group is the Mack Mine located in a small cove at the foot of the mountain and 1½ miles south-southeast of the village of Rincon. At the Victor Mine, a few very fine aquamarine crystals were found, sea green in color, and up to 2 inches in length; also a number of needle-like prisms of specimen value only. In the gem pockets, some morganite was recovered but was small and of no value; one crystal recorded measured only ¾ by 1 inch. The Clark Mine also produced very small quantities of morganite from gem pockets. At the Mack Mine, a number of slender hexagonal prisms of facet-grade beryl, pale greenish-blue to light blue, were recovered from a series of small irregular pockets which honey-combed the thin ledge within its upper six inches. Atop the mountain to the east of these mines, some exploratory work has taken place on a few of the numerous pegmatites which may be seen there; it is reported that some gem aquamarine has been found.

In the Ramona District, a group of dikes located along the western slopes of Hatfield Creek Valley, about 3½ miles east-northeast of the center of Ramona, have provided aquamarine and morganite from various mines and prospect pits. Good morganite has come only from the ABC Mine which is located on the extreme northwestern edge of the pegmatite area overlooking a small canyon in which a branch of Hatfield Creek runs along a southerly course, scarcely ½ mile from Highway 78. Bits of corroded morganite have also come from the Little Three Mine but their value for gems has been negligible. The Surprise Mine, now bulldozed over and inaccessible, produced several fine crystals, one of 6 inches in length and 1½ inches in diameter being recorded. Good greenish aquamarine has been found in the Surprise Mine, the Hercules, in lesser amounts in the Little Three and in the Black Panther. Taken as a whole, the importance of this district in respect to gem beryl has been very slight. Further details on mineralization may be consulted under TOURMALINE, GARNET (Spessartite), and TOPAZ.

In the southern part of San Diego County, pink and green beryl has been reported from the Crystal Mine located 8½ miles northwest of Jacumba. There is presently very little known about this locality but the nearest peg-matites which seem to fit the general locality, outcrop on the south slope of a steep narrow ridge overlooking the western side of La Posta Creek, exactly 15 miles northwest of Jacumba.

Baja California Norte. Aquamarine has been obtained from very small pockets in quartz cores in certain pegmatites of the San Pedro Martir Mountains of the interior of this peninsula. In 1911, the geologist Wittich reported finding a number of crystals, the best of which was a transparent greenish prism ¾ inch long and about half that in width. Larger yellowish-green crystals were also obtained but showed only occasional clear spots. This discovery points again to the relatively unexplored nature of the interior of Baja California and the likelihood that careful investigation may someday reveal productive gem-bearing pegmatite.

TOPAZ

Some of the finest gems known to man are yielded by the species topaz but in the minds of many persons, yellow gems are "topazes" and it is difficult to convince them that not all real topaz is yellow nor are all yellow gems genuine topaz. The majority of transparent yellow stones sold as "topaz" are in reality either *citrine*, the yellow variety of quartz, or a synthetic gem of similar color. The name "Brazilian topaz" under which such gems are frequently sold is doubly misleading because genuine topaz of yellow color is found in that country but in such small quantities that demands of the market can not possibly be supplied unless a bit of deception is practised. In North America, yellow topaz is rarely seen but good blue, beautiful warm sherry, and colorless crystals are commonly found in a number of places.

Topaz is aluminum fluosilicate with the formula: $Al_2SiO_4(F,OH)_2$. Gem varieties occur mostly in pockets in granitic pegmatites but small crystals are also seen in gas cavities in rhyolite rocks, as well as in openings in high-temperature vein deposits. One of the outstanding characteristics of topaz is its rarity in massive form, the vast majority of examples being beautifully developed glistening crystals of great perfection, belonging to the Orthorhombic System. Crystals range in size from minute sparkling pinpoints to some which reach hundreds of pounds in weight, but in North American localities, the average is far less. Individuals appear as short stubby prisms, diamond or square-shaped in cross section, terminating in blunt ends beveled by several pyramidal planes. At times the terminal plane is fully developed and crystals then look as if they had been sliced across; at other times, this plane is very small or altogether absent and the terminals are wedge- or chisel-shaped. Perfect crystals are highly lustrous with all faces looking as if they had been polished, however, where chemical activity takes place within the pocket after crystals are formed, faces become etched more or less completely and are then inclined to be lackluster. Sometimes dissolution is so severe that

FIGURE 25. Topaz crystals from various American localities. Upper left: a large milky blue crystal from the Little Three Mine, Ramona, California, measuring 2½ by 2¾ inches by 3¼ inches; upper right: a sharp but flawed pale sherry crystal from a pocket in the granite of the Walker Quarry, North Conway, New Hampshire, measuring 3½ inches by 1¾ inches. The lower crystals are virtually flawless pale brown crystals from pegmatite pockets of the Devil's Head region of Colorado. The largest crystal measures 2¼ inches in length and is slightly etched on all surfaces while the smaller crystal, placed on end to show the markings better, is strongly etched on the basal termination and pyramid faces. Courtesy Smithsonian Institution.

all traces of form are lost and nothing remains except irregular lumps covered with many hillocks with curious angular pits between. A series of topaz crystals showing a variety of forms are illustrated in Figure 25. Almost every crystal of topaz shows evidence of the single highly perfect and easily developed cleavage which lies at right angles to the length of the prism. Usually the base of the crystal is broken at the point where it was attached to pocket walls and this surface is seen to be wonderfully regular and smooth. Few specimens are without several mirror-like reflections inside which are also due to partially developed cleavage planes. Although the hardness of topaz is listed as 8 on the Mohs Scale, some care must be taken with cut stones to prevent them knocking against hard surfaces because they may split along the cleavage plane as neatly as if they had been sawn in two.

Topaz is fairly high in specific gravity, varying between values of 3.5 and 3.6. Several typical readings established on American specimens are as follows: Thomas Mountains, Utah—3.565; Nathrop, Colorado—3.567; Pikes Peak, Colorado—3.567; Stoneham, Maine—3.560.

Refractive indices are medium in value, ranging between extremes of: $a = 1.607$, $\gamma = 1.617$, and $a = 1.629$, $\gamma = 1.637$. Thomas Mountains material gives: $a = 1.6072$, $\beta = 1.6104$, $\gamma = 1.6176$; sherry crystals from Colorado: $a = 1.608$, $\gamma = 1.618$; blue material from Texas gives the same as the last. Birefringence varies from 0.008 to 0.010; topaz is biaxial, positive. The dispersive power is only 0.014 but is offset by the unusual internal clarity which permits development of considerable brilliance in finished gems while the ability to take an almost perfect polish contributes not a little to the final result. The most common colors of North American topaz are blue, grayish-blue, bluish-green, colorless, and in certain localities, a fine reddish-brown or sherry color. The last is extremely attractive but, unfortunately, fades in strong light. The author has several sherry gems kept away from light which are still as beautiful today as they were when cut a number of years ago, but on the other hand, a magnificent sherry gem of almost 200 carats cut for the U.S. National Museum from Colorado material, has faded badly because of continual exposure and is now only faintly tinged with brown. Aside from blue and sherry, bright colors of topaz are rarely seen in North American specimens, some pale straw yellow crystals of small size as well as very pale pinks from Mexico are known but the vivid yellows, browns, and the magnificent rich orange "imperial" colors of Brazilian stones are not met with. Colors in topaz are frequently combined; in Texas blues, for example, not all of the crystal is blue, the coloration being confined to zones parallel to the sides of the prism or passing upward through the crystal in a band which stretches from corner to corner. In such specimens, zones other than blue are colorless. In some New Hampshire crystals, blue, amber, and colorless are all seen in a single individual.

LOCALITIES

Alberta. In 1896, two rolled pebbles were found in the gravels of a small stream west of Jasper House in the Canadian Rocky Mountains; from the name, it is presumed that this locality is in Jasper National Park. One of light bluish-green color measured ¾ by 1 ¼ by ½ inches in size; the other, of faint orange yellow tinge, measured 1 by ½ by ½ inches. Since that year, no other finds have been reported from this area but perhaps further investigation may turn up more and permit tracing the material to its source.

New Brunswick. Crystals up to ¾ inch, some clear and flawless, have been found in cavities in massive quartz which cuts slate near its contact with granite in the district around the confluence of the Burnt Hill Brook and the southwest branch of the Miramichi River in York County.

Maine. In his book: "Gems and Precious Stones of North America," Dr. Kunz mentions topaz from "Harndon Hill" in Stoneham Township, Oxford County. As it turns out, this is in error since the locality is actually upon the summit of Lord's Hill which is about ½ mile to the southeast of Harndon Hill in the southwestern corner of the township. The place from which the crystals came is on the southwest edge of the exact summit of Lord's Hill, and places the locality very close to the boundary between Stoneham and Lowell townships, or about ½ mile east-northeast of the corner made by the junction of Stow and Stoneham townships. The original find brought to light crystals ranging in size from ½ inch to almost 2 ½ inches in diameter, transparent in parts and etched upon the exteriors. Large opaque crystals up to 12 inches in diameter were said to have been found also, some weighing 20 to 40 pounds, coarse and rough on the outside and much filled with flaws and inclusions. Colors of small crystals ranged from pale orangy-brown to blue to colorless, sometimes with two or more of these hues in the same crystal. Pale green is also reported. The color of larger crystals was deeper in shade. Recent visitors to this locality report finding blue aquamarine fragments, massive topaz, apatite, and curved or "ball" muscovite mica in the rubbish thrown out from the old pits.

Topaz is an extremely rare mineral in the pegmatite of Mount Apatite in Minot Township, 4 miles west of Auburn, Androscoggin County (see APATITE), however, one specimen of blue color found many years ago, yielded a fine gem weighing 43.75 carats which is now in the U.S. National Museum.

In Sagadahoc County, a variety of rare minerals, including topaz, are obtained from cavities in pegmatite which outcrop on a long low hill just north of the Cathance River and about 2 ½ miles north of Topsham in Topsham Township. In 1929 a pocket was found in the floor of the Fisher Quarry and from it some very interesting topaz obtained. The main pocket measured approximately 4 by 6 by 6 feet with an upward extension reaching another 6 feet up to the floor of the quarry. Hundreds of crystals were removed but all were so badly etched and dissolved that only two had original faces; the largest crystal measured 4 by 4 by 5 inches and weighed about 3 pounds. The total quantity of topaz was 25 pounds of which half this was made up of six large crystals. Most were colorless but some were slightly tinged with brown and others pale blue. Pale blue and pink beryls were also found, one pink example being about one pound in weight and showing severe etching except on the basal faces which were smooth and bright. Numerous small needles of tourmaline were removed from floor deposits, the largest crystal being nearly ½ inch in diameter. Herderite, a rare phosphate, was found in beautiful crystals, some up to 2 inches in length. Other associated minerals were albite (cleavelandite), slightly smoky quartz, gahnite, apatite, lepidolite, muscovite, columbite, torbernite and cassiterite. The majority of the specimens from this pocket are now in the Mineralogical Museum of Harvard University.

New Hampshire. Perhaps the outstanding New England locality for topaz is that on South Baldface Mountain, 3½ miles west of North Chatham and just south of the boundary between Carroll and Coos counties. The top of Baldface consists of two distinct peaks, one mile apart, the southern being 3569 feet above sea level and the northern being 3591 feet. Both peaks or knobs, are of bare rock laced with small pegmatite bodies in which topaz occurs in pockets. The groundmass between the knobs is Conway biotite-granite partly broken into great blocks. Two prospect pits are on the precipitous northeast shoulder of South Baldface while another is on the southeast slope. All mining here has been of an informal and sporadic nature. Topaz occurs associated with smoky quartz, orthoclase and microcline, biotite, muscovite, and a little phenakite. Pockets range from small to large, one on record was 10 feet high and 2 to 3 feet across the top and 4 to 7 feet across near the bottom. The trend of mineralization seems to be northeast as marked by a series of excavations in this direction. Pegmatites are similar to those noted in Colorado in that they do not consist of long narrow dikes or huge oval masses but only as small roughly spherical bodies in granite. Grain size near the pockets begins to increase at the borders and becomes very coarse toward the center finally climaxing in an opening which is lined with pocket crystals. Sometimes the structure of pocket walls takes on the texture of graphic granite but at other times it is merely a coarsening in grain size. Feldspars within the pockets occasionally show a faint greenish cast, like amazonite, but most are buff in color with well-developed faces. Most quartz is smoky, some quite clear, and occurs in single crystals as well as in parallel groups. Biotite is encountered with sharply developed crystals of hexagonal outline. Phenakite is found as small transparent colorless crystals up to ½ inch in size attached to, or partially embedded in, feldspar, quartz and topaz. Topaz occurs from minute crystals to those as large as 2½ by 3½ inches. The majority are translucent to transparent but often badly flawed with liquid- or gas-filled bubbles of small size. Some are suitable for faceting but most are sought for cabinet specimens because of their perfection of form and the sharpness of the faces (see Fig. 26). Colors range from colorless, the predominant hue, to pale bluish-green but some are pure blue and others faintly yellow. In early days, no brownish crystals were reported, possibly because many which had lain in the ground near the surface had lost their color before discoverers appeared. In any case, recent excavations (about 1950) brought to light many which were brown or brown and blue combined. Below the prospects just described occurs another place where topaz crystals have been found; this is in a thin pegmatite dike on the lower northeast slope of the mountain in which are found small pockets in graphic granite containing topaz. About 1900, Harvard University collected 200 crystals from the Baldface locality, especially from the east slope of South Baldface at an elevation of 2900 feet.

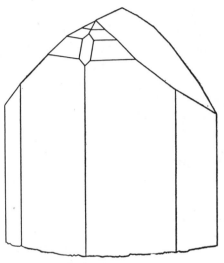

FIGURE 26. Topaz crystal from Baldface Mountain, New Hampshire.

Fine topaz is also obtained from another part of northern New Hampshire, specifically, within a broad area in Coos County which is underlain by coarse reddish to grayish-white biotite-granite. Noted localities are Greens Ledge in the western part of Milan Township, located exactly 3 miles slightly west of south of West Milan, and Victors Head located 1¾ miles north-northwest of Percy in the northern part of Stark Township. Pocket granite occurs in many areas in Stark Township, in a few places in Lancaster, Kilkenny, Dummer, Millsfield, Milan, Odell, Berlin, Strafford, and in Northcumberland townships. Throughout the region, topaz is often found loose in the thin topsoil covering the rocky ridges or else occurs in the pockets, slumped to the bottom along with other pocket material and from which it is excavated as a jumbled mass of debris mixed more or less intimately with clays, infiltrated topsoils, etc.

Greens Ledges have furnished hundreds of topaz crystals in the last several decades from a series of pockets occurring at an elevation of 2000 feet. Crystals range in size from less than an inch in diameter to some reaching several inches in length and almost as much in diameter. Some pockets have been very productive, one on record produced 56 crystals, ten of which were perfect and averaged about ½ inch in diameter and one inch in length; the pocket was only 14 inches long and 9 by 6 inches across. Crystals were mostly pale yellow in color but sherry and blue as well as colorless crystals were also found. Most were transparent and some clean enough to afford faceted gems. Some pockets contained very perfect crystals but in others the crystals were found completely etched or even partly destroyed. In some instances massive topaz has been found in the rock adjoining the pockets but is valueless for gems. Topaz pockets on Victors Head follow the same pattern noted above but occur at an elevation of 1700 feet. In all localities, topaz is accompanied by several or all of the following minerals: amethyst, sometimes fine, smoky quartz, microcline and albite, molybdenite, limonite, sericite, muscovite, beryl, chlorite, pyrite, and fluorite.

In the early 1950's, a new New Hampshire locality for topaz was discovered at the Lovejoy gravel pits about 2½ miles northwest of Conway, Carroll County. The granite at this place is badly decomposed and though retaining its original structure, can be crumbled easily into individual grains thus making it useful for a variety of constructional purposes. At the pits, decomposed granite outcrops over an area of over 150 acres while similar but solid rock is also noted at Redstone, about 3 miles north of Conway in a quarry at the base of Redstone Ledge, immediately east of Redstone, providing comparable pocket mineralization. In both localities fissures and cavities occur in the granite lined with smoky quartz crystals up to 10 inches in length, microcline crystals several inches across, and topaz, the largest found so far being a fine, well-formed crystal 3¼ inches in length. One pocket found in the Lovejoy Pits in 1954 yielded 15 crystals. In form, the crystals are the usual squarish prisms capped with chisel-shaped terminals; all are more or less transparent but contain numerous inclusions. Clear areas are confined to the tips from which flawless gems of perhaps 5 to 10 carats weight can be cut. Topaz crystals from one pocket were distinctly brownish-yellow in tinge but another pocket nearby yielded only colorless crystals. As previously noted in localities further north in Coos County, graphic granite forms pocket walls and is an indication, in digging, that a pocket is being approached. A crystal from the Redstone locality is illustrated in Figure 25.

Connecticut. The famous old tungsten mine in Trumbull Township, Fairfield County, long noted for a variety of interesting minerals also produced some gem quality clear blue topaz crystals. Good crystals were found in cavities in massive quartz both in the workings of the mine at Long Hill, located 1 mile north of the railroad station of the same name, and in a quartz vein near the mine.

Virginia. Blue topaz, occasionally in faced crystals, but usually in large formless masses has been obtained from the Morefield Mine, located on a shallow wooded slope not far from State Highway 628 and about 4 miles east-northeast of Amelia, Amelia County. One huge mass of topaz, completely cloudy and unfit for gems, measured 44 inches in length and weighed about 500 pounds! Smaller masses and rare crystals were sometimes clear enough in spots to furnish gems. At the Rutherford Mine, known as the source of the world's best amazonite, blue topaz was found, though rarely, in crystals and crystalline masses and sometimes capable of being cut into gems. Both mines exploit complex pegmatites noted for the variety and beauty of the minerals found in them.

South Carolina. In an unusual massive low-fluorine topaz deposit at the old Brewer Mine, located on Brewer Knob about 3 miles west of Jefferson, Chesterfield County, beautiful facet grade crystals of yellow and blue topaz were said to occur in small cavities. Granular material from this deposit showed the following properties: R.I.: $a = 1.629$, $\beta = 1.631$, $\gamma = 1.638$; birefringence 0.009; specific gravity 3.509.

Georgia. Colorless topaz suitable for cutting into small gems, has been found lining cavities in quartz at the Williams Mica Mine, about 2¼ miles southwest of Ward Gap or 9½ miles northeast of Dahlonega, Lumpkin County.

Texas. Outstanding gem quality blue and colorless topaz occurs in many places in the granitic rocks of Mason County upon a plateau region known as the Llano Uplift. Here is found a series of low hills without any prominent ranges or mountains in a region in which rain is scarce and only the largest streams flow regularly. The elevation of the topaz deposits ranges from 1600 to 1800 feet above sea level. Underlying igneous rock is Precambrian coarse grained reddish granite in which individual feldspar grains may reach as much as 1 inch in diameter but schists and gneisses also occur. In places, this granite contains small pegmatite bodies of irregular form in which topaz-bearing pockets of various size are found. Two productive areas have been discovered, the first and best known is near Streeter on Highway 377, about 8 miles west of Mason, the other near Katemcy in the northern part of the county about 12 miles north of Mason and just east of Highway 87. The discovery of topaz in this region took place in 1904 when R. L. Parker of Streeter picked up a pebble of "quartz" from the bed of a stream on the property of Sam Awalt near Streeter, and struck by its heaviness, sent it away to be identified. In a short time it was returned with the pronouncement that it was topaz. An attempt was made immediately to determine the source and this was found in due time, however, since the enclosing rocks were so hard, mining of pockets was discouraging and efforts were concentrated on recovering loose crystals found in sands and gravels of creek beds and dry washes. Mining was not begun until 1908 and limited work in the next two years on several deposits produced a total of 200 pounds of good crystals; by 1912, some dozen prospect holes had been dug. As of 1913 the following deposits had been established: on the C. J. Worley place ½ mile east of Streeter; on the Dan Blickenbach place about 2½ miles northeast of Streeter; and upon A. Smart's place near Grit.

The old Worley prospect was located in the wash of a dry stream about ¼ mile east of the farmhouse. Work was conducted here for several hundred feet up and down the watercourse. Large boulders filled the streambed and it was necessary to dig around and beneath them in order to recover the heavy topaz crystals which had settled in bottom layers of alluvium. In one spot showing cavities in an outcrop, some blasting was done. Topaz crystals from this locality were tinted fine blue, sometimes deep blue, while others were bluish-green.

In the Katemcy area, discovery of deposits was also due to R. L. Parker and P. H. Parker who first found topaz upon the property of D. E. Amrine. In 1913 prospects were located on the Awalt property and on land belonging to L. McGhee as well as upon the Amrine place, all within a small area about 4 miles south-southwest of Katemcy.

The Awalt prospects were located on low ground between the forks of a dry wash about 250 yards southeast of the house and numbered about a dozen pits. Some gravel covered the area here but primarily large masses of rock were exposed. In the latter were found pegmatite bodies of coarse grain with pockets as much as several feet across and about one foot deep. In the pockets large reddish, grayish, or pale bluish-green (amazonite) feldspar crystals and colorless to smoky quartz crystals were found lining the sides along with some black tourmaline. Topaz crystals from the Awalt property were mostly colorless but of fine quality; some blue material was also found.

The McGhee prospect is about ½ mile northwest of the workings just described in a flat area alongside a dry streambed. No gem pockets were found and all crystals were recovered from alluvium. In the gravel the following minerals occurred with topaz: quartz crystals, red, gray, and amazonite feldspar, muscovite, and small amounts of cassiterite. Topaz from this locality was of very fine quality though mostly colorless but small amounts of bluish-green crystals were also recovered. Some large specimens were found at the diggings, the largest being a 1,296 gram crystal (45.7 oz.) now in the U.S. National Museum. This magnificent specimen is slightly bluish green, showing a large cleavage plane at the base where the crystal had broken, and some well-developed faces although most edges are rounded and surfaces dulled by stream wear. The color is typically concentrated along opposite prism edges.

The Amrine prospects consisted of four pits opened by blasting, several hundred yards southwest of the Awalt prospects. Exposed granite was the usual coarse grained, red material in which pockets were found containing large red feldspar crystals, massive and crystallized quartz, muscovite, black tourmaline, and purple or gray fluorite. Not much good topaz was recovered.

In Mason County, the essentially level terrain has prevented topaz crystals from traveling far after erosion from pockets and consequently they are found in considerable quantity in the lowest layers of alluvium where their higher specific gravity has caused them to settle. Recent efforts in this area have proved that not all alluvial deposits are exhausted by any means, since many crystals have been found by private parties who pay an admission fee to dig upon certain properties. Topaz from Mason County is currently offered from $.50 to $1.25 per gram for fine blue facet grade material. Very fine gems have been cut from Texas topaz as witness one example of 333.5 carats cut by Hugh Leiper and prepared from a crystal originally weighing 700 carats and measuring about 1¼ by 2¼ inches. The gem is now in the possession of Porter Rankin of Midland, Texas, for whom it was specially cut. In 1957, an untouched area was prospected on the Davenport Ranch, 7.1 miles northwest of Mason and immediately west of the Grit country store on Highway 29. Among other crystals, a fine specimen of 180 grams has been found here.

Idaho. A fairly large topaz was reported in 1896 from a gold placer about "100 miles north of Boise." This could possibly place the locality in the New Meadows area in Adams County where some gem quality corundum has been found. The crystal was described as similar in habit to the famous specimens from Alabaschka in the Ural Mountains of the USSR. It was stated to be green in color, to weigh 1,110 carats, and to measure 2 inches in length and 1¾ inches in diameter. It was found associated with loose amethyst crystals resting upon the bedrock beneath the gold bearing gravels. Another report states that a colorless topaz crystal was found in 1919 at a locality 5 miles northwest of Moulton, just east of Almo in Cassia County. Still another report, equally vague, stated that a clear blue topaz of "large size" was found in gold bearing gravel in a tributary of Paddy Creek in the Warren District of Idaho County.

Wyoming. Many beautiful small transparent colorless topaz crystals, said to resemble those from the Thomas Mountains of Utah, have been found at the headwaters of the Bighorn River in the northern part of the state. Unfortunately, details are lacking on this occurrence.

New Mexico. Gas cavities in rhyolite beds at the western base of Round, or, Maverick Mountain, north of Diamond Creek in the Taylor Creek District of Catron and Sierra counties, have furnished small clear colorless topaz of some specimen value.

Colorado. Outstanding topaz crystals come from a number of places in this state under geological circumstances similar to those observed in Texas and New Hampshire; one occurrence is also listed in which topaz occurs in gas cavities in rhyolite instead of in pockets in pegmatite. The majority of crystals have been obtained from pegmatite in Pikes Peak granite, a coarse-grained reddish rock containing reddish potash feldspar, quartz, hornblende, and biotite mica. The area covered by outcrops of this granite is truly enormous—over 1,000 square miles—and promises the production of fine gemstones for many years to come including amazonite and quartz as well as topaz. Pikes Peak granite weathers easily leaving behind in many places, typical rounded boulders or outcroppings of spherical shape. Much is so soft that ordinary picks and shovels can be used to dig it away. Although pockets in pegmatite may be found any place where this rock outcrops, certain areas have been more productive than others and remarks are accordingly confined to them.

The finest topaz has come from the Devil's Head region in the western part of Douglas County. Devil's Head, formerly called Platte Mountain, a large isolated peak 9,348 feet high, is accessible by road from several directions and is frequently visited by collecting parties although little commercial work is ever done. The most productive area is located south of the summit atop a ridge below the main access highway. Originally, topaz was found in a long pegmatite body which some persons believe to be actually a more or less continuous pegmatite dike. Discovery of topaz at this locality dates back to at least 1883 at which time it was reported by Walter B. Smith. The last extensive work was accomplished by Over and Montgomery in 1934 when numerous excellent crystals were uncovered. The largest pocket found measured 1 by 1 by 4 feet and contained smoky quartz, microcline feldspar, limonite, hematite, cassiterite, and fluorite in addition to topaz. The latter occurred in small to fist-size individuals broken loose from their moorings along the walls and completely etched, sometimes very deeply. Most were nearly perfect internally with surprisingly few inclusions. The largest crystal measured about 3¼ by 3¼ by 4⅜ inches and weighed 1160 grams or 5800 carats. It was largely flawless though badly etched, and of beautiful rich reddish-brown color. A smaller sherry crystal was cut into a faceted gem of 235 carats for the U.S. National Museum but after exposure to daylight for some months, it faded to colorless. Many other crystals of smaller size were also found. Probably several hundred pounds of gem grade material has been mined in this area since the locality was first discovered. Old accounts state that up to 1890 over 3000 gems were cut from Devil's Head topaz, two exceptional stones of 125 and 193 carats being mentioned. Several typical crystals of topaz from this region are shown in Figure 25.

Better known for its magnificent amazonite and smoky quartz crystal groups, the Florissant area north of the community of the same name in Teller County, has also produced much topaz. Specimens from here are sometimes labeled "Crystal Peak" because this is the name of the highest of the rounded granite knobs which protrude above the gently rolling terrain characteristic of this area. The productive area is very large, covering at least three square miles extending northward from a point about 2 miles northeast of the town of Lake George, and easily reached by several roads from Florissant and Lake George. Now under lease, about 800 acres are open to collecting upon payment of a daily fee, which, in 1957, was $1.25 per person. Elevation averages about 9000 feet above sea level in rolling wooded terrain free of underbrush in most places while Crystal Peak rises to 9668 feet. The underlying reddish granite is somewhat coarser in grain than elsewhere and is much decomposed so that it may be dug away with ordinary hand tools to as deep as 10 to 20 feet below the surface. Pegmatites are difficult to discover since most are effectively covered by topsoil but good indications of their presence are scattered pieces of white massive core quartz which resist decay far better than feldspar. The discovery of topaz at this locality is credited to a Mr. Transue in 1884 and was the second discovery of this gemstone in this state. For several years production was estimated at $4000 or more, but the total to date must be several times that. Crystals up to 3½ inches in size have been found here in typical pegmatite pockets. In form, pockets are more drawn out than those noted in other topaz deposits, perhaps because the pegmatites themselves are narrower also. Granite adjacent to pockets gives little hint of pocket development, merely showing a sudden increase in grain size until irregular masses of quartz and feldspar, about 1 inch in diameter, are found surrounding pocket openings. Feldspar crystals vary from small individuals of only ½ inch in size to some which may be as much as 6 inches thick and over a foot long. Quartz is ordinarily of the smoky variety and so dark in hue that it is difficult to see through a crystal only 1 inch in diameter. Their form is very characteristic, long tapering individuals coming almost to a point being the rule. Some are glassy in luster but others are etched or covered by tenacious coatings of scaly reddish hematite. Topaz crystals are mainly colorless but a few are slightly yellowish or bluish, while in respect to associations, a large number are found implanted upon crystals of feldspar. The most productive place for topaz appears to be a small area about ½ mile northwest of Crystal Peak.

Good topaz has come from pegmatite pockets in the Tarryall Mountains of southeast Park County but crystals have not been as large or as suited for gems as those from other localities. Crystals range up to about 1 inch in length and are colorless or pale blue.

Some gem quality topaz has also been obtained from pockets in pegmatite in the Crystal Park area of western El Paso County. The rather level section which comprises the "park" is at an altitude of about 8,600 feet at the base of Cameron Cone, Mount Arthur, and Mount Garfield, and is accessible by toll road from Adams Crossing on the highway between Colorado Springs and Manitou Springs. Pegmatites are sprinkled heavily over this area and may be found in the form of dikes, lenses, or irregular bodies. Cavities reach as much as three feet in size and are lined with the usual pegmatite pocket minerals of the Pikes Peak granite. Some blue topaz crystals up to ¾ pound in weight have come from this area as well as from upper Glen Cove to the west and close to the border of Teller and El Paso counties. A fine blue topaz gem cut from Glen Cove material is shown in Figure 27.

Some topaz is found in pockets in pegmatite on Stove Mountain several miles south of Manitou Springs and immediately north of St. Peter's Dome in El Paso County. The collecting area is reached by the Gold Camp Road which runs south from the highway between Colorado Springs and Manitou Springs.

FIGURE 27. A pale blue topaz gem cut in pear fashion from a large clear crystal found by Edwin Over in the Pike's Peak Region of Colorado. The gem is 2⅛ inches in length and weighs 368.5 carats and was cut by the author for the U.S. National Museum. Courtesy Smithsonian Institution.

Very small topaz crystals occur in gas cavities in rhyolite flows at Ruby Mountain, a low hill rising about 200 feet above the Arkansas River across from Nathrop, Chaffee County. Locally the rhyolites are white, gray, or pink, and form distinctly banded flows of considerable thickness in which horizons are found containing numerous small cavities. Within these openings are found beautifully formed topaz crystals, seldom over ½ inch in size, along with deep red spessartite. When first removed from the cavities, topaz crystals are yellow but with exposure, this color fades to pale blue, very faint yellow, or even to colorless. This locality is chiefly of interest to mineral collectors although some of the largest crystals can be cut into small brilliant gems.

Utah. One of the favorite mineral hunting grounds in the Western United States is in the topaz-bearing rhyolites which outcrop at the southern base of the Thomas Mountains in Juab County. Beautifully developed sparkling clear crystals of colorless and sherry topaz are found here in gas cavities in gray spongy rhyolite. Many of these have been cut for collections but the majority are far too small to be of commercial value since they seldom exceed a fraction of an inch in size and cannot furnish flawless gems over several carats weight. The best collecting area is a small depression called Topaz Cove which lies at the base of the mountains immediately north of Thomas Pass on Highway 149 leading from Jericho. Rhyolite cavities are lined with many small quartz crystals dotted here and there with sharp upright crystals of topaz, accompanied at times by pseudobrookite, hematite, fluorite, calcite, bixbyite, garnet, and very rarely, by minute deep red hexagonal tablets of a peculiar variety of beryl. In the northeastern portion of the range, 3 to 4 miles south of Dugway Road, topaz is also found in a similar rhyolite, however, most of these are gray in color due to containing numerous included grains of quartz. A few are both large and clear, much larger in fact than those found at the southern end of the range. Opaque crystals may reach as much as 2 inches in length while clear specimens, usually slightly etched, may be as much as 1 inch long and about ½ inch in diameter. Less than one half mile east of this locality, some highly unusual crystals of pale rose-red were found weathered out upon the surface accompanied by many rough opaque "sand" topaz crystals.

California. Important commercial quantities of cuttable and specimen grade topaz have been obtained from two mines in San Diego County. The first is the Emeralite No. 2 Mine, or, as it is also known, the Mountain Lily or Ware Mine, the last taken from the name of the owner and operator, J. W. Ware, formerly a jeweler of San Diego. The total production was said to have been several hundred pounds of crystals, mostly blue although some were pale green, ranging in size from less than ½ inch across to one green crystal which weighed 3¼ pounds. A large crystal measuring 2⅞ inches tall, 3¼ by 2½ inches across the base, and weighing 12 ounces is in the Warner Collection of the California Institute of Technology at Pasadena. This crystal is well-formed, showing a flat termination with several large sloping faces, and is pale blue in color but the coloration is confined to a cylindrical zone around the outside of the prism while the interior is colorless. Only the smaller crystals from this mine were sufficiently clear to afford faceted gems. The largest flawless cut stone of record is reported to be a beautiful blue 17 carat pear-shaped gem. Associated with topaz in the pockets were found some exceptionally fine tourmaline crystals, small in size, but of such a lovely and distinctive greenish-blue color that they led to naming the mine "Emeralite."

The second source of topaz, and probably the most important, is the Little Three Mine which is an opencut exploiting an exposed sheet of pegmatite lying on the south flank of a hill overlooking Hatfield Creek, about 3¾ miles east-northeast of Ramona. This area contains a number of gem mines; among them, the Hercules, Surprise, Black Panther, and ABC, all situated on several pegmatites concentrated in a small district between the forks of Hatfield Creek. The mine is presently under the ownership and operated by Louis B. Spaulding of Ramona. It is reached by tar road from Ramona and unimproved dirt road into the mine property. The pegmatite sheet averages several feet in thickness although in places it may be as much as 8 feet; the strike is northwest to southeast and the dip is southwest at an angle of about

FIGURE 28. A view of the Little Three Mine, Ramona, California; taken about 1914. The large boulder upon which the workman is seated is dark igneous rock which rests upon the lighter-colored pegmatite. The latter covers the slope in blanket fashion. Pockets at the upper part have been opened for tourmaline and topaz. Courtesy U.S. Geological Survey.

20°. The Little Three pegmatite is shown in Figure 28. Although this mine was opened many years ago, operations were only resumed by Spaulding in 1956. Since then a series of small pockets has been opened yielding large green tourmaline crystals of specimen grade, smoky quartz and feldspar groups, and blue and colorless topaz crystals. The largest topaz found recently is a single crystal showing a large basal plane and covered in part by minute scales of lepidolite; the color is pale blue. Only smaller crystals are useful for gems because larger specimens are invariably flawed and filled with minute inclusions. A typical Little Three topaz is illustrated in Figure 25, while a drawing of a crystal is shown in Figure 29. Fuller descriptions of this and the Ware Mine will be found under TOURMALINE and BERYL.

Durango. Large quantities of small topaz crystals occur in the tin washings of this state where they are found associated with *wood tin* (cassiterite). Both minerals are heavy and consequently lodge in the lowest portions of alluvium. Crystals are mostly colorless but many appear pale orange to red because of inclusions of microscopic rutile needles; the size seldom exceeds ⅜ inch in length.

Zacatecas. Fine colorless crystals occur upon the Hacienda del Tepetate in the Pinos area in the extreme southeastern part of the state and provide perfectly transparent and flawless facet material. Crystals range from about ¼ by ¼ inches to ½ by 1½ inches in size, while one report mentions a crystal 3 inches in length. Occasionally one turns up which is pinkish but the vast majority are colorless. The occurrence is like that of the Thomas Mountains of Utah, i.e., in cavities in rhyolite. Similar crystals are reported in rhyolite outcrops along the Continental Divide from Zacatecas to the neighboring state of San Luis Potosi. Other localities in the Pinos area are the Arroyos de San Juan de las Herreras, the Cerro de la Cruz, and in the Cerros de San Miguel de los Pinos, 9 kilometers southeast of the city of Pinos.

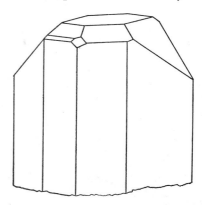

FIGURE 29. Topaz crystal showing the habit commonly observed at the Little Three Mine, Ramona, California.

San Luis Potosi. In the area near Cerritos, topaz has come from near Tepozan and the Sierra de Cambra. In the region around the city of San Luis Potosi, from the Hacienda de Canoas, the Mesa de Santa Cruz, and the Mesa de San Jose Buenavista.

Guanajuato. From the Hacienda la Quemada in the Ciudad Gonzales District; from the Canada de Marfil in the Guanajuato District; from the Hacienda de Tlachiquera near Leon in the Leon de los Aldamas District.

Hidalgo. From the Cerro del Nado southward of Apulco in the Tulancingo District.

Guerrero. From near Coyuca de Benitez in the Tabares District.

OPAL

The rainbow is imprisoned in opal. Weak, brittle, sensitive to heat and easily scratched, opal seems a poor candidate for an important place in the ranks of gems, yet nowhere else is seen the indescribable pure hues of dazzling intensity which leap forth from fine specimens. Despite its inherent faults, opal's beauty is supreme, and today, as for thousands of years past, it occupies a special niche in the hall of gems. Opal was well known to the ancients, the noted Roman naturalist Pliny was eloquent about its charms; even its name implies great antiquity, for the ancient peoples of India who spoke the now extinct Sanskrit tongue, called the gem *upala*, meaning "precious stone." This term was modified slightly by the Greeks and passed to the Romans who called it *opalus*, providing, obviously, the root *opal* which we use today.

According to latest researches, opal can be conveniently divided into two broad types depending on the kind of inner structure observed in each, that is, *common opal*, and *hyaline* or *clear opal*. This seems an arbitrary classification but recent x-ray studies of opal structure show that common opal, which is poorly translucent, contains scarcely any detectable crystal structure while highly translucent to transparent material, displays patches or islands of well-defined crystalline quartz. It is in fact this very feature which is now believed to explain the gorgeous spectral colors observed in opal. Examination of color patches under a microscope shows numerous thread-like parallel lines, sometimes as several sets crossing each other in a three-dimensional network. The nature of these geometrical figures was not recognized up to now but it seems plain from x-ray work that they consist of two rare forms of quartz, tridymite and cristobalite, which have partially crystallized during solidification of the opal. The production of color is due to the manner in which light is reflected from the tridymite and cristobalite grids; their spacing is such that light of only one wavelength is reflected, all others passing through to be lost somewhere inside the gem. Since every color of the spectrum has its own wavelength, it is easy to see that only the purest possible hues, unmixed with others, can return to the eye. This accounts for the intensity of hue which is so pronounced a feature of this gemstone. It is interesting to note that many feldspar gems also exhibit similar reflected color, essentially due to the same cause, i.e., the formation of minute crystal colonies of another mineral species within the host.

Regardless of the presence of crystalline bodies within opal, the latter is generally regarded as being amorphous and therefore unable to grow in crystals or to exhibit those properties which every crystalline substance possesses. Opal is like a solidified jelly, not of gelatin certainly, but of silica carried by water and deposited wherever space was found. Thus it occurs in crevices and cracks, in open spaces in volcanic rocks, a very common mode of occurrence it may be added, and frequently replacing wood to form what is known as *opalized wood* or *wood opal*. In cavities, opal is also found as rounded growths like bunches of grapes or solidified into miniature stalactites and stalagmites dripping from roof to floor. At other times it is found as thin films or crevice fillings or forming seams a foot or more in thickness. Opal is most frequently associated with volcanic rocks or with volcanic activity, also with hot springs as in Yellowstone Park where it forms terraces, basins, and cones of *siliceous sinter* or *geyserite*.

The varieties of opal are legion; one writer assembled 148 terms describing opal or affixing names to its varieties, however, the accepted terms are few in number and this text will confine itself to them. The supreme form of opal is of course *precious opal*, a term reserved strictly for specimens which show play of color. Precious opal may be further subdivided into *white opal*, or material of whitish background color, and *black opal*, material in which the background is either gray, bluish-gray, or black. The *fire opal* of Mexico noted chiefly for bright red coloration in transparent material may also show play of color in addition to the reddish-yellow, orange, red, or brownish-red body color characteristic of this variety. Fire opal is highly translucent and frequently quite transparent. Completely colorless and transparent opal is called *hyalite* or *water opal*, and looks like nothing more than congealed droplets of glass. Some of the Mexican opal is precious hyalite since some pieces show fine play of color in an absolutely colorless groundmass. *Common opal* is a catch-all term applied indiscriminately to any opal which does not display play of color and which otherwise does not fall under some definite classification. Sometimes opal is so porous that it appears chalky white and completely opaque, this kind is known as *cachalong* and is commonly met with in connection with agate nodules where it frequently forms bands in the agate or around the outside. A special type of cachalong is called *hydrophane* because of its affinity for water which it soaks up in amazing quantities, gradually growing more and more clear until it is highly translucent. Some hydrophane shows play of color *after* soaking. If common opal is penetrated with dendritic growths it receives the label *moss opal* in allusion to the form of these growths. The markings in moss opal are due to the same cause which forms mossy growths in agate and jasper, that is, the infiltration of manganese or iron salts. The term *prase opal* or *chloropal* is sometimes used to designate a greenish variety of common opal but chloropal is a particularly poor varietal name because it is the accepted name for a distinct mineral species, a hydrous iron silicate.

The composition of opal is silica, SiO_2, but as said before, lacking definite crystal structure except in patches or islands. All opal contains water amounting in extreme cases to as much as 10% by weight. The presence of water contributes translucency while its absence imparts greater opacity. Water is lost whenever specimens are removed from the ground and subjected to the dry atmosphere of homes and shops but this seems not to be particularly harmful in common opal but sometimes causes disaster in the case of translucent precious varieties. The gorgeously colorful opal of Nevada for example, frequently cracks after removal from the ground and does this in spite of whatever precautions are taken. The cracking or crazing begins on the outside of the specimen in clear portions, extending in time below the surface to an appreciable distance. It is believed that as the water leaves the spongy opal structure, stresses are set up in the silica framework which the gemstone attempts to relieve by cracking. The hardness of opal varies between 5½ and 6½ but it is extremely brittle, breaking almost as easily as hard candy. Fracture surfaces are very characteristic, showing beautifully the shell-like formation of a true conchoidal fracture. The luster varies from glassy to resinous, and in combination with the conchoidal fracture is almost sufficient to accurately identify opal in the field. Being soft and brittle, as well as sensitive to changes in temperature, owners of opal gems must treat them with utmost care. They should not be allowed to rub against any hard substances, particularly other gemstones, nor must they be worn on the hands when washing lest the sudden application of heat or cold cause them to crack.

The specific gravity of opal averages 2.10 but may vary between 1.9 and 2.2 depending upon the porosity or the presence of impurities. The range of Mexican opal is between 1.97 and 2.06. Refractive indices vary from 1.444 to 1.464, showing single refraction only and of course no dichroism even in the most highly colored specimens. An unusually low refractive index was obtained by the author on a pale orangy-red fire opal from Queretaro, Mexico, weighing 56.23 carats, the value being: 1.433, considerably less than any recorded. A perfectly colorless hyalite from San Luis Potosi, Mexico, gave 1.451.

The colors of opal are many and varied, especially in common varieties. Fire opal from Mexico ranges from colorless to faintly straw yellow body color, through reddish-yellow, orange, red, and to brownish-red and reddish-brown. Virgin Valley, Nevada, opal shows perfectly white to slightly creamy tints in opaque portions to very slightly yellow in transparent parts. The black opal from this famous locality is most curious, ranging in color from deep blackish-brown to dead black but transparent in thin sections. Some of these black specimens frequently show deep smoldering red flames, like dying embers in a fire grate. Wood opal frequently shows brown, dead white, yellow, red, and sometimes odd colors such as green and pink. Some of the opalized logs from Washington may show a half dozen colors in a specimen no more than 6 inches across. Common opal may also show pronounced banding in differing colors corresponding to several stages of deposition.

LOCALITIES

Greenland. In the Umanak District, precious opal has been found along with hyalite at Ujaragsugssuk on Hare Island; some wood opal has been noted here also. Common opal is frequently associated with zeolites, chalcedony and agate in the basalts of Nangisat and Kuanersuit at the southwestern extremity of Disko Island. At Godhavn, common opal is found in geodes with chalcedony and as separate nodules in basalt at Per Dams Skib; the color is white with a bluish tinge.

Nova Scotia. Fine specimens of cachalong have been found in volcanic rocks at Cape Split and Cape Blomidon, Kings County.

British Columbia. Opalized and silicified wood is found in the Kamloops petrified forest (see QUARTZ). The wood is found in the form of logs and wood fragments, some very large in size. Fire opal said to be similar to that of Queretaro, Mexico is found in the bed and along the banks of Deadman's Creek near Kamloops. White, pale green, and apple green common opal occurs in Tertiary rocks at Savona Mountain in the Ashcroft Mining Division. Common opal also occurs at Agate Mountain in the Similkameen Mining Division; finely laminated common opal is found in Tertiary argillite and sandstones at the Horse Fly Mine, Horse Fly River, Quesnel Mining Division; also in the neighborhood of Fourmile Creek, Slocan Lake, in the Slocan Mining Division. Good specimens of hyalite occur in basalt near Hihhum Lake, Bonaparte River, Clinton Mining Division.

New Jersey. Old mineral locality references for the United States sometimes refer to a mineral called "isopyre." This material was originally found in the vicinity of Dover, Morris County, where it occurred as vein fillings in magnetite ore. It was compact, dark green in color, almost black, and sometimes showed red spots. For many years it had been considered a distinct mineral species but eventually proved to be merely highly impure common opal. Some small quantities were cut as cabochon gems.

Cachalong opal of dead-white to pinkish or creamy tones frequently occurs associated with quartz and agate in cavities in lava throughout northern New Jersey. Especially fine specimens taking an excellent polish have been obtained from the large quarry in Prospect Park, Paterson, Passaic County; also at Great Notch in the same county and many other places.

Nebraska. Some fine moss opal is found as nodules in limestone near Angora, Morrill County. The locality is 2 miles east of Angora Hill from Highway 19. In the limestone, each nodule is encased by chalky material which gradually becomes impregnated with opal as the interior is reached. The opal varies from white opaque to gray translucent showing delicate dead-black dendritic markings of considerable beauty. In general the nodules are rounded and several inches in diameter, but irregular forms also occur. The deposit was once mined commercially and the remains of a horizontal tunnel and associated dumps may be seen on the side of a low hill. The opal-bearing limestone covers a considerable area and other deposits may eventually be found in the vicinity. In Cherry County, opalized wood has been found in washes, gullies, and stream beds in the vicinity of Valentine.

Kansas. Colorless, white, or grayish translucent opal is widespread throughout the Ogallala Formation of Tertiary age in Clark, Ellis, Wallace, Logan, Ness, and Rawlins counties. It occurs in the form of nodules and irregular masses in white cherty calcareous rocks; opalized bones are also found in the same formations. Much of the opal contains dendritic growths as in the Nebraska specimens described above. A good locality is an old road cut about 5 miles south of Wallace in Wallace County.

Colorado. Moss opal has been found in gravel along the south fork of the Republican River in southern Yuma County about 20 miles north of Burlington. Much opal has been found in the lavas and volcanic debris of Specimen Mountain located on the line between Jackson and Larimer counties in Rocky Mountain National Park. Although most is common opaque white opal, some transparent specimens are found of inferior gem quality. In these the color may be yellowish or orange to red. At the locality, the opal is associated with various chalcedonies and jaspers.

Fine opalized wood has been found upon Opal Hill, a rounded eminence located 4 miles southwest of Fruita in Mesa County. White opaque specimens are mainly found but blue, green, brown, yellow, and banded varieties also occur. Similar material is found in Glade Park and Pinon Mesa near Fruita. Opalized wood is widespread along the Colorado River valley and side canyons westward from Grand Junction into Utah.

Wyoming. In Yellowstone Park, common opal is found on Specimen Ridge and Amethyst Mountain in the area between the Lamar River and Yellowstone River; also at various places in the Grand Canyon of the Yellowstone; also as seams in volcanic rocks on the northern flanks of Mt. Washburn. Good wood opal occurs on a high volcanic ridge behind Terrace Point on the Southeast Arm of Yellowstone Lake. As in all National Parks, collecting specimens is forbidden.

Texas. Precious milk opal occurs as thin seam fillings and veinlets in a dense, hard purplish to reddish-brown rhyolite upon the Woodward Ranch, located 16 miles south of Alpine, Brewster County. Blue and green flames of color predominate in a ground mass of milky opal but orange and red are also noted; the individual flashes are very small. The opal is sparingly distributed in the rock and next to impossible to remove in pieces of any size. The compact nature of the opal and rock mixture suggests cutting cabochons from the most colorful parts in the style in which the "ironstone" opal of Australia is treated.

New Mexico. White, gray, green, and other colored opalized woods occur in volcanic ash and tuff near Battleship Rock in the Jemez Sulphur District of Sandoval County; wood opal has also been found in the Rio Puerco District and in the Cochiti District; very fine specimens of the precious variety are reported from Calla Canyon in the last district. Milk-white opal occurs east of Isleta Pueblo in Bernalillo County. In Socorro County, fine examples of wood opal, some logs reaching as much as 50 pounds in weight, are found in sands and gravels at the north end of the Fra Cristobal Range on the eastern side of Elephant Butte Reservoir. Numerous root, limb, and stem sections occur here in colors ranging from translucent grayish tones to milky-white, also brown, black, yellowish, and mottled in several of the above colors. Similar wood with beautifully preserved cellular structure is found just south of the east end of Bernardo Bridge across the

Figure 35. An amazonite crystal from the Crystal Peak area north of Florissant, Teller County, Colorado. The large single crystal is partially capped with white microcline and overgrown upon the base with blades of iron-stained cleavelandite. Size: about 3½ inches tall and 3 inches in width.

Figure 50. *Upper* — a multi-colored double-terminated tourmaline crystal from the Tourmaline King Mine at Pala, California. The lower termination is almost flat while the upper is composed of a number of pyramidal faces characteristic of the habit of tourmaline from this mine. The center is deep raspberry-red material of excellent carving quality.

Lower — Crystals and crystal sections of gem tourmaline from the Himalaya Mine at Mesa Grande, California. The large specimen in the center is almost flawless while the combination of red and green is a characteristic feature of tourmaline from this famous mine.

Figure 56. *Left* — A blue tourmaline crystal with attached cleavelandite blades from the Tourmaline Queen Mine at Pala, California.

Figure 57. *Right* — A magnificent multiple growth crystal of deep raspberry-red tourmaline from the Tourmaline King Mine at Pala, San Diego County, California. The crystal is 5½ inches tall and about 3 inches wide at the top. Tourmaline crystals of such large size seldom produce clear material for facet cutting but were prized for carving purposes.

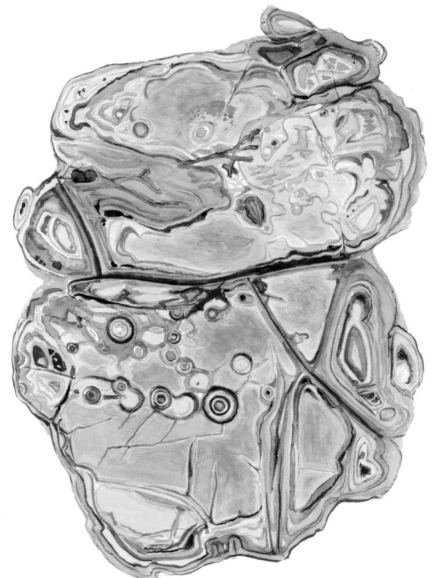

Figure 64. A nodule of variscite from Fairfield, Utah, sliced through and polished.

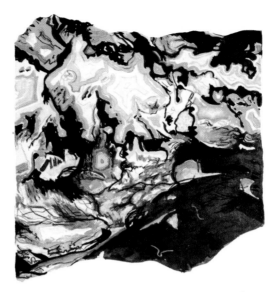

Figure 88. Moss agate from Ochoco Mountain, Crook County, Oregon. Actual size.

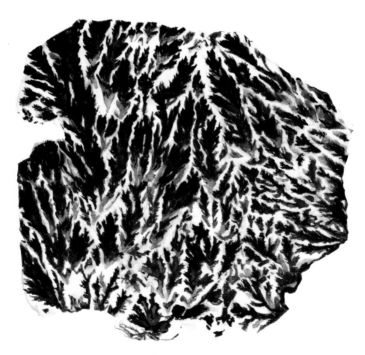

Figure 89. A thin slab of plume agate from a deposit near Deming, New Mexico. Actual size.

Figure 106. An exceptionally fine polished slab of fortification agate from the deposits near Gallego in Chihuahua, Mexico. Actual size.

Rio Grande River, in the same general field. The colors follow the same general patterns and hues but specimens are larger, one of 3 feet in length and 1 foot in diameter has been recorded. This opalized wood field also extends southward into Sierra County along the Fra Cristobal Range while an eastward extension may exist in the broad Jornada Valley east of Truth or Consequences where many fine opalized wood specimens have also been found. In Grant County, precious opal in good specimens has been reported from points in the Rita District and Central District; in the latter a peculiar "button opal" is said to occur about ½ mile from Fort Bayard Station in volcanic rock. The interiors are stated to be pure white while the outside rinds are composed of black chalcedony. In Hidalgo County, moss opal has been found in the vicinity of Playas Lake.

South Dakota. Excellent wood opal is frequently found along hillsides, knolls, and stream banks in the valley of the Missouri River north of Mobridge in Corson and Campbell counties; also in the vicinity of Little Eagle in Corson County along the Grand River and about 20 miles northwest of Mobridge.

Montana. Fine hyalite and beautiful reddish-yellow translucent common opal occur near the summit of Mount Blackmore, Gallatin County. One of the nearby peaks, Hyalite Peak (10,110 feet) has been named after the occurrence. The opal from this locality was once seriously considered for gem purposes and the name *blackmorite* proposed for it.

Idaho. This state is sometimes called the "Gem State" in allusion to the several important gemstones which are found within its boundaries, particularly very fine precious opal whose quality has often been likened to that of the famous Hungarian opal. All of the occurrences are in basaltic rocks and the life of each opal-mining venture in the past has been short because of the difficulty of mining in these tough rocks. At the surface, where rocks are disintegrated to some extent, it is easy to extract opal nodules without damage, however, as workings progress in depth, the basalt becomes fresher and much tougher, and the problem of removing the opal masses without shattering involves so much hand labor that the operation as a whole quickly becomes uneconomical. There are probably many deposits among those to be described which still contain much precious opal—for those who have the time and the inclination to painstakingly dig for them.

In southeastern Kootenai County, common opal is found near Setters; some ranges from translucent to almost transparent and occurs in yellow, greenish-yellow, and resin-brown colors.

One of the well-known precious opal fields lies squarely upon the boundary between Idaho and Washington near Whelan in Latah County very close to Moscow. The precious material was discovered in 1890 in a decomposed basalt during digging of a well and set off a miniature "rush" which brought in many people anxious to try their hands and test their fortunes in opal mining. Within months after the discovery was made public, a small town, now vanished, was set up nearby and named Gem City. During the summer and fall of 1891, over $5,000 of very fine material was mined, said to be the equal of the best Hungarian specimens. A gem weighing only 3½ carats was once held at the unrealistic price of $500 while a rough mass weighing 2 ounces was priced at $1,200. The deposits were worked intensively from 1891 to 1893, mainly from the Washington side, but the striking of hard rock discouraged mining and the locality drifted into obscurity. In 1904, a brief resurgence took place but since then no further mining here has been done.

Precious opal has been found in basalt bluffs overlooking the Clearwater River opposite Silcott in Nez Perce County.

Opalized wood of high quality occurs in a well-defined horizon of volcanic ash and other sediments about 500 feet above the junction of Fourth of July Creek and Mann's Creek in Fourth of July Canyon, 16 miles northwest of Weiser in Washington County; the same horizon has yielded similar material in Weiser Cove near Weiser, also near Mesa in Adams County to the north of Weiser.

Opaque white opal attractively stained and spotted with bright red cinnabar occurs in the cinnabar mines of the Yellow Pine District, Valley County.

In 1902, very beautiful precious opal along with much common opal, was found on the west side of Panther Creek Valley in Lemhi County. The opal was found in a large porphyry dike which runs parallel to the creek some 6 miles below its head at an altitude of 7,000 feet above sea level. The dike forms a low ridge partly covered with debris running parallel with the creek and measures about 150 feet in width and 1½ miles in length. Opal nodules occur abundantly as cavity fillings ranging in color from milky, bluish-gray or bluish-white, green, brown, pink, etc., and in all degrees of transparency. The discoverer of the deposit, S. V. Le Sieur of Provo, Utah, obtained a fine green piece which weighed 60 carats and another of brownish color of 150 carats. Aside from these early examples of large size, the vast majority of precious opal nodules have not exceeded 10 carats. The precious types were said to be unusually brittle but of very fine color, the flashes being very broad and brilliant. Common opal has also been found in Lemhi County near May in yellow, flesh-pink, and black masses.

A little precious opal has been recovered from a deposit above Black Canyon Dam near Emmett in Gem County. Sandstone cemented with films of precious opal has been collected from Neocene lake bed sediments on both sides of Moore Creek in Boise County near Idaho City.

In 1893, attention was drawn to deposits of precious opal in basalt in an area centered about Squaw Creek Canyon about 8 miles southwest of Nampa in Owhyee County. One of the deposits is on top of a small sage-brush-covered hill capped by opal-bearing basalt at an elevation of 3500 feet above sea level just below the junction of Squaw Creek and Little Squaw Creek and about 3 miles away from the Snake River. The basalt is part of a flow which enters Squaw Creek Canyon and covers rhyolite bedrocks. The rock is honeycombed with gas cavities, most of which are empty but some filled with opal; of the opal fillings, most are ordinary milk white material of no value but some are very fine precious opal of gorgeous coloration. Other cavities are filled with chalcedony and chalcedony with opal, some-times banded in conformance with cavity walls or in layers and then form-ing true onyx. One of the larger workings in this area is located 3 miles west of what was then known as Enterprise, and consists of two sets of workings in a small valley. Opencuts and a tunnel of 40 feet in length are located on the west side. Opal is found in a whitish decomposed rhyolite in which occur blocks and rounded masses of perlitic rhyolite. The opal fills seams and veinlets, as crack and joint fillings, and in nodular masses, both in the rhyolite and in the perlite. Another deposit is located about 2 miles south-southeast of a place formerly known as Sommer Camp, and about 4 miles west of Enterprise. About 6 pits within a 200 yards of each other have been sunk into decomposed whitish rhyolite interbedded with brownish glassy rhyolite. Much chalcedony and common milk opal were found along with precious material.

In the extreme southwestern part of Owhyee County, precious opal occurs as seams and cavity fillings in basalt on the Brace Brothers Ranch near Cliffs, about 40 miles from Boise. The rock is very hard and removing opals without shattering is almost impossible. About 25 miles west of Mountain Home along Castle Creek in the same county, opal claims were once filed at a point about 6 miles east of Oreana. Although some good opal was found, the difficulty of removing it from the rock without shattering it into useless fragments prevented profitable mining.

Some of the finest opalized wood in the world has been obtained from a unique deposit along Clover Creek east of Bliss, Lincoln County. Logs of an extinct species of oak were found encased in hardened volcanic ash that had to be blasted in order to free the wood. Specimens reached as much as 12 inches in diameter but the average was closer to 4 inches to 6 inches. Ranging from buff to brown and with black markings, Clover Creek wood is notable for the beautifully preserved structure of the original wood. Each pore and radial streak so characteristic of present-day oak wood is faithfully preserved in opal. Some specimens were "quarter-sawed" like oak used in furniture but in most cases, logs were simply sawn across into slabs and polished. Many years ago, tons of this material were collected under the direction of Warren E. Foote, a noted mineral dealer of Philadelphia. So far as is known, none of this opal wood has been collected from this locality in recent years although many museums exhibit fine specimens. It is said that some precious opal has been found as "float" fragments at this locality but no one has traced it to its original rock.

Washington. Perhaps the most remarkable opalized woods in the entire continent are found in the vast semi-arid region of south central Washington where huge logs of gaily-colored common opal represent all that remains of an ancient forest. This portion of the state is overlaid by layers of volcanic ash and a variety of sediments which comprise the Latah Formation, generally middle Eocene in age, or, in some places, upper Miocene. The Latah Formation contains many trees whose descendants are well-known to us today. Arranged in order of abundance they include: redwood (Sequoia), oak (over 10 varieties), swamp cypress (Taxodium), elm, maple, willow, cedar, poplar, chestnut, alder, birch, persimmon, and laurel. These pieces of petrified wood testify that over all this country was spread a lush woodland very much like that seen today in the Southeastern United States. Uprooted and literally dashed to pieces in ancient floods, its trees eventually came to rest as driftwood upon the shores of huge inland seas. In time these were buried under volcanic ash and slowly but surely replaced by silica in a state of enduring preservation. Accumulated as driftwood, opalized logs are understandably more abundant in those areas corresponding to ancient lake beaches but numerous specimens are found sprinkled widely over many square miles where they have been carried by erosion. To find good material collectors take advantage of this fact by searching along canyons and gullies which have sliced through the elevated table-lands. When chips and fragments are found, these are tracked back up the hillsides and the source log from which they came is usually discovered buried in the ground. Logs sometimes reach enormous dimensions, specimens up to 5 feet in diameter are recorded although most are far smaller. When free of cracks and flaws, smaller specimens are sawed across and polished as slabs showing a complete cross-section with annual rings and pore markings. Much material has also been employed for bookends and other coarse items of lapidary work. Throughout the Latah formation, wood opal occurs in two distinct horizons vertically separated by almost 1000 feet, the upper being marked by dark sediments while the lower, containing the best material, is composed of whitish sediments. In all cases a marked feature is the association of lava flows which appear as cappings over the sediments and perhaps have much to do with the circulation of ground waters responsible for transporting and depositing silica in the buried logs.

The most prolific belt of wood opal localities comprises the Horse Heaven Hills, a range of eroded table-lands which begin in the west near Glenwood in Klickitat County and curve northward in a shallow arc through the southern part of Yakima County, thence eastward to terminate at the Columbia River in Benton County, a distance of almost 120 miles. Very fine specimens have been obtained from the rolling hills immediately north and northwest of Roosevelt on the Columbia River in Klickitat County, also north of Bickleton. In Benton County good material has been found near Prosser and Mabton. Further to the north in Yakima County, very fine specimens are found on the slopes of Yakima Ridge particularly to the south of Cairn Hope Peak and about 1 mile northwest of Goldcreek where the eastern extension of the ridge enters Benton County. The Rattlesnake Hills in Yakima County lying immediately south of Yakima Ridge and also extending eastward into Benton County, produce much fine wood. The Saddle Mountains in the southern part of Kittitas County, especially near Vantage and Crab Creek Canyon south of this town, furnish exceptional specimens.

In Grant County, logs of opalized wood are found in lava along the east side of Moses Coulee and in Grand Coulee (now filled with water). Other examples have been found at Trinidad.

In Douglas County, common opal of green color has been found in the vicinity of Waterville; large nodules of brownish common opal have been found embedded in diatomaceous earth near Quincy in Grant County. The precious opal locality near Whelan has been mentioned under Idaho and will not be described further here.

Oregon. Good wood opal has been found in the northern part of Harney County in the alluvium upon the slopes of Silvies Canyon in Myrtle Park. This locality is reached by taking Highway 395 18 miles north from Burns and thence west for 7 miles to Silvies Canyon. In Malheur County, some fine opalized wood has been found along Sucker Creek from Homedale upstream to Rockville. In Baker County, some fine white and black banded opalized wood has been found at Pleasant Valley. Near Durkee is an old locality for precious opal but little work was done here although some very fine specimens were once obtained.

Outstanding specimens of hyalite and other translucent to transparent varieties of opal occur on Opal Butte south of Parkers Mill in the southwestern corner of Morrow County. Opal Butte, also called Peters Butte, was prospected in 1889 and the first claim filed in 1890. Although some very fine common opal was found here, one mass of 12 inches in diameter being recorded, mining efforts were suspended after one season's work and no formal mining attempted since that time.

A precious opal locality of some interest in recent years is that atop Hart Mountain to the northeast of Plush in Lake County. Hart Mountain is a basalt-capped mesa which slopes away gently to the east but exposes steep cliffs to the west facing Plush Valley; the volcanic rocks are of Tertiary age and contain precious and common opal as well as chalcedony in gas cavities.

FIGURE 30. Looking west across the mouth of Virgin Creek and up Beet Creek in Virgin Valley, Nevada. This photograph, taken in August 1913, shows the old Ebeling Ranch on the right. The old Mathewson or Dow opal claims were located near the high mesa on the left while the Stone Tree claims were located in the low hills between the two higher mesas. In the distance may be seen the light-colored beds of volcanic tuff conglomerate, ash sands, and ash, capped by dark basalt. Courtesy U.S. Geological Survey.

Originally discovered lying loose in the soil, some attempt at mining opal was made but was soon discouraged by the toughness of the underlying rock. This locality is accessible by road from the eastern side.

Fine precious opal is occasionally found as small seams and veins in the thunderegg "plume beds" of Priday Ranch near Madras, Jefferson County (see QUARTZ).

Utah. The westward extension of the opalized wood field along the Colorado River of western Colorado lies in Grand County and exactly the same sort of material is found in the river valley.

Nevada. Few important mineral or gemstone collections are without at least one example of Virgin Valley precious opal, but only a handful of persons other than mineralogists and collectors are even aware of the existence of these very important deposits. Though incomparably beautiful in respect to play of color and unmatched in terms of size, Virgin Valley opal is seldom used for gems because of its unfortunate tendency to crack. If some way could be developed to keep gems intact—and many methods have been tried! —Virgin Valley opal would immediately become a universal gem favorite.

FIGURE 31. The old Monarch Claim of Deb Roop in Virgin Valley, Nevada in August 1913. Mr. Roop is in the foreground digging away a large opalized log embedded in the soft clayey volcanic ash deposits. Courtesy U.S. Geological Survey.

Despite inapplicability to commercial jewelry purposes, at least several hundred thousand dollars worth has been sold to museums and private collectors since the discovery of the deposit in the early part of this century.

Virgin Valley, as shown in Figure 30, is a shallow depression situated among rolling sparsely-vegetated hills in the high desert regions of Humboldt County in northern Nevada. It is reached by road from Denio or Quinn Crossing in Nevada, or from Cedarville in California. The general location is 20 miles southwest of Denio at the end of a road which turns off south from Highway 8A a few miles east of the Summit Lake Indian Reservation road. Of little value for anything except cattle grazing, the valley did not come into the news until after a precious opal specimen was picked by a cowboy in either 1905 or 1906. Some persons believe that the original discovery was made by Marsden Nanson, a mining engineer who was passing through the area on horseback and found opal lying upon the ground. In any case, the word was soon passed and prospectors as well as local residents took to the field and staked virtually all of the productive ground. An early working is illustrated in Figure 31. From 1908 when the first important quantities of opal were produced to about 1920, numerous claims were filed and much opal removed from workings which were chiefly shallow pits sunk upon the productive strata. During this early period of exploration and discovery, the two most important mines, the Bonanza (1908) and the Rainbow Ridge (1912) were staked and exploited.

Following 1920, a period of inactivity set in which was not broken until the Rainbow Ridge Mine was acquired by Glenn and Keith Hodson in 1949 and the Bonanza in 1955. The Bonanza is stated by the Hodsons to be in poor condition inside and much reconditioning would be necessary before active mining could be commenced, however, the Rainbow Ridge Mine which has been worked by them each summer season since its purchase, has been cleaned out and systematically operated in an efficient manner. From this mine has come numerous fine specimens of precious opal including the Hodson Opal which weighs about 7 pounds.

In 1955 a new discovery was made of precious opal on the east side of Virgin Valley and is important because it extends the possibilities of opal-bearing formations into an area which has hitherto been regarded as completely barren, all of the important mines having been located only upon the western side. The prospect at this point is called the Green Fire Mine and is unlike the other mines in that opal occurs as seams and irregular masses instead of replacements of wood, up to now, the only mode of precious opal occurrence noted in the Valley.

Virgin Valley opal occurs in a series of beds composed of volcanic ashes and tuffs of varying compactness and coherence, weathering easily into rounded knolls cut along the sides by narrow, steep-walled ravines. The strata of several hundred feet thickness are divided into three beds of different character. The lower beds consist of white, greenish, and bright red layers frequently eroded deeply along the exposed edges, the middle beds show brownish and gray sediments forming low rounded knolls and hills, while the upper beds consist of soft cream-colored ash deposits capped by porous dark-gray lavas along their rims. These strata are shown in Figure 30. From fossil evidence, it appears that the formations are Miocene in age. The precious opal occurs in ash or tuff of gray to greenish-gray color with a hard clayey consistency near the surface where it is dry, to a sticky gumbo-like material at depth where moisture is present. Sand, pebbles, and cobbles of rock including quartz, rhyolite, and obsidian, occur in the opal-bearing horizons. Precious opal is invariably associated with petrified wood in all deposits on the western side of the valley but this association appears to be absent in the Green Fire properties on the eastern side. Petrified wood is abundant in the form of logs, limbs, twigs, bark, and roots, replaced in whole or in part by either chalcedony, common opal, or precious opal. The wood is in various stages of petrification from partly silicified lignite of deep black color to material completely replaced by silica. The precious opal is found either by itself, wholly replacing wood, or in conjunction with common opal or chalcedony. It is also frequently observed forming bright streaks and films filling cracks or covering the exteriors of ordinary petrified wood. Still more rarely, it fills openings in clay or forms irregular nodules. Although the structure of the original wood is often faithfully preserved by chalcedony and common opal, precious opal which appears to be of later development, seldom preserves any trace except the exterior shape of the wood fragment. In addition to wood, some fine examples of spruce and pine cones preserved in precious opal have been uncovered in the deposits, however, these are much rarer. A pine cone replaced by opal is illustrated in Figure 32. In respect to translucency and color, a remarkable variety is exhibited, ranging from specimens which are completely jet black and opaque to those which are like limpid drops, of jelly, faintly tinted with straw yellow. Sometimes limb sections show a core of black material which gradually lightens to transparent brown as the exterior is approached, and finally changes into clear and almost colorless material on the exterior. Flames of dazzling intensity may occur in any of these zones. The black

FIGURE 32. An unusual specimen of transparent opal, part of which is precious, showing with an opalized pine cone. This specimen was found on Deb Roop's Monarch Claim in Virgin Valley in August 1913. Courtesy U.S. Geological Survey.

coloration appears to be due to organic matter left behind, perhaps from the original wood; when tested by heat, water is given off from such specimens as well as a strong pyroligneous acid odor. Some of the black material shows no play of color but beautiful sheets of red flame are noted in others, as in the Roebling Opal. Common opal is found with the precious variety and occurs in various shades of purple, reddish-brown, gray, and white.

The predominant play of color is red and occurs either pure or admixed with orange and yellow, often in brilliant broad patches; particularly fine in black opals. The greens are very pure in hue, rich and vivid; in certain lights they shift toward yellow-green or blue-green. Blue is pure but uncommon. The purples are similar to those observed in certain clear Australian opal, never in distinct patches but more like a gentle glow throughout the specimen. Orange and yellow are rather common, occasionally in broad sheets of flame but mostly in wispy veils and shreds.

Each specimen of Virgin Valley opal shows layers arranged concentrically around the core corresponding to the cylindrical outlines of the original limb section as shown in Figure 33. There seems little doubt that the notorious tendency to crack is related to differing amounts of water contained in each layer and the varying degrees of openness in the internal structure which must be more like a spongy mass than completely solid. The toughest material appears to be milk-white in color, or, at the other end of the scale, material which is completely opaque black; each type is found in nodule cores. Conversely, the material most susceptible to fracture is highly translucent to transparent and occurs on the exterior. Although the first type

FIGURE 33. Upper left: opal in trachyte matrix from Queretaro, Mexico. Upper right: limb section of black opal from Virgin Valley, Nevada. Bottom: two specimens from Virgin Valley. The left hand cut gem is hyalite from San Luis Potosi, Mexico; the right hand gem is a fine cherry red fire opal from Queretaro which measures almost 1 inch in diameter and weighs 56.23 carats.

mentioned may not crack after the passage of many years, the second frequently begins to develop minute fissures which extend themselves laterally to interconnect until the entire surface is reticulated like a serpent's skin. In extreme cases, the cracks are so minute and so numerous that the entire outer layer may be rubbed off with the fingers, crumbling away into a mass of sand in which each grain sparkles and flashes with color. It would seem in these types that the internal structure is more open, permitting water to be released more readily and causing shrinkage which can only be relieved by cracking, much in the same way that mud cracks when thoroughly dried. Many attempts to prevent cracking have been made but generally with little success; some persons keep specimens immersed in water, glycerine, mineral oil, or other liquids with the idea of "curing" the opals so that internal strains may be relieved gradually. Cut gems have also been subjected to a variety of treatments but any method has failed to produce consistent results and has led to no firm conclusions upon which further experimentation may be guided.

The principal mines in the valley are located along the western edge in an area several miles wide and about 9 miles in length, however, the discovery of the Green Fire deposit on the eastern side indicates that opal mineralization may be far more widespread than originally believed. In general, the elevations of the several workings range from 5,100 to 5,400 feet above sea level although the local elevations are only several hundred feet above the valley floor. In the center of the depression, Virgin Creek flows northward to join Beet Creek at the head of a narrow canyon below which point it is called Thousand Creek. One mile south of the junction of both creeks, are located several hot springs upon the former site of the McGee Ranch, later used as a CCC Camp, and still more lately as a camping ground for visitors to the valley. From this point as a reference, four groups of claims may be located. The principal group comprises the old Cracker Jack, Bonanza, Opal Queen, and Opal Queen Extension properties, located about 3 miles to the southwest. The second group is about 5 miles south, the third about 5 miles southwest, and the fourth about 1½ miles west-northwest. The old Big Horn claim is 1 mile northwest and the G. W. Brown claim 3½ miles west-northwest; also many others of lesser importance along the west side of the valley. The Rainbow Ridge Mine is several miles west-northwest upon a low hill marked at its base by a stone cabin occupied by the Hodsons during their annual mining operations every summer. This mine, presently the only one producing substantial quantities of fine material, consists of an adit at the base of the hill from which extend laterals comprising in all over 1000 feet of tunnel. In mining, it is difficult to predict when precious material may be met for its distribution in the productive layers is far from regular. However, the waste is carefully watched for signs of precious opal for it has been found that specimens tend to appear in "nests" and where there is one, there may be others. In general, only one horizon within the ash beds will contain precious opal and mining is simply a question of following this horizon in all directions to systematically cover the ground. In the Bonanza, it is said that two opal-bearing horizons separated vertically by a distance of 75 feet were encountered.

Many outstanding specimens of precious opal have been found in Virgin Valley but perhaps the most famous is that known as the Roebling Opal after its purchaser, Colonel Washington A. Roebling, who left his comprehensive and world renowned mineral collection to the U.S. National Museum, including his opal. Discovered sometime in 1917, or perhaps a bit earlier, this magnificent specimen of dead black color was held by the Rainbow Ridge Mining Company, at a price reputed to be a quarter-million dollars. However, many persons say that the Colonel paid far less for it, one person placing the sale price at as low as several thousand dollars; the actual price seems to be unknown but probably lies somewhere in the tens of thousands. The Roebling Opal weighs 16.95 ounces troy, or 2665 carats; it is a section of a limb

FIGURE 34. The famous Roebling Opal from Virgin Valley, Nevada; weight 18.6 ounces. This specimen is an opalized section of limb showing some traces of the original rough exterior. The body color is intense velvety black which when illuminated shows beautiful large flames of deep red. After almost 40 years on exhibition in the U.S. National Museum it has not appreciably deteriorated contrary to the popular impression that *all* Virgin Valley opals do so in time. Courtesy Smithsonian Institution.

measuring slightly under 4 inches in length, 3⅛ inches in width, and 1 3/16 inches thick and consists entirely of deep black precious material coated on the outside with a brownish skin. Figure 34 illustrating this specimen gives no indication whatsoever of the magnificent deep red flames which seem to leap forth from the interior when strongly illuminated. After years of exhibition, this specimen *remains completely intact, showing no sign of deterioration!* In 1952, the Hodsons uncovered an enormous mass of precious opal from the Rainbow Ridge Mine weighing 7 pounds but covered in spots by gray clay which, if removed, would lower the actual weight of precious material to an estimated 6½ pounds. The size is 9½ inches by 5½ inches by 4½ inches, the shape that of a long slightly tapering limb; it is composed entirely of precious material except for the small amount of adhering clay and is translucent to transparent throughout. Every portion exhibits decided play of color with individual patches up to ⅛ inch wide and as much as one inch long in the form of narrow scintillating ribbons of color. The principal hues observed in this specimen are blue-green, red, yellow, yellow-green, and here and there touches of blue. It is valued at $50,000. After the discovery of the Hodson Opal, another large mass weighing slightly over 6 pounds was found by a visitor in an old mine shaft and is variously valued at from $30,000 to $75,000. The famous "Grubstake Opal" in the American Museum of Natural History is a polished slab of precious opal measuring 4 inches by 2 ½ inches by ¾ inch and showing extremely fine play of color. This splendid piece was found by an old Nevada prospector who brought it to a general store to leave as security or "grubstake" for purchases of food and camping supplies. After taking his stock he melted into the desert and was never heard from again. Eventually the opal mass found its way into the J. Pierpont Morgan Collection.

In other parts of Nevada, common opal is fairly widespread. Clear material in nodular form is found 30 miles south of Vya in Washoe County, a short distance west of Highway 34. Here it occurs in a light-colored rhyolite in nodules ranging from opaque white to transparent cream to reddish. Some specimens show traces of play of color while others contain dendritic markings, however, the majority of the material is completely undistinguished.

Fine specimens of bright cinnabar in opaque white to cream-colored common opal have been obtained from a quicksilver mine south of Beatty in Nye County; similar material occurs at the Rand Mine ten miles from Midas in Elko County.

Opalized wood is found in depression called the "Sump Hole" located 1 mile east of Highway 3A about 13 miles southwest of Coaldale in Esmeralda County. Logs and fragments of opalized wood have been found throughout the clays and other sedimentary formations in the depression and in the area immediately surrounding. The wood often shows beautiful grain and takes a fine polish. The colors are generally shades of brown but others occur also. Large opalized wood trunk sections are found near Montezuma Mountain just west of Goldfield in this same county. In the extreme southern part of Churchill County, about 7 miles north-northwest of Rawhide, excellent opal wood is found in a small canyon in the northern part of the Walker River Indian Reservation. The locality is reached by proceeding north by road from Rawhide a distance of 6 miles, and then turning west on a secondary road for 2 miles.

California. Opalized wood has been found in numerous places throughout the state but seldom in outstanding quality. Good material has come from the gold gravels of Nevada City in Nevada County, as in Sailor Flat and Blue Tent Mining Camp, where fine logs occurred in ancient stream bed gravels. Large trees of opalized wood are found west of Calistoga in Sonoma County. Precious opal has been reported from the Weise Ranch between Glen Ellen and Kenwood in Sonoma County, where it was said to occur in kaolin. In Napa County, a seam of green common opal 10 inches thick was uncovered in the Lone Pine chromite mine 3½ miles from Knoxville. Similar material has been reported from the chrysoprase mines near Lindsay in Tulare County (see QUARTZ). Some precious opal has been mined from basalt at the end of Red Rock Canyon in Kern County; the entrance to this canyon is 18 miles north of Mojave.

In San Bernardino County, a deposit of precious and common opal was extensively worked by the American Opal Company at the head of an eastern branch of Blacks Canyon near Opal Mountain (elev. 3973 ft.), approximately 20 miles northwest of Barstow. Work at this locality commenced about 1909 and lasted for three years or perhaps more. In 1912, a small crew was employed mining and shipping about 500 pounds of matrix and rough opal every two weeks. A shaft of 200 feet in depth was sunk and the deposit exploited at the bottom by means of numerous drifts and tunnels. The best opal, occurring in a white volcanic tuff, was said to occur at ground water level, about 200 feet below the surface. Common opal has also been found nearby over a rather wide area which begins about 18 miles north of Hinkley and is reached by turning off Highway 91/466 at that town and taking a secondary road north. Clear honey color to cherry red opal like the fire opal of Mexico is found in tuffs laid down in beds beneath a capping of black basalt. The collecting area extends for 6 miles on either side of the secondary road. Also found in the immediate vicinity are agate geodes and colorful jaspers.

A very small quantity of precious and common opal has been found in the vicinity of Lead Pipe Springs in San Bernardino County associated with thundereggs in red rhyolite. Nodules reach several inches in diameter and normally contain fillings of chalcedony and agate but sometimes precious opal in masses up to ¾ of an inch across are found in them also. Common white opal is found about 1½ miles northeast of the springs on the north side of a steep hill in the form of nodules or balls occurring at the contact of tuff beds and red rhyolite. The major portion are white in color but greenish, yellow, and reddish types also occur. The balls range in size from 1 to 5 inches in diameter. This locality was exploited about 1912 by F. M. Myrick of Randsburgh, who did much prospecting in the desert areas of this county. According to Mr. Myrick, it was sometimes necessary to break open several hundred thundereggs in order to find a single piece of opal. When precious opal was found, however, it showed excellent flashes of red, blue, and green against a background of gray to milky white.

Chihuahua. Very pure and clean fractureless masses of pale salmon common opal have been found near Sisoquichic in the Sierra de Tarahumare in the western part of this state. Dendritic opal in commercial quantities occurs in the south; some is reddish to brownish in color and some cherry color and clear. In the past 8 or 9 years good cherry opal averaging about 15 per cent transparent gem grade has been mined in the Creel area of the west. Some of this material verges toward yellowish colors as well as bright red but one is of the precious variety. Precious opal has been reported from Villa Ojinaga and Hacienda Santa Isabel in the Iturbide District.

Coahuila. Wood opal occurs in the Fortuna Mine and others in the Sierra Mojada in the Monclova District.

Durango. Wood opal occurs at the San Francisco del Mezquital Mine in the Mezquital area.

San Luis Potosi. Precious opal has been mined from time to time from places in the Cerro della Enramada in the municipality of Valle de Reyes in the Santa Maria de Rio area; hyalite occurs at Puerto Blanco and the Hacienda San Pedro in this same area. Good hyalite of facet grade occurs in cavities in rhyolite on the Cerro del Tepozan about 32 km. from San Luis in the Cerritos area.

Guanajuato. Precious opal has been found in the Sierra de Santa Rosa, Rancho de Enmedio and south of El Cubo in the Guanajuato District; also upon Cerro Campuzano in the municipality of Huanimaro in the Cuitzeo de Abasolo District.

Jalisco. Opal has been found in recent years near Guamar and at Guanimero but not in commercial quantities.

Queretaro. Virtually all opal labeled as "Mexican" whether it be precious or the clear cherry red type known as "fire" opal, comes from this state. Much precious material has been found here and in its own distinctive way, possesses unrivaled beauty. In spite of being mined and sold for over 100 years, much confusion has existed about the nature of Mexican opal while its merits have been debated by many gemologists. In general, this opal enjoys a lesser reputation than that from Australia no doubt due in part to the oft-repeated statement that it tends to crack with age. This denunciation has been repeated so often and in language so similar that one suspects the original blackening of character has been parroted by one author after another. The proof of the pudding insofar as dehydration and cracking are concerned, lies in the hundreds of gems which are still in fine condition after having been exposed to dry atmospheres for many years. The reputation of Mexican stones has not been helped by the avarice of miners and local dealers who have sold much material fit for little else than consignment to the scrap heap; like fine gems from any locality, true gem quality precious opal from Mexico is scarce and valuable—it is not peddled on street corners or in bus and railway terminals. Connoisseurs of opal agree that Mexican opal cannot be compared to others since its several varieties possess a characteristic limpidity and color distribution which are completely different. Indeed so distinctive are they that one familiar with them has no difficulty identifying them wherever they may be encountered.

Precious opal was cut and polished by the Aztecs long before America was discovered. To them it was known by the tongue-twisting name of "vitzitziltecpatl," or "humming bird stone" in allusion to the flashing colors resembling the plumage of these birds, and like other gemstones, held in high regard because of its beauty and rarity. The famous *Aztec Sun God Opal* formerly the property of the eminent gem collector Phillip Henry Hope, and now on display in the Chicago Natural History Museum, is believed to be the work of an ancient Aztec lapidary. Another gem, the *Aguila Azteca*, or Aztec Eagle, is also believed to be authentic native work. This carving of an eagle's head executed in precious opal weighs 32 carats and was once in the collection of Emperor Maxmilian. Worked opal gems of considerable antiquity have been found in the mountains southeast of Lake Chapala near Jiquilpan, Michoacan. Fra Sahugun, an early chronicler writing of the exploits of the Spanish Conquistadores, describes precious opal so clearly and accurately that little doubt remains as to its identity and that the Indians knew it well.

For many years after the Conquest, the sources of precious opal remained unknown, however, in 1855 a servant on the Hacienda Esperanza discovered one of the rhyolite flows in which precious opal occurs and procured a few specimens of good material. Serious attempts at mining did not take place until some years later when the famous Santa Maria Iris Mine was opened upon an opal-bearing rhyolite flow. This working is on the side of the road leading from Queretaro to Cadereyta and is merely an opencut from which blocks of soft pinkish to reddish rhyolite are quarried, to be broken up later into pieces averaging about 2 inches across (see Figure 33). During the process of reducing the rhyolite into smaller sizes numerous round patches of glassy opal are encountered and carefully chipped free from the matrix. As in all the rhyolite flows in this area, gas pockets occur which may or may not be filled with opal and other silica minerals, and may or may not contain gem quality material. In most cases, the opal filling extends from wall to wall and is unavoidably shattered when the rock is broken up, however, this is not of serious concern because the very finest opals are found as shrunken masses lying loosely attached in the cavities or even entirely free of all connection to the walls. Such masses have been likened to a prune in appearance for their exterior is often wrinkled and irregular in form. The body color of such specimens is mostly very pale straw or blue whilst throughout each stone magnificent vivid patches of flame are clearly visible even in its unpolished state. Precious opal of lesser quality is found associated with common opal of various colors such as yellow, orange, red, brown, and also milky white, either filling cavities completely or resting on the bottom in horizontal layers. Frequently clear opal encloses a central sphere of opaque white material. In size, nodules range from mere specks to several inches across, a good average being about one inch in diameter. Fine quality material of light body color in masses up to several inches across occurs in very large cavities interlayered with white to pale red or brown common opal. In recent years, very little fine opal has come from the Queretaro mines except from the Carbonera, a working located not far from San Juan del Rio and accessible from the village of Tequisquiapan by a poor road.

It is the practise of the opal miners to take the week's production of opal into the city of Queretaro where entire families devote themselves to the cutting and polishing of gemstones. The stones are sold to the cutters who in turn prepare them into finished gems with crude but effective equipment. Most gems are disposed of to visiting buyers at fairly reasonable prices but by the time gems are resold in the larger cities or sent abroad, the price has doubled several times. Clear stones are generally cut as high cabochons with or without matrix attached, the gems of pure material naturally being worth far more. Transparent specimens without play of color are faceted and make very attractive if fragile gems. Some specimens of a cloudy nature are heat-treated under the delusion that milkiness can be dispelled and play of color heightened. It is very doubtful whether the slight improvement this treatment affords is worth the risk of cracking what might otherwise be an acceptable stone. In any case, the method employed involves placing the cut gems in a sand bath where they are slowly heated, probably to a temperature not exceeding 300 to 400 degrees F. The effect of this treatment appears primarily to darken the rhyolite matrix but embrittles the opal to such an extent that extreme care must be used in handling. Some milky types respond to this treatment by turning gray or black and are then sold as "black opals." In general, these are very drab in appearance and scarcely worth keeping.

Queretaro opal occurs in many basic hues and degrees of limpidity but generally speaking, their transparency is the prime characteristic which serves to distinguish this material from opal of other countries. Another feature which is unique to Mexican opals, is the arrangement of color flashes within the gems. These most often appear as small but distinct flakes arranged vertically to the banding; pinpoint colors and very large broad flashes are almost unknown. Clear types free of inclusions make very fine faceted gems of surprising brilliance despite the low refractive index. Opal from Mexican localities basically ranges from almost colorless through pale straw, gradually assuming reddish tints through orange and thence into deep pure red. The so-called "cherry" opal is red with a touch of brown. The admixture of this color also produces increasing cloudiness until some masses of opal look like translucent chocolate candy. Very dark browns, grays, and natural blacks also occur as well as intense and opaque whites and some which shade from this latter hue into a delicate tinge of bluish-milk. As a general rule, play of color appears most frequently in opals of slightly yellow color or those of milky cast but good precious material may be of any body color. At times, clear masses are found in which needles of an unidentified mineral grow upon the rhyolite cavity walls and form inclusions within the opal.

Special names given by the Mexicans to several outstanding types of precious opal are both colorful and descriptive. The *lechosos* are those which are milky in cast, taking their name from the Spanish word for milk. These are found in all degrees of diaphaneity, from those which are virtually opaque to those in which only the slightest bluish-white haze fills the gem. Astonishingly beautiful colors are frequently observed in lechosos, often taking the form of a mosaic composed of even, regularly-spaced patches of dazzling color. The paler types strongly resemble the classic gems of Hungary. *Azules* are virtually transparent stones in which vivid flecks of red and green appear suspended in a pale bluish haze. The Mexican opal, *par excellence*, however, is the *lluvisnando*, a highly descriptive term derived from the Spanish *lluvisnar*—"to sprinkle with rain." The body color is an extremely pale honey yellow, sometimes faintly blue, and exceptionally transparent; in the depths of each gem may be seen narrow sheets of intense color descending like a shower of rain drops through the rays of the setting sun. Sometimes the individual darts of flame are small, at other times fairly coarse, but in any case, once seen, a good *lluvisnando* is not easily forgotten. There are few opal gems anywhere which can compare in beauty with this finest of the Mexican kinds.

In recapitulation, precious opal occurs in Queretaro at the following places: upon the Hacienda La Esperanza and Hacienda La Jurada in the Toliman District; at the Mina La Purisma in the Amelaco District; in the Arroyo de Ramos and upon the Hacienda Foentesuela in the municipality of Moconi in the Cadereyta District; upon the Hacienda Tesquisquiapan, Hacienda La Llave, and at the Mina Carbonera in the San Juan Del Rio District.

Hidalgo. Good quality precious opal has come from the Barranca de Tepezala in the Cerro de las Fajas in reddish rhyolite rocks which are exposed at various places in the Atotonilco District. Similar material has also been reported from the Barranca Agua Dulce in the Tulancingo District and from within the municipality of Zimapan in the district of the same name.

Michoacan. Precious opal in small quantities occurs upon the Hacienda

San Isidro in the municipality of Contepec and upon the Cerro Agustino in the municipality of Maravatio in the Maravatio District.

Mexico. Wood opal is found at the Puebla de San Lucas in the municipality of Chiautla in the Texcoco District of this state.

Distrito Federal. Wood opal occurs upon the Hacienda de Aspeita in the municipality of Atzcapotzalco.

Puebla. In the municipality of Naupan around Copila, wood opal occurs in some abundance. This locality is in the Huachinango District.

Tlaxcala. Wood opal occurs in various places in the Cerro de las Silicatas in the Hidalgo District.

Guerrero. An especially fine type of precious opal has been reported from near Huitzuco, which, from its description, appears similar to the black opal of Australia, viz: "fine rich green and red play of color in a gray background and another type in which intense red reflections are noted against a dark gray to black body color." At San Nicolas de Oro, opal of pale yellow, pale red and with reflections of red, green, and yellow, occurs in feldspar porphyry. Near Coacoyula milk opal with good color play has been found in highly silicified rhyolite but not in commercial quantities.

Oaxaca. Good gem quality precious opal has been reported in nodules in red rhyolite near Tlaxiaco.

Honduras. The existence of important deposits of common and precious opal in this country has long been known, however, very few specimens appear upon the market and very few persons even know that fine opal showing excellent color play is found in Honduras. The deposits appear to be both large and widespread and the potential for future successful mining is most attractive. The most important fields are in the western part of Honduras near Gracias, Intibucat, and Erandique, the latter being of especial significance. Erandique is about 80 miles due west of Tegucigalpa in high country well over one mile above sea level just north of the northern border of El Salvador. Opal is found in beds or belts of dark brittle trachyte, also in the country rocks next to the contacts. Common opal is very abundant, forming veins which dip steeply into the earth and run in a northeast-southwest direction. Precious opal occurs as narrow seams in the common material, sometimes forming alternate layers with common material. At times the bandings are so close together that it is possible to cut gems showing stripes of common opal alternating with stripes of beautiful precious opal. Near Erandique, the principal excavations have been made upon a trachyte hill rising to 250 feet above the surrounding terrain and extending over a distance of several miles. Opal has been found wherever openings have been made in the hill. Some specimens of the precious variety from Erandique rival in beauty and quality the best from any other locality. Connoisseurs who have examined Honduran gems state that they most closely resemble Hungarian stones, that is, the body colors incline toward misty whites of high translucency in which medium size patches of color of fine brilliance and clarity are observed. Some reports disparage their durability, stating that the colors tend to fade and cracks develop.

Qualified persons examining the opal fields have stated that many places between Intibucat and Las Pedras appear very favorable inasmuch as trachytic rocks are common and much common opal has been observed in them. The deposits in the vicinity of La Pasale and Yucusapa and the mountain of Santa Rosa also appear to offer much promise. The valley leading from Tambla toward the pass of Guayoca is also promising while within ½ mile of Tambla are found very large beds of common opal in a variety of colors. Near Guayoca, banded opal showing alternate layers of opaque and translucent white material very much like onyx occurs in some abundance in red glassy trachyte; petrified wood is also abundant in the vicinity. Beautiful white opal showing red flames has been found in the deposits and indicates the existence of other precious varieties.

Near Choluteca some excellent precious opal has been uncovered. Within several miles of Goascoran is located a mine which once produced the precious variety showing good play of color. A remarkable fine red opal with purplish bands occurs in large quantities about 5 miles east of Villa San Antonio on the plains of Comayagua where it forms veins up to several inches thickness in gray porphyry. Comayagua is located about 60 miles northwest of Tegucigalpa.

Plotting the localities mentioned above upon a map indicates that an area in which opal-bearing volcanic rocks occur in Honduras covers at least several hundred square miles. The general region covered in the Department of Gracias is roughly trapezoidal in shape and bounded as follows: beginning at Gracias in the northwest of the area, proceed south to Erandique, thence southeastward to Goascoran very close to the border of San Salvador, thence north to Comayagua, thence west to return to Gracias. In major respects, the rock types are very similar to those bearing opal in Mexico and it may not be far wrong to predict that important deposits will someday be discovered all along the belt of volcanic rocks which extends from Mexico southeastward toward Panama.

Cuba. Fist-size and larger specimens of fine moss opal have been found eroding from white cherty rocks along the banks of the Yucatan River at La Cieba, 8 miles north of Camaguey, Camaguey Province. The opal is stated to be pale gray in color and penetrated by very fine black dendritic markings of great delicacy and sharpness.

Guadeloupe. Common opal occurs at many points in the volcanic rocks of this Lesser Antilles island.

Martinique. Common opal is also frequently discovered on this island

and others of the chain extending southward from the eastern part of the Virgin Islands to terminate north of Trinidad. Volcanic rocks are very common in all of these islands, forming, in fact, the principal elevations; although very little exploration for gemstones has been done upon members of this archipelago there is no reason to assume that a variety of quartz and opal gems is lacking. In this respect, refer to the petrified wood occurrences on Antigua Island (see QUARTZ).

CHAPTER III

Important Gemstones

GEMSTONES of considerable importance in commerce, comprising both crystalline and massive minerals suitable for many applications in jewelry and ornament:

FROM PEGMATITES PRINCIPALLY:
    The Feldspar Group
    Spodumene
    Tourmaline
FROM IGNEOUS ROCKS:
    Sodalite and Cancrinite
FROM VOLCANIC ROCKS:
    Olivine

FROM VEIN DEPOSITS:
    Turquois
    Variscite
FROM METAMORPHIC ROCKS:
    Jade (Nephrite and Jadeite)
    Rhodonite
    Idocrase (Vesuvianite)
    The Garnet Group

THE FELDSPAR GROUP

SOME of the most fascinating gems known to man are cut from several closely-related mineral species collectively called the *feldspars*. Moonstone is perhaps the best known, but others like amazonite, sunstone, and labradorite, are also familiar to many and frequently used in jewelry or in objects of ornamentation. In nature, feldspar is so common that if all members of this group were considered merely varieties of one mineral species, then that species would be almost as common in the earth's crust as quartz—the mineral generally accorded this distinction. North America is particularly fortunate in the variety and quantity of feldspar gemstones found within its borders.

The Feldspar Group consists of two potassium feldspar species: *orthoclase* and *microcline*, and a sub-group called the *Plagioclase Series*. The latter consists of a sodium-rich species called *albite* ($NaAlSi_3O_8$) at one end of the

132

series; and then oligoclase, andesine, labradorite, bytownite, as sodium is gradually replaced by calcium, with calcium-rich *anorthite* ($CaAlSi_3O_8$) at the other. The exact place of any plagioclase is difficult to determine unless careful tests are made to establish just how much sodium or calcium, or both, are present.

The potassium feldspar species, orthoclase and microcline, are identical in composition, being potassium aluminum silicates with the formula: $KAlSi_3O_8$. However, due to differences in internal atomic arrangement, they crystallize in distinct fashions and otherwise display variations in properties. Orthoclase provides moonstones and sunstones, while microcline is principally noted for its beautiful bright green variety called *amazonite*, a large crystal of which is illustrated in Figure 35. A special term, *perthite*, is applied to braid-like or criss-crossed intergrowths of several feldspar species such as in microcline-albite perthite. This peculiar mixture of species is distinctive and often beautiful; in amazonite, for example, it may result in bright green microcline being attractively flecked with pure white albite. Perthite derives its name from Perth, Ontario, where it occurs in abundance in flesh-red masses. The group name, feldspar, has been handed down to us from an old German name—feldspat(h)—meaning literally "field spar." Orthoclase is taken from the Greek words for "right" and "cleave" in allusion to its cleavage planes which intersect each other at right angles. Microcline cleaves *almost* at right angles and hence its meaning, also from the Greek, comes from the words "small" and "incline"—small inclination. The gem variety of microcline—amazonite—is named after the Amazon River, but this was done over 200 years ago and we must pardon the unfamiliarity with Brazilian geography of the person bestowing this title since this mineral has never been found on this river and most probably came from somewhere in Minas Gerais in the interior. A variety of orthoclase—*sanidine*—is peculiar to volcanic rocks where it occurs in flat tabular crystals, sometimes clear and of facet grade, or showing a bluish sheen and hence properly called moonstone. Its name is derived from the Greek words meaning "board-like" in allusion to the form of the crystals.

Since plagioclase species show a decided departure from right angle cleavage, the sub-group name was taken from the Greek words meaning "oblique" and "cleavage." Albite, one of the principal members of this group, is named after the Latin word for "white" because it is most often found in this hue. Oligoclase means in Greek "little" and "cleave" because it was thought to have a less perfect cleavage than albite. Labradorite and bytownite are both named after Canadian localities, Labrador in the first instance, where this species is found in unparalleled perfection, and Bytown (now Ottawa). It is amusing to note that the feldspar originally coming from Bytown was subsequently proved *not* to be bytownite even though named after this place.

Note: Figure 35 is in the color section following page 112.

In respect to general names used to describe gem varieties, *moonstone* of course alludes to the beautiful play of silvery or bluish light in and upon cut specimens, while *sunstone* is a type of aventurine with brilliant reflections which someone thought to be sun-like in their intensity. *Peristerite* is the name given to certain iridescent albites from Canada in which a variety of colors is seen; the name is derived from the Greek for "pigeon" in allusion to the many colors seen on the neck of this fowl.

Although orthoclase and microcline are identical chemically, the first belongs to the Monoclinic System and the second to the Triclinic. It is extremely difficult to distinguish the two in hand specimens except when the unmistakably green variety of microcline is being judged. Although orthoclase shows two perfect and easily-developed cleavages intersecting at 90°, microcline shows almost as much viz.: 89° 30′—a difference too small to be sure of in field tests. When perfectly crystallized, both species exhibit squarish blocky prisms with beveled edges, generally much corroded on the faces and seldom smooth and shiny. An idealized crystal is drawn in Figure 36. Both are unfortunately very fragile because of the perfect cleavages and the low hardness (from 6 to 6½) and considerable care must be exercised in cutting gems to avoid inadvertent breakage. Fracture surfaces are irregular and inclined toward greasy in luster; broken pieces, however, are seldom without numerous brilliantly-reflective cleavage surfaces. It is easily possible, for example, to cleave a block of either mineral, several inches across, and leave a surface almost perfectly flat. Both minerals show specific gravities close to 2.56. Both are biaxial, negative, showing the following refractive indices, for orthoclase: $\alpha = 1.518$, $\gamma = 1.526$; for microcline: $\alpha = 1.522$, $\gamma = 1.530$. The birefringence equals 0.008 for both. The color dispersion is very low, about 0.012. Ordinarily, both species are white, grayish, or creamy in color, but smoky and yellow tints are commonly observed in transparent material. Amazonite is the only variety in which a pronounced shade occurs.

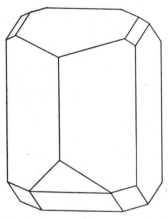

FIGURE 36. An orthoclase crystal.

Plagioclase feldspars are Triclinic in crystallization and are principally found in igneous and plutonic rocks but important amounts also occur in metamorphic rocks such as gneisses and schists. Albite and oligoclase are very common in pegmatites while labradorite often occurs in enormous masses in plutonic rocks such as gabbro. Species of the plagioclase sub-group give us a beautiful example of how certain elements can replace each other to gradually alter the characteristics, for example, albite, which is selected as the sodium-rich end-member, shows the lowest specific gravity and refractive indices of the group, however, as replacement occurs, these properties increase in value until the other end-member, anorthite, is reached, showing markedly higher figures:

Species		Refractive Indices		Specific Gravity
		α	γ	
Albite	Sodium-rich	1.526	1.536	2.62
Oligoclase		1.539	1.548	2.65
Andesine		1.550	1.558	2.68
Labradorite		1.560	1.568	2.70
Bytownite		1.568	1.578	2.73
Anorthite	Calcium-rich	1.576	1.588	2.76

It is to be noted that the birefringence varies from 0.010 in pure albite through 0.008 in the middle to 0.012 in pure anorthite. All species are biaxial but the optic sign which is positive in albite, changes to negative in oligoclase, returns to positive for andesine, and reverts again to negative in anorthite. The color dispersion is again low—about 0.012.

One of the most remarkable features of the plagioclase species is their tendency to twin repeatedly. Striations caused by such twinning are most apparent in the bladed variety of albite called *cleavelandite,* a common mineral near and in gem pockets in pegmatite, and in labradorite where it appears as thin streaks showing differences in color from the remainder of the crystal grain. It is also frequently observed in oligoclase and bytownite.

Plagioclase varies considerably in hue but if pure, would be white in massive form or colorless in transparent specimens. Facet-grade albite and oligoclase are colorless except some of the latter from North Carolina tends to be slightly greenish in tinge. Oligoclase often receives a reddish or orange cast from numerous spangles of hematite or goethite occurring as inclusions in sunstones. Labradorite also contains many inclusions and is nearly always gray to black in massive form on this account, on the other hand, clear facet-grade material is yellowish or straw color.

LOCALITIES

Greenland. A number of feldspar gemstone localities are known on the island, principally along the West Coast. In the Upernivik District, clear, poorly-formed crystals of faint brownish orthoclase are found in graphite at Lango; crystals reach 2¼ inches in diameter and are stated to be transparent. Aventurine feldspar is found in granite directly north of Godhavn between that settlement and Disko Fjord at a place called Kagsiarik; aventurescent microcline, semi-transparent, reddish and grayish in color is found in small veins at Uperniviks Naes, a promontory less than ¼ mile east of Godhavn

on Disko Island; also at Kiporkarfik near Godhavn and sparingly with labradorite in pegmatite at Sermersok valley near Kivigtut on Disko Island. Aventurine feldspar also ocurs in pegmatite on a small island called Kjod, about ¼
mile immediately south of Godhavn. Similar material is found at Nangisat,
a peninsula which protrudes into the central part of Disko Fjord. In the
Egedesminde District, adularescent feldspar showing sky-blue reflections occurs on the island of Maneetsok, about 5 miles north of the settlement of
Egedesminde. Beautiful peristerite showing blue reflections occurs at Nia-
quornaq; small fragments of labradorite are found at Eqalugssuit; highly
translucent microcline of violet-gray body color showing blue reflections and
associated with biotite occurs at Tinuktekasak; albite showing blue reflections
is reported from a pegmatite on Sungausak Peninsula, 25 miles southwest of
Egedesminde and just east of the Bjornenaes Islands.

In the Holsteinborg District, labradorite occurs at numerous places from
Simiutak Island at the mouth of Sondre Stromfjord south along the West
Coast to Kangamiut at the mouth of Evighed's Fjord; near the latter place it
has been observed on a small sandpit called Sandhullet; labradorite has also
been found on Umanarsuk Island 5 miles south of the village of Holsteinborg;
beautiful microcline moonstone and aventurine have been noted generally
within the district.

In the Godthaab District, gem varieties of feldspar are widespread and
abundant. Albite peristerite showing fine blue reflections against a whitish-
gray body color occurs with biotite in a pegmatite in granite at Kanajorssuit
(Store Ulkebugt) north of Godthaab on the northwest shore of Godthaab
Fjord. At Hjortetakken, reddish-gray peristerite occurs associated with biotite in a pegmatite and displays fine sky-blue reflections; similar material is
found at Aliortoq in Karajat Fjord, 15 miles south-southeast of Godthaab but
is said to be a soda-orthoclase rather than albite. The material from the latter
place occurs in cleavage fragments up to 4 inches across associated with hornblende, it is fairly transparent, and shows a pale blue adularescence; its specific gravity is 2.5 to 2.553. Pearl gray labradorite occurs at Kasigianguit on the
south shore of Ameralik Fjord, about 20 miles east-northeast of Godthaab.
Peristerite is also found at Kuanebucht several miles south of Godthaab; at
Vildmansnaes, and upon Thor Halleson's Varde; adularescent orthoclase
occurs on Store Malene on the peninsula several miles southeast of Godthaab;
labradorite is reported from Qasigianguit.

In the Frederikshaab District, labradorite and soda-orthoclase moonstone
are found in veins in granite at Kugnat Mountain at the entrance to Arsuk
Fjord.

In the Juliannehaab District, beautiful adularescent feldspars are found
extensively at the head of Kangerdluarsuk Fjord about 12 miles northeast of
the settlement of Julianehaab where it forms a constituent mineral of the

augite-syenite; also at Narssarsuk where a fine semi-transparent brown to colorless feldspar showing lovely blue reflections of fine quality occurs in pegmatites; also at Amitsoq and specifically at Siorarssuit in Kangerdluarsuk Fjord. Peristerite is found at Ninasarnaussaq; fine deep green amazonite occurs in large amounts with quartz and biotite at Nunarssuit and at Nalagutoq on Semersoq. The mountain called Nunasugsuk at the head of Kangerdluarsuk Fjord and the flat-topped mountain called Redekammen between Igaliko and Tunigdliarfik Fjords also produce fine adularescent feldspars associated with a variety of rare minerals.

In East Greenland, reddish-white albite showing fine peristerism is found at Kap Arends.

Labrador. Known to the Eskimos as "fire rock" and worn ornamentally by their chiefs, the beautiful labradorite of this grim and forbidding sub-Arctic province was first introduced to Europe by Moravian missionaries in the year 1770. There is little doubt that this peerless feldspar gemstone made a lasting impression on these hardy souls for no one who has observed the rich pure blue, like that seen on the wings of certain Brazilian butterflies, or the equally lovely green, gold, bronze, and copper, fails to marvel at this minor miracle of nature. The effect is of course most pronounced in polished specimens, especially when skilfully cut into slabs to exactly coincide with the crystal plane along which the colors appear, but even in the rough, good pieces flash with dazzling colors.

Labradorite occurs as large to very large crystal grains in the gabbros and anorthosites of Eastern Labrador, especially in the vicinity of Nain but also over a considerable area as far north as 57°8′ N. along the coast and inland for 30 miles. The Isle of Saint Paul is often referred to as the classic locality and is near Nain about midway along the eastern coastline of Labrador but actually the best and most easily accessible material has been taken in recent years from quarries upon the island known to the Eskimo as Nepoktulegatsuk, or, if this tongue-twisting name is too much, as Tabor's Island. The mineral rights upon this island were held as late as 1935 by Sir Wilfred Grenfell, the famous statesman-missionary of Labrador who did so much to develop the resources of this land and to better the welfare of its native inhabitants. Tabor's Island is about 12 miles from Nain and is completely uninhabited, anyone venturing there for minerals being forced to proceed by boat and pitch camp upon its inhospitable rock shores. A large rock mass, incised with the inscription "Grenfell Quarry," marks the place where the finest material occurs. Labradorite is usually obtained by drilling and blasting with light explosive charges to avoid excessive shattering. Statistics on production are skimpy but it is known that 50 tons were mined from this quarry in 1935. Much labradorite has also been obtained by collecting drift boulders from near this locality and elsewhere. Inland, beautiful large crystal masses are observed on the northeast side of Lake Michikamau and on the islands in Lake Ossokmanuan at the headwaters of the Hamilton River, the enclosing rock being anorthosite. Near Nain, good material has been obtained from Ford's Harbor and Black Island.

In place, labradorite occurs as individual crystals, frequently striated by twinning, as much as 24 inches across and associated with pyroxene and hypersthene. Lesser amounts of olivine, hornblende, biotite, and apatite are also present. In composition, labradorite from this area ranges from andesine to labradorite. Minute rod-like inclusions are common within crystals and assume directions related to the crystal structure; brown platy inclusions are sometimes large enough to show pronounced aventurescence and then give *sunstone labradorite*. These impurities lend a very dark grayish to almost black coloration. Very large polished slabs have been prepared from the better and more solid crystals, for example, a slab measuring 3 by 3 feet is in the American Museum of Natural History. Unfortunately, much of the material which is sold in the United States today is frequently very badly shattered and difficult to cut into flawless cabochons.

Quebec. In Papineau County, some very fine peristerite occurs in a small quarry on Lot 2, Range V of West Portland Township in the Lievre River district. Basic colors of the albite are gray to pink; the quarry is situated on a pegmatite 50 feet in width. Perhaps some of the finest albite peristerite in Canada is found at the Villeneuve Mine located on Lot 31, Range I in Villeneuve Township. The basic color is pure white but pink, green, and gold flash across the surface and result in an especially handsome gemstone when polished. In Wakefield Township, Gatineau Co., considerable amazonite was found in the Leduc Quarry years ago, and crystals as much as 18 inches across are recorded. This quarry is located on Lot 25 East ½, Range VII. Much pale green amazonite has come from a quarry on Lot 14, Range XIV in Hull Township, lying 3 miles by road from Kirk Ferry Station on the Canadian Pacific Railroad. In Terrebonne County, some excellent blue labradorite in crystal grains measuring up to several inches across occurs at various places near St. Jerome and St. Morin. Similar but finer-grained material is found at Chateau Richer in Montmorency County. Far to the north in New Quebec Territory, fine amazonite of good color is reported from pegmatites on some of the islands of the Paint Hills Group.

Ontario. Since as far back as 1850, beautiful peristerite has been recorded from Lot 9, Concession IX in Bathurst Township, Lanark County occurring in a pegmatite dike mined by opencast methods. From the same county, flesh-red perthite occurs in pegmatite dikes on Lot 3, Concession VI in North Burgess Township. This is the first locality from which this laminated feldspar was particularly noticed and given its name. The perthite from here is further distinguished by its small golden spangles which occur in streaks and thus qualify it as an aventurine. In Renfrew County, some deep green amazonite but only in small quantity has been found in a pegmatite outcropping on Lot 23, Concession XV, Lyndoch Township. Amazonite is found in Hastings County at the Woodcox Mine located on Lots 16, 17, Concession VIII, Monteagle Township. Very fine peristerite appears in pegmatite on the north half of Lot 24, Concession VI in the same township. Both amazonite and peristerite occur at the MacDonald Mine near Hybla, 15 miles north of Bancroft. In Frontenac County, peristerite is found at the Burnham Mine, Lot 3, Concession X, in Portland Township. Pink peristerite corresponding to oligoclase-andesine occurs in wall zones of a large pegmatitic body at the Richardson Mine located on lots 4, 5, 6, and 7, Concession XXI, Cardiff Township, Haliburton County. The workings are 3.8 miles by road east of Wilberforce. In the same county, aventurescent peristerite is obtained from near Drag Lake in Dudley Township. This material is pale brownish in color and exhibits bluish adularescence. In Peterborough County, peristerite albite is found on the north shore of Stoney Lake near the mouth of Eel Creek, Burleigh Township. Amazonite occurs in the Nipissing District of Ontario on Lot 6, Concession A, and Lot 7, Concession B, in Cameron Township. Beautiful yellowish and highly translucent peristerite is found at Sundridge, Strong Township, Parry Sound District; Sundridge is on Highway 11. Flesh-red aventurine feldspar, said to be very fine, is reported from a pegmatite dike traversing gneiss 20 miles east of French River on the shore of (Georgian Bay) Lake Huron in the Sudbury District.

New York. Beautiful peristerite albite yielding handsome gems has been found at the famous Newcomb tourmaline locality in Essex County (see TOURMALINE). The albite occurs in massive form with some in crystals more than 2 inches across and showing fine adularescence. An unusual aventurescent albite given a deep red color by platy hematite inclusions occurs at the Fisher Hill Mine, Mineville, Essex County. The hematite plates are rather small and the luster is silky rather than spangled as in ordinary sunstone. Gem quality blue adularescent microcline occurring in metamorphic limestone of the Grenville series has been found in an outcrop located one mile west of Olmstedville along the Olmstedville-Minerva Highway in Essex County. It is found associated with pyroxenes and amphiboles, also scapolite and idocrase. Some clean unfractured pieces were found which yielded gems of 5 carats.

Labradorite of good quality, very compact, and colorful, has been found extensively in place and as drift boulders throughout Essex and Lewis Counties; some of the boulders have been carried by glacial action as far south as New Jersey and have been reported in many New York counties such as Green, Lewis, Orange, Schoharie, St. Lawrence, and Warren. It is especially abundant in Essex County, large numbers of boulders found in one of the streams causing it to be named the Opalescent River. This stream rises just west of Mount Marcy in the Adirondack Mountains and flows southward to Tahawus and thence west to join the headwaters of the Hudson River near Newcomb. New York labradorite shows principally blue and green reflections but reds and bronzes are found in specimens which have somewhat weathered. Large amounts were once quarried at Keeseville, Essex County, where it was prepared for monumental and building purposes under the name "Au Sable Granite." It does not have the broad crystal grains noted in the Canadian material and consequently is far less suited for gem purposes but makes a very satisfactory material for coarse objects of ornament. The basic color, as may be expected, is dark gray.

New Jersey. Some very good sunstone in the form of bright orange patches in dark brownish red and black gabbro has come from the dumps of the Alan Wood Iron Mine atop Mine Hill near Dover, Morris County. The hematite inclusions are quite small and the effect is less spangly than silky. Numerous interlocked aventurescent feldspar grains up to an inch across have been found in masses measuring 6 inches or more across.

Pennsylvania. In Bucks County, fine blue orthoclase moonstone has been found at the Vanartsdalen Quarry located 2 miles north of Neshaminy Falls, and ¾ mile west of Nashaminy Creek on a small brook in Southampton Township. The orthoclase, basically gray or black in color, occurred in cleavage masses in Franklin limestone and was once called "chesterlite." In Chester County, where most of the famous localities lie, numerous townships have provided gem varieties of feldspar. Brilliant oligoclase sunstone, some very fine and comparable to Norwegian material, has been found in pegmatite near Pierce's Paper Mill, ½ mile southeast of Kennett Square in Kennett Township. The locality is on the east branch of Red Clay Creek. Fine labradorite said to be as good as the Canadian material also occurred here. Oligoclase sunstone also was found on Cloud's Farm, 2 miles southeast of Kennett Square, on a small brook entering the east branch of Red Clay Creek; similar material was taken from a quarry near Fairville and others nearby. In Delaware County, amazonite was discovered loose in the soil at Mineral Hill, one mile west of Media; albite moonstone and orthoclase sunstone have also been obtained here, the latter of grayish color with numerous very small spangles of hematite. In Middletown Township, oligoclase sunstone, albite moonstone, and amazonite were obtained from a cut along the Pennsylvania Railroad east of Lenni Station. Orthoclase sunstone, amazonite, albite moonstone, and oligoclase sunstone occurred together in a small feldspar quarry about one mile west of Media, or about ¾ mile northeast of Black Horse. Transparent oligoclase suitable for faceting has been found on Dismal Run about one mile north of Lenni. Albite moonstone and oligoclase sunstone occur generally in a swarm of pegmatite dikes in the area southwest of Black

Horse extending as far as Chrome Run and bordered on the south by the Pennsylvania Railroad. In Newton Township, oligoclase moonstone was collected from road cuts and exposed dikes one mile west of Newton Square. Very fine transparent oligoclase came from Mendenhall's Quarry about one mile southwest of Chadd's Ford in Pennsbury Township. In Ridley Township, Ward's Quarry on the east side of Crum Creek, about ½ mile south of Crum Lynne railroad station, furnished amazonite. In Thornbury Township, greenish gray albite moonstone has been found at Glen Mills; also in pegmatite dikes on Ridley Creek in Upper Providence Township just east of Sycamore Mills. In this latter township, orthoclase sunstone and colorless transparent oligoclase have been taken from a pegmatite dike at Blue Hill, about 2½ miles northwest of Media.

Virginia. Splendid moonstone, similar in quality to that of Ceylon, has been recently recovered (1958) from the gravels of a small creek on the O. W. Harris' Mica Mine Farm near Oliver, Goochland Co. The farm turnoff is 7.7 miles west of Highway 1 along State Highway 738. The creek in which the moonstone is found rises immediately behind the farm buildings and flows about one mile to empty into the Little River. On its western side, about ¾ mile from the farm buildings, is the Saunders Mica Mine (inoperative). Underlying rock in the immediate vicinity is foliated schistose gneiss composed primarily of mica, feldspar, and quartz in which occur streaks of extremely crude reddish garnet crystals, well-formed small stout crystals of blue kyanite, and very rarely, small masses of rutile. Moonstone, tentatively identified as orthoclase, forms streaks, lenses, and "eyes" in the gneiss, the eyes sometimes reaching as much as 6 inches thick and 18 inches in length and providing the major portion of the fragments found in the stream gravels. Within each feldspar mass also occurs coarse quartz and mica in formless grains, however, the feldspar predominates. Being easily cleaved, moonstone masses have been thoroughly shattered and distributed along the gravel beds through which the creek flows. A considerable area along the creek bed and associated slopes in underlaid by a mantle of moonstone-bearing gravel several inches to a foot or more thick over which lies an overburden of several feet of clay, sand, and topsoil.

The moonstone is found in lightly waterworn angular fragments ranging from mere chips to pieces several inches in diameter although the latter are generally severely shattered, partly altered into kaolin, and largely full of impurities. The smaller clear pieces, some being virtually transparent and suitable even for faceted gems, provide beautiful cabochons up to 1 inch in diameter displaying strong silvery reflections when properly cut. Refractive indices determined on a Rayner refractometer are unusually low in value: $\alpha = 1.518$ $\gamma = 1.524$; birefringence 0.006.

The total extent of the deposit is not known nor is it established that the moonstone-bearing rocks exist only on the Harris Farm. It is entirely possible that similar deposits may be found for some distance north and south along the general trend of the rock formations in this section of Virginia. If systematically worked by hydraulic methods, considerable moonstone may be recovered from the Harris deposit, however, samplings of the creek bed indicate that of the total gravel only about 5% is feldspar while gem moonstone comprises perhaps 5% of the latter.

The finest amazonite that the world has ever known comes from two extensively mined pegmatite dikes near Amelia, Amelia County. This mine, once known as the Allen and now as the Rutherford is located 1¼ miles north of Amelia in a pasture upon the Keener Farm (see Figure 37).

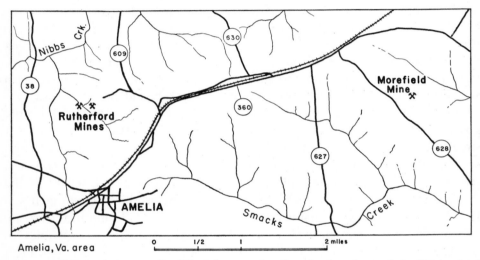

FIGURE 37. Map of the Amelia, Virginia area showing the locations of the Rutherford and Morefield mines, noted for their production of amazonite and other desirable gem minerals.

Another working, the Morefield Mine, some miles away, also has produced quantities of amazonite but not of such fine grade.

At the Rutherford Mine, two distinct parallel pegmatites have been worked for mica, feldspar, gemstones, and mineral specimens. The upper excavation in the Keener pasture is noted for its splendid amazonite and mica, while another deep opencut marks the major mining operation carried out upon the other dike. Both pegmatites appear to be irregular in thickness and branch out into the surrounding rock from central stocks of about 5 to 6 feet in thickness. Intensive exploration by members of the U.S. Geological

Survey in the years 1943-1945, including diamond-drilling, indicates the likelihood that both dikes continue to some depth. At the upper workings where the best amazonite occurs, mining was carried out by means of shafts and tunnels, now caved in and waterfilled. It was found that the dike was strongly zoned, showing a quartz core sheathed with large masses of amazonite followed by much cleavelandite and other forms of albite, also microcline and muscovite mica in books which sometimes reached 18 inches or more across. The cleavelandite crystallizations from this deposit are generally conceded to be the finest of their kind, individual crystals reaching as much as 8 inches in length and ¾ of an inch thick and found criss-crossing each other in a reticulated network. Gem quality spessartite garnet and other rare minerals such as microlite occur in spaces between blades while cavities in the quartz provide quartz crystals and rarely small amounts of amethyst. Some blue topaz occurs in the cleavelandite zone. In places, large masses of albite furnished beautiful specimens showing bright blue chatoyancy. Cut gems are very effective since the pure white color is an excellent foil for the intense blue reflections. Blocks and pieces of moonstone are collected even now from the extensive dumps of the lower mine but none from the dumps of the upper workings which have been bulldozed over. Under a microscope the Rutherford albite shows numerous gas-filled inclusions; the refractive indices are: $\alpha = 1.528$, $\beta = 1.532$, $\gamma = 1.539$.

Amazonite occurs in very large masses, individual crystal grains sometimes reaching 12 inches across, however, faced crystals such as occur in cavities in the Colorado localities are almost unknown. Near the surface, material is cracked rather badly and decidedly bleached, but with depth, the solidity improves and color becomes far more intense. This superb amazonite was much prized, especially in the cutting center of Idar-Oberstein, Germany, where large quantities were shipped during mining. Much of the amazonite is perthitic, showing bright white albite streaks which contrast well with the deep green. In later mining, an unusually translucent type of amazonite was found which assumed an extraordinary color almost like turquois blue. This material is highly translucent, pieces of ½ inch or more in thickness easily permitting a glow of light to pass through them. One of the drawbacks of such amazonite, however, is its highly perfect cleavage which permits thin laminae to split off almost like mica. All amazonite from this locality displays strong pearly schiller reflections from cleavage surfaces.

The Rutherford mines were worked as early as 1873. The amazonite mine was operated by the American Gem & Pearl Company of New York City from 1912 to 1932 and in this time, yielded about 15 tons of gem amazonite valued at $60,000. The last systematic work was done in 1943 for a period of five months but was abandoned because of dewatering problems. In

1957, W. D. Baltzley operating as the Piedmont Mining Company, Inc. of Powhatan, Virginia, leased the property and commenced bulldozing and drag-lining of the upper mine with the view of exposing the dike beneath its 12 to 15 feet of overburden. However, preliminary work showed extensive heavy ground which collapsed inward as the mine was dewatered necessitating abandoning the operation. In 1958, work was transferred to the lower mine which was quickly dewatered and the pegmatite body exposed. Although worked primarily for mica, important quantities of spessartite garnet, amazonite and beautiful albite moonstone are being recovered. A visit to the mine in early 1959 showed a large exposure of solid moonstone in the floor of the opencut at the northeast end.

Several beautiful cut specimens of moonstone from the Rutherford Mines, measuring up to ¾ inch in length, are in the collections of the U.S. National Museum; they are flawless, show a silvery luster, and in every way resemble Ceylon moonstones except for a somewhat greater cloudiness. It is not certain whether these are albite or microcline or from which of the two workings they came.

The next most important mine in this area is the Morefield Mine, named after its owner, Silas Morefield of Winterham, Amelia County. The pegmatite upon which mining operations have been carried out is located about 4 miles northeast of Amelia just off State Highway 628 (see Figure 37). It was opened by Mr. Morefield in 1929 who mined in opencut fashion up to 1931, leasing it several times thereafter until it again returned to his control in 1943. During one of the lease periods, a shaft was sunk to considerable depth to explore the dike and much material was taken out and cast upon the dumps. A large quantity of amazonite has come from the single pegmatite dike which varies from 3 to 5 feet in thickness and dips nearly vertically. Associated with the amazonite are large topaz masses of colorless to blue color, beryl, phenakite, and many other rare or interesting minerals. Generally speaking the amazonite is fair to good material, firm, and free from cracks in the larger pieces obtained from the deepest workings. It is not as deep in color as the best material from the Rutherford Mine, nor has it the same degree of translucency. From the period 1929 to 1941, approximately 450 to 500 tons of feldspar have been taken from this mine, much of it amazonite, and valued in toto at about $3300. Additional minerals of economic value were produced by the owner from 1943 to 1944.

Amazonite has also been removed from the Richeson (formerly the Berry) Mica Mine, located 1¼ miles north 35° east of Amelia close to the bed of the Richmond & Danville Branch of the Southern Railroad. Visible remains of previous work consist of a slumped pit 35 feet in diameter and 15 feet deep. Further away at the Herbb No. 2 Mine in Powhatan County, considerable amazonite in large blocky masses was encountered during opencast mining for mica. This mine is 3.6 miles northeast of Flat Rock and is reached by State Highway 613 from Flat Rock. This pegmatite is similar in many respects to the Rutherford and Morefield pegmatites but did not yield such handsome and valuable specimens. The dike varies in thickness from 4 to 25 feet and has a large quartz core around which was found the amazonite. The latter is rather pale but may improve if workings in depth are carried out. Grayish moonstone has been obtained from the Champion Mine located about 2½ miles north-northeast of Amelia in Amelia County. This mine is along State Highway 630 about one mile north of its intersection with State Highway 620. Blue moonstone has also been reported from the Irish Creek tin deposits located several miles south of Vesuvius, Nelson County, and about the same distance southwest of Montebello. The tin mineral, cassiterite, was mined from a pegmatite in which feldspar was a common gangue mineral.

North Carolina. In 1887 a most unusual transparent feldspar was found at a depth of 380 feet in the Hawk Mica Mine which is located 4.5 miles east-northeast of Bakersville at the junction of Soapstone Branch and the left fork of Cane Creek, one mile northeast of Hawk, Mitchell County. This material was later shown to be oligoclase, S. G. $= 2.651$; R. I.: $\alpha = 1.537$, $\gamma = 1.547$ (appr.). Clear sections occurred only in the centers of large whitish crystal grains. From this oligoclase very brilliant and attractive faceted gems and cabochons were cut, ranging in color from colorless to faintly green and resembling some varieties of aquamarine. Flawless areas were large enough to yield gems of about ⅜ inch in size; one such specimen in the author's collection is an octagonal step cut weighing 4.13 carats. The largest piece of clear material found here, though not flawless, measured 3 by 2 by 1 inches and was faint green in color. Similar material has been reported from the Plumtree Mine located on Plumtree Creek, about .8 mile northeast of Plumtree in Avery County. Colorless to faintly bluish-green transparent oligoclase also comes from the Gibbs Mine located on the west bank of the South Toe River, 1.9 miles due east of Bowditch in Yancey County and reached by road from that community.

Oligoclase sunstone has been reported from a quarry near Statesville, Iredell County; it was said to be grayish-brown in color due to hematite inclusions, but the spots of aventurescence were very small. Oligoclase sunstone was also found many years ago upon the property of W. G. Bowman about one mile north of Bakersville, Mitchell County, at the base of Meadlock Mountain.

Amazonite has been reported from the McChone Mines, located ½ mile east-southeast of Chalk Mountain, or 1½ miles southwest of Spruce Pine in Mitchell County. Some amazonite is also reported from the Ray Mica

Mine which is 1.7 miles northeast of Vixen or 2.3 miles south-southeast of Burnsville, Yancey County.

Wisconsin. Albite peristerite is found in pegmatite dikes cutting the granites of the Wausau area surrounding the city of Wausau, Marathon County. The individual grains measure only several inches across but are found in aggregates of considerable size. Adularescence is bluish to greenish and very similar in appearance to that observed in peristerites from Canada. This material found some use in the past for coarse ornamental stonework but has not been heretofore considered for gems. Some of the albite shows a body color inclining toward orange; other material is grayish.

Colorado. The marvelously crystallized amazonite, smoky quartz, and topaz from Colorado have excited the admiration of mineral and gem collectors for many years. All of these gemstones, plus other species, come from a region which has been rather vaguely labeled as "Pike's Peak." This geographical description is misleading since very little material of mineralogical interest comes from this mountain, rather, it is from pockets in pegmatites which cut the Pike's Peak *granite* that desirable mineralizations come.

FIGURE 38. An early photograph (1913) of one of the amazonite pegmatites in the Florissant area of Teller County, Colorado. This pegmatite is about 4 feet thick and shows upon its exposed face a number of blocky crystals of amazonite plus smoky quartz and biotite. Photo taken at the old J. D. Endicott mines about 5 miles north-northwest of Florissant in the gap northwest of Crystal Peak. Courtesy U.S. Geological Survey.

An especially productive area known variously as the Crystal Peak or Florissant area, begins about 2 miles north of Florissant in Teller County and when visited in 1957 was found to be under lease to a company organized as the Crystal Gem Mines. Some work was being done along a dike called "Pocket No. 7" involving the use of explosives as well as bulldozing. It was said that amazonite indications continued to the bottom of the opencut (about 5 feet), and that they seem to continue laterally as well as in depth. Figure 38 shows an exposed dike discovered in 1913 prior to its excavation and gives some idea of the appearance.

In the Florissant area, all dikes seem to be commonly oriented and also dip at shallow angles below the surface. Pockets are almost always flattened openings of disk-like shape with only several inches or perhaps as much as a foot of space between the hanging wall and the floor of the pocket. It is in such openings that amazonite crystals appear although it should be stated that most cavities are solidly filled with clay, topsoil, etc., leaving little if any air space. Undisturbed pockets show groups of amazonite crystals of typical blocky form penetrated here and there by smoky quartz crystals, intensely black in color, and tapering to a narrow point. Many of the latter are quite clear and flawless inside but are so dark that only small stones may be cut if some degree of brilliance is expected. Specimen groups of amazonite crystals sprinkled with shiny black quartz crystals are highly prized and bring good prices at any time they are offered. A fine fist-sized specimen may bring from $10 to $20 while larger groups are valued at $50 up to $100. A splendid crystal from this locality is illustrated in Figure 35. Unfortunately, such groups are very scarce because late-stage pocket activity has often resulted in complete disintegration of the walls and shattering of crystals. In most pockets, broken quartz and single crystals of feldspar are the rule, and though handsome in themselves, or useful for cutting, are far less desirable than a complete group. In size, amazonite crystals range from small smooth-faced individuals of ½ inch to giant specimens of 6 by 6 by 10 inches. Smoky quartz crystals also vary widely in size, the largest being about 18 to 20 inches in length though seldom as perfectly formed as the smaller. Associated with the amazonite are found several iron minerals such as limonite, goethite, siderite, hematite, and pyrite; also fluorite, mica, and rarely topaz. Not all dikes produce green microcline, many are found in which ordinary white to grayish crystals occur. Sometimes these are curiously etched and overgrown along the edges with additional material as if a second phase of mineralization began sometime after the first had stopped. Some pockets are very extensively permeated by micaceous hematite which enters every nook and cranny and seriously discolors all specimens. Some of it may be caught up during growth of quartz crystals, resulting in a decided coppery hue near the surface of crystal faces.

Amazonite from this locality varies in color from faint green to deep green, sometimes deep blue-green. Crystals are frequently white inside and only the exterior is colored. Much is good gem material but in general does not compare in quality to Virginia material in respect to flawlessness and translucency. Because of inaccessibility until recent years, major production from this area took place some time after 1900 and terminated about 1938. Although cavities may range from inches to feet across, one enormous one was found in 1910 which produced $3500 worth of crystals from a space measuring 15 by 15 by 6 feet.

Another famous area within the Pike's Peak granite region is that known as Crystal Park. This is a mountain meadow which lies at the foot of Cameron Cone, about 5 miles south of Manitou Springs in Teller County. Cameron Cone (10,709 ft.) is 6 miles west of Colorado Springs and about 2 miles southwest of Manitou Springs. The area extends for several square miles and averages about 8600 feet in elevation. The slopes of Cameron Cone as well as Bear Creek Canyon several miles to the south have all been productive of amazonite and other minerals from pegmatite pockets. Much smoky quartz and some topaz has been found in cavities which here seldom exceed about 3 feet in width, however, amazonite crystals reach about the same size noted from other localities in the Pike's Peak granite region.

Amazonite in considerable quantity has come from the Devil's Head area about 18 miles due north of Woodland Park. The latter community is in Teller County but Devil's Head (9348 ft.) is in the southern part of Douglas County. This locality, formerly known as Platte Mountain, is most famous for its topaz. Principal collecting areas are south of the peak upon a steep-walled ridge and within reasonable walking distance from roads. First discovered in 1880, hundreds of pockets have been found and excavated, the last important one being found by Over and Montgomery in 1934 when some splendid topaz crystals were recovered (see Topaz). Etched amazonite of fine blue-green color came from this pocket and provided some of the most colorful material yet found in the state. The crystals from this find were not large reaching only several inches across at most.

Amazonite, smoky quartz, topaz, and other minerals occur in pockets in pegmatite on the slopes of Stove Mountain in Teller County, about ten miles southwest of Colorado Springs; similar material found under the same circumstances occurs on St. Peter's Dome, a conical mountain located directly west of Cheyenne Mountain in El Paso County immediately south of Stove Mountain. A little amazonite is found in pegmatite pockets in the Pine Creek area of Douglas County where it is found with large smoky quartz crystals, some of the latter reaching 12 inches in length and of good faceting quality. The amazonite grades into creamy white; much is broken and iron-stained. The Pine Creek area begins about 11 miles west of Sedalia and lies several miles north of the community of Pine Creek.

Idaho. Transparent andesine, some suitable for faceted gems, occurs as loose grains eroded from lava at Crystal Butte, 18 miles north of Saint Anthony, and 8 miles southeast of Ivan, Fremont County. The crystal grains are said to reach a length of several inches, strewing the surface of this volcanic cone and giving it its name. The color varies from pale yellow to colorless. Another locality in this county is given as Mack's Butte upon which occur clear crystals of an unstated feldspar species from ⅛ to 1 inch in thickness.

Oregon. Sanidine and sanidine-sunstone occur near Lakeview, Lake County in the form of grains weathered from lava.

California. Labradorite in facet grade and also in beautiful sunstone types has long been known from Modoc County and frequently appears upon the gemstone market. Clear straw-yellow fragments often reach lengths of from ½ to 1¼ inches and thicknesses up to ½ inch. Many are completely flawless and produce fine gems. The sunstone type is noted for bright coppery reflections which at one time were thought to be flaky metallic copper inclusions, however, the spangles are now known to be goethite. Inclusions are exceedingly small, averaging only 0.01 to 0.03 mm. in diameter. The properties of this labradorite approach bytownite.

Sanidine occurs in the lava flows south of Little Lake in Inyo County but rarely in pieces over 1 inch in length. Crystal grains are usually much flattened and elongated. In Mono County, similar material has been found weathering from lava just north of Mono Lake on the road leading from Mono Lake community to Bodie.

Arizona. Andesine and andesine-sunstone showing bright coppery reflections have been reported from the Altar Mountains within the Apache Indian Reservation near Globe. In color and other characteristics, it strongly resembles labradorite from Modoc County, California. The refractive index has been given as 1.550.

Utah. Fine facet grade yellow labradorite in small squarish fragments is found littering the top and sides of an upthrust mass of lava in the center of an alkali flat, ½ mile northeast of Clear Lake railroad station, Millard County. The country rock is a crumbly andesite in which the labradorite grains are abundantly distributed. One collector reporting his experiences at this locality stated that a party of four persons gathered a pint of fragments in a three hour period, their size ranging from about ¼ inch to over 1 inch, all pieces being rectangular in outline and usually frosted on the exterior. Much is flawless and produces fine straw-yellow brilliant gems. This locality has been known for many years and material appears frequently upon the market. In 1947, cut stones sold in Salt Lake City for $3 to $6 per carat.

New Mexico. One of the finest moonstones in North America occurs in an obscure locality on the west slope of the Black Range in Grant County. The species approximates sanidine in composition, furnishing gem quality material from within the interior of large white crystals associated with quartz in a series of small pegmatite bodies scattered throughout a granite porphyry intrusive in quartz-latite. Pegmatite bodies consist essentially of feldspar and quartz but accessory albite, biotite and sphene are also present. Large crystals are completely opaque on the exterior and it is necessary to cob away this material before the clear glassy sanidine is exposed. The body color is a very distinctive smoky gray or brown. Strong bright blue adularescence occurs only along one direction, and in intensity rivals that observed in Ceylon moonstones; in some pieces a silvery adularescence rather than blue is present. Most of the material is cracked and veiled with inclusions and large flawless gems are impossible to obtain. Old reports on New Mexico localities indicate that labradorite has been found in basalt near Abiquiu in Rio Arriba County, as "comparatively large" crystals showing blue reflections. Another moonstone is reported from volcanic rock near Jemez in Sandoval County; it is said to be of magnificent blue color and occurs as grains in a porphyry.

Texas. Clear facet grade labradorite, in grains up to ¾ inch diameter, occurs loose in the soil on the Woodward Ranch, 17 miles south of Alpine in Brewster County.

Chihuahua. In the western part of this state, clear straw-yellow orthoclase of the sanidine variety is found lying on the ground as loose fragments reportedly weathered from lava flows. One Texas mineral dealer has imported several hundred pounds in the last few years for sale as faceting and carbochon material. Much larger pieces are available as compared to that obtained from other localities, for example, in the American Museum of Natural History, collections include a brilliant-cut gem of 7.50 carats and an emerald-cut gem of 23.43 carats.

Guanajuato. Clear facet grade sanidine occurs at Penas de Quinteros and in the Sierra de Santa Rosa in the Guanajuato District.

SPODUMENE

First found in important quantities in gem grade in the pegmatites of the Pala District, California, spodumene provides an unusual and beautiful gem when faceted into brilliants or stepcut stones. After the initial discovery near Pala, a number of other gem-bearing pegmatites in the immediate neighborhood were found to contain spodumene along with gem-quality tourmaline and beryl. From the standpoint of quality and size, the best gem spodumene in all the world still comes from this area although important quantities have been uncovered in Brazil and Madagascar. Nowhere else are found such richly colored specimens as those from the Vanderburg Mine on Hiriart Hill near Pala, nor can any other locality boast their equal in size. Perhaps the best-known variety is a lovely pink to pale purple and violet kind known as *kunzite*, although from the standpoint of beauty if not for size, the emerald-green *hiddenite* variety from a small area in North Carolina is scarcely less famous. It is truly unfortunate that spodumene has several serious drawbacks insofar as suitability for gems is concerned; the tendency for pink or lilac varieties to fade to almost colorless hues when exposed to daylight certainly militates against their use in ordinary jewelry. Furthermore, as any experienced gem cutter will acknowledge, spodumene is devilish in its behavior during cutting. Possessing two perfect cleavages, both easily developed, the greatest lapidary skill is exacted in bringing a gem to a successful conclusion. For this reason alone, finished stones represent in number many less than those begun, while the painstaking labor required during cutting demands high lapidary fees. Notwithstanding all these deterrents to popularity, gems of spodumene are eagerly sought by collectors and museums who pay good prices to obtain fine examples.

The varieties of spodumene acquire their distinctions solely on the basis of color. Pink, lilac, and purplish to amethyst types take the name of *kunzite*. *Hiddenite* is properly reserved only for those of true emerald-green color and not for pale yellowish-green kinds which bear no special varietal name.

FIGURE 39. The late Dr. George F. Kunz, after whom the purplish variety of spodumene was named, examining a fine kunzite crystal from the Pala Chief Mine near Pala, California. The transparency and flawlessness of the crystal are shown by the image of a finger appearing above the thumb. Courtesy Martin Ehrmann, Beverley Hills, California.

Colorless to yellow types are called *triphane*. The name kunzite was affixed to the California gemstones in honor of Dr. G. F. Kunz, the noted gem expert and Vice President of Tiffany's of New York City at that time. Dr. Kunz is seen in Figure 39 examining one of the early crystals of spodumene recovered from the Pala District. It is interesting to recall that the identification of spodumene from this locality is popularly accredited to Dr. Kunz but an article in the now-defunct Mineral Collector Magazine, Volume XIII, No. 2, April 1906, indicates that perhaps this mineral was first identified by W. S. Valiant of Rutgers College, New Jersey. Entitled "Addenda and

Corrigenda," the article written by Valiant, discusses the matter of naming the spodumene from Pala. It was pointed out that a sample had been sent him by Dr. W. V. Nichols of Oceanside, California, was promptly identified as "spodumene of fine gem quality," and returned immediately by mail. It was not until three months later that the official announcement came from New York City heralding the discovery of a new gemstone. If all this is true, and there seems no reason to disbelieve Mr. Valiant, then the credit is due that gentleman, with perhaps the honor of naming the gem properly falling to his lot also.

The matter of naming hiddenite seems less controversial because W. E. Hidden discovered this variety in 1879 near Stony Point, North Carolina and it has since borne his name. Triphane is derived from Greek, meaning, obscurely it might be added, that the mineral "appeared threefold" in terms of luster as observed from three different points of view. Spodumene seems more haply named since its Greek derivation means "burned to ashes" because it forms an ash-like mass when heated to destruction.

Spodumene is common only in lithia-rich pegmatites and is rarely found elsewhere. Crystallizing in the Monoclinic System, it is lithium aluminum silicate with the formula: $LiAlSi_2O_6$. In most cases it occurs in long lath-like crystals of flattened rectangular cross-section, dead-white and opaque to translucent gray in color. A distinctive feature are the striations on the sides of the prisms which in ordinary kinds, appear like a series of fine grooves but in gem crystals are coarse and deep. Under usual circumstances, spodumene is found in pegmatites firmly embedded and completely enclosed in the massive quartz and feldspar of the cores. Crystals of this sort seldom produce gem material except from a few glassy spots near their centers. On the other hand, should pegmatites contain pockets, then it is easily possible for these openings to contain magnificent gem-quality crystals suspended in the clay and debris filling such cavities. This is the mode of occurrence in California where the largest examples have been found. Examination of all such crystals shows that true crystal faces are absent, the entire exterior being covered by deep grooves, etch marks, and surfaces brilliantly reflective as if fused or melted as shown in Figure 40 which illustrates a suite of typical gem crystals from California. It is theorized that these highly irregular shards and splinters are but remnants of much larger crystals whose imprints may be clearly seen in the massive quartz still surrounding the places where pockets were excavated in such mines as the Pala Chief and San Pedro in the Pala District. Each of these imprints is filled with pink powdery montmorillonite, presumably derived from the alteration of spodumene, and sometimes small splinters of this mineral can still be found in the clay if it is carefully scraped away. Associated with spodumene in the California pockets were found morganite and aquamarine, a series of phosphate minerals, principally triphylite, small needles of deep purple tourmaline, some apatite, and the usual magnificent crystallizations of quartz and feldspar. Most of the pockets found contained a solid filling of firm brownish red clay, very sticky and difficult to remove. Spodumene crystals were found in this clay as well as in the floor debris consisting of pink and white clays, broken fragments of

FIGURE 40. Three magnificent crystals of spodumene from the Pala Chief Mine near Pala, California. The longest crystal, pink in color, measures 12¼ inches in length. The crystal on the right of rich purplish-pink hue is 8¼ inches in length, while the third crystal, an almost colorless example, measures 5¾ inches in length. The typically striated prism sides and etched surfaces of gem spodumene are shown extremely well in this photograph. Courtesy Smithsonian Institution.

cleavelandite feldspar, highly irregular quartz crystals, etc., sometimes rather firmly cemented together.

The occurrence of hiddenite in North Carolina is considerably different in many respects but is still a matter of crystallization within pockets in pegmatite. A fuller description will be given under the locality.

The workability of gem spodumene is seriously affected by the two cleavages which are parallel to the length of the crystal and intersect each other at angles of 87° and 93°. One of the cleavage planes is parallel to the breadth and the other roughly parallel to the edge of each crystal. Partially developed cleavages are frequently present in all gem varieties and reveal themselves as brilliantly reflective streaks or planes, or sometimes as thin sheets of reddish discoloration where pocket clay has entered. Twinning is common and some cutters believe that twinned crystals are under stress and hence cleave more readily during cutting. The hardness is ordinarily listed as from 6.5 to 7 but lapidary experience has shown it to vary markedly as follows: parallel to a cleavage plane—6.5, across the prism—about 7.0, across the ends of crystals—about 7.5. The luster of gem crystals is glassy and brilliant. Shattered or impure examples often show a pearly luster upon cleavage planes. The specific gravity varies from 3.17 to 3.19 but may reach 3.23. Refractive indices vary considerably with color, rising steadily as the color intensifies. Colorless material gives: $a = 1.654$, $\gamma = 1.669$; kunzite shows: $a = 1.660$, $\gamma = 1.675$; hiddenite shows: $a = 1.6623$, $\gamma = 1.6765$. The birefringence remains in all cases, close to 0.015. Dispersion is modest, only 0.017. The optical sign is positive.

Gem-quality material varies from colorless to rich hues but the latter is rarely observed. Kunzite is ordinarily some shade of very faint to rather deep pink. At times the basic pink takes on a violet cast of some intensity, causing cut gems to look much like paler types of amethyst. Very fine violet kunzite of exceptional depth and purity of hue has been found at the Vanderberg Mine in Pala and is unmatched in this respect by any spodumene heretofore known. True hiddenite is almost emerald-green in color but is somewhat more yellowish than that gemstone. Pale yellow-green hues are also commonly observed but seldom intense. A peculiar bluish to grayish green kunzite occurs in the Vanderberg Mine, some specimens looking like aquamarine. Being biaxial, spodumene exhibits its strongest colors along the crystal axes which emerge near the ends of crystal prisms. The effect is very striking in kunzite crystals which often appear virtually colorless unless observed through the ends. Pleiochroism is strong to distinct, according to intensity of color. Kunzite shows in the dichroscope, colorless, some shade of violet pink and a shade of purplish pink; hiddenite shows emerald-green, bluish green, and yellowish green. Yellow and yellowish green specimens show slight but distinct changes in the basic color plus one colorless direction. In cutting, the best color can be realized only if the gem is cut to place the table facet across the principal crystal axis. Since most crystals are narrow, this means that large gems of rich coloration cannot be obtained from any but the largest crystals. Placing the gem so that the table facet is parallel to the broad face of the crystal affords a larger stone but one which shows good color only at its ends.

LOCALITIES

Maine. Large flattened rectangular crystals have been mined from the Lower Nevel Quarry Pit on the northeast slope of Plumbago Mountain in Newry Township, Oxford County. Grayish to greenish crystals are filled with numerous inclusions parallel to the length of the prism and, when cut, afford distinct though not sharp, catseye gems. Crystals vary from 12 to 24 inches in length, up to 8 inches in width, and 3 inches thick. Small spots sometime occur clear enough to cut into colorless faceted gems. Small bits of facet-grade pink spodumene have been found at the Black Mountain Mica Mine in Rumford Township, Oxford County.

Massachusetts. Fibrous purplish spodumene of distinct color and capable of cutting into attractive chatoyant gems has been found at the Barrus Farm near Lithia, in northwestern Hampshire County.

Connecticut. Material similar to the above has also come from the Strickland Quarry on the west face of Collins Hill several miles east of Portland in Middlesex County; also facet-grade material but only as very small fragments from the interior of much larger crystals. In 1886, a crystal measuring 8 by 12 inches yielded a clear area of 1½ by 1 inches.

North Carolina. Hiddenite, the beautiful emerald-green gem variety of spodumene is found only in a limited area in Alexander County. Its discovery came about as a pleasant surprise incidental to searching underground for emeralds which had formerly been found as crystals lying loose in the topsoil in a cultivated field upon the old Warren Farm, near Salem Church, Sharpe's Township. This locality has long been identified with Stony Point, the nearest community, but is now known as Hiddenite. The mine workings, now abandoned and caved in, are located one mile north of Hiddenite about 300 yards from the highway between Taylorsville and Statesville, or about 15 miles northwest of Statesville. However, the owners of the property now permit collecting from the old dumps upon payment of a daily fee.

The history of this mine is most interesting and bears retelling. Upon the Warren Farm, six long narrow crystals of emerald, then completely unrecognized, were found during plowing and labeled picturesquely if inaccurately, "green bolts." Because of his announced interest in the minerals of North Carolina, W. E. Hidden, after whom this variety was named, was soon informed of these unusual crystals. Upon discovering them to be emerald, he obtained the necessary rights to the property and set to work a corps of men to excavate a series of trenches designed to intersect the vein from which the crystals had weathered. Some five weeks of fruitless effort were spent this way during July and August of 1880 before a vein containing small prisms of emerald was found at a depth of eight feet. This "blind vein" as it was called, was found to contain besides emerald, an unusual green mineral in the form of thin transparent blades, much etched, and perfectly clear. These were found to outnumber emerald crystals by fifty-to-one and at first it was supposed that they were either kyanite or diopside. In due time they were identified as spodumene and because of their unique nature, were deemed worthy of bearing their own varietal name, hiddenite, which, rightly enough, was selected to honor their discoverer.

Despite the lack of large numbers of emerald crystals, the occurrence of hiddenite plus other pocket minerals such as splendid quartz and rutile crystals, more than offset this deficiency. Work was prosecuted vigorously for some years until the depth and difficulty of mining created undue expense and gave an unprofitable turn to the enterprise. Initial opencut work proved the existence of about 80 mineralized veinlets in a space of 40 feet square but the ingress of water forced the driving of a drainage tunnel before further work in depth could be done. This tunnel was driven to a distance of 261 feet to intersect a vertical shaft sunk in the mineralized zone to a depth of 56 feet. The various workings eventually covered an area of about 20 to 50 feet wide by 150 feet in length at the surface. Early surface excavation was made easy by an overburden of red clayey soil about 15 feet deep although this proved troublesome later due to slumping in wet weather. The country rock was found to be much contorted and metamorphosed gneiss of Pre-Cambrian age. It is grayish in color and contains fine grains of quartz, biotite, and garnet. During the 1880's, Hidden organized the Emerald and Hiddenite Mining Company, capitalized nominally at $200,000 and with a paid in capital of $20,000, to exploit the deposit. A force of 20 to 30 men was kept constantly at work during this early profitable period.

When first produced, hiddenite developed a tremendous native appeal as an American gem and all specimens as well as cut gems sold readily. Shortly after organized mining, for example, a 2½ carat cut gem was sold for $500, with other gems receiving $32 to $100 per carat when they were available. None of the crystals was large, the best specimen of record being only slightly less than 2½ inches long, ½ inch wide and about ⅓ inch thick. This magnificent specimen is a beautiful rich green with its terminal end flawless, and it is estimated to be capable of cutting into a 5½ carat gem. This crystal found its way into the Bement Collection and eventually into the American Museum of Natural History when that collection was purchased by J. P. Morgan and donated to the museum. In this institution is also a fine matrix specimen showing a ¼ inch x 1¼ inch crystal on gneiss with pyrite and bright red rutile. Other loose crystals up to 1¼ inch are also included. The J. P. Morgan gift also furnished a cut stone of 9.29 carats, the largest cut hiddenite known.

At the time of discovery, hiddenite was proclaimed to be the first instance of spodumene in gem quality but later events proved this to be wrong, the discovery of gem quality yellowish spodumene in Brazil antedating the North Carolina discovery by several years (1877). The magnificent color of hiddenite is due to small amounts of chromium, the same coloring agent which gives emerald its characteristic hue. The deposit is entirely unique since chromium is normally absent wherever spodumene is found. The color is unaffected by light or heat; hiddenite has been subjected to the blowpipe flame and though losing color when hot, returns to the original hue when cold. This same property is also characteristic of emerald and ruby, both gemstones owing their color to the presence of chromium. As is true of other spodumene varieties, hiddenite caused considerable difficulties in cutting until the New York lapidaries learned how to treat this completely different gemstone. In appearance, hiddenite crystals are unmistakable. Each one looks like a miniature Roman sword, with the handle end being that affixed to the cavity walls and the thicker and pointed end, that which protrudes into the cavity and provides the termination. The color is pale green, almost colorless at the butt end, darkening rapidly as the point is approached. Near the termination is not only the richest shade of green but also the most flawless area and hence that most suitable for gems. The sides of the crystals are grooved parallel to the length while the terminations are etched into curious rounded or pointed hillocks, pointing to partial destruction by solution after crystals had reached full growth. Figure 41 represents a series of crystals

FIGURE 41. Hiddenite crystals found at the noted emerald and hiddenite locality near Hiddenite, North Carolina. The crystal at the top, only several inches in length, shows the typical severe etching noted in most gem quality spodumene crystals. Courtesy Smithsonian Institution.

obtained during the most recent working of the mine while Figure 42 is a drawing of a typical crystal.

After many years of inactivity, the workings at Hiddenite were re-opened by Burnham S. Colburn and his brother William B. Colburn of Biltmore, North Carolina, in 1926 to 1927 for specimens only and again produced a quantity of hiddenite and emerald. Using modern equipment and constantly employing the services of a few men, they worked this mine for nearly 2 years. None of the hiddenite was worthy of cutting and none was cut. A few found weighed over 50 cts. At this time, observations were made by unusually competent mineralogists and give us the most accurate description of the nature of this deposit. The gem minerals occur in pockets in a series of pegmatites which range from paperthin veinlets to some as much as one foot thick. Cavities range in size from minute openings to those several feet across, varying widely in mineral content but generally containing either beryl or hiddenite, or sometimes both. One pocket was found during mining which contained 20 crystals of hiddenite, many twinned and all etched. The color was fine green but most were too flawed for cutting. A large number of slivers and partially dissolved fragments were obtained from the pocket debris. A few good matrix specimens showing hiddenites still attached to the walls were taken out also. In rare cases, a few crystals were found in which etching had been very slight, leaving faces geometrically perfect and mostly smooth. Associated with hiddenite were some fine colorless to faintly amethystine quartz crystals, many containing liquid inclusions. One of the latter weighed 25 pounds but another crystal showed the largest liquid-filled cavity, an opening within the crystal of 2½ inches in length. The amethyst occurs as an overgrowth upon colorless quartz.

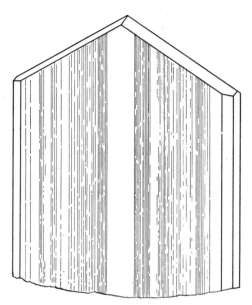

FIGURE 42. A typical hiddenite crystal from North Carolina. Compare the form of this crystal with the kunzites shown in Figure 41.

In regard to the quartz crystals containing liquid-filled cavities, it is interesting to recall that in the early days, crystals of the self-same type caused Mr. Hidden considerable anguish because he had failed to appreciate the fact that water freezes, whether entrapped in quartz crystals or not. It seems that he had collected a large quantity of magnificent specimens which he had laid upon the porch of his cabin for want of a better storage place. One night, the mountain air chilled below freezing and upon coming out in the morning, Mr. Hidden found all his splendid crystals reduced to a pile of glassy fragments, burst asunder by the expansion of the freezing water in the numerous entrapped bubbles.

Other minerals found in the gem pockets are albite and orthoclase feldspar, emerald, black tourmaline, garnet, muscovite, rutile, apatite, pyrite, calcite, aragonite, siderite, ankerite, arsenopyrite, nontronite, and amphibole.

The locality just discussed is not the only place in this area where hiddenite has been found and at times mined. Both emerald and hiddenite have been found upon the Osborne-Lackey place, 1/5 mile northwest of the original locality. It is recorded that about 50 emerald crystals were found here as well as a few of hiddenite but these were very pale and inferior in quality. At another place, about ½ mile west of Hiddenite, some work was accomplished in 1907 on a similar deposit by the American Gem Mining Syndicate. This was followed by an opening called the Ellis Prospect, ¼ mile east of Hiddenite. Hiddenite occurred in both but only in important quantities at the Ellis Prospect where it is stated that about 200 carats of crystals were obtained. One crystal weighed ten carats but though one half was deep emerald green, the other half was colorless. The vein filling at this prospect consisted of quartz, calcite, dolomite, muscovite, rutile, black tourmaline, emerald and aquamarine varieties of beryl, pyrite, chalcopyrite, and monazite.

Gem quality spodumene of pale yellowish-green color has been found in the McChone Mines located 1 mile south 30° west of Spruce Pine in Mitchell County. In a pegmatite quarried at these workings were found decomposed spodumene crystals up to 1 by 3 inches containing small clear sections suitable for faceting. Some fragments reached 1/4 by 1/5 by 1/3 inch in size.

South Dakota. In the Black Hills occur a series of enormous pegmatite dikes in which gigantic crystals of spodumene are frequently found. Upon occasion, these contain small areas clear enough for faceting into gems although the color is usually a rather unattractive green. Material of this kind has been found in the Helen Beryl Mine near Custer, Pennington County. One specimen seen by the author showed a network of opaque whitish material with small clear spots, one of which was about ¼ inch in diameter.

California. The premier world localities for gem spodumene, especially the beautiful kunzite variety, are contained within a relatively narrow belt of pegmatite dikes which begin in southern Riverside County and extend southward into the Rincon District of San Diego County. Nowhere else has this gemstone been found in such perfection, quality, and size.

History accords to Frederick M. Sickler the honor of being the discoverer of gem spodumene in Southern California. According to his own statement, he first found colorless to very pale pink kunzite as float upon what is now known as the White Queen Mine atop Hiriart Hill in the Pala District of San Diego County. Although dismissed at first as some curious variety of tourmaline (probably on account of the vertical striations which are so characteristic of this mineral and which resemble those seen on tourmaline) it was not until he and his son found more in the Katerina Mine that their curiosity was sufficiently aroused to send some away for identification. This took place in early 1902 although the initial discovery was said by Sickler to have taken place some years previously. In the latter part of 1902, the mineral in question was confirmed as spodumene of gem quality and resulted in an intensive prospecting of the entire area by the Sicklers, two Basque prospectors—Bernardo Hiriart and Pedro Peilitch (or Feilitch), Frank A. Salmons, and John Giddens. Within a few months, all likely-looking outcrops had been staked on Hiriart Hill and Pala Chief Mountain, the next eminence to the west. One of the early leading producers of kunzite, the Pala Chief Mine, was located on the west edge of the summit of Pala Chief Mountain in May 1903. These mines are shown on the map in Figure 43.

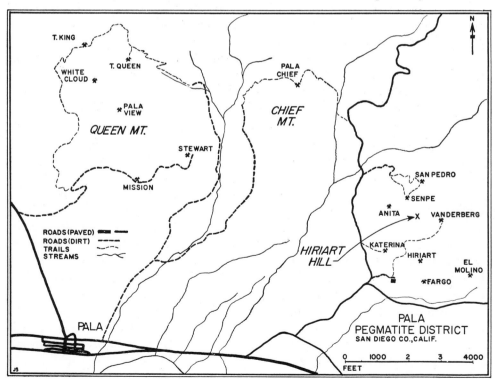

FIGURE 43. Map of the Pala District, San Diego County, California, showing the principal roads, trails, and mines.

At about the same time, Bert Simmons, another prospector working further to the north, located the Fano-Simmons Mine on the southeast slope of Coahuila Mountain in Riverside County. When this prospect proved to contain gem minerals, among them kunzite, a company entitled the Fano Kunzite-Tourmaline Mining Company was formed and active work commenced. This mine soon lapsed into obscurity, perhaps because of exhaustion of easily-accessible gem pockets, and nothing of importance seems to have been done since. This mine may be the same as that now known as the Williamson Mine.

In the Pala District, numerous prospects were opened up until the entire top and flanks of Hiriart Hill were segmented into claims and spotted with dump heaps glistening with white feldspar. Similar openings were made upon numerous dikes on Pala Chief Mountain and also upon Tourmaline Queen Mountain further to the west. However, no gem spodumene of any consequence has been found on the latter although wonderful tourmaline and beryl have come from the several mines opened up on its flanks. Active mining and prospecting continued until 1914 when rich markets were lost due to unsettled world conditions and oversupply of gemstones, resulting in an abrupt termination of the industry. Since then, only small informal operations have taken place and nothing significant produced until the purchase of the Hiriart Hill claims by George Ashley of Pala. The transfer of title took place in July 1947, when Frederick M. Sickler turned over the following claims to their new owner: San Pedro, Anita, Katerina, Vanderberg, Fargo, K. C. Naylor, White Queen, El Molino, and Hiriart. In 1948 the San Pedro, Anita, and Senpe claims were sold by Ashley to Charles Reynolds of Lilac, California. In addition, the Fargo, El Molino, and White Queen claims were sold to Norman E. Dawson of San Marcos, California. Notable success has attended the mining efforts of Ashley and Reynolds, both striking pockets shortly after commencing work.

Hiriart Hill, the locale of the principal spodumene deposits, is a rounded rock mass rising 900 feet above the alluvial fan at its base. Its crest reaches an elevation of 1766 feet above sea level and is located 2.3 miles northeast of the Indian village of Pala. It is accessible by tar road from the village which runs along its western side while private dirt roads skirt its base along the south and east. Much of its surface is covered by extremely thick brush which greatly interferes with prospecting by causing difficulty in passage and preventing a view of the ground. The basic rocks are gabbros of dark color which tend to weather more rapidly than the dike rocks and thus cause the latter to stand out in relief. The entire hill is crisscrossed by a network of pegmatites of varying dimensions ranging from mere stringers to those as much as 20 to 30 feet in thickness and thousands of feet in length. All dip westerly at angles of about 20°. Several thousand feet immediately to the

FIGURE 44. A rarely photographed sight—a gem pocket in the process of being cleaned out. In this instance, the photograph was taken of a pocket of kunzite crystals found in the Vanderberg Mine on Hiriart Hill, Pala, California, and shows the jumbled mass of crumbly feldspar, clay minerals, and etched kunzite (dark colored) which fill the pocket. It is to be noted that in this case, the term "pocket" is somewhat misleading since there proved to be no open space when this miniature bonanza was unearthed.
Courtesy George Ashley.

northwest across the intervening valley floor, are the Little Chief and Pala Chief mountains, similar in all essentials to Hiriart Hill.

The first work done by Ashley was in the Katerina, an underground working situated in a thick pegmatite low on the southwest flank of Hiriart Hill. In 1947 a series of five small pockets were struck which yielded about a "hatful" of spodumene, mostly fair to good grade in both quality and color. The last pocket was the best, producing above average material of good purplish color. Most pieces were small but some were of good size, one crystal of two pounds weight being recovered. From one of the best specimens, a fine gem of excellent color was cut, finishing into 93½ carats. Associated minerals in these typical pegmatite gem pockets were: clear quartz crystals of curious turreted form, pale straw yellow in color and very fine in quality; small quantities of beryl adjacent to the pockets but not within them; and the usual feldspar crystals and very small quantities of rare

FIGURE 45. Vanderberg Mine, Hiriart Hill, Pala, California. The huge mass of light-colored rock is all part of a single pegmatite body which outcrops near the summit of the hill. In the rear of the small tunnel has been found pockets containing superb kunzite.
Courtesy George Ashley.

minerals. As in all pockets found upon this hill, red and pink clays fill the pockets and contain the loose crystals of spodumene (see Figure 44).

The next working attacked by Ashley was the Vanderberg, an opencut located upon the northeast shoulder of Hiriart Hill overlooking a steep declivity. Ashley bulldozed a jeep trail to this pegmatite and commenced active work which included running a short drift into the most promising section of the dike (see Figure 45). His efforts were rewarded by discovery of several pockets of the most magnificent kunzite ever brought to light in the history of gems. The best Madagascar and Brazil spodumenes cannot compare to the breathtaking beauty of the kunzites removed from this mine, nor can they compare in respect to their degree of internal perfection and large size. The color is easily the most striking feature since it is a deep pure bluish purple, like the best hue in amethyst but more vivid and transparent. In addition, most unusual greenish-blue spodumene was obtained from one pocket, quite unlike anything ever found before. Some idea of the richness of a

FIGURE 46. The astonishing contents of a single gem pocket uncovered in the Vanderberg Mine on Hiriart Hill, Pala, California. This pile of kunzite crystals weighed a total of 130 pounds. Courtesy George Ashley.

pocket may be obtained from the figure of 130 pounds of gem-quality spodumene recovered from a single pocket—every sliver richly colored and at least 10 per cent flawless faceting grade material. This astounding find is pictured in Figure 46. From among larger pieces in this batch, Mr. Ashley has cut a deep amethyst-color gem of 177 carats, another magnificent stone of 215 carats, and a third weighing 107 carats. Like all kunzites, however, these stones will fade if continually exposed to strong light, the sequence of shades being from bluish to normal purple, thence to pink, and finally to almost colorless. Gems which have been kept away from continuous exposure, however, preserve their color indefinitely. The largest crystal obtained from this pocket is a bluntly pointed stout lathlike crystal of 2½ pounds with its sides striated vertically with many fine grooves. Much of it is flawless gem stock. From the standpoint of cutting, the best piece found was a crystal which measured about 7 inches in length, 3 inches in width, and about ⅞ inch in thickness with an estimated weight of ¾ pound. The largest crystals are illustrated in Figure 47 showing them shortly after they had been extracted. Accessory minerals found in the Vanderberg pockets included clear to cloudy gray quartz crystals, bluish translucent apatite, and some fine peach-colored morganite beryl capable of cutting gems of from 6-8 carats from clear sections.

The San Pedro mine is located upon the northwest shoulder of Hiriart Hill where it tunnels into a huge pegmatite outcrop which provides a con-

FIGURE 47. George Ashley's helper holding a board on which are spread a few of the exceptional dark amethystine kunzite crystals found in the Vanderberg Mine on Hiriart Hill near Pala, California. The major portion of each crystal proved to be flawless material of intense coloration and easily the finest gem quality spodumene found at any locality in the world. Courtesy George Ashley.

spicuous white rib running down the hillside until it plunges beneath the ground at its base. Soon after acquiring this mine, Reynolds commenced work in a favorable section and was rewarded by striking an enormous gem pocket from which he eventually extracted at least 280 pounds of spodumene! The total value of this find has been estimated at from $20,000 to $30,000. All of the crystals occurred as typical etched and corroded fragments suspended in a dense reddish-brown clay which completely filled the opening. The largest spodumene crystal, still in the possession of Reynolds, is a magnificent slablike specimen, weighing five pounds and measuring approximately 11¼ inches in length, 3¼ inches wide, and 1¼ inches thick. One end is a decided pink for several inches which gradually fades in intensity to be replaced by very pale yellowish green continuing to the other end. Other large crystals from this pocket exceeded one pound in weight while many dozens of specimens were found of about ½ pound each. From one of the better colored pieces, a fine pendeloque gem was cut weighing several hundred carats.

The earliest locality in this district to achieve lasting fame, was the Pala Chief Mine opened originally along the outcrop of a thick, gently dipping pegmatite which showed signs of producing gem quality tourmaline. This was found, it is true, but shortly after work began, beautiful crystals of vivid pink kunzite were discovered also. The association of both minerals in large sized specimens and in gem quality is unusual and occurs nowhere else in the district. Kunzite crystals from the Pala Chief are remarkable for their tendency to form beautifully regular blades tipped at one end with a blunt point while the sides are striated by a multitude of fine grooves. Coloration is also distinctive, being a slightly purplish pink of medium intensity and easily apparent even through the sides of the crystals. In 1912, crystals of 47.4 and 45 ounces were taken out and went into the A. F. Holden collection. The larger of these samples measured 11 inches in length. The Morgan Collection acquired several fine specimens as follows: a crystal 9 inches tall, 5 inches wide, and about ¾ inch thick; another, 7 inches tall, 5 inches wide, and also about ¾ inch thick. All were of gem quality. Some fine crystals in the collection of the U.S. National Museum are shown in Figure 40. In 1914, about 20 pounds of fine kunzite crystals were produced including a number of fine large specimens suitable for museums. Shortly afterward the mine was shut down and no major work has been accomplished since. This property is now a patented claim held by the F. A. Salmons Estate. Important faceted gems from this mine may be seen in the American Museum of Natural History and include: a tear-shaped gem of 191.83 carats, an oval of 118.50 carats, and a square gem, faceted top and bottom like a double-rose cut, weighing 224.10 carats. The Warner Collection in the California Institute of Technology at Pasadena includes several magnificent, very regular crystals of "Roman sword" outline as follows: one of 10¾ inches in length, 3 inches wide and 1 inch thick, beautifully deep in color and virtually flawless, another of 8 inches length, 2⅛ inches wide and ½ inch thick and of about the same degree of perfection.

Very minor and completely insignificant amounts of gem quality spodumene, mainly of the kunzite variety, have come from the Victor Mine and Clark Mine at Rincon, the Ware Mine on Aguanga Mountain, the Esmeralda, Himalaya and San Diego mines at Mesa Grande, and also from the Vista Chief and Mountain Belle mines in Moosa Canyon, all in San Diego County.

TOURMALINE

No other gemstone intrigues the gem or mineral collector so much as tourmaline. Sensitive to the slightest changes in chemical composition, this complex borosilicate displays an astonishing range of color, sometimes exhibiting as many as four or five distinct hues in a single crystal. To the mineral collector, few species can surpass the resplendence of its shining crystals which often form long narrow individuals descriptively called "pencils." As a gem, it has become increasingly popular in clear faceted specimens which are obtainable in virtually every color of the rainbow. Fascinating catseyes are cut from crystals which display strong silky chatoyancy from numerous minute tubes while flawed material in a variety of vivid colors is popular for cabochons and tumbled baroques. Pink tourmaline is a favorite of the Chinese to whom it has religious significance and shops selling Oriental art objects frequently include small carvings and beads of this material. In addition to ornamental uses, tourmaline possesses the peculiar property of *piezoelectricity*, developing an electrical charge at the instant a wafer sliced from a crystal is severely compressed. The pronounced display of this property has led to extensive employment in high pressure gauges in which it has been found to be uniquely useful.

As a gemstone, tourmaline is a relative newcomer to the Western World although European miners have long been familiar with the opaque black variety known as *schorl,* a kind which is both widespread and abundant in many classes of rocks. It is said that the species name was taken from the Singhalese word "turmali," a term applied indiscriminately by the natives of Ceylon to a variety of minor gemstones found in the gem-bearing gravels of their island. In any case, a parcel of tourmaline brought from the East to Europe in 1703, resulted in the first application of the name and this species title has remained in effect up to the present. The derivation of *schorl* is obscure but seems to have been applied by Medieval German miners to several nonmetallic minerals encountered during mining but later reserved for black tourmaline alone. At the opposite extreme, the rare colorless variety known as *achroite,* takes its name from the Greek word for "without color." The red variety is called *rubellite,* an obvious derivation from the Latin word "ruber" meaning "red." Dark blue kinds are called *indicolite* after their resemblance in color to the dyestuff indigo. Brownish types are known as *dravite* after their occurrences in the Drave District of Carinthia, Austria. Purplish-red kinds are sometimes labeled *siberite* after Siberia where certain pegmatite deposits yielded magnificent gem specimens of this color. Pink material is sometimes called *elbaite* after the famous occurrence on the island of Elba. No particular qualifying names are given to other hues except for the much to be deplored term "Brazilian emerald," sometimes applied to transparent green tourmaline from that country. This misleading appellation is all the more reprehensible because true emerald occurs in Brazil.

The chemistry and crystal structure of tourmaline have long fascinated students of mineralogy. For many years explanations were sought to account for the wide variation in color and the diversity of forms in which this mineral is found. Some investigators believe that it should be regarded as a series of closely related species rather than a mineral occurring in several varieties marked by important differences in mode of occurrence, chemistry, and crystal habit. The former view is adopted here and accordingly the tourmaline series may be divided into the following members:

Species	Composition
Black tourmaline (schorl)	$NaFe_3B_3Al_3(Al_3Si_6O_{27})(OH)_4$
Brown tourmaline (dravite)	$NaMg_3B_3Al_3(Al_3Si_6O_{27})(OH)_4$
White tourmaline (lime-dravite)	$CaMg_3B_3Al_3(Al_3Si_6O_{27})(O,OH)_4$
Colored tourmaline (lithia)	$Na(Al,Fe,Mn,Li,Mg)_3B_3Al_3(Al_3Si_6O_{27})(O,OH,F)_4$

The above should be regarded only as typical formulas since an enormous range of variation is possible in the prefixed elements whose combinations account for corresponding changes, in hue, crystal habit, density, refractive index, and many other outward and inner changes. Although some gem material is obtained from black tourmaline and brown tourmaline of the dravite type, the so-called "lithia" or colored tourmaline provides virtually every scrap of cuttable material used in the gem trade. Black tourmaline is by far the most abundant however, and occurs in many geologic and mineralogic situations; it is common in schists and gneisses where it has formed metamorphic action upon impurities and is especially abundant in pegmatites of the granitic type. In the latter it is most frequently observed along the wall and border zones where it forms rosettes or "sunbursts" radiating outward from points along the edges of the pegmatite. Sometimes these crystals continue development along with other minerals of the intermediate and core zones and consequently appear in cavities or pockets within the core. If mineralizing solutions are low in iron and contain instead some of the elements noted above in the first part of the colored tourmaline formula, a striking change in both color and clarity takes place as the crystals change from dead-black to green or blue and thence into the vividly-colored transparent crystals typical of "gem pockets" in pegmatite (see Figure 48). On the other hand, no such transformation is observed in dravite tourmaline which is characteristically a mineral of metamorphosed limestones or dolomites or of the contact zones between such rock masses and enclosing granitic, gneissic, or schistic rocks. The colors of gem tourmaline have been the subject of considerable debate for many years, some authorities claiming the element lithium as the cause. However, recent investigations indicate that green colors owe their existence to the presence of small amounts of iron while pinks and reds emanate from the presence of manganese plus caesium and lithium rather than lithium alone. The exact role of the latter element in causing color is not clear. Brown crystals found in pegmatites and not of the dravite type, apparently owe their color not to an admixture of red and green but rather

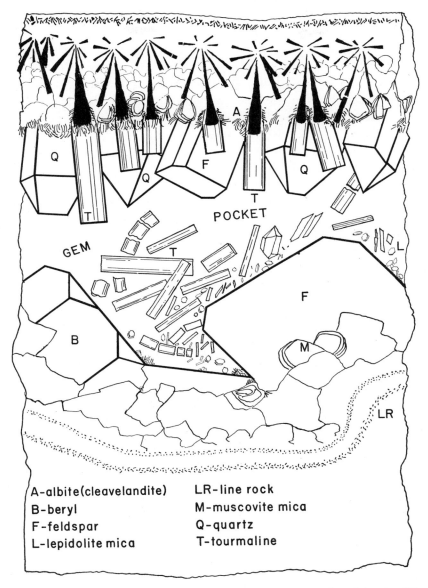

A-albite(cleavelandite)
B-beryl
F-feldspar
L-lepidolite mica

LR-line rock
M-muscovite mica
Q-quartz
T-tourmaline

FIGURE 48. A cross-section through a typical "gem pocket" as found in the Himalaya Mine, Mesa Grande, California. On the diagram, the space labeled "gem pocket" is ordinarily filled with sticky red clay but is sometimes empty. The roof of the pocket is studded with fine sharp crystals of quartz, colored tourmaline, feldspar, and mica. The bottom is covered with many small and large tourmaline crystals, often doubly-terminated, mica booklets, pieces of feldspar, curiously twisted quartz crystals, etc., and the whole generally cemented together with white, pink, or brownish-yellow clay minerals.

to finely divided matter in a state of suspension. Chemically there appears to be complete gradation from green gem quality tourmaline to that which is utterly black; in the latter, the composition is rich in iron and poor in manganese and lithium. In any case, all evidence points to excessive iron acting as a "poisoning" agent, inducing extremely dark and dull colors whenever present in more than trace amounts. In pegmatites, black tourmaline is seen in thin sections to be colored, some examples crushed to powder show deep blue, others dark purplish-red. Changing color by subjecting tourmaline crystals to heat treatment is often mentioned in gem literature, however, for all practical purposes, very little change, if any, can be noted in the vast majority of cases. Since recent studies indicate that color-causing elements are essential parts of the tourmaline crystal lattice, application of heat can do no more than cause a temporary expansion of the structure with a slight color change which returns to the original hue when heat is withdrawn.

Tourmaline crystallizes in the Hexagonal System, forming typical elongated crystal prisms like rounded triangles in cross section, and striated with numerous fine grooves resembling those seen upon phonograph records. Grooving is absolutely parallel and is so distinctive a characteristic that many tourmaline crystals can be recognized through this feature alone (see Figure 49). On the other hand, this mode of crystallization so characteristic of crystals growing in pegmatite pockets is seldom observed in those which grow completely enclosed by other minerals. Thus in the black specimens encased by feldspar along the wall and border zones of pegmatites, prisms tend to be six-sided and lack the "phonograph record" grooving. Dravites from metamorphic limestones also grow this way. Within gem pockets, crystals of small size—"needles" and "pencils"—also tend to be six-sided but gradually become more corpulent with increasing size until very large crystals, say two to three inches or more in diameter, are virtually circular in cross-section (see Figure 49).

The atomic structure of tourmaline is *hemimorphic*, that is, the atoms are arranged in such a manner that each end of the crystal grows in different fashion. Thus, when doubly-terminated crystals are found, one end is ordinarily capped by a simple flat plane with perhaps traces of beveling by pyramidal planes, while the other end is most often drastically beveled, sometimes to a sharp point. Such a crystal is illustrated in Figure 50 where it is seen resting upon the flat end while the pointed end, terminated by a series of pyramidal faces, is on top. This peculiar atomic structure gives rise to the property of piezoelectricity mentioned previously, and also the property of *pyroelectricity*, or the generation of electrical charges by the application of heat. The latter property is so pronounced that gems placed on exhibit in sunlight become completely covered by dust particles attracted by electrical charges generated by the sun's warmth.

Note: Figure 50 is in the color section following page 112.

The formation of tourmaline in pockets is shown in Figure 48, a sketch of a typical pocket found in the pegmatite of the Himalaya Mine at Mesa Grande, California. Ideally, such pockets would be air-filled openings lined by splendant crystals of tourmaline, quartz, feldspar, beryl, etc., however, they seldom are. The surge of mineralization which causes the growth of such perfect crystals seldom stops at the "ideal" point. In most cases, it continues with some violence after crystallization has been started, shattering the enclosing quartz into numerous shards and slivers, breaking off tourmaline crystals, and otherwise behaving like a witch's cauldron at high heat. Altera-

FIGURE 49. Tourmaline crystals from San Diego County, California. The two large crystals at the upper right are very dark green specimens from the Little Three Mine, Ramona. In the foreground are a doubly-terminated crystal and a pink crystal partly imbedded in a feldspar crystal from the Himalaya Mine at Mesa Grande. The light-colored specimen in the center is a pink crystal from the Tourmaline King Mine at Pala; all the rest are from the Tourmaline Queen Mine also at Pala. One of the latter specimen in which the core of the crystal is pale aquamarine blue but the exterior is black giving the entire crystal the appearance of being solid black.

tion and etching of existing minerals proceeds at such a pace that sometimes much of the original mineralization is utterly destroyed. In the Stewart Lithia Mine at Pala, California, many places are seen in the pegmatite where prisms of what appear to be pink tourmaline are found in reality to be nothing more than a greasy soft clay mineral called halloysite. At the Himalaya Mine, tourmaline crystals are frequently altered to pink opaque masses of scaly lepidolite which retain faithfully the external form of the original crystal even to the grooves. Late stage "churning" inside gem pockets accounts for the curious distorted doubly-terminated quartz and tourmaline crystals which could not have formed had they not been broken away from their original anchorages. Referring again to Figure 48, the sequence of color observed in the crystals of tourmaline in this pocket are typically: black at the base where iron disappears from crystallizing solutions, fine green, then lastly pink at the termination. If such a crystal is cut across, it will be seen that concentric layers of color corresponding to the different phases of mineralization occur throughout the crystal. Each section of color is like a sleeve fitted over the preceding one and as shown diagrammatically in Figure 51 explains both

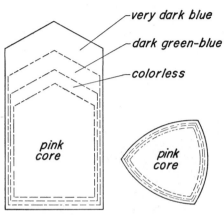

very dark blue

dark green-blue

colorless

pink core

pink core

COLOR ZONING in TOURMALINE

Figure 51. If a tourmaline crystal of several colors is carefully cut into sections, zoning such as that shown above may well appear. The above example is a crystal from the Tourmaline Queen Mine at Pala, California. Not all colored crystals will exhibit such decided changes in hue, many show only a vague blending from one part of the crystal to the other.

"cylindrical" color zoning and color zoning along the length of the crystal. In general each gem pocket represents a similar series of chemical events and all tourmalines from it will show essentially the same colors arranged in similar zones. However, marked differences are noted from pocket to pocket, sometimes furnishing tourmaline crystals so widely different in color and pattern that one could easily believe they did not come from the same mine. Even here, the *general* patterning and coloration is still so distinctive that experts familiar with the mines in one district can unhesitatingly sort out a parcel of crystals with complete accuracy, identifying the origin in each case.

When free of flaws, gem quality tourmaline crystals are fairly tough with a hardness of from 7 to 7½. Due to internal strain, many tend to fracture across the prism or develop "checking" upon external zones. Sometimes internal strain related to changes in chemical composition causes exterior zones to spall off leaving rounded or lenticular cores called "nodules," much prized by cutters because they are invariably of superb cutting quality and uniformly colored. Nodules are frequently encountered in the gem tourmaline deposits of Maine and California. Tourmaline possesses conchoidal to irregular fracture, the purest specimens showing exceptionally smooth and brilliant broken surfaces reminiscent of obsidian. The gross range of specific gravity is from slightly below 3.00 to almost 3.30 although most gem specimens fall between 3.00 and 3.12. Colorless or faintly colored material averages from 3.08 to 3.12; green from 3.04 to 3.10; blue from 3.09 to 3.11; pink and red from 3.00 to 3.06; yellow from 3.08 to 3.10; brown from 3.00 to 3.09. Black tourmaline ranges from 3.1 to 3.2. The correlation of specific gravity and refractive index has been investigated rather thoroughly. In general, specimens of low gravity show low refractive indices, and vice versa, however, the relationship between color and refractive indices, if any, remains to be proved although there is some indication that material of pale color such as light pink or light green is accompanied by lower indices than darker types. The range of indices falls between: $\omega = 1.616-1.634$, and $\epsilon = 1.630-1.652$. A series of 20 faceted gems in a wide variety of color from several Southern California mines were tested by the author and the lowest values were measured on a pale yellow-green specimen from the Himalaya Mine, giving: $\omega = 1.634$, $\epsilon = 1.620$, birefringence 0.016. The highest values recorded also were measured upon a pale blue and green gem from this mine as follows: $\omega = 1.647$, $\epsilon = 1.628$; birefringence 0.019. The largest birefringence was obtained upon a dark greenish-brown specimen from the Little Three Mine at Ramona, California: $\omega = 1.647$, $\epsilon = 1.620$, birefringence 0.027. Tourmaline is uniaxial, negative.

Perhaps of all hues, green is most commonly found in gem tourmaline, followed by pink and red. Each of these basic hues occurs in many nuances, and frequently in combination with other colors. A wide variety of brownish-green shades are commonly noted also. The property of dichroism in colored specimens is very pronounced, even faintly-colored crystals often show marked changes in the windows of a dichroscope. Some of the dichroic color combinations which may be expected are:

APPARENT COLOR	DICHROIC COLORS	
Dark green	rich green	olive green
Red	yellow red	pure red
Red	pale red	pure red
Pink	pale pink	pink
Pink	colorless	pink
Pink	pink	pale yellow
Pale blue	colorless	pale blue
Medium blue	pale grayish-blue	dark purplish-blue
Dark blue	dark intense blue	blue, almost black
Brown	brown	dark reddish-brown

Because of their shape, clear facet grade tourmaline crystals are cut mostly into oblong stepcut gems, oriented in such a way that the darkest color observed parallel to the principal crystal axis (see Figure 5) is minimized. This is frequently necessary in green gems which tend to assume disagreeable tints if cut the wrong way, however, some pale green gems are more effective if deliberately cut contrary to the rule given above since the direction along the crystal axis may show a lovely rich yellow-green color much more attractive than that observed through the sides of the crystal. Pink gems are most often cut this way for the same reason. However, when a gem is fashioned in accordance with this scheme, the best recovery of rough weight is through a brilliant cut rather than some form of stepcut. Some of the finest gems of all are those cut from crystals in which abrupt color changes take place along the prism, the so-called "bicolors," usually red and green. These seem more vivid when side by side and fine specimens are highly prized but unfortunately very few are flawless, pink sections containing minute inclusions while the division between the hues is frequently marked by small fissures and cracks. Catseye gems of truly good quality are very rare, the common types containing coarse air-filled tubes which are in reality *negative* crystals, and which tend to fill with polishing powder during the final stages of cutting. Catseye material tends to appear only on the extremities of crystals, that is, upon the ends which protrude into pockets. The finest material shows strong silky chatoyance arising from extremely fine tubes too small to be seen clearly without magnification. Aside from ordinary ornamental cuts, some crystals showing strong cylindrical color zoning are cut into slices and polished on both sides to display to best effect the lovely hues which often contrast markedly. Slices of this sort are obtained from so-called "watermelon" crystals in which the largest part of the core is red or pink, sheathed by a zone of pale pink or almost colorless material, and then covered on the exterior with a thin zone of green.

LOCALITIES

North West Territories. Numerous pegmatite dikes occur in the Yellowknife region of the Mackenzie District, northeast of Yellowknife and also in the Beaulieu area. Many have been noted near Lac De Gras and Aylmer Lake as far as 210 miles northeast of Yellowknife. These dikes have been explored mainly for tantalite and columbite although lithium minerals and beryl also occur in a number of them. Blue-green and red gem quality tourmalines in small pencil crystals have been obtained from several while the general mineralization appears favorable for further discoveries, possibly of greater gem importance. Blue-green crystals are reported from dikes in the Bore Group of claims at the south end of Sproule Lake, 34 miles northeast of Yellowknife. Pegmatites showing mineralization appropriate for gem tourmaline occur on the north side of Hearne Channel in the east arm of Great Slave Lake, 72 miles east-southeast of Yellowknife; another group of similar character lies 5 miles southwest of the north end of Buckham Lake or about 50 miles east of Yellowknife. Red and green gem material in minor amounts has been obtained from dikes in the Prelude Lake area located immediately north of this lake or about 17 miles northeast of Yellowknife.

Ontario. Very rarely some brown dravite tourmaline similar in all respects to that found in New York State, occurs in the metamorphic limestones of the Grenville series.

Quebec. Brown dravite occasionally clear enough to cut very small faceted gems has been found in the Grenville limestones of this province as in lot 10, Concession XI, Chatham Township, Argenteuil County where it occurs as fine crystals in flesh-red limestone. Similar crystals in the same association have been noted near Calumet Falls in Litchfield Township, Pontiac County.

Maine. The tourmaline of Maine has long been famous for its exceptional clarity and purity of color. Green shades tend to assume a unique and distinctive tinge of blue through the sides and a pure rich green through the ends of crystal prisms, a combination which cannot help but produce the finest cut gems known of this color. The disagreeable olive so commonly noted in green crystals from other localities is largely absent. Many fine gems of other colors have also been cut from Maine tourmalines, notably from Mt. Mica, Mt. Apatite, and from the Berry Quarry in Poland Township.

In Oxford County, the northernmost occurrence of noteworthy tourmaline is at the old Dunton Tourmaline Mine located atop the east spur of Plumbago Mountain in Newry Township and is reached by a steep trail which ascends the eastern face from the highway at the base. The Dunton workings exploit a complex pegmatite yielding a variety of rare and unusual minerals including large watermelon tourmaline crystals found solidly frozen in quartz. Although these colorful crystals provided numerous prized mineral specimens, they proved almost totally unfit for gems and such clear facet grade material as has been found at the workings, generally occurs in the form of small indicolite prisms lining cavities in quartz. It is interesting to note that a number of the large frozen crystals reached the extraordinary dimensions of 4 to 5 inches in diameter and as much as 24 inches in length.

Slender gem quality green pencils have been found in considerable quantity in small pockets in the Harvard Quarry pegmatite located at the lip of the steep western slope of Noyes Mountain, about ½ mile east of Mud Pond and slightly over 2 miles northwest of the village of Nobles Corner, Greenwood Township, Oxford County. Tamminen's Quarry located about ½ mile south of the Harvard Quarry is said to have produced small quantities of gem quality green tourmaline from pockets in the pegmatite.

In the mid season of 1954, a magnificent assemblage of gem quality tourmaline crystals of exceptionally fine color were removed by Stanley Perham from a feldspar and mica quarry operated by himself and called the B.B. No. 7 Pit, located near Nobles Corner in Norway Township, Oxford County. During the course of ordinary work, favorable signs of pocket mineralization were observed and followed and a pocket eventually uncovered. Approximately 14,000 carats of crystals were found, of which 5,000 carats consisted of large crystals and crystal fragments, and about 3,000 carats in smaller sizes. Another 4,000 carats of indicolite was stated to be suitable for small faceted gems and cabochons. The remaining 2,000 carats were specimen material only. Many of the crystals were terminated but a large number were merely broken cross-sections of much longer prisms. The prevailing color was a fine blue-green through the sides of crystals and yellow-green down the length. The largest piece of gem quality weighed 137.47 carats and was found broken into two sections which, when cut, yielded these magnificent green gems: two rectangular stepcuts of 23.67 and 10.91 carats, a triangular stepcut of 6.77 carats, and a small navette shaped gem of 1.78 carats. One large non-gem crystal weighed 738.5 carats and was stated to be of fine green color. Many other very small crystals were also found but aside from a few which were pink, the predominant colors were green and blue.

The Bennett Quarry located about ½ mile north of the Bennett Farm-house and about 3 miles west of the village of Buckfield, Buckfield Township, Oxford County, has furnished a small quantity of fine green tourmaline pencils from pockets found in a large pegmatite dike. Further south in the same county, red tourmaline frozen in pegmatite and giving the locality its name has been found on top of Mt. Rubellite, a low spur at the north end of Greenwood Hill in Hebron Township. The quarry is located about 1½ miles northeast of the village of Hebron. None of the tourmaline found at this locality proved worthy of cutting. About 2½ miles almost due north of Hebron village, small quantities of pink and green gem quality tourmaline have been found in pockets in the pegmatite of Mills Quarry on Number Four Hill, a small rounded eminence located close to the line between Hebron and Paris townships.

FIGURE 52. A large single crystal of green tourmaline, portions of which were gem quality, found many years ago at Mount Mica, Maine. The height of the crystal is 6 inches and the diameter about 3 inches. Courtesy U.S. Geological Survey.

The incomparable Mount Mica tourmaline deposit is the prime locality of Oxford County, and indeed surpasses any other tourmaline occurrence in the eastern half of the continent. The locality, presently a gaping pit filled with water, lies atop a small low hill rising to 900 feet, about 1½ miles east of the village of Paris in Paris Township. Gem crystals were originally found lying in topsoil by two neighborhood lads, Elijah S. Hamlin and Ezekial Holmes, in the fall of 1820. The day after the initial discovery was marked by a heavy snowfall which prevented further search and it was necessary for the impatient boys to wait until the following spring before they could return to the spot. The results of this visit were most gratifying, for more than 30 crystals or rare beauty and transparency were found along with masses of lepidolite and splendid crystals of quartz. The first large pocket was found in 1822 after two younger brothers of Hamlin opened the dike by the use of explosives. These operations were attended with astonishing success for a soft place, exposed by the removal of rock, yielded to the pick and a pocket of about two bushels volume was laid bare. In the bottom were found about 20 crystals, one of magnificent green color and more that 2½ inches in length and almost 2 inches in diameter. Many other equally fine specimens and crystals were found and it is said that an oxcart was needed to haul away the finds. From 1822 to 1864, Mt. Mica was visited by many mineralogists and interested persons resulting in a most unsystematic exploration of the deposits with many specimens taken away and forever lost to the world of science. However, in the last year mentioned, organized operations were begun which, with many interruptions, have carried on the work of mining the deposits almost up to the present date. Several specimens of tourmaline from Mount Mica are illustrated in figures 52 and 53.

FIGURE 53. Largest crystal of tourmaline found at Mount Mica, Maine; length 15½ inches, maximum width 7 inches; weight 31½ pounds. This crystal is transparent to translucent grass green at the tip while the middle and lower flanks of the top section are made up of numerous small colorless to pale pink or brownish prisms ranging from ⅛ inch to ¼ inch in diameter. Courtesy U.S. Geological Survey.

At Mt. Mica, the summit of the hill is now occupied by a large opencut, one edge of which is the steep face of the actual quarry and the other, piles of waste rock removed from the cut. The working face extends about 200 feet in a northwest-southeast direction more or less parallel to the strike of the pegmatite and varies from 20 to 30 feet in depth. Country rock is banded mica gneiss interlayed with schist. The dip is about 20 degrees below the horizontal necessitating the removal of the country rock overburden in order to expose the mineralized top half of the pegmatite. The pocket horizon varies from several feet to as much as 7 feet in thickness and contains numerous pockets ranging in size from several inches in diameter to one which was uncovered many years ago large enough to accommodate entry by a man. The total number of openings found up to October, 1907, was stated to be about 430, however, most proved barren of tourmaline. Generally, pockets were roofed by cleavelandite and quartz crystals, clear and smoky, while the floors contained a jumbled mass of crumbled feldspar, cookeite, loose scales of lepidolite, and much montmorillonite clay derived from the alteration of feldspar in late stages of pocket formation. Almost all tourmaline crystals were found detached from the walls and lying in the floor debris.

The importance of this deposit as well as some idea of the splendor of its tourmaline is perhaps best gained by a review of productive years:

1871—A. C. Hamlin opened a pocket which yielded the finest achroite found up to that time; one crystal was 4½ inches long and 1½ inches in diameter, white at the apex but changing to a smoky hue near the bottom; both ends were tipped with green; this crystal is now in the Mineralogical Museum of Harvard University.

1886—Several pockets were found producing an estimated $5000 worth of gem and specimen material; the largest transparent crystal of record was found by Samuel R. Carter, and measured 10 inches long, 2¼ inches diameter, 41 ounces in weight but was broken into 4 pieces of which the middle portions were of fine gem quality. This crystal and 50 others came from a pocket 4 feet in diameter. Cut gems from this lot were as follows: brilliant rich grass-green gems of 34½ carats, another of 27½ carats; also a deep blue-green gem of 8 carats and a fine yellowish-green specimen of 7½ carats. No pink or red crystals were found this year.

1893—A fine piece of green tourmaline uncovered this year was cut into a magnificent bluish-green gem of 69¼ carats now in the U.S. National Museum. The rough piece sold for $1000.

1895—A remarkable pocket provided splendid green crystals of unusual perfection yielding cut stones of 57, 34, 17, and 12 carats weight. The 57-carat gem was acquired by the Isaac Lea Collection and is now in the U.S. National Museum; the 34-carat (34.03) gem was purchased for the J. P. Morgan collection and is now in the American Museum of Natural History.

1896—A large pocket was opened in July, measuring from 5 to 6 feet in length and from 3 to 4 feet in width and although the walls were studded with numerous red, green, and white crystals, all were stated by Loren B. Merrill, the operator at the time, to be "decayed." Another cavity was found to the rear of the first in August but again yielded nothing of great value. Still another was opened close to the last and proved to contain several fine crystals, one of which measured 7 inches long and 3 inches wide at the base, green in color, lighter at the base and terminated with rich red. This specimen is in the Harvard Museum.

1898—About 8 pockets were found during August, September, and

October; two red and green crystals of 9 inches in length and more than 3 inches in diameter provided fine cabinet specimens; fine gem quality crystals of bluish-green and red yielded gems of considerable value. One magnificent crystal was 6 inches long and over 1 inch in diameter of fine transparent blue, terminating at the base in a band of red 1 inch wide.

1910—Loren B. Merrill found a flawless section of a green tourmaline crystal which weighed 422 carats and measured 2 3/8 inches in length and 1 3/16 inches in diameter; both ends were rounded in a typical nodular form. For many years Merrill cherished this gem as his most prized possession but at one time agreed to have it cut in half, one part to be faceted and the other kept in its rough state and both parts eventually to go to the Harvard Museum. However, this scheme was never carried out and after that gentleman's death, the nodule passed into the possession of Stanley I. Perham who advertised it as the largest flawless nodule of tourmaline ever found at Mt. Mica. About 1934 this specimen was acquired by Stephen Varni of New York who placed it on the market urging prospective purchasers to buy the complete piece instead of forcing him to divide it into smaller, more saleable sections. The final disposition of the unique specimen is unknown to the author.

In Androscoggin County, several feldspar quarries have produced considerable amounts of fine gem grade tourmaline. The most productive locality is that of Mt. Apatite, named after its exceptionally beautiful crystallized purple apatite, and located 1 1/4 miles east-northeast of the village of Minot in Minot Township. At this locality it appears that the entire flattish top of the hill is underlain by a sheet of pegmatite which numbers tens of feet in thickness and may extend as deep as 75 feet. Pale green gem tourmaline crystals were first found here in 1868 lying loose in an outcrop upon a farm. In 1883, crystals were found in place and in that year about 1500 crystals and fragments were removed from a pit measuring 20 by 8 by 8 feet. Specimens ranged in size from about 1/2 inch to one crystal which was 4 1/8 inches long. This working was operated intermittently for a number of years, the last time in 1902. In 1907, further mining took place a short distance away from the original discovery site. Figure 54 shows one of the early excavations at this locality. Tourmaline in this pegmatite was found in pockets generally less than 12 inches in diameter, although one pocket of record measured 4 by 5 by 6 feet. In color, crystals proved lighter in tone than from other Maine localities, and in respect to hue included: colorless, pink, blue, lilac pale green, light red, bluish-pink, and some in which several colors were combined in one specimen. Later operations uncovered a few crystals of fine green color, said to be almost "emerald green." The largest of the green crystals found in later years measured about 1 1/2 inches in length and 3/4 inch in diameter. A splendid blue-green gem cut in emerald style is in the American Museum of

FIGURE 54. The J.S. Towne feldspar quarry on Mount Apatite, Maine. Photo taken in June 1913. The exposed rock is pegmatite and from near the bottom of the excavation yielded several pockets containing gemmy apatite and tourmaline crystals. Courtesy U.S. Geological Survey.

Natural History and measures ¼ inch by ¾ inch; its weight is 11.87 carats.

Not far from Mt. Apatite is the Berry Quarry, located at the north end of a low hill about 1¼ miles southeast of Minot and several hundred yards southwest of the Little Androscoggin River in Poland Township, Androscoggin Co. The best gem tourmaline was recovered by F. L. Havey during 1910-1912, when a number of productive pockets were opened. In 1912, 11 pounds of gemmy crystals, many suitable for faceting, were taken from a single opening. Crystals ranged in size from small pencils to those more than an inch thick and several inches long. Green proved to be the predominant color, especially the much desired blue-green shade.

In Sagadahoc County, the Willes Feldspar Quarry located 2 miles northwest of Cathance Station in Topsham Township, has occasionally yielded gem beryls and transparent tourmaline of green color from small pockets.

Connecticut. The famous Strickland Quarry near the summit of Collins Hill, Portland Township, Middlesex County, has long been noted for its rare pegmatite minerals, including gem quality tourmaline. The quarry is located approximately 2½ miles northeast of Portland or about 1.4 miles north-northeast of the junction of Highways 6A and 17. Pockets proved to be rather small although one of 4 by 1½ by 1½ feet was found. Tourmaline crystals were mainly green, varying from olive green to pale greenish-blue. One crystal, weighing several pounds, provided fine cut gems from clear beautiful greenish-blue to bluish-green fragments. Another transparent crystal 7 inches long is now in the collection of the Wesleyan University, Middletown, Conn.

One of the noted gem tourmaline localities of the Eastern United States is the Gillette Quarry located on the steep eastern bank of the Connecticut River, approximately 5 miles south-southeast of Middle Haddam in Haddam Township, Middlesex County. Originally opened for feldspar in 1899, the quarry quickly gained a reputation for fine green tourmalines, transparent glassy quartz crystals of slightly brownish-yellow cast, beryl and other minerals ordinarily associated with secondary mineralization in pegmatites. The pegmatite dike dips at a very steep angle to the west and along its western edge occurs a narrow pocket zone from which the gem minerals have been obtained. Although not large, some pockets were unusually rich in crystals of tourmaline, one pocket on record produced 600! Crystals generally ranged from slender needles to stout pencils but others up to 9 inches in length have been found. A series of 105 crystals up to 1 by 9 inches are in the Morgan Collection in the American Museum of Natural History of which the largest is a bicolor, green and red. Other fine crystals recorded are: an 8 inch crystal, doubly-terminated, mostly green with one end yellow; a 6 inch crystal, doubly-terminated, 1½ inches thick; and an odd slender prism only ⅛ inch thick but fully 7 inches in length, pale green and almost flawless. In general, crystals are chiefly valuable for specimens since they rarely contain clear areas large enough to cut more than small gems, perhaps of several carats average weight. However, some very fine chatoyant green crystals have been found and proved eminently suitable for catseye gems.

New York. St. Lawrence County has provided a number of good crystals of the dravite species from openings in metamorphic limestones. A noted locality is upon the old Reese Farm near Richville, DeKalb Township. Locally, the limestone carries impurities such as tremolite, pyroxene and tourmaline, the latter occurring as cinnamon brown crystals ranging in size from small pencils to stout prisms an inch or more in diameter and several inches in length. Upon rare occasions, cavities are found containing small, highly perfect, transparent crystals of gem quality. The majority of crystals, however, are completely enclosed in limestone and provide clear faceting material only from small spots. One crystal from the Reese Farm was 2½ inches long and 1 inch in diameter, perfectly terminated at both ends. Similar yellowish crystals have been found about 3 miles northeast of Richville, while a noted locality for colorless and white dravite is located about 5 miles north of this town. The Bement Collection once contained an achroite from this place which is said to have been over 1 inch long and so clear that a gem of 10 carats could have been cut from it, however, another account states that this crystal was in reality pale yellow rather than colorless. Yellow crystals, rarely clear enough to facet small gems, occur in outcrops of metamorphic limestone of gray color on the north side of the Oswegatchie River about 2 miles southeast of Gouverneur across the river from Hailesboro. A number of localities near Gouverneur furnished many hundreds of similar crystals ranging from 1 to 6 inches in length, rich in faces, and sometimes doubly terminated, however, seldom could a gem over one carat be cut from them.

In Essex County, a noted brown tourmaline locality was one exploited on the south shore of Lake Harris about 1 mile east of Newcomb Post Office. The crystals, often of large size (one of 8 inches in length and 4 inches in width is on record), occur in coarsely crystalline Grenville limestone associated with green tourmaline, blue apatite, sphene, zircon, muscovite mica, smoky quartz, scapolite, albite, graphite, tremolite, pyroxene, and pyrite. All dravite was remarkably fresh in appearance, of rich brown color, and some perfectly transparent. A few entirely flawless crystals were found but these did not exceed ¼ inch in length. One observer estimated that hundreds of fine gems ranging in size from 1 to 10 carats could have been cut from the material uncovered. The dichroism noted in this tourmaline is very dark brown and paler red-brown.

The possibility of finding similar crystals elsewhere in the Grenville limestones is borne out by a recent discovery. In 1954 a road cut along the south shore of Brant Lake in the south portion of the town of Horicon, Warren County, revealed a number of fine brown tourmaline crystals associated with graphite, diopside, pyrite, apatite, muscovite, rutile, and calcite. Crystals were much more slender than the Newcomb type, showing simple hexagonal prisms covered with sharp faces. The color was deep chocolate brown while some of the smaller and more slender crystals proved clear enough to cut stones of perhaps one carat. Di hroism strong: brown and dark greenish-brown. The largest crystal found measured 7 inches in length and 1 inch in diameter but was not of gem quality.

South Dakota. Various complex pegmatites in the Keystone area of Pennington County furnish very small quantities of colored tourmaline, however, good transparent material is virtually unknown due to the absence of pockets in which the best specimens must invariably occur. Some of the frozen crystals show red and pink colors and may have some application in cabochon work. Green crystals of at least 2 inches in length have been reported from the Bob Ingersoll Mine near Keystone.

Colorado. Just after the turn of the century, C. A. Beghtol of Canon City worked several pegmatites for gem tourmaline in the Royal Gorge area near Canon City, Fremont County. Gem crystals were found at two places: the Royal Gorge No. 1 Mine, 5 miles north 70° west of Canon City, and the Royal Gorge No. 2 Mine, 4 miles northwest of Canon City. The No. 1 Mine is in the east wall of a canyon entering Royal Gorge from the north about 200 yards distant from its rim. Tourmaline occurred in a pegmatite 4 feet in thickness but very short in length and soon pinching out after work was commenced. One pocket was found nearly a foot deep from which a number of very fine pink, green and nearly colorless crystals of gem quality were obtained. The No. 2 Mine is on a plateau north of the Gorge and about 2 miles removed from its edge. It is on a low oval hill about 200 yards east of the Mica Hill Mine. Tourmaline found here was generally frozen in granular lepidolite but a few good specimens were obtained from very small openings.

In Gunnison County, colored tourmaline of gem grade has been found in several pegmatites of the Quartz Creek district, an extensive area of about 29 square miles containing 1,803 pegmatites. Many of the pegmatites have been mined for beryl, lepidolite, scrap mica, tantalum and columbium minerals, and monazite. Out of this large number of pegmatites, however, only 10 contain colored tourmaline and few of these produce any gem quality material. The Quartz Creek pegmatites are accessible by road from Parlin and lie between that town and Ohio City.

New Mexico. Small transparent deep green tourmaline crystals, none over ⅛ inch diameter, occur in the pegmatite of the Canary Bird Mine, located ¾ mile southeast of Persimmon Peak or 1½ miles southwest of Las Tablas, Rio Arriba County.

California. By far the largest quantity and greatest value of gem tourmaline in the Western Hemisphere has been produced from a series of mines located in southern Riverside County and San Diego County. The sheer volume of magnificent crystals in bewildering variety of color and form that came from these mines in the days of active work in the earlier years of the Century, makes all other North American deposits taken together pale into insignificance. In some cases, production from a single mine was reckoned in *tons!* In terms of total production, the following table compiled from the Precious Stones chapters of the annual Mineral Resources of the United States, indicates the growth, peak production, and decline of tourmaline mining in the United States. The figures for California are not separated but it may be assumed safely that the major portion is Californian, with perhaps several thousands of dollars per annum being deductible for New England production. The figures given in the table are probably accurate only in the mid-period when systematic collection of production data was in effect. A large number of very small mines and prospects in California produced significant quantities of tourmaline which were absorbed through non-trade channels and hence never reported. Furthermore, a considerable quantity is produced from time to time by informal mining operations and also remains unreported. The total of $797,205 shown on the table for the period concerned, is probably closer to $2,000,000.

TOURMALINE PRODUCTION IN THE UNITED STATES—1896 to 1948 *

YEAR	VALUE $	POUNDS	REMARKS
1895	3,160		
1896	3,000		
1897	9,125		
1898	4,000		
1899	2,000		
1900	2,500		
1901	15,000		
1902	30,000		
1903	45,000		
1904	40,000		
1905	50,000		
1906	72,500*		* Estimated.
1907	84,120*	2,140	* Estimated. The bulk of this production was from California, mainly from the Himalaya Mine, also from Mesa Grande Gold & Gem Mining Co., and from the Pala Chief Mine.
1908	90,000*	3,300	* Estimated. The Calif. prod. was mainly from Mesa Grande, also from Ramona, Rincon, and Pala.
1909	133,192*	1,548	* Estimated.
1910	46,500*		* Estimated.
1911	16,445		Most of this production was from Poland, Maine.
1912	28,200*		* Estimated. Most of this prod. was from Poland, Maine.
1913	7,630		
1914	7,980		
1915	10,969		
1916	50,807		
1917	12,452		
1918	6,206		
1919	17,700*		* Most of this production was from Mt. Apatite, Me.
1920	4,869		
1921	1,450		
*	*		* From 1921 to 1932 no Precious Stones Chapters were included in Mineral Resources for the U.S.
1940	2,400		* Includes kunzite, beryl, and rock crystal as well as tourmaline. This production was from Calif. only.

YEAR	VALUE $	POUNDS	REMARKS
1943			Tourmaline and pink beryl produced from the Pala district; no value or quantity given.
1946			Small amounts of aquamarine, kunzite, and tourmaline were produced in San Diego Co.; no figures given.
1947			Kunzite, topaz, tourmaline produced in small amounts from California; no figures given.
1948			Good crystals of green tourmaline from Pala were produced in small quantities this year.

TOTAL $797,205

* Statistics compiled from Precious Stones Chapters of Mineral Resources of the U.S., also from the Minerals Yearbooks. Does not include 1954 production from the BB No. 7 Mine, nor the 1958 production from the Himalaya Mine; the latter is estimated to be about $15,000.

Vague accounts place the initial discovery of gem tourmaline in California in the year of 1872 when Henry Hamilton found loose crystals on the southeast slope of Thomas Mountain in Riverside County. The first official announcement came in 1884 in the Fourth Annual Report of the State Mineralogist when it was stated that rubellite was found in the "San Bernardino Range" of Southern California. The description leaves little doubt that the tourmaline referred to comprised the rosettes and sprays of rubellite found embedded in fine granular lepidolite in the Stewart Lithia Mine at Pala, San Diego County. There followed a further series of vague reports up to 1893 when an occurrence on "one of the San Jacinto Mountains in Riverside county" was mentioned. The famous Himalaya Mine at Mesa Grande in San Diego County, was officially located in 1898 although there is abundant evidence that its pink tourmaline had been known for some time before by local inhabitants. Mining began here in the closing months of that year and proved to be immediately and fabulously successful. The adjacent San Diego Mine, located upon the southward extension of the same pegmatite bodies, was opened by 1901. In this same year, prospecting in the Pala area located the kunzite-bearing pegmatite of Hiriart Hill and led to intensive local search for other profitable pegmatite. The Tourmaline Queen Mine was located in 1903, also the Tourmaline King and the Ed. Fletcher Jr. Mine known earlier as the Schuyler. This group of claims was staked on the mountain which is now named Tourmaline Queen Mountain. Following in the same year, came the location of the Pala Chief Mine on Pala Chief Mountain. In 1902 and 1903, the Mountain Lily Mine, now known as the Emeralite Mine No. 2, or Ware Mine and the adjacent Gem Mine No. 1, were discovered atop the crest of Aguanga Mountain in San Diego County. Several small and unimportant mines near Rincon were opened in 1903 also. The Ramona mines were located within a matter of months in this same year, except for the Prospect Mine which was not staked until 1904. In the Mesa Grande area, further prospecting resulted in the opening of the Esmeralda Mine in the early part of 1904.

After the initial discovery period, production rose steeply until a peak was reached in 1910. Enormous quantities of tourmaline were produced in carving and cabochon grade, flawless facet grade, and in specimen grade. During 1904 alone, Kunz records that about six tons of tourmaline were shipped from the Himalaya Mine to New York, including 300 to 400 pounds of the finest grade nodules and pencils! For some years prior to 1912, the Chinese and Japanese absorbed a very large proportion of carving and cabochon grade pink material but as a result of domestic difficulties in China which led to the fall of the reigning dynasty, exports were drastically curtailed. The onset of World War I prevented further resumption of trade while the development of Brazilian sources took over much of the market formerly supplied by Californian mines. All of these factors influenced the almost overnight cessation of mining which has never regained its former importance. In 1913, J. W. Ware operated the Mountain Lily Mine at Aguanga and reported the discovery of beautiful "nile green" tourmaline. In 1914, the famous Tourmaline King Mine was sold to R. M. Wilke of Palo Alto who carried on a very thorough program of exploration but with disappointing results. In the late 1930's, J. W. Hilton and associates located a number of claims in the Rincon area but apparently none were productive. The Clark Mine in this area was mined briefly and largely without financial success in 1942 for quartz crystals. At some time in the early 1930's, the Anita Mine near Sage in the extreme southern part of Riverside County was located and operated briefly. Intermittent and largely unsuccessful operations of a one- to two-man nature were conducted during the late 1940's and early 1950's at the Emeralite Mine, the El Molino, and others in San Diego County. Interest in lithium in connection with atomic energy caused a brief flurry of mining preparations at the Stewart Lithia Mine in 1954-1955 but after some development of access roads, nothing further was done. The currently productive Himalaya Mine at Mesa Grande to be discussed more fully later, was acquired in the early 1950's by Ralph R. Potter and the adjacent property, the San Diego Mine, by Fred J. Rynerson sometime before. Virtually all of the mines in both Riverside and San Diego counties are in extremely poor condition, except those in which work is in progress. Many are badly caved in, filled with rubbish, inaccessible, and otherwise unfit for systematic mining without extensive rehabilitation.

The tourmaline mines of Riverside County, the northernmost in the Southern California region, are shrouded in mystery and their locations are far from certain. The Fano-Simmons Mine which is described by Kunz as being "about 3 miles north of the Coahuila Indian Reservation" may be the same as the workings now known as the Williamson Mine, located 1.7 miles south-southwest of the summit of Coahuila Mountain at the head of a small narrow valley on the south slope of the mountain. Kunz recorded that about 25 pounds of all grades of tourmaline had been produced at this mine up to the time of a visit by representatives of the California State Mining Bureau in 1904. The Columbia Gem Mine, according to Kunz's account, is located "about half a mile northwest of the road leading from Coahuila to the Hemet reservoir, and near the summit of the divide crossed by this road." The only road which corresponds with this fragmentary description is that leading from Anza eastward climbing the western flank of Lookout Mountain and joining Highway 74, 7 miles east of Anza by road. From this latter junction, the mine should be about ½ mile west-northwest near the top of the southeast spur of Thomas Mountain. Some very beautiful tourmaline was said to have been obtained from this mine. The Columbian Mine, renamed the Desert Rose, was worked for a short period in 1951 but only one green tourmaline crystal and some rich pink rose quartz were recovered. The last mine of consequence in this county is the Anita noted for several enormous green tourmaline crystals which were obtained from pockets in an almost horizontal pegmatite. The pegmatite is considerably shattered, and outcrops at the edge of a cultivated field, 1.55 miles west slightly northwest of the summit of Red Mountain. It is reached by a dirt road which turns eastward from Highway 79, 2¼ miles north of Sage. Several pockets were found in the pegmatite, yielding principally olive-green tourmaline, some fine pink, and other crystals which were exceedingly deep blue, virtually black. The latter were needle-like and associated with clear quartz in certain pockets. A locally-famous large green crystal is said to have been taken out of a pocket in two pieces, of which the termination was said "to just fit into a coffee can," or, just under 5 inches in diameter.

In Southern Riverside County, the principal pegmatite areas are poorly defined but embrace at least the major portions of Red, Little, and Coahuila Mountains, a continuous range of sage brush and partly forested hills bounded on the east of Bautista Canyon, and a parallel range just east of this canyon. The last includes Rouse Hill, Thomas Mountain, and Lookout Mountain. A number of prospects may be seen from the air on the west flanks of Coahuila Mountain but are inaccessible except by foot over extremely rugged terrain. This entire area has been more or less thoroughly prospected but probably some attractive pegmatites have had to be ignored because of access and working difficulties. Before leaving Riverside County, it may be worthwhile to mention that some gem quality red and pink tourmalines were once found in a novel occurrence at the Jensen Quarry at Crestmore near Riverside. This quarry and several others nearby are noted primarily for the great variety of interesting minerals in metamorphic limestone. Gem tourmaline was found in a pegmatite dike which had cut through the metamorphosed rocks but had no relationship to them. A pocket in the dike yielded about one half pound of crystals, including some of watermelon color.

Immediately south of the border of Riverside County, a pegmatite area extends along the north side of Chihuahua Valley southeastward to Hot Springs Mountain, the highest peak in San Diego County, located 4 miles northeast of Warner Springs. The mines in this valley are sometimes called the Panama-Pacific Exposition Group. The northernmost mine is the French Pete Mine, located 2 miles south-southeast of Beauty Peak and reached by poor dirt road from the northwestern end of Chihuahua Valley. This small working produced a few small pencil crystals of greenish and dark blue color. The Pearson Mine and associated prospects, exploit a series of pegmatites which form conspicuous straight outcrops on the gradually sloping eastern side of Chihuahua Valley. Since this entire area is very wild and almost unpopulated, it is difficult to fix positions, but if a topographic map (Warner Springs Quadrangle) is referred to, the Pearson Mine may be located at Lat. 33° —23.5′ N., Long. 116° —37.9′ W. The mine consists of a series of openings and shallow underground workings in a pegmatite which dips northeast and strikes southeast along the valley wall. Some very interesting small pencils of extremely dark purplish-blue tourmaline have been found in recent years, often in handsome groups with smoky quartz crystals and slender pale aquamarine crystals. The tourmaline is of specimen value only. Long thin pencils of black tourmaline of considerable mineralogical interest have been found in small pockets in a pegmatite located in the northern corner of Lost Valley, Lat. 33° — 22.38′ N., Long. 116° — 33.4′ W. The Peter Cabat Mine has produced small amounts of pale pink and good blue tourmaline crystals, none of large size but some said to be of good gem quality. This mine is located squarely on the summit of a steepsided ridge, 1.7 miles north, slightly west of the intersection of Lost Valley Truck Trail and Puerta La Cruz Truck Trail, or about 5 miles in the same direction from Warner Springs. Other pegmatite prospects are located in the general area to the east of Warner Springs, and it is said that some provided very small quantities of gem tourmaline in years past.

Southwest of the last mentioned pegmatite area, occurs another embracing much of Palomar Mountain and its outlying ridges, notably Aguanga Mountain, a steep-sided spur extending southeast from the highest point on Palomar Mountain proper. Along the summit of this ridge is the noted Emeralite No. 2 Mine or Ware Mine, named after its most successful operator. The pegmatite here is noted principally for its production of fine blue and greenish-blue topaz crystals, most of which came from a large pocket discovered 50 feet inside the northern adit (see also BERYL and TOPAZ). The pegmatite is horizontal and varies in thickness from 10 inches to as much as 36 inches but averages close to 24 inches. It is only a dozen or so feet below the surface of the ridge. In many small pockets which proved to be nothing more than angular depressions between shattered masses of pegmatite, were discovered undoubtedly the most uniquely colored tourmaline found in the county. The hue is a delightful vivid blue, slightly greenish, and comparable to the color of blue topaz or fine aquamarine. Unfortunately, only rather small pencils of this magnificent hue have been found, the largest recovered by Norman Dawson, the latest operator, being only several inches in length and a little over 1/4 inch in thickness. The largest gems cut from this material do not exceed several carats. The dichroism of this material is very slight and consequently finished gems are vividly colored and brilliant. Other colors have also been found in this mine, such as fine green, from whence came the name "emeralite," pink, and crystals of several colors together.

The famous Pala mines are located in the northern part of San Diego County, several miles south of the Riverside County line, and exploit a series of pegmatites which occur on three prominent rounded hills situated as follows: Hiriart Hill, 2.4 miles east-northeast of the Indian village of Pala; Pala Chief Mountain, 2.1 miles northeast; and Tourmaline Queen Mountain, 1.9 miles directly north of the village. Hiriart Mountain is noted almost solely for its magnificent spodumene since little tourmaline of consequence has been found in its mines. Minute pencils of deep purplish-blue, almost black, have been found in the San Pedro, Senpe, and others on this hill, while dark greenish-blue, deep blue, and bluish-green pencils have come from the Fargo Mine located low on its southern flank, south of the summit, and also from the El Molino Mine located low on the southeast flank. A crystal from the El Molino in the author's possession, shows a pale grayish-blue interior and a very dark greenish-blue skin and terminal capping. A number of Pala mines are plotted on the map in Figure 43.

The Pala Chief Mine on the mountain of the same name, is a most unusual mine for this district because both fine tourmaline and spodumene occur in the same pegmatite. The extensive underground workings exploit a pegmatite sill which is almost horizontal and underlies a shelf-like flat, several hundred feet west of the mountain summit. The tunnel entrances and access benches face west and overlook the valley of Trujillo Creek. The pegmatite averages about 10 to 15 feet in thickness and shows a confused structure in much of the southern end where small pockets containing spodumene and tourmaline, as well as curious quartz crystals filled with kaolin inclusions, have been found in recent years. The opposite or northwestern end of the pegmatite is more simple in structure and in places, yielded very fine and large crystals of tourmaline, frequently several inches in diameter and somewhat more in length. The general color pattern was watermelon, that is, cores of crystals were pink to pale red, while the exteriors were dark, somewhat olive green. Many small and finely-colored pencils of facet grade quality were found, some showing vivid and beautiful colors in pinks, greens, greenish-blues, and other combinations. The large size of crystals is attested to by a brilliant cut rubellite of 113.8 carats from this mine now in the American Museum of Natural History. Like so many gems cut from this variety, this too contains slight flaws and feathers.

Immediately to the west of Pala Chief Mountain lies Tourmaline Queen Mountain, a rounded brush-covered hill rising to an elevation of 1922 feet. Relatively few but large pegmatites outcrop on the slopes, all dipping to the southwest. On the southeast flank, several hundred feet above the valley floor is the Stewart Lithia Mine which exploits an enormous complexly mineralized pegmatite. At one time this mine supplied much of the world's lepidolite mica which was refined for the sake of its lithium. Huge masses were obtained from a central lens where the lepidolite occurs associated with cleavelandite, quartz, rare phosphate minerals, tourmaline, etc. It is estimated that this pegmatite is almost 100 feet in thickness with a core almost 75 feet thick. Exceptionally fine pink tourmaline in pencils and sometimes in large crystals over an inch in diameter and several inches long were obtained from pockets along the borders of the core. One area within the core provided the finest green crystals from any locality in California but these were generally small transparent pencils only ⅛ to ¼ inch in thickness, and several inches long. The color was a true rich green devoid of disagreeable olive tints. Gems cut from this type are exceptionally colorful and brilliant. The pink crystals referred to before are also noted for their color which tends decidedly to orange-pink rather than the purplish-pink which the vast majority of tourmalines of this hue exhibit elsewhere in the county. The Stewart Lithia Mine is noted among mineral collectors for the handsome specimens of bright red tourmaline needles radiating in sprays and rosettes within a groundmass of extremely fine granular pale purplish-pink lepidolite.

Near the Stewart is the Mission Mine, just to the west, and the Alvarado and Douglass mines to the east and lower on the slope. None of these have produced much tourmaline. To the north are the Canyon Cut and North Star mines which prospect the northward extension of the Stewart dike. It is said that some few fine large tourmalines were found in the pegmatite at the Canyon Cut but little evidence appears either within the workings or in the dump. The position of these workings is shown in the photograph of Tourmaline Queen Mountain in Figure 55.

Approximately 1000 feet directly east of the summit of Tourmaline Queen Mountain is the mine which lent its name to this prominence. The peg-

FIGURE 55. A view of Tourmaline Queen Mountain in the background in the Pala District of San Diego County, California. The thin white streak at the upper right of the mountain is the Tourmaline Queen pegmatite with the mine located at the point where white streaks follow the slope.

matite exposed here, appears as a long outcrop along the eastern wall of the mountain, and although prospected by shallow opencuts along its southern portion, has evidently proved productive only at its northern extremity where the underground workings are located. In thickness, the dike ranges from about 6 to 20 feet, the thicker portions generally being most favorably mineralized. Gem pockets appear along well-defined mineralized "streaks" which run down the dip at several places. In common with other California gem mines, pockets in the Tourmaline Queen are encountered between the edge of a quartz core and the lower half of the pegmatite, the pocket roofs always consisting of coarse quartz crystals and blocky feldspar crystals showing much corrosion and etching upon the faces. Nearby but not within the pockets proper, are large irregular masses of very compact and fine grained lepidolite. Enormous black tourmaline crystals begin from small nuclei near the hanging walls of the dike and steadily grow in size as they descend downward until they reach diameters of several inches at the edges of pockets. At the points where they penetrate through the quartz crystals lining the roof, they assume color and transparency, crystallizing in large crystals of wonderful quality within the pockets. Sometimes these crystals remain rooted among the quartz crystals and provide magnificent specimen groups if carefully and intelligently removed. Most frequently, however, large crystals are found broken by the violence of late stage activity within pockets, and are then found loose and sometimes doubly-terminated. Similar mishaps to quartz also provide an abundance of distorted crystals but some become very clear and of gem quality after detachment. Floors of pockets are filled with mixtures of cleavelandite blades, fragments of feldspar, quartz shards, flakes and small masses of lepidolite, pink montmorillonite, and streaks and veinings of felted microscopic tourmaline needles. Within this debris are often found numerous fine gem quality tourmaline pencils, often doubly-terminated, as well as some of the larger crystals detached from the roof. Any open spaces left in the pocket after the cessation of chemical activity, fill with an unusually tenacious sticky dark brownish-red clay, believed to be derived from alteration of enclosing rocks and infiltrated into pockets through cracks and seams. This clay causes much difficulty in cleaning out pockets and frequently encloses fine bits of gem material which are then inadvertently thrown out on the dumps.

Many of the large tourmaline crystals from the Queen contain cores of bright to deep pink and even red material, highly transparent and eminently suitable for exceptionally fine carvings or even small faceted gems. Although some are entirely pink, the majority are sheathed in a thin pale to very dark blue coating which masks somewhat the basic color. This blue material represents the very last stages of tourmaline mineralization and as a consequence many pencils and smaller crystals are found composed entirely of pale blue-gray to blue material. The color distribution within such crystals is shown diagrammatically in Figure 51. One mineralized streak within the Queen pegmatite is noted for its production of tourmaline of blue color. The outermost portion of this streak, very close to the southern adit, produced a large number of most peculiar "black-skinned" crystals from a pocket several feet across. One in the author's collection measures 2 inches in diameter and 2½ inches in length, and is doubly terminated on one end by a simple basal plane and upon the other by a series of very small pyramidal hillocks forming a thin zone of catseye material. A smaller specimen which was cut open and polished, shows the "black-skin" to be in reality a 1/16 inch thick layer of deep indigo material. The center portion is pale aquamarine blue, a most unusual and rare color in this species, while this is sheathed in turn by a thin zone of achroite next to the skin. Further down the dip, this same mineralized streak opened into two pockets which produced a number of blue crystals of similar internal color but sheathed in dark blue material instead of indigo. A crystal of this type is shown in Figure 56. A number of Tourmaline Queen crystals are illustrated in Figure 49. Altogether, the Tourmaline Queen Mine has perhaps produced several tons of tourmalines as well as many quartz and morganite beryl crystals from its pockets.

Perhaps some of the largest and most magnificent crystals and crystal

Note: Figures 56 and 57 are in the color section following page 112.

groups of tourmaline from any world locality have come from the Tourmaline King and the adjoining Ed. Fletcher Jr. Mine, located high on the north slope of Tourmaline King Mountain, about 1000 feet northwest of the summit. In a dike similar in many respects to that seen in the Queen except more steeply dipping, an enormous quantity of rich raspberry red crystals were removed from a series of pockets which were encountered a few feet inside the outcrop and ran up and down the dip for a distance of perhaps 100 feet. The crystals frequently reached dimensions of 3 inches in diameter and lengths up to 5 inches and even longer, the interiors consisting of rich vivid rubellite of exceptional color and lacking generally any trace of purplish tinge, while the exteriors consisted of many smaller pale pink crystals forming overgrowths. A fine specimen of this type is illustrated in color in Figure 57. Most of the very large crystal groups of tourmaline on a matrix of quartz, seen in prominent museums, came from this series of pockets. Like the crystals of the Queen, many pink specimens from the King were found to be covered with a thin sheath of blue or green material. This coating is scarcely noticeable in large crystals but in smaller specimens, and in pencils, it appears as a decided cylinder in which is seen a thin core of pink material. At times, this coating becomes greenish and smaller crystals then show watermelon patterns. Almost all of the production of large crystals from the Tourmaline King was purchased by Chinese and Japanese agents for no other tourmaline of this shade was so highly prized for carving. The American Museum of Natural History includes the following crystals in the Morgan Collection: one single prism with typical overgrowths of small pencils, 8 inches tall and 3½ inches in diameter at the swelling top; another 4 inches tall and 3½ inches thick; the last, 8 inches tall, and from 2 to 2½ inches thick, associated with cleavelandite and lepidolite scales. Figure 50 illustrates in color another type from this mine, this time a doubly-terminated crystal in which the red color appears only as an ill-defined cloud within a mass of greenish-blue material.

In the Rincon District of San Diego County, only the Victor Mine produced any colored tourmaline. The mine is located exactly 2 miles south-southeast of Rincon. The Victor Mine opened a pegmatite which lies like a blanket on the hillside permitting the miners to peel off the top half and expose a series of small pockets containing various minerals, including tourmaline. Pink, violet, green, and colorless "pencil" crystals were found along with some in which the core was pink and the exterior pale green, however, nothing outstanding was discovered in respect to quality or quantity.

The Mesa Grande district lies southeast of Rincon, in high, rolling, partly-wooded terrain about 3 miles southwest of Lake Henshaw. From several fabulously rich dikes has come an astonishing quantity of vividly-colored tourmaline crystals, generally smaller in size than those of the Pala District, but compensating in variety of color and sheer quantity for what they lack in size. The most productive workings are upon Gem Hill, a rounded knob which rises to 4058 feet above sea level and located 2.75 miles northwest of the Mesa Grande Store. The San Diego Mine occupies the portion of the dikes located about 900 feet north of the summit of Gem Hill while the Himalaya Mine takes up the remainder, being located about 1800 feet north. Both mines exploit the deposit through a series of inclines, tunnels, and cross-connecting drifts which exit on the east face of the hill although many openings are now slumped shut. The Himalaya additionally is exploited by a main tunnel which exits upon the shallow western slope. Ralph Potter, the owner and operator of this mine, has succeeded in clearing out this tunnel to over a distance of 500 feet and has produced large quantities of magnificent crystals from the pocket zone. The richness of the pegmatites in Gem Hill would lead one to believe them to be of large size, however, it is surprising to learn that each of the two parallel dikes range only from several inches to 3 feet in thickness with the average depth only about 20 inches.

Numerous pockets occur in well-defined streaks which follow the dip and are separated laterally by sections of barren rock sometimes 50 feet in width. The extreme northern end within the boundaries of the Himalaya property proved to contain the most prolific streak which was exploited at an early stage of mining by an opencut. Early after initial operations, as shown in Figure 58, the increasing depth of overburden forced underground mining and accordingly a main tunnel was driven from the west slope to intersect the dike, and a series of inclines extended upward along mineralized streaks until the outcrop on the eastern face of the hill was encountered. Numerous laterals were driven to connect adjacent inclines in order to systematically excavate pocket-bearing portions of the dike. The San Diego Mine could not profitably attack the pegmatites from the western slope and accordingly all work was done from the steep eastern face of the hill; efforts consisted of tunnels, inclines, and laterals connecting the inclines. Numerous well picked over dumps surround Gem Hill below both mines but still yield crystals and fragments by careful and laborious screening.

Figure 48 illustrates a typical gem pocket as found at either the Himalaya or San Diego mines. In pocket-rich portions, similar openings would occur every few feet, very wide in thicker sections of the dike, but sometimes only a few inches across in thin portions. The majority of pockets were crammed with tourmaline crystals and crystal fragments in such profusion that it seemed as if someone had painstakingly fitted them in to fill all possible spaces. In each pocket, the remaining space is usually filled with typical dark reddish-brown clay at the top, and with pocket debris at the bottom consisting of numerous pencils of tourmaline, often of facet grade, bits of feldspar, cleavelandite, quartz crystals, lepidolite, frequently in beautiful six-sided flakes, and white to pink clays. A few pockets were found in which activity

FIGURE 58. The west cut of the Himalaya Mine, Mesa Grande, California, taken about 1912. On the left may be seen slabs of barren pegmatite left undisturbed by the miners. The fantastically rich sections were followed beneath the ground in the center trench and later exploited by tunnels and inclines from the other side of the hill as well as a point some feet below the site shown here. Courtesy U.S. Geological Survey.

had been arrested at an early stage and consequently the crystals of tourmaline and other minerals remained in pristine condition; such pockets contained neither introduced clay or pink or white pocket clays and were hollow in their centers. The size of tourmaline crystals at Gem Hill ranges from needle-like individuals to those an inch or more in diameter and as much as 7 inches in length. However, the latter are comparatively rare and the average is closer to about ⅜ inch diameter and 2 inches in length.

The coloration of crystals from this deposit is fantastic in its variety but pink and green are predominant. In order to show the proportions, a sample lot of 500 crystals was examined and the following percentages determined: pink—34%; green—20%; multicolored crystals, mainly pink and green together—23%; red—6%; brown—6%; black—2% or less; blues—less than 1%. Thus it can be seen that red and green occur in 54% of the crystals while if multicolored crystals combining these colors are added, the percentage rises to 77%. A suite of typical crystals and crystal fragments is shown in color in Figure 50. Warm yellow-green is characteristic and serves immediately to distinguish Gem Hill specimens from all others of similar hue found elsewhere in the county. Color zoning is common but pronounced only along the length of the crystals, cross-sections showing only slight changes in hue between the basic color and the skin color. Exceptions are noted of course, as in the dark-skinned crystals recovered from the lower dike which proved to be larger than the average size just noted, about 1½ inches in diameter, and sheathed in a thin dark olive-green skin which seems almost black. Some of these crystals, furthermore, show cores totally unlike the ordinary crystals, some sections being dark olive-green, others yellow-green, some pink, red, and even colorless. It is said that crystals of this type furnished the largest flawless red nodules found in the Gem Hill mines. In respect to zoning along the length of crystals, an outstanding and specially characteristic kind is that where the lower portion of the crystal is bright pink and the upper part bright green. It is from exceptionally perfect specimens of this kind that bicolored gems are cut. The upper green portion is frequently penetrated by numerous tubes, which if sufficiently fine, afford good catseyes.

Virtually all of the faceting material has come from nodules which have broken away from the parent crystal and are found embedded in the debris of the pocket floor. Within crystals, nodules occur just below the crystal terminations, or if the crystal is partly green, just below the color boundary. Some idea of size is had when the famous California tourmaline specimens of the Warner Collection are examined. This collection is housed in the California Institute of Technology in Pasadena, California, and contains 28 enormous crystals of tourmaline from various San Diego Co. localities, averaging 1 pound in weight, as well as many cut stones. Outstanding examples from the Himalaya Mine are a 100 carat green catseye, a 31 carat flawless brilliant of unique orange shade, and a square stepcut green gem of 35 carats.

Several other mines and prospects are located on the flanks of Gem Hill but so far as is known, production from them has been very small. One rather extensive working is located on the eastern flank of the hill about ¼ mile southeast of the San Diego Mine main tunnel; the dumps show much quartz and numerous crystals of this mineral but no tourmaline. The pegmatite at this place is higher than those entered by the principal mines and shows nowhere along its length any signs of favorable mineralization. Another shallow pit located about 900 feet southwest of the summit of Gem Hill enters a pegmatite of about 6 feet in thickness but dump material contains nothing of gem interest. The Cota Mine exploits a dike low on the western flank of Gem Hill slightly over ½ mile west of the summit and several hundred feet below the access road to the Himalaya Mine.

Approximately 1.4 miles west-northwest of Gem Hill is located the noted Esmeralda Mine from which have been obtained fine morganite and aquamarine beryl and modest quantities of gem tourmaline. This mine is on top of a steepsided ridge lodged in the triangle between the Mesa Grande Truck Trail and the Lusardi Truck Trail and is accessible by road from Mesa Grande Schoolhouse. The dike is a peculiar, near-vertical pegmatite which, in one place, swells enormously and it is at this point that a series of pockets were removed, containing large quartz crystals, citrine crystals, pink and dark greenish-blue tourmaline, and beryl. The dark blue tourmaline crystals are unique, occurring in small pockets within coarse blocky feldspar and massive quartz adjacent to the main quartz core. Their color is very rich and lovely, but only crystals of ¼ inch in diameter or less are sufficiently pale to afford attractive faceted gems. Pencils have been obtained from about ⅛ to ¾ inch in diameter and from ½ to 4 inches in length. Some exhibit exceedingly deep indigo blue shades while others are dark wine red or a peculiar grayish-purple. Color zoning is not pronounced as a rule, but when observed, is noticeable only along the prism length.

The Banner Mine Southeast of Mesa Grande in the Julian district, has produced a very few green tourmaline pencils of gem grade from within small vuggy pockets in masses of lepidolite and cleavelandite. This mine is located in a side canyon leading south from near the foot of Banner Grade on Highway 78.

The Ramona gem pegmatites are located in a small area centered 4 miles east-northeast of the center of the town with dikes outcropping on the southerly slopes of several rock-strewn hills which overlook cultivated fields lying between Hatfield Creek and its northern branch. The ABC Mine, located about one mile upstream on the northern branch from its junction with Hatfield Creek, exploited a pegmatite of about 4 feet thickness which lies exposed upon a hillside. Only very dark and dingy olive green tourmaline pencils and stubby crystals measuring several inches long and somewhat less in width came from this deposit. Some are clear but far too dark to afford attractive gems. One mile northeast of the creek junction mentioned, are located the Little Three Mine, the Black Panther, the Hercules, the Spaulding and the now obliterated Surprise Mine. The Little Three Mine is noted for its enormous dark green tourmaline crystals, the largest of which was stated to be 15 pounds in weight. Many others have been found which measured several inches in diameter and from 4 to 6 inches in height. A crystal in the author's collection illustrated in Figure 49, measures 2¾ inches in diameter and 2 inches in height and is basically deep green in hue with a dark brownish band near the termination and a lighter green band above this. Dichroism is intense, being dark green and greenish-brown and consequently causing faceted gems to be disagreeable in tone. A few pink pencils have been found in the Little Three pegmatite but in most cases, this color is confined to the tips.

Just below the opencast workings of the Little Three, occurs another dike which has been recently opened in one place upon a pocket. Disappointingly, only exceedingly dark olive-green crystals were found closely resembling those from the ABC Mine. The other mines in this area have produced very little gem tourmaline although considerable quantities of cuttable dead black crystals have been found in the pockets associated with quartz, cleavelandite, and spessartite garnet.

Baja California Norte. Few gemstones of any description have been found in this sparsely-populated and mostly desert region. Following the discovery of tourmaline in San Diego County, California, immediately to the north, interest was naturally directed toward the adjacent area in Baja California Norte in which the central spine of mountains consist of essentially the same rock formations. Shortly after the turn of the century, small quantities of dark wine red gem tourmaline were recovered from pegmatites in the Sierra de Cacupah near the boundary of California. Unfortunately, exact information on the area is lacking although rumor has it that the pegmatite containing the tourmaline was found outcropping on a low hill in pine-forested terrain. More is known, however, about several occurrences about 275 miles south of Ensenada near the towns of Calamahi and San Borja. As a result of explorations in this area, a German geologist found two pegmatite districts in which colored tourmaline occurred under most unusual circumstances. Instead of being in pockets, the gem quality pencils, mainly pink in color, were found forming sprays and masses of small crystals in strongly folded black biotite schists. The nearness of pegmatites led to the conclusion that tourmaline-rich solutions had somehow been diverted from the pegmatites and injected along seams and joints in the schists.

The first of these localities is within a broad area of dark biotite schist in the mountainous terrain between Calamahi and San Borja. The schists are intruded in many places by feldspar-quartz dikes containing considerable black tourmaline. Schists containing gem tourmaline are to one side of the main area and extend into the arroyos of San Pedro. Here only small lenses and "eyes" of pegmatite are found and it is with these that gemmy tourmaline is associated. Some crystals show both pink and green and others are completely green, but pink is the predominant color. The largest were 4 inches in length but none were more than translucent. Despite their unsuitability for gems, their mere existence points to the possibility that further prospecting may uncover productive deposits in this region. The belt in which these occurrences were noted is said to extend for a distance of about ¾ mile.

The second locality is located about 16 miles north of the first, in the center of the Sierra San Borja and close to the divide between the Pacific Ocean watershed and that of the Gulf of California. The occurrence is exactly the same but the schists are more compressed and folded. An interesting associate of the tourmalines is deep blue sapphire which occurs as small rude crystals, smaller individuals showing paler colors and some degree of translucency. The sapphire crystals range in size from very small up to about ¼ inch in length and about ⅛ inch thick.

Sonora. Some green tourmaline of gem grade has recently been reported from an unspecified locality in the southern part of this state.

SODALITE AND CANCRINITE

Though unrelated, sodalite and cancrinite are treated together because gem-quality specimens invariably occur side by side in all North American localities. In some instances, the mottled effect of bright blue sodalite next to deep orange-yellow cancrinite provides extremely handsome ornamental material. Sodalite was named many years ago after the sodium in its composition while cancrinite honors a famous Russian diplomat of bygone days: Baron Cancrin. Sodalite occurs in quantity at several localities in Canada where it was once quarried commercially but only with partial financial success. This early failure toward commercialization has not affected its popularity among American amateurs, who buy appreciable quantities every year. Sodalite and cancrinite are not very durable chemically or physically, and must not be used as gems set in jewelry subjected to hard wear.

In composition sodalite is a sodium aluminum silicate with chlorine, with the rather complex formula: $Na_4Al_3Si_3O_{12}Cl$. It occurs only in nepheline rocks of igneous origin formed from magmas rich in sodium. Crystals are quite rare and in North America at least, only massive material consisting of small to large intergrown grains is found in significant quantity. It seldom occurs in pure masses being often mottled and veined with nephelite, plagioclase feldspar, black biotite mica, cancrinite and other minerals. Hardness varies between 5½ and 6 but since it possesses a large number of dodecahedral cleavage planes, it is relatively fragile and gives the impression of being even softer. Broken sections show conchoidal to uneven surfaces of slightly greasy luster. The specific gravity is low, 2.2 to 2.4. Belonging to the Isometric System, it shows accordingly only one refractive index. Textbook values give $n = 1.4827$ but an exceptionally pure specimen from Canada faceted into a small transparent gem and presently in the author's collection, shows only $n = 1.480$. Since sodalite is singly refractive there can be no dichroism. Sodalite varies from almost opaque to transparent, but the latter degree of diaphaneity is found only in very small patches in some of the darker material from the Princess Quarry in Canada.

Cancrinite possesses a chemical formula like a mathematical nightmare: $3H_2O \cdot 4NA_2O \cdot CaO \cdot 4AL_2O_3 \cdot 9SiO_2 \cdot 2CO_2$. This is more a listing of constituents than a formula but shows that it is essentially a silicate of sodium, calcium, aluminum, carbon, and oxygen and contains water. As mentioned before, cancrinite occurs associated with sodalite under identical conditions, and like that mineral is found in similar granular form. Cancrinite belongs to the Hexagonal System and like sodalite, seldom appears in distinct crystals. The hardness is low, varying between 5 and 6, while the presence of several prismatic cleavages imparts a further degree of fragility. The fracture is uneven, displaying a greasy to glassy luster. The specific gravity ranges from 2.42 to 2.50. Refractive indices are: $\omega = 1.515\text{-}1.524$, $\epsilon = 1.491\text{-}1.502$; birefringence 0.023; uniaxial, negative. Only material of deep orange-yellow color is useful for gemstones, other shades being too pale or too dull. In spite of rather strong coloration, there appears to be no dichroism. Cancrinite is not found in transparent material but all of it seems more or less translucent. Both sodalite and cancrinite are attacked and dissolved by hydrochloric acid.

The usefulness of sodalite and cancrinite in lapidary work is limited to cabochons although very small faceted gems not exceeding a fraction of a carat, can be cut from clear grains of sodalite. Both minerals have been used in many ornamental applications such as bookends, ashtrays, paperweights, desk pen sets, or simply as attractive polished slabs. Recently, sodalite has been employed in tumbled gems and is now appearing on the market in baroques for mounting into inexpensive bangle jewelry.

LOCALITIES

Greenland. Very deep blue sodalite occurs in eruptive rock on the south side of Arsuk Island slightly south of Moffy's Harbor in Arsuk Fjord in the Frederikshaab District; also in nepheline-syenite at Gronnedal.

Ontario. The principal locality for sodalite is the now inactive Princess Quarry on Lot 25, Concession XIV, Dungannon Township, Hastings Co. Sodalite in solid streaks and as disseminated grains in nepheline-systenite outcrops over a distance of 250 feet with a maximum width of from 40 to 50 feet. This has been stated to be a conservative estimate and that actually sodalite occurs beyond these boundaries. The quarry cut is over 200 feet long and is located some 300 feet north of the Bancroft-Hermon Road in the side of a low ridge. Large masses of handsomely mottled rock from the Princess Quarry were once sold under the name of "Princess Marble" although scarcely anything less related in chemical composition to real marble could be imagined. In 1906, fully 130 tons were shipped to England where it was used as ornamental stone trim for the interior of Sir Ernest Cassell's house in Park Lane, Hyde Park.

At the locality, still privately held, sodalite and its associated minerals form a very tough rock which must be bored and blasted to remove. Associated minerals consist of streaks of white to bright red plagioclase feldspar, nephelite, biotite, magnetite, and small spots and patches of cancrinite.

Sodalite is frequently encountered in the broad belt of nepheline-syenites passing through the townships of Glamorgan, Haliburton Co., and eastward through Faraday, Dungannon, and Monteagle townships in Hastings Co., and Raglan Township and as far as Lake Clear in Brudenell Township, Renfrew Co. The usual occurrence is ragged patches and masses of varying size, sometimes beautifully developed along cracks and fissures in enclosing rocks. Exposures showing large masses of beautifully colored sodalite have been observed on Lots 25 and 29, Concession XIII, Dungannon Township. Some work was done some years ago on Lot 25 where the overburden was removed and the rock blasted to reveal several large patches of good material. Spotty material associated with cancrinite occurs on Cancrinite Hill (see below). Sodalite and cancrinite localized along fractures in pegmatite, occur in the Goulding-Keene Quarry on the west side of the York River, immediately north of the Bancroft-Hermon Road, on Lot 12, Concession XI, Dungannon Township. Another quarry is located on Lot 23, Concession XIV in the same township but shows only small amounts of these minerals. Minor quantities have been noted also in Haliburton and Peterborough counties. In Renfrew County, at Craigmont, Raglan Township, patches of deep blue material occur in nepheline-syenite associated with beautiful salmon colored nephelite and gray palgioclase feldspar and yield exceptionally handsome material.

Productive sources of fine yellow cancrinite in Canada are few but it is known from almost all the sodalite occurrences. In Hastings County, a considerable quantity occurs at Monck Road in Faraday Township; also 2 miles from Bancroft in Dungannon Township ½ mile south of the Princess Quarry where it occurs on Lot 25 in Concessions XIII and XIV on the south slope of an eminence called Cancrinite Hill. Fine amber-yellow material is reported from the nephelite quarries at Blue Mountain, Methuen Township, Peterborough County. Like sodalite, cancrinite also fades with exposure.

Quebec. Sodalite has been noted at Brome, Brome County, but only in small quantity.

British Columbia. Much specimen and cutting grade sodalite has been obtained from a locality at Kicking Horse Pass, a declivity which crosses the Rocky Mountains at the boundary between the Yoho National Park in British Columbia and Banff National Park immediately to the east in Alberta. Nepheline-syenites containing sodalite are said to extend over an area of about 32 square miles on the Pacific slope of the mountains to the southwest of the pass. Exposures are found on the Ice River, a tributary of the Beaverfoot River.

North West Territories. Sodalite is present in an oval body of nepheline-syenite and related rocks which outcrop over a distance of 5 miles at Big-spruce Lake on Snare River, northwest of Yellowknife. There is no information as to the suitability of this material for gemstone purposes.

Maine. An old but now completely extinct locality is that at Litchfield, Kennebec County. Small outcrops of soda-rich syenite locally called litch-fieldite, contained beautiful masses of bright blue sodalite and vivid yellow cancrinite but the greatest quantity of cuttable material was obtained from boulders which had broken loose from the parent body through the action of glaciation and erosion. In Litchfield Township, one outcrop occurs approximately 1000 feet north of Spears Corner and another about 2000 feet southwest. Spears Corner is about 5½ miles west of Gardiner, Kennebec County. Drift boulders have been found over considerable distances from these outcrops, generally toward the southwest, in Litchfield and West Gardiner townships. Dennis Hill in Litchfield Township has provided much good material in the past. In another section of the state, sodalite in thin seams and in small boulders, has been reported from Straw Hill, Newfield Township, York County, about 4 miles from Limerick.

Arkansas. Blue sodalite is a rare constituent of the rocks near Magnet Cove, in Hot Springs County. It has been found as granular masses of several inches in diameter in quarry pits on the south border of the Cove, about ¾ mile northeast of Cove Station and about 1½ miles southwest of Magnet Post Office.

OLIVINE
(*Peridot*)

Olivine has enjoyed the esteem of mankind for many thousands of years, an ancient deposit on St. Johns Island in the Red Sea being mentioned by the famous Roman naturalist Pliny in his *Natural History* written about A.D. 70. The celebrated bright green crystals from this island have provided beautiful gems up to the present day and there is no indication that the deposit is exhausted. Bright green crystals, often of enormous size, also occur in the Mogok District of Burma and may well have been used by the peoples of the Far East for some very large cut gems originating from old Indian collections seem too large to have been cut from St. Johns material. In North America, gem quality olivine occurs in considerable quantity in a number of places but never in large sizes. Nevertheless it has been much used in jewelry from the day of its discovery and even now, almost any lapidary magazine carries advertisements offering rough or cut stones for sale.

Olivine receives its name from the typical olive-green color of many specimens while the name *peridot*, ordinarily assigned to the bright yellow-green gem variety, is taken from the French but from whence that language received the term is uncertain. A golden-yellow kind *chrysolite*, is named for the Greek words for "golden" "stone"; *forsterite* (see below) is named after J. Forster, a mineralogist, and *fayalite*, is named after the island of Fayal in the Azores.

In mineralogy, olivine is the species name for a series of closely related Orthorhombic magnesium-iron silicates in which the magnesium end member is called forsterite while the opposite extreme, iron silicate, is termed fayalite. These relationships are expressed in the general formula: $(Mg,Fe)_2SiO_4$. The magnesium end member, forsterite, generally assumes some shade of yellow, while iron-rich fayalite is either dark brown or black. The gem variety peridot includes those members of the series whose composition is rich in magnesium. Peridot is generally some shade of green and owes its color to iron whose compositional ratio is about one part to five parts of magnesium. Yellowish-green olivine is sometimes called chrysolite but since this name has been variously applied to totally unrelated minerals, it has fallen into disfavor and is now little used.

Olivine and its gem variety peridot are most frequently found in dark volcanic rocks in small to large formless grains or granular aggregates. The latter often reach several inches in diameter and are sometimes called, though erroneously, "olivine bombs." True volcanic "bombs" are masses of liquid lava which are thrown out by explosions to harden in flight, eventually landing upon the slopes of the cinder cone where they form much of the debris. Although peridot is frequently found in these masses it is as inclusions rather than as separate missiles. Figure 59 shows typical granular aggregations of peridot at the noted San Carlos locality in Arizona. In every locality mentioned below, peridot is found only in small grains, sometimes freshly eroded from enclosing rocks and then angular or blocky in form, or worn considerably by windblasting and then well rounded and covered with many fine pits. Peridot is not very hard, only 6½ to 7, but it is tough. One fair and one poor cleavage may be detected by close examination but these are developed with difficulty and the usual fracture surface is merely conchoidal, showing a bright, somewhat oily luster. Hardness and toughness vary according to crystal direction and cause much difficulty in cutting, sometimes one facet polishing to perfection and another next to it failing to respond to any treatment the lapidary can devise. The specific gravity varies over a wide range for the entire olivine series from 3.2 for forsterite to 4.3 for fayalite, however peridot is much more restricted, generally falling between 3.32 to 3.50. Refractive indices rise as the iron content increases and for this reason vary from low values for bright green peridot as follows: $\alpha = 1.645$, $\gamma = 1.683$, to high values for darker and more iron-rich kinds as $\alpha = 1.668$, $\gamma = 1.706$. The large birefringence is fairly constant at 0.038 and along with the faint pleiochroism in various shades of green, serves to distinguish this

FIGURE 59. Peridot inclusions in basalt along the northwest wall of Peridot Canyon, ½ mile above its mouth, San Carlos Indian Reservation, Arizona. Beneath the hammer head may be seen a curving inclusion of peridot consisting of many loose small grains of clear material. Courtesy U.S. Geological Survey.

gemstone from others which resemble it. Two specimens from San Carlos gave the following indices: $a = 1.650$, $\gamma = 1.688$ and $a = 1.651$, $\gamma = 1.689$. Pleiochroism in these is faint greenish-yellow and green. Olivine is biaxial; the optic sign varies from positive in forsterite to negative in fayalite.

American peridot gems are seldom large in size due to the lack of flawless material in anything but small grains. Gems of 5 carats or more are most unusual, the majority being less than 2 carats. A fine 9 carat gem and several others almost as large are exhibited in the U.S. National Museum. In the last several years, tumbling techniques for polishing have been applied to the small peridot grains of Arizona with a high degree of success. The finished product is brilliantly smooth and is used in some quantity for making baroque jewelry.

LOCALITIES

British Columbia. About 1915, gem quality peridot was found as grains in volcanic bombs upon the exact summit of Timothy Mountain between two extinct cinder cones. The underlying andesite and trachyte are intruded by basalt which contains peridot. Numerous bombs were found sprinkled over the ground in this area and from them excellent dark green stones were obtained, some of the individual pieces weighing as much as 10 carats. Timothy Mountain lies east-northeast of the town of Lac LaHache along Highway 2-97 in south central British Columbia.

Arizona. The most productive locality for peridot in North America is in a small area in Gila County, 2½ miles southwest of the Indian village of San Carlos in the reservation of the same name. San Carlos lies 16 miles north of Coolidge Dam and is easily accessible by good road. The place where peridot occurs is on the summit and sides of a flat tableland called Peridot Mesa. The mesa is capped by a basalt flow of from 10 to 100 feet thick, covering tuffs, siltstones, and gravels of an earlier geologic time. Roughly rectangular in outline, the mesa is about 1½ to 2 miles in width in a north-south direction and somewhat more east to west. Peridot found in place is firmly embedded in basalt and when the latter is fresh and unaltered, all attempts to dislodge pieces are doomed to failure unless explosives or breaking up the rock with sledge hammers are tried. This is a wasteful procedure, however, since the peridot is shattered in the process. Sometimes when the peridot occurs in aggregates, or "bombs," the entire mass is crisscrossed with joints and fissures and it is then easy to dislodge individual grains. Such aggregates average from 3 inches to 8 inches in diameter, although early visitors to the locality mention some of 15 inches or more in diameter, and one exceptional mass of this much in width and 30 inches in length! Each aggregation is encased in a thin shell of spongy basalt. Peridot comes to hand much more easily in other places on the mesa especially in the gullies and canyons which lead down the sides. Here the forces of weathering have decomposed the basalt to the point where individual grains of peridot are set free and lie loose upon the ground or in the talus of the hillsides. Practically all commercial material is derived from such sources. Estimates of peridot content in the basalt place the quantity at 25 percent to 40 percent of the total volume, thus assuring a plentiful supply for many years to come.

Individual grains of peridot vary considerably in size from some as small as sand and utterly worthless to others which measure from ¼ to ½ inch or even larger. One specimen found in 1904 measured 1½ inches in length and weighed 1½ ounces. This is an impressive peridot regardless of locality! When broken from the enclosing rock, each grain is fresh, sharp, and lustrous, but soon after exposure begins to dull, and, in time, the entire exterior becomes frosted. Peridots found in the soil are well-rounded, possibly due to a combination of mechanical abrasion and chemical attack. Among such loose grains occur dark brownish-olive hypersthene fragments, identical in appearance except for color, and green diopside fragments which are difficult to distinguish from the peridot except for their color which verges more toward pure green than that noted in peridot which is decidedly yellowish. Both minerals are extremely rare. The hypersthene is sometimes clear enough to cut faceted gems but they could scarcely qualify as beautiful, however, in some examples, minute gold colored inclusions lie in parallel arrangement and permit cutting cabochons showing weak catseyes.

In accordance with policies governing Indian reservations, mineral rights on the San Carlos Reservation were awarded some years ago to the present Indian residents and to this day they control and regulate the gathering of peridots. In recent years, other occupations have proven more profitable and have led to decline in production. Gathering peridot fragments is seldom systematically carried out and when a few pounds have been collected, they are sold to trading posts, to tourists, or to dealers in Globe. Prices paid for rough in recent years have ranged from $3 to $5 per pound but only about one pound in ten is worth cutting even into small stones. Finished gems sell for about $5 per carat with the average weight running from 1 to 3 carats but not always without flaws. The largest stone cut in recent years was one of 15 carats but a huge specimen of 22 carats is said to have been cut many years ago. The color varies from shades of yellowish- to brownish-green, some very fine and equal to peridot from any locality.

The second locality for peridot in Arizona is that in Buell Park, Apache County, about ten miles due north of Fort Defiance and almost on the boundary between Arizona and New Mexico. Buell Park is a saucer-shaped depression about two miles wide and roughly circular in outline. Near its southeastern rim a narrow curving ridge rises abruptly from the smooth contours of the bowl and proves to be a type of volcanic rock in which peridot is exceptionally abundant. Receiving its name from this abundance, Peridot Ridge as it is called, extends to about 1¾ miles in length and curves sharply toward the north at its eastern end. Peridot granules are found in disintegrated rock along the flanks of the ridge and for a considerable distance over adjacent areas. Peridot also occurs abundantly in the very small hill in the floor of Buell Park and is of double interest because of the large numbers of pyrope garnet grains which also occur here. Minerals associated with the peridot of Buell Park are pyrope garnet, emerald-green diopside, calcite, ilmenite, limonite, enstatite, augite, biotite, and large amounts of serpentine. From 20% to 60% of the peridot grains are ¼ inch or less in size but larger ones up to 1 inch across or even more are known to occur but seldom clear and flawless. The color of peridot from this locality is the same as from San Carlos and similar small gems can be cut from large enough pieces.

New Mexico. In Dona Ana County, a peculiar shallow circular depression called the Kilbourne Hole, has all the earmarks of being the mouth of a long-extinct volcano. Pale green nodular masses of peridot occur in the basalt rim of the crater, especially near Afton. In size, these nodules average up to 2 inches in diameter and consist of shattered angular fragments of peridot, some of which are large enough to cut into small but handsome gems. In some instances, peridot and augite are found in aggregations up to 10 inches in diameter along the north rim of the Hole but these seldom yield gem material.

Mexico. Olivine nodules in basalt have been reported from near Camargo, Chihuahua but no information is available as to the presence of gem quality peridot.

TURQUOIS

So distinctive is the sky-blue or robin's egg blue of turquois that the name of this mineral is frequently used to describe any color which resembles it. It is for color and color alone that turquois is prized since in its usual massive form it is nearly opaque and little would be gained by employing faceted cuts or other forms designed to take advantage of optical properties. Unfortunately, very little turquois of this highly prized shade is mined, the majority leans decidedly toward greenish tones while some is actually more green than blue. Though hardly expensive as compared to diamond or sapphire, good turquois is not cheap; however, a large number of color grades permits extensive employment in all classes of jewelry from the cheapest to the most expensive. Anyone who has taken a trip through the Southwestern United States has not failed to notice the hundreds of turquois-set jewelry pieces displayed in souvenir establishments along the way. The material used in such pieces is seldom the best, the finest turquois finding its way like other prized gemstones into standard trade channels for use in high class jewelry. The name of this mineral is derived from the French word Turquie for Turkey, and more particularly from the French designation of the gemstone itself—*pierre turquoise*, in allusion to the belief that it came from this Mid-East country. Spelling turquois with a final *e* in the French style is proper but modern usage leans toward the shorter form used here.

The history of turquois is so closely intermeshed with that of the peoples in lands where this gemstone was found, that no one can say with certainty when it was first used. The Aztecs placed the highest esteem on turquois; when chieftains and nobles died, pieces were interred with them; images of gods always showed turquois as part of their regalia, while among the living, maces and other marks of authority were skilfully inlaid with hundreds of bits of turquois in mosaic patterns. The masters of the Aztec civilization led by Montezuma himself, always wore necklaces and ornaments of this gemstone to signify rank and to indicate alliance with the deities of their religion. Perhaps the finest remaining examples of Indian artistry are the ceremonial masks carved from wood or even made of human skulls, covered completely by inlays of turquois, shell, and other materials. Fortunately, splendid examples of this form of art have been preserved and may be viewed in this country in the Museum of the American Indian in New York City. Turquois was one of the materials exacted as tribute from neighboring states by the central Aztec government. Since little occurs in Mexico proper, it is reasonable to assume that the subjugated tribes required to pay this tribute were forced to obtain turquois from Arizona and New Mexico, the nearest places from which substantial supplies could be gotten. The miners of turquois did not undervalue their product by any means for when the Spaniards made their first exploratory trips into the Southwestern part of what is now the United States, they found it esteemed just as highly as it was in Mexico. In fact, this esteem has clung tenaciously up to the present but of course is modified somewhat by the more plentiful supply of what once used to be a scarce commodity. Up until recently, each Navajo had to have a piece of turquois in his immediate possession in the belief that it brought him closer to his gods and warded off enemies or prevented harm in general. Since the God of Gambling, Noholipi, owed his remarkable luck to a piece of turquois, what could be more sensible than to have one also when playing cards? Fending off evil spirits from a house was accomplished by setting a piece in the door lintel; thanks for past crops and assurance of equally good ones in the future were brought about by mixing a bit of powdered turquois in corn meal, in fact, there was hardly any phase of Indian life in which turquois did not enter to some degree. Among the Yaquis, Navajos, and Pueblos, turquois was considered money, possibly because every piece represented a certain amount of mining labor by some individual and thus was in effect a wage. Not too many years ago before turquois became as common as it is now, each Indian customarily "banked" extra money in turquois ornaments or jewelry, and when times were hard, he could take part of his hoard to the trading post in exchange for the necessities of life. It was in those days that a fair trade for a horse could be nothing more than a string of fine turquois pieces! Indians of the Southwest still use this "pawn" system to obtain funds in emergencies.

Today, turquois is always thought of in connection with silver in the land of the Navajo but it has not always been thus. One authority states that before 1880 no silver whatsoever was employed until some white man persuaded a Navajo craftsman to work up silver-turquois jewelry made from coins. From this inauspicious beginning sprang up the present lively industry in which turquois plays so prominent a part. Modern Indian silverwork by the more skilled craftsmen is extremely beautiful both in respect to design and execution. In addition to turquois, pieces of abalone shell, jet and other materials are used in inlay work but the greatest reliance is still placed upon the effect of bright sky-blue bits of polished turquois set off by the gleam of plain silver. Figure 60 shows several items of Indian jewelry using silver set with turquois. Compared to the sophistication of modern jewelry in the European tradition, Indian work is certainly crude but the very traces of

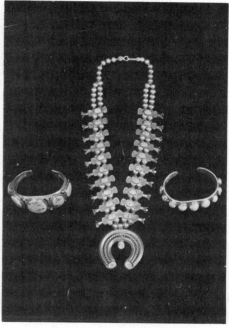

FIGURE 60. Several examples of Navajo turquois and silver. The necklace on the left consists of four strands of crudely and partly polished nuggets terminated by loops of polished turquois cylinders and also several of freshwater pearl shell and coral. The spacers between nuggets are also pearl shell. The jewelry on the right shows a beautiful necklace of separate links fashioned in modified "squash blossom" pattern which is terminated by a horseshoe pendant. The bracelets are heavy gauge silver set crudely but effectively with large turquois cabachons. Courtesy Mrs. T. R. Cooley.

barbarism typified in native motifs, and the boldness and directness of design add much to its attractiveness. Certain tribes specialize in certain types of work and it is said that a connoisseur of Indian jewelry can tell at a glance where a piece was made if not the name of the craftsman who made it. For example, the Navajos prefer simple massive silver pieces in which broad areas of the precious metal are exposed and only a few large stones employed to complement the design; their specialty is metal work and not lapidary work. On the other hand, the Zunis revel in the use of many small bits of polished turquois set in geometrical patterns and used in such profusion that the silver is almost hidden from view. If a piece of silver is seen in which as many as 30 to 100 stones of perhaps the size of a match head or pea are employed, the chances are that the work is Zuni. The latter tribe and the Navajo divide jewelry work among themselves in order to share their talents. This is well exemplified in the "channel" work which is so popular now. In this style, the Navajos cast or fabricate silver pieces in which many recesses are left while the Zunis cut turquois, abalone shell, jet, and coral gems to fit these recesses, later flatting and polishing the top. The final result looks like mosaic work or jewelry finished in the technique known as champlevé. The Hopi are relative late-comers in Indian silver work and have made rapid strides in the craft only since 1946. Their work is characterized by the sparing use of turquois "pointing up" designs which rely for their effect mainly upon the silverwork itself. In addition to the substantial amounts of turquois consumed in Indian jewelry, large quantities are funneled into established trade channels or sold to amateur gem cutters. Poor grades of material, too porous or earthy for ordinary methods of lapidary work, are now being impregnated with paraffin, or still more lately, with colorless plastics driven into the pores under high pressure and then "cured."

Chemically, turquois $(CuAl_6(PO_4)_4(OH)_8 \cdot 4H_2O)$ is a hydrated basic phosphate of copper and aluminum in which some iron substitutes for aluminum. Theoretically this substitution could continue by degrees until no aluminum remains and the opposite end member of the series, *chalcosiderite*, $(CuFe_6(PO_4)_4(OH)_8 \cdot 4H_2O)$ is formed. In nature, however, specimens corresponding only to the ends of the series have been found, i.e., turquois with *some* iron or chalcosiderite with *some* aluminum. In addition, it has been found that sometimes iron also substitutes for part of the copper as in material from Los Cerillos, New Mexico and from Columbus, Nevada. In 1953 a new mineral, *faustite* $(ZnAl_6(PO_4)_4(OH)_8 \cdot 5H_2O)$, was described from a locality in Nevada in which it appeared that zinc has substituted for copper and thus suggests that an entirely new series between turquois and faustite could exist based upon this exchange of elements.

For practical purposes chalcosiderite can be eliminated from further discussion since it appears only in small transparent green crystals not at all like turquois in its usual massive form and far more rare in any case. However, faustite found at the Nevada locality occurs as apple-green vein fillings, or as nuggets or nodules enclosed in montmorillonite clays and alarmingly like turquois in all important respects except the obvious one of color; further comparison of properties will be made below. In any case, analysts of this new mineral point out the possibility that some "odd colored" turquoises may actually be faustites. Both minerals are of secondary origin forming near the surface through the action of infiltrating water upon aluminous igneous or sedimentary rocks and obtaining copper or zinc from metalliferous deposits in which these elements are present. This mode of formation results in both minerals depositing as fillings in cracks and fissures, or producing stalactitic or concretionary aggregates of cryptocrystalline structure. Frequently concretions occur as rounded nodules or "nuggets" which are kidney-shaped on the outside. From these are ordinarily obtained the most compact and hence the best polishing material although very large nodules tend to be earthy and porous. Leaving faustite for the moment since so little is known about it, turquois occurs mainly in altered trachytes and rhyolites although much has come from seams and veinlets in altered porphyry, monzonite, and granite. It is found almost wholly in arid regions, very little being recovered from any locality in a wet climate. Common associates are limonite, kaolin, sericite, quartz, and chalcedony. Faustite and turquois fill seams and fissures solidly and must be painstakingly cobbed by hand from enclosing rock but at other times, both occur as nodules embedded in kaolin or sericite from which they may be easily separated. Several modes of turquois formation are shown in Figure 61. All turquois (and faustite) is porous to some degree but the most compact types, usually of better color, are far more

FIGURE 61. Turquois from the Western United States. On the right are a number of thin polished slabs removed from a single nodule showing the change from mottled to solid patterns as the interior of the nodule is reached. The matrix specimens show seam turquois imbedded in rust-stained quartz and feldspar rock. Courtesy Smithsonian Institution.

desirable because they take a superior polish, are harder, and are less subject to discoloration due to absorption of oils or greases.

Turquois (and presumably faustite) crystallizes in the Triclinic System but crystals as such are extremely rare, the only known locality in North America being in Virginia where minute individuals have been found. Massive turquois varies from 5 to 6 in hardness, faustite is about 5½. Variations occur according to compactness, the better grades being considerably harder. It is relatively tough as may be expected from its cryptocrystalline structure but sometimes is brittle in dense material. Fracture surfaces vary from irregular to subconchoidal with a dull earthy luster in very porous material to a waxy luster in good grades. The specific gravity of massive types varies again with compactness and may be as low as 2.6 or as high as 2.8; faustite is 2.92. Refractive indices are: $\alpha = 1.61$, $\beta = 1.62$, $\gamma = 1.65$; birefringence 0.04; positive, biaxial. Faustite has had only a general index determined, i.e., $n = 1.613$. Upon a refractometer, turquois also gives only a hazy index reading in the neighborhood of 1.62 but even this is difficult to see unless perfectly polished compact material is used. The best blue color is probably seen only in material which approaches ideal composition, that is, free of iron, and at the same time is unusually compact in structure. As more iron appears the color tends to assume greenish tints while added porosity results in paling of whatever basic hue is present. Faustite is stated to be more yellow-green than the greenest turquois, the color of specimens collected so far being apple-green. All shades of color may be present in one specimen of turquois but by and large, the material from one locality is apt to be fairly uniform. Nodular masses often exhibit *spiderweb* markings which consist of vein matter or limonite-stained quartz or clay filling the spaces between the smaller nodules which make up the whole. Sometimes turquois becomes brecciated and such material then provides very attractive gems since the blue of the turquois appears as small angular patches, like a mosaic, outlined in dark brown. Combinations of turquois with matrix rock are called *turquois matrix*.

Turquois gems, like pearl and opal gems, demand some care from their owners if they are to remain unharmed. Their softness is obviously good reason for protecting them from hard knocks or rubbing against other gemstones in the jewel box. Far more serious than mere mechanical abrasion however, is the insidious damage brought about by chemical attack from perfume, oils, perspiration, soap lather, and many other substances which are found in modern households. All of these will cause discoloration in time and may eventually result in replacement of the prized blue color by some dingy grayish or brownish shade of green. Improvement of color in freshly-mined stones is a common practice and perhaps has some merit if suitable additives are used, however, the difficulties in the past have stemmed from the indiscriminate use of oils and greases which slowly but surely react to cause disagreeable discoloration. The impregnation of earthy or porous types with melted paraffin has become a common practice today especially in the treatment of turquois from the Globe-Miami district of Arizona and certain exceptionally porous types from Nevada. The first step is to cut and polish the gems. These are then immersed in paraffin which has been melted in a double boiler and maintained at just below the boiling point. Stones are permitted to soak for one to two hours, then removed from the paraffin bath and the excess wax wiped off. When cool, they are buffed by hand between folds of flannel cloth. Those who practice this form of adulteration claim that paraffin is very stable and causes no discoloration with age, however, since paraffin is a petroleum derivative it cannot help but absorb various organic compounds which may themselves cause impairment of hue. In favor of the process, it may be said that colors are very much heightened and much material otherwise unsuitable for lapidary work is salvaged and sold for prices which permit wider use in inexpensive jewelry.

LOCALITIES

New Jersey. In 1904 turquois was found at the bottom of an 1100 foot incline in the Bridgewater Mine of the American Copper Company on First Watchung Mountain, 3 miles north of Somerville, Somerset County. Pieces as large as silver dollars and several times as thick were taken from veinlets and seams; the quality was said to be good.

Virginia. A small incline in a copper prospect near Lynch Station, Campbell County, provided the first and only crystallized turquois in North America (and in the world!). As the story goes, the original miner had noticed bright blue stains in a quartz vein which spelled "copper" and proceeded to mine with the expectation of striking a lode of this metal. Testing soon showed the blue mineral not to be ordinary copper ore and all further attempts at mining were given up. As it turned out, the mineral was turquois which formed velvety masses of minute sparkling crystals along seams and cracks in quartz; as mineral specimens these were worth far more than any copper ore in existence. Readers may experience some mental anguish in knowing that at least a bushel of the richest "ore" was burned and ruined in smelting attempts.

Alabama. Fine blue turquois in small amounts has been found on the old Hobbs property close to the north line of Sec. 3, T20S, R7S, and a little south of Pleasant Grove Church in Jefferson County. Another occurrence is in a railroad cut about 2½ miles due north of Pleasant Grove Church near Erin, Clay County, where it forms thin light green to yellow-green veins in schists of Carboniferous age. A small amount has also been found in the neighborhood of old copper mines near Idaho where some mining was done but apparently turquois was not found in profitable quantities.

Texas. Minor amounts of turquois have been mined from four places in the Sierra Blanca Mountains about 8 miles northwest of Sierra Blanca in Hudspeth County. In 1884 turquois was reported from north of El Paso. The Texas Turquois Company of El Paso mined at a locality about 5 miles west of Van Horn in Culberson County. Old workings of modest size, are located upon the smaller hills on the northeastern side of the Carrizozo Mountains about 1 mile north of the Texas & Pacific Railroad. The enclosing rocks are Algonkian in age and appear to be fine-grained rhyolite or rhyolite porphyry which has been broken and fractured. Turquois along with limonite appears as fissure and vein fillings. Colors range from greenish to pure blue while the quality appears equal to standard turquois from other states. About one mile south, turquois has been found in a small dike of altered porphyry intruded into black siliceous slate in a prospect at the Maltby silver-copper mine.

Colorado. The oldest and deepest turquois mine in the state is the King Mine located along the sides of a small mesa called Pinon Mountain, 1½ miles west of the Rio Grande River in Conejos County, and 10 miles east of Manassa. The mine is often identified with the town of Lajara which is 13 miles west-northwest. The deposits on Pinon Mountain were known long before the white man appeared as evidenced by numerous stone hammers, deerhorns used for picks, etc., which were left behind by prehistoric Indian miners in the slumped pits. The mine was rediscovered in 1890 but active work did not commence until 1900 when the Colorado Turquois Mining Company acquired the property. In 1909 the mine was leased to several individuals who set up a lapidary shop in Colorado Springs to handle the output. Since that time it has been in almost continuous operation.

The main workings consist of an opencut measuring 330 to 180 feet across and 65 feet deep. Nearby are the Nellie Bly, Last Chance, Lajara, Sunset, Arkansas, and Mexico claims which exploit a common network of turquois veins. The basic rock of the hill is altered trachyte and rhyolite capped by a ledge of brownish or grayish chert about 20 feet thick. Turquois forms paperthin to ¼ inch thick veinlets but in places where veins swell, nuggets occur encased in kaolin, sericite, and limonite-stained quartz. The finest material ranges from pale blue to sky blue and is very hard, compact, and uniform, however, excellent matrix material and nuggets of spiderweb pattern are also found. The largest recent example of a spiderweb nugget was unearthed in 1941 and weighed 10¾ pounds before trimming and 8¾ pounds afterwards. It measures 7 inches in length by 3½ inches thick and received an offer of $1,000. This splendid piece is now exhibited in the museum of the Colorado State Bureau of Mines in Denver. The same mineralized streak which produced this nugget yielded a total of 700 pounds of very good turquois. In 1947 the estimated production of the King Mine was stated as 2,000 pounds valued at about $30,000.

In Saguache County, a highly important deposit mined actively in recent years is located 8 miles northwest by road of the town of Villa Grove. The Hall Mine, as it is called, is at an altitude of 10,000 feet upon the southwest slope of Turquois Hill. Turquois was first recognized here in 1893 although copper mining had been carried on in the vicinity for some years previously. In 1903, nuggets found on the surface near the copper mines led to active exploration but formal work did not commence until about 1936. More recently the use of bulldozers has expedited mining and in 1956, an estimated annual production of $33,000 was achieved. At the mine, turquois occurs in veins and nodules in an altered felsite porphyry locally penetrated by quartz latites. All gradations of solidity occur from copper-stained kaolin to earthy and porous material to topnotch hard blue material. A curious feature is the encasement of turquois in concentric shells of kaolin which can be peeled off like onion layers, each shell showing sharp boundaries of color. In this deposit, colors range from greenish-gray through yellowish-green to all shades of blue. Fine sky blue predominates, tending to be found in nodules of uniform texture in which a minimum of spiderweb veining is noted. Turquois from this mine in its finest grade is the best from any Colorado locality.

In Lake County, about 7 miles northwest of Leadville, some good material has been produced from the Turquois Chief and Poor Boy mines. From 1935 to 1937, about 1,000 pounds were produced. The country rock is an altered and highly mineralized granite which has been worked locally for various metals as at the old Iron Mask Mine, adjacent to the turquois claims.

In Mineral County, some turquois has been found as gravel in West Willow Creek between the Commodore and Amethyst Mines in the Creede district but as yet its source is unknown. Similarly, turquois has been found on the surface at various points near Cripple Creek in Teller County.

New Mexico. Of all Western States, New Mexico is credited with having produced the most turquois, one authority even going so far as to state that its estimated total production up to 1915 exceeded $5,000,000, however, it is certain that Nevada, Colorado, and Arizona, each exceed it now in terms of annual production. The principal districts in which turquois is found are the Cerrillos Hills in Santa Fe County, the Burro Mountains and Little Hachita Mountains of Grant County, and the Jarilla Hills of Otero County. Other deposits are known but are far less important. In virtually every district, turquois was discovered by white men prospecting among the evidences of ancient Indian workings. The extent of aboriginal workings is nowhere more pronounced than in the fantastic workings upon Mount Chalchihuitl in the Cerrillos Hills.

In these hills, located about 6 miles north-northeast of Cerrillos and about 20 miles south-southwest of Santa Fe, two principal groups of mines are found, the first, already noted, is Mount Chalchihuitl, the second, a series of workings on Turquois Hill about 3 miles distant. Mount Chalchihuitl is a low eminence in the middle of the Cerrillos Hills, perhaps several hundred feet high, the whole north side of which has been quarried or honeycombed until nothing now remains but a huge pit measuring about 200 feet across and from 35 to 130 feet deep. Below this excavation are spread extensive dumps which one observer estimated as covering 2 ½ acres. This is easily the largest and perhaps also the oldest turquois mine on the continent. Persons who have visited this locality have expressed astonishment and awe that so much earth and rock could have been removed by Indians using only the crudest hand tools and working under truly appalling conditions far under-ground. Considering the vast amount of turquois uncovered in old Indian village sites, it seems plain that it could only have come from some grand scale working such as Mount Chalchihuitl. It also seems clear that this mine must be very old if the age of artifacts found in Indian graves is any criterion, authorities reckoning that mining may have commenced as early as 1,000 years ago. At a late Basket Maker Indian village site in Chaco Canyon, for example, pendants of turquois have been found along with other artifacts dating back to 670 A.D. In 950 to 1150 A.D., turquois mining must have been in full swing for in the Pueblo Bonito of Chaco Canyon, a community of the era, the Hyde Expedition collected over 50,000 turquois objects. A small burial room yielded the amazing total of 24,932 beads, pendants, and other pieces of turquois, while one skeleton had buried with it 5,891 objects alone!

Upon Turquois Hill, two important mines, the Castilian and the Tiffany, were worked extensively during the late 1880's as well as additional claims in the immediate neighborhood. All of these properties were acquired by the American Turquois Company of New York City and worked up to about 1910 with good results, especially the Tiffany. At about the same time, further prospecting revealed other deposits outside the area controlled by this company as well as near Mount Chalchihuitl. In 1950 a little turquois was reported from the Tiffany Mine but for all practical purposes, the district is now considered dormant.

In the Cerrillos District, country rock consists principally of monzonite porphyry exposed by the erosion of overlying Cretaceous sediments. Tur-quois appears along seams and cracks in the rock and also in the form of kaolin-enclosed nodules. Color varies from green to greenish-blue and to fine sky-blue, some of the best material being equal to the Persian. Much of the turquois is spiderweb pattern, criss-crossed by thin veinlets of limonite which is derived from the alteration of pyrite. The highest quality material from the Tiffany Mine was produced in such abundance that it was believed to be largely instrumental in replacing Persian turquois on the American market. The total valuation of material from this mine alone was estimated at over $2,000,000. The American Museum has in its collections the Bernheimer turquois nugget from Cerrillos measuring 3 by 4 inches in size; also several carved hearts weighing 34.17 and 52.37 carats respectively.

The Burro Mountains of Grant County contain several deposits which once produced considerable fine turquois but are now largely exhausted and currently inactive. Evidences of prehistoric Indian mining were also discovered here but it was not until 1875 that the first locality, the Calliate Claim, was staked by John E. Coleman, locally known as "Turquois John." It is said that this gentleman stumbled upon the ancient workings while in the mountains on a hunting trip.

The principal rock underlying the mines is Precambrian granite intruded by quartz monzonite and quartz monzonite porphyry. Turquois is found both in the granite and in porphyries traversing granite. Fractures are widespread forming zones along which turquois mineralization has occurred. The most important mine in the district, the Azure, exploits such a zone which in this instance is some 40 to 60 feet wide, consisting of badly shattered granite partially altered into kaolin and sericite. Turquois occurs from paperthin veinlets to seams at least 1½ inches thick but usually from ⅛ inch to ⅜ inch thick. Nuggets are found in thicker seams embedded in kaolin and sericite. Nodules yield the finest gem material, especially those removed from mineralized zones which have undergone severest alteration. Some nodules are penetrated by quartz crystals or associated with grayish to olive-green masses of halloysite. The finest material came from the "Elizabeth Pocket," a soft section of the mineralized zone which extended 150 feet along the vein system and measured about 40 feet wide and 50 feet deep.

The Azure Mine is located 10 miles southwest of Silver City and 1½ miles north of the mining camp of Tyrone (Leopold). It was opened in 1891 by the Azure Mining Company of New York City and under intensive mining produced between $2,000,000 and $4,000,000 of turquois up to about 1914. The Elizabeth Pocket was entered in 1893 and accounted for much of the value, producing the largest quantity of turquois ever known from a single pocket. One pure nugget weighed 1500 carats. The best material from this mine was said to be the equal of any Persian material, the pride of the company in its product led them to inscribe a small circle upon the base of each cut stone as a distinctive trademark to let every one know that the turquois had come from the famous Azure Mine. The output included pure turquois, turquois matrix, and some material mottled in several shades of blue. Odd colors such as reddish-brown, chocolate brown, and even violet were found in addition to bluish-green, light and dark green, and paler blue shades. The deposit was worked opencut for 600 feet along the mineralized zones, reaching depths of 60 feet and widths of from 100 to 200 feet. Lower parts of the ore body were reached by tunneling. About 150 yards east of this mine a new deposit was opened in 1908 along a fracture zone in granite, however, this was soon exhausted after a brief period of mining.

The Parker Mine is located ½ mile southeast of the Azure Mine and was worked by the American Gem & Turquois Company by means of tunnels and opencuts. Another deposit was also worked some 200 yards to the northwest. In these deposits the turquois is emplaced along the contact between quartz monzonite porphyry and altered granite. A number of prospects and smaller mines were worked in the immediate vicinity of those discussed above, as for example: a locality ½ mile south of the Azure Mine on the west side of St. Louis Canyon where some good material was found; a few miles southwest of Leopold along the road leading to Silver City; at two places near the old Burro Chief Copper Mine about ¾ mile south-southeast of the Azure where the turquois was greenish in color and originally mistaken for an ore of copper and not at all good in quality; a few miles south of the Big Burro Mountains in the Cow Spring District where some good seam turquois was found; on the south side of the Burro Mountains in the White Signal District at several places; also at a depth of 410 feet in the Copper King Mine.

In the Hachita District of Grant County, turquois deposits are found in the Little Hachita Mountains about 6 miles west of Hachita at elevations ranging from 5,000 to 5,400 feet. Among a series of small knobs and ridges is one which is prominent and is called Turquois Mountain; like other New Mexican localities, deposits on its flanks had been extensively worked by prehistoric Indians. The first modern development took place sometime between 1885 and 1888 when the lure of gold brought prospectors here. In 1892 W. E. Hidden of North Carolina emerald and spodumene (hiddenite) fame, did a little work but was disappointed in the lack of good material. In 1908, the first intensive work began and in the next few years mining was in full swing. In this region are found sandstones, slates, and limestones, associated with rhyolite, trachyte, and andesite, the turquois occurring in altered portions of the trachyte and andesite. The old Robinson and Porterfield mines include the Azure, Cameo, Galilee, and Aztec Claims. The Azure claim consists of two sets of workings on Turquois Mountain, one at the northeast end and the other a short distance to the southwest. The first deposit produced turquois in seams up to ½ inch thick locally emplaced along the contact of an altered trachyte and monzonite porphyry especially along zones where it was much fractured and iron stained. Color ranges from dark sky-blue to greenish blue and pale blue; pale material is quite soft. The principal yield was turquois matrix. The second workings produced some hard turquois of fine blue color. The Cameo Claim is about one mile west-northwest of the northeast end of

Turquois Mountain and exploits a vertical veinlet of fine blue turquois emplaced in altered trachyte. The Galilee Claim is 3/5 mile southwest of Turquois Mountain and is an opencut situated upon two main veinlets of turquois filling iron-stained fracture zones in the rock. The Aztec Claim lies 1½ miles south-southwest of Turquois Mountain and has been worked by means of a tunnel following turquois seams embedded in joints. Some nuggets, as well as seam material, have been taken from this deposit.

Also in the Hachita District may be mentioned the American Turquois Company Mine located a few hundred yards west of the Cameo Claim and worked by shaft and opencut along a deposit consisting of good blue turquois veinlets in iron-stained altered trachyte; the M. M. Crocker Claims, two in number, one located on the southwest end of Turquois Mountain and the other on a small knob ½ mile west-southwest of the mountain; the R. S. Chamberlain Mine on the east side of the northeast end of Turquois Mountain exploiting an extensive prehistoric Indian working along the contact between trachyte and monzonite; also several minor occurrences as follows: ⅓ mile south of Turquois Mountain; and on the Le Feve Claim slightly over ½ mile south-southwest of the mountain.

In the Jarilla District of Otero County, turquois was first discovered by W. E. Hidden in 1892 who came upon extensive ancient Indian workings. The Jarillas are a low range of hills rising out of a sandy desert in the western part of the county, 50 miles north-northeast of El Paso, Texas. In 1898, some years after work had been carried on in this district, good material was mined from the De Meules property, but little was produced from the district as a whole although a number of claims were eventually located. Turquois was found in seams and crevices in trachyte associated with kaolin, and limonite near the surface and with pyrite, chalcopyrite, gypsum, jarosite, and kaolin at depth. Turquois from this locality is said to fade after exposure, perhaps due to the evaporation of water.

Arizona. This state has never been a heavy producer and in recent years has fallen far behind in total annual production. In 1954 it is estimated that only $13,000 worth of turquois came from all districts. Most Arizona turquois now comes from the extensive porphyry-copper mines in the Globe-Miami District of Gila County where it occurs as veins in the ore bodies. The Castle Dome Mine situated on the south slope of Porphyry Mountain 5 miles west of Miami, was opened in 1943 and now produces about 4,000,000 pounds of copper every month. Turquois is fairly abundant throughout the leached capping over the orebody and also in the ore itself which in this case is primarily chalcocite. Veinlets of turquois occur up to ½ inch thick forming plates several inches across, while nodules or nuggets up to ½ inch thick occur in places associated with clay minerals and sericite. All qualities occur from soft and earthy material found along the walls of open fractures, to good hard blue, the best being nugget and seam material. The color in soft types ranges from almost white to pale blue, while compact material is greenish-blue to pale blue. At one time the company collected the turquois and sold it for gem material but in recent years this practice has been abandoned; miners are now given the privilege of collecting turquois during off-duty hours and selling it to augment their incomes.

In the Sleeping Beauty Mine in the same district, much turquois was found during initial stripping operations to expose the ore body and one authority estimates that several hundred pounds were obtained in this fashion. The quality is more earthy and porous than that from the Castle Dome Mine but some good material is found from time to time. Locally this turquois is sometimes treated with paraffin to improve its color.

In Cochise County, considerable turquois has been won from a deposit on the west flank and summit of Turquois Ridge, also known as Turquois Hill or Turquois Mountain, at an elevation of 5,400 feet, ¾ mile northwest of Courtland. The latter community is about 15 miles northeast of Tombstone. There are four principal groups of workings in which numerous cuts and over 1500 feet of tunnels have been driven. Turquois occurs here as veins and nuggets embedded in sericite and kaolin associated with limonite in Cambrian quartzite and profoundly altered granite. This deposit was discovered in 1890 when prehistoric diggings were investigated; since then it has been worked more or less continuously up to the present. In the late 1920's a wide and rich stringer of turquois was found which yielded almost 80 pounds of material valued at $8,000 to $9,000; one solid mass weighed 3 pounds alone.

In Mohave County, several important deposits lie along the hills and peaks on the southwestern side of the Cerbrat Range to the east and south of Mineral Park. This district is about 15 miles northwest of Kingman and several miles east of Highway 93/466. The initial discovery was made prior to 1883 in which year some good material appeared upon the market. In 1886 several claims were staked but production did not begin in earnest until 1898 when promising leads were followed. In recent years, the Southwest Gem & Jewelry Company mined 200 pounds (1947-1948) and 75-100 pounds (1949) from its Cerbrat Ranch property. The Mineral Park region consists principally of Precambrian gneisses and schists intruded by granites and granite or quartz porphyries. Turquois forms seams and veins in the porphyry and streaks and patches in quartz veins as well as nodules and nuggets embedded in kaolin minerals in the larger veins. All gradations from hard gem material to porous material and even copper-stained kaolin are found. The best is rich blue, hard and compact, and takes a fine polish. Matrix stones are sometimes very good, forming pleasing contrasts between the blue turquois and the limonite-stained material which forms the webs of contrasting color. Prior to 1899 blocks of blue-veined rock were shipped to New York for working into pedestals, mantels, and other ornamental objects.

The principal deposits of the Mineral Park District are located as follows: upon Ithaca Peak, 1 mile east of Mineral Park; Aztec Mountain, 1 mile south of Ithaca Peak; and at the end of a range of hills ⅓ mile south-southwest of Mineral Park; also on a mountain 4/5 mile south-southeast of Mineral Park. The Ithaca Peak locality is shown in Figure 62.

FIGURE 62. The Monte Cristo Claim of the Aztec Turquois Company on the southeast end of Ithaca Peak in the Mineral Park region of Arizona. Photograph taken about 1914. Courtesy U.S. Geological Survey.

Nevada. For some years, this state has led all others in the production of turquois, one authority recently counting 38 mines in this state alone! In 1938 total production reached 8,000 pounds valued from $.50 to $40 per pound with an average value of $3 per pound. In 1940, the Fox Turquois Mine near Cortez in Lander County, as the principal contributor, placed upon the market 7,928 pounds of good material which sold for $11,405, representing the major share of the state total for that year which amounted to about $20,000. In 1941, $28,000 was produced with the Smith (Cortez) Mine contributing the major portion. This mine was again first in 1942 when 13,033 pounds valued at $32,000 were marketed. Other sections produced another $4,000 for a statewide total of $36,000. In 1945, the Pedro Claim produced 3,601 pounds of cobbed mine-run material. In 1946, the Nevada Turquois Company of Mina reported $20,000 worth from its properties while the Pedro Claim near Battle Mountain produced nearly as much. In summary, from 1940 to 1946 inclusive, a total of $124,000 worth of turquois was mined from the state. After 1946 production slumped badly but in the 1950's resumed at a high tempo which continues to date.

The earliest significant production came from a series of mines in the region encompassing the eastern part of Esmeralda County and the adjoining western part of Nye County. The Royal Blue, a famous mine enjoying even today a fine reputation for excellent material, is located in Nye County about 12 miles north-northwest of Millers very close to the boundary of Esmeralda County. The turquois deposits lie upon the eastern scarp of a plateau at 5,400 feet elevation and have been worked by tunnels, shafts, and an open-cut. Turquois occurs in fracture zones in partly altered trachyte and porphyry as seams and veins up to 1 inch in thickness. In thicker places, nodules are also found but seldom exceed 1 inch in diameter. The best material is generally obtained from hard limonite-stained rock while soft and pale-colored material of considerable porosity is obtained from trachyte. The color ranges from pale to dark blue with much being free of undesirable greenish tinges. The best is said to equal any turquois found in America. Fine matrix specimens also occur, showing rich mottling of turquois set off by dark brown hairline veinlets of limonite-impregnated material.

The old Oscar Wehrend Prospect is located ⅓ mile north of the Royal Blue Mine and produces turquois seam material and nodules from kaolinized trachyte. The W. Petry Mine is on top of a small hill 10½ miles northwest of Millers among the eastern foothills of the Monte Cristo Range. The underlying rock is fine-grained rhyolite, altered and kaolinized, and penetrated by paperthin to ½ inch thick seams of turquois following numerous cracks in the rock. The best material is fairly dark blue but pale blue is common; good matrix material is also present.

The Myers and Bona Mine is 13 miles west-northwest of Millers in Esmeralda County and is located on the northeast face of a small steep hill upon the western slope of the Monte Cristo Range. The enclosing rock is altered quartz porphyry in which bands of black slate are interlaminated, the turquois occurring along the contact between the two rock types. Nodules from ¼ inch to 2 inches in diameter as well as seam material up to ½ inch thick have been found, the former occurring scattered through the rock or in enlarged places in veins. The best turquois is hard and fine blue, probably as good as any material from other places in the United States.

The Montezuma Mine is located on the north side of a small hill 12 miles northeast of Redlich or about 20 miles by road east of Sodaville, and is in the eastern part of Esmeralda County. Several outcrops occur on the hill in addition to the principal workings mentioned above. Turquois is found as seams, veins, and nodules in altered trachyte, the nodules varying from less than an inch to more than an inch in diameter. Colors range from fine blue to dark greenish-blue to pale blue. The best turquois resembles Royal Blue Mine material but the largest production in the past has been low-grade.

The Moqui-Aztec or S. Simmons Mine is about 1 mile southwest of the Montezuma on the south side of a ridge lying at an elevation of 6,250 feet.

Prior to 1908 the mine was worked by means of tunnels and opencuts; considerable pale blue material being obtained as well as some fine spiderweb. Country rock is fine-grained kaolinized quartz-porphyry in which the turquois fills seams or forms nodules in thick seams but some also occurs in massive fractured quartz.

The Smith Black Matrix Mine is located upon one of a small number of hills about 3 miles northeast of Klondike, a railroad station in Esmeralda County lying between Tonopah and Goldfield. Regional rocks are limestones and shales of Cambrian age with dark jaspery-like phases in which occur superthin to ¾ inch thick seams of turquois. In some places the jaspery rock has been shattered and then the turquois is found cementing the brecciated fragments together, sometimes in areas as much as two inches in width. Many larger pieces of turquois contain angular fragments of the black jasperoid material. Limonite stains the rock extensively, particularly near the turquois. The unusual occurrence of turquois in black matrix provides unique and beautiful gems which are not matched from other localities. Some gems are cut to show blue to green turquois streaks in black rock while other pieces are mainly turquois but contain fragments of the host rock in pleasing patterns strongly contrasting in color.

Turquois has been found in two places in the Columbus District upon the old variscite claims of the Los Angeles Gem Company, about 2 miles northwest of Columbus. At one locality it appears in dark gray cherty rhyolite and at the other, in dark jasperoid or silicified limestone. The latter mode of occurrence provides matrix gems similar to those coming from the Smith Black Matrix Mine.

In 1910, turquois was found on the Carr-Lovejoy variscite claims 9 miles north-northeast of Blair Junction in Esmeralda County. Another variscite property, the Rick & Botts Claims 4 miles northeast of Coaldale, in the foothills of the Monte Cristo Range of Esmeralda County, yielded turquois from veinlets and seams in altered quartz porphyry (see Figure 66). The seams are generally thin but some nuggets up to 1 inch in diameter have been found. The Sigmund Claim, located 3½ miles south of Redlich, has produced seam turquois and nuggets of fine blue color. Turquois of poor quality has been found upon the Dunwoody variscite claims 8 miles southwest of Sodaville, Esmeralda County. Seams and veins up to ¾ inch thick are found in fracture zones in altered porphyry and rhyolite.

Other minor occurrences in this region are: very beautiful pure dark blue turquois and turquois matrix at a locality at Belmont in Nye County; in 1898 turquois occurring as veins and nodules in trachyte with limonite was discovered by G. Simmons at an ancient "village site" at a place 18 miles east of Vanderbilt, California; in 1901 turquois was discovered on Cactus Mountain, 50 miles east of Butler in Nye County; during 1910 turquois was found at several places near Goldfield during the search for gold; pale green tur-quois was discovered in the Mizpah vein at Goldfield at a level of 600 feet as-sociated with black manganese oxides and kaolinite; in 1957 turquois of un-stated quality was vaguely reported from the region southeast and southwest of Tonopah.

In Clark County near Crescent Peak, deposits of some importance were once worked by J. R. Wood of New York City. The spoil from ancient workings, including various hand tools, led to the discovery of the mine which is located 3 miles east-southeast of Crescent in rough country im-mediately south of Crescent Peak. The locality lies a few miles south of Highway 68 connecting Nipton, California, with Searchlight, Nevada, and is about halfway between. The rock in the turquois-bearing areas is altered porphyry, granitic or monzonitic in composition. A large proportion of the turquois occurs as nuggets in fractured zones in the rock embedded in whitish clay minerals. Nodules are so firmly encased in clay shells that they must be chipped or ground off to determine the quality of the material inside. In general, the quality is good, blue being the predominant color; the texture is also fine and the hardness high. Other turquois workings in the vicinity were opened by Smithson & Phillips about one mile east of the Wood Mine on the east side of the divide extending south from Crescent Peak. Another prospect is located 1 mile south of Crescent near the head of a small valley. At this point the country rock is dark granular quartz monzonite or granite cut by fine-grained rhyolite.

In Lyon County, turquois has been produced from two workings near Yerington. The first mine is about 8 miles west-northwest of Yerington on the western slope of a ridge west of the Walker River and has been worked by shaft and opencut. The country rock is altered monzonite in which tur-quois fills seams and veins or forms nodules. Color ranges from dark blue through greenish-blue to green; the best grade being slightly translucent and of good general quality. The second locality is about 1½ miles north-northwest of Yerington near a copper vein in the low hills of the Walker River Valley. Turquois as seams and nodules in altered granitic porphyry and trachyte has been found here at several points within one hundred yards of each other.

In Lincoln County, light blue turquois was reported in 1897 from the foot of Sugar Loaf Peak in a dike cutting mica schist whose outcrop showed evidence of prehistoric work. In Mineral County, turquois was discovered in 1915 near Rand, about 18 miles south of Rawhide. In the Candelaria District of this county, the Reik Mine has produced important quantities of good material.

In 1957, Lander County came to the forefront in the news when it was announced that an enormous nugget of turquois weighing 152 pounds had been mined near Battle Mountain in July, 1954. Subsequently this astonishing mass of turquois was eclipsed by a phenomenal nugget of 178 pounds (42,720 carats) discovered on December 10, 1956 in the floor of a drift in the Number 8 Mine located in the extreme northeastern corner of Lander County in the Lynn District, about 30 miles northeast of the community of Battle Mountain, and about 7 to 8 miles south of Boulder Mountain. This property is only a mile or so from the border of Elko County. Originally the nugget weighed considerably more than 200 pounds but its size proved too great to permit it to pass through any of the underground openings available, accordingly the outside was carefully cobbed to separate waste material and to remove accessory masses of turquois loosely attached to the central nugget. It was reduced in weight to its present figure after sandblasting to clean off the brownish clay in which all nuggets are embedded in this mine. This tremendous mass is virtually pure turquois of spiderweb pattern, compact in texture and essentially solid. The largest found anywhere in the world, this nugget was mined by John F. Sabin and W. L. Edger, owners and operators of the Number 8 Mine.

The Number 8 Mine (there are 8 claims within the immediate vicinity) is located atop a low grade copper deposit which was mined briefly for copper some years ago but abandoned after a few carloads of ore had been shipped. Country rock is typical porphyry such as is found elsewhere in the West in which many low grade copper deposits occur. Turquois is found in more or less continuous seams of ½ inch thick and perhaps several inches wide extending at times in unbroken sheets for 7 or 8 feet along the vein. In "pockets" or places where veins have thickened, nuggets are found varying from pea-size to walnut-size and of course much larger on occasion. According to Mr. Sabin, the configuration of the enclosing rock can disclose signs of pocketing since it twists or curves as a pocket is approached while ordinarily if the rock is untwisted only seam turquois is met with. Within pockets, nuggets are found enclosed in brownish clay, probably kaolin, which proves extraordinarily tenacious. The simplest method of cleaning has been to tumble nuggets in a cement mixer to wear off this coating and to permit examination of the interior quality, thus assisting in its sale.

A typical sample provided by Mr. Sabin shows considerable variation in color, quality and in pattern, some material being uniform turquois while other types are spiderwebs consisting of fine networks of brownish hairline markings dividing the turquois into spherical, sometimes angular segments. Spiderweb segments vary from 1/16 inch across to as much as 1/4 inch across but in every case are very regular in their geometry and make a pleasing design. Rarely, an exceptionally hard limonitic matrix is found which takes a fine polish along with the turquois, providing exceptionally handsome gems. Other spiderweb pieces show black veinlets and also provide attractive stones when cut and polished. Most of the turquois is rather porous, some pieces sticking decidedly to the tongue when wetted. Much of the No. 8 Mine material is disposed of to large dealers in Mexico, Arizona, and New Mexico who cut and polish it chiefly for the tourist trade. Because of its porosity, it is greatly improved by treatment with pure paraffin and it is understood that most is processed in this fashion after cutting.

In 1914, J. F. Campbell opened a turquois deposit located in the Hot Springs mining district on the east side of Reese River Valley about 35 miles south of Battle Mountain.

The famous Cortez Mine also known as the Smith Mine, located near the old mining camp of Cortez in Lander County was discovered by a Shoshone Indian by the name of Johnny Francis several years prior to 1914. In this year the claim was leased to an individual who took out 500 pounds of turquois of various grades. The property was later acquired by E. C. Smith and McGraw of Pasadena under the name of the Cortez Turquois Company and successfully operated by them for a number of years. In early days of mining, the Cortez yielded a fine nugget weighing about 5 pounds; another large specimen measuring across the fracture face 5 by 2½ inches was broken in blasting. However, the largest nuggets from this mine are not the best, inclining toward earthiness and pale coloration.

Fine turquois is obtained from Copper Basin, about 8 miles south-southwest of Battle Mountain in Lander County, especially from the Blue Gem Turquois Mine. Although other deposits exist in the immediate vicinity this has been the only one to prove productive. The Blue Gem was active in the early 1950's but ceased substantial production in 1954 when some material was culled from the dumps.

Not far from the Cortez area are the Super X Mine and the Badger Mine located in the Indian Creek area south of Tenabo, both produced substantial quantities of excellent material but are currently inactive.

In Eureka County, the Copper King Mine in the Maggie Creek District yields the interesting mineral faustite which has been described as the zinc analogue of turquois. The Maggie Creek District is in the Tuscarora Mountains about 10 miles northwest of Carlin. Faustite occurs as apple-green seams and veinlets about ¼ inch thick cutting through argillaceous cherts and shales. It is always intimately associated with montmorillonite clays and is found enclosed as nuggets in this mineral wherever seams become thicker. The nearest turquois deposit is the Number 8 Mine described previously. Faustite closely resembles turquois in all major respects; it is hard, breaks with a slightly conchoidal to smooth fracture, possesses a smooth feel, and even has comparable physical properties.

California. At one time considerable turquois was obtained from mines in San Bernardino County and in very small quantities elsewhere, but of late, very little turquois of any type is produced from this state. The so-called Manvel District in San Bernardino County occupies a desolate region in the northeastern part of the county at the southern base of the Silurian Hills, and is about 5½ miles by dirt road from Halloran Springs on Highway 91/466. The turquois mines are all within a range of hills called the Turquois Mountains and consist of a series of claims once owned by the Toltec Gem Mining Company and the Himalaya Mining Company both of New York. The Toltec Gem Mining Company's claims were subdivided into three groups known as East Camp, Middle Camp, and West Camp, all within a few miles of each other. Near the West Camp are the claims of the Himalaya Mining Company located at the head of Riggs Wash or about 12 miles east-northeast of Silver Lake. A photograph of the Himalaya mine appears in Figure 63. The bedrock near the turquois mines consist of

FIGURE 63. The long-abandoned workings of the Himalaya Mining Company's turquois claim located 12 miles north 60° east of Silver Lake in San Bernardino County, California. The wanderings of turquois seams have been followed by a series of "gopher holes." Courtesy U.S. Geological Survey.

coarse-grained porphyry granites and monzonite porphyries occurring in the form of dikes, and much decomposed along zones of turquois mineralization. Gem material occurs in the form of veins and nodules sometimes emplaced in light-colored matrix but at other times in rock which is heavily stained with limonite. The nuggets seldom reached over 1 inch in diameter but occasionally larger specimens were found for one account of the mine mentions a fine quality cabochon weighing 203 carats and measuring 1¼ by 1¾ inches cut from Himalaya material. The best turquois in the Manvel District ranges from pale blue to fairly dark blue; poorer grades are decidedly greenish in cast. In 1920, the yield from these mines was estimated at $20,000.

Further south in San Bernardino County, turquois was obtained in small quantities from the Gove Mine located about 2 miles west of the Cottonwood Siding on the Santa Fe Railroad. Country rock is principally biotite gneiss which has been intruded by a belt of rhyolite or porphyry, the latter severely crushed and altered in part to kaolin. Turquois is found at the contact between this rock and the biotite gneiss in seams and nuggets.

In other places in San Bernardino County, turquois was mined from an unspecified point in the Solo Mining District; from the Goldstone Camp 30 miles north of Barstow where it occurred as thin seams in black matrix; from an indefinite locality near Goffs; from near Barnwell in the New York Mountains; and an apple-green type from near Victor.

In Imperial County, some material of bluish-green color in the form of seams and nodules has been found about 2 miles east of Midway Well on the trail to the True Friend and Silver Mom Mines on the east slope of the Chocolate Mountains.

Baja California Norte. Small veinlets of turquois and quartz traverse shattered dioritic rocks about 2 miles south of El Aguajito, a small ranch and waystop lying between the town of Rosario and the Mission of San Fernando at a point somewhat north of 30° north latitude, or about 185 miles south of Ensenada along the principal road. The most recently operated mine at this deposit is called La Turquesa and has produced a fair quantity of good material from opencuts and underground workings. Not far away are two other outcrops which appear to be identical in mineralization; these are north of the Mission and at about 115° west longitude. In addition to the La Turquesa, the Vincent, Hermosa, and the Preciosa have been operated nearby. The local area appears to be mineralized with copper and perhaps this explains the presence of turquois. At none of these localities does turquois occur in large pieces or in nodular form.

Sonora. A vague report states that two deposits of turquois were found by J. Owen in volcanic rock in the La Barranea copper mining district in 1901.

Zacatecas. In the Santa Rosa District in the Sierra de Santa Rosa, turquois of good quality and color has been found as seams and nodules in the silver-lead mine near Bonanza but for some years had been thrown over the dumps unrecognized. When it was finally identified, a small quantity was mined for gem material from the tunnel known as the Socovan de las Turquesas. In the Mazapil District, good turquois has been mined from the Santa Isabel Mine and the Todos Santos Mine.

VARISCITE

One of the most beautiful of all North American gemstones, variscite is distinctive in that it is found nowhere else in masses large enough to cut. Known for some years from a number of localities in Europe and elsewhere, it suddenly sprang into importance when large deposits were discovered in 1894 near Fairfield, Utah. In the ensuing years, other deposits were found in the same state and also in the neighboring state of Nevada. Since then, at least one hundred tons of nodules and vein sections have been mined from all deposits combined and distributed to mineral collectors and lapidaries. A sliced and polished nodule from Fairfield, Utah, is illustrated in Figure 64.

Upon rare occasion, variscite is found in minute transparent crystals but the greatest quantity occurs in cryptocrystalline masses, either as rounded or oval nodules, or as fillings in seams and openings in enclosing rock. It somewhat resembles turquois in the rough but its bright shades of yellowish-green are distinctive and no confusion should arise between the two. Variscite receives its name from Variscia, the ancient district which is now known as Voigtland in Germany and in which place it was first found. When first discovered in America in commercial quantities, its distributors coined the name *amatrice*, a contraction of American-matrix, in the hope that this would prove a more palatable title to the public who were expected to buy the finished gems. In view of the confusion that is always aroused by such names, this title, fortunately, did not gain popularity, and, along with another similar label: *utahlite*, was soon discarded. Other names given at one time or another are: *lucinite*, after the Lucin, Utah locality, and *chlor-utahlite*.

Variscite is closely related to strengite, another phosphate mineral of similar composition and crystallization, and forms with it a mineral series varying according to the proportion of aluminum or iron in the composition. The end members of this series are: variscite $(Al(PO_4) \cdot 2H_2O)$ and strengite $(Fe(Po_4) \cdot 2H_2O)$.

For all practical purposes, variscite found in gem quality in the several localities in the Western United States, is virtually without iron and thus shows no grading into strengite.

All variscite deposits in the West appear to have formed under the same conditions, that is, by seepage of phosphate-impregnated waters through aluminous rocks to form hydrous aluminum phosphates along seams and crevices in deeper formations. Invariably, variscite and the bewildering variety of other phosphates which have formed from its alteration, are found as fillings in shear zones or places where earth movements have caused underlying rocks to fracture into blocky fragments of varying size. Cracks and fissures radiating outward from such zones are also frequently impregnated.

Note: Figure 64 is in the color section following page 112.

A considerable quantity of cryptocrystalline quartz accompanies the phosphates and is found in the form of chalcedony veinlets or as impregnations in limestones causing their conversion into cherts. Two distinct modes of variscite formation are found, the first being simple filling of crevices and fissures, the second being the formation of oval or spherical nodules, with or without hollow centers.

Variscite is found crystallized only in minute transparent vivid green individuals lining cavities within otherwise solid material. These belong to the Orthorhombic System and consist of small rectangular tablets with simple beveled edges. Because of variation in compactness, the hardness varies from much below the published value of 4.5 to somewhat above. Its cryptocrystalline nature lends some degree of toughness to variscite but it is far from being very durable. When cut, it should not be used in rings but may be quite satisfactory in earrings, brooches, pendants, and beads. Broken surfaces vary from irregular to conchoidal, showing a dull earthy luster in the softer types and somewhat waxy in the most compact. The specific gravity generally falls in the range between 2.2 to 2.5 but considerable variation downward can be expected according to solidity. Crystals show a specific gravity of 2.57 as compared to a representative figure of 2.53 for ordinary massive material from Lucin. Crystals from the latter locality have also furnished the following refractive index readings: $a = 1.563$, $\beta = 1.588$, $\gamma = 1.594$; biaxial, negative.

The color of variscite is generally some light to dark shade of rich yellowish green, but very pale to almost white shades are known, as well as those of purest deep green. Variscite seldom shows large unbroken stretches of pure color since the centers of nodules and seam fillings always tend to be more compact and hence deeper in color, shading off into paler tints near the edges. Frequently, green areas are penetrated by tubular growths of other phosphates which appear as "eyes" when the rough is sliced across and polished. Such specimens are more highly prized than plain material. In large measure, the beauty of variscite is attributable to the number of alteration minerals which have formed at its expense; as Figure 64 shows, much of the attractiveness of this specimen would be lost without the rich yellows, reddish and brownish ochreous tints, olives, grays, and blue-greens of these additional species.

Variscite is treated easily with standard lapidary techniques but its porosity and the contrasting hardness of the several minerals ordinarily met with in any piece of considerable size require some precautions. It cannot be sawn with oil for example, since all oils and greases tend to soak into the pores and discolor it badly. Prolonged polishing of surfaces must be guarded against also, since this merely tends to cut away the softer minerals and leave the harder species standing in relief. In spite of these defects however, there are few minerals in the entire world which can compare in interest and beauty to resplendent polished nodules of variscite or more elaborate objects such as the bowl shown in Figure 65.

Figure 65. A beautifully carved variscite bowl (foreground), measuring about 3½ inches in diameter, from the workshop of George Ashley, Pala, California. The larger bowl, also by Ashley, is made from banded amethyst and chalcedony from the Creede District, Colorado. Courtesy George Ashley.

LOCALITIES

Utah. Three groups of variscite deposits are known in this state, the first being the famous Fairfield locality, discovered in October, 1894; the second, the Lucin deposit, first worked in 1902, and the last, the Amatrice Mine in Tooele County, discovered in 1905.

The deposit near Fairfield, Utah County, also known as the Utahlite Mine is a short distance north of the north fork of the south fork of Clay Canyon about ¾ mile above the road and clay pit, 2.8 miles from Fairfield South, and 5½ miles west of Fairfield. The country rock is black limestone in which variscite and numerous associated rare minerals occur as nodules and concretions in brecciated zones. Nodules are generally oval, somewhat flattened, and embedded in a matrix of quartz and calcite. Although many are regular in form, others may bulge in places, or even consist of several smaller nodules grown together. The greater number of smaller nodules are made up almost entirely of yellow earthy crandallite with some colorless calcite, often surrounding a rough-walled central cavity. Crandallite also envelops solid nodules and is freqently interlayered with grayish mixtures of crandallite and deltaite. In some nodules, small cavities of irregular form are lined with calcite or with white fibrous crusts of dennisonite, lehiite, and other phosphate minerals. A few cavities contain plume-like crystals of dehrnite and lewis-tonite. The attractive "eyes" often seen penetrating variscite are composed of a core of millisite with an outer ring of greenish wardite, followed by an exterior zone of transparent colorless gordonite. All in all, each of these fascinating nodules is an impressive ready-made collection of rare phosphate minerals and, quite aside from intriguing patterns and beautiful colorations, is doubly treasured on this account. The following is a partial list of the minerals so far identified in these nodules: crandallite, deltaite, dehrnite, englishite, gordonite, lehiite, lewistonite, millisite, montgomeryite, overite, sterrettite, and wardite. It is currently held that most of these phosphates are alteration products resulting from the reaction of alkaline solutions upon original larger masses of variscite.

Production of variscite from the Fairfield locality reached its peak in the years 1909 to 1911 when thousands of pounds of nodules were sent to the market. Since that time, mining has been sporadic, the last reliable figures giving an output of "several hundred" pounds in 1942. The total to date can only be guessed but must amount to many tons. The most highly prized nodules are those in which bright green opaque to slightly translucent varis-cite predominates and the pattern is complete. This perfection tends to be confined to those nodules of 4 inches or more in diameter, with the propor-tion of variscite increasing as the nodule increases in size. The largest nod-ules seldom exceed 12 inches in diameter; those of 10 inches are also seen but the most common sizes range from 3 to 6 inches.

The next locality to be considered is that near Lucin in Box Elder County. This deposit was opened by C. J. Burke in 1902 and is situated on the northern portion of a hill named Utahlite Hill about 5 miles northwest of Lucin in the extreme western portion of Box Elder County not far from the Nevada line. The locality is reached by road from Lucin, proceeding north for 3.4 miles then turning west for 4.4 miles for a total distance of 7.8 miles. Interestingly enough, the original discovery was staked as a gold claim but since none was found, the claim was abandoned and the locality lost. It was subsequently rediscovered in 1905 but was not officially claimed until 1909 when papers were filed by Frank Edison and Ed. Bird. Utahlite Hill is about one mile long in a northwesterly to southeasterly direction and about one half mile wide, with the low summit upon which the claims are located rising to a total altitude of about 5000 feet although the hill itself is only 300 feet above the surrounding terrain. Four claims were originally located to cover the most promising outcrops which appear on the summit next to small rocky prominences. The country rock is Pennsylvanian quartzite, locally containing lime, with variscite and associated phosphates occurring in sheared and brecciated zones which parallel the bedding of overlying Carboniferous limestone. The latter grades upward into quartzite which is barren of variscite. The phosphate minerals, presumably formed under the same conditions as noted in the Fairfield deposit, consist of variscite and many others previously noted, accompanied by considerable chalcedony. Limonite and crushed chert are abundant, also fresh pyrite enclosed in variscite. Gem material occurs in balls, nodules, seams and veins, the latter ranging from paper-thin to several inches thick. Concretionary forms are often separated from the enclosing rock by considerable quantities of chalky filling. In places, small to large angular fragments of chert and limestone are solidly cemented together with variscite in the shear zone mentioned above.

Color and pattern of Lucin variscite are similar to those of Fairfield but green hues are inclined to be deeper in shade. The color ranges from very pale green to bright grass green, many pieces often being pure in color and permitting uniform cabochons of at least an inch across to be cut. Some of the darker and more compact material is noticeably translucent. Matrix specimens derived from brecciated zones often show variscite 6 inches to as much as 10 inches across, veined by other minerals, but still primarily variscite. It is recorded that one block of pure variscite from one of the claims measured 4 to 6 inches thick and weighed several pounds. Larger pieces have been found in recent years. Variscite is sometimes found here filling spaces between angular fragments of white quartz, and, when polished, affording very handsome specimens, however, the vast difference in hardness between these minerals makes it extremely difficult to obtain a uniform polish. This deposit is also of interest in that much material of deep color is found to be honeycombed with small cavities lined with glistening, perfectly formed crystals of variscite. Too small to be of use as gems, they are valued chiefly for their rarity. It is interesting to note that if variscite from this locality is heated strongly enough to drive off its combined water (below 160° C), a remarkable color change takes place, the usual green hue being replaced by deep lavender.

The third locality for variscite in Utah is the Amatrice Mine located upon a small knob among the foothills of the Stansbury Mountains, 10 miles south 65° west of Tooele in Tooele County, or about 9 miles west of Stockton. The small knob has been labeled Amatrice Hill, and stands about 200 feet above the surrounding terrain with its summit at an elevation of about 5700 feet. The variscite occurs here, as in the other localities, in fissured and brecciated zones in limestone and quartzite. The summit of Amatrice Hill consists of hard, dense, dark brown calcareous quartzite, while the eastern slope is siliceous, sandy or cherty limestone of light to dark gray color. Variscite occurs in this limestone in concretionary nodules but also fills spaces between broken fragments of rock. Three variscite-bearing mineralized zones are known to exist upon the hill, each labeled according to the type of material obtained therefrom; i. e., the "jade" zone, noted for dark material, the "cobweb" zone, for variscite crossed by a webbing of other minerals but for the "appleblossom" zone, unfortunately, there seems no sensible explanation. Surface evidence of loose material indicates that streaks of variscite occur elsewhere on the hill.

Nodular and seam deposits at this locality appear in a bewildering variety of form, while even in the variscite itself, there is much variation in shade from pale to dark green. Some of the lightest tones are almost white and as opaque as chalk while the other extreme is marked by fairly translucent material of great density and deep color. In each deposit discussed so far, the most compact material, and hence that capable of taking the best polish, is dark green somewhat translucent variscite. The most highly prized specimens from this locality are beautifully patterned seam sections showing considerable variety of color.

Nevada. Four distinct groups of variscite deposits occur in this state, three in Esmeralda County, and the fourth in Mineral County. The principal group and the first to be discovered (about 1908), is in the eastern foothills of the Candelaria Mountains in Esmeralda County near Mina County and close to the workings of the old Norton Bell Silver Mine on the summit of the mountain immediately south of the mining town of Candelaria and about one mile west of the Mount Diablo Silver Mine. The variscite workings are on the eastern part of the hill, about a mile south of Candelaria, at an elevation of approximately 6500 feet above sea level. Two localities are stated to be within this group, another authority giving their positions as: (1) about 1½ miles northwest of the deserted mining camp of Columbus, and (2), about 2 miles west of Rock Hill Siding. Both are said to be two miles apart in a northeast-southwest direction.

Rock formations in the vicinity of the deposits are mostly siliceous or cherty limestones and slate, rhyolite tuffs, altered rhyolites, sandstones and shales. Small altered trachyte dikes are also present. Unlike the Utah occurrences, the variscite occurs here in brecciated contacts between rhyolite and trachyte but in the usual seams, veins, irregular masses, and nodules. Mineralized zones appear to be concentrated along fissures and joints in the country rock. Seam variscite occurs in fillings varying from paperthin to 2 to 3 inches thick while variscite-impregnated zones may extend laterally for several feet into the country rock. Where more room has been provided in the enclosing rock, nodules of the usual form occur instead of seams. The Emerald Claim in this group was noted for its production of beautiful deep green variscite streaked handsomely with jet black veinings. The range of color from all claims is from very pale chalky green to deep green with variations in shade within single masses. Large unbroken areas are scarce, and flawless stones of substantial size are difficult to obtain.

Another important pair of occurrences in the Monte Cristo Mountains of Esmeralda County, lie from 3 to 6 miles northeast of Coaldale and also somewhat further east, about 9 to 11 miles north-northeast of Blair Junction. The first series of mines has been called the Coaldale Group, and the second, the Blair Junction Group. The principal workings in the Coaldale Group lie 4 miles northeast of Coaldale on the south side of the mountains at elevations ranging from 6100 to 6700 feet above sea level and extend for a distance of about three fourths of a mile along a rocky canyon. The Morning Glory and Saint Patrick claims lie along a hill on the southeast side of the canyon while the Bonnie Blue Bell and Bluebird claims traverse the canyon in an east-west direction. The Bonnie Blue Bell claim on the northwest side of the canyon as shown in Figure 66, is of more than passing interest since turquois has been found upon it as well as variscite. The country rock is a hard, chert-like altered rhyolite, gray to black in color, and outcropping in the form of ledges. The Blair Junction Group consists of nine claims lying at altitudes ranging from 6200 to 6600 feet above sea level, along the northeast side and along the summit of a ridge. Country rock in this area is a dull gray to black, chertlike altered rhyolite. Variscite occurs in seams, veins, and also in nodules; its

FIGURE 66. A photograph taken in May 1910, showing the old variscite-turquois claims of Wilson, Capps & Riek, 4 miles north 50° east of Coaldale. The camp has been pitched on the Bonnie Blue Bell Claim. Esmeralda County, Nevada. Courtesy U.S. Geological Survey.

character is like that observed in other Nevada localities and includes the black-veined types mentioned before.

The last group of variscite deposits are located about 8 miles southwest of Sodaville, Mineral County, in the eastern end of the Excelsior Mountains. Six claims were originally staked out along the sides and the head of a steep rocky gulch whose depths vary from 300 to 600 feet. The elevations of the claims range from 5300 to 6300 feet above sea level. The gulch containing the claims proceeds along a southeast course, opening out upon a gently sloping alluvial fan which extends toward Rhodes Salt Marsh. As in the Monte Cristo occurrences, variscite is found in brecciated zones in dark colored rhyolites. Seam types are most common but some nodules have been produced. A greenish turquois has been found nearby in an altered porphyry close to the rhyolite.

JADE
(*Nephrite and Jadeite*)

From the standpoint of mineralogy, nephrite and jadeite are distinct minerals which bear little chemical resemblance to each other but since both occur in fine-grained to fibrous massive forms and lend themselves to similar lapidary treatment, they often are considered simply as "jade" and treated accordingly. However, the distinctions between them are numerous despite superficial resemblance, and it is proposed to treat them separately in the subsections which follow.

Collectively, the term "jade" has been applied not only to *jadeite,* a Pyroxene, and *nephrite,* a mineral close to actinolite and a member of the Amphibole Group, but also to such minerals as serpentine which enjoys the name "new jade" in China, plus other fine-grained minerals which look like the first two mentioned. To be entirely correct, at least in Western eyes, only jadeite and nephrite should be labeled "jade." Of the two species, jadeite is subject to considerable variation in composition and accordingly it is subdivided into the following subspecies:

Jadeite: Essentially a silicate of sodium and aluminum.

Diopside-jadeite: Intermediate between jadeite and diopside; essentially a silicate of sodium, calcium, and aluminum.

Chloromelanite: Intermediate between jadeite and acmite, or jadeite, acmite, and diopside; essentially a silicate of sodium, calcium, magnesium, iron, and aluminum. The presence of iron causes the color to become very dark green, sometimes almost black and accounts for the name of this subspecies which means, from the Greek, "greenish-black."

The entire question of mining and distribution of jade in North America has excited the interest of archeologists and ethnologists for many years. In fact, the absence of any known localities up until very recent years, led to the intriguing speculation that stocks of jade were brought all the way from the Asiatic localities by means of a chain-link trade route to Siberia, over the Bering Straits into Alaska, and thence eastward through the Canadian Arctic, and southward along the Pacific coast to Mexico and Central America. The utter absence of any visible trade in this commodity along any of the routes mentioned and the fact that all tribes were obviously still using jade in appreciable quantities when white men were present to observe such things, should have led to the conclusion that supplies were locally derived. The fog about the origin of jade in North America gradually lifted as Alaskan and Pacific Northwest sources were discovered, but the failure to discover where the huge quantities of jadeite used by the Aztecs, Mixtecs, Toltecs, and other Indian races of Mexico and Central America came from was still as much a mystery as ever. Finally, in 1952 one source of jadeite was discovered in the Motagua River valley of Guatemala! The identity of this jadeite with that in many artifacts has been proved but other types are known only in artifact form and their sources remain undiscovered. However, since jades occur primarily in strongly metamorphosed rocks, particularly those of basic composition, it has been predicted that more sources will eventually be located in Central America in areas where such rocks abound. In fact, similar rocks occur over wide areas parallel to the Pacific Coast of the United States and Canada, and many of the jade boulders found in the various streams of this region undoubtedly have been detached from deposits somewhere in the wild and inaccessible mountains upstream. It is interesting to note in this connection, that the source of Fraser River nephrite is still unknown.

The uses of jade among aboriginal inhabitants depended greatly upon the extent to which their civilizations were developed. In the more primitive races and tribes, jade was prized only for its toughness; it made splendid adzes and other cutting tools which had to be used with much driving power to make them effective. Since it could not be chipped like quartz, obsidian, flint, chert and other brittle minerals, its reduction to final form required long abrasive operations usually involving rubbing against quartzose rocks such as sandstone, or using loose sand upon wood. On the other hand, slicing large blocks, drilling holes, carving, and other advanced lapidary operations were regularly carried out only by the highly-skilled artisans of the cultured races of Mexico and Central America. Among these Indians, a degree of art was reached which compares favorably to that manifested in some of the early Chinese works, but of course it never reached the sublime perfection achieved by these masters. Furthermore, the Aztecs, Mixtecs, and others, regarded jadeite in a different light than did the more primitive tribes. To them it had religious, cultural, and official significance but to the primitive races, it was first and foremost a raw material for very necessary tools and weapons.

In hand specimens, nephrite and jadeite are distinguished because of differences in fracture; nephrite has an exceedingly close fibrous structure which imparts a splintery surface to fracture faces; on the other hand, jadeite is composed of stubby, bladed crystal grains, generally easy to see with the naked eye, and imparting a granular or glistening sugary character to fracture surfaces. Although most jadeite crystals are quite small, some become rather coarse as in the peculiar pale greenish material from Guatemala in which individual crystals reach as much as ½ inch across. Differing structures in both minerals also affect translucency: in jadeite, specimens often appear almost transparent while in nephrite the fibrous structure retards light and the effect is one of feeble translucency in the purer types but scarcely any in impure kinds. Jadeite tends to be free of coarse inclusions but nephrite is often darkened by black spots and streaks. Furthermore, the surface finish of nephrite is inclined to be glossy rather than brilliant while jadeite often shows a pitted or "lemon peel" texture on polished surfaces due to variations in hardness within individual crystal grains, however, despite this drawback, the polish is usually far more brilliant than that of nephrite.

NEPHRITE

Of the two jade minerals found in North America, nephrite occurs in far greater quantity insofar as raw material is concerned. The discovery in 1936 of excellent quality green material in Wyoming in the form of "float" boulders and pebbles set off a "jade rush" which even today has not fully abated although the tremendous area in which specimens have been found has been virtually swept bare. Later discoveries in California as well as a revival of interest during World War II in the deposits of the Kobuk River area of Alaska has kept nephrite jade in the forefront as a typically American gemstone much esteemed and much worked by the gem-cutting fraternity.

Nephrite is an intermediate species between actinolite and tremolite in composition, and like them is also a member of the large and important rock-forming Amphibole Group. Actinolite is, ideally, calcium magnesium iron silicate while tremolite is free of iron and is therefore calcium magnesium silicate. The compositions of both species show that iron can substitute for magnesium to provide a host of minerals intermediate between the two end members: actinolite ($Ca_2(Mg,Fe)_5Si_8O_{22}(OH)_2$) and tremolite ($Ca_2Mg_5Si_8O_{22}(OH)_2$).

Nephrite is typically a product of metamorphic action and is generally found associated with gneisses, schists, serpentines, and metamorphosed limestones. It is especially common at points of contact between rocks of dissimilar character in strongly metamorphosed zones. Occurring as lenses, sheets and nodules, nephrite is so much more durable than its enclosing rocks that it ordinarily remains after these have weathered away. Consequently it often appears many miles from original points of formation, as waterworn or windblasted pebbles and boulders, carried thence by streams, rivers, and shifting soils. When waterworn or windblasted by surface sand, it often assumes a high gloss approaching a true polish and is easily recognized on this account. At other times, when such abrasive agencies are not active, its exterior alters badly and completely hides its inner nature. Many such fragments have been found in Wyoming, requiring in each instance, a hammer blow to chip off a corner to reveal the character of the material within. As a member of the actinolite-tremolite series, nephrite also forms crystal belonging to the Monoclinic System, however, these are so minute that they are rarely visible to the naked eye. Under the microscope, nephrite is shown to consist of exceedingly long thin fibers, closely interlocked, and generally oriented in bunches in some common direction. The toughest kinds are those in which the crystals are so fine and so randomly oriented that the material appears to be like hardened lard, smooth and translucent. As the fibers become more straight, they tend to split apart more readily. Fracture surfaces vary from dull in very fine grained kinds to splintery in those in which some degree of lamination is present. The nephrite from the Pacific shore of Monterey County, California, for example, is frequently so full of inclusions of a mica-like nature, that fracture surfaces tend to be flat with a decided silvery luster. Aside from jadeite and rhodonite, nephrite has no close competitor in toughness, exceeding even jadeite in this important property.

The specific gravity of nephrite varies over a considerable range because of the frequency and quantity of inclusions of foreign minerals, but purer types generally fall between 2.90 and 3.00. Very dark kinds with black inclusions of heavy iron minerals, may be considerably above the latter value. Refractive indices determined by microscopic methods show $a = 1.60\text{-}1.63$, $\gamma = 1.62\text{-}1.65$; birefringence 0.02; biaxial, negative. However, due to its finely fibrous nature, ordinary refractometer determinations made upon nephrite will show only vague readings lying somewhere between 1.60 and 1.65. In color, most nephrite is some shade of green, ranging from rather pure yellowish-green to olive-green to greenish-black. The so-called "black" nephrite such as is found in Wyoming is actually very dark olive-green in color but this cannot be checked readily unless a very thin sliver is held before a strong light source. Unbroken color in nephrite is rather rare, most is mottled with streaks of slightly different shade or flecked with dark colored "flow-like" inclusions. Probably the best colored material to be taken from any source in North America is the bright pure green found in some of the boulders in Wyoming, but even this material is rarely free of small black specks or other inclusions. However, compared to the best nephrite from Asiatic sources, it is still very fine quality. Typical North American nephrite specimens are shown in Figure 67.

FIGURE 67. North American nephrite specimens. The large slab in the background is dark green Alaskan jade showing several streaks of chatoyant grayish-green material near the top. Leaning against it is a slab of Wyoming nephrite showing a rind of altered material and small black specks scattered throughout the bright green unaltered material within the core. On the right is a rough specimen of similar material. The lower left and lower right specimens are also from Wyoming while the rounded pebble in the center is from a beach deposit in Monterey County, California.

LOCALITIES

Greenland. Earlier mineralogists did not often recognize the essential properties of the several jade minerals and were apt to mistake other similar minerals for jade. Thus Karl Giesecke in his mineralogical travels in Greenland in the opening years of the 19th Century, gives several localities where "jade" was found by him. However, the associated minerals indicate that it was probably serpentine that he found and not jade.

The northernmost locality, one of three along the west coast, is southwest of Christianshaab in the Disko Bay area. The locality is called Kakarsuit and is not far from the settlement. The rock is mica schist penetrated by veins and seams containing actinolite, amphibole, tremolite, sahlite (hedenbergite), and nephrite, along with dolomite and limestone. Serpentine and massive steatite are found here also, the latter being employed by the Eskimos for carving into various utensils. Further south near Godthaab, impure beds of talcose rock within granite occur on the Kuanebucht, several miles southeast of the town of Godthaab. Nephrite occurs here as rounded lumps of greenish color embedded in the talc. The third locality is a rather vague reference to an occurrence in the Kitsugsut Islands about ten miles northwest of Cape Desolation in southwest Greenland, the associated minerals being actinolite and chlorite embedded in hornblende schist.

Wisconsin. In 1958, dark green nephrite boulders were reported from the gravels of Rib Creek near Wausau, Marathon Co. The refractive index of this material is stated as 1.62 and the specific gravity as 2.96.

Alaska. In 1883 a Naval lieutenant by the name of George M. Stoney noted jade tools in the possession of the Eskimos living along the Arctic coasts of Alaska. The expedition of which he was member, granted him permission to explore the Kobuk River for along its banks at some point far upstream jade was said to occur. Forming a small party of himself and a few Eskimos as guides, he proceeded upstream to about 90 miles above the delta mouth. Time ran out however, and he had to return to meet his ship. Next year, in 1884, he was back at his own request, better prepared, and determined to reach the mysterious source of jade. At a place 150 miles upstream, the Eskimos pointed out Jade Mountain some eight miles across the floor of the valley but inspired by superstitious fears, refused to go any further. Undaunted, Lt. Stoney took several seamen and made the trek without the help of the natives. He ascended the mountain and found upon it a green mineral which had the appearance of jade, however, when these were submitted to the Smithsonian Institution upon the return of the expedition to the United States, he was much disappointed to learn that he had brought back only serpentine. More determined than ever, Lt. Stoney again received permission to return in 1885, planning to ascend the river, build a log cabin, and stay the winter until the return of the ship in the summer of 1886. All of this he did, building his cabin near a jade-bearing creek which is now named Cosmos Creek in honor of the name he gave to his miniature settlement—"Fort Cosmos." During this period he again ascended Jade Mountain and this time found true nephrite jade in abundance, earning the honor of being the first to discover nephrite in place in North America. Since this early discovery, many parties have made the laborious and time-consuming trip to the area in which jade is found and worked the deposits sporadically for jade and for the valuable asbestos which occurs in some quantity in the same rock formations. However, the first scientific study of the area did not take place until

Alaska Department of Mines personnel were sent to examine the deposits at various times from 1943 to 1945. The results of their investigations showed asbestos and jade occurring in a series of ultrabasic rocks presumed to be altered peridotites, injected into schists and limestones over a broad area about 40 miles in length, north of and roughly parallel to the Kobuk River. The ultrabasic rocks consist mainly of serpentine in which asbestos and nephrite are common. The asbestos is both of the chrysotile (serpentine) and tremolite varieties. Magnesite, antigorite, and magnetite are accessory minerals, the last appearing frequently as black specks in jade.

The broad valley through which the Kobuk River flows westward on its way to Hotham Inlet and Kotzebue Sound on the Bering Sea, rises very gradually, and at Kobuk Village it is still only 1000 feet above sea level. Immediately north of the river at this point is a low range of mountains, not over 5,000 feet in elevation, sliced through by a series of powerful streams which rise in the Schwatka Mountains further north. It is in these low rounded mountains, sometimes called the Jade Hills, that the in place deposits are found, while almost every stream bed in the vicinity contains rounded boulders of nephrite derived from deposits located in these hills. Figure 68

FIGURE 68. A huge mass of serpentine, nephrite, and asbestos perched on the tundra atop Jade Mountain in the Kobuk region of Alaska. Though such large masses are far from gem quality, lenses of good nephrite occur within them and may be removed with much effort. The weathering of this form of rock results in the release of nephrite which eventually is water-worn to the form shown in Figure 69. Courtesy Ross Hastie, Cincinnati, Ohio.

shows a view of the typical regional terrain. Important alluvial deposits occur in the Shungnak River whose gravel jade seems to be derived from an outcrop on the east flank of Bismark Mountain about 9 miles upstream from where the Shungnak empties into the Kobuk. Outcrops of jade-bearing rocks also occur in a belt which runs west to east commencing on the north flank of

Shungnak Mountain to the north flank of Cosmos Mountain, crossing Cosmos and Wesley creeks, and terminating near the headwaters of Camp Creek. The famed Asbestos Mountain—Dahl Creek area begins at the junction of Stockley Creek and Dahl Creek, extending northward to the summit of Asbestos Mountain and thence easterly for a short distance. The Kogoluktuk area embraces a small outcrop on the summit of a steep hill lying between Lynx Creek and California Creek, both of which empty into the Kogoluktuk River, which, in turn, empties into the Kobuk. Small outcrops exist on the west flank of Ferguson Peak at the 1000-foot level and not far from California Creek. The classic locality for nephrite however, is at Jade Mountain in the Jade Hills where much material has been removed from the bed of Jade Creek. This locality lies about 30 miles due west of Kobuk

Figure 69. Ross Hastie with a fine quality nephrite boulder unearthed from the bed of Dahl Creek in the Kobuk region of Alaska. The smoothness of the boulder surface is characteristic and aids in distinguishing jade from rocks of similar color and appearance. Courtesy Ross Hastie, Cincinnati, Ohio.

Village. Figure 69 shows a beautifully smooth boulder of fine quality nephrite in the bed of this creek. The above list of localities is probably far from complete since qualified observers believe that outcrops containing nephrite may be found over a considerably larger area if this region should ever be thoroughly explored.

The quality of Alaskan nephrite is very variable, much found in outcrops being schistose and utterly worthless. The best material has always come from the streambeds where natural tumbling processes have permitted only the most compact material to survive. Jade Creek nephrite occurs as smooth boulders, almost polished, but frequently stained to about ¼ inch below the surface by the decomposition of the iron content or possibly by the infiltration of iron oxides. The same type of dark brown staining is noted along cracks and fissures in the interior of boulders which are later sectioned on diamond saws. Pure unaltered material, however, is finely fibrous, translucent, and frequently penetrated by seams up to ½ inch thick of straight fiber actinolite which is pale greenish gray in color and strongly chatoyant (see Figure 67). By careful cutting, interesting catseyes may be made from such material. The color of the nephrite itself is generally some shade of deep green of good intensity. Many specimens are streaked with lighter and darker shades of green, some streaks being rather yellowish in cast. Black inclusions of magnetite are frequently met with. In contrast to the Jade Creek nephrite, that from the Shungnak River gravels is said to be more grayish but of good texture. The Dahl Creek material is dark green and contains numerous black specks. All in all, very little Kobuk nephrite is as fine in texture or as vivid in color at the best Wyoming material. The specific gravity of Kobuk nephrite ranges from 2.92 to 3.01.

The exploitation of Alaska nephrite began with the Eskimos at some distant time in the past. A determination of age by means of tree rings in the Eskimo village ruins of Ambler Island in the Ambler River, showed this village to be at least 230 years old, which places the numerous nephrite artifacts found therein at least that far back in age. Kobuk River material has been identified in artifacts found in the hands of natives all along the Pacific coast of Alaska and British Columbia, and to the north into Canada along the shores of the Arctic Ocean. This wide distribution indicates that the locality has been known for many hundreds of years. In more modern times, the difficulties of transportation to the several localities along the Kobuk River have kept out many who would be interested in gathering jade, while the even greater task of taking the boulders to civilization has been an appalling prospect even to the hardiest. During World War II, in order to exploit the strategically important asbestos which is found in commercial amounts in the area, an airfield was leveled near Kobuk Village to solve the transportation problem. In 1944 the first significant commercial exploration of the deposits began, some 11 tons of jade and 200 tons of asbestos being taken out by boat and by air in the following year. The work was done by the Arctic Circle Exploration Company of Fairbanks, Alaska, who staked claims and operated mines for asbestos and creek diggings for alluvial jade. It is said that some jade was sold to Chinese agents and compared favorably in quality and color to the better grades of New Zealand nephrite. In the summer of 1946, the company shipped out 13¾ tons of nephrite, realizing as much as $5.00 per pound for some grades up to a high of $55.00 per pound for exceptional material. The following year, an estimated $25,000 to $30,000 worth of boulders weighing from 200 to 1500 pounds were assembled at the claims for shipment to China. Visitors to the jade deposits at that time, stated that many boulders of excellent quality jade remained behind because they were far too big to move while their exceeding toughness made it almost impossible to drill and blast them into more manageable pieces.

Since 1947, however, nephrite has been mined rather steadily under the stimulus of increasing sales of polished jade in jewelry and gift shops throughout Alaska, as well as sales of raw and polished material to export markets. In a visit to this area in 1957, Bureau of Mines personnel investigated jade mining at Shungnak and found the Empire Jade Company to be active in the Jade Mountain area. Aside from the mining of jade, this company restricts its activities to the cutting of boulders into sizes suitable for 24 inch saws. In some instances, they polish jade into book ends and sets for earrings and tie clasps. Most of their raw material is sold during winter when mining is curtailed, principally in Alaska and in the United States, and it is stated that five stockpiles of raw jade have been established in a number of places, including 7 tons at Seattle under bond, at Hong Kong, Paris, and elsewhere. Much material is sent to Germany for cutting, polishing, and in some instances, carving. The cut and most of the carved material is then sent to New Zealand for retail sales. In this connection, it may be mentioned again, that the better grades of this nephrite are very similar to those of that country and could be easily mistaken for the New Zealand *punamu* or *greenstone* nephrite. In 1956, the author visited Hong Kong and at that time was struck with the considerable quantity of nephrite being sold in locally-manufactured jewelry which had all the earmarks of either New Zealand or Alaska jade; from the above it appears that this material may be actually Alaskan jade. In 1957, gift shops in Nome and Fairbanks were selling elephants carved from Jade Mountain material. Carvings ranged in size from 3 to 6 inches, the 3 inch size bringing $40 while the larger ones brought as high as $500 depending on quality and detail of carving as well as the type of tusk insert employed, i.e., ivory, etc.

About 1952, Mr. Joiner of the Empire Jade Company discovered a 20-ton boulder of nephrite containing some quartz, and undertook to deliver this enormous mass to Kotzebue. The first part of each winter was spent in sledding the boulder across the snow until it was finally moved in stages to Kotzebue where it now awaits a buyer. This is undoubtedly one of the largest (if not *the* largest) single masses of nephrite ever mined.

Recently the Native Service Arts and Crafts organization in Alaska has completed the construction of a log cabin lapidary shop at Shungnak designed to accommodate 20 Eskimo lapidaries who will use modern cutting and polishing equipment to produce finished articles for a growing market. No doubt a wider variety of forms, including carvings, will be attempted. Although some Eskimo jade work has been on the market for some years, it has generally been very simple due to the complete unfamiliarity of these people with anything except the crudest methods for working stone and a historical disinterest in art. However, under the training which is being given, future years may see the development of a considerable lapidary industry in Alaska. Recent products of Eskimo origin include short necklaces of rounded and bored nephrite beads of spherical shape alternating with spacers of ivory which also add color contrast. Earrings and tie clasps, cuff links, and other small items of severely plain design have also been produced in quantity. So far as is known, virtually every carved piece of any artistic consequence is not native work but has been carved in Idar/Oberstein, Germany.

North West Territories. Boulders of nephrite have been found in the stream gravels of the Rae River in the Coronation Gulf Region.

Yukon Territory. Boulders of nephrite are occasionally found in the gravels of the upper Lewes River not far from the border of Alaska.

British Columbia. The Selish Indians inhabiting the valley of the Fraser River in south central British Columbia found boulders and pebbles of nephrite in the river gravels and for many years bartered these to tribes not in a position to obtain their own. In more recent years, residents of the Fraser River Valley interested in mineralogy or gem cutting, have continued to find numbers of jade boulders, one of which is recorded as weighing 200 pounds, and said to be of excellent color. In the last several years, many have been obtained from the Bridge River which enters the Fraser from the west near Lillooet, the largest specimen being an enormous boulder of 800 pounds weight. This mass had to be drilled and broken apart into manageable pieces which were then removed by pack horse. The jade-producing stretch in the Bridge River extends from its mouth to at least as far as Monto Mines, about 50 miles upstream. The colors of British Columbia nephrite generally involve some shade of green, about 40 per cent of all specimens being grayish-green to greenish-gray, streaked and mottled, while the remainder are dark green, brownish-green, pale bluish-green, yellowish-green, green and gray mottled and green and black mottled. A very small amount is fine green of good translucency and uniform texture. Inclusions are frequently found, some are soft and cause difficulty in polishing but others are hard and polish satisfactorily with the jade. In the alluvial gravels of the Fraser River, jade occurs in waterworn masses from as far south as Chilliwack, some 63 miles east of Vancouver, to as far north as Lytton. However, recent finds (1957) indicate that this northward limit has been extended upstream and therefore the exact terminus remains unknown. Between Lytton and Hope, the Alexander Bar near Chapman has yielded numerous specimens, a 35 pound boulder being found as recently as 1954. Another productive bar lies several miles north of Lytton. The Thompson River which enters the Fraser from the east also produces jade boulders. The nephrite of this entire area sometimes produces fine material of good color but inclusions of porphyritic texture are frequent and mar the quality. So far, no in place deposits have been found in this region and the source remains unexplained. The specific gravity of British Columbia nephrite ranges from 3.00 to 3.027.

Oregon. Although schists and associated serpentine have been found in the mountainous regions bordering the Pacific Ocean, only one in place deposit of nephrite is known. In Curry County in the southwestern part of the state, nephrite pebbles are found in the talus below Sugarloaf Peak and in the gravels of streams which descend from its slopes. This area is reached by forest service road from Pistol River on the coast. Nephrite, some of which is gemmy and suitable for cutting, occurs in place as lenses and stringers in massive serpentine. Nephrite from this locality is said to be of finer quality than that found along the beaches of Monterey County, California.

Pebbles and boulders of nephrite are occasionally reported from a number of the streams and rivers which drain the west slope of the coastal mountains in western Oregon, however, few of these finds are authenticated and in some cases at least, have turned out to be compact grossularite garnet, sometimes called "Oregon jade."

California. Perhaps the best known locality for nephrite in this state is the Cape San Martin region on the Pacific Coast of Monterey County from which many tons of smoothly-rounded grayish-green boulders and pebbles have been removed from beaches below outcrops containing nephrite in place. The earliest recognition of nephrite at this locality took place in 1936 when Spencer N. Parmalee found a waterworn pebble upon the beach. Struck by its resemblance to oriental material, he subjected it to preliminary testing and satisfied himself that it was nephrite, however, thorough testing and identification were not accomplished until 1939 when samples were submitted to Dr. Austin F. Rogers of Stanford University. Since 1939, many thousands of specimens have been removed from the several localities mainly by amateur collectors although some material has been sold commercially.

The occurrences of nephrite at this locality are of two types, first, as beach pebbles weathered originally from the rocks containing nephrite, and, second, in the rocks themselves. Between Plaskett Point to the north and Cape San Martin to the south, a series of gray schists outcrop in which are intruded peridotite rocks altered to serpentine. The nephrite occurs as lenses and nodules next to the serpentine in rather narrow zones. Nephrite in place occurs 1250 feet southeast of Plaskett Point, in an indentation called Jade Cove. Rolled pebbles are found in this cove and in another beach deposit some 1000 feet further southeast. Another in place deposit and corresponding jade-bearing beach, lies just south of the mouth of Willow Creek about 1200 feet northeast of Cape San Martin. Both localities are several miles apart along Highway 101 which skirts the Pacific shore between Morro Bay and Monterey. The quality of nephrite found at these localities is generally inferior,

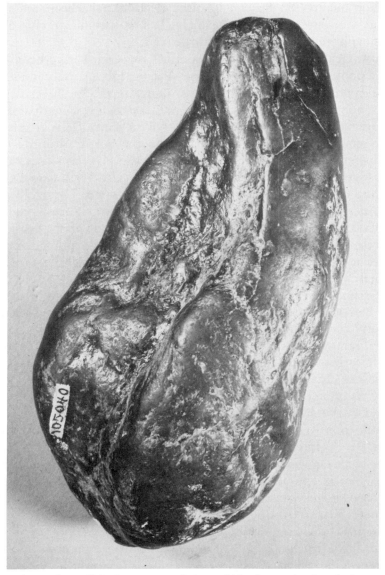

FIGURE 70. A partly polished green nephrite pebble from the beach between Point Sur and the Salmon Creek Ranger Station, Monterey County, California. The twisted structure and schistose character are typical. Size: 6¾ inches in length. Courtesy Smithsonian Institution.

numerous minute inclusions and partings arranged parallel to the bedding causing specimens to fracture easily. The silvery reflection from these inclusions is quite pronounced and is so typical that jade from these localities can be instantly recognized. The color is generally greenish gray and not very pure in hue; translucency is low and, in general, excellent specimens are very rare. The size of individual pebbles varies from an inch or less to 12 inches or more in diameter. A boulder weighing 121 pounds is now on exhibit in the California Academy of Sciences building in Golden Gate Park, San Francisco, California. A waterworn pebble from these deposits is illustrated in Figure 70.

Recently, nephrite boulders up to 3,000 pounds weight have been discovered under the ocean surface just offshore of Jade Cove by a group of collectors who conducted exploratory and recovery operations from moored pontoon rafts using "skin-diving" equipment. Some very large masses of nephrite similar to those found for many years along the shore have been landed in this unique gem-mining operation.

Another locality in Monterey County but one less well known, is said to be in the western Santa Lucia Range between Point Sur and Salmon Creek Ranger Station. Nephrite of good quality is stated to occur here as rolled pebbles and boulders, also in place in serpentine. Occasional pebbles of jade are reported from beaches near Cambria Pines, San Simeon Creek, and Salmon Creek.

In Marin County, nephrite occurs as lenses and thin veins near the contact between schist and serpentine on the east slope of Massa Hill on the Vonsen Ranch, about 5 miles southwest of Petaluma. The hill is composed of schists, serpentine, and sedimentary rocks of the Franciscan Group. Lenses of nephrite seldom exceed several inches in thickness and the deposit is economically unimportant but small quantities of material could be obtained if blasting of the enclosing rock is resorted to. The color ranges from pale olive green to pale bluish-green to dark bluish-green. The central parts of veins provide material of fair translucency while the outer parts yield an almost opaque somewhat chatoyant fibrous material of blue-gray color. The latter has provided some very pleasing gems somewhat resembling gems cut from a fibrous type of serpentine known as *satelite*.

Tulare County has produced commercial quantities of dark green translucent nephrite from a locality on Lewis Hill, about 2 miles northeast of Porterville. This material was identified and worked commercially by Frank Janoko and C. V. Alston of Porterville in 1949. The deposit consists of two distinct lenses of large size, one of which yielded several tons of nephrite with more in sight.

Nephrite from this occurrence is dark oily green in color, streaked with "flow" markings and narrow lenses of yellowish green material and dark spots. Cabochons and polished specimens are characterized by smooth finishes interrupted by rather large pits where softer sections are encountered.

Miscellaneous finds of nephrite have been reported from other counties in California, among them, an enormous boulder weighing 1350 pounds found in the streambed of the upper Trinity River in northeastern Trinity County. This boulder measured 38½ by 27½ by 19 inches and showed color variations from greasy grayish white to green to dark green. In appearance, it was similar to boulders derived from lenses in serpentine and points to the possibility that nephrite may be found in the higher country of Trinity and Siskiyou Counties where metamorphic rocks conducive to the formation of nephrite are known to occur. The localities for jadeite boulders in Williams Creek, 6 miles east of Covelo in Mendocino County, and near Mina on the Eel River in the same county, are also stated to be nephrite localities. Not enough is known about these finds to state which species has actually been found, or whether both have been found. In Santa Barbara County a boulder of nephrite was reported from the gravels of a creek near Los Olivos on the south slope of Figueroa Mountain. In Siskiyou County, nephrite of good quality has been identified from the Chan Jade Mine on Indian Creek in the famous idocrase-producing region (see IDOCRASE). This jade is interesting because some contains small specks of gold. A specimen of this material is in the Museum of the California State Division of Mines in the Ferry Building, San Francisco. Nephrite in place has been recently reported from the north bank of the American River in Eldorado County, northeast of Placerville, and 5.6 miles distant by road.

Wyoming. The most remarkable and easily the most important jade area in the entire Western Hemisphere is that of south central Wyoming. In a vast desert region, thousands of pebbles and boulders of nephrite in all colors and qualities have been picked up from the surface in the few years since its discovery in 1936. It was soon found that although many exposed specimens were beautifully polished by the sand-blasting of ceaseless Upper Plains winds, others buried in the soil were weathered to inconspicuous colors or covered with grayish lichens. Those who knew what they were looking for reaped rich awards, and even today, many professionals and amateurs alike, roam the hills for specimens overlooked by others. A steady influx of new material indicates that finds are constantly being made while the exploration of several in place deposits promises additional material for years to come. Of all North American gemstones, few are held in such high esteem as Wyoming jade. All variations in color occur, from beautiful green to olive green to some which are almost black. Sizes range from nicely polished hand specimens to boulders too large to move without mechanical equipment. Useful for jewelry, for objects of art, and prized for specimens, Wyoming jade will be in demand for many years.

The origin of nephrite in Wyoming is not clearly understood in all cases, due to the very few in place exposures available for examination. In all the vast area under consideration, it is said that only five in place deposits are known. However, in each instance nephrite seems to be associated with ultrabasic serpentine adjacent to schists and granites. A peculiar feature of one in place occurrence is the association of milky quartz crystals with the nephrite. The latter occurs adjacent to the quartz and is penetrated by crystals several inches in length and about ¼ inch in diameter, displaying, in slabbed sections, perfect hexagonal outlines. Another deposit yields dark olive green nephrite in which is found considerable pink thulite and grayish-brown zoisite forming attractively mottled material.

It is difficult to pinpoint localities in which jade has been found, first, because of the understandable reluctance of successful hunters to reveal their favorite grounds, and, second, because this essentially wild and barren country has few landmarks to which accurate reference can be made. A careful study of the literature describing nephrite occurrences in Wyoming shows that "float" has been found over such an enormous area that the only logical conclusion is that jade has been scattered far and wide by ancient erosion and weathering and that all areas contain approximately the same amount of drift material. Lumping together the several smaller areas in which jade has been found, a single broad region can be delineated as follows: beginning at Lander, Fremont County, proceed southwestward to Farson, Sublette County, from Farson proceed eastward to the Red Desert in northeast Sweetwater County, thence east to Seminoe Dam in northern Carbon County, thence northward to Alcova in the southern part of Natrona County, finally westward to Lander, the starting point. The broad region delineated stretches 140 miles east to west and about 60 miles in maximum width. The following areas have been especially productive:

Split Rock Area. Excellent nephrite has been found near the Sweetwater agate beds not far from the corner made by Fremont, Natrona, and Carbon counties. In addition to many surface finds, jade has been found in place at the Long Creek deposit located a few miles north of the junction of Long Creek and Sweetwater River in Fremont County. At this point, a series of low hills consisting of Precambrian gneisses are cut by a dike-like body of hornblende-augite in which nephrite is found. The dike extends over ½ mile, varying in width from 30 to 50 feet and containing a lens of nephrite-bearing rock about 25 feet in length and 15 feet in width. The American Jade Company of Denver, Colorado, was reported to have spent $50,000 developing nephrite claims in this area.

Kortes Dam Area. In 1949, a large deposit of "black" nephrite was discovered near Kortes Dam and northern Carbon County. The dam is upon the North Platte River a few miles below Seminoe Dam. A single slab weighing 1500 pounds was removed from the deposit shortly after work began.

Southwest Lander Area. In this area, the first well-authenticated find of jade was made by Allan Branham in 1939 near Granite Peak, a mountain rising to over 10,000 feet in the southeastern end of the Wind River Range.

However, it has been said that a sheepherder made the initial discovery in 1936 at a point 48 miles southwest of Lander. Remarkable float specimens of beautiful green nephrite have been found in the Warm Springs country in the foothills and slopes of the Wind River Range in the same area. A 50 pound piece was found at the foot of Crooks Mountain. The largest specimens exceeded several thousand pounds while an unverified report mentions a huge mass of 8000 pounds found in 1943 in the same vicinity. Recorded finds of extraordinary size are as follows:

1940	2495 lb.—Southwest Lander Area; in Chicago Natural History Museum.
1941	2000 lb.—Southwest Lander Area; in Chicago Natural History Museum.
1943	460 lb.—Purchased by Donal Hord; carved into his famous statue "Thunder"; now in the San Diego Fine Arts Museum.*
?	3600 lb.—Southwest Lander Area; purchased by Chang Wen Ti of Los Angeles, California.
?	3366 lb.—Large slab measuring 4 ft. by 3 ft. by 12 to 16 inches; fine green; found by Bert A. Rhoads.

* The Hord statue mentioned above, weighs 104 lbs. and measures 20 inches in height. It is fairly uniform dark green nephrite showing some incipient fractures but on the whole, remarkably solid. The surface finish is excellent but was only achieved after much effort on the part of Mr. Hord and his assistant. The subject is a solemn-visaged American Indian sitting cross-legged on rain clouds and drawing thunder from a small drum resting on his shoulder.

In 1944, Allan Branham found brownish-green nephrite in place in the Granite Peak area, uncovering a vein or lens about 4 feet in length and 2½ feet in width. At an unstated time, Hart Robinson found "black" nephrite in place in the same area. One of the characteristics of the finer jade found in this general area is the development of a dark reddish skin on the exterior of rough masses. Alteration in these boulders proceeds to about ¼ inch below the surface and shows beneath the red skin, a brownish zone of altered nephrite followed by a pale green opaque zone next to the bright green material within the core. None show any sign of stream wear, in fact, their angularity indicates prolonged surface attack while buried in the soil. On the other hand, a number of boulders have been found exposed to the effects of wind-driven sand-blasting and display exceptionally smooth polished surfaces. In some cases, wind-blasting has reduced smaller masses to curious angular forms known to geologists as "dreikanters," a German word meaning three-cornered and descriptive of their shape; such pieces may be only a few ounces in weight and less than an inch across.

All qualities of nephrite have been found in the Southwest Lander Area and readers should not receive the impression that each piece is excellent. Duller colors such as grayish-green, brownish-green, and extremely dark, almost black greens are also common. In general, textures are fairly uniform but some pieces show marked "flow" patterns consisting of streaks and lines of varying color caused by differences within the nephrite itself or by numbers of fine inclusions. Bright green material is frequently delicately speckled with small black or pale green inclusions while at the other end of the color scale, in blackish material, an absolutely uniform texture and color is evident. The extremely dark nephrite is particularly superb, polishing to a perfect unbroken glistening surface. Specimens of this color occur in fairly large pieces and should be earnestly considered by jewelers and sculptors for ornamental objects. Compared to similarly-colored Siberian jade, it is at least equal if not superior.

Estimates of Wyoming jade production are sketchy at best since very little of the total produced has ever passed through regular commercial channels where some check could be obtained as to quantity and prices. However, it seems likely that at least 100 tons has been found and possibly much more. Fragmentary records show that in 1943 about $15,000 worth was sold while in 1944 about 3,000 to 4,000 lbs. was produced. The price received for rough material in the summer of this year varied from $1.00 to $10.00 per pound. It is said that Chinese agents purchased a total of 5,890 lbs. of Wyoming nephrite in the summer of 1944 for shipment to China upon cessation of the war. In 1950, about 1500 lbs. were sold for up to $30.00 per pound. Pickings on the gem fields were much less than in previous years and one estimate gave only 200 lbs. as being produced in this year, however, black jade was still plentiful. At the time of writing, Wyoming nephrite was being commonly handled by dealers at various conventions and exhibits arranged by amateur mineral and gem societies. Most dealers showed only a part of their stocks but were in a position to supply larger quantities if required. The finest grades however, were scarce and commanded prices up to $50 per pound (1959).

JADEITE

Jadeite is a member of the large and important Pyroxene Group and like them, crystallizes in the Monoclinic System. Crystals with faces are very rare, having been found only recently in California as tiny individuals lining cavities in massive jadeite. Pure jadeite is sodium aluminum silicate but variations in composition are often found in Mexican material, e.g.: *diopside-jadeite*, and *chloromelanite*. The presence of varying amounts of iron in the latter causes its deep green to almost black color. The formulas of the three are: jadeite $(NaAlSi_2O_6)$, diopside-jadeite $[(Na,Al,Ca,Mg)Si_2O_6]$, and chloromelanite $(Na,Al,Fe)Si_2O_6$.

Jadeite is formed through strong metamorphic action from the alteration of soda-rich rocks enclosed in serpentinous rocks. It appears as lenses, veins, stringers and nodules. Because of its inherent toughness, jadeite survives erosion when softer enclosing rocks have long since disintegrated into powder. For this reason, it has been found spread over considerable distances in alluvial deposits but only rarely is it discovered in place. Waterworn boulders vary in size from several inches to several feet across. Jadeite from a California locality has been reported in blocks weighing several hundred pounds or more. A large boulder found in a Mayan temple in Mexico weighed 200 pounds; another found in Guatemala measured 12 inches across.

The toughness of jadeite is due entirely to its structure; close examination of a typical specimen shows many thousands of minute crystals closely interlocked in every conceivable direction. This structure imparts a tenacity which is seldom equalled by any other mineral. In contrast to its supreme toughness, scratch tests show only a modest degree of hardness, about 6.5 to 7.0 on the Mohs Scale. This combination of properties makes jadeite easy to saw and carve while retaining great strength even in thin sections. The luster of jadeite is dull on fracture surfaces due to the granular structure but close examination shows a multitude of twinkling reflections from the pronounced cleavage surfaces of individual crystal grains. This same cleavage in individual grains sometimes gives rise to a slightly silky luster. Specific gravity varies according to purity but generally falls somewhere between 3.3 and 3.5; exceptionally pure material from Cloverdale, California gives 3.245; material from Clear Creek in the same state gives 3.43. Relatively pure types are translucent, sometimes very much so, but others may be so impure as to be opaque. Refractive indices are medium high in value, determinations on the small pure crystals from Cloverdale furnishing: $\alpha = 1.640$, $\beta = 1.645$, $\gamma = 1.652$; recent values on Clear Creek material are: $\alpha = 1.654 \pm .002$, $\beta = 1.657$, $\gamma = 1.666$; birefringence 0.012; biaxial, positive. Guatemalan jadeite gives: $\alpha = 1.654$, $\gamma = 1.669$; birefringence 0.015. Indices compare closely to averages of 1.65 to 1.68 for Burmese material. It should be remarked however, that properties of American jadeite may vary from those of Burma because the latter is virtually pure soda-jadeite while certain of the California and Guatemala varieties show enough replacement of sodium by calcium and magnesium to warrant calling them diopside-jadeite. In addition, many specimens of jadeite artifacts from ancient temples and cities of ancient Mexico and Central America show mechanical admixtures of albite; unless care is taken to insure purity of samples, readings of specific gravity and refractive index may result in error.

American jadeite varieties are many and frequently colorful but in general lack the intensity of hue noted in Burma material. White, pure or slightly tinged by gray, green, or grayish-blue are common; deep green to almost pure black is known in chloromelanite from Mexico and Central America. Intermediate shades of green, mixed with gray, blue, or yellow are also recognized but are rarely intense or pure in hue. Vivid colors have been found in Mexican artifacts, even the classical emerald green of "Imperial Jade" being found in a few instances.

Up to now, the use of native jadeite has been very restricted because of the non-availability of good material. Very little colorful material occurs at the California localities while anything worthwhile from Mexico and countries further south appears only in the form of beautifully executed artifacts, justly treasured for their archeological value. In Mexico, the national policy in regard to such artifacts requires that they be designated as "national treasures" and their export is strictly prohibited. Although not now economically important, the recently discovered deposit of jadeite in Guatemala may someday supply material to the market, while the possibility exists that other deposits of useful material may eventually be found in that country as well as in Mexico.

LOCALITIES

California. Up until recently, San Benito County was the only place in North America where jadeite was known to exist in rocks of origin. The first report of jadeite was made in an unpublished thesis by R. C. Mielenz in 1936 in which he discussed the geology of a portion of this county and remarked upon the occurrence of jadeite in schistose rocks. In 1950, L. P. Bolander, Jr., reported boulders of jade-like rock in the bed of Clear Creek in the same county, at a point about 6 miles east of the area described by Mielenz. This material was confirmed as jadeite by Dr. G. Switzer in the same year. Shortly after, additional finds were made in the same general area and a miniature "jade rush" took place. Jadeite was eventually located in almost a dozen large exposures in the canyon of Clear Creek on the road between New Idria and Hernandez in the southern part of the county while a large isolated mass near Santa Rita Peak was found recently. Clear Creek is a short stream, several miles in length, emptying into the San Benito River near Hernandez. In this part of San Benito County, jadeite outcrops in an oval body of serpentine, four by twelve miles in size, rimmed by Franciscan sandstone and the Upper Panoche Formation. The jadeite appears as small to large lenses completely enclosed in serpentine and one is recorded of about 50 x 100 feet in size; veins of jadeite also occur near the edges of schist bodies enclosed in the serpentine. Minerals associated with jadeite in lens-like bodies are fibrous prehnite, thomsonite, garnet, sphene, and biotite altering to chlorite while in the vein formations jadeite is associated with analcite and albite within albite-glaucophane-acmite schists. Boulders bearing jadeite are strewn over the creek and valley floors, some reaching five feet in diameter.

Unfortunately, the jadeite is of little economic value because of its generally poor coloration which varies from white to pale grayish green; it also lacks translucency while its streaking by many softer impurities prevents obtaining a good polish. Some good material, however, is found from time to time.

Jadeite has been found in waterworn masses in Mendocino County in the bed of Williams Creek, near Mina and Covelo in the Eel River gravels, and in San Luis Obispo County in the creek bed near Paso Robles. Jadeite in place has been reported in glaucophane schist near Valley Ford, Sonoma County, while another deposit is reported several hundred feet below Leach Lake on the flanks of Leach Lake Mountain in northern Mendocino County.

Mexico. Although no direct source for jadeite has been found in this country, its early history begins here and it is worthwhile to consider Mexico separately because most raw material eventually found its way into its ancient cities to be carved into the many splendid artifacts which are still being uncovered in new excavations.

The early Spanish Conquistadores found the Indians highly prizing a green stone which they called *chalchihuitl*. The conquerors, not very skilled in mineralogy, dubbed the stone "esmeralda," the Spanish equivalent for emerald, and thus started a misconception which took many years to dispel. As a matter of fact, the emeralds of Columbia were not known to the Spanish until a considerable number of years later. Early chroniclers among the freebooters remark upon the reverence accorded jadeite by the natives of the land, apparently comparable to that accorded to nephrite by the Chinese. Divine influences were ascribed as well as protection against disease, relief from pain, and other beneficial results. Jades were placed in the mouths of deceased nobles to function as hearts when they commenced living again in afterlife. Martinus de La Cruz stated that the natives mixed certain herbs and a "green pearl" in crushed jadeite and used this compound as a remedy for fractured heads (!), fever, gout, and even as an agent to revive dying persons. Nothing loathe to turn superstition to good account, the early freebooters extolled the virtues of jadeite in relieving pains in the side or in the region of the kidneys, and sold as many pieces as they could lay their hands on, calling the material "piedra de yjada," or "stone of the loin." In Europe, the stone was given a Latinized name: *Lapis Nephriticum*, or "stone of the kidneys," a title which was eventually shortened to the modern name *nephrite*. The French used "pierre de ejade," which also was shortened to *jade* and thus furnished still another useful term. The third title, jadeite, was last to appear, owing its existence to Damour, the eminent French mineralogist who undertook the study of American jade and Chinese nephrite. The latter mineral appeared in Europe in the 17th Century as a substitute for American jade which had by this time become very scarce. He concluded that two distinct mineral species were involved, the American material he called *jadeite* in contradistinction to the Chinese stone which he called *nephrite*. However, his findings were largely ignored and everyone continued to believe that nephrite came only from Mexico and jadeite from the Far East, an exact reversal of the true state of affairs.

The same eagerness to sell jade for its supposed medicinal value led directly to the loss of the jadeite localities. Within fifty years after the Conquest, practically every scrap of material had fallen into the hands of the Spaniards and was promptly dispatched to Europe. Montezuma and his people, living in the region around what is now known as Mexico City, knew jade only as an item of tribute brought each year by emissaries of neighboring states who, in turn, obtained it from sources still further removed. The conquest resulted in thorough disruption of the jade traffic; either through ignorance or design, no one could tell the Spaniards from whence this precious mineral came. So thoroughly was jade removed from the sight and thoughts of the Indians that within a phenomenally short time, even the knowledge of its existence vanished! This explains why the sources of jadeite have remained until recently one of the most intriguing and furiously debated archeological mysteries of all time. Even today, we have only one certain locality for jadeite and that happens to be in Guatemala; none has been found as yet in Mexico although exploration of certain areas in which serpentine outcrops may still reveal old mines.

The earliest jade objects have been found at sites in Tlatilco, Zacatenco, Ticoman, Gualupita, and El Arbollilo in Mexico, and at Finca Arizona and Kaminaljuyu in Guatemala. Radioactive carbon dating of the Tlatilco site gives an age of about 1500 B.C. indicating the use of jade by the Indians for at least 3000 years. However, the high degree of skill employed in its working by the Olmecs who were believed to have lived at the same time as the Tlatilocs, indicates that its first use may go back considerably further. Authentic jadeites have been found as far north as the state of Sonora and all the way into Panama at the southern extreme. The majority of specimens have come from buried towns and temples in the Mexican states of Guerrero, Oaxaca, Chiapas, Vera Cruz, and Tabasco. Large numbers of carvings, beads, and other jewelry pieces have been found in the dredgings of the famous ceremonial pool of Chichen Itza, also at Monte Alban in Oaxaca, and other places.

The coloration of jadeite from Mexico and Central America is generally not intense although some very fine green has been found almost as translucent and deeply colored as the best imperial jade from Burma. Colors most commonly met with are pearl-gray through various shades to bluish-gray (the so-called "blue" or "Olmec" jade), also greenish-gray, bluish-green, and dark green sometimes almost black. These are most commonly met with in the artifacts of the Olmec Culture. Another type is yellowish green, coarse in grain, but still so coherent that it remains remarkably tough; it is frequently found in artifacts from Mayan and Aztec sites. This kind is also found as small tubular pieces and "jaguar claws" from Olmecan sites. Olmecan lapidaries also had access to supplies of fine green jadeite mottled with white and virtually indistinguishable from similar Burmese material. Much of this was used in the Olmec earplugs which look like miniature hats with open crowns. Other cultures also used this particular type of jadeite since it has been found among the artifacts excavated from their cities and temples. Still another variety of jadeite is more opaque in its translucency being grayish-green in color and closely resembling the *celadon* of Chinese ceramics. This type is common among Mayan artifacts. The latter culture also used an evenly-colored pea-green material as well as bright to dark green jadeite almost indistinguishable from Burmese. Chloromelanite has been found rather widely distributed among all cultures but is most common in Guatemala where it was used for celts, axes, and other utilitarian tools. The color varies from very dark green to black.

Although the best jadeite artifacts are found whenever ancient ruins are systematically and scientifically excavated, a small quantity appears every year in the hands of natives and eventually finds its way into collections. However, much of the present-day "Mexican Jade" is nothing more than massive translucent calcite from the famous quarries of Tecali (see CALCITE), dyed an appropriate green, and sold to unwary tourists. It most often appears as small polished stones set in silver jewelry or as rude carvings, sometimes faithfully copying the forms and spirit of ancient Indian pieces.

Guatemala. Speculations about the origin of jadeite, some of them very wild indeed, were largely laid to rest when quantities of jadeite were found in place in the valley of the Rio Grande Motagua in south central Guatemala. This river, one of the two largest in Guatemala, rises among rugged mountainous terrain and flows eastward to empty into the Gulf of Honduras near the border of Honduras and Guatemala. To its north is the Sierra de las Minas, and further west, the Sierra de Chuacas. Both ranges of mountains have aroused interest in the past because of the abundance of serpentine rocks which are known to exist in them. Furthermore, chips, unworked blocks, and partially to fully finished artifacts found in the Motagua River valley suggested that the source of raw material was not far away.

Finally, in 1952, after considerable research and explorations in the field, Robert Leslie found jadeite in place near Manzanal. The trail led from a large almost spherical boulder found in a plowed field upon the Finca Trujillo between San Cristobal and Acasaguastlan and the hamlet of Cuijo, to an archeological site about two kilometers west of Finca Trujillo and near the village of Manzanal. The boulder was covered completely by fresh unweathered fracture surfaces indicating its use as a supply of smaller workable chips. Exploration near the village revealed jadeite in place in an outcropping directly above the village and about one kilometer distant by trail. The outcropping consists of albite with sparse inclusions of amphibole and some almost colorless grains of jadeite as well as masses of jadeite in place. Covering almost 400 square feet in area, the outcropping and also the trail leading to the village of Manzanal are littered by many chips of greenish jadeite. A broken mass of perhaps 15 pounds in weight of very pale greenish material from Manzanal was brought back and delivered to the U.S. National Museum where same slabs were sawn from it and examined closely. The surfaces of the slabs are quite smooth and the material is coherent from one end to the other. It is exceedingly tough in spite of its peculiar coarsely granular structure which at once distinguishes Guatemalan jadeite from any other kind. The best way to describe this material is to say that it looks like a conglomerate of large crystals reaching up to ½ inch across cemented firmly together with smaller crystals. A polished slab ¼ inch thick shows a high degree of translucency, the conglomerate-like structure being easily apparent.

The composition of jadeite from Manzanal has been established as essentially the same as that from Burma except that the slight traces of chromium noted in the latter are absent in Guatemalan material. The presence of albite as a mechanical impurity is characteristic and serves as an additional means of distinguishing jadeite from these widely separated sources. In all known occurrences such as in Burma, Guatemala, California, Japan, Celebes, etc., jadeite is found enclosed in serpentine and invariably associated with albite but the admixture of this mineral is very slight. In contrast, albite is very common in jadeite from Mexico and Central America causing some types to vary from albitic-jadeite to jadeitic-albite. Other accessory minerals noted are: muscovite, sphene, hornblende, actinolite, zoisite, and chromite, all rare. In chloromelanite, albite is rarely found but garnet is sometimes common, while sphene, analcite, epidote, hornblende, glaucophane have been noted as rare associates.

In his studies of the jades of Mexico and Central America, the late Dr. Foshag of the U.S. National Museum suggested that in addition to the Manzanal locality, other serpentinized rock areas may eventually reveal jadeite quarries. Likely places were listed as follows: In Guatemala—the Sierra de Chuacas along the north of the Rio Grande Motagua; and an area south of the Rio Negro extending from Zacapulas to Santa Rosa; and an area along the western shore of Lake Yzabel. A small area near Tehuitzingo in Puebla was searched by him without success. Another small area near Victoria, San Luis Potosi, is also a possibility. The latter two localities are in Mexico.

RHODONITE

In Tsarist Russia, few ornamental gemstones were so extensively used or so highly prized as their rose-red *orletz*, the name by which rhodonite is known to the people of that country. Our English name recognizes the beauty of this mineral for it is derived from *rhodos*, the Greek word for rose. Massive rhodonite is also much valued by American amateur gem cutters for its lovely pink colors which are often handsomely mottled by delicate veinlets of black creating an effect which must be seen to be appreciated. It is found in large masses of astonishing toughness and is well suited for ornamental projects such as book ends, paper weights, carvings, spheres, in addition to more delicate uses as in cabochons for jewelry. Some of the exceptionally handsome material from Rosamond, California, is illustrated in Figure 71 wherein a box carved from this material as well as a polished slab show the striking effects produced by black veinings. Although rhodonite also occurs in crystals large enough to facet, none have been found in North America and this discussion will confine itself to massive material.

Rhodonite is, ideally, a simple silicate of manganese as shown in the formula: $MnSiO_3$. In many deposits, however, some of the manganese is replaced by minor amounts of iron, calcium or zinc. Rhodonite is a metamorphic mineral appearing mainly in places where manganese ores and other metal deposits have formed. It is usually found in irregular masses or nodules, or as streaks or veins, minutely crystallized and therefore exceedingly tough although its hardness is only $5\frac{1}{2}$ to $6\frac{1}{2}$. Rhodonite fractures with much difficulty, leaving behind grainy surfaces which display small points of light from reflections of cleavage planes. In these respects, it is strikingly similar to jadeite except for its characteristic color. Seldom found in large uniformly-colored masses, most rhodonite is veined and mottled with dead-black or dark brown manganese oxides. Only rarely are distinct crystals found, sometimes, as at Franklin, New Jersey, occurring as coarse squarish prisms solidly encased in metamorphic limestone, or, at other times, as small clear prisms in cavities. The system of crystallization is Triclinic. Although two prismatic cleavages are present, intersecting at angles of about 88° and 92°, these are not troublesome in massive material because the individual crystal grains are both small and tightly interlocked. The specific gravity varies between 3.4 and 3.68, depending on purity and compactness. Refractive indices are: $a = 1.72\text{-}1.73$, $\beta = 1.73\text{-}1.74$, $\gamma = 1.73\text{-}1.744$; birefringence varies from 0.01 to 0.014; biaxial, positive or negative. Refractive indices are difficult to determine on massive material because of its lack of translucency and random arrangement of the many minute crystals, however, upon well polished flat

FIGURE 71. Rhodonite from several localities. The slab to the left and to the carved box to the right are richly-colored material from Rosamond, California. The box measures 5¼ inches by 3¾ inches by 1¾ inches. The upper of the three cabochons is from near Bald Knob, North Carolina, the lower left hand specimen is from the Alice Mine at Butte, Montana, while the remaining cabochon is from material found at the Plainfield. Massachusetts locality.

surfaces, a weak reading falling somewhere between 1.71 and 1.75 may be read with some luck.

The color of rhodonite is distinctive, ranging from pale pure pink to deep pink as the material becomes more compact. In general, translucency also varies for the same reason, deeper colored varieties tending to be more diaphanous. Variations of color within the same specimen are common, sometimes shades from the palest pink to almost red being seen across a distance of several inches. Naturally, the most highly prized colors are the deepest while anyone who has had experience in cutting and polishing rhodonite knows that more deeply colored specimens are also easier to cut and polish to a high luster than is possible in ordinary material. In some instances, rhodonite is rendered impure by other minerals such as chalcedony or idocrase, and is then mottled or curdled in texture, but often in pleasing combinations of gray, green, etc.

LOCALITIES

Alaska. Rhodonite of fair grade occurs in some quantity in a gold-bearing quartz vein at the head of Silver Bay, a narrow inlet several miles southeast of Sitka, Baranof Island, Southeastern Alaska.

British Columbia. Massive material occurs in some of the ore deposits of the Slocan Mining Camp at the southern end of Lake Slocan in the south-eastern part of the province. Massive, deep pink bunches or lenses are found in calcareous rocks in a vein of the Harp Group near Zwicky. Several foot-ball-sized cobbles of rhodonite have been picked up from the gravels of the Fraser River somewhere in the stretch above Chilliwack; this material is stated to be of good cutting grade. Very beautiful rhodonite has been found near the summit of Hill 60 near Cowichan Lake on Vancouver Island.

Massachusetts. One of the earliest recorded localities for rhodonite in North America is that known either as Plainfield or Cummington, with per-haps the latter being applied more often to specimens found as drift boulders in Cummington Township, Hampshire County. The actual in-place deposit is at the contact of Hawley schists and Savoy schists about 6 miles south of Forge Hill and very close to the intersection of the Berkshire Trail highway and the road leading to this highway from Charlemont where it occurs in place and also in numerous boulders which can be recognized from their surface blackness brought about by partial decomposition of the rhodonite into pyrolusite. Rhodonite is intimately associated with quartz veins next to which are found garnet, ankerite, rhodochrosite and other minerals. The color is pale grayish-pink to deep pink but seldom as fine as better grades from Russia, Australia, or Rosamond in California.

New Jersey. Zinc-bearing rhodonite has been found in the Franklin workings of the New Jersey Zinc Company at Franklin, Sussex County; also at the workings of this company at Ogdensburg several miles to the south. The first mentioned locality is world-famous for the splendid crystals which were found as groups embedded in pure white calcite. Some of the more compact massive material has been used sparingly in ornamental applica-tions but most is too fibrous or cleavable to hold together. The color is pale to deep pink. A polished slab of Franklin rhodonite measuring 12 inches by 12 inches is in the American Museum of Natural History as well as a magnificent group of crystals on matrix measuring 12 inches by 18 inches.

North Carolina. A peculiar violet-pink, very fine-grained rhodonite is found in several prospects developed along a manganese ore vein in Allegheny County. This lengthy vein extends over a considerable distance near Bald Knob but the main prospect pit is about 7 miles southeast of Independence, Virginia, and 1½ miles south of the state line between Virginia and North Carolina. The rhodonite forms lenses of pure material up to 4 inches in thickness intergrown with massive brownish spessartite garnet and delicate veinlets of pyrolusite. A cabochon of this material is illustrated in Fig. 71.

Montana. Massive material once occurred in quantity as a gangue mineral in the silver veins of the now-inactive Alice Mine at Butte, Silverbow County. Similar material is common in several of the mines, among them the Rainbow Lode, Allie Brown, and the Wapello Vein in the Lexington Mine. In these deposits, rhodonite associated with rhodochrosite and other ores, forms banded veins below the oxidized zone, sometimes up to 24 inches thick. Rhodonite from the Butte district is extremely fine-grained, pale to bright pink in color, and delicately veined with black; it takes a fine polish. A cabochon made from typical material is illustrated in Fig. 71.

Oregon. A vein of rhodonite 48 inches thick is said to be located near the Oregon Caves on Cave Creek, Josephine County, furnishing flawless slabs of good color, 6 to 8 inches across. Rhodonite, associated with black oxides of manganese, is found beneath a limestone bed. The color is delicate rose pink with gray and greenish-gray mottlings as well as black markings. Boulders of this material have been found in the gravels of Cave Creek and other streams in the vicinity as well as some in adjacent Jackson County.

New Mexico. Showy examples of massive material have been found at the Comstock Mine in the Kingston District of Sierra County.

California. Much good rhodonite has been mined from the Wheeler rhodonite prospect in Siskiyou County, located about 9 miles north of Happy Camp, on the steep eastern slope of Thompson Mountain, between the east fork of Indian Creek and Thompson Creek. The workings are at an elevation of 4,500 feet in wild and mountainous country and consist of an opencut and tunnel exploiting the rhodonite body which here forms a ledge 6 feet thick. The enclosing rock is fine-grained quartzite interbedded with black schist in which occurs delicate pink to deep rose pink material seamed and veined with black markings. Black oxides of manganese are found penetrating joints and seams in the rock and sometimes form pure masses of considerable size. Despite the extent of the deposit, rhodonite is not found in large blocks of even coloration, however, it is even in texture. Many specimens contain dull greenish-gray quartzite inclusions while others in which green inclusions are more vividly hued provide handsome contrasts in pink, black, and green.

A considerable quantity of fine pink rhodonite veined with black has been obtained from the Peters Mine near Taylorsville, Indian Valley, Plumas County. Similar material was obtained from Genessee Valley nearby.

In Tulare County, rhodonite was found at the old Ward Property about 3 miles north of Lemon Cove. This locality is on the north side of a small ravine about ⅓ mile northeast of the Kaweah River and about 1 mile east of the Ward ranch house. Rhodonite occurs in two ledges about 35 feet apart separated by a mass of quartzite. One of the ledges is about 30 feet thick the other about 10 feet, however, both consist principally of quartzite heavily stained with black manganese oxides in which are found stringers of massive rhodonite.

Beach pebbles of rhodonite are found in the cove at the outlet of Lime Kiln Creek on the Pacific coastline of Monterey County, about 8 miles north of Plaskett Point.

One of the outstanding localities for exceptionally deep color rhodonite is that of Portal Ridge in Los Angeles County near Lancaster (Rosamond). Massive, fine-grained, exceptionally tough material occurs in the form of weathered, black-skinned boulders lying on the surface or partially embedded in the soil. Some of the larger specimens reach weights up to at least several hundred pounds but are so tough that any attempt to break them up with sledges meets with failure. All have dead-black exteriors from layers of manganese oxides up to several inches thick. Toward the interior, the black oxides become hard and finally give way to pink, then red rhodonite. This locality yields the finest rhodonite in North America but is rapidly being depleted. Several splendid examples of this material are illustrated in Fig. 71.

Fair quality rhodonite, covered with the usual black manganese compounds, has been found as boulders at the summit of Cajon Pass in the San Bernardino Mountains in the extreme southwestern corner of San Bernardino County, in alluvial material which forms a large fan leading north from the pass toward the desert floor.

Poor to fair rhodonite, heavily veined and laced with black, has been found several miles northeast of Bankhead Springs in the southeastern part of San Diego County. Some fine specimens are reported to occur in the Anza State Park near the Riverside County line.

IDOCRASE
(*Vesuvianite*)

The mineral idocrase furnishes several very attractive gem varieties, principally compact massive types such as the green *californite* from a number of places in the state of California and facet grade material from Laurel, Quebec. Californite is very popular among the amateur cutters of the United States because it is extremely tough, occurs in large pieces and in a variety of attractive colors, and is relatively inexpensive. Much is consumed each year in handmade jewelry, or made into bookends and other more massive objects, and more recently, employed in tumbled baroque gemstones for use in jewelry. Facet material is far more difficult to obtain and only several localities are known to be productive.

The name idocrase is apparently derived from the Greek but its exact connotation is uncertain, on the other hand, the alternate name *vesuvianite* is taken from the well-known occurrence of this mineral in limestone blocks ejected from Mount Vesuvius in Italy and from which place this mineral was first identified. The name *californite* was proposed by G. F. Kunz in 1903 as a commercial name for the mineral and is obviously in honor of the state in which it was found. The title "California jade" has also been used but is misleading and should be dropped. A massive variety of blue color is called *cyprine*.

Idocrase is a hydrous calcium iron magnesium silicate with the formula $Ca_{10}Al_4(Mg,Fe)_2Si_9O_{34}(OH)_4$. In some instances, the purity of idocrase from California is questionable because variations in analyses and in physical properties indicate that grossularite garnet which occurs with it in massive form, is mixed intimately with the idocrase. Crystallizing in the Tetragonal System, idocrase forms distinctive prismatic crystals, short and stubby, of square cross section and capped by 4-sided pyramids at each end as shown in Figure 72. Crystals are rarely of gem quality except at the Laurel locality. The hardness is only 6½, but the compact nature of massive forms imparts a toughness comparing with that of jade. Massive material breaks with a fine sugary surface, or, if the structure is fibrous, with a hackly rough surface. Crystals break with conchoidal fractures of glassy luster. Specific gravity

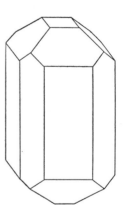

FIGURE 72. An idocrase crystal.

varies considerably (see California, below), but generally falls somewhere between 3.4 and 3.5. Refractive indices for clear material vary from $\omega = 1.706$, $\epsilon = 1.702$ to $\omega = 1.726$, $\epsilon = 1.732$; birefringence 0.004. A yellow faceted gem from Laurel gave $\omega = 1.708$, $\epsilon = 1.700$; birefringence 0.008. The birefringence of idocrase can vary from as little as 0.001 to as much as 0.010; it is to be noted that the optic sign changes from negative for low values of refraction to positive in high values.

The colors of idocrase are many but some shade of yellowish- to olive-green predominates. Brown, yellow, blue, pink, and colorless are also known. The yellow transparent material from Laurel shows very strong dichroism: dark brownish-red and bright, faintly greenish-yellow.

Commercialization of North American idocrase has met with considerable success in the case of massive types but less so for faceting material from Laurel. About 1910, an unsuccessful attempt was made to sell californite to the Chinese as a substitute for jade. In his Consular and Trade Report for October 25, 1911, Consul General S. S. Knabenshue of Tsientsin stated that samples submitted to leading firms in that city found a poor reception because the particular color of green was of no value to them. Since adequate supplies of nephrite from Turkestan and jadeite from Burma were arriving in China daily, there was probably no need at that time to consider substitutes, especially if they bore a resemblance in color to the cheap serpentine known as "Soochow jade" or "new jade." This latter material is much used even today and can be seen in almost every store selling curios in Hong Kong. If present trade laws did not prevent doing so, it may be that californite would meet a better reception in the Chinese jade cutting centers than it did many years ago. Although much californite is rather dull in color some types are very beautiful, especially the translucent chartreuse material from Pulga, California. There is little question that the better grades could sell abroad but it is doubtful that better prices would be received than those now being offered in the amateur gem cutting market. In the case of the clear yellow idocrase from Laurel an attempt to lay it before the public through established jewelry channels was made many years ago, but after limited success, the venture fell through. The famous Canadian firm of Birks, Ltd., jewelers of long-established reputation, obtained the output of idocrase from the Laurel mine and had it cut into brilliants and stepcuts but never in gems more than several carats weight because of size limitations of the material itself. The more publicly-palatable title of *Laurelite* was adopted but even this did not offset the failure of this gem to "catch on."

LOCALITIES

New Brunswick. Green idocrase occurs in masses up to several inches across at Charley Cove on Frye Island, Charlotte County. The material is yellowish-green to slightly brownish-green, almost opaque, badly fractured and is not very attractive.

Quebec. Beautiful purplish-pink massive idocrase of granular texture occurs in the Montreal Chrome Pit, Black Lake, Coleraine Township, Megantic County. Pieces up to several inches across have been found here and should provide striking cabochons, however, much of the material contains minute vugs lined with clear microscopic crystals of idocrase and specimens of this nature should be avoided since such places will fill with polishing powder if an attempt is made to cut them. The color seems due to manganese; the presence of 0.20 percent of this element is shown by analysis.

The noted idocrase locality at Laurel is actually a small pit in forested land requiring the services of a guide to reach. It is near the southern end of Sixteen Island Lake in the north central part of Argenteuil County. Not much has been reported about the mineralization of the deposit since recent visits by competent mineralogists found the excavation filled with water. However, it seems that this is an occurrence within the metamorphic limestone of the Grenville series with additional mineralization provided by intrusion of a feldspar pegmatite. The pegmatite was originally mined for mica and it was during this time that gem quality idocrase was found. From specimens at hand, it appears that this mineral formed rude squarish prisms with vertical striations along the sides, about 2 inches in diameter and perhaps 3 inches to 4 inches in length. Fragments found in the dumps by recent visitors show that all crystals were badly shattered during formation and consequently clear areas over ½ inch cannot be obtained, furthermore, the presence of numerous minute liquid inclusions further restricts the size of flawless facet-grade fragments. When finished, facet gems are a beautiful rich yellow with orange-brown overtones, and distinctive in appearance from other gemstones of similar hue. A fine brilliant-cut gem of ⅜ inch across (weight not stated) is in the American Museum of Natural History. Smaller examples are in the collections of the Royal Ontario Museum of Natural History at Toronto and also in a number of private collections.

New Jersey. The rare blue variety of idocrase, cyprine, was once found in some abundance in the Parker Shaft of the New Jersey Zinc Company on Mine Hill, Franklin, Sussex County. It first appeared in 1922 as a coarsely fibrous massive material mixed with brown garnet, pale pink bustamite, white willemite and calcite which provided most attractive polished slabs. The color varied from blue to blue-green and was said to be almost as intense as lapis lazuli. Blue-green types furnished refractive indices of: $\omega = 1.710$, $\epsilon = 1.698$; sky-blue material gives: $\omega = 1.713$, $\epsilon = 1.705$; green: $\omega = 1.719$, $\epsilon = 1.712$. The specific gravity was given as approximately 3.45. The mine mentioned above is now closed permanently.

Maryland. Small vein-like masses of translucent olive-green idocrase similar to californite occur in a large quarry northwest of Rockville, Montgomery Co. Associated minerals are pink to red massive grossularite garnet, bright green diopside and serpentine. Refractive indices of this material are: $\omega = 1.713$ and $\epsilon = 1.710$; birefringence 0.003. Further details on this locality are given under DIOPSIDE.

Oregon. Boulders of idocrase of the californite variety have been found at the mouth of the Chetco River and also north of this point in Curry County; colors are yellowish-green to pale green.

California. The earliest discovery of californite in this state is attributed to a Chinese prospector by the name of Chan who filed on an outcropping on the south fork of Indian Creek, Siskiyou County, under the impression that it was nephrite jade he had found. The claim is sometimes referred to even now as the Chan Claim. Following this first discovery, other deposits of idocrase have been found in California until the list now numbers 7 localities scattered among 6 counties. In the descriptions below, each of these will be taken up proceeding from north to south.

Characteristically, massive idocrase occurs in metamorphic limestone near its contact with igneous rocks; grossularite garnet is intimately admixed to some degree in all occurrences while serpentine is frequently seen in others. Typical specific gravities of californites are:

Siskiyou County	3.286	color unstated	Kunz
"	3.57	white	Pogue
Butte County	3.410	green	Sterrett
"	3.470	yellow-green	"
"	3.599	white	"
Fresno County	3.359	green	Clarke & Steiger
"	3.586	white	"
"	3.351	green	Sterrett

The above data are remarkable for the fact that white material is significantly and consistently higher in value than green. This is indicative of the presence of grossularite garnet which has a substantially higher gravity (SG = 3.5 or more) than idocrase (SG not more than 3.45). The problem in examining any californite is to distinguish which part of the mixture is true idocrase and which part is white grossularite. Perhaps the term *californite* is actually the most appropriate since the evidence is strong that little of the californite type idocrase is pure. Further, external features are also distinctive and actually bear little resemblance to idocrases from other types of occurrences. It is perhaps best to think of all californites as mixtures of several minerals and let it go at that.

The first and perhaps the most productive locality for californite is the Indian Creek or Happy Camp deposit located at 1700 feet elevation on the south fork of Indian Creek about 10 miles north-northwest of Happy Camp. The locality and early workings are shown in Figure 73. The south fork of Indian Creek runs in a northeasterly direction in a steep narrow canyon, joining the main stream about 2½ miles below the mine. The location of the claim is in Section 7, T.17 N. R7E, H. In the canyon, californite outcrops for over a distance of 300 feet in a north-northwesterly direction on the north side of the creek, about 75 feet above the bed. The country rock is principally serpentine, colored gray, green, or black, and contains californite in pods, lenses, and irregular bodies ranging in size from a few inches to 10 feet in thickness. Openings consist of benches with several short tunnels driven beneath the deposit. Large masses up to 5 x 5 feet across were found in the creek bed in early days, while later exploration of creek gravels showed smaller boulders and pebbles scattered downstream as far as Blue Bar Camp, the lower limit of finds. More material has also been found in O'Meara Creek which enters Indian Creek about two miles above Blue Bar Camp. At the

FIGURE 73. One of the earliest mines for idocrase (californite) along the South Fork of Indian Creek, Siskiyou County, California. Looking north across the creek may be seen several tunnel openings on the idocrase seam embedded in soft serpentine. Many fine boulders of this material have been found in the bed of the creek below the outcrop and for some distance downstream. Courtesy U.S. Geological Survey.

principal outcrop, masses of good color are seldom over 12 inches thick while poorer kinds may be several feet across. Some is quite translucent but much is opaque greenish-gray. Many cracks and seams traverse the masses and flawless blocks of large size are scarce. Californite from this deposit is characterized by a translucent ground mass of grayish olive-green in which are sprinkled small streaks of opaque pale green or yellowish material. White grossularite, very compact and uniform in texture, often highly translucent, is also found in boulders in the stream bed of Indian Creek and has been erroneously called "white californite."

The finest californite from any locality in the state is the beautiful, highly translucent greenish-yellow material from Pulga in Butte County. Some specimens are so clear that one is reminded of certain exceptionally translucent chalcedonies. The color is very pure and vivid and shows no trace of dinginess. The best grade is actually clear enough to facet respectable stones of several carats weight and even larger ones would be feasible if it were not for the fact that so many cracks and seams crisscross the masses that flawless areas over ½ inch across are seldom found. There are two deposits near Pulga but both are close together and only the commercially important one will be treated here. The workings are located on the west side of the north fork of the Feather River about ½ mile northeast of the Big Bar Station of the Western Pacific Railroad and near the small community of Pulga. The deposit was first worked by the North California Mining Company in 1907, and in 1910 considerable quantities of fine material were removed. An opencut and tunnel expose the deposits which outcrop on a steep rocky hillside, almost a cliff, about 200 feet above the railroad tracks at an elevation of 1600 feet above sea level. The country rock is greenish-gray to yellowish-green and greenish-black serpentine, badly crushed and compressed into lenticular masses. Californite occurs in a belt 12 feet wide in the crushed serpentine with lenses, nodules, and streaks, scattered irregularly through the belt. Pure masses range from less than an inch to as much as 3 inches thick. Pebbles and cobbles of vein material are found in gravel at the junction of the north and middle forks of the Feather River. In addition to the chartreuse or greenish-yellow color, bluish-green, gray, some with touches of pink, and darker shades of pure green also occur. Parts of gray, green, and yellow masses are highly translucent. Beautiful pure white grossularite garnet, also very translucent, is found in pieces of the same size as the californite. Some is clear enough to facet gems of up to 10 carats in which sufficient reflection of light is returned from back facets to make them glow with a creamy color. Although unflawed californite is invariably small, its beauty makes it much sought after for cabochons, faceted gems, and tumbled stones.

An interesting californite occurrence is recorded along Traverse Creek, 2½ miles south-southeast of Georgetown, Eldorado County near the crossing of Bear Creek Road over Traverse Creek. Although massive californite from this locality is good cutting quality, a unique type is provided by the occurrence of beautiful perfectly-developed prismatic crystals of idocrase which are found lining vugs in massive material. These crystals are very small but transparent and flawless; two deep green faceted gems but only ⅛ inch in size are in the American Museum of Natural History. At the locality, numerous veins of californite are found scattered throughout an outcrop of serpentine covering an area of several hundred acres. Veins contain lenses and rounded masses of good quality up to 3 feet thick. The principal working is an opencut 15 feet deep and about 50 feet along the strike of the outcrop. The color is the usual yellow-green with colorless to white garnet as an accompanying mineral.

In Fresno County an important deposit is located on the east side of Watts Valley about 1½ miles south of the Hawkins Schoolhouse. The workings are at 2000 feet above sea level or about 700 feet above the level of Watts Creek. This deposit was initially mined many years ago by the

Prethero Brothers and Nat Parker who sent much of their production to Los Angeles for cutting. Californite occurs here as lenses, nodules, and streaks in serpentine but unflawed pieces are seldom over several inches thick. Joints, cracks, and streaks of impurities are numerous. The better grades are translucent, principally green in color with a yellowish tinge but yellowish-green and other shades are known. White grossularite garnet is also present. In Tulare County, two deposits of commercial value are recorded: the first near Lindsay and the other near Exeter. The Lindsay deposit was originally worked for copper and is located on the south side of the ridge south of Lewis Creek at elevations of from 300 to 500 feet above the surrounding level terrain. The country rock is serpentine containing lenses and stringers of californite. The latter is generally green but grades into pale gray and white, and pinkish-white next to the contact with serpentine. Blocks as large as 24 inches across occur here. Lighter colored and more translucent types contain dark green spots whose coloration is attributed to traces of chromium. The texture is exceedingly fine and the toughness of a very high order. Some very good grass-green translucent material has been found at this locality. All workings are opencut, consisting of about a dozen small pits sprinkled over the hillside. At the Exeter locality, a vein of californite of from 2 to 4 inches in thickness encased in magnesite crosses serpentine forming the top of a rounded hill about 500 feet above the valley floor. The white magnesite is pleasingly mixed with the californite, and, as shown in polished seam sections, appears to have cemented together masses of brecciated californite. The color of californite from this locality is predominantly green.

The last locality in California and also the least important, is that at the Crestmore quarries of the Riverside Cement Company located three miles north of Riverside in Riverside County. Pale green californite occurs here in the upper level of the Commercial Quarry in masses and streaks of no great size. A small quantity has been cut but apparently has not been of outstanding quality.

THE GARNET GROUP

In the Mineral Kingdom, garnet is especially abundant in metamorphic rocks but is also common in igneous rocks. In the former it tends to grow in beautiful sharp lustrous crystals much prized by mineral collectors as well as connoisseurs of gemstones, while in igneous rocks it is most apt to form gemmy grains of exceptional clarity and color which however lack good crystal form. North America is blessed with an abundance of garnet in all its colors and forms, important localities for both specimen and gem material being known from the Arctic to Mexico. Especially fine pyrope, even better than that so commonly seen in Bohemian garnet jewelry occurs in abundance in Arizona while bright orange spessartite from California and Virginia is seldom rivalled by material from any other locality in the world.

Because the species almandine and pyrope are most commonly found in gem quality and hence appear most frequently in jewelry, many persons believe all garnet to be red in color; actually nothing could be further from the truth! There are six distinct species of closely-related minerals comprising the Garnet Group, differing from each other in chemical composition and occurring in an astonishing variety of colors. Thus among the several garnet species may be found material in pure black, pure white, and colorless, but also in virtually every color of the spectrum except blue. Though perhaps most abundant in single crystals, garnet is also found in massive forms some of which closely resemble jade or idocrase.

The name garnet has been derived from the Latin word *granatum* which referred to seeds, especially to those of the pomegranate, in which, as readers will recall, hundreds are found surrounded by a bright red pulp and bearing a superficial resemblance to actual garnet crystals. The origin of names for each of the six species will be discussed as each is taken up.

Belonging to the Isometric System, garnet habitually forms rounded crystals rich in faces, sometimes looking like natural jewels which have been cut and polished by the hand of man. The most common geometric forms are the dodecahedron and trapezohedron, either singly or combined and then resulting in even more complex crystals. Several common forms are illustrated in Figure 74. The approximately spherical shape of perfectly formed crystals is echoed in rough specimens which after suffering abrasion, look like crudely-formed sandblasted marbles. The six garnet species may be divided

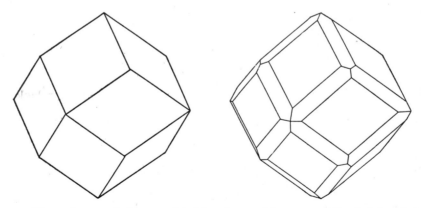

FIGURE 74. Two characteristic crystal habits observed in garnet. The left hand form is known as the dodecahedron while the right hand figure shows each edge of the basic dodecahedron beveled by a trapezohedron. Compare the latter figure with the Stikine River garnet crystals shown in Figure 75.

into two sub-groups within each there may be considerable blending as one or two elements are exchanged in varying proportions:

Almandine	$Fe_3Al_2Si_3O_{12}$	iron aluminum silicate
Pyrope	$Mg_3Al_2Si_3O_{12}$	magnesium aluminum silicate
Spessartite	$Mn_3Al_2Si_3O_{12}$	manganese aluminum silicate
Grossularite	$Ca_3Al_2Si_3O_{12}$	calcium aluminum silicate
Andradite	$Ca_3Fe_2Si_3O_{12}$	calcium iron silicate
Uvarovite	$Ca_3Cr_2Si_3O_{12}$	calcium chromium silicate

The characteristics of the first group are greater hardness and the predominance of red, brown, or orange colors, while those of the second group are generally softer and appear in a wider variety of hues but aside from grossularite, seldom display red or orange coloration.

ALMANDINE

Almandine is by far the most abundant garnet and is typically a mineral of metamorphic rocks, especially schists and gneisses from which it is often removed in beautifully formed dodecahedral crystals completely covered with glistening faces (see Fig. 75). Crystals vary in size from those as small as a pin head to some reaching several feet in diameter as in the Adirondack Mountains of New York. Because most metamorphic rocks are placed under stress even after the constituents have solidified in final form, crystals larger than the size of a pea are seldom found unshattered. For practical purposes, flawless masses of almandine larger than an inch across are extremely rare. *Carbuncle* is the name applied to deep red almandine cut in cabochon form, sometimes with the base hollowed out to lighten the color. Since the carbuncles of Pliny's time were cut and polished at a place called Alabanda, the derivation of this name has come down to us as the species title. The hardness of almandine corresponds to $7\frac{1}{2}$ on the Mohs Scale, which, combined with a good degree of toughness and the complete lack of cleavage planes in this as well as in all species of the group, makes gems cut from it fairly durable. Almandine tends to fracture into angular fragments with smooth glistening surfaces and sharp edges. The luster is glassy and brilliant. The specific gravity varies from 3.85 to 4.20 but the presence of gas or liquid-filled inclusions as well as heavy foreign mineral particles may cause lower or higher values. Refractive indices are also variable, from 1.751 to 1.82 although most gem specimens seldom go below 1.77. Refraction is single; the dispersion is moderate: 0.024. The most common color of almandine is rich red-brown or brownish-red, sometimes so dark that the specimen appears black. Finer grades, perhaps with less iron in their composition, gradually lighten in tone and assume a lovely tinge of purple which is very distinctive.

There is of course no pleiochroism and the distribution of color within crystals is completely uniform. Commercially, almandine is most employed in the form of faceted gems in rings, also as carbuncles, sometimes of very large size. Pale colored kinds are extremely beautiful and make very effective faceted stones for all manner of jewelry. Minute inclusions of needle-like rutile crystals are often thickly distributed throughout some crystals and give rise to asterism when cut in cabochon form. The distribution of these inclusions is governed by the crystal structure in such a way that finished gems may show four-rayed or six-rayed stars depending on how they are cut. Star almandine is abundant in Idaho but only a few examples show truly bright stars.

PYROPE

Pyrope is also much employed in jewelry because of its beautiful deep red color, in fact it is this color which gave this species its name from the Greek word meaning "fiery." The color varies from slightly brownish-red to purplish-red as the composition approaches almandine. When the proportion of almandine reaches one to two of pyrope, the color becomes much paler in tone and a delightful rose-red in hue, furnishing the variety known as *rhodolite*. Here again the name is derived from a descriptive Greek word, this time *rhodos* for "rose." The origin of pyrope differs from other garnet species since it is primarily found in volcanic instead of metamorphic rocks. The lovely specimens from the Arizona-New Mexico field occur in a peculiar breccia of volcanic origin, while the kimberlite plugs of the Arkansas diamond mines contain small irregular grains of pyrope, some of gem quality. Crystals are extremely rare, the majority of specimens being little more than formless masses, sometimes deeply etched or grooved, or, pebble-like in form but smooth and glassy as if exterior layers had chipped off. Most are very small, seldom over ¼ inch in diameter although some reach as much as ½ inch and even larger. Though free from cracks as a rule, small black specks, needle-like inclusions (rutile?), and gas or liquid filled cavities are common internal imperfections. Physical and optical properties of pyrope grade insensibly toward those of almandine as magnesium and iron interchange in the composition. The hardness is close to almandine, perhaps at times slightly softer and therefore varies between 7¼ and 7½. Specific gravity ranges between 3.648 and 3.82. The single refractive index may fall anywhere between 1.730 and 1.77, but most often between 1.74 and the latter value. The dispersion is moderate, 0.024. Pyrope is mostly employed in the form of small faceted gems in jewelry, a statement which is also true of rhodolite, however, in recent years much of the pyrope of Arizona-New Mexico has been tumbled into beautifully brilliant and colorful baroques which may be successfully appliqued to silver jewelry by modern plastic cements.

SPESSARTITE

One of the loveliest of all the garnet group is *spessartite* which is found in gem-quality crystals of pale orange-yellow, orange, orange-red, or deep red color. Unlike similarly hued *grossularite* which always seems to be swirled inside as if melted and then solidified, spessartite is unusually clear internally and therefore provides gems of excellent brilliancy. The name of this species is derived from Spessart, a district in Bavaria where good examples have been found. Spessartite frequently contains considerable almandine and then tends toward brownish or reddish hues, but varieties most closely approximating the ideal formula are more orange or yellow. Practically all gem material is derived from pegmatite dikes where spessartite is often the most abundant garnet; it is found in individual crystals sprinkled throughout border zones inward to the very core where it occurs as fine crystals perched on other minerals in pockets or as etched masses enclosed in spaces between cleavelandite crystal blades. Individual crystals range in size from those as small as a match head to some as large as golf balls.

Somewhat softer than other garnets, the hardness ranges from 7 to 7¼, specific gravity varies from 3.90 to 4.20, and the refractive index falls between 1.79 and 1.81. Spessartite is seldom seen in jewelry on account of its rarity and very few sources offer a steady supply of material. Superficially, spessartite can be confused with similarly colored grossularite (*hessonite*) and at one time all of the spessartite from the Southern California sources was erroneously labeled "hessonite." Recent work has conclusively shown this material to be virtually ideal spessartite in respect to chemical composition.

The three remaining garnet species, *grossularite, andradite,* and *uvarovite,* are more closely related to each other than to any of those previously discussed, each containing calcium as an essential element instead of aluminum.

GROSSULARITE

Grossularite owes its peculiar name to a fancied resemblance of some translucent greenish types to the fruit of the *grossularia* or gooseberry. The commonly used names *hessonite* or *essonite,* applied to brownish or brownish-red facet grade specimens, have been derived from the Greek word for "less" in fanciful allusion to their inferior hardness as compared to zircons of similar color. Sometimes *hyacinth* and *jacinth* are also used to designate grossularite of orange and reddish-brown color but some confusion may result because these terms are more accurately applied to similarly colored zircons. *Cinnamon-stone* is another self-explanatory term for grossularite. Grossularite displays an unusually wide range of color and form, being found in crystals ranging in color from absolutely colorless, through pink, green, yellow, orange, brown, and red. However, virtually all good facet material is found in orange to orange-red and reddish-brown crystals. Massive types occur in translucent white to dead white, greenish, brownish, and sometimes yellowish shades. Grossularite is almost wholly a garnet of metamorphic rocks in which calcium minerals are abundant, thus it is most likely to be encountered in metamorphic limestones but is also found in schists and in contacts between calcareous rocks and igneous bodies. Crystals are frequently of excellent form, usually simple dodecahedrons, and are often found embedded in calcite or perched on walls of crevices in metamorphic rocks; they may reach several inches in diameter but are seldom completely clear and of gem quality. The internal structure of reddish or brownish grossularite is characteristically confused or "swirled" as if the original material had been melted without stirring. When broken, this graininess of structure is reflected upon fracture surfaces. The hardness is not very great, about 7 for clear material and about 6½ for massive kinds, the latter being exceptionally tough on account of their granular structure. The specific gravity varies from 3.42 to 3.80. The single refraction measures from 1.741 to 1.748; the dispersion is moderate at 0.028. In North America, very little grossularite useful for clear faceted gems is found in quantity anywhere but massive forms are abundant associated with idocrase of the californite variety (see IDOCRASE).

ANDRADITE

Perhaps the most spectacular of all garnet gems are provided by members of the *andradite* species enjoying as they do high refractive indices and enormous dispersive powers. The latter property often results in faceted gems twinkling and sparkling with many many bits of color although the effect is sometimes partly masked by deep body color. By far the handsomest andradite is the yellowish-green to emerald-colored variety known as *demantoid* in which dispersion is so pronounced that its resemblance to diamond in this respect led to its being given the Dutch name for diamond, i.e., *demant*. So far as is known, the only important gem material has come from the Ural Mountains of the USSR. A yellow variety of andradite named *topazolite* after its topaz-yellow color, is also frequently mentioned as a gemstone but few specimens large enough to cut have ever been found. The Greek word for "black" has been used to form the varietal name for a black andradite called *melanite*. Beautiful crystallized specimens have been found in California and in Arkansas but are of little use in the lapidary arts. Andradite receives its name from the Portuguese mineralogist d'Andrada who appears to be the first to describe one of its subvarieties. Like grossularite, this species is most frequently found in metamorphic rocks containing calcium; at the Arizona locality for example, crystals occur lining cavities in metamorphic limestone. Andradite is rather soft, only 6½, also rather brittle. Crystals generally show simple dodecahedral development, sometimes with beveled edges, but at other times are modified by numerous small lines and ridges upon the faces. Specific gravity ranges from 3.80 to 3.90; refractive indices vary from 1.82 to 1.89 with a very high dispersion of 0.057, a value comfortably exceeding that of diamond (0.044), and sphene (0.051). The color of Arizona material is deep rich brown in which dark red flashes of dispersive color appear in cut examples.

UVAROVITE

Uvarovite, the last member of the garnet group, is here dismissed with a few words primarily because its crystals are far too small to be cut. If only larger individuals could be found, this exceedingly beautiful emerald-green garnet would quickly assume an important place in the world of gems. Handsome groups of minute crystals have been found in the United States lining crevices in massive chromite but the largest crystals seldom reach as much as ⅛ inch in diameter and even then are not fully clear.

LOCALITIES

Greenland. Almandine of gem quality has been found in numerous places in schists and gneisses of the west coast of Greenland from the Disko Bay region south. Precious garnet associated with chlorite is found in granite which has been intruded by basalt on the island of Tasiusak at 73° − 23′ N., 55° − 50′ W. Similar garnet occurs on the island of Nusak southeast of the above locality; also at various places along the shores of Ikerarsuk Fjord north of Upernivik. Gem quality crystals occur associated with anthophyllite on the island of Ntivdlinguak, a few miles southeast of Upernivik; also at numerous points upon the islands situated about 9 miles north of Upernivik and between that settlement and Tasiusak; also near Taujat on the Svartenhuk Peninsula. Much garnet associated with quartz, orthoclase and graphite in veins in gneiss is found on Lango (island); some is clear and deep red. At Akia on the island of Storo, a few miles east of Umanak in the southeastern arm of Umanak Fjord, beautiful red gem quality almandine occurs in pegmatites associated with quartz and graphite. Much of the garnet occurs in rounded masses without trace of crystal form. Gem material is common and said to be of very high quality; its specific gravity is 4.06.

Precious garnet is found in black micaceous schist associated with hornblende and feldspar on the island of Simiutaluk at the mouth of Atanek Fjord, about 40 miles south of the settlement of Egedesminde.

During the summer of 1942, the author was stationed at the Bluie West Eight air base located in the innermost reaches of Sondre Stromfjord and just north of the Arctic Circle. On the northern shore of the fjord immediately next to the harbor, a small boulder of white mica schist was found in which many beautiful purplish-pink rhodolite grains of gem quality were studded thickly. The size of the grains was only about ⅛ to ¼ inch but each was of unusual transparency and delicacy of color. The refractive index of this rhodolite has been determined as 1.76.

Perhaps the most noted place for Greenland garnet, often mentioned in gem literature but not located with much exactitude, is the region east of Godthaab. Garnet occurs abundantly in micaceous schists between the eastern arm of Ameralik Fjord (Ameragdla), and the southeast extremity of Kangersunek Fjord which is about 10 miles east-northeast of Ameragdla. The area is about 45 miles east-northeast of Godthaab. This garnet was well-known to the natives of Greenland at least as early as the beginning of the 19th Century and when the Danes settled Greenland, it was brought in by Eskimo hunters who penetrated the hinterlands in search of game. Garnet occurs as formless masses in gneiss, mica schist and hornblende schist associated with a peculiar anthophyllite (gedrite) which shows strong and beautiful adularescence (see ACTINOLITE & TREMOLITE). Masses up to 55 pounds in weight have been found. Broken pieces are often coated with white mica plates while occasionally small feldspar crystals are observed within the garnet itself. This material has been used to some extent for gem cutting and one writer records that one exceptional mass furnished a polished specimen of flawless character over 1 inch in diameter. The specific gravity of this almandine is uncommonly low: SG = 3.840 − 3.865.

Alaska. A famous locality for beautiful crystallizations of almandine much prized as mineral specimens, is that variously labeled "Stikine River" or "Wrangell." The locality is actually 1¾ miles southeast of Sergief Island in the mouth of the Stikine River delta on the mainland of Alaska and a considerable distance from Wrangell, a town located on an island and usually the point from which trips to the locality are begun. The deposits outcrop about 300 yards from the water's edge where Garnet Creek empties into the estuary. As shown in Figure 75, finely-formed crystals occur in dark-colored schists consisting of quartz, biotite, muscovite, graphite, and feldspar. Crystals are generally small, less than ¼ inch in diameter, but many are found ¾ to 1

FIGURE 75. Deep red almandine garnet crystals in gray micaceous schist from the noted locality upon the Stikine River estuary near Wrangell, Southeastern Alaska. Each crystal shows well the development of the dodecahedron each of whose edges is beveled by partially developed faces of the trapezohedron. Courtesy Smithsonian Institution.

inch in diameter and even larger. The garnet of this deposit has been known for many years and attempts have been made to mine the crystals for abrasive purposes. The most important mine workings are met as Garnet Creek is ascended, and are marked by a series of opencuts and tunnels. In the deposit, stones from near the surface appear of little use for lapidary work due to extensive cracking but those from deep workings are more solid and have been infrequently used for cabochons. The specific gravity of this garnet is 4.1. All crystal faces are well developed and show a combination of the dodecahedron and trapezohedron.

North West Territories. Beautiful gem quality almandine is found at Alert Harbor, and at Garnet Island, Baffinland. At the latter place, the garnet occurs as irregular masses enclosed in a schist consisting of biotite and feldspar; masses reach as much as 4 inches in diameter but are invariably cracked to such an extent that only small gems can be cut. The color is fine deep red.

Quebec. Massive grossularite garnet containing vugs lined with small transparent crystals of gem grade occurs in metamorphic limestone on Lot 7, Range 1 in Wakefield Township, 21 miles north of Hull on the right bank of the Gatineau River, Gatineau County. Some of the crystals are perfectly colorless and transparent with clear areas large enough to facet gems of several carats, others appear in light yellow to light brown hues. In the United States National Museum is a faceted cushion brilliant of this material, pale yellow in color, and weighing 1.24 carats. Grossularite similar to the foregoing also occurs in Hull Township in this same county. Similar granular cavernous grossularite in which the cavities are lined with small gemmy crystals, occurs in the Southwark Asbestos Pit, located 1½ miles southeast of the town of Black Lake, Coleraine Township, Megantic County.

New York. Large quantities of almandine in the form of rude crystals enclosed by envelopes of black hornblende occur extensively in the gabbro-diorites of Warren County. The thoroughly shattered crystals crumble into angular fragments when removed from the rock and provide in places, clear faceting material of very deep brownish-red color. Although flawless pieces of several grams weight are common, the color is generally too dark to permit cutting gems over several carats in weight, however, when cut to small sizes such gems are very beautiful. The garnet deposits of the North Creek area of Warren County have been mined since 1880 when the importance of this mineral for abrasive purposes was recognized. One of the principal mines is the Barton Mine located ¾ mile north of the summit of Gore Mountain and a little less than 4 miles west-southwest of the town of North Creek. At this place, the garnet-rock is quarried and crushed and the garnet fragments separated by flotation processes from the waste. No effort is made by the company to segregate gem material although much is quarried along with opaque grades ordinarily used for abrasives. Crystals average 2 to 6 inches in diameter, frequently reaching as much as 12 to 24 inches but are always highly fractured. Other localities are: on Ruby Mountain several miles west of North River; on Oven Mountain several miles south of North Creek; on Humphrey Mountain 6½ miles southwest of the southern end of Thirteenth Lake; the Rexford Mine is located 1¼ miles south-southeast of North Creek; the Crehore Mine is on Casey Mountain, 3½ miles northwest of North River. The Barton Mine garnet varies in specific gravity from 3.88 to 4.19 but generally averages between 3.95 and 4.00.

Pennsylvania. Deep blood-red gem almandines have been known for many years from Greens Creek located about 1 mile south of Chester Heights railroad station in Aston Township, Delaware County. Greens Creek is a northeastward-flowing branch of the West Branch of Chester Creek. Garnets have been found loose in the soil and in gravel in the vicinity of an old dam at the mouth of the creek as well as upon the surrounding slopes. This garnet has been erroneously called "pyrope" and is frequently referred to as such in older literature. Crystals occur as groups of crudely-formed individuals or as singles, and range in size from ¼ to 1 inch in diameter; only a few of the total number are gem quality.

Virginia. Some of the finest spessartites the world has ever known were and still are produced from the Rutherford Mines and associated dumps located 1¼ miles north of Amelia, Amelia County. The land upon which the mines are situated is presently controlled by Crawford Keener, the present resident. The No. 1 or upper mine is nearest the farmhouse and was once extensively worked for mica, beautiful amazonite, garnet, and other minerals.

FIGURE 76. Spessartite garnet and black tourmaline. This small but very fine matrix group from the Hercules Mine, Ramona, California, shows several sharp garnet crystals of bright orange color associated with black tourmaline crystals, smoky quartz, and rosettes of cream-colored cleavelandite. The largest garnet crystal is about 1 inch in diameter; the tourmaline is 1¼ inches tall. Above: a round brilliant of Amelia, Virginia spessartite weighing 40.12 carats. Courtesy Smithsonian Institution.

The No. 2 or lower mine is located about 200 feet to the southwest of the No. 1 Mine and produced a similar array of minerals. Spessartite apparently occurred originally as masses devoid of crystal form for no large flat crystal faces are evident but only a series of minute striations in geometric patterns corresponding to the angles of a dodecahedron. Masses are highly irregular in form reflecting the shape of the spaces between blades of cleavelandite in which they grew, and often reach dimensions of several inches. The American Museum of Natural History possesses a polished slab measuring fully 3 by 4 inches! In the earlier days of mining of the No. 1 Mine, masses of spessartite were produced enabling gems to be cut from 1 carat to almost 100 carats in weight. Notable examples are a magnificent red-orange oval faceted stone weighing 96.06 carats in the American Museum of Natural History, accompanied by a suite of other gems numbering 33 altogether. The U.S. National Museum owns cut examples ranging from 5.65 carats to 40.12 carats (see Fig. 76). Although many pieces were clear enough to facet, only the smallest are reasonably free of flaws. Internal imperfections take the form of wispy inclusions consisting of irregular liquid- and gas-filled cavities of minute size. The color of Amelia spessartite varies from an extraordinarily light and pure orange, almost yellow, to various shades of red-orange, red, and brownish-red, but always with an attractive overtone of orange even in the darkest specimens. Although the latest serious mining efforts took place in 1943, recent work on the No. 2 Mine may lead to further production. The dumps in the vicinity continue to yield fragments for diligent searchers, a fine piece of angular outline and almost completely covered by the curious markings referred to above, being found in the Fall of 1957 by Mrs. Carl Gerber of Arlington, Virginia. This specimen weighs slightly over 115 carats and appears clear enough in places to produce small faceted gems of perhaps a carat or so in weight. It was kindly presented to the author in whose collection it now occupies an important place and is the subject of the drawing in Figure 77. Further information on these mines appears under FELDSPAR.

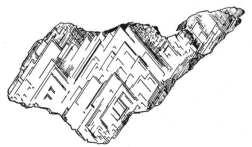

FIGURE 77. Spessartite garnet, Amelia, Virginia. This mass shows numerous striations corresponding to many small crystal faces and is typical of spessartite found in pegmatite bodies which have been subjected to complex mineralization. Such markings are also common on spessartites at Ramona, California. Specimen is about 2 inches in length.

North Carolina. Gem quality pyrope grains of fine red color but small size were found many years ago in the heavy residues of gold-panning operations in Burke, McDowell, and Alexander counties and undoubtedly found their way into the gold-bearing gravels from the peridotitic rocks of the highlands.

Deep pink to rich wine-red almandine crystals have been obtained from a slightly graphitic schist outcropping with pyroxenic rock along Laurel Creek, 8 miles southeast of Morganton, Burke County. The crystals occur in streaks or in scattered individuals in the schist and range in size from a fraction of an inch to some 3 to 4 inches in diameter. All are badly broken but from the solid pieces some facet grade material has been obtained as well as flawed material good enough for cabochons.

When speaking of garnet, the name of North Carolina is automatically linked to rhodolite, the beautiful rose-pink variety of pyrope which is here found in wonderful perfection. The original rhodolite was discovered in the gravels of Cowee Creek, a stream which drains the slopes of Mason Mountain in Macon County, about 8 miles north of Franklin. The varietal name was given by J. H. Pratt and W. E. Hidden who saw in the waterworn pieces not only the rose color or *rhodos* of Greek, but also the similar hue of the blooms of the rhododendron which grows luxuriantly upon the mountain slopes and valleys of the region. The occurrence was first mentioned in 1893 although it seems certain it was known before this, and as the gemstone achieved some degree of fame, further explorations in the vicinity of Cowee Creek revealed rich deposits in Mason's Branch, a short stream which drains into the Little Tennessee River about ½ mile north of Iotla on the Franklin-Bryson City highway. The exhaustion of gravels in Mason's Branch led to prospecting for in-place deposits which were eventually discovered upon Mason Mountain. A quarry was opened on the south flank of the mountain about ½ mile south of its crest, or about 1 mile upstream on Mason's Branch from its junction with the Little Tennessee River. The garnet and ruby areas of Cowee Creek are shown in Figure 15 while further information on the Cowee Creek deposits is given under CORUNDUM.

At the in place locality, garnet is found as rude masses, badly shattered and without trace of crystal form, enclosed in a dike-like body composed of rhodolite, gedrite (anthophyllite), hypersthene, and biotite. The garnet-bearing dike averages from 15 to 20 feet in width and penetrates hornblende gneiss and biotite gneiss. The rhodolite masses reach as much as 6 to 8 inches in size and are associated with glassy gray quartz, some of the garnet masses contain as much as 60 per cent to 70 per cent rhodolite. There are three in place deposits known upon Mason Mountain but aside from the extensively quarried deposit just described, the others are of little importance.

Of all rhodolite collected, the finest material came from stream gravels.

It is said that the largest pieces measured up to 2 inches across but like others of unusual size, showed numerous cracks and inclusions. The best cut gem is stated to be a brilliant of 13⅜ carats but the vast majority seldom exceeded 5 carats. Stream rhodolite from Mason's Branch presents a distinctive appearance because of its highly irregular form and a uniform sandblasted exterior; most fragments are severely flattened and thus not of the best shape for good cutting yield. The specific gravity ranges from 3.837 to 3.838.

Georgia. Deep red almandine crystals have been collected from schistose rocks between Canton and Ball Ground in Cherokee County. A clear gem quality crystal of ¾ inch diameter has been reported. In Paulding County, beautiful deep pure red crystals, largely flawless and reaching as much as ½ inch in diameter, have been found in the vicinity of the Little Bob Copper Mine near Dallas. At a point 6 miles southeast of Dallas, very fine dark red almandine crystals of facet grade occur loose in the soil. Examples up to ⅝ inch diameter have been found but the color is so deep that gems over several carats weight are blackish in hue. The author owns an oval brilliant of this material weighing 10.54 carats which is extremely deep red in color but entirely flawless; the refractive index is 1.79.

Kansas. Small gem quality red pyrope granules occur in an outcrop of igneous rock near Stockdale, Riley County.

South Dakota. Beautiful flawless red almandine pebbles and crystals have been obtained in quantity incident to gold washing in Elephant Gulch, 4 miles west of Custer, Custer County. Crystals take the form of well-developed dodecahedral crystals with smooth faces, the individuals seldom exceed the size of a grain of wheat although a few are found up to ½ inch in diameter. The finest were recovered commercially at the beginning of the century by a local company who cut them into gems which sold for from $.10 to $5 each.

Colorado. Small but beautiful spessartite crystals occur in rhyolite on Ruby Mountain on the east side of the Arkansas River opposite Nathrop in Chaffee County. Prized mainly for specimens, some are large enough to cut as exemplified by a specimen in the American Museum of Natural History which shows a gemmy ½ inch crystal perched on rhyolite. The spessartite is found in gas cavities in the rhyolite associated with topaz crystals, small quartz crystals, and minute sanidine feldspar crystals.

Montana. Small but fine almandine grains occur in abundance in the gravels of the Ruby River in Madison County upstream from the town of Alder. The gravels in the vicinity of Ruby Dam are said to have produced excellent specimens but the principal outcrop and best collecting area appears to be located along the sides of the first large stream which enters the Ruby River watershed from the east several miles upstream from the dam. The enclosing rock is stated to be a schist. The rounded grains are typically red to brownish-red and are very small as a rule, sample stones provided the author averaging from ⅛ to ¼ inch in diameter. The largest known specimen of gem quality is said to have been ¾ inch in diameter. All specimens examined by the author were roughly spherical in form and displayed no trace of crystal faces.

Garnet in the form of rolled pebbles of small size has been found associated with sapphire in the Missouri River gravels in the vicinity of Helena and elsewhere along the river. The color varies from bright red and orange red, to reddish-pink. Although small, the garnet pebbles are of fine quality. The refractive index is 1.770; specific gravity 3.87, the composition intermediate between pyrope and almandine. Further locality information may be found under CORUNDUM.

Idaho. Star almandine crystals occur abundantly at a number of localities, which up to now, provide the only significant sources of this unique gem material in the North American Continent. Perhaps several tons of crystals have been won from stream gravels or removed from the friable schists in which they occur. Asterism is caused by a multitude of exceedingly minute bluish needles of a foreign mineral, probably rutile, which impart a whitish to bluish chatoyancy in specimens which are especially rich in them. Ranging in size from ¼ inch to several inches in diameter, crystals generally take the form of rhombic dodecahedrons modified by trapezohedrons. The faces are seldom smooth, the majority of specimens showing numerous minute striations corresponding to the angles of trapezohedral faces. The enclosing rocks are mica schists, consisting mainly of pale greenish muscovite in very fine scales. Asterism-causing inclusions are confined to the centers of crystals, the exterior zone being mainly clear deep brownish-red to purplish-red almandine, frequently clear enough to cut acceptable faceted gems. Associated with the needle-like inclusions are black spots, possibly magnetite, which are sometimes so abundant that they ruin the crystal for any lapidary purpose. Most specimens are cracked or deeply incised by curious mica-filled worm-like channels which freqently penetrate to the core.

Good Idaho star stones are very beautiful, showing distinct four-rayed stars against very dark backgrounds, however, the vast majority of crystals yield only weak stars. Finished gems range in size from ¼ inch diameter to ¾ inch and up to 20 carats in weight; very solid crystals are sometimes cut in spheres and then show a series of four-rayed stars, six in number corresponding to the symmetry of the axes of the Isometric System. In cases where six-rayed stars are encountered, it is always found that two three-rayed stars are joined as shown by the fact that one is considerably weaker than the other. The Cleveland Museum of Natural History includes within its gem collection a magnificent perfect sphere of garnet measuring 3 inches in diameter and showing four-legged stars perfectly. It is not known where the raw material for this sphere came from but all characteristics point to an Idaho origin.

Asteriated almandine is also found in the gravels of Ruby Gulch, 2 miles south of Fernwood in Benewah County at a point where the gulch empties into the St. Maries River. Here crystals weather from outcropping schists and are found ranging from ½ inch to about 2 inches in size although some occur up to 3 inches in diameter. In the stream gravels, many crystal fragments are found showing only traces of original crystal faces. About 5 miles southeast of Fernwood is the famous Emerald Creek locality which is accessible by road and from which much fine garnet has been obtained in the stream gravels, especially in the East Fork. The Emerald Creek Abrasive Company which is now operating in this area (1958), permits recovery of garnet crystals by collectors after payment of a $3.00 daily fee. Another place is at the headwaters of the North Fork of the Purdue Creek about 4 miles upstream from where it is crossed by the road between Bovill and Clarkia near the boundary between Latah and Shoshone counties.

Recently star almandine has been reported from stream beds near Headquarters, 11 miles north of Pierce in Clearwater County. Crystals apparently occur in local schistose rocks from which they weather and find their way into the soil.

Facet grade almandine specimens were once plentiful in the gold-bearing gravels of Deadwood Gulch in Boise County; crystals and pieces of crystals as large as 1 inch in diameter were found. Purplish almandine of facet grade was also found in gold gravels near Lewiston in Nez Perce County.

Oregon. The so-called "Oregon jade" is in reality massive grossularite garnet. Forming unusually fine-grained masses of exceeding toughness, it was assumed to be some variety of nephrite jade until chemical analyses and other tests clearly established its identity. Although occasionally picked up in many of the rivers draining into the Pacific Ocean in the western part of the state, the greatest number of specimens have been found in gravel bars along the Umpqua River in Douglas County and in the Rogue River in Curry County. Pebbles appear as well-rounded masses up to 5 pounds in weight though some have been found larger. A very wide variety of coloration has been noted, including: white to cream, green, yellow, brownish-yellow, brown, pink, black, and frequently mottled in several colors. The specific gravity of these specimens averages about 3.50. The composition is almost pure grossularite with some idocrase generally present. This material has been picked up frequently at the mouth of the Rogue River near Wedderburn; also in Big Creek near Yachats in Lincoln County, and in Althouse Creek about 1½ miles south of Holland in Josephine County where they are found in piles of boulders left behind by gold-placering operations. Boulders of grossularite up to 12 inches in diameter also occur here as well as pebbles of agate, jasper, and serpentine. As in the California occurrences shortly to be described, grossularite in Oregon is derived from lenses in serpentine rocks outcropping in the mountains paralleling the Pacific Coast.

California. White to pale green massive grossularite occurs associated with idocrase (Californite) at the localities for the latter on Indian Creek in Siskiyou County (see IDOCRASE). Pure white material with idocrase occurs in veins in serpentine along Traverse Creek about 2½ miles south-southeast of Georgetown in Eldorado County. Crevices in the garnet have yielded some small but very fine crystallized specimens. Some of the grossularite from nodular lenses shows beautiful concentric bandings in white, violet, green, and yellow, and takes a fine polish. White opaque material similar to the above is found associated with calcite and idocrase at the locality for the latter on the south side of Watts Valley in Fresno County; also white to pale green from near Selma, 1½ miles from Hawkins Schoolhouse in Tulare County.

Beautifully translucent massive grossularite of pure white color also occurs at the noted idocrase localities near Big Bar, Butte County with some being clear enough to facet into gems of several carats. Further south in Orange County, massive greenish material in the form of worn pebbles has been found near El Toro but nothing further could be learned about this locality.

The most noted garnet occurrences in California center about central San Diego County where exceptionally fine spessartite has been found in crystals lining pockets in pegmatites. In the early days of exploration at the Himalaya Mine on the west slope of Gem Hill near Mesa Grande, some fine light reddish-orange masses yielded flawed but sparkling gems of several carats weight. This occurrence apparently was an isolated one for much mining afterwards failed to uncover any more. In the same way, some good material has been found from time to time in the mines of the Rincon District and in several of the Pala workings. However, the finest material occurs in small pockets in pegmatites outcropping on the western side of the Hatfield Creek Valley 3¾ miles east-northeast of Ramona. Exceptionally fine material of beautiful orange color still comes from the Little Three Mine property. Openings in honeycombed pegmatite range from a fraction of an inch to some several inches in diameter and even larger. In these narrow spaces are found fine transparent trapezohedral crystals up to 1 inch in diameter perched upon matrices of cleavelandite and associated with black etched tourmalines and smoky quartz crystals. A typical specimen of this material is illustrated in Figure 76. Some of the crystals show smooth bright faces but the majority are completely covered by numerous minute striations. Cracks are frequent and for all practical purposes, limit the size of flawless gems which can be cut to 7 carats or less. In spite of their small size, spessartite gems from the Little Three command a ready market for in no other gemstone can such lovely intense orange hues be obtained. It is encouraging to note that the present owner and operator of the Little Three mining property, Louis B. Spaulding of Ramona, is actively engaged in work which may lead to further production. In the past several years he has mined a thin pegmatite in a working known as the Spaulding Mine located several hundred yards to the northeast of the Little Three Mine on the opposite side of Hatfield Creek and removed therefrom several pounds of fine spessartite crystals and fragments of small average size.

The Spaulding Mine has been stripped to expose a pegmatite which dips 20° to the south and strikes approximately east-west. Although showing pockets over a distance of 150 feet, only the extreme eastern portion shows the honeycomb formation conducive to the formation of spessartite.

About 200 feet northwest of the Little Three, the downward extension of the Hercules dike recently yielded some gem quality spessartite in much the same sort of mineralization as noted at the Spaulding Mine.

In addition to the mines just described, several others in the immediate neighborhood have also provided good material, notably the Hercules which is several hundred feet above the Little Three on the same slope, the Surprise, about ¼ mile to the northeast but now obliterated by fill, the Black Panther located about ¼ mile to the west of the Little Three, the Lookout on the eastern edge of the ridge upon which the Hercules and Little Three are located, and other pits and prospects. Several mines are shown in the photograph reproduced in Figure 78.

Some gem grade grossularite of the hessonite variety occurs with gem quality deep olive-green epidote in a peculiar deposit in the McFall Mine, located 7½ miles southeast of Ramona and about 1 mile east of Indian Head Hill on the eastern edge of the San Vicente Grant. Small gems have been cut from this brownish-red garnet but are seldom flawless when over one or two carats in weight.

In the southeastern corner of San Diego County some exceptionally fine hessonite has been mined from metamorphic limestones in a rather broad area located about 8 miles north-northeast from Jacumba very close to the right of way of the San Diego and Arizona Eastern Railroad at Dos Cabezas. At least four properties were worked to some extent in this area. East of Jacumba near Mountain Springs on Highway 80, four prospects for hessonite were worked in the early part of the century. It was said that crystals obtained from all of these deposits were exceptionally large and fine. In 1955 the author was privileged to examine a fine specimen of hessonite brought in from the Dos Cabezas area where it had been found on a hill whose top was littered by numerous fragments of garnet. This piece was a section of a much larger crystal, perhaps originally 2 inches in diameter, and measured about 1½ inches in length and about ¾ inch across. It was essentially flawless, rich deep

FIGURE 78. A general view near Ramona, San Diego County, California, showing three mines which have produced fine spessartite garnet. The highest working at the upper right is the Lookout Mine which produced very little of consequence; next below is the Hercules Mine from which has been mined some very fine spessartite garnet. The workings at the lower left are those of the Little Three Mine, a famous producer of not only spessartite garnet but also of topaz and tourmaline. Courtesy U.S. Geological Survey.

orange-red in color, and could have easily been cut into several gems of about 15 carats each.

Arizona. The famous pyrope garnet field of this state includes a number of localities scattered throughout Apache County, Arizona, and in San Juan County, Utah and McKinley County, New Mexico. In each locality pyrope occurs as small pebbles sprinkled throughout the topsoil or concentrated in small gravel in washes. Despite steady collecting over a period of many years, there are few signs of exhaustion and as many specimens as are wanted can always be purchased upon the market. The collection of stones is generally the prerogative of the local Indians on whose lands some of the deposits occur and it is through their efforts that the market is largely supplied.

Recent geologic and mineralogic investigations in this area show that pyrope occurs in peculiar igneous rocks which outcrop as "pipes" of oval or circular outline. The rocks of the pipes consist of broken masses of sedimentary, igneous and metamorphic rocks, reduced to rubble, and upthrust through the sandstones which form the underlying rocks of much of the northern part of Arizona. It is interesting to note that many of the rubble rocks cannot be related to any known rock types within 100 miles of the garnet field. It is believed that these rocks come from deep within the earth where they have been torn loose and engulfed in the upwelling ignous rocks. About 50 per cent of the volume of the pipes is occupied by sandstone blocks with spaces between them filled with a matrix of serpentine-rich material and small rubble. Within the matrix, garnet occurs as inclusions in crystalline rocks and also scattered throughout the serpentine filling. In the Buell Park locality, described below, the outcrop is also serpentine and has been formerly described as a kimberlite tuff.

Pyrope occurring in granules only range in size from mere specks to angular fragments or rounded masses of ½ inch diameter. The vast majority are ¼ inch or slightly less but nodules up to 1¼ inches diameter have been found. It is remarkable that none of the pieces show the slightest trace of crystal faces. Faceted gems prepared from Arizona pyropes average ½ to 1½ carats in weight but others have been cut up to 5 carats. Flaws and inclusions are very common and consist of irregular liquid- or gas-filled cavities, sometimes of large size, inclusions of foreign minerals such as short thin needles of rutile, black spots of magnetite, and stubby prisms of dark green diopside. Out of a representative sample of 160 stones examined by the author, very few were without inclusions. In respect to color, the sample showed that some shade of dark red prevailed but 15 of the stones were decidedly orange to orange-brown in color, one specimen being so pale that it could easily be mistaken for an orange spessartite. Of the remaining 145 stones, about 45 were a lovely vivid shade of purplish-red and the remainder were dark red, some inclining slightly toward purple and some toward brown. Very few of the total number were pale red, the majority were quite dark and some appeared almost black.

One of the most important deposits in Arizona is the Garnet Ridge field located atop and on the sides of a very low hill about 5 miles in length, with its center located about 5 miles due west of the town of Mexican Water in the extreme northern part of Apache County. There are four pipes which contain garnet while the soil is sprinkled with garnet grains for some distance around them. A large pipe of 800 feet diameter is located on the western side of the ridge near its southern end while the others are in a group about 2 miles to the northeast on the eastern slope of the ridge. This group consist of a very large pipe of 3000 feet by 1200 feet in size and several smaller ones to its southeast. The elevation of Garnet Ridge is about 5500 feet above sea level and presents a generally barren surface of smooth rounded contours. Pipe rocks appear to extend to considerable depth since a boring down to 115 feet failed to run through the deposit.

The Moses Rock field is located 10 miles due north of Mexican Water and is just over the line in San Juan County, Utah. A dike-like body containing pyrope outcrops over a distance of 8000 feet and trends north. Patches of alluvium at the southern end contain granules which have weathered from the outcrop.

Another occurrence known as the Mule Ear deposit lies about 2 miles north of the Moses Rock field along the western edge of Comb Ridge. It is very small in extent as compared to the others and perhaps should be regarded more as a locality than a deposit. A small alluvial field is located at Mexican Water almost on the boundary between Arizona and Utah.

The noted Buell Park area lies almost on the border between Arizona and New Mexico and is located about 10 miles due north of Fort Defiance in McKinley County, New Mexico, and Apache County, Arizona. Abundant garnet grains litter a circular depression called Buell Park which measures about 2 miles in diameter and is 7200 feet above sea level. The floor of the park is underlain by kimberlite tuffs in which garnet is embedded along with peridot. Although the quality of the stones is good, pieces over 3/16 inch diameter are so rare that commercial exploitation has been discouraged. A small hill in the exact center of the depression contains an unusually heavy concentration of garnet and peridot. Also, in McKinley County, New Mexico, fine small pyrope grains occur in soil atop a mesa called Furry Mountain and upon its eastern slope which overlooks Todilto Park.

In another section of Arizona, fine andradite has been found in considerable quantity in an area of contact metamorphic rocks southeast of Stanley in Graham County. The locality is accessible by a poor road which turns south from Highway 70 about 8 miles east of Coolidge Dam. Garnet float is found on either side of the road as the district is approached while much has been collected from occurrences on the southern flank of Quartzite Mountain, Limestone Mountain, and on Crystal Peak. This locality is often referred to as "Stanley Butte" in allusion to a prominent mountain nearby although none of the andradites actually occur upon this mountain. Within the metamorphic rocks, andradite crystals line irregular cavities, crystallizing as solid aggregates with only the tips of the individual crystals protruding. Numerous platey inclusions of a green mineral cause decided chatoyancy upon the faces and impart a grayish-green color to the crystals despite the fact that the garnet itself is decidedly brown. Some of this material has been broken up and tumbled into atractive chatoyant baroque gems. In those crystals with few greenish inclusions, clear areas are found suitable for faceting although flawless gems of over a carat or so are rarely attainable. The author's collection includes a number of stepcut andradite gems from this locality several of which are almost 2 carats in weight and essentially flawless. The remarkable dispersion of andradite is much masked by the yellowish-brown color but vivid sparks of red and bright green are noted nevertheless.

Baja California. Hessonite crystals similar to those from the southeastern portion of San Diego County, California, occur just across the border in contact zones between granites and metamorphic limestones. Excellent transparent specimens have been obtained from the Sierra Juarez and in the Cacupah Mountains not far from Jacumba, California. Somewhat further south upon the peninsula, spessartite of reportedly good gem grade is said to occur in abundance in some of the pegmatites of the Sierra San Pedro Martir. This mountain range forms the central spine of Baja California Norte and reaches elevations in excess of 9000 feet above sea level. Since the rock types forming this range are essentially the same as those containing the famous gem-bearing pegmatites of Southern California, it is reasonable to suppose that similar gemstones will be found when this wild and inaccessible area is thoroughly explored.

In the extreme southern part of Baja California, spessartite is also reported from granitic rocks in the vicinity of the harbor of San Jose del Cabo and is also stated to occur with pyropes (?) in biotite schists nearby. Garnet crystals of an unstated species and ranging in size from ⅛ to ½ inch in diameter occur in aplite near the mining town of El Triunfo south of La Paz. Another reference states that spessartite is found in granite in the high peaks of the Cacachilas Mountains between La Paz and the Gulf of California, occurring as deep red crystals up to ¼ inch diameter; this may be the same locality as the one just mentioned. Pyrope is said to occur in the Puntas Arenas area, also at the Real del Chico, Hacienda de los Priegos.

Durango. Small red garnet pebbles said to be very similar to the pyrope of Arizona and possibly the same species, occur on a small isolated hill near the center of a huge circular depression known as the Bolson de Mapimi in the northeastern corner of this state.

Vera Cruz. Gem quality pyrope in small sizes has been found along the bed of the old F. F. Isthmus railroad in the Las Vegas—Escobar district.

Hidalgo. Similar material occurs near Laguna Haso Chuhuahan and Zimapan—Canhardo.

Michoacan. Small gem quality pyrope grains are found near Villa Madera.

Morelos. Beautiful pink grossularite crystallized in simple dodecahedrons occurs in profusion in metamorphic limestone near its contact with igneous rocks upon the Rancho San Juan, near Xalostoc in the Sierra Tlayacac. The deposit in which the crystals occur associated with wollastonite and idocrase covers an area of 300 by 400 feet and is estimated to contain at least 240,000 tons of material. The unusually compact nature of the garnet-bearing rock has led to its limited use as an ornamental stone because all three associated minerals are about the same in hardness and accept a uniform polish of high luster. Within the mass, grossularite crystals range in size from ½ to 4 inches in diameter but some have been found weighing as much as 4 to 5 pounds. The vast majority are pale pink and only slightly translucent but occasionally some are found which are deep rose pink and contain small clear spots suitable for faceted gems. Sawed and polished slabs of ¼ inch thickness provide handsome exhibit sections, especially when held before a light so that the pink garnet, the yellow idocrase, and pure white granular fibrous wollastonite which encloses both, appear in handsome and striking contrast. An attractive 4 inch sphere of this mixture is in the American Museum of Natural History while the U.S. National Museum owns a faceted gem of deep rose pink transparent pure garnet weighing 1.2 carats. The unique grossularite from this locality has had many names appended to it; for example, it has been called *landerite* after Carlos F. de Landero, *xalostocite* after the locality, and *rosolite* after its color.

CHAPTER IV

Quartz Family Gemstones

Includes numerous crystalline and cryptocrystalline varieties found in sedimentary, igneous, and metamorphic rocks. Many of these are of considerable commercial importance although cut gems prepared from them do not, as a rule, command high prices.

THE FREQUENCY with which varieties of quartz are employed for gems and ornamental objects is understandable when it is considered that of all mineral species, quartz occurs in greatest quantity. There is scarcely any spot on the globe where it cannot be found in some form. Being hard and durable, quartz outlasts many other minerals, and tends, geologically, to exist forever, merely changing its form with each eon of development. The omnipresence of quartz is shown by the forms in which it occurs, many of them deeply interesting to the lover of gems. Clear sparkling crystals suitable for faceted gems line miniature grottos in virtually every kind of rock while massive varieties deposited by precipitation from water, fill cracks and crevices and provide enormous amounts of raw material useful for cabochons, carvings, and many other ornamental applications. Despite their abundance, the finest quartz gemstone varieties are not to be despised for they possess much beauty, are durable, and, in some instances, provide gems so unique that no other species is capable of matching them.

Before launching into a discussion of the principal varieties, it is desirable to mention that quartz occurs in two general forms: as large distinct crystals or crystal grains, or as masses composed of billions of exceedingly minute crystals, too small to see clearly even under strong magnification. The first are conveniently called *crystalline* varieties, while the second are labeled *cryptocrystalline* in allusion to the "secret" or hidden nature of their structures. Both are essentially pure quartz and differ mainly in appearance and mode of growth. Crystalline varieties are those which provide the transparent raw material utilized in faceted gems while cryptocrystalline kinds are only translucent at best and thus find major employment in cabochons, carvings, and other applications in which transparency is not essential. In succeeding paragraphs, crystalline varieties will be taken up first followed by brief discussions of the principal cryptocrystalline varieties.

The name of quartz is of obscure German derivation, having been used by the early miners of that country at least as far back as Agricola's day, but what it meant or from what other word it was derived has not been settled. In any case, when used alone, the term *quartz* to most people means the extremely common milky to grayish material which forms veins and seams in many kinds of rocks. The alternative and somewhat old-fashioned name for quartz is *silica*, directly descended to us from the Latin *silex* or *silicis* meaning "flint." The name of the element *silicon* has been taken from this root while words such as *siliceous* and *silicified* generally refer to the presence of quartz in all manner of natural occurrences. On the other hand, *silicate* refers only to special combinations of silicon and oxygen in the atomic structures of *silicate minerals*.

Transparent colorless quartz is termed *rock crystal*, and, among the several clear varieties used for gems, is the most common and least valued. Rock crystal occurs principally in brilliant shining crystals which may be as small as pinheads or as large as logs. Typical rock crystals are illustrated in Figure 79. Some idea is gained of the huge dimensions in which this variety occurs by visitors to the U.S. National Museum in Washington, D.C. where a flawless sphere of polished rock crystal over 12 inches in diameter is on exhibit. This astonishing example of lapidary art was carved and polished from a single crystal believed to have come from a pegmatite dike near Sakangyi, Burma. Very large examples also occur in North America and will be described in their proper places. A smaller but nonetheless beautiful crystal sphere is shown in Figure 105. Exceptionally brilliant rock crystals of small size are frequently mislabeled with local names employing the term "diamond," e.g.: "Herkimer diamonds," for the sparkling specimens found in Herkimer Co., New York, and "Lake George diamonds" from another locality in the same state, etc. The "rhinestones" of jewelry should be, if this name is properly applied, rock crystal faceted from waterworn quartz pebbles found in the gravels of the Rhine River in Germany, but nowadays, it is indiscriminately applied to a variety of glasses fashioned into imitation gems. The application of the term "crystal" to pressed, cut, or blown glasses is to be deplored since nothing further from the crystalline state can be imagined and indeed some persons naively believe that "crystal" glass purchased for

FIGURE 79. Typical crystalline quartz specimens. Upper: largely flawless rock crystal from Arkansas. Lower: a group of stubby amethyst crystals from Upper Providence Township, Delaware County, Pennsylvania. Courtesy Smithsonian Institution.

the elegant dining table is actually quartz. Although pure quartz sand is the basic material of almost all glasses, its manufacture involves fluxing with metallic salts and the resulting melt loses all resemblance to rock crystal except in respect to transparency. Large masses of genuine rock crystal, however, have been used for carving into dishes, bowls, urns, and many other objects of ornamentation but the labor and skill involved are enormous and few such works of art appear for sale except in the windows of dealers in antiques.

Another transparent quartz, perhaps the best known and certainly the best loved member of the family is *amethyst*. This beautiful purple or violet variety is said to receive its name from the Greek word meaning "not drunk," reflecting the quaint belief that anyone who drank wine from a cup made of amethyst was somehow protected from the unwelcome effects of over-

FIGURE 80. Cut and rough amethysts. The large specimen resembles a pincushion because of the number of individual crystals which dot its surface. Coming from the noted silver distict of Guanajuato Mexico, it measures about 6 inches by 7 inches and is approximately 2 inches in depth. To its left is large single crystal of exceptionally dark amethyst from Four Peaks, Arizona, showing typical etched crystal faces as well as overgrowth of minute fluorapatite crystals. The cut gems in the foreground are from Virginia, Arizona, and North Carolina.

indulgence. As a general rule, amethyst seldom occurs in large flawless crystals and therefore cut gems tend to be rather small. Unequal color distribution is also a common fault and further decreases the likelihood of obtaining large beautiful gems of uniform coloration. Because of these reasons, high-quality amethyst gems over 20 carats in weight, are both rare and expensive. Several examples of amethyst crystals are illustrated in Figures 79 and 80. Yellow crystalline quartz is called *citrine* in allusion to its resemblance to the color of lemon, however, this descriptive and distinctive title is used altogether too infrequently. Because the buying public has been accustomed to the idea that any transparent yellow gemstone is "topaz," it is a widespread practise in the jewelry trade to label faceted citrine as "topaz" or "Brazilian topaz," and it sometimes becomes a rather disturbing duty to inform a lady that the large yellow gem she is wearing is not genuine topaz but merely the yellow variety of clear quartz. This is not to imply that citrine lacks beauty or is in any way to be despised, but it should be cut loose from the misleading appellation "topaz" and permitted to stand alone upon its considerable native merits. Citrine occurs in a large variety of shades which range from very pure yellows to brownish-yellow and some which tend to show mixtures of yellow and orange along with brown. To a lesser degree, the same doubtful trade ethics mentioned above apply to the brown variety of crystalline quartz,

FIGURE 81. The effect of asterism as seen in a specimen of milky rose quartz from Bedford, New York. The star appears when the polished sphere is held at some distance before a pinpoint of light. Courtesy Smithsonian Institution.

correctly known as *smoky quartz* but also frequently mislabeled "smoky topaz." In this variety, the brownish coloration ranges from the merest whisper of hue to coloration in which the tone is so pronounced that a black appearance is imparted. Richer-colored smoky quartz is sometimes called *cairngorm* after an occurrence in the pegmatites of the Cairngorm Mountains of Scotland. Some which is almost black is infrequently called *morion*, a term taken from the old Roman name for this variety— *mormorion*. Smoky quartz crystals often compare in size to rock crystals and hence are capable of providing very large faceted gems or even good-sized carvings. Because of its abundance, however, smoky quartz has little value in cut form and is worth considerably less than either amethyst or citrine.

Another distinctive variety of crystalline quartz is pale to rich pink material known simply as *rose quartz*. It is most frequently found as large masses in cores of pegmatites and is distinguished from other varieties in that it very rarely exhibits crystal faces. Sometimes it occurs clear enough to facet very respectable gems but even the best of these are not very brilliant because of the profusion of microscopic acicular inclusions which impart a decided milky cast. Latest investigations indicate that these fine needles are rutile, which, when arranged correctly within the quartz, give rise to asterism in cabochon gems. The star effect is shown clearly in Figure 81 where a sphere of rose quartz from Bedford, New York, has been placed before a strong pinpoint source of light. A rough specimen and faceted gem are shown in Figure 82. The majority of rose quartz is streaked and veined with whitish

FIGURE 82. A rough and cut specimen of rose quartz. Always slightly milky in character, this variety of quartz seldom provides gems of good brilliance. The rough mass is from Troup County, Georgia while the faceted gem, measuring 1 inch in length and weighing 38 carats, is from Oxford County, Maine.

inclusions but large uncracked masses can often be obtained suitable for carving into figurines, bowls and other objects of art in addition to smaller objects utilized in jewelry.

Crystalline quartz is also noted for another aspect of its character which leads to the growth of crystals in which fantastic and strange, but also beautiful, inclusions are noted. Apparently, as quartz crystals grow, they permit foreign minerals to develop simultaneously upon their surfaces, however the latter are eventually overtaken by the quartz and entombed forever in clear crystal caskets. Perhaps the best known examples are rock crystals in which multitudes of slender glistening needles of rutile are enclosed, furnishing the prized material known as *rutilated quartz*. A polished slab containing such inclusions is a fascinating object, the lustrous needles darting through air-clear quartz in every conceivable direction and never failing to arouse wonder and admiration. In similar fashion, but usually less delicate in texture, is formed clear quartz containing inclusions of black tourmaline or green actinolite. Penetration of quartz by needles of tourmaline is well shown in Figure 83.

FIGURE 83. A polished quartz crystal cross section; Pohndorf Amethyst Mine, Montana. The inclusions are blue tourmaline. Hazy six-sided shadows are smoky quartz "phantoms" representing layers of pigmented material arranged parallel to prism faces of the crystal. Courtesy Smithsonian Institution.

Collectively, all material containing needlelike inclusions is known as *sagenite*, a term derived from the Greek word for "net" in allusion to the criss-cross pattern formed by the needles. The resemblance of these slender needles to arrows inspired the French term *fleches d'amour* or "arrows of love," and in varieties in which the included crystals are exceedingly fine and hairlike, *Venus' hairstone* or *Thetis hairstone*.

At times, included needles are exceedingly fine and abundant imparting to the quartz the hue of the foreign mineral or bringing about some special effect other than mere coloration. For example, some of the quartz from the locality which furnished the specimen illustrated in Figure 83 contains so many black tourmaline needles that the quartz also appears quite black. In other instances, millions of dark grayish-green actinolite inclusions produce the same result, forming the variety known as *prase*. If inclusions are arranged in parallel streaks or sheets and exhibit a decided silky luster, strong chatoyancy results as in the varieties known as *tiger's eye, hawk's eye,* and *falcon's eye.* The first named is bright brownish-yellow and is found in great abundance in Griqualand, Southwest Africa from whence it is exported to lapidaries all over the world. The last two varieties are found in the same

deposit and differ in appearance only in being grayish-green or grayish-blue. All three owe their fibrous structure to the replacement of blue asbestos (crocidolite) by quartz, the yellowish kinds representing asbestos which has been more or less completely altered to iron oxides before being replaced by quartz. Though the replacement is almost complete in each case, enough of the original or altered mineral remains to impart the lustrous sheen so admired in polished specimens. These precise varieties are rare in North America but similar materials, locally called *binghamite* and *silkstone*, occur in iron deposits in Minnesota and will be fully treated in the localities section. Although tiger's eye and its close relatives are only translucent at best, some crystalline quartz such as rose quartz and

FIGURE 84. A large cabochon of sagenitic chalcedony from Nipomo, California, a cabochon of fibrous crystalline quartz from Minnesota, and a splendid cabochon of pure white catseye quartz from Arizona.

rock crystal sometimes contains fine needles which in themselves are highly translucent and permit the perfect display of a single brightly-reflective light streak as in *catseye*. An especially beautiful kind has been recently discovered in Arizona and will be described under that state (see Figure 84). Crystalline

quartz of granular structure also provides attractive gemstones when permeated by numerous minute crystals of foreign minerals. In this class is *aventurine*, or granular quartz sprinkled heavily with small platelets of mica, hematite, or goethite, each minute crystal reflecting a spark of light and imparting
a spangled effect to the whole. Similarly, *dumortierite quartz* contains many
thin needles of dark blue or pink dumortierite which though not brilliantly
reflective, nevertheless impart an attractive coloration.

Cryptocrystalline quartz, as remarked before, is distinguished by the
extreme minuteness of the individual crystals which comprise the whole.
Hand magnifying glasses and even microscopes are powerless in resolving the
form of the crystals which comprise this material, however, recent investigations have shown that the crystals generally grow at right angles to the
layering, forming exceedingly slender rods while the spaces between are filled
with amorphous silica corresponding to opal in all essentials. So different is
this type of quartz from the relatively coarse crystalline kinds that it is given
the general name *chalcedony* and it is this which forms the basic substance of
the almost countless varieties of cryptocrystalline quartz known to mankind.
Because of its porosity, chalcedony often permits ingress by infiltrating solutions carrying metallic salts in solution, or sometimes organic matter, and
when such foreign matter is deposited, the basic chalcedony is stained in
beautiful colors, with or without patterning. Pure, or *common* chalcedony,
is dull grayish, bluish, or milky material which looks much like congealed
wax and as such has little to commend it for gem purposes except in those
kinds in which the color is naturally bright blue. However, as a result of

FIGURE 85. Agate and jasper collected along the banks of the Panama Canal near Cocoli
provided the raw material for these Japanese carvings. The lion is spotted yellow jasper,
the fish is creamy chalcedony tipped with bright red carnelian, while the elephant is
almost pure white chalcedony. The height of the fish is 5 inches.

staining, much otherwise uninteresting chalcedony is lifted to the status of beautiful and desirable gem material. Several carved examples of chalcedony are shown in Figure 85.

Chalcedony in which pronounced color banding occurs is called *agate*. The bands may have much or little opal filling the spaces between quartz fibers; in any case, the porosity often varies markedly from band to band and accounts for variations in color imparted by unfiltrated impurities. Agate showing bands which take abrupt and sharp turns is called *fortification agate* while nodules containing bands of strongly contrasting color, which, when cut across and polished, exhibit circular patterns are called *eye agate*. *Ruin agate* or *breccia agate*, is that in which previously deposited agate was shattered into angular fragments and later repaired by further infusions of chalcedony. *Polka-dot agate* is the descriptive term applied to a type in which spheroids of opaque chalcedony are suspended in translucent material, affording, when cut, interesting dotted patterns. *Onyx* is a variety in which perfectly straight bands of contrasting color occur (see Figure 101) and formerly was much used for cutting into cameos and intaglios. Lately this term has been misapplied to black, artificially-stained chalcedony in which there is no trace of banding at all.

Reddish to yellowish-red chalcedony is called *carnelian* of which the best quality is rich and vivid in color and much used since ancient times for cabochons, beads, small carvings, and numerous other ornamental applications. The name of this variety alludes to its color, being derived from the Latin word for "flesh." Most natural carnelian occurs as nodules or nodule sections of common chalcedony which have been infiltrated by solutions bearing iron salts which later precipitated as reddish oxides. Dark brown to pale brown chalcedony is called *sard*, a term handed down from the ancient Greek name for Sardis, the capital of Lydia in Asia Minor. Sard or carnelian

FIGURE 86. Botryoidal chrysocolla chalcedony from Globe, Arizona. This "old timer" shows highly translucent gem quality blue chalcedony lining an opening in massive chrysocolla. Courtesy George Ashley.

showing pronounced straight bands alternating with white bands is called *sardonyx.*

Although most chalcedony is colored by iron oxides in varying concentrations, compounds of other elements may also impart distinctive and beautiful hues. Handsome warm green chalcedony, often very translucent, results from infusion by nickel silicates and is then called *chrysoprase.* An especially lovely blue-green color is caused by chrysocolla, a copper silicate, and the resulting material labeled, for want of a better name, *chrysocolla agate* or simply *chrysocolla.* The name "blue chrysoprase" has been proposed for this variety but is obviously objectionable and has not been adopted. A fine example of chrysocolla chalcedony is shown in Figure 86.

In the famed *Montana moss agate,* salts of manganese and iron infiltrate grayish translucent chalcedony pebbles, possibly as they lie in moist ground, forming beautiful black and red tree-like or *dendritic* growths. Figure 87 illustrates some polished specimens of this variety and shows the finely-detailed patterns and their more than superficial resemblance to trees, shrubs, and mosses.

The term *moss agate* is generally used to describe all chalcedony containing mossy or dendritic growths but whereas Montana agate appears to have formed by a process of infiltration, other types show every sign of having generated mossy patterns by a process of simultaneous growth of impurities along with enveloping chalcedony. Figure 88 illustrates moss agate from Oregon in which the sharp greenish filaments which so strikingly resemble algae or seaweed, show a completely different mode of formation from moss agate of Montana. The formation of chalcedony bands between the filaments indicates that the latter had actually grown prior to the chalcedony. Some authorities explain this development as resulting from the greenish mineral growing within a jelly-like mass of uncongealed chalcedony which later hardened, but this theory has now been almost universally discredited. A special and particularly beautiful variety formed in this fashion, shows indescribably delicate plumes like the tail feathers of an ostrich, billowing upward through clear chalcedony. This variety has been aptly called *plume agate* and within the English language there seems to be no other more appropriate descriptive term. Especially fine plume agate is obtained in Oregon and Texas and good specimens command high prices when of fine quality. Several examples of this variety are shown in Figures 89 and 102. As a final example of mossy growths in chalcedony, mention should be made of a dark green kind spotted with blood red dots and popularly known as *bloodstone.* Although many books call this material *jasper,* it is actually clear chalcedony in which green mossy growths are so minute and so numerous that they cannot be seen distinctly except under magnification. The red spots are

Note: Figures 88 and 89 are in the color section following page 112.

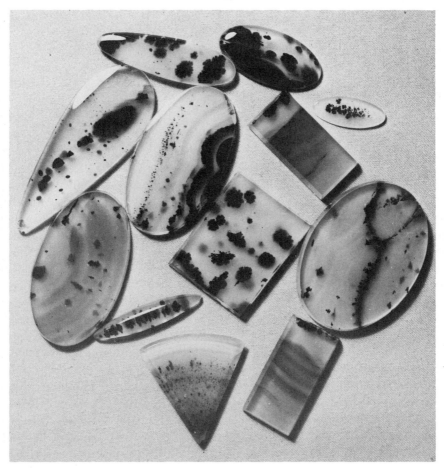

FIGURE 87. Montana moss agate from the famous gravel beds along the Yellowstone River. The beautiful dendritic markings are pure black in color while the chalcedony itself is pale gray and highly translucent. A few cabochons contain streaks of reddish-brown. The drilled pendant at the upper left measures over 2 inches in length.

ascribed to small inclusions of iron oxides which permeate the surrounding green material.

Very similar to the sagenitic quartz mentioned earlier, is chalcedony sagenite or *sagenitic agate*. Exactly the same kind of slender needles of foreign minerals are seen but now penetrating translucent chalcedony instead of clear quartz. Inclusions most often form spherical tufts radiating from focal points along the walls of cavities, the latter being later filled with clear chalcedony in which the needle-like crystals are imprisoned. Sagenitic chalcedony is very beautiful and highly prized when the chalcedony is translucent and the inclusions easily visible. A sagenitic chalcedony from California is illustrated in Figure 84.

A special form of chalcedony called *iris agate* is remarkable in several ways. Outward appearances lead one to believe that it is common chalcedony, highly translucent but uncolored, and apparently of little gem value, however, a thin polished slab of this obviously drab and lifeless material becomes flushed with wondrously pure and vivid rainbow colors as it is held before a light. Although the cause of this remarkable rainbow display is not certainly known, it is theorized that the large number of successive growth bands interferes with the normal functions of light passing through the slab and causes it to split into its spectral colors. One authority believes that thin layers of chalcedony showing alternately high and low refractive indices, possibly due to a variation in opal content between the spindles of quartz, duplicates a diffraction grating and causes the breaking up of light. The number of layers in iris agate ranges from 400 to 15,000 per inch. The best effects are seen in very thin slices, down to 1/32 inch thick or less, but the color display is visible only when the slice is held at arm's length before a pinpoint source of light.

So far, only the relatively pure and translucent varieties of chalcedony have been discussed but silica-bearing solutions from which chalcedony may be deposited also find their way into many other formations in which no large open spaces exist, and like cement in concrete, replace or consolidate foreign material into exceedingly hard and compact masses. The most abundant material of this type is known as *jasper*, and, as may be expected from its mode of formation, occurs in every degree of silification from virtually pure chalcedony to material which cannot take a polish because it is so lacking in quartz. In general, jasper is used to designate those impure kinds of chalcedony in which concentric banding is absent and translucency much impeded by the presence of opaque earthy impurities. Obviously there cannot be a clean-cut division between jasper on one hand and chalcedony on the other, in fact, many specimens are found in which one part is pure chalcedony of the agate variety and next to and grading into it, occurs jasper. An examination of typical jasper structure under a high-powered microscope shows numerous minute spherules of earthy matter acting as nuclei for radial growths of chalcedony-type quartz crystals. When such spherules are easily visible, the variety is termed *orbicular jasper*, or, depending on size and pattern, as "flower," "poppy," or "fish-egg" jasper, etc. Good examples of orbicular jasper are shown in Figure 90. However, the largest portion of all jasper shows mainly a very compact structure which varies little in texture from place to place within the specimen. Jasper frequently forms very large masses, sometimes a number of feet in thickness, but as a rule, most examples are compact and free of earthy or soft inclusions and cracks only in small

FIGURE 90. Orbicular chert from Morgan Hill, California, cut in cabochon form. The two larger gems are the typical "flowering" or "poppy" jasper for which this locality is noted. The top gem is from north of San Francisco; size, 2 inches in length.

areas. Jasper is often associated with other forms of chalcedony in basalts, tuffs, or other formations associated with volcanic activity.

Closely related in structure to jasper, are the fine-grained, quartz-rich masses found in sedimentary rocks known as *chert* and *flint*. Flint is generally nodular in form while chert occurs as large lenses or layers enclosed in limestone, sandstone, and other sedimentary rocks. Because of their high silica content many types of chert and flint polish beautifully. Both forms are believed to result from the permeation of enclosing rocks by solutions carrying silica, causing replacement of the original material by quartz. Pervasive silica solutions also reach whatever fossil animal or plant remains happen to be present in the rocks, and for some unexplained reason, concentrate in them, frequently replacing them completely and faithfully in chalcedony. Peculiarly enough, the enclosing rocks or sediments seem scarcely touched in the process, and, when erosion takes its toll, the replaced fossils are left behind long after the enclosing rocks have disintegrated into soil and washed away. This curious behavior on the part of silica-bearing solutions is responsible for the abundance of *petrified wood* so often noted on the surface in certain areas of the Western United States. This is strikingly shown in Figure 99. The term petrified wood is broadly applied to any wood which has been replaced by mineral matter but *silicified wood* should be used if quartz is the

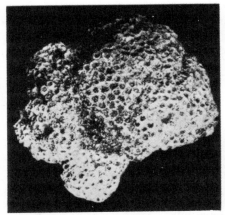
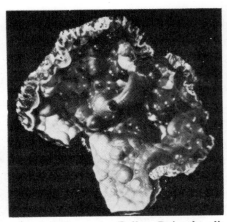

FIGURE 91. Two views of the same silicified coral geode from the Ballast Point locality in Tampa Bay, Florida. The left hand photograph shows the exterior covered by numerous star-like pits left by the coral animals while the right hand view shows the interior. Chalcedony lining is dark in color nearest the wall while the interior surface is coated with a thin opaque layer of porous chalcedony corresponding to cacholong opal in character. Courtesy Robert O. Vernon.

mineral in question. Silica infusions are also responsible for the perfect preservation of many calcareous animal remains, including corals, shells, and even the bones of extinct dinosaurs! Corals may be replaced in part or entirely by chalcedony, good examples being the *silicified coral geodes* of Tampa Bay, Florida, a fine specimen of which is illustrated in Figure 91, and the cream-colored silicified corals found in some of the sedimentary formations along the Panama Canal. The Tampa Bay corals seldom show full replacement, the majority of specimens being hollow and lined with rounded growths of vari-colored chalcedony. On the other hand, the corals of Panama are completely silicified and it is possible in typical specimens to take slices from any

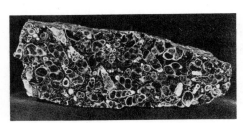

FIGURE 92. A polished specimen of silicified turritella shells from Wyoming. The basic color is dark brown with white markings. Size of specimen: 4¾ inches by 1¾ inches.

place in the specimen showing the fine "star" pattern of the original calcareous skeleton. The latter form of silicified coral has been called *beckite* or *beekite*. In a unique deposit in Wyoming occur masses of small spiral snail shells identified as *turritellas* which have been so faithfully reproduced in silica that even grains of sand which drifted into the shell openings remain preserved in clear chalcedony. This interesting material is popularly known as *turritella agate*. A typical specimen is illustrated in Figure 92. In regard to silicified bone, the most spectacular examples by far are the huge joints of long-extinct dinosaurs in which each marrow cell is reproduced in red carnelian. These intriguing specimens occur over a considerable area in some of the Western United States and also in Canada. Needless to say, all of these organic remains provide excellent lapidary material if the replacement by silica has been thorough.

Though not *varieties* in the strict sense of the word, certain growths of crystalline and cryptocrystalline quartz are prized for the forms in which they occur and not as so much raw material to be cut and polished into gems. Among the most popular are *geodes,* a geological term applied to hollow concretions lined with crystals and often easily separated from the enclosing rock. Geodes are frequently ball-like in form and give no indication from their rough and drab exterior that sparkling crystals may be within. Thousands of these curious concretions occur in sedimentary beds in Illinois and other states nearby, containing milky quartz and rock crystals. Geodes from volcanic rocks often contain amethysts but seldom in crystals large enough to cut faceted gems. Mineral collectors and gem fanciers sometimes saw geodes in half and polish the edges, but in other cases, the geodes are simply broken open, using some care to prevent shattering into small and less attractive fragments. Exterior layers frequently consist of banded chalcedony which may vary in thickness from a fraction of an inch to several inches, and is followed either by rounded growths of chalcedony or deposits of quartz crystals. Sometimes the original cavity becomes completely filled and the formation is then properly called a *nodule.* Every variation from solid nodules to thin-walled geodes are found in nature and several of the most common types in the form of slices sawn from rounded masses are shown in Figure 93.

A special type of nodule called the *thunderegg* is especially abundant in areas of the Western United States underlain by volcanic rocks. The thunderegg, it is said, owes its name to the Warm Spring Indians of Central Oregon who believed these hard, almost spherical chalcedony concretions to be missiles thrown out of the higher volcanoes of the Cascade Mountains whenever the gods inhabiting the lofty heights became angry. However, this interesting superstition is not borne out by fact for although thundereggs have been found in great profusion upon the slopes of hills and mountains and indeed look as if they had been ejected from a volcano, they actually form in and erode from very soft and friable volcanic ash beds. Thundereggs differ considerably from ordinary chalcedony nodules and geodes both in respect to mode of formation and internal structure. Whereas ordinary nodules are chalcedony fillings of gas pockets and cavities in volcanic lavas, thundereggs invariably occur only as concretions in cinder beds or pumice deposits of considerable porosity. Apparently these porous deposits contained no large cavities to speak of and silica borne by solutions merely permeated the cinders

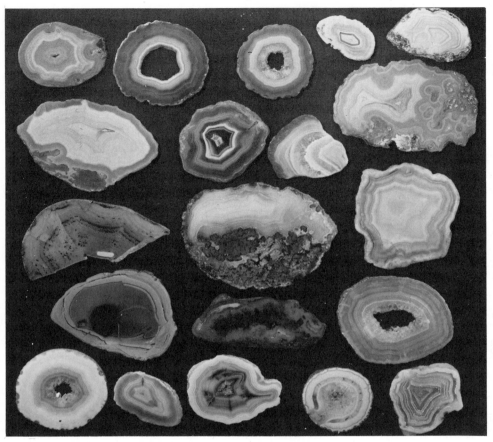

FIGURE 93. Polished agate slices. The variety of color and pattern in agate is almost limitless. The doughnut-shaped slices are from geodes and show linings of small clear quartz crystals.

until favorable points were reached where chalcedony could be deposited. Thus thundereggs are not cavity *fillings*, but merely aggregations of chalcedony. However, at some time before solidification was complete, the center of the concretion split and drew apart, permitting additional material to fill the space so provided. Figure 101 illustrates a typical thunderegg and shows the external rind of silicified ash and the star-shaped translucent core of essentially pure chalcedony which may or may not be mottled, spotted, or banded. The external appearance of thundereggs is also distinctive for each "egg" is covered with rounded warty protuberances totally different from the fairly regular covering noted upon chalcedony nodules derived from gas pocket fillings in lava. The internal patterns of thundereggs are often beautiful, sometimes containing very fine plume, sagenitic, or moss agate or bands of striking color contrast (see Figure 101). Thundereggs have been found in singles, doubles, and even triples, and in sizes ranging from 1½ inches in diameter up to a few enormous specimens of 36 inches across. As a general rule, the size averages from 2 to 5 inches.

The varieties of quartz and chalcedony are virtually endless and unfortunately all cannot be discussed within the space allotted. Some idea of their number may be obtained from the fact that almost 200 varietal names for members of the Quartz Family are known, and indeed entire books have been devoted to discussion of its members! To avoid repetition, further varieties derived from peculiar modes of formation, or found in only restricted areas in North America, will be discussed where appropriate under LOCALITIES.

The chemical composition of quartz consists simply of silicon and oxygen, combined in accordance with the formula: SiO_2. When completely pure as in rock crystal, it is entirely colorless, however, much crystalline quartz receives color from the presence of minute quantities of foreign elements whose exact role in inducing color is even now not fully understood. In amethyst, manganese and titanium are believed to give rise to the lovely violet to purple shades of this gemstone, while in citrine, traces of iron cause the yellow coloration. In smoky quartz, the brownish tinge is attributed to slight changes in crystal structure possibly brought about by the effects of radiation from radioactive minerals. It is interesting to note that in this variety, the color can be driven off by the application of heat and restored by irradiation. Heat treatment of citrine in which a light smoky tint is noted, often brightens specimens considerably by driving off the brownish color. Heat treatment of amethyst is also frequently resorted to but usually with the intention of imparting a very rich reddish-brown color, the resulting stones then being known as "Spanish topaz" or "Madeira topaz," or simply, "burnt amethyst." Some amethyst reacts to heat treatment by losing all traces of color and other types assume a peculiar grayish-green hue which is not observed in natural crystalline quartz. Only recently it has been found that the amethyst of Four Peaks, Arizona behaves in this fashion but the green shade imparted is far less intense than that noted in similar material from Brazil. The color of rose quartz is ascribed to finely-divided rutile. When exposed to sunlight, rose quartz bleaches decidedly but according to some investigators, the original hue will return if specimens are kept in the dark. The color of chalcedony is grayish to bluish when pure, but as remarked before, is often changed to many other hues by the presence of infiltrated minerals.

Quartz belongs to the Hexagonal System, crystallizing ideally in six-sided prisms terminated by pyramid-like faces drawing to a point as shown in Figures 94 and 95. Rock crystal, like those illustrated in Figure 79, grows in simple prisms which vary from short stubby individuals to long narrow crystals in which the sides tend to draw inward by a series of minute steps until the crystal resembles a candle in general form. Smoky quartz and citrine crystals generally observe the same habit (see Figure 94), however, amethyst is peculiar in that it prefers to form groups of crystals, all of about the same size, terminated by nothing but points (See Figures 79 and 80). Slender crystals of this variety are consequently far less common. As mentioned before, rose quartz very rarely exhibits any crystal faces. Twinning is extremely common in quartz, especially the type known as *interpenetrant twinning* in which it seems that two crystals attempted to form in exactly the same place but by a process of mutual adjustment, managed to grow into a twinned crystal. Such crystals show zig-zag markings on their faces and small offsets where one crystal grew slightly more than the other. Twinning occurs in large areas in crystals of colorless quartz, citrine, and smoky quartz, but strangely, in amethyst, the twinning appears repeated many times. It is for this reason that fractured fragments of amethyst often show a series of narrow striations on broken surfaces in the so-called "ripple fracture," each of the lines marking a place where one crystal twinned in respect to the other. The almost universal color banding of amethyst is also connected to twinning for purple and colorless zones occur in geometrically straight bands whose outlines and thickness conform to the twin boundaries.

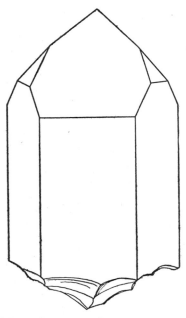

FIGURE 94. One of the most common habits observed in quartz crystals, especially in rock crystal (compare Figure 95). In this example, the six-sided prism is terminated by an over-developed set of rhombohedral faces, and another set much smaller in size.

In comparison to the coarse crystals noted in crystalline quartz varieties, chalcedony crystals are so small that they appear merely as thin fibers or spindles without faces, standing upon their points in endless ranks. When found lining walls of cavities, chalcedony consists of successive bands in each of which the fibers are vertical to the banding. In jasper, on the other hand, the same fibrous crystals radiate outward from countless nuclei and cause the homogenous texture for which this variety is noted. Recent investigations have shown that opal frequently forms between fibers of quartz in chalcedony and affects translucency, refractive index, specific gravity, and the ability of the chalcedony to absorb or reject foreign particles carried in solution. The differing permeability of chalcedony bands is attributed to a combination of quartz fiber size and how much or how little opal is deposited between them. Opaque white bands probably represent exceedingly fine fibers solidly packed by opal, thus accounting for the failure of such bands to assume coloring from either natural or artificial solutions. The use of artificial staining solutions will be discussed briefly in a later paragraph since much Brazilian agate is customarily colored and sold for cutting into inexpensive gems, and probably much American material of uninteresting color could similarly be beautified. Weathered nodules of chalcedony sometimes assume an opaque whiteness which is most pronounced on the exterior; lapidary treatment shows that such white areas are far softer than ordinary material and leads to the conclusion that the original quartz fibers have been largely altered into soft and opaque opal. This alteration is very common in many Mexican agate nodules in which some of the bands show beautiful pastel colors as a result of this whitening. An exceptionally fine polished Mexican agate nodule is illustrated in Figure 106.

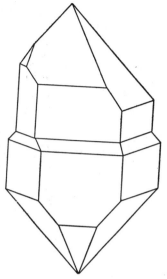

FIGURE 95. A doubly-terminated crystal of quartz from a pegmatite pocket. The step or buttress development is characteristic.

In respect to mode of occurrence, crystals of quartz are found almost solely in open cavities in all classes of rocks. Splendid large rock crystals, smoky quartz and citrine crystals are found in pockets in pegmatites. They are also abundant in open fissures in gneisses and schists, also in sandstones and limestones although they tend to be smaller in the last two rocks. Amethyst occurs in geodes in volcanic rocks and also in openings in quartz fissure veins in schists and gneisses. Amethyst is especially abundant in ore veins containing silver as in the Thunder Bay Region of Ontario and in the famous Mexican silver mines. Rose quartz is almost wholly obtained from large quartz cores in pegmatites. Chalcedony and its numerous subvarieties occur mainly in volcanic rocks such as basalts, diabases, rhyolites, trachytes, and the softer kinds derived from ash deposits, however, it is also abundant in many sedimentary rocks where it has been concentrated by migrating solutions. The latest theories of the origin of chalcedony in volcanic rocks accounts for the concentration of this variety of quartz in nodules and geodes in the following manner. When the lava pours out upon the surface of the earth, gases imprisoned in the fluid mass rise to the upper layers where they form bubbles of varying shapes and sizes. Slight movements of the congealing mass may cause them to stretch out or otherwise deform in directions parallel to the flow. Upon cooling, vaporized minerals contained in the gases deposit upon the walls of the cavities followed by others brought in by very hot water solutions which everywhere permeate the plastic mass. Often the wall rock of the cavities is partly altered in the process and becomes soft, permitting the nodules which form later to be easily detached from the enclosing rock. As the watery solutions enrich themselves in soluble minerals, they pass through the walls of the cavities and cause further deposits along the walls. These initial formations may not be quartz minerals by any means for many instances are noted where calcite, barite, anhydrite, glauberite, and other minerals are deposited before any chalcedony appears. Frequently, crystallized calcite is formed and is later covered by chalcedony layers which then retain perfect imprints of the calcite crystal points. In respect to the chalcedony itself, the nature of the solutions, how long they continued to flow, their impurities, and many other factors, determine the thickness and frequency with which they were deposited. In Figure 106, for example, close examination shows there are at least 100 distinct bandings corresponding to as many cycles of solution activity. If conditions are favorable, chalcedony continues to form until all available space within the cavity is taken up, however, in many instances interruptions occur. Thus nodules and geodes are frequently found in which the exterior layer may be calcite, followed by chalcedony, then perhaps a thin band of crystallized quartz which may be milky, transparent, or even amethystine, and then successive bandings of chalcedony, etc. There is no hard and fast rule apparently, the successive formations both in regard to thickness and composition depending entirely upon what solutions infiltrated the cavity during the course of mineralizing activity.

The hardness of crystalline quartz is 7 on the Mohs Scale but that of chalcedony may appear slightly lower depending on its purity and porosity. Chalcedony frequently appears harder than crystalline quartz but this may be attributed to its fibrous structure which imparts great toughness. Crystalline varieties are far less tough, shattering rather easily with a tendency to split most readily along planes corresponding to those of the terminal faces of crystals. Fracture surfaces in crystalline quartz vary from glassy conchoidal to granular and glistening. Chalcedony also fractures in a conchoidal to splintery manner but the surfaces resulting are invariably dull or waxy in luster. Jasper frequently displays granular dull surfaces which become more nearly conchoidal in form and brighter in luster as the content of silica rises.

In rock crystal, the specific gravity is fairly constant at 2.651; in colored varieties, more variation is noted and values therefore range from 2.647 to 2.656. The porous structure of chalcedony causes lower values generally between 2.58 and 2.64. Poor quality jasper, chert, and other impure forms may show even lesser values, or if the content of heavy minerals is high, somewhat higher values. Refractive indices are double in accordance with the uniaxial nature of quartz, varying as follows: $\omega = 1.543$ to $\epsilon = 1.552$, $\omega = 1.545$ to

$\epsilon = 1.554$; birefringence 0.009. Since the value of the extraordinary ray is larger than the ordinary, the optical sign is positive. Quartz shows little dispersion, only 0.013, and consequently faceted gems show very few flashes of dispersive color unless large in size. The structure of chalcedony, plus the presence of opal, causes slightly lower values of refraction varying between 1.533 and 1.539.

Crystalline quartz is not noted for strong dichroism in colored varieties, nevertheless, richly hued specimens show distinct changes under favorable conditions of observation:

VARIETY	DICHROIC COLORS	
Amethyst	reddish-purple	violet
Rose quartz	faint pink	colorless
"Green" amethyst	pale green	very pale straw yellow
Smoky quartz	reddish-brown	olive brown
Citrine	yellow	paler yellow

Of considerable commercial importance, artificially stained chalcedony finds much employment in inexpensive jewelry, however, very little is treated by domestic firms, the market being almost exclusively supplied by a number of German companies. The dyeing of chalcedony by artificial means is an art of ancient vintage. History records that as far back as Roman days, the inhabitants of the region now centered about Idar-Oberstein in Germany learned how to stain chalcedony and through the intervening years, brought the art to its present highly developed state. Today their descendants still earn much of their living, dyeing the chalcedony of Brazil and Uruguay into a variety of hues, some of which, however, have no duplicates in nature. In the two South American countries mentioned, enormous quantities of ordinary gray chalcedony occur as nodules in volcanic rocks, providing cheaply-produced material known to be largely satisfactory for this purpose. However, not all chalcedony is suitable for dyeing, even some of the Brazilian and Uruguayan material being rejected after testing. As mentioned before, opaque white to cream material refuses to stain naturally, and reacts in the same way to laboratory staining attempts. Gray translucent chalcedony, furthermore, shows surprising degrees of porosity which cannot be predicted by mere visual examination and its reaction to dyeing must be established by the use of small test slivers or slices removed from larger pieces. The subtle shadings of color and color banding exhibited in natural chalcedony are only partially duplicated in the laboratory, since nature has taken her time in imparting colors and had a much larger palette of delicate tints to choose from. As a consequence, artificially colored specimens are characteristically garish in hue, uniformly spread through the piece, and altogether "too perfect" to be real.

In general, the dyeing process consists of cleaning the chalcedony pieces or slices, subjecting them to heat to drive off any water trapped between the pores, and then immersing them in a bath which contains the necessary dyeing agent. Some material has been dyed by ordinary organic dyes but since these are seldom permanent, the colors imparted fade in time. The better method is to employ certain water-soluble metallic salts, which, after lodgement in the pores, can be subjected either to heat or chemical action to decompose them into permanent oxides bearing the desired hue. Thus, a vivid artificial carnelian is obtained by steeping chalcedony in a solution of iron nitrate and then heating the pieces strongly to decompose the nitrate into a permanent oxide of vivid red color. Bright green coloration is similarly imparted by the use of nickel nitrate, a beautiful bluish-green is given by ammonium bichromate and chromic acid, while remarkable blue can be created through the use of ferrocyanide salts. The familiar black onyx so commonly used in rings and pendants is obtained by soaking slabs of chalcedony in sugar solutions and then subjecting them to a further soaking in sulfuric acid. The latter attacks the sugar deposited in the pores and converts it into deep brown carbon. All shades of brown can be obtained by this method depending on the duration of the treatment.

LOCALITIES

Greenland. The principal occurrences of quartz minerals on the West Coast are associated with recent volcanic rocks which outcrop in abundance in the region around Disko Island. In the Umanak District, chalcedony, jasper and other forms of quartz, along with common milky to bluish opal occur in the basalts of Nugssuaq Peninsula at Niakornak on the southern shore of Umanak Fjord. Similar mineralization occurs westward of Niakornak wherever volcanic rocks make their appearance. Eastward, quartz gemstones, particularly geodes consisting of chalcedony or opal enclosing zeolites or sometimes solid chalcedony, occur near Slibestens Fjeld. On the extreme north western tip of Nugssuaq Peninsula at Kaniuak are found geodes, nodules, jaspers, and other quartz varieties. Southwest of Kaniuak lies the small Eskimo community of Nugssuaq surrounded by a series of islets upon which are found many quartz gemstones. Quartz-bearing basalts occur as far south as Nusak. Gray chalcedony occurs as fissure fillings in basalt and as crusts on calcite at Naqerdlok; agate geodes are found in amygdaloidal basalt at Vesterfjeld, also at Kangilia. Chalcedony geodes occur at Angertunek while stalactitic chalcedony is found at Sangmissoq; also gray chalcedony at Naqornarssuk, and bluish-white chalcedony and agate in geodes and fissure fillings at Agatdalen (Agate Valley). Chalcedony is found on the south and west coasts of Ubekendt Island.

In the Disko Island region quartz gemstones occur in numerous places in the basalts. Chalcedony nodules are found at Sefarsuit on the northern tip of Disko Island; abundant bluish chalcedony occurs along the sides of a broad valley leading inland from the northeast coast of the island at a place called Kinguak; brown jasper, green moss agate, and other varieties are found here also. Blue chalcedony and agate in geodes up to 8 inches in diameter are found at Kuganguaq in the Ritenbenk District; also geodes up to 6 inches containing chalcedony and agate in basalt at Asuk, some containing crystals of quartz. Chalcedony crusts line fissures in basalt at Qutdligssat. Much quartz is found along the shores of Disko Fjord, Disko Island; bloodstone is found in small pieces on the beach at Tarajungitsok on the southern coast of the northeast arm of the fjord, also in considerable quantity in the valley of the stream which enters this arm. Chalcedony occurs on the eastern shore of Disko Fjord between its two principal arms; large quantities of chalcedony, agate, jasper, especially bloodstone, are found on the Nangisat Peninsula which projects southward into Disko Fjord; also similar material at the extreme northeastern end of the fjord. At the latter place, chalcedony occurs as seams and nodules, also as geodes lined with quartz crystals. In the Godhavn District, amethyst crystals line chalcedony geodes at Ametystskraenten (Amethyst Slope) in Stordalen; stalactitic chalcedony is found at Marrak; pebbles of green and brown jasper at Equluit and green jasper at Eqalunguit. Nodules and geodes of chalcedony and agate occur in basalts behind Brandevinshavn, a small harbor on the south coast of Disko Island about ¾ mile east of Godhavn. Further east along the coast from this town at Aumarutigsat occur jasper, agate, and other quartz varieties.

Bloodstone, or possibly plasma, is found on the beach as broken masses at Akugdleq, a small bay about 10 miles south of Christianshaab.

In the Frederikshaab District, small cavities in the granite of Kugnat Mountain at the entrance of Arsuk Fjord furnish rock crystals, amethysts, and smoky quartz crystals. Green jasper and bloodstone are found on the peninsula of Tapatsiait several miles directly west of Ivigtut across Arsuk Fjord. Similar material is also found in dikes intruding granite on Ikertunguak Island in Ikersuak Fjord northwest of Juliannehaab in the Juliannehaab District. In this same district, blood red jasper is found as blocks and boulders in breccia in association with sandstone and basalts in the inner reaches of Igaliko Fjord. Clear, deeply etched rock crystals up to 4 inches in length, occur in pegmatites at Narssarssuak; similar crystals up to 4 by 6 inches occur at Igaliko and Iganeq. At Ilua, rose quartz is found in large fragments. In the southern extremity of Greenland, chalcedony is found on Statenhuk Island and other islands north of Cape Farewell on the west coast where it occurs as waterworn pebbles on the beaches. Aventurine quartz is reported from the small island of Aluk about 35 miles northeast of Cape Farewell where it is said to occur in a large pegmatite associated with allanite and mica.

In East Greenland, rose quartz is found on Dronning Louise Island and south of Nagtoralik; agate and chalcedony occur at Kap Dalton and Kap Brewster; brown jasper occurs as large blocks at Geologfjord while agate is found at Knudshoved and at Hold-With-Hope; ordinary chalcedony occurs at Carlshavn.

Alaska. The predominantly volcanic nature of the rocks composing the numerous islands of the Aleutians and the Alaska Peninsula, should produce numerous varieties of quartz, however, very little has been reported up to date. On the Island of Attu, small translucent pale gray chalcedony nodules found on the beaches of the southeast coast have been locally called "moon-stones." Reddish jaspers have been noted along the north coast of Adak Island; the nearby island of Tanaga has produced numerous agate pebbles from various beaches along the northern coast. Gray banded agate has been found on Unalaska Island. Carnelian and chalcedony pebbles are found on the beaches of Popof Island in the Shumagin Group near the village of Sand Point, apparently weathered from basalts which outcrop nearby. On the Alaska Peninsula, small pale red and honey-yellow carnelian pebbles occur in the gravels of the north shore of Becharof Lake near its outlet.

In Northwestern Alaska, dark gray petrified wood occurs as waterworn pebbles on the western shore of Nelson Island next to Etolin Strait.

In Southeastern Alaska, some fine petrified wood occurs on the shores of Glacier Bay but a more exact locality is unspecified. Petrified wood has also been found on Hamilton Bay, Kupreanof Island. Grayish chalcedony nodules and agate nodules weathering from basalt are found on the beaches of Admiralty Island from Gambier Bay southward to Wilson Cove, also in the vicinity of Point Gardner. Agate and jasper are found in Saginaw Bay on Kuiu Island and on the beaches of Zarembo Island.

North West Territories. Pebbles of jasper have been noted at the east end of Great Slave Lake and on Princess Royal Island; chalcedony in geodes occurs in basalts at Dubawnt Lake; agate is found on Southampton Island. Pale to deep pink rose quartz occurs on Amadjak Bay on Baffinland.

Quebec. Olive green jasper in small veins is found on Belanger's Island in the Nastapoka Island Group just off the entrance to Richmond Gulf on the east coast of Hudson Bay. Agate and chalcedony have been reported along the Hamilton and Ungava rivers in New Quebec Territory. Agate pebbles occur in the conglomerates of the Bonaventure formation along the shores of Chaleur Bay (Gaspe Peninsula). A small bed of dark green and reddish-brown jasper traversed by streaks of white chalcedony occurs at River Ouelle in Kamouraska County. Blood-red jasper, often attractively patterned, occurs near Sherbrooke in Sherbrooke Co. Large quantities of rich red jasper are found on Lot 15, Concession X in Hull Township, Gatineau Co.

New Brunswick. Agate and amethyst within chalcedony geodes occur in lavas on the west side of Little Dipper Harbor, at Dalhousie, and upon the Upsalquitch River 7 miles above the forks in Restigouche County. In Victoria County, the gravels of the Tobique River yield small agate, jasper, and chalcedony pebbles. Amethyst is found upon the Washademoak River in Queens County; also at Darling Lake and Hampton in Kings County. Agate, amethyst, and chalcedony geodes occur between North Head and Dark Harbor on Grand Manan Island, Charlotte County.

Nova Scotia. This Province is noted for the numerous varieties of crystalline and cryptocrystalline quartz which occur in geodes, nodules, and fissure fillings in lava sills. Frequently, lava sills form steep cliffs along the shores of the Bay of Fundy and elsewhere; their weathering releases gemstones to the beaches below. Exceptionally fine amethyst crystals in geodes and lining crevices occur in volcanic rocks at Partridge Island and also upon Cape Sharp in Cumberland County. Some amethyst masses over 12 inches across have been found while a magnificent geode of "two gallons" capacity was uncovered at Cape Sharp. Agate, jasper, and chalcedony also occur at both localities while fine agate is found on Two Islands. It is interesting to note that masses of amethyst composed of numerous solidly interlocked crystals occurred so frequently along the shores of the Bay of Fundy that it found some employment in ornamental items. This compact material was sliced into slabs, polished on both sides, and used as insets in boxes, caskets, and clock cases.

In Kings County, exceptionally fine amethyst, carnelian, beautifully-patterned agate, and many other forms of quartz are found eroding from the basalt cliffs of Cape Blomidon and are recovered from the beaches below. Sagenitic quartz occurs at Scotts Bay. Smoky quartz has been found at Ross Creek; red jasper is found at Woodworth Cove on Long Island; fine specimens of agate come from between Cape Split and Cape Blomidon, also from Canada Creek and Harbourville.

Very large smoky quartz crystals were once found in cavities in pegmatite in the vicinity of Paradise River and near Bridgetown and Lawrencetown in Annapolis County. Agate eroded from lava occurs on the beaches of the Bay of Fundy in Annapolis; also carnelian from Trout Cove and on the north shore of Granville; bloodstone in small nodules and irregular fragments is found at the base of Chute cove.

Chalcedony, agate, jasper, and fine amethyst also occur in lavas along the Bay of Fundy shore of Digby Co. A splendid chalcedony geode lined with brilliant sparkling amethyst and weighing 40 pounds was found at Sandy Cove. Other localities in this county are: Cape d'Or, Mink Cove, St. Mary Bay, Digby Neck, and the south side of Nichol's Mountain. Red jasper is found upon Briar Island.

Other occurrences in this province are: smoky quartz near Paces Lake near the head of the Musquodoboit Harbor, Halifax; morion and smoky quartz crystals of large size at Joe Bell Creek, Chester, and near Lake Ramsay in Lunenburg Co.; rose quartz from near Shelburne in Shelburne Co.; and green quartz colored by numerous fine needles of actinolite from Kail's Point. The Lake Ramsay locality mentioned above yielded a fine smoky quartz crystal measuring 26¾ inches in length which now reposes in the Provincial Museum at Halifax.

Ontario. Pale rose quartz occurs in a large quartz pegmatite core on the south half of Lots 30 and 31, Concession XV, Lyndoch Township, Renfrew Co. Rock crystals of perfect clarity have been mined for piezoelectric purposes from a deposit located 500 feet south of the shore of Red Horse Lake and 5000 feet east of Black Rapids in Leeds County. Crystals occur in vugs and pockets in a brecciated quartzite, especially at points where the quartzite has been intruded by pegmatites. Crystals range in size from ¼ inch diameter to some as much as 2 inches in diameter and up to 8 inches in length. In the same general area as the above deposit are found others, principally within a triangular area from the east end of Higley Lake to the east end of Fodey Lake and to the north of the latter point for about 3000 feet. Another deposit is located 2000 feet southeast of the Red Horse Lake deposit.

Banded agate of fine quality occurs in the Algoma District in the extreme eastern part of Lake Superior on the shores of Goulais Bay about 15 miles north of Sault Ste. Marie. Green breccia jasper occurs at the outlet of White Beaver Lake, Montreal River, Timiskaming District. Red jasper, banded with hematite and similar to the *jaspilite* of Michigan, occurs at McInnes Lake in the Patricia District; at Jasper Lake; Hunter Island in the Rainy River District; also east of Lake Nipigon at Whitefish, Kaministikwa River; in the Thunder Bay District, and elsewhere.

Perhaps the finest agate in Canada occurs on the south shore of Michipicoten Island, a rocky, sparsely-wooded island located in the east end of Lake Superior near the Ontario shore. Upon this island are well exposed volcanic rocks of the Keeweenawan Formation in which numerous gas cavities and fissures are filled with many varieties of chalcedony. Recent visitors to the island report finding very large nodules and geodes along the south shore not far from the western extremity of the island. Good chalcedony and agate occur at the eastern corner of the island and abundantly at a point on the south shore 3 miles west of Quebec Harbor. Michipicoten agate is noted for lovely opaque to slightly translucent banding in pastel shades including unusual pale blue, lavender and green. In general, the bands are not as sharply defined as in Mexican agate but some are very striking nevertheless.

Agate and chalcedony similar to that found on Michipicoten Island occur upon several offshore islands which form an arc south of Nipigon Bay in northern Lake Superior. The Osler Series lavas, which in many places are amygdaloidal, overlie Edward Island, the peninsular area of the mainland just to the northeast, Isle St. Ignace, and Simpson Island. Nodules and geodes are found on the beaches and in the soil where they have eroded from lavas, and also in place. In general, the nodules are potato-shaped, average about 1½ inches in diameter, and may be hollow or filled with calcite crystals or beautiful terminated quartz crystals varying in color from colorless to amethystine; some are colored red due to hematite inclusions. A fine exposure of agate-bearing lava is upon the north headland of Pringle Bay.

The Thunder Bay Region of Ontario has long been noted for the enormous quantity of splendidly crystallized amethysts which occur in numerous silver, lead, and zinc veins. There is scarcely an important collection of minerals which does not contain representative specimens. In the Chicago Natural History Museum, for example, a sheet of crystals measuring 12 inches wide by 2½ feet in length is on exhibit. Unfortunately, few of the amethyst crystals are of good gem quality in spite of their abundance, and only a few faceted gems were cut from the clearest and most uniformly-colored individuals. Thunder Bay amethyst crystals range in size from as small as ¼ inch across to a maximum of 5 inches diameter; unbroken sheets of crystal aggregates have been removed from the mines weighing as much as 150 pounds!

The silver-lead-zinc mining region in Thunder Bay District embraces an area 150 miles long and 25 miles wide on the north shore of Lake Superior. The region is underlain by ancient volcanic and sedimentary rocks intruded in places by granite while upper formations consist of various sedimentary strata intruded by lava flows and numerous dikes of diabase. Fissures have formed in favorable places and it is along these that mineralization has taken place. Characteristically, veins contain calcite, barite, fluorite and quartz (clear, smoky and amethystine); also galena, sphalerite, chalcopyrite, pyrite, several silver minerals, gold, and other metalliferous ores in minor amounts.

There are two distinct belts of mines and prospects from which amethyst has been produced along with silver and base metals. The first belt begins at the northern end of Nipigon Bay with several mines in the vicinity of Ozone Siding on the Canadian Pacific R.R., and extends very nearly to the north shore of Black Bay, thence southwest through Pearl in McTavish Township and along the north shore of Thunder Bay in a more or less straight line to its termination in several mines near the eastern end of Arrow Lake. The second belt begins at Pie Island in the southern part of Thunder Bay and extends southwestward through several islands and mainland localities to its termination in Big Trout Bay in Crooks Township.

Due to the large number of amethyst occurrences (at least 65), only those of outstanding interest will be listed: good crystal groups from mining location X-124, 4 miles northeast of Little Gull Lake west of Strange Township; spectacular crystals of clear quartz, some up to 2½ inches diameter, and amethyst from the dumps of the Star Mine on the southern half of Concession V, Lot 5, Strange Township; well-terminated amethyst crystals in seams and as vug linings along the north shore of Sunset Lake in Lismore Township, about ½ mile south of the eastern end of Whitefish Lake; on the east face of Silver Bluff, 1½ miles southeast of Silver Mountain R.R. Station in Strange Township; attractively-banded white and amethystine quartz in mining location R-64 on Silver Mountain in Lybster Township about 2 miles south of Hillside R.R. Station; beautiful amethyst crystals in the vicinity of Echo Lake in the northwest corner of Lot 12, Concession I, Marks Township; large quartz crystals with amethystine tips at the West Beaver Mine in mining location T-140 in O'Connor Township near its southeast corner; good amethyst crystals in Lot 3 of McTavish Township east of Ancliff; splendid clear rock crystals of optical grade in vugs in the silver veins in Lot H, McIntyre Township, about 6 miles east of Port Arthur.

Alberta. Much high quality silicified wood occurs in an extensive area along the Red Deer River Valley centered about 90 miles east of Calgary. This wood closely resembles the Eden Valley material of Wyoming, appearing as small limb sections of creamy-white exterior with dark brown to black cores. This area is also famous for its silicified dinosaur bones which are frequently hollow and lined with small sparkling quartz crystals. This locality is frequently called Drumheller and the wood *Drumheller wood.* The Dinosaur Beds Provincial Park is located 8 miles to the north of Drumheller. Collecting specimens is of course forbidden in this Park but in view of the very large area over which the wood and bone occurs, there is no need to collect within its boundaries. Upon rare occasions, silicified pine cones accompany some of the Drumheller wood.

Fine silicified wood occurs in the vicinity of Ross Coulee and near the elbow of the South Saskatchewan River in the Medicine Hat Division.

British Columbia. Near Penticton, gray chalcedony geodes up to 10 inches in diameter and containing amethyst, occur 8 to 10 miles west along the Green Mountain Road. An abundance of quartz gemstones is found in the vicinity of Princeton in decomposed lavas. The Vermillion Bluffs nearby, provide large amounts of petrified wood, chalcedony casts after wood, agate, and other forms of quartz. A recent noteworthy find at this locality is a large nodule weighing 50 pounds, solidly filled with milky quartz crystals enclosed by a two-inch rind of smoky chalcedony; this nodule measures 17 inches by 12 inches by 8 inches. Much agate and chalcedony occur at Agate Bluffs 8 miles from Princeton while fine material has been picked up from gravels in neighborhood streams such as in Whipsaw Creek, Similkameen River, Wolf Creek and elsewhere. Fine red moss agate has been found at Cloverdale.

The Monte Lake area located 27 miles east of Kamloops on the Vernon Highway has also been unusually productive of chalcedony gemstones eroded from basalts. Petrified wood occurs at McGlashin Lake and in the Kamloops Petrified Wood Forest on Robbins Range. Green jasper occurs on Sunday Summit near Monte Lake while the area around this lake is noted for moss agate, the original material coming from a road cut at the south end. In the vicinity of Kamloops, large and attractive banded agate nodules have been found at Barnhardt's Vale while moss agate in large pieces has been picked up at Douglas Lake some 20 miles south of the town. Fine moss agate is also found in Mission Flats 3 miles west of Kamloops. Agate, chalcedony, jasper, and other quartz gemstones have been found near Savona Mountain, Savona Lake, and at Dufferin Hill. Amethyst-lined geodes and a beautiful translucent blue chalcedony occur in slides just above the highway at Little River fishing camp on the shore of Little Shuswap Lake not far from Squilax. Carnelian occurs as waterworn nodules in the gravels of the Little River nearby. Fine pale blue and gray chalcedony and white-banded agate occur on the north and south sides of Kamloops Lake; the largest specimens are found along the banks of Tranquille and Chris creeks which enter this lake. In the Ashcroft area, agate and chalcedony occur upon the Nicoamen Plateau. Nodules of eye-agate, blue and gray banded agate, and green jasper occur in volcanic rocks at Shaw Springs 9 miles west of Spence's Bridge on the main line of the Canadian Pacific Railroad. The locality is on the south side of the Thompson River where eroded basalt cliffs form talus slopes. In the Thompson River gravels, chalcedony and agate are fairly abundant especially in the stretch from about 5 miles east of Spence's Bridge to Lytton. Good agate and jasper occur in the Fraser River in the vicinity of Lytton while just recently, quartz colored dark blue by inclusions of dumortierite has been found in the form of boulders in the stretch upstream from Chilliwack.

Chalcedony nodules occur on the shores of Ootsa Lake in the Omineca Mining Division; handsome chalcedony, sometimes of large size, is found at Aspen Grove Camp in the Nicola Mining Division; jasper pebbles in conglomerate occur near Atlin Lake in the Boundary District.

Volcanic rocks underlie much of Vancouver Island and in some places, contain gas cavities filled with various types of chalcedony. The west coast of the island is relatively unexplored but reports indicate that hunting for gemstones should be profitable. Jasper and agate are found on the beaches of the island near Victoria and upon beaches 8 miles north of this city. Similar gemstones have been found at Sooke about 20 miles north. In the Queen Charlotte Islands, fine agate occurs near Massett and Skidegate near the north coast of Graham Island.

Maine. In Scribner's Ledge Quarry in Albany Township, Oxford County, superb rose quartz occurs in a pegmatite near the center of its core. This quarry is located about 1 mile north of the North Waterford Pumping Station. Some of this rose quartz has been cut into exceptionally attractive spheres as well as faceted and cabochon gems, and, due to numerous fine inclusions, also displays attractive asterism. A ball of 1½ inches in diameter, showing the star effect well, is in the American Museum of Natural History. Similar material has come from the Bumpus Quarry in the same township, the exact location being 6.4 miles slightly east of south of Bethel and 1.2 miles southwest of the village of Town House.

In the southwestern part of Oxford County, fine amethyst crystals were once found in pockets in pegmatite on Deer Hill in Stow Township. In 1885 or 1886, a superb crystal yielded a faceted gem of 25 carats. The most recent quarrying at this locality in August 1956 brought to light a large pocket measuring 7 by 4 by 3½ feet from which was removed almost a ton of quartz crystals, some pale amethystine in color. Though interesting as mineralogical specimens very little suitable amethyst was found in the lot. Deer Hill is located 4½ miles directly north of the village of Stow, or 1¾ miles east-southeast of North Chatham, N.H. The pegmatite which yielded the amethyst covers much of a spur of Deer Hill immediately south of its summit and has been opened in several places by shallow pits. The country rock is granitic gneiss. Amethyst occurred in small pockets of irregular form strung along the contact between the coarse feldspar and quartz core of the pegmatite. Several thousand fine crystals, some of rich coloration, have been recovered. The American Museum of Natural History boasts a fine oval facetted gem of 40 carats from this locality as well as a fine group of deep purple crystals measuring 4 inches by 5 inches. Elsewhere in Oxford County, amethyst has been dug from pits atop Pleasant Mountain in Denmark Township.

New Hampshire. Some of the most important occurrences for amethyst in the United States are located in Coos County, principally in Stark and Milan townships, but also embracing parts of Lancaster, Kilkenny, Dummer, Millsfield, Odell, Berlin, Strafford, and Northumberland townships. The most productive localities occur a few miles north and south of the stretch of Highway 110 between West Milan and Groveton. Although amethyst crystals, as well as smoky quartz and topaz, have been picked up in a broad area, the best localities may be conveniently located on the Percy, N.H., U.S. Geological Survey Quadrangle (scale 1:62500).

Amethyst occurs loose in the soil or in pockets upon Green's Ledge in the western part of Milan Township; on Diamond Ledges on Long Mountain in the northern part of Stark Township; between North Peak and Square Mountain in Kilkenny Township; upon the south peak of Percy Peak; and upon the western slopes of Hutchins Mountain in Stark Township not far from the border of Northumberland Township. The gemstones occur in pegmatites, which, in this area, are enclosed in reddish- to grayish-white biotite granites. Gemstones have been found only in the higher elevations of the mountains, frequently from 500 to 1000 feet above the lower slopes or the valleys below, but their occurrence at these heights is due more to the thinner soil covering and greater rock exposure than to the absence of pockets at lower levels. Finds on Green's Ledge have been made at an elevation of 1700 feet while on Diamond Ledges, amethyst has been found in abundance only at 2000 feet elevation. The granite on these mountains is easily eroded in the vicinity of pockets and therefore tends to be shattered, releasing pocket contents to the soil covering the slopes. Local collectors have found some intact pockets however, and in them, noted the following minerals in addition to amethyst: smoky quartz, often abundant, feldspar, well crystallized in blocky individuals, topaz; also minor fluorite, molybdenite, knebelite, limonite, albite, sericite, beryl, chlorite, pyrite, and muscovite. Pockets vary in size from several inches in diameter to some over a foot across; a few have been found several feet in diameter.

Much of the amethyst is intergrown with smoky quartz in narrow alternate bands, sometimes as many as ten alternations being noted in a single crystal. In those of pure hue, the intensity of color varies from pale to rich reddish-purple. Clear facet-grade material suitable for gems is not abundant but some very fine stones up to 40 carats weight have been cut. The American Museum of Natural History owns two fine facetted gems weighing respectively, 12.73 and 9.90 carats, both from an unspecified place in Berlin Township. Smoky quartz is far more abundant than amethyst and is also found in much larger crystals. The Diamond Ledges produced a fine example of 14 inches by 20 inches weighing 91 pounds but the average is of course much smaller. Crystals are simply developed as a rule, but some overgrowth of smoky quartz by amethyst in the form of "sceptre" crystals is sometimes noted. Further details on these localities may be consulted under TOPAZ.

Amethyst has also been reported from Mount Crawford and in Surry, Waterville and Westmoreland townships. Some fine gems of rock crystal colored green by acicular inclusions of actinolite have been cut from material obtained at the old Franconia Iron Mine located on the southern flank of Ore Hill, about 1½ miles south of Sugar Hill, Grafton County. Good rose quartz has been mined from the Wenham Mine located about 5½ miles north of Gilsum in Cheshire County.

Vermont. A large deposit of bright red jasper outcrops on the Parrott Farm just off Highway 2, about 9 miles north of Burlington, in Chittenden County. This jasper is similar to the *jaspilite* of Michigan in that it appears cherty in origin and is associated with bright steely-blue specular hematite which appears in numerous hairline cracks and fissures within the otherwise solid material.

A green aventurine of some interest for ornamental purposes occurs in a small saddle on the north side of Round Hill (on the west flank of the

Green Mountains) 3¾ miles southeast of Rutland Station, Rutland County. The basic rock is fine-grained quartzite of foliated schistose structure colored by scales of bright green fuchsite mica but somewhat deadened in color by the presence of minor amounts of chlorite, tourmaline and magnetite.

Massachusetts. Especially fine agate nodules have long been noted from the basalt sills in the vicinity of Deerfield in Franklin County, in fact, this locality has been mentioned in some of the earliest American gem literature. The basalts of the Connecticut River Valley in general, contain gas cavities filled with various quartz gemstones including chalcedony, agate, and agate geodes in which some very attractive amethysts have been found. Some beautifully banded agate was found many years ago about 1 mile east of Deerfield Academy; also in the gravels of the Deerfield River. The Cheapside Quarry at East Deerfield, overlooking the river, has furnished some fine amethyst from chalcedony geodes. Other areas productive of agate are in the vicinity of Amherst, Hampshire County, and Conway in Franklin County. In general the agate nodules are small, perhaps less than several inches in diameter, however, many have been infiltrated with coloring matter and show very handsome bands. Very little agate has been discovered in recent years.

Rhode Island. A variety of quartz gemstones occur in peculiar formations outcropping on Diamond Hill, Cumberland Township. The entire hill is primarily quartz and is honeycombed with cavities and seams along which jasper, agate, and ordinary chalcedony have been deposited.

Not far from Diamond Hill, some very attractive clear quartz shot through with dead-black hornblende needles in sagenitic patterns has been obtained from quarries on Calumet Hill. The finest pieces reached 6 inches across and several hundred pounds were sent to Germany in 1880 for cutting when the quarries were active. Needles of hornblende reached lengths of over 1 inch and lay crisscrossd like jackstraws in clear quartz.

Jasper and carnelian in shaley rock have been found near Pawtuxet south of Providence. Many years ago, some very fine amethyst crystals, some suitable for faceted gems, were found in openings in an agatized quartz rock along the shores of Narragansett Bay near the Bristol-Mt. Hope Ferry. The best locality was reported as lying 100 yards east of the slip. This occurrence has been exhausted for many years and the old ferry has now been replaced by a modern toll bridge connecting the large island on which Newport is situated with the mainland. Good agate, jasper, and chalcedony are sometimes found along the beaches of Mt. Hope Bay.

Connecticut. A few pegmatite quarries in the vicinity of Portland, Middlesex County, have provided crystalline quartz gemstones. Rose quartz occurs at the Pelton Quarry about 1 mile south of Portland Reservoir and northwest of the city; citrine and smoky quartz crystals occur in pockets at

Strickland Quarry on the west slope of Collins Hill, several miles east of Portland.

The southward extension of the volcanic rocks previously noted along the Connecticut River in Massachusetts appears also in this state and extends almost to Long Island Sound, producing the same sort of crystalline and cryptocrystalline quartz gemstones. Basaltic sills run through the western half of the state in northeast to southwest direction and in many places display favorable mineralization. Agate nodules, often beautifully colored and banded but seldom over 3 inches in diameter, occur in basalt debris or in gravels. In Hartford County, agate has been found near Farmington while fine amethyst was found, but only rarely, in the Meriden quarries located 1½ miles northwest of Meriden. "Chalcedonic Balls" as the old literature describes agate nodules, have been found near Torringford and Woodbury in Litchfield County. In New Haven County, trap-rock outcrops between Milford and West Haven have also provided nodules while similar rocks in the neighborhood of Guilford and East Haven are said to have provided good specimens.

New York. Rose quartz occurs in a pegmatite dike which has been quarried for feldspar in the village of Overlook in Saratoga County, 12½ miles north of Batchellerville; this material varies from pale to deep pink; some is clear.

Unusually well-formed and brilliant rock crystals occur in Herkimer County and are widely known as "Herkimer diamonds." Literally millions of these sparkling crystals have been picked up from the soil over a span of many years. Though prized chiefly for mineral collections, a few have been faceted into gems and some necklaces have been made by boring doubly-terminated crystals and threading them on a string. Localities for "diamonds" are centered about Middleville in the southern part of the county where calcareous gray sandstones yield numerous specimens from small cavities. Three principal outcrops and associated soils are known: one belt begins at Middleville on the north side of the road between that town and Newport and extends in a northwesterly direction; a second stretches from Middleville eastward about one mile toward the northern side of the highway to Fairfield; the third, and the most prolific, is located atop a hill between Middleville and Herkimer and extends from Middleville to 3 miles southward. Cavities range from those barely large enough to hold a ¼ inch crystal to some like miniature caverns from which as much as a half bushel of crystals have been obtained. Smaller pockets seem to produce the best crystals. Some crystals contain inclusions of black carbonaceous matter and liquid- or gas-filled bubbles. The finest crystals are those of about ½ inch in diameter although some larger ones are very brilliant also. At one of the sandstone outcrops near Middleville, the owners of the Taber Estate permit collecting for a daily fee of $2 with the privilege of keeping all specimens found.

Silicified corals were once found at Schoharie in Schoharie County and at other points in the vicinity, yielding some material suitable for cutting and polishing. Black silicified coral with white markings was obtained at Catskill.

Small quantities of citrine crystals along with smoky quartz crystals of faceting grade have been obtained from pockets in the pegmatites of Bedford Township, Westchester County. Some fine rose quartz of both faceting and cabochon grade, the latter showing fine asterism, was also obtained. A sphere of this material showing the star effect is shown in Figure 81. The principal production of rose quartz came from the Kinkel Quarry located on the easterly slope of a small hill about ¾ mile southeast of the village of Bedford. When prepared into spheres, Kinkel Quarry rose quartz exhibits 6-rayed stars but some unusual specimens exhibit 12-, 18-, and 24-rayed stars. Citrine and smoky quartz also occur in this quarry but only in pockets in the pegmatite. Nearby, the Hobby Quarry also yielded much rose quartz from the core of a large pegmatite. This working is located about 1½ miles southeast of the Kinkel Quarry along the Mianus River in North Castle. The Baylis Quarry, located about ½ mile west of the Kinkel Quarry, is reputed to have produced the finest rose quartz of the group but none was asteriated. Large smoky quartz crystals also came from this opening.

New Jersey. Beautiful crystalline and cryptocrystalline quartz gemstones occur in the basalt sills of Northern New Jersey. The most productive formations outcrop in Bergen County in the north and pass through Passaic, Essex, Morris, Somerset, Hunterdon and Mercer counties. The Watchung Mountains in the northern counties form gently curving parallel ridges of several hundred feet elevation which trend from northeast to southwest. Many quarries have been opened in the sills and it is at such places that collecting is at its best. Beautifully marked agate, sometimes striped with numerous opaque white bands suspended in translucent chalcedony, is common in fresh rocks while specimens picked up from weathered rocks are often handsomely stained pink, brown, and other colors. Fine amethyst-lined geodes are found also and provide beautiful mineral specimens, however, as a rule, the individual crystals are too small to cut gems over several carats weight. Fine agate, prettily mottled and banded, has been found at Braen's Quarry in Hawthorne, Passaic Co.; also at the large quarry at the end of Planten Avenue in Prospect Park, and the long-abandoned quarry on McBride Avenue just above Passaic Falls in Paterson. Excellent amethyst druses have come from the last two places mentioned. Beautiful finely-banded white to gray agates occur in the quarries at Great Notch just west of Passaic in Passaic Co. Carnelian in small but richly-colored pieces occurs in the gravels of Stirling Brook near Stirling in Morris Co.

Pennsylvania. In Northampton County, catseye quartz, chalcedony and prase were reported many years ago from South Mountain south of Redington, about 5 miles east of Bethlehem in Lower Saucon Township. Deposits of chert, much of which is suited for gem purposes, occur over an area of at least 20 acres in the vicinity of Vera Cruz, Upper Milford Township, Lehigh County. A series of pits reaching depths of 20 feet and widths of 50 feet may be seen near the Pennsylvania Turnpike about 7 miles south of Allentown. The chert is hard, compact material capable of taking a fine polish and occurring in a wide variety of hues including red, brown, yellow, blue and black.

Petrified wood, sometimes well silicified and cuttable, occurs in the Triassic formations of Bucks County as in Neshaminy Creek west of Newtown; ¼ mile southeast of Roelof's Station; 1½ miles north of Woodburne Station; northeast of Leonard's Station; near Rocksville; south and southeast of Holland Station; east of Churchville Station; etc. In Montgomery County, silicified wood occurs ¼ mile east of Morganville Station and also in gravel pits near Maple Glen and Jarrettown. Chalcedony and jasper occur in a large deposit in Cambrian quartzite near Durham, Durham Township, where it was once quarried for crushed rock. Jasper, agate and jasp-agate occur on the old Gotschall Farm 1½ miles north-northwest of Spies Church in Alsace Township, also near the old Boyertown Iron Mines ¼ mile southwest of Boyertown in Colebrookdale Township; chalcedony and jasper occur at Kinsey Hill 1½ miles south of Jacksonwald in Triassic diabase; also at Mertztown in Longswamp Township. Chert, amethyst, chalcedony, and silicified wood occur at Friedensburg in Oley Township; chalcedony, jasper and agate are found on Flint Hill 1 mile south of Bowers Station; amethyst has been found at Green Hill, 1¾ miles northeast of Oley Furnace. Chalcedony and chert occur at Fleetwood in Richmond Township. In Ruscombmanor Township, chalcedony and chert occur on farms ½ to 1 mile east of Pricetown; also 2 miles west of Pricetown; jasper, chalcedony, agate and amethyst were found at Fritztown. Chalcedony and jasper have been reported from Cushion Mountain in Spring Township.

The following localities are in Delaware County. Aston Township: amethyst in clusters and single crystals in a vein which cut across Dutton's Mill Road west of Morgan Station; amethyst in exposures on the south side of Chester Creek, ½ mile west of Crozierville opposite Lenni. Birmingham Township: amethyst on the Brandywine River 1½ miles south of Chadd's Ford. Chester Township: fine groups and crystals of amethyst and smoky quartz in the old Shaw & Esrey Quarry north of the Baltimore & Ohio Railroad about ¼ mile east of Chester Station; amethyst in geodes near Henvi's Quarry north of Chester Creek, east of Upland and near the Waterville Road; amethyst and smoky quartz on Peter Green's Farm south of Chester Creek and ¼ mile west of Upland Station; amethyst in exposures along the road on the east side of Chester Creek opposite Bridgewater Station. Lower Chichester Township: clear colorless and smoky quartz crystals up to 7 inches across on a knoll near the Linwood Mill Dam about 1½ mile north of Trainer Station. Marple Township: amethyst in exposures along Crum Creek near Worrell. Middletown Township: crystals of amethyst in pegmatite, some containing rutile needles, on the Marshall Farm near Dismal Run ½ mile south of Sycamore Mills. Thornbury Township: amethyst at Glen Mills. Upper Chichester Township: amethyst crystals up to 1 inch across in pegmatite about 2 miles north of Boothwyn east of the Chelsea-Boothwyn Road; smoky quartz and amethyst crystals up to 2 inches across on the Armstrong Farm ½ mile north of Boothwyn and east of Chelsea Road; pale amethyst crystals in parallel growth loose in soil on the Bergdoll Farm immediately north of Boothwyn Station and west of the Chelsea Road; fine rutilated quartz crystals loose in soil on the McCay Farm ¼ mile east of Boothwyn Station. Upper Darby Township: large colorless and smoky quartz crystals in pegmatite along the West Chester road ½ mile west of Upper Darby Post Office; fine smoky crystals up to 7 inches by 9 inches in pegmatite in an old sand pit in the northwestern part of Lansdowne. Upper Providence Township: bluish and greenish quartz containing actinolite inclusions, also amethyst in soil at Blue Hill crossroads 2½ miles northwest of Media and ¾ mile northeast of Sycamore Mills; deep purple amethyst crystals in groups up to 2 inches by 10 inches from veins on Crum Creek, 1 mile east of Rose Tree Inn and 1½ miles northeast of Media; deep purple crystals up to 7 pounds occurred on the Morgan Hunter Farm not far from the preceding locality—the splendid group illustrated in Kunz' "Gems and Precious Stones of North America" came from this spot; this group measures 5 inches by 6 inches with crystals up to 4½ inches by 5 inches and is now in the American Museum of Natural History; amethyst on the Copple Farm ½ mile east of Media Reservoir. Figure 79 illustrates a small but handsome group of amethyst crystals from this township.

The following localities are in Chester County. Birmingham Township: rutilated amethyst in exposures in field ¼ mile east of Pocopson Station; clear and smoky quartz crystals in the soil on the west slope of Osborn Hill 2½ miles south of West Chester. East Bradford Township: amethyst crystals loose in soil on fields south and southwest of Sconneltown between Brandywine Creek and Plum Run; one inch amethyst crystals in road cuts 2 miles south of West Chester in a quartz vein. East Marlboro Township: clear quartz crystals up to 4 inches diameter on farms 1 mile southwest of

Willowdale and on the west branch of Red Clay Creek. London Grove Township: colorless and smoky quartz crystals up to 5 inches in diameter in the soil near quarries ¼ mile east of Avondale. Newlin Township: amethyst crystals in the soil on farms south of Glenhall. Pocopson Township: amethyst crystals loose in the soil on farms about ¼ mile west of Pocopson station. Sadsbury Township: amethyst in roadcuts between Parkesburg and Sadsburyville. Valley Township: amethyst and smoky quartz in exposures along Lancaster Turnpike northwest of Coatesville. Westtown Township: amethyst in cavities in rock at Brinton's Quarries about 3 miles south of West Chester on the Birmingham Road. Silicified wood occurs ¾ mile northeast of Sheeder, in fields ¼ mile east of Coventryville.

In Lancaster County, amethyst crystals with a slight smoky tint have been found in fields 1 mile northwest of Mt. Pleasant in Bart Township. Rutilated quartz has been found in crystals at Kinzer in Paradise Township. Silicified wood occurs in fields 2 miles northwest of Churchtown, also in a railroad cut ½ mile southeast of Elizabethtown and in the fields to the east and southwest of this town; also in fields 3 miles northeast and 1 mile north of Bainbridge.

Moss agate of very fine quality has been found from time to time in Rock Springs Run, a small brook about 1¼ miles north-northeast of Rock Springs, Maryland. This locality is about ¼ to ½ mile west of Jenkins Corner in Fulton Township, Lancaster County. It is stated that the moss agate occurs in various exposures in the vicinity, also loose in the soil, or sometimes in the small stream which rises near Jenkins Corner and flows northeasterly and then southerly into Octoraro Creek. The quality is fine, showing black lacey dendrites in gray translucent chalcedony.

In York County, silicified wood occurs in fields 2 miles south and southeast of York Haven. In Cumberland County, beautiful black and white banded agate is said to occur in fields on the south side of Highway 11, 1 mile east of the Carlisle Interchange on the Pennsylvania Turnpike; nodules are several inches in diameter. In Cumberland County, smoky, colorless, and amethystine quartz crystals have been found loose in the soil 1½ miles northwest of Carlisle. Agate and jasper are reported from Caledonia State Park in Franklin and Adams counties. Amethyst and rock crystals have been found loose in the soil in Morrison Cove valley between New Enterprise and Waterside in Bedford County; the crystals are small and said to resemble the "diamonds" of Herkimer County, N.Y. In Westmoreland County, silicified trees have been found 7 miles east of Greensburg.

Maryland. Silicified wood is relatively common in the Potomac Formation of the Lower Cretaceous which outcrops in numerous places around Baltimore and between that city and Washington, D.C. Considerable material has been found in clays and gravels in railroad cuts between these two cities, especially fine wood of cutting grade occurring near Beltsville, Prince Georges County, in old bog-iron mines. The wood so far found has been identified as *cupressinoxylon* and differs only slightly from modern *Sequoia*. Good wood has also come from near Raspeburg several miles northeast of Baltimore while fossil cycads have been found in gravel pits southeast of the city and also in sand pits along the Baltimore to Washington highway.

Virginia. The southwestward extension of the Potomac Formation passes through the District of Columbia into Arlington and Fairfax counties in Virginia and yields considerable silicified wood from gravel pits and other exposures. Perhaps 20 or more logs and limb sections, some as much as 50 to 100 pounds weight, have been found in gravels northwest of the corner of Edsall Road and Shirley Highway but this locality is now built over and inaccessible. The majority of the wood is jet-black inside due to much residual carbonaceous matter and only thin exterior zones are well-silicified. Very rarely, limb sections occur which are completely replaced by chalcedony and hence polishable. A sawn and polished section in the author's collection measures 12 by 3 by 2 inches; the color is pale brown. A polished limb section is shown in Figure 96.

An old report mentions dark red moss agate occurring with steatite in the Bull Run Soapstone Quarry near Centreville, Fairfax Co.

In Page County, good red jasper, sometimes orbicular or mixed with patches of white quartzite, black hematite, and bright green epidote, occurs as loose surface material in fields on Hoak Hill, .9 mile northwest of Ida; similar material occurs along the western slope of the Blue Ridge northeast and northwest of Ida. Some very fine cabochons and polished slabs have been prepared from this material.

A considerable number of fine single amethyst crystals and groups suitable for specimen purposes have been obtained from a number of localities in this state. The exact mode of occurrence of the amethyst is not always clear, some authorities stating that they formed druses in thin cavities along the centerline of quartz veins but other evidence indicates they may be pocket crystals in pegmatites. In either case, the veins or pegmatite dikes always appear intruded in gneissic and schistose rocks of great age which outcrop in the Piedmont Regions of the several Eastern Seaboard States. The most northerly find of amethyst took place in 1902 when a split crystal weighing over 3 pounds and measuring 6 inches by 5 inches was picked up in a cultivated field one mile west of Minnieville in Prince William Co. Not all of the crystal was purple however, this color appearing only in smaller crystals overgrowing a large central individual of ordinary milky quartz. The smaller individuals ranged from ½ inch to 1½ inches in diameter.

In 1915, fine amethysts were discovered upon farmland 4 miles southwest of Trevilians in Louisa County. At that time, the properties described were

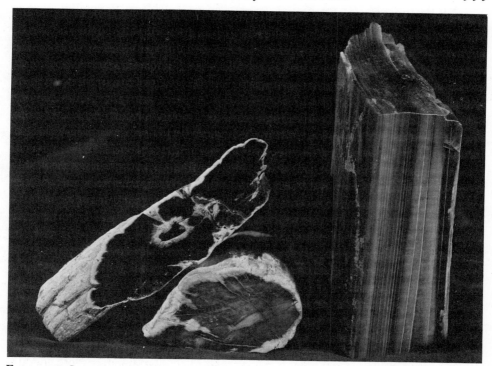

FIGURE 96. Several specimens of silicified wood. The left hand piece showing a dead black core is typical of those found in the Eden Valley area of Wyoming. The small center piece is pale brown in color and is a cypress-like wood found commonly in the gravels along the Eastern Seaboard of the United States, in this instance, from a gravel pit in Fairfax County, Virginia. The beautifully marked specimen on the right, measuring about 6 inches in height, is from Washington.

held by A. J. Rudinger, W. Overton, and J. J. Boxley. On the Rudinger Farm, amethyst crystals were found loose in the soil in two places, and about two quarts of crystals were collected. Most were pale to almost colorless and only a few were deep in hue; the sizes generally fell beneath 1 inch in diameter. Trenching to granite bedrock in one place uncovered a vein of quartz containing vugs from which were recovered about one-half bushel of crystals. These were about the same size as those previously found on the surface but were of deeper color and better quality. In Nelson County, near Lowesville, a shattered pegmatite embedded in decomposed gneiss yielded some exceptional amethyst crystals, one of the largest of which provided a very fine faceted heart-shaped gem weighing 114 carats which was shown at the Jamestown Exposition. The locality is upon a farm, formerly known as the John Saunders Place, situated 2½ miles northeast of Lowesville and 8½ miles west-northwest of Arrington. In 1907, the American Gem & Pearl Co. of New York City obtained rights to the deposits and sank a dozen or more pits within an area of 125 x 300 feet to depths of from 2 to 7 feet. One pocket was found containing 40 pounds of amethyst while many smaller cavities of lesser capacity were removed. Several thousands of fine gems were cut from this material, providing, in larger specimens, gems from 50 to 150 carats in weight. Many were unusually rich in color but some pale stones of pinkish-purple were also found. In adjacent Amherst County, some fine amethyst was picked up many years ago upon Fancy Hill, 1/3 mile north of Sandidges Post Office and 7 miles north-northwest of Amherst. Crystals were found loose in soil in two places upon a ridge, however, no digging was done to find their source. The country rock here is granitic gneiss.

Amethyst, milky, smoky, and colorless quartz crystals, apparently derived from pockets in pegmatite, are found in the topsoil of a broad area near the small community of Rice in Prince Edward Co. Occurrences are centered about the farm of George R. Smith, located about 3 miles due north of Rice and reached by Highway 619. Loose crystals occur in plowed fields on both sides of Sayler's Creek. An examination of the soil shows numerous fragments of reddish, iron-stained coarsely granular quartz, along with much less amounts of opaque white feldspar, sometimes in cleavages several inches across. Fragments of graphic granite confirms the presence of pegmatites. During a visit by the author in 1957, Mr. Smith exhibited several crystals said to be the largest found in the area. One was a single point 4 inches in diameter and 6 inches tall with only the top perfectly developed. Color was evident throughout the crystal but the deepest hue was concentrated near the tip. This specimen weighed 4½ pounds. Another amethyst group of several crystals joined in approximately parallel position, weighs 1⅞ pounds and measures about 3¾ by 4 inches by 3 inches. The several crystals comprising the group are doubly-terminated and again show concentrated color only at the tips, the remainder being ordinary milky color. Although beautifully formed and lustrous, no part is sufficiently clear to afford flawless faceted gems over several carats weight. A third crystal purchased from a farmhand came from an adjacent property and appears quite different in character from those from the Smith Farm. More of this crystal is clear but the color is very pale rose-purple. Not far from the Smith Farm, Silas Morefield of Winterham, Va., had conducted mining some years ago upon surface indications of amethyst, and, from a pocket, obtained about 1000 pounds of all grades of quartz and amethyst but only a small percentage was suitable for fine faceted gems.

Small quantities of amethyst were found in Charlotte County in an area centered about Charlotte Court House and near Brookneal in Campbell County. The old A. W. Donald Plantation 2¼ miles west-northwest of Charlotte Court House yielded some fair facet-grade amethyst in all colors from a series of test pits sunk upon the property in 1912. Amethyst has been reported from the Wingo Place 4 miles south of the court house. Loose crystals have been found upon the land of Lacey Rush about ⅓ mile northeast of Brookneal; some digging was done here many years ago but without much success. This locality is of interest because two large crystals were found here, each nearly 10 inches long and 4 inches in diameter, showing well-defined pale purple color zones parallel to pyramidal faces. The L. H. Clay Place about 10 miles northeast of Brookneal and nearly 3 miles west-southwest of Red House, provided a few crystals gathered from fields 200 to 400 yards northwest of the farmhouse; one crystal was 2½ inches long and ⅞ inch in diameter with one end of good medium color. Amethyst also had been found in fields about ¾ mile southwest of the Clay farmhouse. The country rock in this area is schistose granite. Rock crystals reaching 10 inches by 5 inches in size have been reported from a point 2.2 miles east-southeast of Willis in Floyd County.

North Carolina. In Ashe County, unusually large clear masses of rock crystal were found about 1887 on a spur of Phoenix Mountain near Long Shoal Creek in Chestnut Hill Township; also near the north fork of Piney Creek. From the first locality was obtained a 51 pound crystal fragment while a 20½ pound absolutely clear crystal which sold for $1000 was found at the second. Altogether several dozen crystals were found ranging in weight from 20 to 300 pounds each; one of 285 pounds measured 29 inches in length and 18 inches by 13 inches in cross section with one perfect termination. This specimen sold for $500. Undoubtedly these enormous rock crystals originated in a pocket in a quartz vein in underlying granitic or gneissic rock. Some crystals showed surface layers of green chlorite inclusions much resembling wispy moss and from which handsome cabinet specimens were polished. An exceptional, clear rock crystal yielded a sphere of 5 inches diameter while other specimens were sent abroad to be carved into objects of ornament.

Amethyst in slightly smoky crystals has been found at the head of Honey Creek in Wilkes Co. Bright brick-red, yellow, and banded red and black jaspers have been reported from Reeds Creek in Granville Co.

Fine amethyst crystals were found about 40 years ago in several places in Warren County where they were discovered in the topsoil of plowed fields. An important occurrence was that upon the G. W. Alston property near Inez, 11 miles south of Warrenton, where two places furnished a number of specimens. Quartz veins ranged from one to two feet in thickness and yielded single crystals up to 3 inches in diameter. Colors were good, although much was distributed in bands; all tints from colorless to deep reddish-purple were found. The J. Buxton Williams place about 2 miles south of Inez provided some very small but very fine amethysts from a knoll about ¼ mile northwest of the house near the corner of the family cemetery. About 2 miles southeast of Inez, some specimen grade crystals were found upon the Mrs. J. Connell property.

Petrified wood occurs in the Quaternary gravels of Halifax Co. Amethyst in quartz veins upon the land of G. W. Partin, 5 miles northeast of Raleigh in Wake Co., once (1910) yielded gem quality crystals of from less than an inch to several inches in size.

Iredell County is especially noted for fine amethyst from a number of localities which have provided both cutting material and superb mineral specimens. All of the finds were made about 1900 though some were reported as late as 1910. The A. C. Cook place, 9 miles southeast of Statesville was worked in 1900 by H. S. Williams of New York City. A shaft was sunk to 12 feet upon favorable surface indications and from underground workings numerous mineral specimens and a high percentage of facet material were obtained. Some of the darker material contained minute hairlike rutile needles. The M. G. Martin place, ½ mile west of the Cook Farm also provided some amethyst; also the Brawley place 1½ miles south of Cook's Farm; the J. S. Fisher place 4½ miles west-northwest of Mooresville and 12½ miles south of Statesville; the J. Cornelius place 6 miles west-northwest of Mooresville; and the Walden Farm about 3 miles south of Statesville.

Particularly fine rutilated rock crystals as well as clear and colorless types containing attractive inclusions of byssolite, goethite and chlorite, have been found in the vicinity of Stony Point in Alexander County. Smoky and rutilated quartz has been found in the gravels of Brindletown Creek in Burke County. Amethyst crystals were found upon the J. T. Eudy place near Mount Ulla in Rowan County and at two places upon the farm of N. H. Swicegood about 5 miles northwest of Linwood and 1 mile south of Taro in Davidson County. At the latter place, prospects were located 1/5 mile west and northeast of the farm house. Trenching here in 1909 yielded several pounds of good crystals from the first deposit and about 300 pounds from the second.

Magnificent amethyst crystals have been found in Lincoln County but most were valued as specimens rather than as cutting material. Numerous places where this gemstone occurs are noted in this county as at the Rendlemann place 2 miles northeast of Iron Station where two prospects were opened; the J. P. Lynch place 1¾ miles northeast of Iron Station; the G. W. Goodson place about 1¼ miles southwest of Denver. Clear colorless rutilated crystals of good quality have been found in topsoil of farms about 2 miles west of Cesar in Cleveland County. The deposit from which these crystals came has not been found. Petrified wood occurs in alluvium of Quaternary age in Wayne, Moore, Montgomery, Anson, and Cumberland counties. Fine rutilated quartz has been found near Concord in Cabarrus County. Good quality agate is reported from near Caldwell in Mecklenburg County; also from near Harrisburg and Concord in Cabarrus County; and in Granville and Orange counties. Smoky quartz has been found in the gravels of Beaverdam Creek in Cherokee County.

Important quantities of amethyst destined for cutting into commercial gems were mined from several places in the valley of Tessentee Creek, Smithbridge Township, Macon County. The Connally Mine, located 2 miles northeast of the mouth of Tessentee Creek, was mined by the American Gem & Pearl Company of New York City many years ago. Amethyst crystals occur here in a steeply dipping quartz vein which outcrops upon the side of the hill in gneissic rock. Crystals found in early mining ranged in size from very small to some which were 2 inches in diameter. Crystals were fairly deep in color but color banding was common; no large stones were cut because of the lack of large, flawless, suitably-colored areas. The William Long Prospect is located between the prongs of Tessentee Creek near its headwaters and 4½ miles east of its mouth. At this deposit, the amethyst vein varies from less than an inch to about 8 inches in thickness and consequently crystals reached only 1½ inches in diameter. Many were light in color but some were dark. Other prospect pits are located ⅔ mile east of the William Long Prospect and also about ¾ mile southwest.

South Carolina. Amethyst of specimen and gem grade has been found 1½ miles southeast of Shoals Junction in Greenwood County, also 1 mile southwest of Shoals Junction. Both localities are about 3 miles southeast of Donalds. Amethyst has also been reported from about 4 miles southeast of Donalds; one specimen found here was described as a slab of matrix measuring 8 inches across studded with numerous crystals.

Georgia. Gem grade amethyst occurs in numerous deposits in Rabun and Towns counties in the area along their common boundary as at the Ledbetter Mine, located on Black Creek, 1 mile north of Rabun Gap, Rabun County. About 150 yards northwest of the main workings are several prospect pits from which a little good material was also obtained. The North Georgia Mine is situated about 4 miles by road from Clayton in a west-northwesterly direction upon the south side of the Blue Ridge at an elevation of about 2000 feet. An opencut and tunnel mark the mine while several pits are located nearby. Amethyst occurred here in pockets in quartz seams embedded in gneiss and it is said that good gem material was found. The John A. Wilson Prospect is 4 miles by road southeast of Clayton and again is located upon a quartz vein in gneiss. Excellent rose quartz has come from the quartz core of a mica-bearing pegmatite at the old Kell Mica Mine in Rabun Co. Fist-size amethyst crystals have been found upon Charlie's Creek, near Hiwassee, Towns County.

In Union County, considerable amethyst was once obtained from the

Garrett Mine 1 mile south of Hightower Bald, upon a ridge separating Shoal Branch and Jack's Branch. Amethyst crystals were found lining cavities in a milky quartz vein. Pockets reached only several inches in thickness but often ran along the vein for distances of several feet.

Silicified *oölite*, or limestone in which numerous small spherical concretions have been replaced by silica, occurs in a number of places in the lowest parts of the Knox dolomite. One of the best collecting localities is Fincher Bluff in Murray County, reached by a dirt road leading north from Hooker School; also in road cuts along Highway 225 between Sardis and Spring Place. In Whitfield County, black siliceous oölite and red oölitic jasper occur in cuts along Tarr Creek on the outskirts of Dalton.

Amethyst of good color has been found in the vicinity of the Antioch Mine near Deweyrose, Elbert County. Agates have been obtained from near Round Oak, Jones County, and near Marietta, Cobb County. Rose quartz occurs with milky quartz in a large vein about ¼ mile southeast of Belmont Hills in Cobb County. Rutilated quartz is reported from the Cochran Mine 2½ miles northeast of Ball Ground in Cherokee County. Banded red, yellow, brown, and white agate is found near Kingston in Bartow County; moss agate has been found near Cordele in Crisp County. Reddish jasper occurs near Roundoak in Jones County. Jasper is also found in the vicinity of Saltpeter Cave in the southern part of Bartow County south of Kingston.

Amethyst crystals are found in cavities in quartz outcrops on the Benny Ray farm 2 miles east of Buckhead in Morgan County. The discovery of this material took place in 1941 and from pockets in the 100 feet long outcrop, almost 300 pounds of crystals were obtained. A large specimen showing a number of crystals on matrix is on exhibit in the State Capitol Museum in Atlanta. Loose crystals of amethyst have also been found upon the Homer Kellin farm, 1 mile north of Fayetteville, Fayette County.

Very fine rose quartz of gem quality and suitable for faceted gems, carvings, cabochons, or spheres showing asterism, has been found in the quartz core of a large pegmatite dike at the Minerals Processing Company's Mine, 8 miles due south of La Grange and 1 mile south of Smith's Crossroads on the west side of Highway 219 in Troup County. The pegmatite outcrops over a distance of 400 feet and has been mined extensively for beryl, some of gem quality, and mica. Though not as deep in color as the rose quartz of South Dakota, it is highly translucent in large sections and shows a faint sheen from its rutile inclusions. At the mine, it occurs as clear places in massive milky quartz, providing blocks of essentially flawless material several inches across. One specimen in the possession of the author is 5 inches long and contains a clear place from which a sphere of 1½ inches diameter could be cut (see Figure 82). The color is uniform light pink with a somewhat yellowish cast.

Alabama. Colorful compact chert, some so fine grained as to pass for chalcedony, occurs upon a small mountain southeast of Gurley in the western end of Jackson County. Agates and chert are found in a series of pits along Highway 128, 1 mile west of Blountsville, Blount County. Siliceous oölite occurs in a chert quarry about 5 miles north of Centreville, Bibb County along Highway 5. Chalcedony has been reported from veins in the buhrstone of the Eocene Claiborne formation in Clarke County.

Florida. A world-famed locality for silicified coral is located in an arm of Tampa Bay in Hillsborough County, and in spite of being known since at least 1825, continues to produce in some abundance the fascinating hollow casts or geodes for which it is noted. Many specimens of this coral have found their way into collections everywhere and in view of the long period of time in which they have been gathered, the total production must now be reckoned in tons! The sources of the coral are the sediments in the bottom of the northeastern arm of Tampa Bay, or Hillsborough Bay. Two specific points have provided the bulk of the material: Davis Island, an artificial piece of land created by dredging the bay and now connected to the mainland, and Ballast Point, a slight projection of land on the western side of Hillsborough Bay. While Davis Island was being created, an enormous quantity of coral was brought up by the dredges but is now no longer available since this piece of property is completely built over by an extension of the City of Tampa. On the other hand, Ballast Point and its immediate vicinity continues to provide suitable material from the tidal flats. Undoubtedly there is much more available on the bottom since Tampa Bay at this point stretches nearly 4 miles across.

When first removed from the water, Tampa Bay corals look like ordinary dead corals and may be completely or partially encrusted with weeds, barnacles, and other marine growths. However, if empty, as many of them are, their lightness betrays them since the interior hollow often takes up most of the volume. Adhering growths may be cleaned off easily and after treatment, look like that illustrated in Figure 91. The second part of this photograph shows a typical geode interior, the rounded growths being translucent chalcedony of particularly hard and dense character. The finest specimens have been obtained by digging in the muck and sand off Ballast Point at low tide, even going so far as to wade out in the water to reach undisturbed ground. Although shattered fragments of branches and limbs of coral are relatively common, large spherical corals such as shown in the illustration are not easy to find. The vast majority are altered into chalcedony immediately below their surfaces and therefore the internal structure of the original coral is reproduced only on the outside; however, on rare occasions, solid pieces are found in which the small "stars" of the coral animals are finely preserved.

Interiors of geodes provide a wide and interesting variety of forms.

Perhaps the most common is a globular development of waxy translucent chalcedony. Frequently, this botryoidal chalcedony is covered with an opal-like coating of pure white opaque material which resembles *cachalong opal*, and, when wetted, absorbs water rapidly, becoming translucent in the process. More rarely, geodes are lined with sparkling quartz crystals of less than ⅛ inch diameter which partake of the color of the chalcedony beneath and thus appear to be brown, gray, black, or whatever the color happens to be. A few such specimens may have several chambers in which one may be lined with crystals and another merely with smooth chalcedony. Some geodes exhibit curious stalactitic growths which look much like the columns seen in some limestone caves (see Figure 91).

Chalcedony linings are very variable in color although the predominant colors are either dark gray, black, and rich brown. Some specimens have been found in which the chalcedony is virtually colorless and highly translucent. At times, reddish-brown linings resemble carnelian but are never vivid in hue. Banding is rare, the chalcedony forming only uniform masses of little color contrast.

Due to the thinness of walls, Tampa Bay geodes are not well suited for cabochons or other gems but some very fine tumbled gems, circular cross-sections, and completely polished small branches have found some vogue in inexpensive jewelry. In general, the geodes are prized mostly for their specimen value because there are few petrifactions in the Mineral Kingdom which are as attractive as cut and polished Tampa Bay coral geodes. In size, specimens range from small fragments of an inch or so in length and perhaps about ¼ inch to ½ inch thick, to some magnificent spherical geodes as much as 12 inches across; however, anything over 6 inches in diameter must be considered a rarity. The average size of standard specimen geodes is from 3 inches to 4 inches across.

The last several years have brought the welcome news that chalcedony replacements of coral and fossils are not confined to Tampa Bay. Several important finds have been made in the vicinity of Tarpon Springs in Pinella County and at Bailey's Bluff just south of New Port Richey in Pasco County where a 100 pound mass of gray chalcedony was unearthed as well as many other smaller specimens of silicified coral. Even more recently, good specimens have been collected from the banks of a canal upon the L. H. Wear Ranch near Kathleen, about 7 miles northeast of Lakeland, Polk Co.

Mississippi. Grayish banded agate occurs as waterworn masses in a gravel pit 4 miles east of Wesson, Copiah Co.; petrified palm wood is reported from Wayne County 7 miles northwest of Waynesboro; dark gray banded agate has been reported from Bell Creek in Harrison County, about 18 miles northwest of Gulfport.

Louisiana. Silicified wood is relatively common in this state and the following species have been identified from the Jackson Eocene, Vicksburg Oligocene, Catahoula, and Fleming formations: laurel, in brown, black, red, and yellow wood; palm, black, with "eyes" of contrasting hue; also birch, poplar, oak and hickory. Brown and gray banded agate along with large pieces of petrified wood is found in the gravels of the Ouachita River about 12 miles south of Monroe in Ouachita Parish; also on the Amite River in Livingston Parish, and on the Tickfaw River in Tangipahoa Parish. Jasper, chalcedony, and carnelian are also found in each of these areas. Silicified palm wood has been found in Rapides Parish and has been identified as two species of *Palmoxylon*. Well silicified and polishable palm wood is found in gravels and sands near Leesville in Vernon Parish. Enormous quantities of silicified wood in the form of large logs have been found in various places in De Soto Parish; one log weighed 1500 pounds.

Arkansas. There is scarcely a collection of minerals which does not contain representative specimens of the sparkling clear quartz crystals found in abundance in Western Arkansas. Beautifully formed, naturally sporting a wonderful gloss, and occurring in almost any size desired, they have long attracted attention and admiration.

The majority of crystals occur in openings in quartz veins penetrating Blakely and Crystal Mountain sandstones of Ordovician age but some veins are imbedded in Paleozoic shale, sandstone, and chert exposed along the central belt of the Ouachita Mountains of west central Arkansas. Veins are mainly massive milky quartz with thin disklike cavities lined with wonderfully clear colorless crystals of simple habit. Sometimes calcite, feldspar, and chlorite accompany the quartz along with much clay infiltrated into the openings. Crystals occur over an area of considerable length extending for almost 150 miles in a southwesterly direction from near Little Rock to Broken Bow in northern McCurtain County, Oklahoma. However, the best crystals occur only in Arkansas in a belt about 15 miles wide beginning in the east at Paron in Saline County and terminating in the west about 5 miles southwest of Mount Ida in Montgomery County. The deposits are mostly along the crests of mountains. Pockets are variable in size and may reach as much as 4 by 10 by 30 feet with single crystals weighing up to 600 pounds. A pocket of these dimensions was excavated at the Dierks No. 4 Mine in the West Chance Area, 2 miles west of the village of Chance in Garland County. Such large crystals are almost always entirely milky and absolutely clear material is obtained only from much smaller crystals as a rule. An enormous sheet of crystals is on exhibit in the United States National Museum and consists of three adjoining sections of sandstone studded with thousands of transparent crystals up to 4 inches in length. The dimensions of the entire sheet are 8 feet tall, 6 feet wide and from 10 inches to 14 inches thick. Many crystals are short and squat, especially when grown together upon slabs, others, however, are long enough to merit the local name of "candles," being about 6 times as long as they are thick. Small crystals may be even more slender as for example those from the Collier Creek Mine in the Crystal Mountains which are appropriately designated "pincushion quartz." Doubly-terminated crystals are common and originate from wall cystals which have broken off and later rehealed as quartz mineralization continued in pockets. The vast majority of crystals are absolutely colorless when clear but milky when filled with many inclusions. Crystals attached to matrix are clear at the points but become milky at their bases as shown in the group illustrated in Figure 79. A substantial amount of smoky quartz crystals have been obtained from Arkansas deposits ranging in color from the barest trace of tint to some which are deep brown and even black.

At least 60 significant mines and prospects are known in the district but are concentrated in several principal groups. The easternmost group consists of 8 mines within a 6-mile radius of the town of Paron, almost in the center of Saline County. The next group to the west is in the Jessieville area in Garland County, encompassing numerous mines surrounding this town, some of which are located in adjoining Saline and Perry counties. Immediately west of this area is another group in the Miller Mountains area centered about 9 miles due west of the village of Chance in Garland County. Further west is the Fisher Mountain area located several miles south of Mount Ida in Montgomery County. Several isolated prospects and mines are also located 7 miles southeast of Mena in Polk County. The greatest concentration, however, is in the Jessieville area where over 25 mines and prospects are located.

No self-respecting craftsman interested in placing a keen edge on cutting tools would be without an "Arkansas Stone," a pure white porous rock consisting of millions of minute quartz crystals cemented with chalcedony and known to mineralogists as *novaculite*. In Arkansas, novaculite is found associated with shales, into which it grades through siliceous layers resembling chert, in beds totaling approximately 900 feet in depth in the Novaculite Mountains of Hot Springs County. Novaculite is sometimes useful for gem cutting, especially when compact in form and stained attractively by iron and manganese oxides. In some examples, these impurities form handsome dendritic markings and veinings while an especially attractive material consists of brecciated novaculite in which many small angular fragments are cemented together by chalcedony and brightly colored in various shades of red, yellow, orange, brown, gray, green and black.

Ohio. Colorful chert from the famed Flint Ridge deposits sees increasing use in the lapidary arts today. The beds begin about 3 miles southeast of Newark and extend to about 12 miles northwest of Zanesville, a distance of about 8 miles in which the deposits average about ¼ mile in width. Flint Ridge "flint" as it is often called is found as layers in the Vanport member of the Allegheny formation of the Pennsylvanian. It is believed that this material is derived from limey debris originally deposited at the bottom of a salt sea and later hardened into limestone. Still later, certain portions of the strata were infused with silica solutions and converted into chert. Tests of Flint Ridge chert show it to be 98 per cent silica plus 2 per cent water and minute amounts of impurities, mainly iron compounds to which are attributed the many attractive colors. Hundreds of old pits blending into a single continuous belt of excavations, are exposed on Flint Ridge in Hopewell and Franklin townships of Licking County and overlap into Muskingum County. The bed of chert averages 5 to 6 feet in thickness but shows extreme variations of from 1 to 10 feet. The chert is dense, hard, and of high quality though some is so porous that it polishes with difficulty. Colors range from milky white through pink, red, green, blue, and gray. Selected pieces of strong color have been used extensively by local cutters for cabochons and other lapidary work. Within the beds occur cavities lined with smoky quartz crystals, amethyst, rock crystals, while in seams are found practically every variety of cryptocrystalline quartz such as agate, carnelian, jasper, etc.

Indiana. Quartz-lined geodes of little lapidary value but forming interesting and beautiful mineral specimens occur in abundance in gravel along the sides of Bear Creek just north of Trevlac in Brown County. Examples are specially abundant along Salt Creek near Heltonsville and at Guthrie in Lawrence County; geodes reaching 14 inches in diameter have been found at these localities.

Waterworn agate and jasper pebbles are found in the gravels of Maumee River in Allen County and in many other places where alluvium has been exposed in pits and excavations.

Illinois. Quartz geodes occur abundantly in the Warsaw formation near Warsaw, Hamilton and Nauvoo in western Illinois. Most are found as round balls eroded from steep-walled creek banks or rolled into stream beds. Some reach diameters of 12 inches and 80 per cent contain rock crystal or milky quartz although others are completely solid. A few contain calcite and dolomite crystals in addition to quartz. About 10 per cent of all geodes are lined with grayish botryoidal chalcedony. On rare occasions amethyst is found, but it is pale and of no value for gems.

Michigan. In the early days of the tourist trade in the isolated portion of Michigan known as the Keeweenaw Peninsula, numerous waterworn agate pebbles were found upon the Lake Superior beaches and served as the raw material from which various items of inexpensive jewelry were made for sale to visitors. Pebbles were often polished and drilled at one end for suspension from necklaces, or placed in bottles of water to show to better advantage their handsome markings. Most if not all of the actual lapidary work was accomplished in Germany where the pebbles were sent for polishing and drilling. The occurrence is extensive, ranging from Ontario to the north, including the offshore islands, and reappearing in the Keeweenaw Peninsula and parts of Minnesota. In every case, the agate pebbles represent eroded silica fillings of gas cavities in volcanic rocks and are still found embedded in them wherever favorable exposures occur.

Keeweenaw agate is classed as *Lake Superior Agate,* a name popularly used to identify the characteristic chalcedonic material from the volcanic rocks just mentioned. Most specimens are small in size, and, where they have traveled some distance, are usually only broken waterworn fragments of larger nodules. The average size is probably less than 2 inches although some up to 10 inches across and weighing as much as 14 pounds have been recorded. On the peninsula, nodules and fragments occur along the beaches, in gravels, and in place in the volcanic rock ridges. Excellent specimens have been found on Manitou Island just east of the tip of the peninsula, also on the tip itself and upon various beaches extending westward along the north shore to Eagle Harbor, Gratiot, and beyond into Minnesota. Agate is found in place on the north shore of Manganese Lake near the tip of the peninsula. The region around Copper Harbor has produced agate from in place deposits along the central highway and from places off the beaten path. Agate harbor is named after its steady production of agate pebbles from nearby beach gravels.

Isle Royale in the north part of Lake Superior and only 8 miles offshore from the Mainland, also produces a variety of quartz gemstones but being a National Park, collecting is strictly forbidden. Carnelian is found in small specimens on the beaches at the head of Siskowit Bay; agate nodules up to 8 inches diameter have been found in the Greenstone Range from Blake Point to Washington Harbor; also upon the north shore of Tobin Harbor toward Blake Point and on nearby islands; Agate Beach near the southwest end of the island at McGinty Cove has yielded some fine material in years past; a few agate nodules have been obtained from along old lake beaches inland from McCargo Cove; many small but finely marked pebbles occur on the beaches at the head of Siskowit Bay. All of the Isle Royale specimens are very similar to those found on the Keeweenaw Peninsula in that they are reddish to brownish in color and show similar patterns.

A small quantity of excellent chrysocolla-impregnated chalcedony has been found as fillings between pebbles of conglomerate in the peculiar copper deposits of the Allouez Mine in Allouez in the western part of Keeweenaw County, Keeweenaw Peninsula. The color is beautiful turquois-blue. A fine cabochon measuring 1¼ inches by ⅞ inch is in the author's collection.

The versatility of quartz as a gemstone is nowhere better exemplified than in the dark red jaspery chert found in numerous iron deposits of Keeweenaw Peninsula. Apparently chalcedony has been deposited adjacent to hematite iron ores and from them has derived its red color. In many places, the basic jaspery material is laced with bands of dark steel-gray hematite of the variety known as *specularite*, and the mixture, when well polished, presents a handsome and unusual effect. The distinctive nature of this gemstone has caused it to be called *jaspillite* or *jaspilite*. Between Negaunee and Ishpeming, a knoll known as Jasper Hill consists almost entirely of jaspilite. Here it is found folded, bent, and twisted in the most fanciful patterns and is capable of being prepared into fine cabochons, bookends, spheres, and other ornamental items. Jaspilite is abundant throughout the Porcupine Mountains of Ontonagan County and in this general area as at Michigamme Mine, near Michigamme in Baraga County; and in the Old Lake Shaft, Section Seven Mine, Section 16 Mine, Holmes Mine, Cliffs Shaft Mine, and Morris-Lloyd Mine, etc. in Marquette County.

Though more famed for calcified corals extensively used for ornamental purposes (see CALCITE), Michigan also produces a few silicified corals of cutting grade. Most specimens are found in the Niagaran dolomite and excellent pieces have been obtained from near Raber in Mackinac County, in the vicinity of Scott's Quarry east of Trout Lake in Chippewa County; and in the vicinity of Whitedale in Schoolcraft County. Very few specimens are completely silicified however, and some care must be taken to select only those which appear to be solid silica replacements. The best types are apparently those which have weathered out of limestone.

Very attractive mottled and banded reddish chert is found in the Traverse limestone north of Norwood in Charlevoix County. Chert nodules are also abundant in the Bayport limestone quarries in Arenac and Huron counties. Chert and flint occur in the Niagaran dolomite in the Northern Peninsula exposed in the Scott's Quarry near Trout Lake and the old quarries at Manistique.

Wisconsin. Recently, quartzite masses of various colors containing a variety of inclusions which suit them for lapidary applications, have been found in the central part of Wood County associated with sandstone. A brownish-red true aventurine is the most colorful material brought to light so far, and shows, in polished slabs, good twinkling reflections from numerous scales of a reddish mineral presumed to be goethite. This material is quite attractive and if found in larger pieces, may lend itself to important ornamental uses.

The entire state of Wisconsin is underlain by gravel beds bearing Lake Superior Agate and excellent specimens have been found in many places. The best chances of success attend searches in gravel pits in the northwestern part of the state.

Minnesota. Like Wisconsin, Minnesota is also underlain by agate-bearing gravels from which numerous fine specimens continue to be obtained. Many have been found in the vicinity of Gunflint Lake in Cook County very close to the Ontario-Minnesota boundary. Lake Superior agate nodules are found in place in volcanic rocks near the shore about 14 miles east of Grand Marais in Cook County. The rock here is filled with round masses of beautifully-banded agate of various colors ranging in size from about ½ inch to 2 inches in diameter; exceptional specimens up to 3 inches have been found also. Agate occurs in gravel pits of Morrison County; also in pits near Cloquet, southwest of Duluth, in Swift and in Stevens Counties, etc. Similar material has been noted in place in basalt in Gooseberry Falls State Park along Highway 61 on the north shore of Lake Superior in Lake County.

Large quantities of silicified algae from the Sudan Formation occur in the Mesabi Range in St. Louis County as upon the dumps of the Mary Ellen Mine along Highway 35 about 1 mile west of Biwabwik, also at the Corsica Mine about 2 miles west of town. This cherty material is basically red but other colors such as swirls of gray, white, brown, black, and yellow are also found. An extremely bright yellow type as well as pure white have been reported. Blocks may exceed several hundred pounds in weight although very little of the total is suited for polishing.

A beautiful gemstone unique to Minnesota is the crystalline quartz replacement of fibrous goethite locally named *binghamite* in honor of William J. Bingham of St. Paul, who, with his son, discovered this attractive material in 1936. When polished, this material exhibits a decided chatoyancy arising from light reflections from millions of exceedingly fine fibers embedded in quartz. Some are stained mahogany-red by hematite and others yellow by limonite. Since the fibers tend to be oriented in parallel, some very fine cats-eye gems have been cut from better pieces of rough. Almost any treatment which observes some care in placing the fibers parallel to the finished surface will produce effective gems or objects of ornament. An example of this variety is shown in Figure 84. More recently, a similar material called *silkstone* has made its appearance upon the market and is found in the same places as binghamite. However, the fibers in silkstone do not show the straightness characteristic of binghamite. Essentially both materials are the same, but binghamite averages about 98 per cent quartz while silkstone is less and for this reason, it is more difficult to polish although it too is very handsome when finished. Both gemstones occur sparsely in quartz veins cutting iron ore formations of the Cayuna Range near Crosby and Ironton in Crow County. Specimens have been found in the dumps of the Arco Mine, Evergreen Mine (now known as the Portsmouth), and elsewhere. Veins containing the fibrous gemstone are relatively rare and blocks suitable for lapidary work do not exceed 6 inches thick as a rule. Some good material has also been found on the No. 2 Dump of the Hanna Company mines.

Iowa. Hundreds of tons of quartz-lined geodes have been carted off from the famed Keokuk beds which outcrop in a broad area near the confluence of the Mississippi River and Des Moines River where the states of Iowa, Illinois, and Missouri join. The beds are mainly sedimentary rocks such as limestones, shales and clays with geodes occurring abundantly in the blue clayey shales and more abundantly still in an impure siliceous dolomitic limestone near the base of the formation. Shales containing geodes of smaller size are found below the limestone.

The occurrence of geodes in Iowa has been officially recognized by the creation of Geode State Park, a plot of land on which the Keokuk beds outcrop, located several miles southeast of Lowell and close to the Skunk River on the border between Henry and Des Moines counties.

Petrified wood fragments are found in gravels at various places near Emmetsburg and Graettinger in Palo Alto County. Beautifully banded colored chert occurs in the Mississippian limestone at the southern edge of Mt. Pleasant in Henry County; hues include white, ivory, brown, red, gray, and a dark grayish-blue.

Iowa has achieved some measure of fame for its Lake Superior agate pebbles which have been supplied for decades by the gravel beds along the Mississippi River Valley. An especially noted collecting area lies immediately south of Muscatine in the county of the same name, where a large alluvial flat has been exploited for many years for the sake of its sand and gravel.

The size of pebbles found at these beds ranges from ¼ inch diameter to a few extremely rare specimens as "large as a cocoanut," according to one authority, who goes on to say that pebbles of ½ inch diameter probably account for 90 per cent of all agate found and the remaining 10 per cent represent larger sizes. Many specimens examined prove to be merely worn fragments of larger nodules, perhaps originally several inches in diameter, however, smaller nodules are frequently whole. The beds at Muscatine have been erroneously heralded as being prolific and some accounts give the impression that large quantities of agate can be picked up in an afternoon. Unfortunately, this is far from the truth if one is interested in collecting worthwhile specimens for the latter are actually few in number and scarce in sizes over one inch.

The types of banding or patterns in the agate nodules at Muscatine are many and varied but consist mainly of several well-recognized kinds. Fortification agate consisting of dark brownish-red to yellowish-red translucent chalcedony interspersed with opaque white bands is fairly common. Nodules of this type are also greenish-brown in color, fairly translucent, and show beautiful contrasts between bands. Onyx types are also common and show perfectly straight bands in various contrasting colors. A large number are found containing solid white or milky quartz centers, surrounded by brownish-red chalcedony or other colored material. Moss, tube, sagenite, and other types of agate have been found also but are quite rare as compared to the common fortification types. Predominant colors are various shades of brownish-red to fairly bright red; also caramel brown and olive green-brown. Vivid colors are decidedly rare.

Missouri. Quartz geodes of the Keokuk formation occur in shales exposed along bluffs on the sides of the Fox River near St. Francisville in Clark County. Lake Superior type agate has been found in the Mississippi River gravels as far south as La Grange in Lewis Co. Compact chert suitable for cutting has been found in Dade and Benton counties where beds have been exposed by road grading operations along the tops of a number of low hills especially at the western edge of the Ozark Mountains.

North Dakota. Translucent moss agate similar to that found in Montana occurs in the gravels of the Yellowstone River and the Missouri River in Williams and McKenzie counties in the extreme northwestern part of the state. Silicified wood capable of taking a good polish is found in the "badlands" near Medora in Billings County with some log sections reaching large size. Chalcedony, agate and jasper are sprinkled over the surface of hills and washes in an area 11 miles north of Mott in Hettinger County. Chalcedony pebbles are found near Dickinson in Stark Co. Small, completely silicified pine cones, about walnut size, have been found in the Hell Creek formation of Upper Cretaceous age near Wade on the Cannonball River, 55 miles southwest of Bismark near the center of Grant County. Unique silicified wood showing numerous borings made by marine teredo worms has been found in gravel pits in the vicinity of Mandan in Morton County. Agate also occurs in these deposits, especially near Mandan and Bismark.

South Dakota. Agate and chalcedony are widespread in gravel pits in the entire eastern part of the state. In Minnehaha County, an attractive conglomerate completely silicified into a hard, compact quartzite has been quarried extensively for building stone and manufacture into ornamental items. In the trade it is known as *Sioux Falls Jasper.* Exposures of this stone may be seen in the vicinity of Dell Rapids and at the Dells of the Sioux River just south of the city of Sioux Falls. Various colors such as chocolate, brownish-red, brick-red, and yellow are exhibited by the numerous rounded pebbles comprising the rock.

Translucent chalcedony nodules showing black dendritic patterns and similar in appearance to those of the Yellowstone River in Montana, occur in the gravels of the tributaries of the Little Missouri River in Harding County close to the Montana border. Moss agate occurs in seams in limestone atop Fox Ridge in northern Meade County about 5 miles east-southeast of Maurine but little has proven to be of good quality. In this same county, banded red and gray chert of fine polishing quality occurs in Carboniferous limestone of the Morrison formation in the vicinity of Deadwood in the Black Hills.

South Dakota is primarily noted for its beautiful banded agate nodules which are so distinctive in appearance that they have been given the name *Fairburn agate* after a prolific locality near the community of the same name in Custer County. Fairburn agate occurs in strikingly contrasted bands of color creating specimens which are equal in beauty to any found elsewhere. The color patterns are generally yellowish-brown with narrow opaque white bands or dark red with white bands; another beautiful combination shows salmon pink bands alternating with white. Other colors include black, yellow, grayish-blue, and milky-pink. Nodules range in size from an inch or two across to some enormous masses weighing close to 40 pounds, however, the vast majority are far smaller.

Fairburn agate occurs in a broad elliptical area which encompasses the Cheyenne River in southwestern South Dakota and to the north, begins near Creston in Pennington County, and terminates in the south near Orella in Sioux County, Nebraska. The belt reaches its maximum width of about 15 miles near Red Shirt in Shannon County. Fairburn agate appears to be derived from weathering of overlying strata of the Chadron formation, the latter overlying directly the shales of the Pierre formation. Outcrops of both formations are most intensively searched for nodules since these seem to be the horizons in which most Fairburn agate is found. All pieces are waterworn and it is therefore assumed that they eroded from rocks which are no longer in existence but were later incorporated in the formations mentioned. One of the best collecting areas has been 15 miles east of the town of Fairburn in Custer County, however, other places have recently come to the fore and produce as much good material. Some fine agate has been found in the badlands around Scenic in Pennington County, associated with petrified wood, jasper, and other chalcedonic gemstones. The badlands near Interior in Washabaugh County are also sprinkled with numerous pieces of agate, chalcedony, jasper, etc. Palm wood, cycad wood, carnelian, and fine orbicular jasper showing small red or yellow spherules in translucent chalcedony have also been found here. In Custer County, some good chalcedonic gemstones have been found just south of the State Game Farm on Highway 16 east of Custer; also in Custer State Park.

Amethyst is occasionally found lining chalcedony geodes which weather from outcrops along the banks of Whitewood Creek near Whitewood in Lawrence County; similar geodes are found in Spearfish Canyon near Spearfish. The geodes occur in shales of the Inglewood formation and vary in size from as small as ½ inch to some reaching 6 inches in diameter. Amethyst is also reported from Warrens Gulch, Box Elder Creek, and Bear Butte Creek in the Black Hills of Pennington County. The Badlands National Monument, prior to its attaining this status, provided silicified coral of good polishing grade. Specimens from this locality show rounded exteriors dimpled with the typical star patterns of individual coral animals and from its appearance, has been called "petrified sponge" by the local residents. Similar coral is found outside the Monument limits where collecting is permitted.

Silicified cycad stumps have been found in numbers in the Cycad National Monument south of Minnekahta in Fall River County, however, this area is inaccessible by automobile and is rarely visited. Although originally many stumps of this interesting fossil plant were collected, recent visitors state that nothing is to be seen there now. The cycad is a very old plant which resembles a cross between a palm and a fern, that is, it possesses a central trunk from whose top grows graceful fronds resembling in appearance those seen on ordinary ferns but actually far different in important respects. In cycads, the stems of individual fronds are bound together to form the central stem and a polished cross-section of a petrified specimen often shows clearly diamond-like markings where fronds emerged. The only fossil cycads found now come from the immediate vicinity of Parker Peak which is a mile or two east of Highway 18 and a little over 2 miles south of Minnekahta; prevailing colors are dark shades of brown with lighter markings corresponding to structural features of the plant. The area between Parker Peak and Hot Springs (the latter about 12 miles east of Minnekahta) has also produced cycad wood from washes and draws. A coal-black silicified wood sometimes furnishing good polishing material occurs in large pieces in gravel of the Little White River (also known as the South Fork of the White River) in an area west of Mission in Todd County. Fine polished examples resemble black obsidian.

Agate nodules sometimes reaching as much as 12 inches in diameter occur in the debris of the floor of Hells Canyon in Custer County. Hells Canyon runs southwest to northeast in the Custer National Forest and is accessible by road from Highway 16. At this locality, nodules and geodes are found in place in the Minnelusa formation, a sandstone bed which outcrops along the walls of the Canyon for several miles.

Perhaps the best known source of rose quartz in the Western Hemisphere is the Scott Rose Quartz Quarry located in a canyon upon a branch of French Creek about 6 miles southeast of Custer, Custer County. Rose quartz is quarried from an enormous milky quartz core of a pegmatite body which measures about 1200 feet in length and about 50 feet in width. The height of the present quarry face is about 75 feet.

This deposit has been in the hands of the Scott Family since 1881 and has been worked on and off since that time. Prior to World War II, much quartz was sent to China to be employed in carvings while a lesser amount of quality material was sent to the cutting centers of Germany. The best grades were cut and polished for use in beads, necklaces, inexpensive jewelry, and such ornamental items as vases, trays and paperweights. Cheaper grades were used in monumental work such as tombstones, facings for fireplaces, and, when crushed, for stucco. Rose quartz has also been found in the Black Hills in other pegmatite bodies and can be observed in a few of them along Highway 89 northeast of Custer and also upon the secondary road behind Mt. Rushmore connecting Highway 16 with Alternate Highway 16.

Nebraska. The Platte River gravels near this river's junction with the Missouri River in Douglas County have provided many agate, moss agate, moss opal, wood opal, and chert pebbles from gravel exposures or from gravel pits. The productive area is along both sides of the Platte River to 75 miles upstream from the point mentioned above. Petrified wood is found in gravels near Johnson, Nemaha County, while agate and jasper are found in gravel pits near Fairbury and Stelle in Jefferson County.

Agate specimens of the Fairburn type have been found in the vicinity of Orella in the northeast corner of Sioux County and undoubtedly represent more of the same material found further north in South Dakota. An interesting chert found in the sand hills and gravel beds of Morrill County near Bayard, appears in the form of rounded pebbles which are gray or black on the exterior, but when broken open, show concentric bands of yellowish-brown, red, orange, or mixed colors. Agate, chalcedony, jasper and petrified wood have been picked up from the hills surrounding Chappell in Deuel County.

Kansas. Chalcedony and agate pebbles occur in the gravels of the Big Blue River and its branches, also upon adjacent hills and in washes in Marshall County while similar material is found in gravel pits along the Republican River in Cloud County. Lake Superior type agate occurs in glacial drift near McLouth in Jefferson County; petrified wood is reported from the northwest part of Ottawa County north of Ada.

Various forms of chalcedony, including agate, are reported from a broad area in the western part of the state where they occur in the gravels of Smoky Hill River, Arkansas River, Cimarron River, Pawnee River, Solomon River, and Medicine Lodge River. The best collecting grounds along the Smoky Hill River lie in Trego, Gove, Logan and Wallace counties; specimens may be picked up along the sides and tops of hills and bluffs on either side of the valley. The best stretch along the Medicine Lodge River is in Barber County.

Moss agate has been found a few miles north of Ashland near Mt. Cassino in Clark County. Chert of various colors and of good cutting quality occurs in the chalk beds of Cherokee, Logan, Norton and Phillips counties; colors are mostly yellow, red and orange-red, sometimes handsomely marked by black dendrites of manganese.

Oklahoma. Petrified wood, chalcedony, jasper, agate and moss agate occur over virtually all of Woods County. Much material is found west and south of Alva. Good collecting areas are also centered about Buffalo in adjacent Harper County. Similar material occurs in some abundance in Tillman and Beckham counties and in numerous other places in the southwestern counties; attractive silicified wood has come from north of Mangum in Greer County.

Texas. Fine silicified wood said to resemble Arizona material is reported from the Palo Duro Canyon southeast of Amarillo in Armstrong County. Banded chert is found in limestone in McCulloch County; also in San Saba County. Chalcedony is found in Hinton Creek northeast of Barton in San Saba County.

A peculiar quartz showing blue gleams like precious opal occurs in the form of small grains embedded in an igneous rock known as *llanite* named after its occurrence in Llano County. The rock is a reddish porphyry consisting primarily of reddish microcline, some albite and orthoclase, quartz, and small flakes of biotite mica. Llanite occurs in dikes intruded into Valley Spring gneiss near the northern border of the county between the town of Llano and Wilbern's Glen. One dike describes a hook from the south slope of Babyhead Mountain just north of Babyhead and swings eastward to Wilbern's Gap and thence southward for about 2 miles. A series of llanite dikes also extend from about 1 ¾ miles south-southeast of Babyhead and progress due south through the summit of Miller Mountain.

Numerous localities for silicified wood occur in a belt of counties which follow the curve of the Gulf Coast some miles inland from the sea. Prospecting in the general area may result in discovering additional localities beyond the few mentioned here. Petrified wood has been found near New Braunfels in Comal County; over a wide area near Smithville in Bastrop County; near La Grange in Fayette County; fine specimens in the vicinity of Gonzales and along Peach Creek in Gonzales County; abundant in water-rolled fragments in gravel beds about 10 miles west of Columbus and Weimar in Colorado; especially fine from near Moulton and the general area surrounding this community in Lavaca County; fragments are very common in the Quaternary formations of Brazos County; also in Uvalde County; beautiful palm logs showing every pore and marking occur in the Catahoula Formation around Three Rivers in Live Oak County; also further southwest to Laredo in Webb County. San Patrico County has produced some moss agate from the vicinity of Mathis. Worm-bored silicified wood occurs in the Rio Grande River near Laredo in Webb County. In Duval County, much wood has been picked up in the area south and west of Freer.

Enormous quantities of moss agate and various types of jasper have been found as waterworn pebbles in the gravels of the Rio Grande River and in gravel deposits along its valley from Eagle Pass southward to Laredo and beyond. Many show fine patterns of moss in reds, browns, and yellows suspended in clear chalcedony, however, due to the abundance of inclusions, they give the impression that ordinary jasper is the material being examined. A few specimens are found in which the chalcedony is very clear and exhibits markings similar to those noted in Montana agate. A great deal of this material has been recovered from gravels excavated for fill for the Falcon Dam thrown across the Rio Grande River near the western tip of Starr County. Rio Grande River agate pebbles are completely waterworn and perfectly rounded, and range in size from several inches to as much as 6 inches in diameter. The distribution of mossy growths within chalcedony is remarkably uniform but in some places, inclusions are so dense that an earthy character is imparted and specimens become difficult to polish to a uniform finish. Along with the material just described, almost every gravel deposit along the Rio Grande River for 40 miles up and down stream from Laredo contains petrified wood; some agatized coral has also been found. One collector broadens the area of productivity by saying that cutting material is found as far downstream as Hidalgo County; taking all distances into consideration, chalcedony gemstones may be collected along the river over a distance of almost 150 miles.

Carnelian is found near Van Horn in Hudspeth County while amethyst is reported from the Sierra Blanca of the same county. Chalcedony nodules occur in volcanic rocks along the southern edge of the Quitman Mountains. Jasper is found near Fort Davis in Jeff Davis County. Agate is abundant between Marfa and the Chinati Mountains in Presidio County and is also found between Davis and these mountains. Much of it is milky to gray banded and is found in nodules ranging from the size of a pea to a few as much as 8 inches in diameter. Presidio County has recently yielded a fine chalcedony gemstone called *bouquet agate,* named for the likeness of its spreading sprays of brightly-hued inclusions in clear grayish to whitish chalcedony to bunches of flowers. Some of the inclusions are also globular and being found in several colors, further heighten the resemblance. This material is found on the Bishop and Mallard ranches south of Marfa where collecting is permitted upon payment of a modest daily fee.

Texas Plume Agate from the Woodward Ranch in Brewster County, is so characteristic in appearance that calling this material by this name is instant identification to an experienced collector. The commonest kind displays beautifully detailed black plumes spreading through clear to milky chalcedony filling flattened rounded nodules. Nodules are peculiarly rough on their exteriors, as if sandblasted, and give no indication of their contents. Plume patterns lie flat within each nodule and for this reason it is necessary to saw the nodules much like one slices a biscuit. Nodules are found ranging from less than an inch in size, to some which are 6 inches across or more but the average is probably about 2 inches. Notable exceptions are a 225 lb.

nodule found about 1955, and one of 90 pounds found in 1957 which is stated to be of superb quality. Both red and black plumes often occur together in the same specimen either in separate patches or with black plumes capped by red plumes. Black plumes are inclined to be very thickly developed and are ordinarily opaque except when sliced thinly; in contrast, red plumes are far more translucent. The basic chalcedony in which the plumes grow varies from almost colorless, highly translucent material, to that which is virtually opaque and white, pinkish, or creamy-white in color.

The growth of plumes is directly connected to the development of the chalcedony itself as shown in nodules which are partly hollow. In these, the cavities are lined with small chalcedony balls, marking in each case, the emergence of plume points. Unfortunately, many nodules containing such hollows are useless for gems because so little unblemished material remains for cutting. It is generally difficult if not impossible to judge the contents of a plume nodule from its exterior except to repeat that those with partial hollows showing the botryoidal growths of chalcedony are generally unfit for cutting. In addition to plume inclusions, some nodules also contain earthy brown inclusions which tend to undercut and thus cannot be used for gems. The only place known to produce plume nodules is a single lava flow in the Alpine area in Brewster County, the major portion of the agate-bearing formation being upon the ranch of J. Frank Woodward about 16 miles south of Alpine on Highway 118. Collecting upon the ranch property is permitted after paying a poundage fee for all material retained. In addition to these famous nodules, other forms of chalcedony occur in abundance upon the ranch property, notably moss agate found in lumps up to 100 pounds weight in the Sierra de Aguaja near the mouth of Santa Helena Canyon. Very colorful jasper also occurs, mottled principally in vivid red and yellow in a wide and interesting range of patterns. Much jasper is also brecciated, showing numerous angular fragments of opaque material cemented together by bluish translucent chalcedony. The general area around the ranch is productive of other varieties of quartz and searching almost any place seems to produce specimens.

In other parts of Brewster County, much agate, jasper, and chalcedony are found west of the Glass Mountains and also in the Chisos Mountains in the Big Bend National Park, the latter area is of course closed to collecting.

Montana. This state has been famed for many years for the distinctive dendritic chalcedony found in the gravels of the Yellowstone River and popularly known as *Montana Agate*. Once seen, Montana agate is not easily forgotten both on account of the uniform translucent pale gray chalcedony of which it is largely composed and the characteristic black mossy inclusions which form spots, trees, bushes, ferns, and many other imaginative objects and scenes. A number of typical polished cabochons made of this material are illustrated in Figure 87. In addition to the dendritic growths created by in-filtration of manganese oxide, some specimens show bands, clouds, and streaks of bright brownish-orange or reddish-brown iron oxides suspended in clear chalcedony. Sometimes these patterns exist together with black markings and create especially attractive material for cabochons. Montana agate is almost wholly nodular, appearing as rounded waterworn pebbles vaguely resembling potatoes, gray on the outside or covered partly or completely with whitish opaque altered chalcedony. Other specimens are merely broken nodule sections while still others show central fillings of crystalline quartz. In size, nodules range from several inches or less to some which reach as much as 10 inches across.

The Yellowstone River along which the nodules occur, rises in Yellowstone National Park and from thence flows northward and then eastward until it passes Billings in Yellowstone County. The river loses 1000 feet altitude before it reaches Billings but from then on, it falls rapidly and is a swift but not turbulent stream. In most places the bed is occupied by gravels and large cobbles while bedrock shows in only a few places. In Figure 97 the agate producing area is enclosed by dashed lines. The delineation of the area

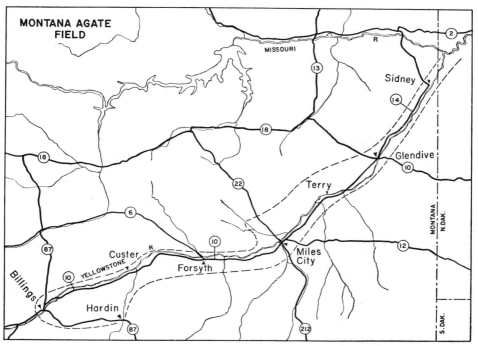

FIGURE 97. The famous Montana agate nodules are found in the area enclosed by dashed lines, a distance of over 250 miles. The most prolific parts of the field extend from Billings to Glendive.

is only approximate since no careful survey has ever been made of surrounding terrain and only informal accounts are available for consultation.

Montana agate is a favorite of every cutter because it handles easily and provides beautiful patterns readily developed by skillful sawing. It is not easy to tell what a pebble contains without slicing through it, but in general, those which are simple translucent chalcedony with few markings, pass light readily when held before a strong source of illumination while those which contain many dendrites or shadings of red or brown appear very dark and therefore pass little if any light. Upon rare occasions, some nodules are found which provide magnificent iris agate but, alas, there is no way of telling these except to test a sliver or thin slice removed from the specimen.

In another part of Montana, black silicified wood occurs near Vaughn, a small village about 11 miles west of Great Falls in Cascade County. Some of the wood shows grain structure but other material is so completely replaced by chalcedony that no texture whatever can be seen. A few specimens exhibit wormholes filled with translucent gray-blue chalcedony.

A famous amethyst and quartz locality in southwestern Jefferson County is located about 2 miles northeast of the Toll Mountain Picnic Grounds and perhaps 2 miles by dirt road from the place where the Toll Mountain road turns north from Highway 10S. At this point, upon a forested ridge, is the Pohndorf Amethyst Mine, named after A. P. Pohndorf of Butte, Montana, a noted mineral dealer and jeweler of many years ago. Amethyst and quartz occur in a large pocket in an irregular pegmatite body 140 feet long and 55 wide emplaced in quartz monzonite, which outcrops near the top of the ridge and has been entered by tunnel (now caved in) from the south. Within the pocket, enormous corroded feldspar crystals of blocky form measuring up to 14 inches in diameter were found lining the walls and were overgrown in places by bunches of hairlike or earthy fibrous masses of black tourmaline, quartz crystals, and much scaly greenish mica in crystals about 1/16 inch in diameter. Many quartz crystals were coated with this mica and some was also encased in surface layers of the crystals. Quartz crystals varied in size from small individuals of less than an inch to one enormous specimen recorded as 36 inches long and 8 inches in diameter. All crystals are tapered toward the termination. Rock crystal, smoky quartz and amethyst were also found but the latter only as sceptre overgrowths upon other quartz crystals. Though small, amethyst crystals were pure in color and fine in quality. Numerous inclusions of hairlike prisms of black tourmaline were so frequently intergrown in outer zones of quartz crystals that the latter appeared quite black. Very attractive cabochons and crystal cross-sections have been cut from this material; a cross-section now in the U.S. National Museum is illustrated in Figure 83. Some of the better quartz crystals with amethyst overgrowths perched on their tops and along their sides, provided extremely handsome and unique specimens and found a ready sale to collectors, however, the amethyst itself was neither available in quantity, or in quality good enough to compete with Brazilian material. Mr. Pohndorf recorded a unique specimen which consisted of a doubly-terminated tourmalinated quartz crystal both ends of which were capped by amethyst overgrowths.

Chalcedony in various forms is found near the summit of Mt. Blackmore in Gallatin County. Silicified wood is found in the vicinity of Miner in southeast Park County. White and red banded agate and chalcedony geodes are found almost on the border between Montana and Wyoming along the rims of the steep-walled canyons of the Doghead Creek area in Big Horn County. The occurrences are near the TX Ranch and are most productive near the junction of Doghead Creek and Big Horn River where seams of chalcedonic gemstones occur in sandstones of Triassic and Jurassic age. Petrified wood, sometimes in fine quality, occurs in the Pliocene marls and sandstone bluffs of Gallatin County on either side of the Madison River near its junction with Elk Creek. Petrified wood is also fairly widespread in the valleys of the Yellowstone, Madison, and Gallatin rivers in Gallatin and Park counties. In Madison County, some rock crystal has been produced from Crystal Butte in the Rochester District west of Twin Bridges. Jasper and chert of good quality occur at Elk Mountain and Finnegan Ridge in sedimentary formations near Cow Camp in Madison County; similar material occurs in the Silver Star District. Excellent petrified wood has been found in the foothills bordering the Jefferson River for a number of miles west of Twin Bridges.

Petrified wood, both silicified and opalized is abundant in the Frying Pan Basin northwest of Dillon in Beaverhead County. Logs reaching lengths of from 5 to 50 feet and diameters of from 1 to 5 feet have been reported.

Wyoming. Enormous logs of perfectly preserved silicified wood occur in a large deposit known as the Crazy Woman Petrified Forest located not far from Crazy Woman Creek on the east side of the Big Horn Mountains in Big Horn County. In Johnson County, silicified wood, agate, chalcedony and other quartz gemstones occur about 12 miles east of Buffalo along both sides of Highway 16. In Converse County, geodes of chalcedony lined with small quartz crystals occur east of Glenrock in the canyon of Boxelder Creek south of its junction with the North Platte River. Natrona County provides cryptocrystalline varieties of quartz from along Poison Spider Creek and several miles north and south of this creek in an area located about 40 miles west of Caspar.

Large quantities of seam moss agate have been mined from extensive deposits at Hartville about 2 miles northwest of Guernsey in Platte County. Much of this material is very beautiful, showing handsome black dendritic markings against a pure white, slightly blue-tinted groundmass of translucent

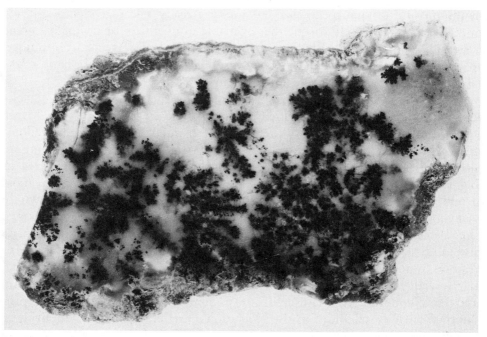

FIGURE 98. A fine polished slab of moss agate. The dendritic growths are believed to be due to infiltrations of black manganese compounds. Courtesy Smithsonian Institution.

opaque chalcedony; a typical example is illustrated in Figure 98. Moss agate occurs in irregular veins of from 1 inch to 24 inches thick cutting almost vertically across bedded limestones at the old Wilde and Deercorn Mine. The latter was opened in 1894, and, at that time, produced mine-run moss agate quoted at $200 per ton. In 1903, more than 7 tons were mined and sent to Germany for cutting; in 1908, about 3½ tons were unearthed including one piece which weighed nearly 1000 pounds.

In Albany County, silicified dinosaur bones occur on the sides of Como Bluff north of Highway 30 and close to the border of Carbon County; various cryptocrystalline quartz gemstones have been found along the foothills of the western slope of the Laramie Mountains about 36 miles northeast of Medicine Bow.

Another well-known name to fanciers of cryptocrystalline quartz is *Sweetwater agate*, a name applied to small dark gray translucent chalcedony nodules in which are found numerous dendritic growths forming starlike patterns. In years past, enormous quantities were gathered from the surface of townships 30 and 31 north, ranges 89, 90, and 91 west in Fremont County. Collecting areas are mostly north of the Sweetwater River. In the area, nodules appear scattered over the surface in valleys, shallow plateaus, washes, and in fact, almost everywhere. As a result of the treeless and brushless nature of the terrain, surface sands are continually shifting and exposing fresh supplies as previous material is gathered up. Many forms are taken by the nodules, some being rounded or oval in cross-section but others flattened and disklike. A few exhibit angular corners and well-defined planes caused by sandblasting (dreikanters). Sizes range from ½ inch to more than 2 inches, but pebbles over 1 inch are uncommon; the color varies from opaque white and gray to highly translucent gray with black dendritic markings. Many are distinctly brownish in cast, like smoky quartz. Dendritic inclusions show a great variety of size and form, varying from small spherical mossy tufts to delicate filaments radiating from a common point. Although very interesting, Sweetwater nodules are generally dull in appearance and can scarcely be classed as fine gem material despite the fact that they have been collected for years.

In other parts of Fremont County, agate occurs along the Wind River from near Riverton and along the valley to the northwest; moss agate is found over a wide area centered about 10 miles northwest of Fort Washakie near Highway 287. Chalcedony is reported as abundant in the limestones and marls north and northwest of the Granite Mountains.

Silicified wood, agate, chalcedony, and other varieties of cryptocrystalline quartz are found in profusion in Sweetwater Co. One of the most noted occurrences of petrified wood in the United States is near Eden in the northeastern part of the county. This interesting material occurs in a wide shallow valley and associated gently-sloping desert uplands extending northeastward for many miles from Eden. Wood has been found along the Big Sandy River and its tributaries upstream from Farson, a few miles from Eden; also up as far as Big Sandy Reservoir and the foothills of the Wind River Mountains to the northeast. The best collecting areas, and also the most inhospitable and inaccessible, are the desert wastes east of Eden over which wood is sprinkled for 40 miles to as far east as the Red Desert. An especially prolific area lies immediately east of Oregon Butte, southeast of Pacific Springs. The majority of Eden Valley wood is dead black but attractively veined with streaks of grayish chalcedony and coated with opaque, partly-altered silica of cream color. A typical specimen is illustrated in Figure 96, and shows the remarkable resemblance to ordinary weathered wood. Eden Valley wood is seldom employed in the lapidary arts but many limb and twig sections are cut across and polished as cabinet specimens. Although ordinary specimens are black, some are translucent brown while others show complete replacement by translucent gray chalcedony. Most of the wood is small, no more than several inches in diameter and from 6 inches to 12 inches in length. Associated with the wood are found interesting growths of dark brown chalcedony showing concentric bandings built up in knobs and hummocks arising from flat bases, and believed to be silica replacements of limey algal deposits. Although easily polished, this curious material is often spotted with small cavities which trap polishing powder and cause disfigurement of finished specimens. Like the wood, it is too somber in hue to be of much value for ornamental purposes.

Agate and chalcedony are found on the slopes of Steamboat Mountain in the Leucite Hills about 15 miles due north of Superior. Silicified turritella shells are abundant on the edges of Delaney Rim about 15 miles southwest of Wamsutter. This interesting material is commonly called *turritella agate* and is found in the form of slabs an inch or two thick consisting of solid masses of spiral *turritella* shells closely packed together and completely replaced by chalcedony. A typical polished specimen is shown in Figure 92. Further west in Uinta County, similar material, along with silicified algae, occurs in a ledge which caps the mountain buttes along Highway 30 between Blacks Fork Creek southwest of Granger and the latter community. This area extends eastward into Sweetwater Co.

The area encompassed by Sweetwater, Uinta, and Lincoln counties in the southwestern corner of Wyoming contains many chalcedony occurrences only a few of which have been examined closely. Large amounts of chalcedony, petrified wood, jasper, and other forms of cryptocrystalline quartz eroded from the Green River Formations appear as loose pebbles and fragments in washes and on rises where loose sand has been blown away by desert winds. A broad and profitable collecting belt begins about 20 miles east of Green River in Sweetwater County and extends a dozen miles or more on either side of Highway 30 to sweep southwestward to Fort Bridger in Uinta County. Northward, the entire eastern portion of Lincoln County, especially along the badlands of the Green River, along Ham's Fork, etc., and adjacent areas in Sweetwater County to the East, affords excellent hunting.

No discussion of Wyoming would be complete without including localities within the confines of Yellowstone National Park. Although collecting is strictly forbidden in this wonderland of natural marvels, mineralized formations observed in the Park extend outward on all sides and can provide material at least as good as any observed inside its boundaries. This is particularly true of the famous fossil wood forests found in the northeast corner of the Park. Explorations outside the park boundaries to the east have shown that the same volcanic debris formations in which are found an astonishing number of silicified trees also exist in the Shoshone National Forest in Park County, Wyoming.

While on the subject of petrified wood, the noted fossil forests on Specimen Ridge and Amethyst Mountain in Yellowstone Park should be discussed. Both of these mountains blend into a single ridge which is about 8 miles in length and perhaps 5 miles in width lying between Yellowstone River and Lamar River, a swift-flowing tributary which enters the Yellowstone from the east. The forest is located on the northeastern flank of Amethyst Mountain and is reached by trail from the paved road connecting Tower Junction and Cooke Entrance. The trail crosses, or actually wades, the Lamar River and then ascends the slopes to the forests. At the point where the river is reached, and for several miles up and down stream, numerous fragments of petrified wood, gray chalcedony, and jasper of poor grade occur in abundance in the gravels of Lamar River. Fragments range from several inches to as much as 12 inches in length and consist of black, somewhat earthy and poorly silicified wood with lighter markings, to some which is dark brown and completely silicified. In the bluffs of Amethyst Mountain may be observed an astounding progression of fossil forests each successively engulfed by sandstones, shales, and conglomerates derived principally from volcanic material. The total depth of the fossil forest strata is over 2000 feet but the best exposures appear at higher elevations. About 500 feet above the Lamar River Valley, the trunks are both numerous and in a fine state of preservation. As one early observer stated: "In the steeper middle portion of the mountain face, rows of upright trunks stand out on the ledges like the columns of a ruined temple. On the more gentle slopes farther down, but where it is still too steep to support vegetation, save a few pines, the petrified trunks fairly cover the surface, and were at first supposed by us to be the shattered remains of recent forest." At the locality, prostrate trunks of from 40 to 50 feet in length are common and not a few as much as 5 to 6 feet in diameter. Standing trunks are rather short and many show silicified roots penetrating the now solidified earth in which they originally grew. In many instances the wood is completely replaced by quartz or opal but some hollow trunks contain linings of beautiful quartz and calcite crystals. Such hollow trunks are really casts of the spaces left behind when original trees were burned and completely destroyed by engulfing hot lavas. Later, silica was brought in by watery solutions and infiltrated every crevice in the fossil horizon, including the tiniest cracks in the wood, the rocks enclosing the wood, and also the adjacent layers above and below. Some of the casts show no trace whatsoever of woody structure except that impressed upon the hot lava by the tree bark. Casts are frequently lined with common gray translucent chalcedony, sometimes banded with opaque white layers and encrusted internally with crystals of colorless or milky quartz. In many instances, amethyst, rarely dark in color, is found inside the casts and it is from the occurrence of this quartz variety that the name of Amethyst Mountain has been derived. The mineralogical and geological wonders of the forests and adjacent areas led to the equally descriptive naming of local creeks which drain the ridge i.e.: Agate, Quartz, Crystal, Jasper, and Amethyst creeks.

Prior to the establishment of the park, numerous specimens were collected from Amethyst Mountain. It is recorded that A. E. Foote, the noted mineral dealer of Philadelphia of many years ago, sold a hollow log section of gray chalcedony lined with amethysts, which measured 24 inches in length and 15 inches in diameter. In summary, the gemstones found at this locality include: amethyst, rock crystal, chalcedony, carnelian, chrysoprase (?), prase, banded agate, chert (probably impure jasper), opal, and red, yellow, gray, blue, and black jaspers.

In extent, the petrified forests of Yellowstone Park are not confined to the immediate vicinity of Specimen Ridge and Amethyst Mountain but apparently proceed from these classic localities to as far east as the park boundary including Hoodoo Basin at the headwaters of the Lamar River and the headwaters of Cache Creek where extensive deposits of wood have been noted 10 miles from its mouth. Further south, silicified forests crop up in appropriate horizons almost to the southern park boundary, specimens being found at the mouth of Beaverdam Creek where it empties into the Southeast Arm of Yellowstone Lake, the Yellowstone River Valley for some miles upstream from Southeast Arm, and Grouse Creek near its mouth on the South Arm. Directly east of Specimen Ridge and Amethyst Mountain, much wood has been noted on the slopes of Mount Norris along Soda Butte Creek opposite Soda Butte Ranger Station; also on Thunderer Mountain, the northeast extension of Mount Norris. Wood has also been noted on the flanks of Bison Peak south of Slough Creek Ranger Station; also along the headwaters of Hellroaring Creek; in the valley of Miller Creek; along Pelican Creek; and on the sides of the plateau between Calfee Creek and Miller Creek near their confluence with the Lamar River. Wood has also been observed near Undine Falls and Wraith Falls about 5 miles southeast of Mammoth Hot Springs on the road to Tower Falls. Petrified wood is found 1½ miles west of Tower Falls Ranger Station and 1½ miles east of Gallatin Ranger Station and on the north side of Specimen Creek in the northwest corner of the park.

The Yellowstone River Valley in the park also boasts its share of localities but most are inaccessible due to the steepness of the canyon walls. Just above the falls, geodes and thundereggs occur in a large slide on the walls of the gorge about 300 yards northeast of Artist Point in an area of severely altered rhyolites on the rim of the Grand Canyon of the Yellowstone. Thundereggs up to several inches in diameter are found loosely imbedded in clayey material. Geodes up to 10 inches diameter have been reported from along Alum Creek; also along the west bank of the Yellowstone River above the Lower Falls. Jasper, gray chalcedony, and seam opal occur on the western and northern flanks of Mount Washburn. Chalcedony and green jasper are found in the valley of Elk Creek several miles above its confluence with the Yellowstone River. Small agate pebbles comprise part of the beach gravels of Yellowstone Lake, particularly in the southern end.

Colorado. Fine jasper, agate, petrified wood, and dinosaur bone are found near Kalouse in northeastern Weld County. Some of the agate resembles that found near Fairburn, S. Dak. Similar material has been recorded from the valley of the South Platte River extending from Morgan County to Logan and Sedgwick counties.

Agate, chalcedony, jasper, and geodes are found in volcanic breccia and associated debris on Specimen Mountain in Rocky Mountain National Park. The locality lies just north of Poudre Lake at Milner Pass and is almost exactly on the boundary between Jackson and Larimer counties. Some of the geodes from this occurrence reach 6 inches in diameter. Small amethyst crystals suitable for cutting into faceted gems have been found in pockets in quartz veins penetrating decomposed granite at the Pennoyer Amethyst Mine in the Red Feather Lakes district of Larimer Co.; many crystals show sceptre development of violet quartz over thin stems of colorless quartz; size ranges from 1 inch to 3 inches but few clear places are found and flawless gems over 5 carats can rarely be cut. In Grand County, fine moss agate and chrysoprase are reported from Middle Park but details are lacking; moss agate occurs on Willow Creek and near Hot Sulphur Springs; fossilized wood also occurs several miles northwest of the springs; moss agate is also found on Williams Fork, 2 miles from the Colorado River, while yellow, red, green and brown jasper occurs at the junction of this creek with the Colorado River. Moss agate has been found in the East End Mine at Central City, Gilpin County. In Clear Creek County, amethyst occurs at several points, e.g., pale but clear crystals in the ore veins of mines on Red Elephant Mountain in the Lawson-Dumont mining district; fine deep color crystals in the mine dumps along Trail Creek, the latter emptying into Clear Creek about 2 miles northwest of Idaho Springs; light but clear crystals along Silver Creek, the latter joining Clear Creek about 6 miles west of Idaho Springs.

Brownish and yellowish petrified wood commonly occurs in gravel along the foothills of the Rocky Mountains in Adams, Arapahoe, Elbert, and Douglas Counties and has even been found in gravel pits within the city limits of Denver. Woods are dominantly tropical and subtropical but temperate species such as ash, walnut and various conifers are found also. In Douglas County, large specimens occur 1 mile south of Parker and a log measuring 50 feet in length and 6 feet in diameter is recorded from this area. In Elbert County, sections of logs and limbs are found in the gravels of Kiowa Creek, between Cherry and Running creeks, and near the sources of Kiowa and Bijou creeks. The Platte River gravels in this county also provide many specimens of silicified and sometimes opalized wood; a good place to hunt is a short distance southeast of Elbert. In El Paso County, gravel beds around Peyton and other places furnish wood. In Prowers County, silicified wood of fair quality has been found abundantly in an area about 18 miles south of Lamar. Petrified wood from this area has been known since 1867 but aside from its curiosity value, its unattractive colors militate against use in ornamentation. In Douglas County, striped jasper is reported from near Larkspur.

A famous locality for chalcedony gemstones is situated at the base of Austin Bluffs, about 4 miles northeast of Colorado Springs in El Paso County. At one time very fine chalcedony, agate, jasper, and carnelian were found here in the debris at the base of the bluffs where they had fallen after weathering from seams in limestone.

Rather than repeat the numerous localities within the Pikes Peak Granite Area of Park, Teller, Jefferson, Douglas, and El Paso Counties where quartz varieties occur within pegmatite pockets, the reader is referred to Colorado Localities under FELDSPAR and TOPAZ.

In Park County, agate was mined many years ago at Thirty One Mile Mountain about 7 miles west of Guffey. Between Guffey and Hartsel are found many quartz gemstones, for example, moss agate and other varieties occur near the saltworks southeast of Fairplay in South Park while agate, jasper and petrified wood occur in the gravels of the South Platte River near Hartsel.

Silicified dinosaur bone and other forms of chalcedony occur at Garden Park, 7 miles due north of Canon City, Fremont County. The deposits are located in the rough hills on the west side of Oil Creek and on the south side of Garden Park where soft shales of the upper Morrison Formation are exposed and yield numerous specimens of bone. Some of the bone is hard and polishes well, showing nicely the cellular structure of the marrow, however, much is also unsuited for anything except specimens. Fine agate nodules, small but beautifully colored and banded, also occur here but in a horizon lower than that yielding bone. Agate, jasper, and geodes also occur on Felch Creek, a tributary of Oil Creek. About 6½ miles south of Canon City lies another famous but now depleted deposit of agate found as veins in Ordovician limestones upon Curio Hill. Material has been mined here by the use of explosives since all available surface pieces have long since been picked up. The agate is banded in beautiful red and brown hues interspersed with thin bands of white. A deposit of cloudy amethyst suitable for cabochon work was mined about 1908 at a point 1 mile south of Twelvemile Park and 12 miles northwest of Canon City where amethyst occurs in quartz veins penetrating biotite granite-gneiss. Although found in cavities, crystals are so crowded together that few are well-developed. Rose quartz was once mined in quantity from the Wild Rose Claim located 6 miles due north of Texas Creek and ⅓ mile west of the junction of Echo Canyon and East Gulch. At this place, a large pegmatite body outcrops on a steep mountainside and has provided rose quartz from its core; some of the material was reported as highly translucent and flawless in pieces up to 2 inches across.

Pegmatites atop Mt. Antero and White Mt. in Chaffee County, have furnished fine quartz crystals as well as other pocket minerals; an exceptional rock crystal provided the raw material for a fine sphere measuring 5½ inches in diameter which is now in the Chicago Natural History Museum. Additional information on these localities appears under BERYL. Also in this county, transparent rock crystals up to 6 inches in diameter and penetrated by dark green epidote needles have been found at the Calumet Iron Mine about ¼ mile south of the abandoned mining town of Calumet City.

In Saguache County, fine agate and chalcedony occur in volcanic rocks exposed near La Garita Creek in the southern part of the county. In Rio Grande County, fine plume agate occurs in geodes in a restricted area on the eastern slopes of Twin Mountains northwest of Del Norte while other quartz gemstones are found in soil for several miles around this locality. Jasper occurs as waterworn pebbles in the stream gravels of the Rio Grande River; amethyst-lined geodes are reported from a point on the river 15 miles north of Loma.

Mineral County is noted chiefly for the abundance of massive amethyst in the silver mines of the Creede District. The town of Creede is at 9000 feet elevation on Willow Creek, a short distance above the latter's junction with the Rio Grande River and in the immediate area, is surrounded by ten mines almost all of which produce massive amethyst from their dumps. Good material has been obtained from the Commodore Mine, about 1½ miles from Creede on the west side of the west branch of Willow Creek; also from the Eunice Mine located high on the west slope of Mammoth Mountain on the east branch of Willow Creek, but productive of only small quantities of amethyst; the P&E mine and Amethyst Mine, located 2 miles north of Creede on the west side of the west branch; also, from the Happy Thought Mine just north of the Amethyst Mine. In all of the silver veins, amethyst has been found as linings and fillings consisting of layers of pale amethystine quartz interspersed with thin layers of bluish-gray chalcedony, small grains of sphalerite, and ordinary milky quartz. Each layer shows numerous amethyst crystals arranged with points facing inward toward the center of the vein, forming, as the miners put it, the so-called "comb structure." Strange as it seems, this attractive material is the gangue of silver ores, and of course was discarded in enormous quantities. Locally, the amethystine material is inelegantly called "sowbelly." Although much has been used for ornamental items, many small cracks and fissures between crystals cause some difficulties in achieving satisfactory surface finishes, moreover, attractive, deeply-colored material is rare, the major portion being very pale in color.

Also in Mineral County, agate and other types of chalcedony are found near the highway leading to Wolf Creek Pass at a point 6 miles west of the summit, while banded, moss, and other varieties of agate, occur near Wagon Wheel Gap in the Embargo Mining District.

Deposits of dinosaur bone replaced by carnelian occur in the extreme western part of Moffat County along the Yampa and Green Rivers and are largely preserved for posterity in the Dinosaur National Monument whose boundaries take in parts of Moffat County and Uintah County in the neighboring state of Utah. The monument covers many square miles in area and from east to west measures over 40 miles and over 20 in width. As its name implies, the park is a huge graveyard for ancient reptiles which roamed this land untold thousands of years ago. In one place, a remarkable skeleton of a dinosaur was found which measured 80 feet in length and 15 feet in height, every bone of which is preserved in imperishable chalcedony. Cross sections of bones show faithful replacement of the cell structure, each open pore being filled with brownish-red carnelian while the webs are marked either by black or white chalcedony. Much bone is too porous to be useful for cutting but a small percentage is very solid and polishes well, however, unless individual bone cells are firmly cemented to each other, thin sections tend to fall apart readily. For this reason, a great deal of the material is unsuited for cutting into cabochons and can only be used in larger items in which the strength of the mass is preserved.

Further south in Mesa County, fair to good quality dinosaur bone is found eroding from sediments of the Morrison Formation on a low bare ridge called Dinosaur Ridge, about 4 miles directly west of Fruita, and has been identified as belonging to *brontosaurs* and *allosaurs* of the Mesozoic period. As in the Dinosaur Monument, specimens look like ordinary weathered bones and one could easily mistake them for those of a recent animal were it not for their enormous size and great weight.

Also in Mesa County, petrified wood is found south of Fruita while superb banded and moss agates occur upon Pinon Mesa and in surrounding areas. Dinosaur bones occur at the base of cliffs at Goodman's Point near Cortez, also upon the slopes of Ute Peak and McElmo Creek Valley in Montezuma County.

New Mexico. In the Petaca District of Rio Arriba County occurs a remarkably pure and colorful stone known as the Pedernal Chert. Its principal hues are creamy-white with flecks and stainings of red, yellow and black. All of it is sound and free of cracks while some is so fully replaced by chalcedony as to be translucent. Masses free of cracks up to 2 or 3 feet across have been observed along the outcrop of the deposit which extends from Cerro Pedernal to west of San Pedro Mountain. Also in this county, granular quartz enclosing numerous needles of dumortierite and suited for lapidary purposes outcrops on the steep west slope of La Madera Mountain. Most of the quartz veins containing dumortierite are exposed in two steep gulches near the base of the mountain about ½ mile southeast of La Madera. Both dark blue and violet dumortierite occur associated with specular hematite.

Jasper is abundant in San Juan County between San Juan River and Chaco River where it is estimated that 70 per cent of the pebbles of the Ojo Alamo Formation consist of jasper, chert, or pink and white quartzite. Chalcedony occurs in various places in the Chaco Canyon area. Petrified wood is locally abundant north of Chaco Canyon and along the Bloomfield-Cuba highway near the common corner of San Juan, Sandoval and Rio Arriba counties. In McKinley County, jasper occurs near Willow Springs northeast of San Mateo; logs of petrified wood are found in the Zuni Mountains southeast of Gallup and in the Navajo Reservation north of Gallup. Silicified wood is found along the Rio Puerco Valley and in the Jemez District of Sandoval County where jasper also occurs. Agate is found in the Nacimiento Mountains of this county. In Santa Fe County, chalcedony occurs in the Cerrillos District while well-preserved petrified wood is found upon Sweet's Ranch about 3 miles east of Cerrillos where a large area containing numerous logs of large size has long been known; one log measured 6 feet in diameter and 135 feet in length. Petrified wood is also abundant northwest of Las Vegas in San Miguel County. Jasper, chalcedony, agate and silicified wood occur in the Rio Puerco Valley in Bernalillo County. The southeastward extension of the Zuni Mountains in Valencia County also provides petrified wood from many places.

Jasper, agate, and other quartz gemstones occur near Joseph in Socorro County; similar material is found in the Joyita Hills, at Mockingbird Gap, and in the Socorro Peaks. At the latter place, dendritic jasper of considerable beauty is reported. In the same county, nodules of chalcedony are abundant in the Magdalena Mountains. Chalcedony and jasper occur abundantly in the Mogollon District of Catron County; also in the Taylor Creek area. Moss agate has been found in the volcanic tuffs along the south edge of the Plains of San Augustin.

Sierra County is noted for the abundance and high quality of its many varieties of quartz occurring within its borders. Jasper, agate, chalcedony and petrified wood are profuse in the Jornada Valley about 13 miles east of Truth Or Consequences (formerly known as Hot Springs) while excellent jasper is found near Cutter across from the Aleman Ranch in the valley. The west side of the Caballo Mountains just north of Truth Or Consequences also produces agate. Dendritic jasper occurs at Mockingbird Gap in the San Andres Mountains on the western side of Jornada Valley. Agate is found near the road from Elephant Butte to Engle and also near the latter community. Gray, brown, chocolate, and cream colored chert occurs in the Derry and Lake Valley districts. Petrified wood is found west of Truth Or

Consequences on the northeast flank of Mud Springs Mountains. Fossilized palm wood is found in the Black Mountains west of this city.

Rock crystals, some of as much as 12 inches in length and containing interesting inclusions of green chlorite have been taken from the Quickstrike Mine in the Organ District of Dona Ana County; various quartz gemstones also occur in the southern part of the Caballos Mountains at the point where they enter this county. In Grant County, jasper, agate, chalcedony, plus other cryptocrystalline quartz varieties occur in the Burro Mountains, also at Cap Rock Mountain, on the west side of the Mimbres Mountains, and generally in the Central District. White-and-pink chert occurs in the Fierro-Hanover, Juniper and Meerschaum districts of this county. In Hidalgo County, moss, fortification, and plum agate are found in the vicinity of Playas Dry Lake near Hachita in the Hatchet Mountains. Various forms of chalcedony occur in the Lordsburg District and also in the Peloncillo and Pyramid Mountains.

Chalcedony, jasper, and many other types of cryptocrystalline quartz occur near Deming (see Figure 89) and in the Cooks Peak area; sagenitic agate and blue chalcedony are found near the gap between Florida and Little Florida mountains. Narrow seams of quartz permeated by dark blue dumortierite, very handsome in appearance, have been found in a quartzite ledge outcropping for 1000 feet in the Tres Hermanas Mountains about 12 miles northwest of Columbus.

Arizona. The Petrified Forest National Monument northeast of Holbrook and situated upon the border between Navajo and Apache counties, is generally conceded to contain the most colorful examples of silicified logs in existence. Nowhere else in the entire world is found such an abundance of high quality material—virtually tens of thousands of tons of compact cryptocrystalline quartz cast faithfully in the forms of trees which flourished many thousands of years ago. Yet this wonder which every year attracts hordes of admiring visitors was once threatened with annihilation and was saved only by the determined action of civic-minded persons residing in the immediate area and elsewhere in the country.

The wonders of the forest were not lost upon the local Indians for legend records that the Navajos called the logs *yeitsobitsin,* or "bones of Yeitso"—a monster who was destroyed by the Sun and whose blood congealed to form lava flows. To the Piutes, the trunks were the spent weapons of Shinarav the great Wolf God and their localized accumulations, the scenes of great battles. In a more practical vein, local Indians utilized the high-quality chalcedony for making arrow and spear points, and later, to trade to visiting white men. The first white man to lay eyes upon the Forest proper was Captain Sitgreaves who, in 1851, passed by 6 miles north of the Zuni River along the present border of the Park. The North Forest was discovered by Whipple and Marcou during their traverse of Northern Arizona in 1853. The unusual abundance of wood along its banks prompted them to name the northern tributary of the Rio Puerco River, Lithodendron Creek, a name which it still retains. As the forests became better known, their marvels were advertised far and wide and it was not long before determined visitors took the not inconsiderable trouble to visit the area, and naturally, each took away at least *one* specimen of wood! By 1890, ravages of collectors in the area had reached such proportions that alarm was beginning to be expressed in many quarters. Hundreds of tons of wood destined for ornamental purposes were carted to the railroad which had now entered the Territory and shipped off to major Eastern cities. One of the largest consumers of silicified wood was Drake & Company of Sioux Falls, South Dakota, who installed massive grinding and polishing equipment large enough to handle the enormous logs. In 1887, sections of wood measuring 25, 24, 17½, and 13 inches in diameter were cut and polished to mirrorlike perfection from pieces selected from a stockpile of 180 tons of wood! It was estimated that Arizona material worth $100,000 was processed in that year. However, the climax did not come until Armstrong Abrasive Company of Chicago announced its intent to erect a crushing plant in the forest area to reduce the logs to abrasive powders and grits even going so far as to send a dismantled plant from Chicago to Adamana Railway Station for this purpose. Fortunately, this disaster was forestalled by the sudden appearance of cheap Canadian emery upon the market, forcing the company to abandon its plans for an Arizona mill.

Public outcry had by now reached such proportions that the then Territory of Arizona adopted a memorial to Congress which reviewed the beauties of the wood, pointed out depredations, and requested that the Commissioner of the General Land Office be directed to withdraw from entry all of the public land covered by the forest. This memorial was aimed specifically at preserving the so-called "Chalcedony Park" near Holbrook. It was further requested that after withdrawal, the land be set aside permanently in the form of a National Park. Several years passed by without action after this letter had been sent to Congress, but in 1899, the Smithsonian Institution was asked for information concerning the area by the Commissioner of the General Land Office, to which request they quickly replied, including much information about the forests and ending with the recommendation that immediate preservative action be taken. Accordingly, Professor L. F. Ward, a paleontologist upon the Smithsonian Staff, was sent to examine the forest and to report upon the advisability of setting it aside as a park. He reported his results later in 1899, and strongly recommended to the Director of the U.S. Geological Survey that not only was preservative action necessary but that it should be taken quickly. However, it was not until 1906 that the Petrified Forest National Monument was formally established and the controversial tract of land permanently set aside. Originally, the monument encompassed an irregular rectangular area of about 44,000 acres below Adamana on the Puerco River in Apache County. In 1932, an additional 50,000 acres were annexed from a section of the Painted Desert on the north and contains what is now known as the Black Forest.

In the Navajo Country and over much of northern Arizona silicified wood is a characteristic feature of Triassic sediments and is found wherever the Shinarump conglomerate and the Chinle formations are exposed by erosion. The most common fossilized tree species belong to extinct members of the Pine Family, particularly to the fossil species *Araucarioxylon arizonicum* and *Woodworthia arizonica* resembling the araucaria pine of modern horticulture. Other species are *Podozamites arizonica*, a type of cycad and a member of the family *Gnetales* called *Scilderia adamanica* (a joint fir). Thirty-five other species of flora have been identified and include Upper Triassic species as follows: cycads, ferns, fungi, horsetail rushes, and gingkos.

Logs are distributed irregularly, occurring in groups of unassorted large and small trees, all lying flat and trending in various directions. Root balls are still attached to some but it is remarkable that none show branches or limbs. The logs are usually encrusted with sand or gravel cemented tenaciously by silica, or, less commonly, by calcareous cement. Exposed logs are mostly broken into segments arranged in proper order but others are split into rails. Surface fractures are commonly smooth and even. The majority of trees are composed entirely of silica but a few are replaced by copper ores, some by limonite, and others are so poorly preserved that coal and lignite may still be found in their interiors. Some formations contain logs which are replaced by uranium minerals and of course these too are highly regarded but not for their lapidary value! The coloration of ordinary silicified material consists chiefly of patches and clouds of red, yellow, purple, blue, and white, but rarely are colors very vivid. Black manganese stainings commonly occur upon the bark and often penetrate some distance within the logs creating very handsome scenic effects when specimens are polished. The woody structure is frequently beautifully preserved. On rare occasions, logs are found with central openings lined with amethyst or rock crystals. In respect to size, one of the most astonishing examples is that crossing a gully within the monument and now known as the Agate Bridge. This tree is 110 feet long and is remarkable in that it is still one piece. Throughout the monument, logs over 50 feet in length are abundant while sections measuring from 3 to 19 feet in length may be counted in the hundreds. Scattered chips are innumerable. In the North Forest where logs are well exposed, a number measure from 30 to 40 feet in length and from 3 to 4 feet in diameter; the largest is 70 feet long and measures 6½ feet across its swelling butt. Several views within the Petrified Forest are shown in Figure 99.

FIGURE 99. Scenes in the Petrified Forest National Monument. The upper view is taken in the area of the monument know as the Third Forest and shows clearly the eroded terrain which exposes the sedimentary layers of the geologic formations. The lower photograph is a close-up of several log sections; note how the logs fracture across with almost mathematical perfection. Courtesy Petrified Forest National Monument.

The wood-bearing formations of the northern part of the state are widely distributed and as a consequence, much wood is found in a number of very important localities aside from those in the Monument and adjacent areas. An extensive forest of beautifully silicified logs is located at Willow Springs, 9 miles northwest of Moenkopi in Coconino County. Another is located near Lees Ferry on the Colorado River close to the mouth of the Paria River in the northern part of this same county. Another forest is on the border between Utah and Arizona in the canyon of Nokai Creek which flows north to join the Colorado River about 10 miles east of Dunns. A forest of rather poor wood is immediately southwest of Ganado in Apache County while halfway between this village and Chinle to the north is still another forest in Beautiful Valley. The latter is one of the outstanding localities of the state. North of Chinle and immediately below the southwestern slope of Round Rock (elev. 6020 ft.) is another important deposit. Round Rock is about 12 miles west-southwest of the village of the same name. Fine quality wood is also abundant in a forest which extends southwest of Tanner Springs in Tanner Wash., north of Pinto Siding on the Santa Fe Railroad in Apache County.

In Apache County, dendritic agate has been found in a broad area along the road between Navajo and Highway 666, or between this point and Sanders and Witch Well. Dendritic agate has been found also near Concho and west of St. Johns. In Coconino County, a bed of cuttable banded jasper (chert?) occurs at the base of the Chinle formation in the Echo Cliffs near Cedar Ridge; the color is reddish and individual bands of jasper are several inches thick.

Mohave County contains many localities for quartz gemstones but little material is truly fine in quality. Agate and chalcedony are found on the eastern flank of the foothills along the eastern bank of the Colorado River near its exit from Lake Mead; the locality is about 3 miles south-southeast of the dam. The ancient river terraces along the banks of the Colorado River provide numerous cryptocrystalline quartz varieties wherever gravels are exposed as in the area between Topock and Oatman, about $7\frac{1}{2}$ miles north of Topock and east of the road connecting these towns. Near Sitgreaves or Meadow Creek Pass, on the road from Kingman to Goldroad, fire agate in flat grapelike growths up to 5 inches across as well as other chalcedonies are found by digging in the topsoil. The pass is $22\frac{1}{2}$ miles from Kingman. Chalcedony is found in rhyolite near Schaffer's Springs between Kingman and Oatman. Agate occurs in the gravels of the Big Sandy River about 12 miles north of Wikieup. The bed of Burro Creek near its crossing by Highway 93 about 47 miles northwest of Congress Junction, yields amethystine chalcedony, jasper, chert and obsidian; specimens are also found west of the highway about $6\frac{1}{2}$ miles northwest of Burro Creek Bridge.

Vari-colored agate in large sizes, occurs on and near the road from Perkinsville to Jerome and 9 miles from the latter in Yavapai County; a ledge of agate said to be "ten feet thick" (!) is located along the Chino Valley-Perkinsville Road, 13½ miles east of Chino Valley. In Gila County, the south bank of the Gila River below Coolidge Dam on the San Carlos Reservoir has furnished agate of several types including a peculiar kind which sometimes encloses native copper. Jasper of good grade has been found in the gravels of Cherry Creek Wash about 15 miles northeast of the east end of the Roosevelt Reservoir. Colored seam agate is found in a broad area centered about 5 miles west-southwest of Payson.

Gila County is noted chiefly for its chrysocolla-stained chalcedony which has been found in abundance in several copper mines of the Globe District. Exceptional material once came from the upper levels of the Live Oak Mine and from the Keystone Mine about 6½ miles due west of Globe; also fine material from the Bulldog Tunnel of the Inspiration Mine at Miami. In copper deposits, chrysocolla chalcedony is found most commonly as seams, veinlets, and rounded nodules in the weathered upper portions of the ore bodies. All gradations can be found, from vividly-colored translucent material of characteristic greenish-blue hue, to opaque material which contains scarcely any silica and is almost pure chrysocolla (copper silicate). When pure, chrysocolla is like opal, that is, it is very weak and brittle and fractures with similar conchoidal surfaces of waxy luster. It is utterly useless for gems but the slight quantities present in the chalcedony of the Globe mines is sufficient to transform this material into a valuable gemstone. Much of the chalcedony contains sprays and rosettes of minute glistening fibrous malachite crystals, which, on account of their decided softness as compared to the chalcedony, cause considerable cutting difficulties. The finest material is completely free of visible inclusions and has no cloudy color distribution, spots, cavities, or other blemishes and is so translucent that small faceted gems may be cut. A fine mass of chrysocolla chalcedony obtained in the early days of mining in this district is illustrated in Figure 86; it measures about 8 inches across and is of fine bright greenish-blue color. George Ashley, who owns this specimen, is also the possessor of a rounded nodule of magnificent quality almost 24 inches in length. Chrysocolla chalcedony is highly prized cutting material and sells readily at several dollars a pound for indifferent material to as much as $20 to $50 per pound for best grades while extremely clear and vividly-colored material may sell for even more. Occasionally, chrysocolla chalcedony is found encrusted by small jewel-like rock crystals, and though not useful for cutting, provides specimens much in demand by mineral collectors.

Another important quartz variety, amethyst, occurs in considerable quantity in a large deposit in the Four Peaks of Maricopa County. Named after a like number of steep-sided mountains aligned in a north-south row about 45 miles east-northeast of Phoenix and almost 9¾ miles directly west of Roosevelt Dam, the amethyst deposit lies at the western base of the second peak from the south at an elevation of 6500 feet above sea level; the highest peak of the group reaches 7691 feet. The mine is reached from Roosevelt Dam by a Forestry Service road and thereafter by a long foot trail. Mining has taken place by tunnelling within a mineralized zone in Mazatzal quartzite along which occurs a series of amethyst-lined pockets. Cavities are irregular in form and vary considerably both in width and in depth, however, most are generally less than ten feet long and a foot in depth although one large pocket measured 4 feet from floor to ceiling. Crystals occur attached to the pocket walls or loose in the pocket debris; the latter show extensive signs of corrosion and are assumed to be remnants of wall druses which were attacked by intense hydrothermal activity during late stages of pocket development. Many severely etched crystals are covered with gray coatings of minute fluorapatite crystals along with small hematite crystals of steel-gray color. A typical crystal is shown in Figure 80. Many of the pockets are filled completely with clays in which are found detached crystals plus apatite, hematite, and a white greasy substance which is probably another clay mineral. Crystals range in size from 1 inch to 8 inches in diameter but few are sufficiently clear to provide gems except from small sections near the tips. The color is very sharply zoned and often so intense that cut gems appear inky purple. A peculiarity of this amethyst is its change to pale green color when subjected to heat. Experiments have shown that the color change can be brought about with minimum hazard of cracking by subjecting amethyst crystals to a temperature of 350°C for one week. Higher temperatures will cause color changes in less time but cracking is almost certain to follow.

Maricopa County is also noted for huge deposits of bright red jasper which occur on both sides of Camp Creek, 18.6 miles north of Cave Creek on the road to Seven Springs. This material is known locally as *Cave Creek jasper* and has been extensively used in many larger items of ornament as well as for cabochons and tumbled gems. Close examination shows grayish translucent areas of crystalline quartz spotted throughout with small, flower-like rosettes of exceedingly fine quartz needles heavily impregnated by iron oxides. Since the grain size as a whole seems very coarse as compared to ordinary chalcedonic jaspers, this material is perhaps closer in structure to ordinary quartz than to chalcedony. However, since it seems identical in all essential respects to the orbicular jasper from California it is probably derived from chert. At the locality, blocks up to 40-50 pounds are obtainable but their quality varies greatly in proportion to the content of iron oxides. In the finest material, some of which is truly excellent, the principal hue is vivid red but earthy types tend to be dingy purplish-red. Orbicular patterns are a distinctive and beautiful feature, showing circular bands of contrasting shades of red, sometimes outlined with blue-black circlets of specular hematite. In some instances individual "flowers" are suspended in translucent gray quartzite which is further beautified by spangles of brilliantly reflecting hematite of bronzy color. This material ranks among the finest jasper-like quartz gemstones of North America. Very fine jasper, similar to that just described, occurs in quantity as float material along the Cave Creek-New River Road about 4 miles southwest of Cave Creek.

Jasper and other forms of chalcedony are found in the beds of Skunk Creek, New River and Agua Fria River near Rock Springs along Highway 69 between Phoenix and Prescott in Yavapai and Maricopa counties. Fire agate occurs on the slopes of Saddle Mountain 22 miles northwest of Hassayampa, Maricopa County. In this same county, chalcedony geodes are found about 1½ miles by trail directly south of Port of Phoenix on the shores of Canyon Lake Reservoir.

In 1956, collectors at the well-known Crystal Peak quartz locality in Yuma County, found a pocket of quartz crystals which contained numerous silky inclusions of an unidentified nature and from which exceptionally handsome chatoyant cabochons and catseyes have been cut. The author can recall of no chatoyant quartz from any locality in the world in which the inclusions are so fine and so brilliantly reflective. The quartz itself is absolutely colorless while the pure white inclusions impart in finished gems a unique sheen of great beauty. Crystals from this pocket reached about the same size as those taken from other pockets which ordinarily produce the clear rock crystals for which this locality is noted, that is, about ½ inch to 2 inches in diameter and from about 1 inch to 6 inches in length. Inclusions are arranged as a series of phantoms with individual fibers oriented at right angles to rhombohedral faces and occupying triangular segments within the crystal prism. A fine circular catseye measuring 9/16 inch in diameter and weighing 12.27 carats was cut from a piece kindly supplied by Dan Brock of Los Angeles, the discoverer of this material (see Figure 84). In addition to this unusual quartz, Crystal Peak is also noted for limpid rock crystals found in cavities in veins of massive milky quartz which here outcrop abundantly. The locality is 10 miles southeast of Quartzite in the Plomosa Mountains and is reached by turning east from Highway 95, 9 miles south of Quartzite, and then proceeding east for another 7.2 miles.

Also in Yuma County, a colorful chert known locally as *opalite*, but named improperly since it is not at all related to opal, is found upon the flanks of a hill 4½ miles west of the junction of Highway 95 with the road which leads from this highway to Cibola. Large quantities of jasper occur sprinkled over the ground in an area south of Brenda on Highway 60-70, about 17 miles east of Quartzite. Plume and moss agate occur in the Muggins

Mountains east of Yuma about 6 miles northwest of Wellton and about the same distance northeast of Ligurta.

In Pinal County, agate and jasper are found in the vicinity of the Martinez Silver Mine at the Head of Martinez Canyon several miles northeast of Florence; also on the south side of Copper Reef Mountain and the north side of the headwater basin of Deer Creek in the Stanley Region of Graham County. In Greenlee County, much chalcedony in all its varieties is found over wide areas. Petrified wood occurs in washes and draws fringing Highway 75 between Clifton and Duncan; fire agate, carnelian, banded agate, and jasper are found at York about 15 miles south of Clifton; chalcedony geodes occur on the Mule Creek Road 14 miles southeast of Clifton; bright red agate occurs at the foot of Mulligan Peak and surrounding areas in Ward Canyon about 15 miles east of Clifton; a purplish agate is found in Limestone Canyon along the San Francisco River 7 miles northeast of Clifton. Good collecting for cryptocrystalline quartz varieties is also possible along Highway 666 between Safford and Guthrie; much pinkish and pastel colored agate occurs in small nodules in the Peloncillo Mountains while agate and jasper are found upon Ash Spring Mountain and in Ash Spring Canyon.

In Pima County, banded agate, moss and plume are found on small hills several miles southwest of Cortaro. Petrified wood is abundant in many places in the Chiricahua Mountains of eastern Cochise County.

Utah. Jasper and agate are found on the north slope of the Drum Mountains in Tooele County. Fine fortification agate and other chalcedony varieties occur in seams and veins in the low hills about 13 miles directly south of Levan, Juab County; good plume agate is reported from near Jericho. Silicified dinosaur bone, agate, chalcedony, petrified wood and silicified shales providing cutting material occur in exposed sedimentary layers of the Cutler Formation 5 miles north of Moab in Grand County; near Cisco in the hills along the Colorado River are found agatized clams, some almost 5 inches in length, silicified dinosaur bone, jasper, and petrified wood logs reaching 12 inches in diameter.

In Emery County, the San Rafael Swell, located about 30 miles southwest of Green River along Highway 24, has long provided an abundance of silicified wood, dinosaur bone, chalcedony, agate and jasper. The Morrison formation, well exposed about 4½ miles south of Woodside, also provides all of the above materials in the form of scattered surface fragments. Much of the area of both Grand and Emery counties is wild, unexplored desert and extremely warm in summer; needless to say, collecting is subject to many difficulties.

In Wayne County, petrified wood and small but fine pebbles of agate are found sprinkled over several square miles in a wild and inaccessible area located about 3 miles west of Hanksville. In Beaver County, black agate marked with blue bands has been found just south of Beaver in Blue Valley. Beautiful lustrous dark smoky quartz crystals occur in pockets in pegmatites in the Mineral Mountains east of Milford in Beaver County. A few of the crystals have been faceted into gems but most have found their way into the cabinets of mineral collectors. Petrified wood is abundant in the wild Circle Cliffs area in the central eastern part of Garfield County. The petrified forest in these mountains is said to be one of the finest in the United States and logs of from 10 to 12 feet in diameter have been reported.

Large chalcedony geodes, some up to 24 inches in diameter, are found in the immediate vicinity of Newcastle in Iron County. In Washington County, large vein fillings and geodes of common grayish chalcedony occur in basaltic rocks around the community of Central. One cavity in basalt was said to have furnished over 500 pounds of material. Fine red and yellow moss agate is reported from the area surrounding Cedar Breaks National Monument.

Idaho. Agate and jasper occur in various creek beds and bases of bluffs along the Salmon River in Idaho County; the stretch between Riggins and White Bird is said to be productive; similar material occurs in Slate Creek and McKinsey Creek. Chalcedony forms veins in the Parker Mountain District of Lemhi County; good quality brown petrified wood occurs in the gold-bearing gravels of the Richardson placers at Leesburg. In Washington County, several kinds of agate and chalcedony are found in Grouse Creek and Hog Creek, in an area 5 miles north of Eaton. Some fine iris agate has been found in Hog Creek and also at Weiser Cove near Weiser. Large chalcedony geodes up to 12 inches in diameter and lined with fine amethyst crystals are found eroding from Tertiary basalts over a wide area in Custer and Blaine counties; many have been picked up in the upper valley of the Big Lost River and in the low hills near the junction of its north fork with the main stream. An interesting plume agate containing dark grayish-yellow marcasite inclusions occurs at Graveyard Point southwest of Nampa in Canyon County. *Tempskya* fern wood has been found on Willow Creek not far from Firth in Bingham County; one specimen on record measured 22 inches tall and 11 inches in diameter.

The Tertiary basalts outcropping in Custer County also cover large areas in Blaine County and yield similar quartz-lined geodes; an especially noted place for amethyst-lined specimens is along Pole Creek. Red and yellow jasper as well as other forms of chalcedony are abundant in Blaine County in the area east of Little Wood River. Chalcedony is common in the basalts of Owyhee County; also in various silver mines as the Oro Fino, De Lamar, etc. Chalcedony geodes occur 3 to 4 miles north of the Nevada line along Highway 93 in Twin Falls County. A beautiful massive fine-grained quartz heavily impregnated with fibrous malachite and cuprite and compact enough to polish, has been found in the Hummingbird Mine in Paris Canyon near Montpelier in Bear Lake County.

Washington. In Okanogon County, moss agate and chalcedony are found in the gravels of the Nespelem River immediately north of the town of the same name. Kittitas County is famous for its huge petrified forests containing both silicified and opalized wood; those containing chiefly opalized wood are treated under OPAL. The unique gingko trees of ancient geological age which occur so abundantly in Washington have been preserved for posterity in the Gingko Petrified Forest State Park located high on the bluffs over-looking the Columbia River Valley, about 5 miles west of Vantage. The park museum contains a very fine exhibit of polished and rough specimens as well as explanations of the geological history of the area. Locally, petrified gingko trees are found embedded in pillow basalts and ash beds covering an area of 6 square miles. Apparently the trees grew upon a succession of lava flows which engulfed each preceding generation and consequently produced wood-bearing beds which now measure about 800 feet in total depth. In this respect, they are much like the forests described under Yellowstone Park, Wyoming. Other forests occur southward from Vantage along the Columbia River. In the western part of the county petrified wood is abundant in many places, e.g., along the west bank of the Yakima River between Roza Creek and Yakima Canyon; at Roza Creek, Squaw Creek, Lookout Point, Umptanum, and Yakima Canyon. Another important forest is southwest of the city of Yakima upon Slide Ranch in Yakima County. In Grant County, forests are located near Corfu and Smyrna; another is a few miles north of Quincy and near the village of Palisades in Moses Coulee. A polished specimen of silicified wood from this county is shown in Figure 96.

Kittitas County is also noted for blue chalcedony nodules which erode abundantly from basalt flows in the region northeast of Cle Elum. Geodes and nodules are found atop Crystal Mountain about 2½ miles by trail from Liberty; also generally in a 2 square miles area centered about 1 mile north-east of Liberty where many specimens are found in stream beds and in talus slopes along steep-walled canyons. Fine nodules occur on the summit of Red Top Mountain located about 1 mile west of Highway 97 in the area just mentioned. Similar material is found on the Middle Fork of the Tean-away River.

In Grant County, agate pebbles occur in the gravels of the Columbia River in the vicinity of Vantage and are also found on gravel bars for many miles downstream; similar material is found on the elevated gravel bars along the east bank of the river near Ringgold in Franklin County. In Klickitat County, agate, carnelian, jasper and petrified wood are abundant in an area centered about 2 miles west of Warwick; also about 20 miles northeast of Goldendale.

In the western half of the state, fine chalcedony gemstones occur on almost every gravel beach of the ocean and inland waters surrounding the Olympic Peninsula; also upon the beaches of the San Juan Islands in the northern part of Puget Sound. Agate Beach along the Straits of Juan De Fuca in Jefferson County is of course named for quartz gemstones, but the name is a misnomer since it is jasper (chert) which is prevalent and not agate. Some of the jasper from this and other beach localities shows handsome orbicular markings whose colors contrast well against the prevalent red background. The beaches north of Queets have provided good examples. In Grays Harbor County, beaches north of Moclips and the gravels of streams entering the ocean in this area provide good stones. A most unique occurrence of chalcedonized clams and oysters is noted in an area about 10 miles north of Oakville in this county, where these interesting fossils are found weathering from steep banks along various rural roads.

In Pacific County, agate, chalcedony, and carnelian occur between Adna and Raymond in almost every gravel bed and stream along Highway 12 over a distance of nearly 40 miles. Agate and chalcedony replacements of various shells are reported from the gravels of the Willapa River near Lebam. *Gastropod* (snail) shells have been found here completely replaced by gray chalcedony sometimes slightly tinged with carnelian and one example of record measured 1¼ inches by 1⅛ inches by 1 inch; a clam shell of similar material measured 1¼ inches by 1 inch by ¾ inch. In addition, beautifully preserved *ammonite* shells and silicified clams are found in eroded steep banks of Green's Creek between Raymond and Menlo.

Chalcedony converted into carnelian by infusion of iron oxides is abundant in the gravels of the North Fork of the Chehalis River in Lewis County. The most prolific area is centered directly north of Forest or about 7 miles southeast of Chehalis. Much carnelian occurs in large pieces associated with chalcedony geodes and geode fragments, fossilized wood and other quartz gemstones. Similar material is found in gravels over a large area around Chehalis and Centralia and appears to be derived from weathered basalts in the mountains to the east. Good material is also found on Lucas Creek, a tributary of the Newaukum River in the central part of the county; also in gravels and cuts near Mary's Corner south of Chehalis. A variety of clear chalcedony containing red spots of cinnabar is reported in good specimens from the mercury mines near Morton.

In Cowlitz County, fine amethyst-lined geodes, sometimes up to 8 inches by 14 inches in size, have been reported with chalcedony, carnelian, and fortification agates, in an area centered about 4 miles east of Cloverdale. In northeast Skamania County, agate, jasper, carnelian, and other quartz gemstones occur in an area of volcanic rocks centered about Table Mountain and extending for many miles to the west and northwest; almost all of the county north of a line between Mount St. Helens and Mount Adams yields similar material.

Oregon. Few regions in the world can compare to Central Oregon in richness in quartz gemstones. Over a wide, semi-arid area embracing hundreds of square miles, are found enormous quantities of agate, chalcedony, and other varieties of cryptocrystalline quartz embedded in or eroding from rhyolite and other light-colored igneous rocks; in contrast, very little quartz is found associated with darker lavas such as basalt. The famous Oregon thundereggs, for example, are found only in veins or seams of rhyolitic perlite. In a study made in behalf of the state, one authority estimated production of quartz gemstones in 1937 as $250,000 annually but pointed out that as foreign sources of supply were cut off as a result of World War II, annual production jumped to about $1,000,000 by 1947. Current production figures are not available but it may be safely assumed that present annual production is valued somewhere between the figures given above. In any case, Oregon gemstones are continually upon the market, well-known to everyone, and, in view of their beauty, always in demand. Because of their great number, only the most important localities will be discussed, however, the major productive areas of the state are shown on the map in Figure 100.

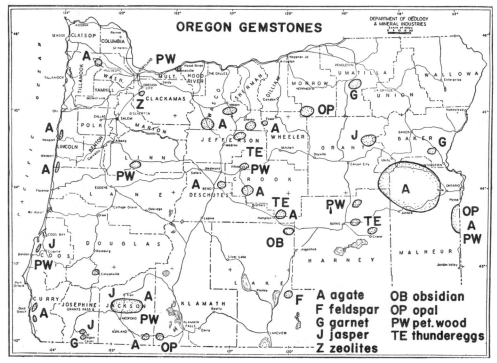

FIGURE 100. A Map of Oregon showing a few of the principal gemstone areas. Courtesy Oregon Department of Geology and Mineral Industries.

That part of Oregon west of the Cascade Mountains furnishes quartz gemstones similar to those noted further north in the corresponding Pacific Slope region of Washington. Almost every gravel bed in the streams and rivers entering the Pacific Ocean as well as the ocean beaches themselves, provide jaspers, agate, and other attractive cutting materials. Carnelian is found in the gravels of the Nehalem River in Clatsop County; also in the northern part of this stream in Columbia County between Vernonia and Clear Creek.

In Benton County, agate and jasper are found in the Willamette River gravels; a good place to search is 8 miles south of Corvallis. In Lincoln County, worm-bored petrified wood has been occasionally picked up from the beaches north of Newport; typical specimens show dark-colored wood dotted with wormholes filled with light gray chalcedony. In size, they range from masses only several inches across to some weighing 20 pounds. All such logs are waterworn and are believed to have been thrown up on the beach from a submerged deposit. All of the coastal beaches of this county yield many quartz varieties. A famous spot near Yachats has produced some very fine clear chalcedony showing beautiful growth markings as well as sagenitic inclusions; also orbicular jasper, petrified wood, silicified coral, and the peculiar water-filled chalcedony geodes known as *enhydros*. In these, the water is sometimes visible from the outside or can be detected by shaking the specimen. A beach 2 miles north of the mouth of China Creek is a good place to hunt; also a beach 10 miles south of Yachats; Cummings Creek beach 3 miles south of Yachats and Ten Mile Creek beach about 8 miles south are also productive places. A 5 inch nodule of magnificent sagenitic chalcedony was found some years ago at Yachats and provided over $300 worth of polished slices.

Chalcedony, agate, jasper, and carnelian occur in the gravels of the north and south Umpqua River in Douglas County. On the North Umpqua River about 22 miles east of Roseburg, silicified wood showing teredo worm borings is sometimes found in stream gravels in specimens weighing over 500 pounds and completely riddled with chalcedony-filled teredo holes, which, in some cases, even show worms inside. A beautiful orbicular jasper (chert) occurs on a branch of Davis Creek about 12 miles east of Roseburg and is noted for perfectly spherical concretions of white opal-like silica embedded in grayish translucent fibrous quartz; however, individual orbs are loosely held and care must be exercised in polishing to prevent shaking them loose. Thin seams of bright green chrysoprase occur in the massive nickel ores mined on Nickel Mountain near Riddle.

Very fine moss agate resembling that from the Yellowstone River of Montana is abundant in gravel beds about 4 miles north of Central Point, also further north to the Rogue River and eastward to Eagle Point and to as far as 15 miles east of Eagle Point. Much material is found in Butte Creek near Eagle Point but the best is said to come from the area around the junction of Butte Creek and Antelope Creek. Agate nodules and carnelian are found on Greensprings Mountain east of Ashland. Green and white jasper and various kinds of agate occur at Big Butte. Good petrified wood is found in many small streams descending the north slope of Table Rock Mountain, about 12 miles north of Medford. In Curry County, Pacific beaches at the mouths of the Chetco and Rogue rivers produce rolled agate and jasper pebbles; the Rogue River gravels near Agness about 200 miles upstream from Gold Beach in the picturesque canyon of the river, provide agate, chalcedony, carnelian, and other quartz varieties as well as pebbles of grossularite garnet.

In Wasco County, petrified wood and interesting silicified pine cones are found near Mosier. An unusual jaspery material which appears to be silica-rich sediment from the bottom of ancient Lake Wasco has been placed upon the market recently and the name *wascoite* proposed for this material because no other classification seems to fit. It is predominantly brown in color, often occurring in large pieces; and shows a large variety of patterns which most closely resemble petrified wood. Occasionally, wascoite contains fossils and a most unusual specimen containing a small fish resembling the modern sunfish (Centrarchidae) is in the collection of C. & M. Springer of Bend, Oregon. Some places in this material are clear while others show streaks and veinings of yellow jasper along with opaque grayish chalcedony.

The region near Antelope has long been noted for a large variety of cryptocrystalline quartz gemstones which are found here in especial abundance although much of the area is privately held and general collecting forbidden. One of the outstanding varieties which has come from here is iris agate of which many thousands of dollars worth has been collected as loose fragments on the surface and as casts after wood in basaltic rocks. Sections are cut across the layering to show the iris effect and in rare instances, unbroken slabs of 3 inches by 6 inches with beautiful bands of rainbow color are obtainable. This iris agate is generally not as translucent as that observed in similar chalcedony from Montana, Texas, and Mexico. For several miles immediately surrounding Antelope, chalcedony geodes are found as well as moss agate in large pieces. One of the largest of the latter, a huge boulder weighing 3 tons, was found in an open field near the community and when discovered, measured approximately 5 by 4 by 3 feet. Being impossible to remove *in toto*, pieces were chipped off with sledge hammers until it was eventually consumed. Another moss agate found in the general area measured 36 inches in diameter and weighed several hundred pounds. This material shows fine red mossy filaments suspended in chalcedony as well as areas of pale green, yellow and brown. Mossy inclusions are frequently so numerous, that some persons have called this material *jasper* or *jasp-agate*.

About 1 ¼ miles east of Antelope, red jasper is found in the county road metal quarry and upon Brown's Ranch in the immediate vicinity; agate, wood, and jasper occur 10½ miles east of Antelope near the state quarry along the highway from Antelope to Clarno; green moss agate occurs about 6.8 miles south of Antelope on the road to Ashwood. In the Warm Springs Indian Reservation north of Madras, an interesting brecciated jasper consisting of sharp angular fragments of yellow and red material cemented together with veins of translucent bluish chalcedony occurs as vein and drift material. On the south slope of the Mutton Mountains in the Reservation, large chalcedony geodes occur in some abundance; one specimen measured 24 inches in diameter. Fine agate also occurs north of the mountains near Wapinitia. Silicified and opalized wood are found near the headwaters of Mill Creek about 13½ miles up the Mill Creek Road in the southwest corner of the county. In Sherman County material similar to wascoite is found 5 miles south of Rufus and also along Highway 97 about 5 miles south of Biggs. Agate occurs near the Orofino Mine near Starkey southwest of La Grande in Union County. Silicified *Tempskya* wood occurs in rolled masses in the gold-bearing gravels of the Greenhorn District in Baker County and was assumed for some years to be some sort of petrified palm, however, after identification by the University of Michigan, its true identity was announced. *Tempskya* is a fossil fern of Cretaceous age whose genus is now extinct. Several types have been described from North America but the Oregon species, *Tempskya knowltoni*, differs considerably from the others. Silicified rolled masses found along with other boulders in the gravels of the district named, consist of numerous "false stems" matted together with rootlets and measuring 6 inches to 8 inches across. Polished specimens show each stem and other structural details clearly; the colors are chiefly warm brownish-yellow and brownish-red, resembling superficially jasper in appearance. Pieces up to 30 to 50 pounds weight have been recovered.

Also in Baker County, chalcedony geodes lined with small quartz crystals are found eroding from volcanic rocks east of Baker, along the Richland Valley through which flows the Powder River. The triangular area between Baker, Richland, and Durkee, is a prolific hunting ground for all manner of quartz gemstones. Dark green jasper, sometimes called "plasma" or "Oregon jade," is found in Shirttail Creek near Durkee; also fossil wood, agate and chalcedony. Near Milepost 393 along Highway 30 near Huntington, large geodes containing quartz crystals are found loose in the topsoil.

In Malheur County, petrified wood, agate, and other varieties of chalcedony are sprinkled over a broad area surrounding Brogan and Ironsides, and Unity in Baker County. Jasper occurs in rhyolite about halfway between Unity and Ironside. Sucker Creek north of Rockville in the eastern part of the county has produced fossil wood and other cryptocrystalline quartz varieties while similar material occurs near Nigger Rock about 10 miles northwest of Owhyee Dam. Very beautiful and colorful chert is found in the Jordan Valley close to the Idaho Border. The patterns in this material are endless in variety although specimens lacking some degree of chalkiness are difficult to find.

Much petrified wood and chalcedony in interesting and beautiful variations is found in Harney County. An important bed of thunderegg nodules is near Warm Springs Reservoir about 40 miles east of Burns and almost on the border between Harney and Malheur counties. Thundereggs are found a few miles south of Buchanan west of Burns; also on the east side of the Steen Mountains just west of Alvord Ranch on the road between Folly Farm and Denio; they are found in washes and gullies leading from mountain foothills.

In Lake County, agate, jasper, and other forms of chalcedony are abundant on the western slopes of Hart Mountain just northeast of Plush; geodes, thundereggs and opal are found here also. The area about Quartz Pass near Quartz Mountain also produces a variety of cryptocrystalline material. Thundereggs are found in Crane Canyon about 8 miles south of Lakeview and in the general area extending southward into California.

Oregon's Crook County is one of the most important areas in the state both in respect to quantity and quality of chalcedony gemstones. Agate, jasper, petrified wood, and other chalcedony gemstones are found in the western half of the county upon elevated ground between Highway 20 and Highway 26. Fine brown moss agate occurs on McAllister Butte near Ochoco River. At Bear Creek south of Prineville is found an agate noted for its dark green filmy moss suspended in almost colorless chalcedony and forming seams and veins several inches thick and of fine cutting quality. Occasionally small cavities lined with minute quartz crystals occur in this material. A sawed slab is illustrated in color in Figure 88. Similar material is found on Ochoco Mountain and is noted for green inclusions which resemble miniature fir trees. The Bear Creek locality is about 2 miles south of the junction of Crooked River and Bear Creek on the eastern slope of Taylor Butte west of Bear Creek or about 19 miles south of Prineville along Highway 27.

The Ochoco nodule beds are noted for their thundereggs which contain agate, plume agate, and rarely opal. Located on Wild Cat Mountain east of Prineville, most productive areas are owned or controlled by citizens of this community who exact a small daily collecting fee. Similar beds are located on Stevens Mountain further to the east. Ochoco jasper is found on the beaches of Ochoco Lake above Ochoco Dam and about 5 miles east of

Prineville along Highway 26. The best collecting area is across the lake from the boat landing.

Crook County is best known for its superb plume agate which occurs as seam and vein fillings from 1 inch to 3 inches or more in thickness and in which the major portion of the material is highly translucent whitish chalcedony with plumes growing at right angles to the wall. The plumes appear as fantastically delicate and detailed traceries which arise from the base of the slab and seem to float in milky liquid. Some collectors slice material into slabs scarcely 1/16 inch in thickness, especially if the plumes are dense, and then polish both sides. Pieces of this sort are kept as specimens only and serve no ornamental purpose but other types, particularly those in which individual tree-like growths appear with considerable space between them, are frequently cut in cabochon form to artistically frame the growth in the center of the completed gem.

At Powell Butte in the Prineville area, some of the finest plumes ever known were found in chalcedony vein fillings eroded from volcanic rocks. All loose material has long since been picked up and actual quarrying is now required to recover more. Within clear, slightly yellowish chalcedony, grow coarse to fine plumes in black, red, orange, or brownish-red colors along with some moss agate. One magnificent specimen worth describing showed bright orange-red plumes of complex pattern which rose to a height of 3 inches in clear pale yellow chalcedony and formed twisting, branching filaments terminating in wisps of great delicacy and beauty. The so-called *flame plume agate* or *Carey plume agate*, is mined on a steep hillside on the Carey Ranch where it occurs in pieces and chunks up to several pounds weight. It is found by digging through loose soil and debris, material being recovered from as far down as 8 to 10 feet below the surface; it is believed to be derived from a chalcedonic ledge further up the hill whose enclosing rocks disintegrated completely and released the agate to the soil. For many years this deposit was worked only by the owners but recently (1958) it has been thrown open to the public on a fee basis of $3 per person per day.

Beautiful examples of small red or black plumes suspended in clear chalcedony occur in the Eagle Rock area located near Eagle Rock (mountain), 11 miles southeast of Prineville. This material is sometimes called *Crooked River dendritic agate* and occurs in the form of seam and vein fillings in volcanic rock exposed at the locality in two pits of about 100 feet diameter each. This deposit is also on private property and collecting calls for prior arrangements with owners. These deposits were discovered in 1949, and, up to date, have yielded an estimated 6000 pounds of material of which much contained only very small dendritic growths and only a small fraction contained top grade plumes.

Jefferson County is also noted for its cryptocrystalline quartz, some varieties of which are both unique and beautiful. A fossil fern known as *Osmundites oregonensis* is found upon one of the branches of the John Day River about 15 miles southeast of Antelope. Numerous types of chalcedony, including thundereggs, are found in the rectangular area bounded by Hay Creek, Madras, Willowdale, and Ashwood, an especially fruitful place for thundereggs being located several miles northeast of the latter. A beautiful chert, attractively banded and colored and capable of taking an excellent polish, is found near Horse Heaven Mine, 22 miles east of Ashwood near the John Day River, and has been called locally *morrisonite*.

FIGURE 101. A "thunderegg" from the Priday Ranch deposit near Madras, Oregon. The oval nodule, measuring 3 inches by 3½ inches, has been sliced through the center and smoothly polished to show the handsome onyx markings within. The exterior is brownish-red silicified volcanic ash which has shrunk in the center to provide an opening for further deposits of chalcedony.
Courtesy Smithsonian Institution.

Perhaps the most famous locality in Jefferson County, and one which attracts hundreds of collectors each year, is the thunderegg deposit of the former Priday Ranch located about 4 miles southeast of Willowdale or about 12 miles northeast of Madras. The term *Priday Ranch thunderegg* is commonly used to describe these interesting and distinctive nodules, most of which are cut in half and then polished to show the patterns within. Figure 101 illustrates a polished nodule half showing strongly banded onyx filling. The present owners of the property charge a daily collecting fee based upon the amount of material removed, however, the collecting season is closed during winter months. At the grounds, several distinct horizons or beds of nodules embedded in friable volcanic rocks are situated short distances apart. One of the beds yields nodules in which the chalcedony is predominantly bluish-gray, sometimes spotted with white specks or banded with white layers; greenish mossy inclusions are also found in this type. Another bed furnishes thundereggs in which beautiful mossy or flower-like inclusions are found in clear chalcedony and from these, very fine cabochons are cut. Several such specimens are illustrated in Figure 102. Not far from the thunder-egg deposits is found a deposit of opaque white chalcedony spotted by perfectly spherical colored inclusions measuring from 1/16 inch to 1/8 inch in diameter. The circular dots are yellow, red, brown, or brownish-black

FIGURE 102. Cabochons of Priday Ranch plume and lace agate. The large cabochon measures a little over 2 inches in length.

and contrast handsomely to the white chalcedony in cut gems. Locally, it has been called *polka dot agate*.

In Klamath County, agate and other quartz varieties occur in gravels of the Klamath River. An exceptionally handsome form of jasper called *Crater Lake Flower Jasper* occurs as cobbles in gold-bearing gravels in the area immediately south of Crater Lake National Park. This material is essentially clear chalcedony in which numerous jaspery growth or inclusions form clusters resembling bunches of flowers; it may be said to be a form of plume but lacks the delicacy which typifies ordinary plume agate. Red and yellow colors predominate with the red tending to be very vivid. Much is so earthy however, that care must be exercised in selecting good pieces to cut.

Nevada. In Washoe County, a fossil forest containing a few enormous silicified trees is situated about 8 miles north of the ghost town of Leadville, very close to the border of Humboldt County and not far from Highway 34.

One stump found here measured almost 15 feet in diameter. Petrified wood from this deposit is predominantly light to dark brown in color.

Pershing County is noted for its fine *dumortierite quartz* which occurs in two large deposits formerly extensively mined for use in high-temperature ceramic applications. Much material has been mined from deposits on the west slope of Lincoln Hill in the Rochester Mining District where dumortierite impregnates numerous veinlets of quartz which cut Triassic rhyolites. The predominant color of the dumortierite fibers is an unusual rose pink, the blue material most ordinarily found elsewhere being conspicuous by its absence. Veinlets range from a fraction of an inch to some as much as 6 inches in thickness, the narrower veinlets being very densely permeated by dumortierite while the thicker veins contain more quartz. Some of the quartz contains dumortierite needles of so fine a character that superficially it resembles ordinary rose quartz. One of the most handsome types contains long parallel or slightly divergent bunches of dumortierite needles which impart a decided chatoyancy in finished gems or even provide fair catseyes. Several such gems are in the author's collection and a splendid polished slab of 5 inches by 4 inches is on view in the United States National Museum. The second extensive dumortierite deposit is found in the Gypsy Queen Canyon, 6 miles north of Oreana where blue is the predominant color imparted to the quartz although some pink material occurs also. At this locality, quartz veins containing medium blue to very dark purplish-blue dumortierite, cut through schistose rocks and provide large blocks of suitable lapidary material. The quartz-dumortierite mixtures average 3.30 in specific gravity while the refractive indices of the dumortierite alone are: $\alpha = 1.677$, $\beta = 1.685$, $\gamma = 1.690$. Dumortierite quartzes are difficult to polish as a rule, but the pink types from Lincoln Hill are an exception, assuming a fine lustrous polish without undue lapidary effort.

In Lander County, a pretty chert, locally but misleadingly called *opalite*, occurs near Ivanhoe about 45 miles northeast of Battle Mountain almost on the northern border of the county. In Churchill County, petrified wood, agate, chalcedony, and jasper are found in gravel beds near the west end of Lahontan Dam and along the northwestern shore of Lahontan Reservoir. In Lyon County, jasper and agate are present in the topsoils of foothills and washes along the western side of the hills located about 5 to 6 miles south of Fernley between this town and Lahontan Reservoir. Chert occurs in the low hills just east of Goldfield in Esmeralda County; agate and jasper are common in the Monte Cristo Mountains in the northern corner of this county. In Nye County, pale amethyst crystals line cavities in rhyolitic rocks at Bullfrog, about 8 miles west of Rhyolite; amethyst is also present in the dumps of a number of abandoned gold mines in this area. Colorful chert is common in the vicinity of the old mining camp of Atlanta along Highway 93 north of Pioche in Lincoln County.

California. Seldom heard of today, is a unique gemstone which once enjoyed considerable vogue when the great gold mines of the Mother Lode country of California were disgorging thousands of tons of gold-bearing quartz. This gemstone is nothing more or less than milky quartz in which bright yellow native gold provides a handsome contrast. Years ago, fine specimens of gold quartz sold readily on the basis of estimated gold content, plus an added premium for the whiteness and purity of the quartz, the distribution of the gold veinlets, and the absence of brown pyrite stains. Kunz states that during one period, the vogue for gold quartz reached such heights that sales amounted to at least $100,000 in one year. To be valued for gem purposes, gold quartz must be dead white, well streaked or veined with bright yellow gold and free of disfiguring stains or cracks. The finest material was originally supplied by mines in Butte, Calaveras, El Dorado, Mariposa, Nevada, Placer, Sierra, Tolumne, and Yuba counties. During the peak of popularity, jewelers were willing to buy gold quartz for as much as $20 to $30 per estimated ounce of gold despite the fact that pure gold could then be bought for only $16.50 per ounce. Variations in richness caused quartz specimens to bring as little as $3 per ounce or as much as $40 per ounce. Ornaments or cut gems of gold quartz are rarely seen today.

In Del Norte County, agate, jasper, and petrified wood are found on the beaches near Crescent City. In Siskiyou County, carnelian is found along Jenny Creek northeast of Hornbrook. Modoc County supplies agate and jasper from deposits near the summit of the road between Pine Creek and Fort Bidwell; also from along the shores of Goose Lake, especially at its south end. Much fine material has also been obtained from a number of streams draining the eastern slope of the Warner Mountains between Fort Bidwell and Cedarville.

Petrified wood and jasper are found on Adobe Creek about 2½ miles east of Petaluma in Sonoma County. Clear rock crystals containing interesting green chlorite inclusions are found in Shady Run, Placer County. Similar crystals, sometimes containing phantos, have been found in the gold-bearing gravels near Placerville in El Dorado County. In Alpine County, a series of volcanic rocks immediately south of Markleeville in the Loope District provide an abundance of jasper. The area surrounding the crest of Sonora Pass along Highway 108 provides agate and other chalcedonic varieties.

Much of the western half of California is noted for sedimentary formations in which occur colorful chert of fine cutting quality and in quantities large enough to supply any reasonable demand. Silicification of the sediments has been so extensive that few signs remain of original layering. The resulting chert includes a large variety of plain types of various colors but the best known and most highly prized is that in which many small "flowers" or spherules occur and is commonly known as *orbicular jasper*. The extent of these beds is not always fully appreciated for although California provides the largest quantity of material, similar formations extend north into Oregon and Washington. It is entirely possible that much of the so-called "jasper" found up and down the Pacific Coast of the United States is actually chalcedonic quartz derived from chert-bearing sedimentary beds and not eroded from volcanic rocks as would ordinarily be the case. In California, rocks of the so-called Franciscan Group contain many chert beds and it is from some of these that most material useful in the lapidary arts is obtained.

In the San Francisco Bay Region, chert is especially common and is characterized by high silica content and vivid coloration, viz.: shades of red, yellow, brown, green, and more rarely, blue. In many localities, the development of spherules is pronounced (see Figure 90). In varieties in which spherules are small, the local name *kinradite* is sometimes applied, a title derived from a J. J. Kinrade who did much to publicize a deposit of this material in Marin County. The richness of this chert in silica has resulted not only in conversion into compact material of polishing grade, but in many instances, has caused the loss of all traces of original sedimentary character. It is for this reason that some kind of chert may be found in which chalcedony is abundant, even to the extent that brecciated material is veined with blue chalcedony and larger seams solidly filled. In other cases, especially in the orbicular types, some of the silica appears in the form of spicules of quartz and is actually crystalline rather than cryptocrystalline. The cause of color is generally due to the presence of iron and manganese oxides, the former being so abundant at times that seams of metallic-lustered hematite are present.

The principal chert beds of the San Francisco Region are the Ingleside Chert, about 530 feet in thickness, and the Sausalito Chert of about 900 feet in depth; both are separated by about 1000 feet of Marin Sandstone. In Marin County, fine specimens have been obtained for many years from an outcrop located about one mile south of Sausalito on the southeast corner of the Marin Peninsula. Across the Golden Gate, within the city limits of San Francisco, and one mile northeast of the Cliff House on a promontory called Land's End, spherulitic cherts occur consisting almost entirely of red, brown, and green orbs sprinkled sparsely throughout uniformly colored material. Spherules range in size from microscopic to almost an inch in diameter, each comprising generally, a red center surrounded with alternate rings of dark and light colors. Ingleside and Sausalito cherts consist largely of silica but iron oxide is sometimes present to as much as 10 per cent. Other productive areas in the San Francisco Region are Point Bonita in Marin County;

the base of the Golden Gate Bridge in the city of San Francisco where large quantities of fine material were found during the sinking of the foundations; and Coyote Point, a promontory jutting into South San Francisco Bay directly east of San Mateo Junior College and 300 yards north of the yacht harbor. The underlying rocks at the latter place are virtually all chert but much material is unfit for ornamental use, however, fine examples of brecciated material, flowering types, and other pattern combinations have been found along the beach at low tide. In San Mateo County, much orbicular chert has been found in the beach shingle of Pescador Beach about 45 miles south of San Francisco.

In Santa Clara County, Franciscan chert provides exceptionally handsome cutting material locally dubbed *poppy jasper* or *flowering jasper,* in allusion to the presence of bright red, yellow, green and brown spherules which resemble flowers. An examination of typical material shows a rather coarse structure of minute quartz rods growing radially from the centers of the spherules with each quartz rod impregnated by microscopic bodies of iron oxides of various colors. The most noted locality is popularly called "Morgan Hill" after the largest community in the vicinity although the deposit is actually adjacent to the bed of Llagas Creek, about 7 miles northwest of Gilroy. This deposit was discovered in 1935 after float pieces picked up some distance away were traced to their source. As the locality, a chert bed measuring 10 feet in depth penetrates a small hill and since 1935 has been quarried extensively to supply the constant demand. Although occurring in fairly large blocks, Morgan Hill chert is frequently criss-crossed by open seams and joints which trap polishing powder and cause disfigurement of finished pieces. The finest specimens exhibit flower-like orbs, averaging about ¼ inch to ⅜ inch in diameter and gaudily colored in reds, yellows, oranges, greens, and browns. The basic material is frequently a rich brown against which isolated orbs contrast well; other specimens show a multitude of orbs connected by curved contour lines and markings in interesting and complex patterns. Chert from this deposit has been extensively employed for book ends, ash trays, paperweights, and other larger items of lapidary work while smaller and more compact pieces have been used in tumbled gems and cabochons for jewelry. Several cabochons in the author's collection are illustrated in Figure 90.

Also in Santa Clara County, a grayish cherty material handsomely streaked with intense orange cinnabar stains, occurs in the New Almaden mercury mine near the town of the same name. Specimens are not very large but the swirled patterns caused by the brightly-colored cinnabar inclusions contrast well to the gray of the chert and provide very handsome cutting material.

In Amador County, fine large specimens of rock crystal, many worn to rounded cobbles, occur in streambeds in the vicinity of Oleta and Volcano; amethyst, smoky and rose quartz are found also. Calaveras County is world-famed for exceptionally large and flawless rock crystals which occur abundantly in gold-bearing gravels in the Mokelumne Hill area. The gold gravels are peculiar in that they represent well-defined ancient stream channels buried beneath enormous flows of basalt and preserved perfectly since the day raging volcanoes suddenly spewed forth their lavas upon this land. Found to be exceptionally rich in gold, these buried watercourses were mined intensively by shaft and tunnel until all of the profitable ground was excavated. During mining, very large masses of rock crystal were encountered, many flawless and eminently suited for lapidary applications. In some instances, individual crystals showed scarcely any signs of streamwear, indicating that their ancient source was not far away. The Tunnel Ridge Channel, as it has been called, located about 2½ miles south of Mokelumne Hill, has produced an enormous quantity of fine specimens. Over the last 20 years, it is estimated that the several mines exploiting this ancient river bed have produced over $150,000 worth of rock crystal. The Eclipse Mine, formerly known as the Infernal, is about 3 miles south of Mokelumne Hill and exploits an ancient channel about 200 feet wide containing uncemented gravel consisting primarily of well-rounded quartz pebbles, many large boulders of country rock, and clay, overlaid by cemented conglomerate, and further capped with basaltic lava. Much fine rock crystal has been won from this mine as well as gold. The Green Mountain Mine, formerly known as the McSorley, delves into an ancient channel of from 100 to 200 feet in width in which the beds of loose gravel are from 5 to 10 feet deep. Beautifully clear rock crystals of excellent external form were found in abundance and sold for optical and jewelry purposes both in the United States and in Europe. During World War II, most of the rock crystal production was purchased for piezoelectric application. Many of the crystals were large, some over 24 inches long and from 10 to 12 inches in diameter, slightly rounded by abrasion but otherwise perfect. The Rough Diamond Mine, lying between the Eclipse and Green Mountain, has also produced some large and fine crystals. Past records show that in 1897, the Green Mountain Mine produced an enormous crystal, almost flawless, weighing over 2200 pounds; the measurements were: 50 inches long, 42 by 38 inches in girth, however, it was not a single crystal but rather a group of which the largest individual measured 14 by 16 by 24 inches. When mined it was estimated that a sphere of 12 inches to 14 inches diameter could be cut from it, but history records no such sphere and it is assumed that flaws revealed by sectioning caused its owners to change their plans. In 1944, a 610 pound crystal was mined in the district and in the same year, the Calaveras Crystal Mining Company sent 1000 pounds of quartz for piezoelectric purposes to Washington, D.C. for the government stockpile but an agreement on price could not be reached and the material was returned. The American Museum of Natural History has in its collections a 6 inch sphere cut from one of the Mokelumne Hill rock crystals.

In Mono County, fine cutting grade dumortierite quartz is reported from the Champion Sillimanite Mine on White Mountain (see LAZULITE and AUGELITE).

In Contra Costa County, interesting blue-gray chalcedony nodules of almost spherical form occur in the lavas of the Moraga formation on the hills east of Berkeley. Productive deposits have been exposed by road and ditch cuts along Skyline Boulevard north from the intersection of Fish Ranch Road. Nodules vary in size from about 1 to 4 inches in diameter. In some instances, the banding shows iris structure and beautiful rainbow effects have been noted in some thin polished slabs.

In Monterey County, exceptionally handsome brecciated jasper occurs as an outcropping seam in the steep wall of Stone Canyon about 18 miles northeast of Bradley and accessible therefrom by road. The supply is seemingly inexhaustible and although many tons have been removed, much more remains. The prevailing color is yellow but interesting veinings and mottlings of brown, red, orange, and dead black are also present. One form, so distinctive that it can be recognized at once, consists of numerous angular patches of slightly olive-yellow jasper from ¼ to ½ inch across cemented together with cloudy white or slightly bluish chalcedony. Much of the material can be removed in large flawless blocks and appears eminently suited for larger lapidary projects.

In Fresno County, some very good orbicular chert with spherules of about ⅛ inch diameter occurs in Jacolito Canyon about 3½ miles south of Coalinga.

Tulare County is noted for fine chrysoprase which has been mined from a number of deposits and which at one time was of considerable economic importance. The best specimens are a lovely warm green, highly translucent, and probably unequalled in quality by material from any other locality in the world. In this county, chrysoprase is said to have been discovered in 1878 at the Venice Hill locality near Exeter by George W. Smith. One of the finest pieces ever found was picked up from the ground near the locality and proved to be a beautiful specimen measuring 3½ by 1½ inches. The Venice Hill mines are located on a group of small hills rising 100 to 300 feet above the surrounding plain in the NE. ¼ Section, 8 T., 18 S., Range 26 E., Mount Diablo Meridian. The hills extend to a distance of 2 miles north and south and about 1 mile from east to west; two prominent hills are included in the group of which the northernmost contain the mines along its southeast slope. The basic rock is serpentine. The second important locality is near Lindsay and was opened by the Himalaya Mining Company of New York City many years ago. Old chrysoprase pits are located along the northern end of a low hill near its summit about 1 mile east-southeast of Lindsay. The serpentine mass comprising the hill is about ⅓ mile in length and rises about 60 feet above the surrounding terrain. Veinlets of chalcedony cut through the serpentine and are slightly colored by nickel minerals but not sufficiently to be of good gem quality. Considerable greenish to yellowish common opal has been found also. The third locality, and also that which has produced the best material, is located 8 miles southeast of Porterville about ½ mile south of Deer Creek and was also mined by the Himalaya Mining Company many years ago. Located upon a rough knob of serpentine, veins of nickel-stained chalcedony can be traced some distance to the north along the top of the hill. The serpentine is frequently weathered badly next to the chrysoprase veins and is often impregnated with nickel minerals, however, in some places, it is firm and hard and approaches noble serpentine in quality. Chrysoprase is found as veinlets measuring ¼ to 8 or 10 inches in thickness. The color is very variable from vein to vein and even within various parts of the same vein with good material generally confined to the thinner veins or thinner parts of thick veins. Much chrysoprase was originally obtained by plowing at the base of the hill to recover fragments borne there by weathering. In 1906, about 3 tons were shipped from the mines, of which 300 pounds was said to be cuttable and retained for domestic use while poorer material was sent to Germany for employment in mosaic work. As at the other localities, common opal stained by nickel minerals was also abundant and in one place on the north side of the hill, some exceptional material was produced which was called *chrysopal* and used to some extent in lapidary applications. Beautiful specimens of chrysoprase have also been obtained from a serpentine hill just east of Plano and about 1½ to 2 miles south of Porterville.

In Kern County, the scheelite mines of the Greenhorn Mountains produce clear colorless and slightly smoky quartz crystals containing slender inclusions of dark green epidote; individual crystals up to 10 pounds in weight have been recorded. When the epidote is sufficiently fine and evenly distributed, interesting and beautiful cabochons can be cut from the material. For further details on these localities see SCHEELITE. Another popular collecting locality in this county is the narrow defile leading from Cache Creek Canyon called Horse Canyon. Cache Creek Canyon opens southward to the desert floor about 2 miles east of Monolith on Highway 466 but the actual collecting locality is about 7 miles up the canyon from its mouth and about 3 miles southwest of Cache Peak (elev. 6708 ft.), the highest peak in the vicinity. Moss agate of unique beauty is principally found here and is so characteristic that the name *Horse Canyon agate* is customarily used. The majority of agate is milky white with concentric fortification banding or

FIGURE 103. Cryptocrystalline quartz cabochons from a number of localities in California. Top: clear chalcedony containing slender hairlike inclusions. Upper left: dendritic chert, to its right, a brecciated chert marked with red veinings. Lower left: opaque patches of jaspery material cemented together with translucent greenish chalcedony. Bottom: a peculiar plaid-like chalcedony strongly resembling petrified wood but actually a silicified material of uncertain origin most closely resembling chert. The three cabochons on the right are "lace" and "tube" agate from the noted Horse Canyon deposit.

sometimes perfectly straight bands. Delicate veils of pale green mossy or lacy inclusions are suspended in clear chalcedony while in other types, tubular inclusions are common (see Figure 103). Most of the material occurs as seam and vein fillings and is not large in size although a single mass of over 69 pounds has been recorded. In the vicinity, jasper and petrified wood are also found. In other places in Kern County, agate, petrified wood, chert and jasper are found in the foothills of Castle Butte in an area immediately southeast and several miles north of Highway 466.

In San Bernardino County, fine sagenitic agate is found near Owl's Head

Springs in Owl's Head Canyon and in Wingate Canyon. Petrified wood is found in place and as float in Sperry Wash along a road which strikes east from Highway 127 where the latter crosses the Amargosa River a few miles southeast of the southern entrance to Death Valley National Monument. Red and white palm wood has been found here as well as black root and limb sections and some wood which is orange in color; also pink and tan cycad wood. An extensive area productive of many varieties of chalcedonic quartz lies in low hills and washes northeast of Eagle Crags about 40 miles north of Barstow. Beautiful bright blue chalcedony in thundereggs occurs in beds near Lead Pipe Springs, a locality discovered by F. M. Myrick in 1911 and worked by him in 1913. The springs are reached by poor roads from Granite Wells about 22 miles east of Atolia but the actual collecting grounds are about 2 miles northeast of the Springs. Lead Pipe Springs nodules consist of bright brownish-red silicified volcanic ash against which the blue to slightly purplish-blue chalcedony shows in pleasing contrast. Nodules range in size from an inch or two to some as much as 6 inches in diameter. Clear chalcedony, dotted with bright red inclusions of cinnabar, occur 15 miles northwest of Lead Pipe Springs and has been called *myrickite* in honor of the discoverer of this material.

The Calico Mountains north of Yermo also produce many quartz gemstones, mainly varieties of chalcedony; Mule Canyon in their southern part is a popular collecting locality, especially at the head of the canyon. The Kramer Hills about 30 miles north of Adelanto and along the Highway 395, have also produced much chalcedony in various forms. Similar gemstones occur west of Pisgah Crater south of Highway 66 and about 35 miles east of Daggett. Petrified palm wood and root sections, jasper and agate occur west of the road connecting Goffs and Lanfair and about 12 miles north of Goffs.

In Los Angeles County, chalcedonies are found in a deep canyon branching off Escondido Canyon, a locality reached by taking the Escondido Canyon Road from between Agua Dulce Canyon and Acton. Exceptional green moss agate, said to compare to the best from India and Oregon, has been found as well as sagenitic agate, bloodstone, various forms of jasper, banded agate, and even amethyst in geodes. Occurrences are in pillow basalts outcropping on private property whose owner charges a daily collecting fee. Basalt flows surrounding Calabasas on Highway 101, about 8 miles north of Malibu Beach, also produce agate, including sagenitic types, jasper, etc. The so-called "moonstones" found on the beaches of Los Angeles and adjacent counties, are merely translucent chalcedony.

In Riverside County, good *fire agate*, is found in the Mule Mountains southeast of Wiley Well in the southeast corner of the county. Ordinarily, this form of chalcedony appears as delicate, slightly pinkish translucent to opaque growths vaguely resembling flowers and called accordingly, *chal-*

cedony roses. In some, the presence of exceedingly minute platey crystals of goethite sprinkled over layers of chalcedony, causes beautiful iridescence and leads to such kinds being called fire agate. The finest material is found as botryoidal growths within cavities in larger "roses." Superficially, fire agate appears dull reddish-brown in color and quite uninteresting, however, when surface layers are carefully ground away to expose the iridescent layers, the rainbow colors of the latter begin to appear in increasing strength. By skillful work, the lapidary is able to remove intervening material until only the thinnest possible layer of chalcedony covers the iridescent goethite. At this time the specimen is polished to bring out most fully the beautiful glowing red, green, brown, and orange colors typical of this material. Though not spectacular, polished fire agates are very attractive and are seeing increasing use in inexpensive jewelry. The best locality for this material ap-

FIGURE 104. Pale smoky yellow quartz crystal of remarkable clarity from the Tourmaline Queen Mine, Pala, California. This almost flawless crystal measures almost 9 inches in length and 5 inches in diameter. The gems below have been cut from similar material, the largest gem on the right, cut in double brilliant fashion measuring slightly over 2 inches in diameter and weighing a little over 500 carats.

pears to be along the southwest side of the mountains about 3 miles south of Wiley Well and about 1 mile north of the Imperial County line. The hills surrounding Wiley Well also produce many kinds of chalcedonic gemstones and this entire area has been much visited by collectors. Rose quartz, sometimes of good grade, occurs in the cores of some of the pegmatites on Coahuila, Red, and Thomas mountains in the southern part of the County. Further details on these pegmatites as well as those in San Diego County may be consulted under TOURMALINE, BERYL, and SPODUMENE.

In San Diego County, the pegmatites producing the gemstones mentioned above, also produce many fine quartz crystals including colorless to slightly straw yellow specimens and exceptional smoky crystals of rich color. Especially fine examples have come from the mines of the Pala District; a typical clear crystal as well as several large stones faceted from flawless sections are shown in Figure 104. A fine sphere cut from Pala material is shown in Figure 105. Pale Rose quartz occurs in large amounts in the core of a pegmatite on the northwest slope of Pala Mountain several hundred feet above its base. Rose quartz was also mined from the Rose Quartz Mine located several miles south of the Esmeralda Mine (see TOURMALINE) on the lip of the Temescal Valley near Mesa Grande.

In Imperial County, many chalcedonic quartzes have been found in the Palo Verde Mountains in the northeast corner of the county, also in the Chocolate Mountains, an area now closed to collecting, and in the Cargo Muchacho Mountains in the southeast corner. Much dumortierite quartz of very deep blue color is found as boulders in a broad area centered about 10 to 12 miles north of Ogilby. The masses are often black-coated and lie scattered about along the beds of washes, especially on both sides of Indian Pass and in the Cargo Muchacho Mountains generally. At the Indian Pass locality, petrified palm root is also found. The dumortierite quartz from this area is not as fine as that from Nevada or Arizona.

Sonora. Small chalcedony geodes lined with beautiful and colorful agate, occur in streambeds near Oputo, a small town on the Rio De Bavispe about 25 miles southeast of Nacozari.

Chihuahua. After examining specimens of agate from many deposits in North and South America, as well as from Europe and other continents, the author cannot recall of any which excel in beauty those found in this Mexican State. Chihuahua agate nodules are naturally endowed with hues so vivid that no artificial staining is needed, indeed, some specimens are so gorgeously colored that it is difficult to believe that they have *not* been tampered with. Figure 106 has been drawn in color to illustrate a fine nodule slice which represents but one form these fascinating nodules can take and is a faithful representation of the original in the author's collection. Chihuahua agate is a relative newcomer to the gem market, being unknown except

Note: Figure 106 is in the color section following page 112.

FIGURE 105. A perfect 6 inch sphere of quartz made by George Ashley of Pala, California, from one of the clear crystals mined by him from the kunzite pegmatites of Hiriart Hill near Pala. The sphere has been cleverly photographed so that Hiriart Hill which appears in the background, along with Mr. Ashley's house, is sharply in focus.
Courtesy George Ashley.

to a few range riders until 1945 when quantities were gathered from the surface for shipment to the United States.

The initial collection of agate nodules eroded from volcanic rocks simply consisted of agate-seekers walking over the productive areas and gathering up the loose specimens. It is believed that the first material of this sort came from the Gallego and Sueco Ranches located about one hour's drive south of Villa Ahumada, along the main highway from Juarez to Chihuahua City. Much of this material had assumed gorgeous coloration after untold years of exposure upon the surface and connoisseurs generally agree that it included some of the finest agate ever found. Needless to say, most of these nodules have long since been skimmed off by local collectors who sell them to dealers. Some nodules containing clear chalcedony, exhibit strong iris effects and were formerly found among the material gathered from the Gallego area. Nowadays, a small quantity of agate is found by digging or searching washes and gullies after infrequent rain showers. The largest nodule of record from this area weighs 69 pounds and is now in the possession of the Southern Gem & Mineral Company of El Paso, Texas.

The agate of the Sueco Ranch is similar to the Gallego material except that less iris is found and more of the nodules are hollow. It has been estimated that 80 per cent of the Sueco nodules and 50 per cent of the large nodules from Gallego are hollow (geodes) but small nodules from the latter ranch show cavities only 20 per cent of the time. Of all nodules found, only 10 per cent are 2 inches or more in diameter while the remainder range from less than 2 inches to as little as ¾ inch in diameter. Upon both ranches, owners prohibit collecting since their primary revenue is derived from cattle-raising and anything disrupting this pursuit is looked upon with much disfavor. Mountainous areas on both ranches contain much agate still in place but these deposits may never be exploited properly unless the property owners change their views.

One of the finest agate varieties from Chihuahua is a lovely rich purple kind, a color most unusual in any form of chalcedony and not even reproduced in dyed material. This type has been found to the east of Gallego and occurs only within a small area. South of the Gallego and Sueco Ranches, much agate, similar in form and color, has been removed from the Borunda Ranch area, sometimes known as Ojo Laguna, lying about 20 miles south of Gallego. Truly colorful and valuable material from this area averages only 20 per cent of the total recovered. Current supplies to the market are produced by opencut mining upon some of the nodule-bearing outcrops.

The area beginning south of the Villa Ahumada and ending just south of Ojo Laguna is approximately 70 miles in length and is the most important agate producing district of Mexico. Deposits of agate nodules are found in widely-scattered surface patches but in-place occurrences are relatively few in number. Nearly all of the agate is banded but some fine moss agate and red jasper have also been found. The first significant deposit lies a short distance southeast of Villa Ahumada followed by another concentration discovered some years ago near the village of Moctezuma. Some very fine material has come from the latter place but most lacks color and compares unfavorably with agate from Gallego, Sueco, or Ojo Laguna. West of Villa Ahumada is found an interesting material called *lace agate* in which ribbon- and flower-like patterns are enclosed in translucent chalcedony, however, the majority of the material is essentially banded agate. Approximately 15 per cent is colorful and suited for fine gems. This material is obtained by blasting chalcedony-bearing rhyolite, and, unfortunately, much of the material is fractured in the process. Also west of Villa Ahumada, an agate best described as *flame agate* has been mined in recent years. Unlike most agate, it shows few pronounced bandings but contains, instead, long streaks or "flames" of bright red color enclosed in highly translucent colorless chalcedony. The same deposit produces a material containing clusters of colored spots which the Mexican miners call *fisheye agate*. Chalcedony masses from this mine are produced in individual pieces up to 47 pounds in weight. Not far away, is found an area from which has been gathered much blue chalcedony in all shades from light to dark blue but probably less than 5 per cent is deep fine blue. Most is without banding, seldom over an inch or two in size, and eminently suited for tumbling.

A beautiful and spectacular plume agate has lately reached the market from a deposit in northeastern Chihuahua in amounts estimated as totalling 15,000 pounds in the last several years. Much material contains small cavities as is usually the case with plume agates, but a small percentage is solid and of high quality. The most interesting types consist of golden or white inclusions in clear chalcedony masses, the latter sometimes reaching the market in flawless blocks up to 14 inches in length. Black plumes are also found as well as a kind in which the inclusions are more globular and form the so-called "flowering" agates.

Isolated patches of agate-bearing rhyolites occur south of the areas just described and do not end until Hidalgo del Parral is reached, almost 250 miles as the crow flies from Villa Ahumada. South of the city of Chihuahua, some agate has been mined also but only in small amounts. Agate of good quality is found northeast of Aldama, a community located about 20 miles northeast of Chihuahua; also west of Ciudad Camargo; southwest of Valle de Zaragoza; and west of Valle de Rosario. The last two localities are 50 to 75 miles southwest of Ciudad Camargo respectively. Some fine red plume agate has been obtained recently from a deposit southeast of Reforma. Considerable quantities of banded and other varieties of agate have been found in the Casa Grande area but little is of good color. Casa Grande is located about 80 miles west-southwest of Villa Ahumada in the northeastern part of the state.

Sinaloa. Small crystals of amethyst, loose or forming druses, occur in fissures in rock in a deposit near Culiacan. Early records indicate that much amethyst was obtained by the Jesuit Fathers from about 1685 to 1760 from a deposit to the northeast of Sinaloa de Leyva.

Durango. Considerable quantities of petrified wood, agate, and other varieties of chalcedonic quartz are reported from the hills and mountains surrounding the Bolson de Mapimi in the northeastern corner of the state. The Nazas River near Rodeo has yielded good plume and black agate. Rodeo is on the main highway between Chihuahua and Victoria de Durango. Petrified wood occurs near Mezquital, a small town about 40 miles south-southeast of Victoria de Durango.

Zacatecas. The mercury mines of this state sometimes provide gray chalcedony in which spots and streaks of vivid red cinnabar render the material suitable for ornamental purposes.

San Luis Potosi. Jasper occurs in the Mina Cerro del Leon near Reyes in the Santa Maria del Rio District.

Nayarit. Green jasper is found in the Sierra de Juanacate; amethyst is mined near Zapilote in the Santiago Ixcuintla District.

Jalisco. Agate is reported from the Teocaltiche District in the northern part of the state and also in the area extending southwestward as far as Yahualica, a distance of about 40 miles.

Guanajuato. In the immediate vicinity of the city of Guanajuato occur a series of rich silver veins from whose central portions have come enormous quantities of drusy amethyst. Crystals are generally small and of little value for anything except tumbled gems although fine specimens are prized by mineral collectors. In the mines, many of them hundreds of years old, amethyst occurs associated with white calcite and various metal sulfides. In some places, sheets of small crystals are found beautifully encrusted by pink and white apophyllite. Amethyst crystals are often peculiarly dark at the base and lighter toward the tips. Wall linings of cavities, uniformly covered by crystals of about ¾ inch in length and about ¼ inch thick, are commonly found in sheets over a foot across; an example of this material is shown in Figure 80. The principal mines are all within a five-mile circle of Guanajuato and exploit various veins of which the Veta Madre or "Mother Lode" is the largest. The Valenciana Mine has been an especially prolific producer of amethyst as well as the Guanajuato, Santa Rosa and Calvillo mines.

Hidalgo. Jasper occurs in quantity in the Pachuca District at the Del Monte Mine, the Cuesta de San Bernardo and along the highway between Guadelupe and Zacaultipan. Amethyst is found in openings in the silver veins in the mines of the Pachuca District. Some chalcedony is also encountered in these ore bodies. Mines specially noted for their amethyst are the Real del Monte and the Dolores. Petrified wood occurs near the Salitera Mine and on the Hacienda de Yextho in the Huichapan District.

Michoacan. Jasper and agate occur near Tlalpujahua and the Espiritu Santo Mine in the Maravatio District.

Morelos. Green jasper occurs near Puebla Ayala in the Morelos District.

Veracruz. Early Spanish chronicles record rock crystal mines worked by the Aztecs in the mountains along the Gulf of Mexico between Veracruz and the Coatzualco River.

Tlaxcala. Petrified wood is found in the Sierra de las Silicates in the vicinity of Tlaxcala.

Guerrero. Jasper and agate occur in the Ollas de Chilapa in the Alvarez District. Much amethyst, some of good faceting grade, occurs in the Municipio de Balsas; cabochon grade material has been mined extensively in the Barranca de los Ocotes not far from Taxco de Alarcon; facet grade material comes from the Sierra Madre del Sur not far from the small village of Amatillan. This material was first worked intensively in modern times in 1933 when much of the production was absorbed by the famous silversmiths of Taxco. Silver jewelry set with amethyst cabochons is commonly displayed in many shops in Mexico and even in those in the United States which specialize in Mexican arts and crafts.

Baja California Norte. Tourmalinated quartz is abundant at the sphene locality (see SPHENE) at Pino Solo south of Ojos Negros where it occurs as core material in a series of weathered pegmatite dikes. Unfortunately, the vast majority of specimens are too dark and flawed to be of much value but occasionally a fine piece is found. The tourmaline needles range in size from slender threads to some which are as thick as darning needles; their color is black. Abundant moss agate and mossy jasper is reported from the eastern slopes of the flat-topped hills forming the western boundaries of interior valleys in the vicinity of El Marmol, the place noted for its calcite onyx quarries (see CALCITE).

Guatemala. Deposits of clear rock crystals suitable for electronic purposes have been found in the Department of Baja Verapaz, north of Guatemala City. The crystals occur in pockets within quartz veins penetrating gneisses and schists. The average weight of single crystals is reported to be from ½ to 1 pound.

El Salvador. Amethyst of fine quality is said to occur in Goascoran but the exact locality is not specified.

Panama. The wealth of the Republic of Panama and the Canal Zone in cryptocrystalline quartz varieties, much of which are of gem quality, is just now beginning to be realized. In addition, some fine amethyst has been found in chalcedony geodes near the Madden Dam in the Canal Zone but the exact locality seems not to have been discovered as yet. It is estimated that over half of the Republic is covered with igneous rocks, mostly extrusive types associated with volcanic activity. Very little granite or schist is found but sedimentary rocks are common, including those formed of volcanic ash and other debris. Most of the volcanic rocks are relatively recent in age while some of the extinct volcanoes in the Isthmus look so fresh that they seem to have stopped activity only yesterday. Principal rock types are andesite, basalt, and rhyolite, plus many tuffs and sedimentary ash beds in which are found boulders and fragments of lava and much silica. Exploration of the Isthmus is difficult because of the truly wet tropical climate which encourages everywhere a lush growth of vegetation, and in favorable places, supports almost impenetrable jungles, however, some areas can be penetrated more easily than others if watercourses are followed. Conspicuous rock outcrops are lacking because of their rapid decomposition and tenacious coverage by vegetation. If the quantity of agate, chalcedony, jasper, and petrified wood found near the Canal is any indication, enormous quantities must await the determined prospector within the hundreds of square miles of land which up to now has been examined only cursorily.

Much gem material was excavated from the volcanic ash formations during the construction of the Panama Canal. The principal cuts were made in the Pacific side and the debris dumped in low places to fill noxious mangrove swamps noted as breeding places of malarial mosquitoes. Thus, from Gamboa on Gatun Lake, to Balboa on the Pacific side, quartz gemstones may be obtained in many places if one troubles to locate old fill dumps and to dig in them. Unfortunately, most dumps have been obscured by heavy underbrush or used as sites for buildings since level land in the mountainous Isthmus is very limited. Large dumps were laid down at Mile 36 just southeast of the ghost town of Empire along the southern side of the canal; also on the northern side just west of Gold Hill. A large dump now densely covered with vegetation but still accessible to the determined collector, was emplaced immediately to the west of the Miraflores Locks on the north side of the Canal, and when active, was called the Cardenas Dump. A small but unusually rich dump is located also on the north side directly across from Corozal and at the point where the canal leaves hilly terrain and enters the tidal flats and mangrove swamps of the Pacific side. This place is several miles southeast of Cocoli and is accessible by car over a poor road which turns off the highway connecting the locks and Cocoli a short distance from the latter place. Much material has also been sprinkled about on the shores of the Bay of Panama, an especially fruitful place being the tidal flats along the point leading to FarFan.

Much of the jasper, agate, and chalcedony found in the Isthmus represents vein and seam fillings in lavas and tuffs but the exact place of origin has not been found. Significantly, most specimens are somewhat waterworn and indicate weathering from formations which may not now be in existence. Near the Culebra Cut where constant work is in progress on the north side to arrest slides, fresh basalt is exposed but shows only zeolite minerals in cavities plus a small amount of ordinary fresh gray chalcedony. Some of the sedimentary formations nearby contain large logs of poorly silicified wood which retain much of their carbon and therefore prove totally unfit for cutting. Better material is found in stream beds and in cuts near the junction of the Trans-Isthmian Highway and the turnoff to Gamboa on the western side of the Canal. Palm wood of brown color has been found here in waterworn fragments as well as several other unidentified tree species. Also found here are silicified coral and a bewildering variety of jasper, but very little chalcedony or agate. All material is deeply altered and largely unfit for cutting because of porosity. The hills near Madden Lake commonly provide masses of chalcedony and agate which from their configuration show that they have formed as cores within pockets lined originally with calcite crystals. During the construction of Madden Dam, chalcedony geodes lined with quartz crystals, including amethyst, were found in the bed of the Chagres River. A huge geode half is on the lawn in front of the local Canal Zone Police Station and consists of a 2 inch thick lining of gray chalcedony coated in the interior with large milky quartz crystals. If memory serves correctly, this geode half is about 20 inches in diameter.

Aside from petrified wood, the usual Canal Zone chalcedony consists of highly translucent material showing very little banding but frequently containing green mossy inclusions ranging from those which are so small that they form what appears to be green jasper or bloodstone, to those which are large and wispy forming material very similar to the Oregon moss agates. Much ordinary chalcedony is converted into carnelian, sometimes of very fine quality, while a unique black agate found in abundance, represents infusion by some as yet unidentified substance, possibly an organic compound. Very fine specimens of both types are found in the Cocoli dump and near FarFan. Strongly-banded agate is very rare but at least one fine specimen was found by the author near Empire. Green moss agate lumps and masses of jasper many pounds in weight have been discovered in various dumps but such pieces are seldom all of good quality throughout. Blue chalcedony replacing wood is reported from the Cerro Azul in Panama Province, Republic of Panama.

Cuba. A famous locality for chalcedony is situated in the immediate vicinity of Madruga about 66 kilometers southeast of Havana in Havana Province. Chalcedony occurs here as vein fillings and as geodes in serpentine and chalk in an area of 6 square kilometers centered about Madruga. Some of the hollow chalcedony masses contain beautiful stalactitic growths which have caused them to be prized as mineral specimens. Masses of chalcedony reach as much as 25 pounds in weight. Specific localities are Chivo Hill, Copey Hill and Jiquima Hill. In the vicinity, agate and jasper are also found. Beautiful agate occurs in commercial quality and quantity at a place 7 miles south of Bayamo in Oriente Province; also 2 miles southeast of Jibacoa, a small town about 16 miles southeast of Manzanillo.

Jamaica. Agate and jasper pebbles derived from the weathering of conglomerates are found in beautiful specimens, sometimes of large size, near the old mines in Upper Clarendon, in alluvial deposits on Hollis'

Savanna, on the savannas of Vere and also in Hector's River Valley, Manchester, and elsewhere. Much colorful banded chert is found as pebbles in various places upon the Island.

Puerto Rico. Amethyst similar to Uruguayan, occurs in chalcedony geodes in limestone about 2 miles southeast of the town of Aguada in the northwestern part of the Island. This same area also produces ordinary grayish chalcedony but nothing of outstanding interest is reported. Chalcedony occurs abundantly throughout the Barrio Piedras Blanca near Aguada. Jasper is found in the Barrio Lejas in association with manganese ores in the southern part of the Island of Juana Diaz; also near the Barrio Bartolo Lares associated with similar ores.

Antigua. Beautiful silicified wood retaining perfectly the structure of the original is found in beds of impure flinty or cherty limestone. These beds have been known since at least 1723 for one geologic work of this date mentions their existence. Many specimens of the wood have been widely distributed in Europe but this material is little known in the United States. Tree species represented are mainly dicotyledons and monocotyledons but no conifers have been found. In a paper dated 1883, sixteen species were described of which five were palms and the remainder dicotyledons. Beautiful examples of petrified wood are found at Corbizon Point, along the north shore of Willoughby Bay, and throughout the central plain of the island especially in the middle part where they are frequently found lying upon the surface in fragments of varying size. Many years ago, a log 12 inches in diameter and 14 feet in length was unearthed. Silicified wood is also plentiful at Bellevue and Cassada Gardens. Silicified shells and corals, the latter especially fine, are also found in the limestones at Wetherill's Bay and at Hodge's Bay; also at High Point and Willoughby Bay. Corals show perfectly the markings of each organism and furnish fine cutting material which has seen extensive use in European cutting centers and is the material which has been known for many years as *beekite* or *beckite*.

Guadeloupe. Chalcedony occurs generally throughout the island but is stated to be abundant in the neighborhood of Ste. Anne; silicified wood is also found in many places but the Savane des Salines is mentioned as a specific locality.

CHAPTER V

Rare and Unusual Gemstones

GEMSTONES which occur in forms suitable for faceted and cabochon gems and other ornamental applications, but which are seldom seen in standard jewelry:

PRINCIPALLY FROM PEGMATITES:
Chrysoberyl
Rutile
Petalite
Pollucite
Phenakite
Axinite
Microlite
Stibiotantalite
Beryllonite
Apatite
Amblygonite
Brazilianite
Lazulite

FROM VARIOUS IGNEOUS ROCKS:
Cassiterite
Diaspore
Enstatite, Hypersthene
Zircon

FROM ORE VEINS AND QUARTZ VEINS:
Algodonite and Domeykite
Sphalerite
Niccolite, Smaltite,
Cobaltite, Breithauptite
Zincite
Rhodochrosite
Willemite
Friedelite
Hodgkinsonite
Sphene
Augelite
Scheelite

FROM METAMORPHIC LIMESTONES:
Diopside
Anthophyllite, Actinolite,
Tremolite
Scapolite
Danburite
Chondrodite

FROM SERPENTINE:
Benitoite

FROM SCHISTS AND GNEISSES:
Iolite
Andalusite
Kyanite
Epidote and Piedmontite
Staurolite

FROM SEDIMENTARY DEPOSITS:
Colemanite
Barite
Celestite

FROM OUTER SPACE:
Tektite

407

CHRYSOBERYL

Although an important gemstone in other parts of the world, chryso-beryl has been found only in very minor amounts in North America. It is primarily a pegmatite mineral but despite the abundance of these formations in this continent, almost all crystals found have proved to be of mineralogical interest only.

LOCALITIES

Maine. Several localities are known in Oxford County. Many years ago a fine crystal ½ inch by 2 inches was found in pegmatite on the steep south slope of Hedgehog Hill in Peru Township; from this specimen a perfect one carat gem was cut of greenish-yellow color. In Hartford Township some chrysoberyl was found in the debris at the southwest base of Ragged Jack Mountain, 2 miles due south of the southern end of Worthley Pond, where it had evidently weathered from a pegmatite further up the slope. Crystals reached 2 inches in length and show transparent spots of pale wine yellow suitable for faceting. Some examples showed the prized bluish sheen of true catseye.

New York. An old locality for chrysoberyl is recorded from a pegma-tite not far from Saratoga Springs, Saratoga County. This dike was worked as early as 1821 and then was "lost" for many years until rediscovered about 1955. The locality is immediately west of a small pond just north of the township road which crosses Highway 9 leading north from Saratoga Springs. The pond is about ½ mile west of the intersection of the township road with Highway 9. The occurrence is in a small pegmatite dike which is only several feet thick and tapers toward either end. Individual crystals from here reached ¾ by 1½ inches in size, occasionally showing small clear areas.

RUTILE

Rutile is best known to gem collectors as the coppery needles which penetrate clear quartz to form the variety known as *sagenite,* or more poetically, *fleches d'amour,* the French term for "arrows of Love." Another equally romantic name is *Venus hairstone,* applied to a kind in which golden needles lie thick and tress-like. The gossamer threads in quartz are actually individual crystals which, by some freak of nature, have grown along one axis until they are thousands of times longer than usual. In contrast to this freakish form, rutile found elsewhere ranges from slender darning-needle prisms to stout squarish individuals which bear no resemblance whatsoever to those found in quartz. The latter are never clear enough to cut, but those of more slender habit sometimes are and then afford beautiful deep red gems of steely luster. In all of North America, such material is found only in Alexander County, North Carolina.

When pure, rutile is simple titanium dioxide with the formula TiO_2 and crystallizes in the Tetragonal System. For practical purposes, the ideal state of purity is never reached in nature since small quantities of iron or other elements are always present. In North Carolina, loose rutile crystals of wonderful transparency and deep ruby color have been found in a number of places where they weather from the enclosing schists underlying the area. It is most likely that these originated in cavities, since it is in openings in pegmatite that identical crystallizations accompany emerald and green spodumene at the famous Hiddenite locality. Such crystals are very beautiful in themselves; they appear as slender striated pencils crossing each other in flat nets

FIGURE 107. Reticulated rutile crystals from Hiddenite, North Carolina. Many of these crystals are completely transparent.

or ladder-like arrangements. Figure 107 shows a typical reticulated group of North Carolina rutiles. Although many are transparent, their usefulness for gems is impaired by hollow tubes which run down their centers and make each crystal a thin-walled cylinder. Others are suitable in all respects and can be faceted successfully.

The hardness of rutile varies from 6 to 6½, and although it is brittle, it is not easily broken. The fracture surfaces are conchoidal and display the adamantine luster so characteristic of this mineral. In spite of the fair degree of hardness, rutile is polished with difficulty, tending to chip along sharp edges and develop striations on facet surfaces. For this reason, plus the scarcity of clear material of pale red color, faceted gems are rarely seen even in the most complete collections.

Rutile is very high in specific gravity; between 4.20 and 4.30. Its refractive indices are also high: $\omega = 2.62$, $\epsilon = 2.90$; birefringence 0.38; uniaxial, positive. Peculiarly enough, the high indices are troublesome because they give rise to the strong adamantine luster which is almost metallic in its brightness. This reflection from the surface of cut gems often masks the true color which would otherwise be rich red. Dichroism is strong, showing in one direction deep red, and in the other, extremely dark red, sometimes almost black.

North Carolina. Magnificent crystals of rutile, perfectly clear and of deep red color, have been found in limonite and quartz near Liberty Church, Alexander Co. Accounts of early finds mention some crystals which reached as much as 6 inches in length and ⅔ inch in diameter although the majority were much less. Similar specimens have been found near Millholland's Mill, at White Plains, near Taylorsville and Stony Point. The locality at Hiddenite is the same which yielded emeralds and the green variety of spodumene known as *hiddenite*. These gemstones were found in cavities in pegmatite along with beautifully sharp lustrous crystals of rutile, the latter in singles and in flat reticulated masses. Sometimes rutile was the predominant mineral in a pocket, almost nothing else but a little quartz being found. Further details concerning this locality can be consulted under SPODUMENE and BERYL.

PETALITE

This curious gemstone, noted for nothing so much as its rarity in clear form, is lithium aluminum silicate. Ordinarily it occurs in laminated white masses in complex pegmatite bodies but is nowhere common except in a few occurrences in Africa. The name is derived from the Greek word for "leaf" in allusion to its cleavage. Sometimes transparent material is called *castorite*, but this name is now seldom encountered; for its derivation see POLLUCITE.

Crystallizing in the Monoclinic System, petalite is very rare in crystals, the usual form being glassy to pearly masses which have few distinguishing marks about them. Its formula is $LiAl(Si_2O_5)_2$. An easily developed and perfect cleavage causes most masses to shatter so thoroughly that only small clear areas are obtainable for cutting into transparent faceted gems. This perfect cleavage sometimes causes confusion with spodumene with which it is frequently associated in pegmatites. It is brittle but fairly hard, 6 to 6½, and possesses low specific gravity, ranging from 2.39 to 2.46. Refractive indices are $a = 1.504$, $\beta = 1.510$, $\gamma = 1.516$; birefringence 0.012; biaxial, positive.

Maine. The only locality in North America from which suitable cutting material came is a pegmatite quarry at the base of Noyes Mountain, Greenwood Township, Oxford County. Occurring in considerable quantity in massive form, it was first thought to be spodumene and it is said that 8 tons were removed before its true identity was established.

POLLUCITE

Another rare mineral sometimes used for gems is pollucite, a hydrous cesium aluminum silicate with the formula: $Cs_4Al_4Si_9O_{26} \cdot H_2O$. It is found only in a few pegmatite bodies where it occurs in granular masses, generally opaque white in color but sometimes clear and capable of being cut into faceted gems. For all practical purposes, the entire supply of gem material has come from one quarry in Maine although small clear sections are known to occur in massive pollucite from other localities. If pollucite were more abundant it would become a valuable ore of cesium, but at the moment it is mainly a mineralogical curiosity and to the connoisseur of gemstones, a desirable addition to his collection on account of its rarity. Pollucite was originally named *pollux* and another mineral now called petalite, was named *castor* since both were thought to be inseparable companions in pegmatite bodies rich in lithium just as the Heavenly Twins of astronomy or of Greek mythology, Castor and Pollux were also inseparable.

Crystals of pollucite are extremely scarce, those that have been found forming in cubes in accordance with the Isometric crystallization of this mineral. Although brittle, pollucite is surprisingly hard. Textbook values range from as low as $5\frac{1}{4}$ to a high of $6\frac{1}{2}$ but lapidary treatment shows abrasive reactions similar to quartz, and hence a hardness closer to 7. Pollucite shows no trace of cleavage, massive specimens invariably breaking with conchoidal fractures with a peculiar dull waxy luster. In the field, it is difficult to distinguish pollucite from ordinary massive varieties of crystalline quartz but the waxy luster mentioned is sufficiently distinct to be helpful. Pollucite from a number of Maine localities shows variations in specific gravity ranging from 2.94 to 2.98, the higher values indicative of a higher content of cesium. Since this mineral belongs to the Isometric System, the refraction is single, varying in value from specimen to specimen only in accordance with the relative proportions of cesium and aluminum. Higher indices are noted with higher percentages of cesium, the general range being $n = 1.507$-1.526, but the gem material from the famous Buckfield locality is fairly constant at $n = 1.520$. Transparent material varies from colorless to faintly pink or yellow but seldom without a slight milkiness from submicroscopic inclusions or structural irregularities. Common massive material is usually brilliant snow white to grayish, depending on the fineness of the particles, and shows a slight pearly luster. Visible inclusions in clear material are of two types, both highly interesting: the first and most prominent, are pure white "snowflakes" about 1/64 inch in diameter with bulges in their centers; the second are exceedingly fine silvery needles arranged at random and not at all plentiful. These can be barely distinguished with a ten power loupe in good light. The snowflake inclusions seem to be oriented in specific directions but the needles are not. The presence of the larger inclusions in field specimens suspected to be pollucite, is a valuable means of identification.

Pollucite seldom occurs in large clear sections and most finished stones, are therefore less than several carats in weight. The author has two stones, a pinkish step cut gem of 3/8 inch by 5/16 inch, weighing 3.85 carats, and another oval mixed cut, quite colorless, weighing 1.60 carats. The first is from Buckfield and is remarkable for its snowflake inclusions; the second is from Newry (Plumbago Mountain) and shows only minute needle-like inclusions. These appear also in the Buckfield stone but are overshadowed by the larger inclusions.

LOCALITIES

Maine. Virtually all of our gem quality pollucite has been removed from transparent portions of large masses found in pegmatite at Dudley's Ledge in Buckfield. Here on the north slope of a small conical hill about 2 ½ miles southwest of the village of Buckfield and about ¼ mile south of Highway 117 in Buckfield Township, Oxford County, are several openings which were made for feldspar many years ago by Perien Dudley and W. S. Robinson. Pollucite occurred in granular masses associated with beryl, both ordinary and cesium-bearing, colored tourmaline, amblygonite, arsenopyrite, lollingite, and cassiterite as well as the usual quartz, feldspar, and mica. Some of the masses reached 8 inches to 10 inches across. In other parts of Oxford County, pollucite has been found in granular masses in Greenwood Township at the western base of Noyes Mountain near the south end of Hicks Pond; also at Hebron, Mt. Mica, Newry, and other places. At times some small fragments of transparent material have come from these places.

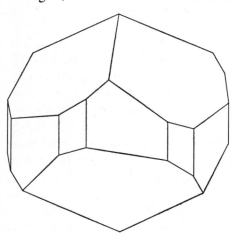

FIGURE 108. Phenakite crystal from Mount Antero, Colorado.

PHENAKITE

Named for the Greek word "to deceive," phenakite ordinarily occurs in colorless crystals long mistaken for quartz or even white tourmaline. It is true that its crystals bear a slight resemblance to both these minerals but in all major respects there is no relationship. Phenakite is frequently found in collections of cut gems as a curiosity only, however, it takes an excellent polish and finished gems are often quite brilliant.

Phenakite is beryllium silicate, Be_2SiO_4, and, like many other beryllium minerals, is found mainly in small cavities in pegmatites associated with quartz, feldspar, and topaz. Belonging to the Hexagonal System, its well-developed crystals are capped by low pyramids while the numerous prismatic faces cause some individuals to become almost circular in outline (see Figure 108). Most crystals are compressed along the vertical axis and therefore tabular in general appearance. Small crystals are often transparent but larger crystals are flawed and clouded by many inclusions near the centers, leaving only the rims clear enough to facet. Phenakite is hard, between $7\frac{1}{2}$ and 8, and also surprisingly tough. Fracture surfaces are conchoidal and the luster glassy. Specific gravity ranges between 2.97 and 3.0. Refractive indices are medium in value: $\omega = 1.651\text{-}1.666$, $\epsilon = 1.653\text{-}1.668$; birefringence 0.015; uniaxial, positive. The majority of phenakite crystals are perfectly colorless but pale yellow crystals are also known. Flawless cut gems seldom exceed several carats in weight.

FIGURE 109. Translucent to transparent twinned phenakite crystals from a gem pocket found in the noted Mount Antero region of Colorado. Associated minerals are feldspar and mica. The largest crystal is about ½ inch across. Courtesy Smithsonian Institution.

LOCALITIES

Maine. The noted topaz locality atop Lord's Hill in the southwestern corner of Stoneham Township, Oxford County, produced small quantities of phenakite crystals from pockets in pegmatite.

New Hampshire. Small crystals have been found in pockets in pegmatite associated with topaz on Baldface Mountain, near Chatham, Carroll County (see TOPAZ).

Virginia. The Morefield Mine, 4 miles northeast of Amelia, Amelia County, is reported to have produced transparent crystals from a complex pegmatite noted primarily for its amazonite (see FELDSPAR). Crystals were stated to be well-formed and ranged in size from ½ inch to as much as 2 inches in length.

Colorado. Good clear crystals have often been found in pockets in numerous pegmatites atop Mount Antero and White Mountain in Chaffee County. Associated minerals are quartz, feldspar and the blue aquamarines for which this locality is noted. Crystals range from opaque white to colorless or sometimes slightly tinged with yellow. Both single and twin crystals occur, ranging from minute prisms to individuals over an inch in diameter. The crystals from this region are noted for their prismatic habit, being much less flattened than those from other places (see Figure 109). Another well-known locality is Crystal Peak, north of Florissant in Teller County, where phenakite occurs as flat rhombohedral crystals in pegmatite pockets associated with amazonite, topaz, quartz and other minerals. For further information on the above localities, refer to BERYL and TOPAZ.

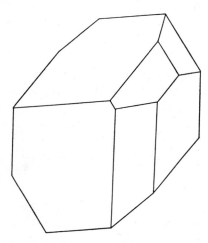

FIGURE 110. A simple axinite crystal. It is difficult in a drawing to show the thinness of these crystals but it is sufficient to say that in this crystal, the depth near the center is only a fraction of the width.

AXINITE

Often mentioned in gem literature, axinite is found in surprisingly few collections, and, likely as not, in very poor examples. Although widely distributed and not especially uncommon as a mineral, transparent crystals of sufficient size for cutting are very rare, and on this account, the supply of faceting rough has never kept up with the demand. Most crystals suitable for cutting are generally some shade of brown and strongly absorptive of light, resulting in rather dark finished gems of more interest to the collector than to the admirer of beauty. Axinite crystals are thin, wafer-like, and extremely sharp-edged, a habit which is so characteristic that the species name has been derived from the Greek word for "axe" in allusion to their form. A typical axinite crystal is drawn in Figure 110.

Axinite is a boro-silicate of aluminum and calcium with iron and manganese appearing in varying amounts; the formula is as follows: $H(Ca,Mn,Fe)_3Al_2B(SiO_4)_4$. It is commonly found in veins in granitic rocks or in metamorphic rocks near contacts with granite masses. Crystals are seldom perfectly transparent, being filled with veils of bubbles or numerous small fractures; inclusions of foreign minerals are frequent also. Hardness is medium, ranging from about 6½ to 7. One good cleavage is present but not easily develop ; ordinary fracture surfaces are conchoidal with glassy luster. The specific gravity varies between 3.27 and 3.29 but gem material is closer to the upper value. Refractive indices are: $a = 1.678$, $\beta = 1.685$, $\gamma = 1.688$; birefringence 0.010; biaxial, negative. Gem material is listed in some references as narrower in range, namely: $a = 1.674$, $\gamma = 1.684$. The pleiochroism of axinite is one of its marked characteristics and collectors are able to identify specimens at a glance by noting the changing colors as cut gems are rotated in the light. Under a dichroscope, the following colors have been noted in dark brown gems from Luning, Nevada: straw yellow, deep purplish-red, dark reddish brown.

LOCALITIES

New Jersey. Many years ago, some splendid crystals of clear yellow axinite were found in the northern underground workings of the New Jersey Zinc Company's mine at Mine Hill, Franklin, Sussex County. These crystals were stated to be an inch across and perfectly transparent.

Nevada. Bladed aggregates, sometimes several inches across, of plum-colored axinite have been found in the mines of the Luning District, Mineral County. In these masses, clear spots occur large enough for small faceted gems.

California. Transparent waterworn gem quality crystals have been found in the gold-bearing gravels of the Feather River in Yuba County. A specimen in the author's collection is a partly-rounded crystal about ¾ inch long and 1/2 inch wide and about 3/16 inch thick. A stone of several carats could easily be cut from it. Its pleiochroism is marked but differs somewhat from that noted in Luning, Nevada material; the colors are: pale yellow, pale violet, and brownish-orange. The body color is pale brown. Similar crystals have also been reported from gravels in the vicinity of Yankee Hill, Butte County, just to the north of Yuba County.

Magnificent large brown axinite crystals associated with dark grayish-green fibrous actinolite (byssolite) and sphene occur in cavities in a pegmatite about 2 miles north of Coarse Gold, Madera County (some say 5 miles northeast of this town). From an unspecified locality near Springerville in this same county, some astonishingly fine specimens of axinite were obtained some years ago, providing what are probably the world's finest crystallized examples of this mineral. One matrix group in the possession of the United States National Museum is about 5 inches across and shows magnificent perfect crystals, some well over an inch across and at least ¼ inch thick, resting upon a matrix of rock associated with actinolite. The color is rich brown and at least one of the crystals is almost flawless. The occurrence was exploited

FIGURE 111. A splendid group of transparent brown axinite crystals of superb gem quality from near Madera, California, and possibly the finest of their kind known. The typical "axe" shape of the individual crystals is apparent. Specimen size, 7 inches by 5 inches; largest crystals approximately 2¾ inches long; associated mineral is green fibrous actinolite (byssolite). Courtesy Smithsonian Institution.

in great secrecy and no one seems able or willing to tell where it is. Figure 111 is a photograph of the specimen referred to.

Glassy, sharp crystals of axinite, said to be of gem quality, were found many years ago in a prospect in Moosa Canyon near Escondido, San Diego County. A very late report indicates that fine axinite crystals containing clear gem areas were found near Fallbrook in San Diego County by Bud Francis, however, details concerning the occurrence are not available at this time.

Baja California. Some large tabular crystals of pale brownish to plum color axinite have been obtained from a pegmatite near Gavilanes, a small community about 45 miles south of the border town of Tecate. The pegmatite contains considerable scheelite for which mineral it was mined extensively some years ago. The axinite crystals are mostly covered with granular deposits of an unidentified pale-brownish mineral which also appears as inclusions in the interior of the crystals. Parts of these crystals are suitable for faceting.

MICROLITE

Among the rarest of all North American gemstones must be counted this complex oxide of tantalum which has been found in clear facet grade crystals only at the famous Rutherford Mines near Amelia, Virginia. At the mines, numbers of small octahedral crystals and irregular masses of olive-green to brown color have been found occupying cavities between blades of cleavelandite in the pegmatite dikes. Microlite was originally identified from a pegmatite at Chesterfield, Massachusetts where it occurred in such small crystals that the Greek word for small—*mikros*—seemed a logical root for the species name, however, this name is no longer appropriate since Amelia specimens sometimes reach several inches across.

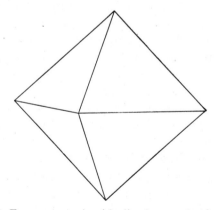

FIGURE 112. An idealized crystal of microlite, in this case, a perfect octahedron.

Microlite and the closely-related tantalum mineral pyrochlore, form a series of Isometric minerals of great chemical complexity, and for the sake of simplicity, only that of microlite will be given: $(Na,Ca)_2Ta_2O_6(O,OH,F)$. Although octahedral crystals of microlite occurred frequently in the Amelia dikes, the major portion of material suitable for gems came from irregular masses found between blades of snow-white cleavelandite near the core of the dikes. The hardness of gem material is about 6. Specific gravity varies from 5.9 to 6.0; index of refraction is single: n = 1.98 to 2.02. Color varies from reddish-yellow to amber brown.

Formless crystalline lumps have been found as much as 4 pounds in weight but the majority of masses and crystals did not exceed from ¼ inch to ½ inch across. In 1885, W. E. Hidden recorded a perfectly transparent crystal of garnet red color which weighed 0.877 grams before cutting; when finished it yielded a fine brilliant gem of great beauty but unfortunately, the weight was not recorded. This gem was said to resemble a red zircon. Flawless crystals up to ⅜ inch in size have also been mentioned by Hidden while another authority states that crystals of mineralogical value only sometimes reached as much as 2¼ inches in diameter. The crystal form is shown in Figure 112.

Additional details on the Rutherford Mines are furnished under FELD-SPAR.

STIBIOTANTALITE

Odd and very rare gems are sometimes obtained from clear crystals of stibiotantalite which occur associated with tourmaline, quartz, lepidolite, beryl, etc., in the gem pockets of the famous Himalaya Mine at Mesa Grande, San Diego County, California. Even here, the first recorded locality for this mineral in America, specimens are extremely uncommon and are eagerly sought upon the dumps by local collectors. One of the most notable features of this gemstone is its power of refraction which exceeds that of diamond, however, its color, softness, and other attributes, prevents any confusion on that score.

Chemically, stibiotantalite is an oxide of antimony and tantalum but at Mesa Grande a considerable percentage of columbium invariably substitutes for tantalum. The formula is therefore: $Sb(Ta,Cb)O_4$. Additionally, small amounts of bismuth substitute for part of the antimony. The hardness is only 5½ but crystals are not easily broken in spite of rough treatment when thrown upon the dumps during mining. The fracture is granular to slightly conchoidal, the luster resinous to adamantine. In accordance with relative proportions of tantalum and columbium, the specific gravity and refractive indices vary considerably:

Tantalum-rich:	SG = 6.818	$\alpha = 2.3742$	$\beta = 2.4039$	$\gamma = 2.4568$
Columbium-rich	SG = 6.299	$\alpha = 2.3977$	$\beta = 2.4190$	$\gamma = 2.4588$

Stibiotantalite crystallizes in the Orthorhombic System and possesses the unique property of pyroelectricity due to its hemimorphic nature. The majority of crystals are approximately rectangular in outline, very flat in proportion to their width, and hence seldom thick enough to afford even small stones. The wide faces are covered with minute parallel grooves (see Figure 113). The color is mostly some shade of brownish-yellow to olive-yellow showing patches of reddish-brown, or completely brown in the case of larger and thicker crystals. In size, crystals may vary from paper-thin wafers about ¼ inch across to thick broad tablets 2 inches or more in length. Occasionally doubly-terminated specimens are found, also single crystals implanted upon pink tourmalines. The majority are found loose in the central filling of gem pockets. Examination of crystals under a dichroscope shows distinct pleiochroism: greenish-yellow, brownish- to reddish-yellow, reddish-brown (see TOURMALINE for further details on the locality).

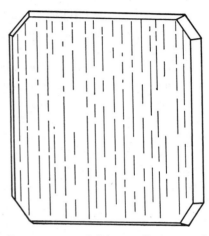

FIGURE 113. Stibiotantalite crystal from the Himalaya Mine at Mesa Grande, California. These crystals are very thin tablets covered on broad faces by numerous shallow striations.

BERYLLONITE

Up until several decades ago, beryl-lonite was somewhat of an engima. The classic locality at the foot of McKean Mountain in Stoneham Township, Oxford County, Maine, was the only place it had ever been found in the entire world. Here, in soil amid broken feldspar, smoky quartz crystals, mica, apatite, triplite, beryl, cassiterite and other minerals, obviously the products of a disintegrated pegmatite "pocket," were found crystals and fragments of a strange colorless mineral which proved to be a new species. When the true nature of this mineral was determined, it set off an intensive search of the mountainside to discover the dike from which the pocket debris had come. Unfortunately, all efforts came to naught and even today the exact source of beryllonite, as this mineral was later named, remains a mystery. Thus, when it was also found on the eastern knoll of Plumbago Mountain in Newry Township, Oxford County, some aspects of its origin were cleared up, including where it occurred in pegmatites and with what other minerals. Beryllonite is named after the beryllium in its composition.

Beryllonite is a phosphate of beryllium and sodium with the formula: $NaBe(PO_4)$. It crystallizes in the Monoclinic System and forms crude tabular crystals and platey masses lacking color and frequently transparent through-out. A few crystals have been found which display a large number of faces and cause the crystals to assume a rounded appearance. At Newry, opaque white crystals have been found adjacent to core units of pegmatites associated with herderite, eosphorite, albite, and tourmaline. Hardness varies from 5 ½ to 6 depending upon the direction of test. A perfect and easily developed cleavage is conspicuous in most specimens either upon the surface or within where it is marked by numbers of partial separations which shine like polished silver; two other cleavages, but far less perfect and developed only with difficulty, are also present. Elsewhere, the fracture is conchoidal with glassy luster. The specific gravity is low and appears constant inasmuch as determinations on both Stoneham and Newry specimens agreed on a value of 2.81. Refractive indices are low: $a = 1.5520$, $\beta = 1.5579$, $\gamma = 1.561$; birefringence 0.009; biaxial, negative. Because of its low refraction and dispersion (0.010), plus its softness and complete lack of color, cut stones are distinguished by nothing but their rarity. Beryllonite is distinguished from similar-appearing colorless gems by the long tubelike inclusions which are frequently found even in specimens which seem quite clear; these inclusions are oriented at right angles to the principal cleavage plane.

LOCALITIES

Maine. The original locality for beryllonite is at the base of McKean Mountain in Stoneham Township, Oxford County. It is to be noted that on the Maine-New Hampshire Fryeburg Quadrangle topographic map (Scale 1:62500), the name of the mountain is spelled: "Joe McKeen Hill" and its summit is actually located about 1 mile south of the southern border of Stoneham Township. Assuming this to be the hill in question, the locality would be about 2 ¾ miles west-southwest of the community of North Lovell, or near the northern end of Horseshoe Pond. Crystal fragments from Stoneham range in size from about ¼ to some almost 2 inches across. The author has a fragment which measures 1 by ⅞ by ⅝ inch in size and another, largely clear, 1 by 1 by ⅜ inch. However, flawless gems of perhaps one or two carats only can be cut from clear places in each fragment.

Much after the discovery at Stoneham, beryllonite was found in the Nevel Quarry on the east face of the eastern spur or knoll of Plumbago Mountain in Newry Township in 1926 or 1927. However, all crystals from this locality were white and opaque although one of 3 ⅛ inches by 2 inches by 1 ½ inches in size was reported. No recent finds of beryllonite have been made at either locality.

APATITE

Apatite is frequently seen in collections but seldom in jewelry, and although beautiful cut gems of considerable brilliance and dispersion can be had in a variety of colors, its low hardness and fragile nature prevent more extensive use. Apatite is difficult to cut and polish and consequently fine examples are not easy to acquire, commanding a good price in recompense for the labor involved in their cutting. It is unfortunate that a greater degree of hardness is not present in this gemstone for few others can match the lovely color of the violet crystals from Maine, the shades of green observed in Canadian specimens, and the deep pure yellow of the splendid crystals from Cerro Mercado, Mexico. Scarcely any apatite is cut in other than facet form but some fibrous varieties produce good catseyes. Because it was mistaken for several different minerals, apatite was named after the Greek word "to deceive."

Apatite is a general name applied to a series of minerals which crystallize in the Hexagonal System and are closely allied chemically. All are phosphates of calcium but with the exception of the particular species under discussion here, *fluorapatite*, none produce good gem material. Fluorapatite is calcium fluophosphate and is assigned the following formula: $Ca_5(PO_4)_3F$. It forms short to long prismatic crystals of hexagonal outline sometimes complicated with numerous additional faces, occurring in cavities in pegmatite, solidly embedded in metamorphic limestone, or in certain ore bodies. Crystals growing freely in cavities are usually very brilliant and smoothly faced but those embedded in limestone are dull and curiously rounded as if they had been passed through an intensely hot flame which caused the edges to fuse slightly. Apatite is not particularly soft, hardness 5, but it is exceedingly brittle and sensitive to heat changes; these complicate its cutting and lead to the lapidary difficulties mentioned before. A poor cleavage exists across the prism but is seldom very pronounced or easily developed; in most cases, crystals fracture readily along the length and across the sides of prisms leaving squarish fragments with bright, glassy to greasy, conchoidal fracture surfaces. Specific gravity of facet material varies from 3.15 to 3.22. Apatite is uniaxial negative, exhibiting refractive indices as follows: $\omega = 1.6357$, $\epsilon = 1.6328$; birefringence 0.0029. Variations occur according to changes in chemical composition. Yellow apatite from Mexico gives: $\omega = 1.634$, $\epsilon = 1.630$; birefringence 0.004. Green apatite from Canada shows: $\omega = 1.632$, $\epsilon = 1.629$; birefringence 0.003; purple apatite from Maine shows: $\omega = 1.633$, $\epsilon = 1.630$; birefringence 0.003. In color, apatite varies from colorless to medium shades of green, blue, purple, yellow, etc.; reddish and pinkish tints occur also. In general, yellow shades are vivid and pure, also purple, but green shades are inclined to be somewhat dull and oily. Dichroism is surprisingly marked even in pale colors; green material from Canada shows green and pale yellow; yellow apatite from Mexico shows rich yellow and faint green; purple apatite from Mount Apatite, Maine, shows blue-purple and red-purple.

Ontario. Squarish fragments of gem quality green to brown apatite from much larger crystals have come from the Liscombe Mine, on the western slope of a ridge ¾ mile southwest of Wilberforce, Monmouth Township, Haliburton County. The pits are located on Lot 34, Concession XV. On this property are found a series of veins composed of phlogopite mica, pyroxene, calcite, and green apatite, the latter in large, beautiful, doubly-terminated hexagonal prisms completely embedded in calcite. Smaller examples in matrix or as free crystals grace mineral collections all over the world (see Figure 114). Stones of several carats or more can be cut from some of

FIGURE 114. A typical Renfrew, Ontario apatite crystal measuring 6 inches long and about 2 inches in diameter; color dark olive green. Although the hexagonal cross-section is apparent in the photograph, none of the crystal faces are very sharp and the "fused" edges so commonly observed in the Renfrew apatites are present. The darker areas to the left are clear and from such places it is possible to cut small faceted gems. Courtesy Smithsonian Institution.

the clear pieces; the U.S. National Museum possesses a fine stepcut gem of 9 carats. The green is slightly grayish blue in cast but attractive and fairly intense. Other mines in the immediate vicinity of Wilberforce also produced similar crystals of apatite as for example, the Montgomery-Marshall property on Lot 9, Concession XXI, Cardiff Township, ½ mile south of the Wilberforce-Bancroft highway. Other important deposits lie in Faraday Township. Further to the east in Renfrew County, are many other localities. Outstanding crystals occur at the Smart Mine, on Lot 31, Concession X, Sebastopol

Township; at the Meany Mine on Lot 31, Concession XI in the same township.

Maine. Probably the finest purple apatites found any place in the world came from the pegmatites of Mount Apatite in Androscoggin County. The low wooded hill, which comprises this "mount," is located 6 miles west of Auburn and is easily reached by good roads. The feldspar quarries were opened on the southeastern portion of the hill and consist of a series of shallow pits exploiting a flat-lying pegmatite of considerable thickness. Figure 115 shows one of the quarries in 1913 when considerable activity was taking place. In the center of this pegmatite was found a series of pockets which in addition to apatite, yielded gem tourmaline, beryl, quartz, and other rare and desirable species. In these pockets, apatite occurs as perfectly formed brilliant crystals, singly or in groups lining the walls. Although some openings were fairly large, apatite crystals were principally obtained from minute pockets sometimes only several inches across. Figure 116 illustrates the portion of the pegmatite in which pockets occur and shows a pocket which has been excavated. Apatites from this locality are simple hexagonal, short, stubby prisms. All faces are sharply developed and perfectly smooth while the interiors of crystals are completely transparent except where cracks intervene. Silvery cookeite mica in small sparkling scales is commonly grown upon the apatite, sometimes completely covering the crystals. In size, individuals range from the size of a pin-

FIGURE 115. The H. N. Greenlaw Quarry on Mount Apatite, Maine in 1913. Behind the men and slightly to the right appears a small gem pocket. Courtesy U.S. Geological Survey.

FIGURE 116. The P. P. Pulsifer Quarry atop Mount Apatite, Maine during 1913. Near the center of the picture is a gem pocket in which fine purple apatite was found. The pegmatite is principally whitish feldspar penetrated by irregular masses of gray quartz. Courtesy U.S. Geological Survey.

head to some over ½ inch long and ¾ inch wide. The finest single crystal came from the Pulsifer Pit and measured 1½ inches by 1¾ inches across the top and a little over 1½ inches in depth. The color is fine amethyst, generally clear except for a few cloudy spots. It weighs slightly over 100 grams. This crystal, along with others from Mount Apatite is now in the U.S. National Museum and is illustrated in Figure 117. Although purple is the most spec-

FIGURE 117. The famous Roebling purple apatite crystal from the Pulsifer Quarry, Mount Apatite, Maine. This beautifully-formed specimen is the largest single crystal found at this noted locality and measures 1½ inches by 1¾ inches by 1½ inches; its weight is slightly over 100 grams. Silvery cookeite mica covers part of the base. Courtesy Smithsonian Institution.

tacular color observed in apatite from Mount Apatite, others are known, viz: light pink, light blue, blue green.

Very fine purple crystals have also come from the Harvard Quarry on the western lip of Noyes Mountain, just southwest of its summit, in Greenwood Township, Oxford County. Fine clear specimens up to ¾ inch across were removed from pockets in pegmatite where they were found associated with cream-colored cookeite. The American Museum of Natural History owns a brilliant cut gem from this locality measuring ⅜ inch across. Minor occurrences of similar apatite have been recorded from the Berry Quarry located on a low hill about 1½ miles southeast of Minot on the west side of the Androscoggin River in Poland, Androscoggin County, where apatite occurred in gem pockets in pegmatite; also from the Tiger Bill Quarry on Long Tom Mountain in Greenwood Township, Oxford County where some excellent blue crystals were found and in Sagadahoc County at the Thomas Feldspar Quarry in Phippsburg Township where green and blue crystals resembling beryl were found in pegmatite pockets. This last locality is 1.3 miles south 17° west of the village of Parker Head.

New Hampshire. Small gem quality crystals of purplish apatite up to ¼ inch by ½ inch were found in pockets in pegmatite at the Charles Davis Mine located one mile northwest of North Groton, Grafton County. In Carroll County, gem quality apatite is occasionally found associated with smoky quartz, amethyst, and rock crystal, in cavities in granite at the Redstone Red Quarry at Redstone Station, Conway Township.

Massachusetts. Beautiful transparent oil-green crystals have been found at the asbestos mine at Pelham, Hampshire County. One crystal of 3 inches by 2 inches was recorded from this locality and said to have been clear in many places.

Connecticut. The pegmatites of the Portland Area have yielded small purple crystals similar to those from Maine, but other colors occur also.

Perfect pink, pale green, violet, and colorless crystals have been found at the Strickland Quarry on Collins Hill, 2 miles east northeast of Portland in Middlesex County and have seen some employment in gems. Beautiful deep green gemmy crystals are reported to occur in small pegmatites at Oneco, Stony Creek, Branford, and New London.

New York. Gemmy yellow apatite crystals were found at the Tilly Foster Iron Mine near Brewster, Putnam County, the American Museum of Natural History possessing a fine matrix group showing crystals up to ¾ inch by 1 inch on a slab measuring 4 inches by 6 inches. Red, yellow, or green, small transparent apatite crystals were found in salmon colored metamorphic limestone at quarries in the immediate vicinity of Hailesboro, St. Lawrence County.

Pennsylvania. Transparent bottle-green crystals and masses were once found in soil in London Grove Township, Chester County, about ¼ mile northwest of Avondale. Crystals were believed to come from weathered metamorphic limestone which outcrops in this area. Similar material has been reported from 1 mile southwest of Chatham in the same township; also in quarries along the Pennsylvania Railroad, ¼ mile northwest of Avondale.

Georgia. Pale greenish-yellow transparent apatite occurs in pegmatite in the Mitchell Creek Mica Mine, located 7½ miles southeast of Thomaston in Upson County. The occurrence is a curious one since the apatite is found partly or wholly included in muscovite mica as gem quality crystals of small size. The collection of the American Museum of Natural History includes several brilliants of ¼ inch and ⅜ inch in diameter and bright yellow in color from an indefinite locality near Holly Springs, Cherokee County.

South Dakota. Excellent gemmy purple crystals were once found in a pegmatite prospect near Glendale in the Black Hills. The several large deposits in the Custer area sometimes provide massive blue apatite which has been cut from time to time into pretty cabochons.

California. Some fine, deep pink, very simple prismatic crystals of apatite have been found in pockets at the Himalaya and San Diego tourmaline mines near Mesa Grande, San Diego County. Those who have had such crystals in their possession state that it is necessary to keep them away from direct sunlight to avoid bleaching. In spite of such precautions, the pink color eventually fades until only a pale brownish pink tinge remains. This unusual color is said to be due to the presence of minute quantities of neodymium. Apatite is also found in pegmatites in other San Diego County mines but is seldom suitable for gems. Peculiar yellowish olive-green tabular crystals occur in sericite-filled pockets in the Clark Mine pegmatite on the southeast slope of Rincon Mountain, near Rincon. Some of these show clear yellow segments which may facet small gems.

Durango. One of the world's classic localities for gem apatite is that at the iron mines of Cerro Mercado near the city of Durango. These deposits were known as early as 1552 but aside from limited mining and smelting attempts, the ore was not systematically processed until a railroad line was built to the city. Allegedly the low mountain containing the ore deposits was named after a certain Senor Mercado who prospected it for silver but found to his disgust that it was nothing but iron ore. Cerro Mercado extends several thousand feet in length and rises several hundred feet above the valley floor just north of the city of Durango. It is composed mainly of latitic rocks with rhyolite tuffs and rhyolites interspersed with large bodies of martite (hematite), the latter providing the commercial source of iron. Accessory minerals consist of goethite, limonite, magnetite, apatite, dahllite, hedenbergite, sepiolite, quartz, chalcedony, hyalite, titanite, calcite and barite. The apatite crys-

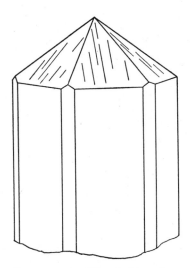

FIGURE 118. The habit taken by the bright yellow facet quality apatite crystals from Durango, Mexico.

tals, called *amarillas* ("yellows") by the miners, are found in small numbers at the Penascos de La Industria on the west base of the mountain, in greater numbers and in finer crystals at Cueva de la Marmaja upon the south slope of the west end, and at various places in the tunnels known as Socovons 1 and 2; also on the north slope of the mountain. The method of mining consists mainly of blasting down the rock along the slopes and removing the easily broken ore in wheelbarrows. Apatite crystals occur loosely embedded in vuggy portions of the ore and are readily removed. The miners collect the crystals and take them home, saving them for the day when a buyer from the United States arrives.

Crystals almost always form hexagonal prisms whose edges are beveled by other prisms; the terminations are simple hexagonal pyramids frequently striated or grooved and dull in luster compared to the brilliant smoothness of the sides (see Figure 118). Internal cracks are frequent, showing up in abundance in the large crystals which may be as much as 2 inches in diameter and several inches in length. Smaller crystals, usually not over ¾ inch in diameter, contain flawless faceting areas of beautiful uniform bright yellow color. Gems over 15 carats in weight and absolutely flawless have been cut from this material but the average cut weight is closer to 7 or 8 carats. The author has a gem weighing 9.46 carats in his collection and has recently cut one of 19.8 carats for the collection of the Smithsonian Institution.

AMBLYGONITE

Almost unheard of as a transparent gemstone until several years ago when a meager supply reached the United States from Brazil, amblygonite has heretofore been popularly regarded only as an opaque to translucent compact mineral found in lithium-bearing pegmatites. However, in 1940 or 1941, clear crystals were found in Maine and from some small fragments, faceted gems were prepared. This antedates the Brazilian discovery by a number of years and the honor of being the first to furnish facet-grade amblygonite must go to this locality. The name of this species is derived from two Greek words meaning "blunt" and "angle" in allusion to the low angles observed on crystals. Amblygonite is also known as *hebronite* after the occurrence of a sodium-rich variety in Hebron, Maine; also as *montebrasite* after a locality in France. In its clear form, amblygonite has little to commend it as a gemstone; it is generally pale in hue and neither very hard nor remarkably brilliant.

Amblygonite is a lithium aluminum fluo-phosphate with varying amounts of sodium replacing part of the lithium and fluorine replacing hydroxyl; this is reflected in its formula: $(Li,Na)Al(PO_4)(F,OH)$. As the substitution becomes greater, the properties change somewhat and the resulting compound is labeled *montebrasite;* carrying the process even further results in a third mineral, *natromontebrasite.* Since the exact position in the series of any specimen is difficult to determine without careful analysis, the name amblygonite is generally adopted as a convenient label and is more particularly adopted for the fluorine end of the series. Amblygonite is almost wholly found within lithium-rich pegmatites of granitic origin where it occurs in medium to large individual crystal masses belonging to the Triclinic System but seldom with any trace of crystal faces. Masses are often huge, sometimes a single accumulation of rude interlocked crystals being tons in weight. Bearing a superficial resemblance to feldspar when fractured, it can be distinguished by its considerably heavier weight, feldspar averaging about 2.55 in specific gravity while amblygonite is about 3.0. Massive material is tough despite the low hardness of from 5½ to 6 and the presence of one perfect cleavage along with several others which are less easily developed. Clear material on the other hand, shows development of perfect cleavage in almost every specimen and is also comparatively brittle. Massive amblygonite is dull to pearly in luster while clear material is vitreous. Specific gravity ranges from 3.0 for compact types to 3.11 for transparent amblygonite. Refractive indices determined on clear gem material from Maine are as follows: $a = 1.616$, $\gamma = 1.643$; birefringence 0.027; biaxial, positive.

The color of massive amblygonite ranges from pure white to creamy white, very pale blue as from San Diego County, and yellowish, pinkish, grayish, and greenish. Clear facet-grade material from Brazil ranges from very pale straw yellow, to yellow, to greenish-yellow; that from Maine is pale greenish-yellow. The dichroism of a typical yellow Brazilian stone showed a faint but distinct variation from colorless to pale yellow.

LOCALITIES

Maine. Magnificent crystals were uncovered during 1940-1941 in the course of opening a new pit upon the eastern flank of Plumbago Mountain, Newry Township, Oxford County. This pit is located about 200 yards east of the old Nevel pollucite quarry. In the pegmatite, crystals were found protruding into pockets, some of the openings being almost 24 inches across. Associated minerals were quartz, beryl, triphylite, pale lilac apatite, and small amounts of eosphorite, cassiterite, and rhodochrosite. For their outstanding degree of perfection, the crystals were unusually large, reaching as much as 4¼ inches by 3¼ inches by 1½ inches in size, squarish in outline and slablike in form. The crystals were largely transparent but far from flawless because of many inclusions. The majority were preserved as found and only some small fragments were cut into gems, one of which, a colorless emerald-cut gem measuring ¼ inch by ⅜ inch, now reposes in the American Museum of Natural History. The specific gravity of this material is 3.032.

California. Massive amblygonite is common in the pegmatites of San Diego County occurring in large gatherings and rounded nodules in the Stewart Lithia Mine and Tourmaline Queen Mine at Pala. This material is sufficiently compact to be cut and polished into ornamental objects.

BRAZILIANITE

The discovery of brazilianite in the early 1940's created considerable interest because not only was it a new mineral but also one which instantly proved suited for cutting into brilliant gems of pleasing rich chartreuse-yellow color. First described in 1945 and named after the land of its origin, it was subsequently found in small quantities in several New England localities, sometimes in pieces large enough to afford gems.

Brazilianite, like so many other phosphate minerals, occurs principally in pegmatites. It is a basic phosphate of sodium and aluminum with the formula: $NaAl_3(PO_4)_2(OH)_4$. Belonging to the Monoclinic System, its bright shiny crystals show a multiplicity of faces which join to form wedge-shaped individuals. Crystals several inches across have been found in Brazil but those from native localities are no more than one inch in size or slightly over. The hardness is rather low for a gemstone, only 5½; the fracture is conchoidal but seldom without traces of the one very perfect cleavage. The specific gravity ranges from 2.978 to 2.985. Refractive indices are fairly high: $a = 1.602$, $\beta = 1.609$, $\gamma = 1.623$; birefringence 0.021, positive. As is typical of many yellow gemstones, brazilianite shows scarcely perceptible pleiochroism, only slight differences in basic hue being apparent in the dichroscope. The color is rather unique among gemstones resembling only the yellow apatite from Durango, Mexico. However, the latter is truly yellow whereas brazilianite is definitely tinged with green.

LOCALITIES

New Hampshire. The most important locality is the famous Palermo Mine No. 1, located one mile southwest of North Groton in Grafton County. Brazilianite is found here from time to time at the contacts between the quartz core and surrounding intermediate zones where it occurs associated with whitlockite, apatite, and quartz. In habit, the crystals resemble some Brazilian examples, being four-sided spear-shaped crystals of very pale yellow color and brilliant. Most individuals failed to exceed ¼ inch in size but a few have

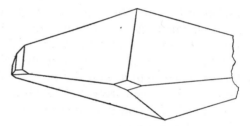

FIGURE 119. Brazilianite crystal from Palermo Quarry, New Hampshire.

been found as much as 1 inch long (see Figure 119). Small flawless crystals have also been reported from the Charles Davis Mine located about one mile northwest of North Groton. The best specimen found here was a flawless, very pale yellow crystal measuring about ⅜ by ⅝ inch perched upon a piece of cavity wall rock.

LAZULITE

The name lazulite is often confused with lapis lazuli and indeed the confusion does not stop here since both are of about the same color and occur in similar granular masses. Both names have been derived from an ancient term describing the blue of the sky—*azul*. Lazulite is far rarer than lapis lazuli but appreciable quantities have been found in North America and it deserves more recognition than it has received. Although soft and therefore not very durable, it occurs in compact masses which take a high polish and exhibit lovely blues ranging from light to intense blue.

Lazulite is a complex basic phosphate of aluminum, magnesium and iron, with the formula: $(Mg,Fe)Al_2(PO_4)_2(OH)_2$. It occurs in alumina-rich metamorphic rocks, in quartz in such rocks, and also in pegmatites. Fine crystals are found in some localities, particularly where this mineral is associated with quartz, but most gem material is derived from granular masses suitable only for cabochons. Crystallizing in the Monoclinic System, its rare crystals are found resembling doubly-terminated pyramids. There are several poor to good cleavage planes evident even in massive material and for this reason, it is possible to distinguish this mineral from the similar-appearing lapis-lazuli in which there are none. Hardness is 5½ to 6; fracture surfaces are splintery to uneven; the luster is dull. Specific gravity varies widely since most material is admixed with other minerals, but in general, it lies somewhere between 3.12 and 3.16. Since the ratio of iron to magnesium varies, refractive indices vary also, ranging between the following limits: $a = 1.604$-1.626, $\beta = 1.626$-1.654, $\gamma = 1.637$-1.663; birefringence from 0.033 to 0.037; biaxial, negative. The lower values are for magnesium-rich lazulite while the higher values are for a mineral in which the ratio between iron and magnesium is equal. A mineral in which the iron exceeds magnesium is named *scorzalite* but this end member of the series to which lazulite belongs has not been recorded as yet from any North American locality. The color of lazulite is azure blue, also sky blue, bluish-white and deep pure blue or bluish-green. A specimen from White Mountain, California showed strong trichroism as follows: colorless, greenish-blue, dark blue, the latter of an especially pure and rich shade.

LOCALITIES

Manitoba. Massive deep blue lazulite is found in narrow veins traversing milky quartz, ¾ mile east of the mouth of the Churchill River, near Churchill on the western shore of Hudson Bay.

New Hampshire. Beautiful massive lazulite of dark to pale blue color occurs with other pegmatite minerals at the famous Palermo Quarry near North Groton, Grafton County. A cabochon measuring 1¾ inches by 1¼ inches is in the author's collection (Figure 120) and shows lazulite in finely granular swirled masses of several colors, principally greenish blue but also pale pure opaque blue with smaller streaks of intense blue. The polish is glassy and far superior to that which may be expected from lapis lazuli. Lazulite similar to the Palermo material is also found from time to time at the Charles Davis Mine, ¾ mile west of North Groton. In Sullivan County, the Smith Mica Mine near Newport at Chandler's Mill, also produces small masses of lazulite.

North Carolina. Dark blue crystals and masses occur in quartz associated with kyanite and muscovite at Crowders Mountain and Clubbs Mountain in Gaston County; also massive in quartz at Coffee Gap in the Laura-town Mountains, Stokes County.

California. The largest masses of pure lazulite found so far in North America have come from the unique Champion Spark Plug Company's andalusite mine on the west slope of White Mountain, Mono County. The mine is located about 20 miles south of the California/Nevada border at an elevation of 9500 feet and is accessible only by pack trail. A large body of quartzite containing anda-lusite provides an interesting associa-tion of several rare minerals including

FIGURE 120. A cabochon of lazulite from the Palermo Quarry, New Hampshire. The color is generally blue with streaks and mottlings of darker and lighter shades. Size, about 1¾ inches in length.

augelite and genuine lapis lazuli although the latter is only found in ex-ceedingly small veinlets of no cutting value. Solid masses of lazulite up to 6 inches thick, coarsely crystalline in nature, are found here in milky quartz. One such mass weighing over a pound is in the possession of the author. The color is very dark blue where pure, lightening somewhat in hue where other minerals form an admixture. Like the material from New Hamp-shire, a fine polish is easily obtained.

Recently, lazulite has been found in quartz at some unspecified locality on the west slope of the Ritter Range in the extreme northeastern portion of Madera County. Some of this has been cut into attractive dark blue cabo-chons from masses said to reach several inches across. Some typical crystals of bipyramidal habit are also found at this locality.

New Mexico. Lazulite suitable for ornamental purposes is said to occur in quartz in Rucca Canyon north of the east end of Soledad Canyon, Dona Ana County.

CASSITERITE

Although transparent crystals of the tin mineral, cassiterite, furnish beautiful and durable faceted gems, only a peculiar massive variety known as *wood tin* has so far been found suitable for cutting in North America, occurring in some abundance in Mexico. Wood tin receives its name from its color and concentric bandings which strikingly resemble the grain of darker woods. Cabochons cut from this material provide interesting if not especially attractive gems and find some demand among collectors of the unusual. When well-polished, wood tin displays a peculiar silvery luster which is quite similar to that seen on certain rough diamonds. The name of cassiterite has been derived from the old Greek word for tin—*kassiteros*. A specimen of Mexican wood tin is illustrated in Figure 121.

FIGURE 121. A nodule of cassiterite or "wood tin" from one of the alluvial deposits in the State of Durango, Mexico.

Cassiterite is a valued ore of tin of which it is the oxide: SnO_2. In its purest form, it grows in squarish prisms reflecting its Tetragonal System symmetry. The vast majority of crystals are opaque black or brown but sometimes, as in Bolivia, transparent pale yellow, brown, or even colorless specimens are found. In Mexico, wood tin occurs lining small cavities of several inches across in rhyolitic rocks, forming rounded banded masses associated with topaz crystals, hematite, hyalite, chalcedony, fluorite, and wolframite. Since the enclosing rocks are easily decomposed, much of the cassiterite is found as nodules or "guijoles," as the Mexican miners call them, in the gravels of washes and streams. These nodules form interesting specimens showing rounded forms like miniature cauliflowers within which are many fine concentric bands of contrasting color. The predominant hues are some shade of brown, dull olive-green, brownish-red, and brownish-yellow. In size, nodules range from those as small as a pea to some enormous masses weighing over 50 pounds but the average is probably several ounces. Cassiterite possesses a specific gravity from 6.8 to 7.1 and is consequently far denser than any other ordinary gemstone. In the Mexican placer mines this property causes wood tin to concentrate in the deepest gravels, and, accordingly, it is sought for in the lowest parts of alluvial deposits.

LOCALITIES

Mexico in General. The following states contain wood tin deposits many of which yield cuttable material: Durango, Zacatecas, San Luis Potosi, Jalisco, Guanajuato, Queretaro, Hidalgo, Aguascalientes, and Puebla.

Durango. Commercial quantities have been obtained from Cacaria or

Canatlan, the Sierra de San Francisco, Sierra de Sacrificios, and various places in the municipalities of San Juan de Dios, Santiago Papasquiaro, and Tamazula.

Guanajuato. From the municipalities of San Miguel Allende, Ciudad Gonzales, Dolores Hidalgo, Leon, and San Felipe.

Jalisco. From Lagos to Teocaltiche along the tin belt of the Sierra de El Laurel; this belt extends into the adjacent state of Aguascalientes.

San Luis Potosi. Various deposits are located in the municipalities of Guadalcazar, Santa Maria del Rio, Venado, and San Luis Potosi.

Zacatecas. In the municipalities of Jerez, Pinos, Sombrerete and Villanueva.

DIASPORE

In spite of its relative abundance, diaspore is seldom found in crystals large enough to facet gems. In fact, it seems doubtful that any has ever been cut although its suitability as a gemstone has been mentioned in gemological literature a number of times in the past. Being transparent, light in color, and quite hard, there seems no reason why it should not make an acceptable gem. Diaspore is often found associated with corundum and emery deposits where it appears as tabular crystals resulting from the alteration of the corundum. In some localities, very fine specimens have been found and certainly, if we are to believe old accounts, their size and quality made them eminently suited for cutting into brilliant faceted gems. Diaspore owes its name to the Greek word for "scatter," for when crystals are heated they burst apart violently into small fragments.

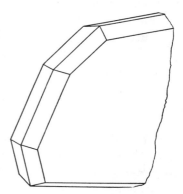

FIGURE 122. A bladed diaspore crystal from Chester, Massachusetts.

Diaspore is hydrogen aluminum oxide with the formula: $HAlO_2$; both manganese and iron substitute for the aluminum in small amounts. The most common occurrence is with corundum and emery as crusts lining crevices or enveloping masses of corundum. Belonging to the Orthorhombic System, diaspore forms tabular crystals (see Figure 122) with a perfect cleavage parallel to the broadest faces of the tablets. Several other cleavages are present also. Hardness varies between $6\frac{1}{2}$ and 7; crystals are very brittle. The luster is brilliant to pearly on cleavage faces. Specific gravity ranges from 3.3 to 3.5; clear crystals showing 3.44. Refractive indices are: $\alpha = 1.702$, $\beta = 1.722$, $\gamma = 1.750$; birefringence 0.48; biaxial, positive. Clear crystals are frequently of beautiful fine brown color but yellowish, lilac and pink are also known. Pleiochroism is strong, one authority noting the following colors in a single crystal: violet-blue, reddish, and pale green.

LOCALITIES

Massachusetts. In the past, the old emery mines at Chester in Hampden County, furnished magnificent specimens but only a few crystals were large and clear enough to cut. Some material is still obtainable from the extensive dumps which surround the workings. Diaspore crystals occurred here as bladed to tabular individuals of beautiful blue or violet color grouped upon the impure form of corundum known as emery.

Pennsylvania. Possibly the finest diaspore crystals known came from the old corundum locality at Corundum Hill, Newlin Township, Chester County, situated about 2 miles northeast of Unionville. Perfectly transparent crystals measuring from ½ to 2 inches in length and about ¼ inch in thickness were found. They ranged in color from colorless to pale brown, and resembled strongly the hues seen in certain topazes. Masses of diaspore up to 2 inches thick were also found consisting of numerous bladed crystals of poor form often showing clear spots. In every instance, diaspore was found associated intimately with large lenses of corundum.

ENSTATITE, HYPERSTHENE

Enstatite and hypersthene are closely related silicates of magnesium and iron occurring abundantly in a variety of igneous rocks. Enstatite is noted for clear green specimens of facet grade, especially those which are found associated with diamond in the famous mines of South Africa. Hypersthene is rarely clear but translucent kinds often provide cabochon material showing strong bronzy reflections of considerable beauty and interest. This effect is due to numerous platey inclusions arranged in parallel layers within each crystal or to a partial alteration or decomposition which proceeds only along certain planes. A similar effect is noted in the *bronzite* variety of enstatite, and it is the strong submetallic brownish luster which has given this variety its name. The resistance of enstatite to fusion before the flame of the blowpipe caused it to be named after the Greek word for "opponent." The Greek word meaning "strong above others" was used to fabricate the name for hypersthene because the latter mineral, though similar to some Amphiboles and confused readily for them, possessed certain superior qualities.

Of the two species, enstatite is the simplest in composition, being essentially a magnesium silicate, however, as iron substitutes for part of the magnesium, the composition becomes more complex, properties change, and the species hypersthene is reached. The formulas are: Enstatite ($Mg_2Si_2O_6$), Hypersthene [$(Mg,Fe)_2Si_2O_6$]. Both species crystallize in the Orthorhombic System but are rarely found in well-formed crystals, the usual mode of formation being small irregular interlocked granules. Two perfect cleavages crossing each other almost at right angles ($87°$ and $93°$) are present in both species and serve as a ready means of distinguishing them from similar-appearing actinolite, tremolite, and anthophyllite. Unfortunately, cleavages are easily started and cause considerable difficulty in lapidary work, the tendency for many specimens being to fall apart under cutting treatment. The luster is mainly glassy except in those varieties which contain inclusions causing submetallic luster. Specific gravity varies from a low of 3.1 for fairly pure enstatite to a high of 3.9 for hypersthene rich in iron. Refractive indices also vary; the following being typical of an enstatite containing a small amount of iron $a = 1.661$, $\beta = 1.666$, $\gamma = 1.671$; birefringence 0.010. A hypersthene with considerably more iron may give: $a = 1.692$, $\beta = 1.702$, $\gamma = 1.705$; birefringence 0.013. Both species are biaxial; the optic sign is plus in enstatite but swings to minus as the composition of hypersthene is approached. Colors range from grayish hues through many shades of light to dark green, sometimes fine in certain enstatites, but most greens are decidedly blackish in cast. Other specimens exhibit brown to very dark brown and almost black colors. Fairly pure and vivid hues are generally absent except in transparent varieties. Pleiochroism is weak in enstatite but becomes strong as the iron content increases; a rich-brown specimen shows: intense brownish-red, medium yellow-green, orange-yellow. A dark green hypersthene from Arizona gives: deep yellow-green, dirty olive-green, and complete darkness in a third direction.

LOCALITIES

Greenland. In the Upernivik District at a place called Upernaviarssuk, bronzite occurs in large grains over 1 inch in diameter displaying a strong bronzy luster. At Auvaitsersarfik in the Godthaab District, fine bronzy enstatite is found in grains up to 3 inches across associated with biotite, quartz, labradorite, and sometimes garnet.

Labrador. Associated with the world-famed labradorite in this province is found a deep brown, almost black hypersthene which has been mentioned as a worthy gemstone in its own right. Numerous inclusions impart a strong coppery luster which contrasts well with the velvety black background color. It is said that at one time it was highly esteemed in France where lapidaries referred to it as *Paulite* in allusion to its supposed occurrence upon the Island of St. Paul off the coast of Labrador. Despite the tons of labradorite which have been imported into the United States in the last decade, the author cannot recall ever having seen rough hypersthene from Labrador offered for sale. Cut specimens have been examined and are rather attractive. The reader is referred to FELDSPAR for further information on labradorite localities. The coppery inclusions in hypersthene are probably minute scales of goethite or hematite but their exact nature has not been determined.

North Carolina. The altered variety of enstatite known as bronzite is found in several places in this state. The first is a well-known occurrence near Webster, Jackson County. A bronzite–diopside rock given the name *websterite* occurs here enclosed in a large outcrop of dunite. In the websterite are found masses of bronzite consisting of coarse grains up to several inches across with strong bronzy luster. Unfortunately, most grains are badly shattered and very weak, causing much difficulty in polishing. This deposit is of very little commercial significance. Bronzite also occurs in small quantities at the corundum mines in the Buck Creek area, near Cullakanee in Clay County, however, very little has been found suitable for cutting.

Arizona. Dark green to black hypersthene fragments are found associated with the peridots on the San Carlos Indian Reservation. In size, they vary from ¼ inch to some over 1 inch across. Larger specimens which appear black actually show in thin sections, an extremely deep greenish-brown color. Occasionally, small platey inclusions give a faint metallic reflection in polished specimens.

ZIRCON

Zircon is another gemstone which is of great importance elsewhere but in the entire North American Continent, it has been found in gem grade only in very small amounts. Readers are probably familiar with cut specimens which are common stock items in jewelry stores but these come mainly from southeastern Asia and from Ceylon. Of the localities discussed below, those in Canada yield only brownish-red types while the one locality in Colorado, furnishes very small crystals in a variety of colors.

Zircon is zirconium silicate, $ZrSiO_4$, crystallizing in the Tetragonal System in simple four-sided prisms of square cross-section, terminated at each end by four-sided pyramids. Crystals vary from exceedingly small individuals, scarcely larger than a pin head, to some which weigh many pounds. The hardness varies from 6½ to 7½; the specific gravity varies from 3.95 to 4.10 in certain peculiar types of greenish hue, to higher values for ordinary gem material, viz. : 4.65 to 4.70. An intermediate kind, also of dull greenish color, falls somewhere between, giving values of 4.1 to 4.6. As may be expected, wide variations in refractive index are also noted. Dull greens or *low zircons* show $\omega = 1.79$, $\epsilon = 1.84$; *intermediate zircons* range between these values and the following which are characteristic of ordinary gem grade or *high zircon*, viz. : $\omega = 1.920\text{-}1.931$, $\epsilon = 1.967\text{-}1.993$. The birefringence is very large, 0.059, giving a "fuzzy" appearance to the back facets in a cut gem as they are viewed through the table facet. Zircon is uniaxial, positive.

Colors vary widely but the most common are some shade of red or brown and combinations thereof; also yellow, orange, and green. Blue and colorless are rarely, if ever, found in nature and are ordinarily derived by heat treatment of brownish or reddish types. Dichroism is generally weak except in blue where it is strong: reddish or brownish gems show dichroic colors of red and brown; blue shows blue and colorless; yellow produces yellow and brownish-yellow; green specimens show scarcely any change.

LOCALITIES

Ontario. The zircon crystals of this province have long been prized because of their extraordinary size. In earlier mining, crystals up to a foot in length and several inches in circumference were found. Perhaps the largest single crystal of record is one of 15 pounds weight. Unfortunately in all of these crystals, size means little because all are minutely shattered and clear gem material has been obtainable only from a very small portion of the tips. As a consequence, gems have been cut up to, but seldom over, one carat in weight. In Hastings County, zircon occurs in the nepheline-syenite of Dungannon Township on Lots 12 and 13 Concession XI. In Renfrew County from which most of the remarkable crystals have come, zircon appears on Lot 31, Concession X in Sebastopol Township; also in splendid crystals at the Smart Mine, at Short's Claim on the north Shore of Lake Clear, and possibly upon Turner's Island in this lake. The last locality is the one from which all of the very largest crystals are claimed to come but recent advice from Canada indicates that close examination of the several pits on Turner's Island leads strongly to the conclusion that no zircon of any consequence has ever occurred here. It is believed that the person who furnished the world-renowned specimens to the market had some secret place from which he obtained them but in order to prevent others from finding this locality, he labeled them as coming from Lake Clear. In Brudenell Township, fine crystals have come from various localities, some of which have provided gems up to one carat in weight of a bright orange-red color. A typical Renfrew County zircon crystal is shown in Figure 123.

In Lanark County, fine zircon crystals, though not large, have come from two pits located 4 miles directly south of Perth. Crystals range in size from less than ⅛ inch to 1¼ inches and ½ inch to ¾ inch in diameter. Clear material is sometimes found at the tips. This zircon heat treats to completely colorless material. In this connection, experiments on heat treatment of Cana-

FIGURE 123. A dark brown zircon crystal partly imbedded in a mixture of calcite and biotite mica from Renfew, Ontario. The square prism is characteristic of zircons from this locality. Dark spots are often clear enough to provide very small faceted gems. The crystal is 2¾ inches in length. Courtesy Smithsonian Institution.

dian zircon show paling of color occurs at 800° F. and is complete if specimens are held at this temperature long enough. Zircon from this locality shows specific gravities of 4.646-4.658 in untreated material, and 4.659-4.667 after heat treatment; it is very pure and contains only slight traces of hafnium.

Quebec. In Argenteuil County, small crystals of red zircon no larger than ½ inch in size occur on Lot 10, Concession V, in Grenville Township. Here they are found in metamorphic limestone associated with wollastonite, pyroxene, graphite, etc. Similar crystals occur in Hull County in Templeton Township, upon lots 12 and 21, Concession XII, also on lots 21 and 23, Concession XIII. Some of the crystals have yielded small but fine gems.

Colorado. In El Paso County, small beautiful zircon crystals occur in quartz, kaolinite, and mica pegmatite on St. Peter's Dome, a mountain located about 7 miles southwest of Colorado Springs. Crystals were found somewhere within the Eureka Tunnel which is northeast of the summit and several hundred yards below the road from Colorado Springs to Rosemont. Crystals are nicely formed but the largest are not over ½ inch in diameter. Colors are pink, green, light wine to honey yellow, and reddish-brown; very small gems can be cut from the smaller and transparent individuals.

ALGODONITE AND DOMEYKITE

Occasionally cut as curiosities for the collector, algodonite and domeykite occur as irregular masses along with other ores in the copper mines of the Keeweenaw Peninsula, Michigan. Cabochons made from these minerals are rather attractive but have no value aside from their unusual nature, furthermore, the bright metallic luster soon tarnishes to dull grayish or brownish color upon continued exposure to the atmosphere.

Algodonite and domeykite are copper arsenides with the following respective formulas: Cu_6As and Cu_3As. Algodonite is 4 in hardness, domeykite from 3 to 3½. Specific gravities are for algodonite, 8.38, for domeykite, 7.2-7.9. Algodonite exhibits a bright steel-gray metallic luster when freshly broken which becomes dull upon exposure; domeykite is similar but tarnishes to yellowish and thence to dark brown.

LOCALITIES

Michigan. Cuttable material has been found in the copper mines near Ahmeek and Mohawk in the western part of Keeweenaw County; also from the Sheldon-Columbia Mine on Portage Lake, Houghton County. In the first-mentioned localities, domeykite is found as silvery masses associated with white quartz by which it is penetrated in fine criss-crossed veinlets. Polishing this material is difficult on account of the great differences in hardness between the quartz and the domeykite. Tarnishing may be delayed by spraying finished pieces with clear lacquer.

SPHALERITE

Dazzling in its dispersion when clear and pale in color, sphalerite is an example of a gemstone often mentioned in gemological literature but rarely seen in good cut specimens. It is a common and important ore of zinc but at one time was discarded by medieval silver and lead miners who thought it to be a kind of galena but found to their disgust that no smelting artifice could make it yield lead. For this reason, it was labeled *blende* or *zinc-blende*, from the German "blenden" meaning "to deceive." It is interesting to note that the name sphalerite reflects the German opinion of this mineral for it is derived from the Greek word for "delusive." Very dark varieties are called *black-jack,* bright red kinds have been called *ruby-zinc* and a colorless variety has been named *cleiophane.* Although thousands of tons are mined every year, sphalerite seldom occurs clear enough to facet and even then, good pale material capable of displaying the high dispersion noted in this species is surprisingly rare. Another reason for the scarcity of attractive cut specimens is the unusual skill required to apply a satisfactory polish during cutting; most museum gems, though clear and light in color, appear dull and lifeless because the surfaces are scratched and striated instead of being perfectly smooth.

Sphalerite, when pure, is simple zinc sulphide: ZnS. Absolutely pure material is colorless but is seldom found because small amounts of iron commonly cause progressive darkening through shades of green, yellow and reddish, finally resulting in so deep a red hue that the mineral appears black. The almost pure sphalerite from Franklin, New Jersey (cleiophane) is very pale green in color and contains only a trace of iron. Crystallizing in the Isometric System, sphalerite is most often found in crystals of triangular cross-section (tetrahedrons) as shown in Figure 124, or as formless grains completely enclosed by other minerals. The hardness is low, only from $3\frac{1}{2}$ to 4, while a series of perfect and easily developed cleavages further contribute to its fragile nature. Because of its high refractive index, its luster is bright and somewhat metallic or adamantine in character. The specific gravity is high, ranging from 4.1 for essentially pure material to 3.9 as iron increasingly substitutes for zinc. Cleiophane from New Jersey is 4.063. Sphalerite is singly refractive and therefore only one refractive index can be measured, however, this value changes according to the presence of iron or other impurities. An unusually pure specimen from Sonora, Mexico measured: $n = 2.3688$ (0.15 percent iron); on the other hand, a specimen in which 17 percent iron was present furnished: $n = 2.47$.

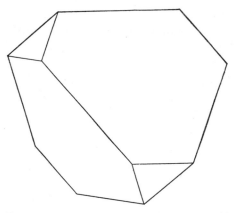

FIGURE 124. A tetrahedral crystal of sphalerite. This drawing is simplified to show clearly the form of the crystal but ordinarily sphalerite crystals are covered with numerous triangular markings and striations.

Gem quality sphalerite varies in color from the lovely pale green of New Jersey cleiophane to olive green as from Sonora, but rich browns, yellows, and reddish shades are also common. Any trace of brown or olive seems to drastically reduce transmission of light and nothing the lapidary can do will overcome this defect. Sphalerite is cut in brilliant style to take advantage of the unusually high dispersion (0.156) but unless the material is fairly light in hue to begin with, dispersive effects will be masked by the body color. Many clear specimens are also cut in step fashion and some flawed material is polished into attractive glistening cabochons. Because of its fragility, sphalerite is useful only as a curious gem for inclusion in the collections of connoisseurs; it has no commercial application.

LOCALITIES

Ontario. Clear resinous brown sphalerite capable of being faceted into gems of several carats weight is found in granular masses in metamorphic limestone near Wiarton, Albemarle Township, Bruce County. At this place it occurs upon Lots 29 and 30, Concession III.

New Jersey. One of the very few places in the world where cleiophane, the almost colorless variety of sphalerite is found, is in the zinc deposits of Franklin and Ogdensburg in Sussex County. The color of cleiophane varies from faintly green to yellowish-green; the latter being more absorptive of light and consequently less brilliant in cut form. Gems up to 15 carats have been cut from the finest material and superficially resemble diamonds in respect to brilliance and dispersion. At the mines, the finest sphalerites occur embedded in curious felted masses of a gray mineral found in pockets in the metamorphic limestone adjacent to the main zinc ore bodies; fine crystals are also recovered from cavities in secondary veins.

Montana. Good transparent gem material occurs in the silver deposits of the Hartley Mine at Neyhart, Cascade County.

Colorado. Transparent greenish crystals occur in a number of zinc mines in the Green Mountain region in the northern part of Eagle and Summit counties as in the Big Four Mine, 16 miles south of Kremmling where ore bodies are emplaced in black limestone.

Sonora. Outstanding world sources of facet grade sphalerite are the Manzanal, Duluth and Chivera mines near Cananea, Sonora. These mines exploit ore bodies yielding principally copper but also much silver, lead, molybdenum, and zinc. In these deposits, sphalerite occurs associated with granular galena in replacement bodies in limestone as large single or twinned transparent crystals as shown in Figure 125. The color varies from pale yellow-green through olive-green to red and brown. Some flawless cleavage fragments have been obtained which furnished gems up to 50 or more carats in weight though seldom uniform in coloration. The best material is pale

FIGURE 125. A group of transparent green sphalerite crystals associated with white dolomite and minor amounts of chalcopyrite from the mines of Cananea, Sonora, Mexico. The size of the specimen is 6 inches by 4 inches while the largest sphalerite crystal measures about 2 inches across. Courtesy Smithsonian Institution.

green but specimens of this color are neither large nor plentiful. Larger pieces show straight narrow bands of red, yellow, green, and reddish-brown, and in cutting, require some care to avoid inclusion of dark areas in finished gems because darker colors drastically reduce brilliancy. The author's collection includes several fine green and reddish-yellow gems over 15 carats in weight cut from Cananea material.

NICCOLITE, SMALTITE, COBALTITE, BREITHAUPTITE

For convenience' sake, these four minerals are discussed simultaneously because they occur together in the famous silver deposits of Ontario. Furthermore, they are related genetically, containing similar elements and forming under similar conditions. All are found in masses which can be polished into attractive cabochons and flats of brilliant metallic luster.

Niccolite is a simple nickel arsenide (NiAs), of very pale copper-red color, which however, tarnishes in time to a grayish to blackish cast. Its hardness varies from 5 to $5\frac{1}{2}$. The specific gravity is fairly constant at about

7.784. Smaltite is also a nickel-arsenic compound but in addition, always contains varying amounts of cobalt which replaces part of the nickel. Its formula is therefore: $(Co,Ni)As_3$. The color ranges from bright metallic white characteristic of fresh cut tin to silvery gray. The hardness is between $5\frac{1}{2}$ and 6. The specific gravity ranges from 6.1 to 6.9. Cobaltite is somewhat more complex chemically, containing some iron replacing cobalt as well as sulfur: $(Co,Fe)AsS$. The color is silvery white inclining to reddish. The hardness is $5\frac{1}{2}$ while the specific gravity is about 6.33. Breithauptite is nickel antimonide, $NiSb$, showing on fresh fracture surfaces a light copper-red color which tarnishes to violet. The hardness is $5\frac{1}{2}$ and the specific gravity 8.23. Very often massive material is veined with white calcite or stringers of native silver

FIGURE 126. To the left, a cabochon of smaltite, to the right, a cabochon of niccolite; the latter is about $1\frac{1}{2}$ inches in length. Both are from Coleman, Ontario.

which add attractive patterns and lend additional interest to finished pieces. Cabochons of niccolite and smaltite are illustrated in Figure 126.

LOCALITIES

Ontario. In Coleman Township, Timiskiming District, each of the species occurs in massive form usually closely associated and sometimes distinguished from each other only with difficulty. The silver veins in this area also contain quartz, calcite, rammelsbergite, and of course, native silver, the object of mining. Especially fine cobaltite has come from the Columbus Claim while good massive smaltite is found in the Hudson Bay Mine, $\frac{1}{4}$ mile northeast of Cobalt.

North West Territories. In another section of Canada, niccolite has been found in fine masses associated with smaltite and chloanthite in veins in augite-diorite, east of the Francois River and about $1\frac{1}{2}$ miles south of Caribou Lake, MacKenzie District.

ZINCITE

The famous ore bodies of Franklin and Ogdensburg, Sussex County, New Jersey, noted for the variety and abundance of rare minerals which are found in them, are the only significant sources of zincite in the world. Zincite, which is named fittingly for its content of zinc, occurs only in abundance in these ore bodies and indeed in such quantity that it becomes an important member of the several zinc-bearing minerals which together provide the concentrate sent to the smelters. Even in the midst of this relative profusion, however, specimens clear enough to afford faceted gems are seldom found, causing zincites to be classed among the rarest of all gems.

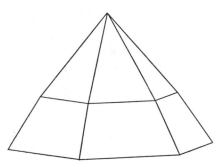

FIGURE 127. A common habit of zincite from Franklin, New Jersey. Since this mineral is hemimorphic, the base of the crystal consists only of a single terminal plane quite unlike the pointed extremity.

Zincite is essentially an oxide of zinc with the formula: ZnO, however, it is invariably contaminated with impurities. Crystallizing in the Hexagonal System, this mineral displays the curious property of *hemimorphism,* as evidenced by the appearance of totally unlike faces on opposite ends of six-sided pyramidal crystals. Perfectly developed crystals show a pyramid on one end but the other is cut off with a flat plane at right angles to the principal crystal axis (see Figure 127). However, crystals are far more rare than massive material which occurs as irregular nodular masses or seamlets sprinkled throughout the white crystalline limestone in which the ores are embedded, or as small granules mixed with patches of willemite and rounded octahedral crystals of franklinite. Ordinary material fractures irregularly and displays a dull to resinous luster but some purer pieces split along the single perfect cleavage plane which zincite possesses and then show from such surfaces, a somewhat higher luster inclining toward adamantine. This cleavage plane is not easy to develop and does not cause undue difficulty in polishing. Although listed as 4 in hardness in most textbooks, cutting and polishing trials show zincite to be closer to 5. The specific gravity is very high for a gemstone, ranging from 5.64 to 5.68, and exceeded only by cassiterite among transparent gem species. It has been noted that purer material tends to increase in specific gravity, hence gem material may reach as much as 5.70. Refractive indices are also very high, again exceeded by only a few gemstones, notably sphalerite and diamond, furnishing the following values: $\omega = 2.013$, $\epsilon = 2.029$; birefringence 0.016; uniaxial, positive. The color of zincite varies from orange-red in exceptionally pure specimens to deep blackish-red in the coarse material most commonly met with in the ore bodies. Faceted gems display an exceptionally rich pure red, intense and pure in hue. In spite of its deep color, little or no dichroism is observed.

New Jersey. Zinc ore bodies at Franklin and Ogdensburg occur at the contacts between Franklin limestone and gneiss and are greatly complicated in mineralogy by the intrusion of pegmatite bodies and dikes of volcanic rocks, and extensive hydrothermal activity, the latter being responsible for the creation of a wide variety of mineral species formed at the expense of those previously in existence. As a result of these mineralogical complications, over 140 species have been recognized from within or adjacent to the ore bodies, a substantial number being unknown elsewhere or occurring only in minor amounts. Zincite is found primarily in massive form except where secondary calcite veins cut the main ore bodies. In such veins well-developed crystals may be found wholly enclosed in limestone or occurring within small cavities. Crystals are generally small although some have been recorded up to 4 inches in length. Most are rude in form but being relatively pure, provide along with adjacent material of similar composition, the bulk of the faceting zincite found to date. Crystals are known only from the Buckwheat Mine, a large opencut on the southern slope of Mine Hill within the city limits of Franklin, also from underground workings leading from this part of the ore body. Unfortunately for collectors of rare minerals and gems, this deposit was exhausted a few years ago and all mining has now ceased. However, massive zincite is still produced in quantity for the Sterling Hill workings, located across the Wallkill River Valley from Ogdensburg, Sparta Township.

The largest known faceted zincite is a magnificent deep red square-cut gem weighing 20.05 carats which the author had the pleasure of cutting for the U.S. National Museum from material obtained from their collections. Another fine example, measuring 3/8 by 5/8 inch and weighing 16.27 carats, is in the American Museum of Natural History. Still another, a 12.7 carat gem, is in the mineral collections of the Philadelphia Academy of Natural Sciences. So far as is known, these three gems constitute the largest of this species in existence.

RHODOCHROSITE

In no other gem is found the warm and vivid pink of fine quality rhodochrosite. Faceted gems are particularly attractive but seldom seen on account of the rarity of clear crystals and the great difficulties attendant to cutting them. Most gem fanciers are acquainted only with the massive banded variety sometimes ambiguously known as *Inca rose* and hailing from Argentina. In the United States, several important localities have furnished excellent clear crystals as well as massive material but by and large, supplies are scanty and the gemstone is commercially unimportant. Rhodochrosite is frequently confused with rhodonite because of the similarity of names, and it is true that in both, the typical rose pink color has led to the derivation of name. However, in rhodochrosite, the species title is formed from two Green words, the first is *rhodos* for rose, and *chrosis* for color.

Ideally, rhodochrosite is manganese carbonate: $MnCO_3$, but it is seldom found completely devoid of iron, calcium, magnesium, or zinc, which often substitute for part of the manganese. In the facet-grade material from the John Reed Mine, Colorado, for example, small percentages of iron, magnesium, and calcium are found in spite of its seeming purity. Opaque pink material from Phillipsburg, Montana, shows about 4.5 per cent of magnesium oxide with a little calcium and even less iron. Rhodochrosite crystallizes in the Rhombohedral division of the Hexagonal System, and, like other rhombohedral carbonates, forms

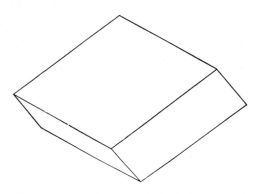

FIGURE 128. The rhombohedral form of rhodochrosite crystals.

sharp-pointed 3-sided crystals (see Figure 128), cleaves readily and perfectly along three intersecting cleavage planes, and optically, shows two widely-separated refractive indices. It is found primarily as a gangue mineral in hydrothermal ore veins, especially those of silver, lead, zinc, and copper where it is associated with calcite, siderite, dolomite, fluorite, barite, etc. Hardness varies between $3\frac{1}{2}$ and 4. Specific gravity varies according to the presence or absence of impurities and is also affected by the structure of the material, massive types being slightly less dense than crystals. Material from the John Reed Mine is 3.71. Refractive indices for pure material are: $\omega = 1.816$, $\epsilon = 1.597$; birefringence 0.219; uniaxial, negative. Indices rise as iron appears but drop somewhat if calcium or magnesium substitute for manganese.

The color of massive rhodochrosite found in North America is pale opaque pink. Fine translucent deep pink, such as that observed in material from Argentina, has not been observed as yet. Clear crystals are beautiful rich pink, often quite dark, with overtones of orange. Dichroic colors are both strong and distinctive: pale straw yellow and rich pink.

LOCALITIES

Colorado. Beautifully transparent sharp rhombohedral crystals occur at the John Reed Mine and others nearby at Alicante, near Leadville, Lake County. Here they occur associated with quartz, fluorite, pyrite, and other metallic sulfides, growing upon walls of cavities. Perfectly clear individuals are rare and those suitable for faceting seldom exceed ½ to ¾ inch in size. The author owns a fine but not flawless stepcut gem from this material weighing 8.10 carats. Similar crystals occur in Park County at the Sweethome Mine in Buckskin Gulch near Alma (see Figure 129). An emerald-cut stone of ¼ by ½ inch from this locality is in the American Museum of Natural History; also a fine matrix specimen from the Thompson Collection showing crystals up to 1 inch upon a cavity lining measuring 9 by 12 by 18 inches.

Montana. Massive pink opaque material furnishing pretty cabochons has been found in quantity at the Emma Mine, Butte, Silverbow County, also from Phillipsburg, Granite County.

WILLEMITE

As a gem mineral, willemite must be counted as a great rarity since it is found in quantity only in the zinc mines of Franklin and Ogdensburg in Sussex County, New Jersey. Among mineral collectors, especially those intrigued by the fluorescent properties of minerals, willemite has long been noted for its brilliant green or yellow glow under the stimulation of ultraviolet light. To the collector of gems, however, it is famed for the beautiful cabochons and faceted gems which may be prepared from suitable material. Mixtures of green willemite, black franklinite, red zincite, and white calcite are sometimes cut and polished into spheres, bookends, paperweights, etc., combining both a handsome appearance and startlingly beautiful fluorescence. In such specimens, the contrast between the vivid green glow of willemite and equally as rich red of the calcite makes this material prized the world over. Willemite is named in honor of King William I, a former ruler of the Netherlands.

In New Jersey, willemite occurs both in massive forms showing no trace of crystal outline, or, far more rarely, in distinct crystals belonging to the Hexagonal System and found lining cavities in carbonate veins in the ore bodies. A brownish opaque variety is named *troostite* after an early American mineralogist, and is often found in rather rude hexagonal prisms, sometimes as much as 6 inches in length and 2 inches in diameter. Clear crystals

FIGURE 129. Transparent rhombohedral rhodochrosite crystals (upper left) perched on a large mass of rock encrusted with malachite and quartz crystals; from Alma, Colorado. Specimen size: 6 inches by 8 inches; crystal size: about 1 inch. Courtesy Smithsonian Institution.

FIGURE 130. Gem grade willemite and several faceted gems from Franklin, New Jersey. The rough mass is a section of a large hexagonal crystal of a bright orange color with many perfectly clear places; size, 2½ inches by 2 inches. The faceted gems weigh from top to bottom, 11.66, 4.95, and 11.05 carats; the larger are about ⅝ inch in diameter. Courtesy Smithsonian Institution.

are usually much smaller and much more rare, ranging in size from needle-like prisms to some which were encountered in the Buckwheat Mine in Franklin, measuring 2 inches long and about the same in width. From these, magnificent orange faceted gems were cut by order of their discoverer, Frederick A. Canfield, who, being connected with the operation of the mine and also an ardent mineralogist, found himself in a most fortunate position to claim all interesting specimens. These clear crystals were noted for the absence of any distinct faces upon their terminations. Similar specimens were found at a later date, also from cavities, but this time of a peculiar yellowish color, quite clear and with an unusual fused appearance along the sides of the prisms. Beautiful examples of transparent crystals and faceted gems of large size may be seen in the collections of the U.S. National Museum (see Figure 130) and the American Museum of Natural History.

Pure willemite is a simple silicate of zinc: Zn_2SiO_4, but at the New Jersey localities it is rarely found without appreciable percentages of manganese, which substitutes for the zinc. Manganese up to 12 per cent has been noted but the average is about 7 per cent, exceptionally pure material showing only traces of manganese and other elements. Willemite is very brittle, breaking with a conchoidal to irregular fracture and displaying a greasy to glassy luster. The hardness is 5 to 5½. An indistinct cleavage is sometimes noted parallel to the basal plane of crystals. Specific gravity varies with impurities from 3.89 to 4.19. Refractive indices also vary according to purity, specimens containing more manganese tending to be higher in value. An unusually pure transparent specimen with only 1.33 per cent impurities, gave: $\omega = 1.691$, $\epsilon = 1.719$; birefringence 0.028; uniaxial, positive. Another, a clear wine-yellow crystal, gave: $\omega = 1.694$, $\epsilon = 1.725$; birefringence 0.031.

In color, willemite may be bright yellow-green, pure white, gray, and pale blue in massive forms, also reddish or brownish due to inclusions. Clear material is ordinarily yellow, orange-yellow, brownish-orange, or a vivid pure yellow-green. The fine gem quality crystals mentioned before have been orange or brownish-yellow only. Gray material sometimes shows small platey inclusions giving a slight aventurescent effect. Red inclusions of hematite, when sufficiently numerous, afford catseyes but the effect is not very strong. All of the greenish varieties of willemite are strongly fluorescent and glow slightly even in daylight.

FRIEDELITE

Among the minerals found at the mines of the New Jersey Zinc Company at Franklin and Ogdensburg, New Jersey, must be included friedelite which here occurs in massive form suitable for limited lapidary purposes. Crystals are also known but are too small to be of value for gems. In appearance, massive friedelite is extremely fine-grained and looks like chocolate-colored chalcedony. Occasionally some fairly translucent material of rich carnelian-red color is found which is suitable for cabochons or even faceted gems although the latter of course do not reflect much light. The name friedelite was affixed to this mineral in honor of Charles Friedel, an eminent French chemist.

Friedelite is a hydrous basic silicate of manganese with the formula: $Mn_8(OH,Cl)_4(SiO_3)_6 \cdot 3H_2O$. Although only about 4 in hardness, it is surprisingly tough because of its exceedingly fine cryptocrystalline structure. In this respect it resembles chalcedony and, like the latter, also breaks with a conchoidal fracture of dull to waxy luster. It generally forms paper thin seams and veins which at times increase to as much as 2 inches or more in thickness, traversing massive calcite-willemite-franklinite ore. Specific gravity ranges from 3.041 to 3.059. Since friedelite belongs to the Hexagonal system there are two principal refractive indices which vary in value between the limits shown: $\omega = 1.654$-1.656, $\epsilon = 1.620$-1.625; birefringence 0.030; uniaxial, negative. Because of its cryptocrystalline nature, massive material shows only a single indistinct reading upon the refractometer; a value of 1.645 was determined upon a bright brownish-red specimen in the author's collection.

Considerable friedelite has been cut and polished into curious and interesting gems, the best being those prepared from fairly translucent material of carnelian red color. Unusually fine pieces were also cut into faceted gems but this form of cutting seldom added much to brilliance. Other pieces have been cut into paperweights, or into polished slabs for mineral collections. The author possesses a floral pendant several inches long, carved in strong relief from dark brown material; this piece is illustrated in Figure 131.

HODGKINSONITE

Another odd mineral found at Franklin, New Jersey, is a pale purplish-pink species called hodgkinsonite. This lengthy name was given in honor of H. H. Hodgkinson, Assistant Underground Superintendent at the New Jersey Zinc Company's mine at Mine Hill, who first found the mineral. In its usual form, it appears as intergrown cleavable crystal grains filling seams and veinlets in massive willemite-

FIGURE 131. A pendant carved from massive dark reddish-brown Friedelite from Franklin, New Jersey. From top to bottom, it measures almost 3 inches.

franklinite ore. None of the veinlets are thick, unfortunately, and large pieces of this attractively-colored mineral are extremely scarce. Wherever the crystal grains are clear, small but pretty gems may be faceted from them. Hodgkinsonite is so rare that few collections contain good specimens and still fewer contain cut examples.

Hodgkinsonite is a basic zinc-manganese silicate with the formula:

$Mn(ZnOH)_2SiO_4$; it usually contains small traces of iron, calcium and magnesium. The system of crystallization is Monoclinic, the extremely rare crystals forming sharply pointed tapered prisms of rectangular cross section. An excellent cleavage is evident in most broken specimens, however, fracture surfaces along other directions are irregular to subconchoidal. The luster is glassy to somewhat greasy. Hardness is less than 5; brittle. Specific gravity is 3.91. Refractive indices are fairly high: $a = 1.724$, $\beta = 1.742$, $\gamma = 1.746$; birefringence 0.022; biaxial, negative. Although the color is invariably pink, a slight purplish cast is apparent. The pleiochroism is distinct showing rich pink, pale purplish-pink, and almost colorless.

Most transparent hodgkinsonite shows interesting inclusions of a colorless mineral in the form of fine needles crossing at random angles; this mineral may be willemite. The thickest vein sections reported have been only several inches across with individual crystal grains up to ¾ inch in diameter. Minute crystals in small cavities have also been found as well as etched individuals up to ⅜ inch diameter in places where veins have thickened. The largest cut stone in the author's collection is about 3/16 inch across, and weighs 0.89 carat.

SPHENE
(*Titanite*)

Some of the most beautiful gems in all of the Mineral Kingdom are cut from clear crystals of sphene. Possessing a high refractive index and a marvelous display of dispersion along with pleasing body colors, cut examples are prized by collectors despite their softness and unsuitability for wear in jewelry. Although relatively abundant in a number of places in North America, good gem material is uncommonly rare. Clear sphenes are almost always cut into faceted gems, the brilliant cut being employed most often to take advantage of the high degree of dispersion. The name of this species is taken from the Greek word for "wedge" in allusion to the shape of the crystals. The alternate name *titanite* refers to the presence of the element titanium in the composition. Some authorities prefer to use the latter as the species name, reserving the label sphene for specimens of light coloration such as those employed for cutting into gems.

Sphene is calcium titanium silicate crystallizing in the Monoclinic System and possessing the formula: $CaTiSiO_5$. It is almost always found in distinct crystals which may be as small as match-heads or as large as dinner plates, but of course, gem material tends to be, unfortunately, on the minute side. Crystals are predominantly wedge-shaped, sometimes very sharp and distinct in form, but at other times somewhat rounded or "fused" in appearance. Twin crystals are common, showing a deep vee-shaped groove along an edge where the two crystals join as shown in Figure 132. Sphene occurs in metamorphic rocks, in marbles, in schists and gneisses, and also in veins in granites. Hardness varies between 5 and 5½; the tenacity is low, causing specimens to break rather easily leaving behind conchoidal fractures of a high luster. A fair cleavage is sometimes seen but is generally absent in gem material. Specific gravity ranges from 3.45 to 3.56 although another authority places the range as between 3.52 and 3.54. Refractive indices are high but vary with changing composition: $a = 1.888$-1.914, $\gamma = 1.990$-2.053; birefringence 0.102-0.139; biaxial, positive. The dispersion is 0.051. Pleiochroism is distinct to strong: a brown specimen from Baja California showed light yellowish-green, deep greenish-yellow, and dark reddish-brown; a green cut stone from the same locality gave: pale green, dark olive green, and pale brown. A green example from Bridgewater, Pennsylvania, exhibited a most remarkable contrast in hues from a deep rich green to dark reddish-brown and deep brownish-orange. A pale orange-yellow specimen from Tilly Foster in New York gave only slight shades of yellow plus one direction in which almost no color was noted; the same weak distinction was noted in a small specimen of brown Ontario sphene which had been heat-treated to dark reddish-orange.

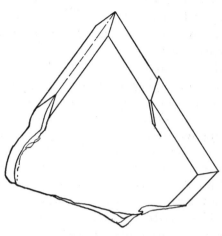

FIGURE 132. A fine example of twinning in sphene. This crystal, whose actual size is 1 inch in length and slightly over ⅛ inch in thickness, was found at the Pino Solo locality in Baja California; all faces are covered completely with many minute pits. The junction of the twins is shown by the dashed line on the left side of the drawing. This crystal is yellow-green in color and gem quality in places.

LOCALITIES

Ontario. Dark chocolate brown sphene in flattened wedge-shaped crystals is a common accessory mineral in the fluorite-apatite-calcite pegmatites of Ontario. There are two principal areas in which these pegmatites are concentrated, the first is near Wilberforce, in southeast Haliburton County, the second on the east side of Lake Clear in Renfrew County. Enormous crystals of sphene, though scarcely suited for gem purposes, came from the Smart Mine in Lot 31, Concession X, Sebastopol Township, Renfrew

County, where a pit for apatite was opened in 1880. Very fine crystals of brilliant hyacinth-red zircon, large apatite crystals, and other minerals accompanied the sphenes which at times were translucent in places and could be faceted. By heat treatment, it is possible to considerably lighten such sphenes to a deep brownish-orange color although they seldom survive this severe test without cracking. The usual method of obtaining suitable pieces is to heat treat a larger piece and then select clear and flawless fragments from among the shattered remnants. Magnificent sphene has been obtained since 1879 from a series of pits on the northern tip of Turner's Island (Island D) in Lake Clear, Sebastopol Township. These mines were originally opened for the sake of their apatite and are no longer worked except once in 1943 when an old working was tested for radioactive minerals. One apatite crystal weighing 700 pounds was removed from this mine as well as a typical dark brown sphene of over one foot in length, now in the collection of Harvard University Museum. Similar occurrences of sphene are found in many places in Grenville, Sebastopol, Eganville, Ross, and Brudenell Townships, Renfrew County. The Elliott Mine in Ross Township has produced much sphene associated with pyroxene. Translucent dark brown sphene suitable for heat treatment but again yielding only very small facet-grade pieces, is found in granite in North Crosby Township, near Westport, Leeds County.

Quebec. Mineralization productive of sphene, apatite, calcite, etc., occurs eastward into Quebec also, as for example at the King Edward Mine in Lot 8, Gore Mountain, on the west shore of Lac Rheaume, Templeton Township, in the northeast corner of Hull County.

New York. Some of the finest sphene from any locality in North America was found during a very brief period in the mining of the magnetite deposits at the Tilly Foster Iron Mine, near Brewster, Putnam County. Although ordinary magnetite deposits found in New York, New Jersey, and Pennsylvania, are ordinarily devoid of interesting minerals, the huge ore body at Tilly Foster contained large masses of metamorphosed limestone which introduced unusual mineral associations, among them sphene, and, as recounted elsewhere, gem quality chondrodite. In the summer of 1891, several hundred beautiful crystals of sphene were uncovered and later acquired by Ernest Schernikow of New York City who distributed them to collectors and museums. In size, they measured from 1 to 2 inches in length; nearly all had smooth faces and were twinned in the fashion typical of this mineral (see Figure 133). Colors were primarily yellow inclining somewhat to orange. Some were large enough to cut into gems from 10 to 15 carats in weight but due to numerous veil-like inclusions, flawless gems could be cut only in much smaller sizes. The famous necklace set of graduated round brilliant cut sphenes of matching color in the U.S. National Museum is probably cut from material from this locality. In 1891, crystals

FIGURE 133. Sphene crystals and cut stones. The pale orange-yellow crystals are from the Tilly Foster Mine, Brewster, New York, and show the typical sharp-edged habit of this species. Cut gems are from the Pino Solo deposit in Baja California Norte, Mexico, and weigh 5.59 and 5.18 carats. Courtesy Smithsonian Institution.

were recovered from the upper portions of the mine in the course of preparation for opencast work, but since that time, no more have been found. Typical rough specimens may be seen in the collections of the American Museum of Natural History, as for example, a loose gemmy crystal of 1½ by 2 inches, and a crystal of 1½ inches perched on matrix measuring 3 by 4 inches.

Pennsylvania. Fine large sphene crystals of greenish-yellow to olive-green color were found many years ago at John Mullen's Quarries on the east side of Chester Creek opposite the Bridgewater Station of the Pennsylvania Railroad in Chester Township, Delaware County. Crystals were found lying loose with quartz crystals in a decomposed mica schist, probably in some sort of pocket since perfectly-developed sphene crystals are seldom found except in such openings. Many measured as much as 1 to 3 inches in length and commonly exhibited twinning. Most were exceptionally clear but some were cracked; larger examples were estimated as capable of being cut into fine gems up to 10 to 20 carats. In Upper Chichester Township of this same county, brilliant green and yellow gem quality crystals up to 1 inch in length were once found near the contact between gabbro and pegmatite along the north side of the Baltimore & Ohio Railroad right of way, just west of the east branch of Naaman's Creek, ⅜ mile southwest of Boothwyn Station.

Baja California Norte. What may eventually be the most important sphene locality in the entire world is a broad area of pegmatite outcrops in a barren desert valley in the center of the peninsula of Baja California some miles southeast of Ensenada. Here in the early 1950's, in a narrow sandy valley sparsely vegetated by desert shrubs, greenish to brown tabular crystals of sphene were found upon the surface quite by accident. The locality embraces a prominent landmark—a single pine tree called Pino Solo at a fork in the road which leads southward from Ojos Negros to Alamo. Upon discovery, several of the crystals were taken to California where they were identified and their considerable value as gemstones verified. Additional prospecting in the area soon afterwards revealed many other fragments sprinkled about the surface but very few as fine as those originally found. Intrigued by the possibility of finding the source of the better quality stones, Elbert McMacken of Escondido, and Edward Swoboda of Los Angeles, California, intensively prospected the vicinity and succeeded in tracking the crystals to a narrow pegmatite which outcropped several hundred yards from the lone pine mentioned. A crew of local laborers were put to work and within several days, many fine crystals were recovered from a greenish micaceous earth found filling the center of the vein. The deposit consisted of a narrow seam or vein containing dark epidote, often handsomely crystallized in single crystals and rosettes, tourmalinated quartz, some white opaque feldspar, kaolin, and the greenish micaceous mineral previously mentioned in which the best formed crystals of sphene were embedded. Both the epidote and sphene crystals were etched on all surfaces and therefore were dull in luster. Hundeds of carats of beautiful sphene were removed from the vein before it eventually pinched off several feet below the surface. The largest crystal proved to be about 2 inches square and at least ½ inch thick; although resinous brown in appearance, it was found to be mostly clear yellow-green material enclosing a central core of exceedingly dark colored sphene which accounted for its somber appearance. Smaller crystals were completely green or greenish-yellow. Most crystals were of simple tabular habit but twinned. Apparently the original crystals grew as brown individuals but as nourishing solutions changed in chemical character, the later layers became paler until the lightest color of all, a fine clear yellow was deposited as a very thin envelope. Because of the variation in color, beautiful clear gems of either deep warm reddish-chocolate hue or smaller ones of green or yellow could be cut. The dispersion so pronounced in sphene appears primarily as red flashes in the brown gems but all colors are seen in those of paler tone.

In 1956, the author carefully examined the Pino Solo area and determined that the underlying granitic rocks, generally badly decomposed and friable, were laced with large numbers of pegmatite bodies ranging from mere lenses of several feet in length to dikes of at least ten feet in width and several hundred feet long. Similar terrain covered the entire valley floor for many miles in all directions. At this time it was confidently predicted that other pegmatites would be found in which gem sphene would be an important constituent since examination of a number of exposed bodies showed the presence of minute crystals in all, and in some, large individuals up to 4 or 5 inches in length but badly decomposed and worthless for any purpose. One such large dike was noted only several yards north of the lone pine alongside of the road. Thus it is gratifying to note that in 1958 another astonishing find of sphene has been made in the same area by Mexican prospectors who with the phenomenal crystal illustrated in Figure 134 recovered

FIGURE 134. A magnificent single crystal of sphene from Pino Solo, Baja California, measuring 4 inches by 5¾ inches by 1⅛ inches and weighing 2925 carats. Numerous places within the crystal are gem quality. Courtesy Charles J. Parsons, CG, FGA.

about 15,000 carats of gem material from one pocket in a large pegmatite. Although the largest crystal measured 4 by 5¾ by 1⅛ inches and weighed 2925 carats, another of 2430 carats appears to contain more flawless material. Neither crystal, however, contains as much gem material in proportion as the numerous smaller crystals won from the same deposit. As of fall of 1958, the large crystal described was in the possession of Martin Ehrmann of Los Angeles who purchased it from the dealer handling the transaction with the Mexican miners. One observer who had an opportunity to closely examine the lot states that several 20-carat gems can be cut from some of the finer crystals. Sphenes of this size would be among the largest known to the world of gems. Fine brilliant cut stones of Baja California sphene up to ⅜ inch diameter are in the collections of the American Museum of Natural History and in the U.S. National Museum. A cut example is illustrated in Figure 133.

AUGELITE

Among the oddities seen only in a few unusually complete gem collections is the rare colorless phosphate augelite. Its name is derived from the Greek word for "luster," alluding to its bright glassy or pearly appearance, the latter caused by development of numerous separations along a perfect cleavage plane.

Augelite is a basic phosphate of aluminum with the formula: $Al_2(PO_4)$ $(OH)_3$. Belonging to the Monoclinic System, it crystallizes in thick tabular individuals but is found more commonly as formless masses. Augelite occurs in veins formed through the agency of hot water solutions but is also frequently observed in certain pegmatite bodies. Hardness varies according to direction within each crystal, exhibiting values from about 4½ to 5. In addition to the perfect cleavage referred to above, another, less perfect, is also present; the net result is that augelite is both fragile and somewhat difficult to cut successfully. Specific gravity is given by one authority as ranging between 2.5 and 2.7; another gives 2.67 for the California material described below. Refractive indices are:

CHANDLER'S MILL, N.H.	NORTH GROTON, N.H.	CALIFORNIA
$\alpha = 1.574$	$\alpha = 1.573$	$\alpha = 1.570$
$\beta = 1.576$	$\beta = 1.576$	
$\gamma = 1.588$	$\gamma = 1.587$	$\gamma = 1.584$

Birefringence is 0.014 in each of the above examples; augelite is biaxial, positive. Mostly colorless, some augelite is also pale yellow and pale rose; in one of the New Hampshire localities, blue examples are found although this color is believed to be due to fine particles of disseminated blue lazulite.

LOCALITIES

New Hampshire. Augelite has been found at two localities in granitic pegmatites. The first is at the Smith Mine at Chandler's Mill, Sullivan County, where pale aquamarine-blue crystals occur associated with lazulite, albite, and quartz. Crystals are embedded and poorly formed, the color, as noted before, is assumed to be due to inclusions of lazulite. The second locality is a famous one among mineralogists—the Palermo Quarry near North Groton, Grafton County.

California. Fine colorless crystals up to ¾ inch across have been found in the Champion Mine on the west slope of White Mountain, Mono County, where it occurs in some abundance (see LAZULITE). At this locality, quartzite has been replaced by lenses of andalusite, the commercial ore of the mine, and the latter is associated with rutile, francolite, strengite, corundum, topaz, lazulite, diaspore, colorless tourmaline, barite, and woodhouseite. Augelite occurs in massive form and as well-formed crystals in limonite matrix. Apparently many of these crystals are under stress within the matrix as they have been known to fly apart spontaneously when removed. Some of the augelite has a slight tinge of yellow. So far as is known, all cut augelites seen in collections within the United States come from material supplied by this mine.

SCHEELITE

Although much better known as a valuable ore of tungsten, scheelite often affords beautiful faceted gems from transparent material. Since the refractive indices and dispersion are high, colorless varieties can be cut into exceptionally brilliant gems which strongly resemble diamonds. Undescribed in gem literature, this interesting mineral is found often enough in gem quality to merit being recognized as a rare and unusually beautiful gemstone. The name of the species honors a Swedish chemist of note, K. W. Scheele, the discoverer of tungstic acid.

Scheelite is calcium tungstate with the formula: $CaWO_4$, and crystallizes in the Tetragonal System. Crystals habitually form 4-sided pyramids, or, when complete, octahedrons slightly elongated along the vertical axes. In the California occurrences described below, modification of form combined with extensive etching, often reduces crystals to rounded lumps bearing little resemblance to any crystal form (see Figure 135). Such specimens have been found loose in cavities and called "nodules" or "nuggets" by the miners. At other localities transparent material is more likely to occur in small crystals of less than an inch in diameter. Large crystals over several pounds in weight have also been found but are seldom clear except at the very tips. The hardness of scheelite is listed as 4½ to 5 but lapidary experience indicates it is closer to 5 or 5½. Several cleavages are present but developed with difficulty. Scheelite is weak and brittle, fracturing easily and leaving behind conchoidal surfaces of glassy to resinous luster; some specimens, notably from California, are somewhat adamantine in luster. The refractive indices are high: $\omega = 1.9208$, $\epsilon = 1.9375$; birefringence 0.017, uniaxial, positive. The dispersion (between 6670 and 4750 Angstroms) is 0.024 for ω and 0.026 for ϵ, high enough to cause considerable flashing of color in faceted gems. Dichroism is very weak, a rich orange-yellow material from Arizona showing orange-yellow and slightly greenish-yellow.

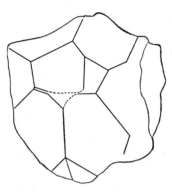

FIGURE 135. A so-called "nodule" of colorless gem quality scheelite from the Greenhorn Mountains of California. A few well-defined faces are present upon the crystal but all edges are somewhat rounded and the mass is frosted more or less completely. The nodule is about ⅝ inch in diameter.

Utah. Beautiful scheelite of rich orange-brown color is found in a tungsten deposit in the Mineral Mountains near Milford, Beaver County. Octahedral crystals with clear tips have been found; the author has cut a gem of about 8 carats from this material.

Arizona. The Boriana Mine in the Hualpai Mountains of Mohave County, is noted for exceptionally large crystals of brownish to yellowish color. A single crystal measuring 3 by 4 inches is in the collection of the Mineralogical Museum of Harvard University; the American Museum of Natural History possesses another of 1½ by 2 inches, clear and flawless on one termination and estimated capable of being cut into a gem of about ¾ inch in diameter. A fine, partly clear brownish crystal from the Cohen Mine in the Cabezas Mountains, is in the U.S. National Museum and measures 5 inches tall and about 4 inches in diameter.

California. Flawless scheelite crystals occur in a group of deposits several miles east of the Greenhorn Mountains State Park in Kern County. The Huckaby Mine is the most noted of the group which exploit these deposits for tungsten and produced in the past many fine colorless to faintly pink etched crystals from pockets in quartz veins. The majority of crystals were rudely formed, often without a single good crystal face, and, at times, merely formless lumps. Within the pockets occurred fine quartz and epidote crystals, the latter often of gem quality and sometimes noted penetrating the clear quartz. This mine and others nearby have ceased operations and the present meager supply of scheelite and epidote is obtained by digging in the extensive dumps. Crystals or "nuggets" of fine scheelite have been found here measuring as much as 2 inches in diameter but the usual size is close to ¼ to ½ inch. Less spectacular specimens are found at the Zellner or Little Acorn Mine and in the Ford Mine in Bull Run Basin; crystals from the latter mine are seldom over ¼ inch. Among cut stones, the U.S. National Museum owns an exceptionally fine mixed cut gem of 18.7 carats; another of ⅜ inch diameter is in the American Museum of Natural History.

The second major locality in California is the series of deposits on the Tungsten Hills northwest of Bishop in Inyo County. Apparently these deposits also produced fine colorless crystals of gem grade since the American Museum of Natural History owns a 20.65 carats brilliant cut gem with this locality on its label.

DIOPSIDE

Among gemstones, diopside is noted mainly for the green faceted gems which some transparent varieties afford, and to a lesser degree, for catseyes which are cut from chatoyant material. Clear diopside is rare in North America but several localities furnishing good specimens are known as well as a few places from which rough suitable for cabochons is obtained.

Diopside is a member of the large Pyroxene Group of minerals, crystallizing in short stubby prisms in the Monoclinic System. With hedenbergite it forms a series of calcium magnesium iron silicates as indicated by these formulas: diopside ($CaMgSi_2O_6$), and hedenbergite ($CaFeSi_2O_6$).

Substitution of iron for magnesium in diopside results in darkening colors and lessened suitability for gems. The minerals of this series occur mostly in zones of strong metamorphism in dolomitic limestone but other types of occurrences are also known. Crystals are common but seldom clear except in small areas. Granular masses showing pearly luster upon individual grains sometimes provide good cabochon or ornamental material. Diopside possesses several cleavages which parallel the sides of crystal prisms and intersect to form angles of 87° and 93°. Luster on cleavage and fracture surfaces is glassy; the fracture is conchoidal. Hardness varies from as low as 5 to as high as 7; very soft kinds are often partly altered. The specific gravity lies between 3.20 and 3.34. Refractive indices are variable but the following may be taken as representative: $\alpha = 1.673$, $\beta = 1.680$, $\gamma = 1.702$; birefringence 0.029; biaxial, positive. Diopside from Richville, New York gives: $\alpha = 1.668$, $\gamma = 1.700$; birefringence 0.032. The usual color of gem varieties is some shade of yellow or dark green, sometimes emerald green if slight traces of chromium are present. Colorless, gray, brown, and grayish- to greenish-blue kinds are also found. Pleiochroism is faint even in strongly colored varieties and shows in green specimens, for example, only slight changes in basic hue.

LOCALITIES

Ontario. The metamorphic limestones of Ontario and Quebec afford large crystals at numerous points but only a few localities are known where clear material suitable for gems occurs. Transparent green crystals, unfortunately much shattered and cleaved and therefore affording only very small gems, come from Lot 1, Concession XXI in Cardiff Township, Haliburton County. Light green gems have been cut from diopside crystals found on Lot 3, Concession IV, Bird's Creek, Herschel Township, Hastings County. Some very fine flawless stones up to 1 carat in weight have been cut from this material. Beautiful but small, emerald-green crystals sometimes occur associated with apatite and other minerals next to a feldspar pegmatite cutting crystalline limestone in North Burgess Township, near Perth, in Lanark County.

Quebec. Large light reddish-brown crystals occur in metamorphosed limestone next to pegmatite in a small pit near Laurel, just south of Sixteen Island Lake, Argenteuil County. Numerous parallel inclusions cause a catseye effect to appear on the surfaces of high rounded cabochons though the band of light is neither narrow nor very bright. Cabochons up to 15 carats can be cut, or, from clear spots, faceted gems up to 2 carats. Greenish-gray material useful for the same purposes is also found here. In Sherbrooke County, beautiful but very small emerald-green diopside crystals are found lining cavities in pyroxenite rock in Orford Township. The specific gravity of this material ranges from 3.13 to 3.15.

New York. The finest transparent diopside crystals, ranking with the best from any world locality, occur in an outcropping of metamorphic dolomite-limestone in a pasture upon the old Calvin Mitchell farm about 3 miles northeast of Richville, DeKalb Township, St. Lawrence County. This locality was known as early as 1884 when several splendid crystals over 3 inches in length and 1 inch in thickness, mostly clear, were recovered from a small pit sunk in the outcrop. It was estimated that gems up to 20 or 30 carats weight could have been cut from these magnificent examples. Diopside crystals from this locality form short stout prisms with glassy prism faces but etched or grooved terminal faces (see Figure 136). In size, individuals range from ½ inch to as much as 4 inches in length. The percentage of facetable material is high. The color, slightly tinged with a smoky cast, is rather unusual for diopside since it partakes of a very light grayish- to yellowish-green, at once distinctive from any other green kind presently known. An outstanding matrix specimen is in the Bement Collection of the American Museum of Natural History and consists of a magnificent single gemmy crystal, 2½ by 4 inches, perched upon a mass of rock,

FIGURE 136. Gem quality green diopside crystals from Richville, New York. The larger crystals are slightly over 1 inch in length. Courtesy Smithsonian Institution.

4 by 5 inches. This museum also includes in its collections a fine and very brilliant emerald-cut stone measuring approximately ⅜ by ½ inch. The author's collection includes a fine rectangular mixed-cut gem of 5.02 carats.

Maryland. Massive diopside mixed with grains and veinlets of flesh pink to brownish-red grossularite garnet, chlorite, opal, and calcite, occurs in considerable quantity in gabbro and serpentine exposed in the Rockville Crushed Stone Quarry near Hunting Hills, Montgomery County. The diopside varies from pale opaque green to deep emerald-green in grains up to several inches across and is more or less altered. Many of the masses show distinct parting with slight pearly luster or schiller on the surfaces. In some masses, the centers of diopside grains show a transition to a black mineral, possibly hedenbergite. The material is quite compact, and attractive book-ends have been cut from some pieces although polishing is not an easy task on account of the considerable differences in hardness among the several minerals present.

New Mexico. Dark green chrome-diopside is reported from the garnet fields of McKinley County. Very little is known about this occurrence although it has been mentioned in several places in old literature. (See GAR-NET).

ANTHOPHYLLITE, ACTINOLITE, TREMOLITE

The several minerals discussed in this section are members of the important group of silicates known as the Amphiboles. Crystals tend to form long prisms showing two excellent cleavages inclined to each other at angles of about 56° and 124°. Some forms produce fibrous aggregates, the best known example being asbestos. Similar formation is seen also in nephrite jade, and, in part, accounts for the exceptional toughness of this gemstone. Nephrite is treated separately although it is very close to tremolite and actinolite in essential properties (see JADE). Clear specimens of actinolite and tremolite sometimes afford small faceted gems while fibrous examples of all three may furnish material suitable for catseyes. Anthophyllite from Greenland provides handsome material exhibiting vivid colors similar to those observed in labradorite and possibly due to the same cause.

Anthophyllite is named after the Greek *anthophyllum*—"a clove," in reference to its usual clove-brown color. The fibrous aggregates of actinolite crystals, frequently radiating from a common central point, reminded early mineralogists of rays and accordingly the Greek word for "ray" was combined with the word for "stone" to form this mineral's name. Tremolite is named after its occurrence in the Val Tremola in Switzerland.

Anthophyllite, actinolite, and tremolite are magnesium silicates which differ chemically in their content of iron and calcium. This is made clear by their formulas: anthophyllite $[(Mg,Fe)_7Si_8O_{22}(OH)_2]$, actinolite $[Ca_2(Mg, Fe)_5Si_8O_{22}(OH)_2]$, and tremolite $[Ca_2Mg_5Si_8O_{22}(OH)_2]$. Anthophyllite crystallizes in the Orthorhombic System but the others crystallize in the Monoclinic. Although actinolite and tremolite are relatively common in metamorphosed impure limestones or dolomites, anthophyllite is comparatively rare except in Greenland where it is abundant in metamorphic rocks along the west coast. Distinct well-terminated crystals are rarely found in any of these species. In all cases the luster is inclined to be glassy, or pearly when many cleavages exist, but also metallic in the case of anthophyllite.

The hardness varies between 5 and 6. The specific gravity of anthophyllite varies between 2.9 and 3.4; that of actinolite and tremolite from 2.9 to 3.3. The refractive indices of anthophyllite vary considerably according to iron content, rising as this element predominates, however, the following are standard values: $a = 1.633$, $\beta = 1.642$, $\gamma = 1.657$; the birefringence is 0.024; biaxial. The optic sign is positive in ordinary material but in the variety *gedrite* (discussed below under GREENLAND), the sign is minus. Actinolite indices are: $a = 1.614$, $\beta = 1.630$, $\gamma = 1.640$; birefringence 0.026. Tremolite indices are: $a = 1.60$, $\beta = 1.61$, $\gamma = 1.62$; birefringence 0.02. The lilac variety known as *hexagonite* gives: $a = 1.600$, $\gamma = 1.627$; birefringence 0.027. Both actinolite and tremolite are biaxial, negative.

Anthophyllite is usually brown in color but grayish and greenish hues are also known. Actinolite and tremolite range from colorless or white, and through various shades of green depending on the iron content; greenish-gray and brown are also known but may be due, in part, to other minerals present in the form of minute rods or flakes. Hexagonite is distinctive pale reddish-purple. Pleiochroism is marked in deep-colored varieties, a dark gray-blue specimen of tremolite showing gray-blue, grayish-green and pale straw-yellow. Hexagonite shows faint but distinct changes in the dichroscope involving very pale pink, deeper pink, and pale purplish-red.

LOCALITIES

Greenland. In his mineralogical travels through Greenland, the famous mineralogist Giesecke described an exceptionally beautiful variety of "hypersthene" in the same locality at which large numbers of gem quality almandine garnets occur. However, Boggild, in his *Mineralogy of Greenland,* states that it is in reality the *gedrite* variety of anthophyllite which Giesecke spoke of. Gedrite occurs as nodular masses in mica schist, a rock very widespread in the area between the eastern arm of Ameralik Fjord and the glacier some ten miles east of this point. The colors displayed by the gedrite are both unusual and beautiful, and are said to resemble most closely those seen in labradorite. Gedrite occurs as small crystals forming radiate masses or as large single crystals of rude four-sided form often striated like tourmaline prisms. The body color varies from brown to black, sometimes greenish, but brown specimens fail to show iridescent colors. Iridescent colors are primarily deep sky-blue, brass-yellow and bronze.

Ontario. Brown tremolite, minutely fissured with flat partings or openings which are brilliantly reflective, has been found at the Richardson Feldspar Quarry located very near the southwest end of the western arm of Desert Lake in the southwest corner of Bedford Township, Frontenac County. This material produces attractive catseyes. Better gems are produced from grayish and bluish tremolites from the Grenville series of metamorphosed limestones as in the quarries in the vicinity of Haliburton and Wilberforce in Haliburton County. Clear tremolite of deep gray-blue color from Wilberforce has been cut into small brilliants of about .5 to .7 carat; also cut has been one type of bright emerald-green color. The latter occurs with diopside of almost the same hue and has been mistaken for this mineral.

New York. Curious crumbly masses of granular pale reddish-purple tremolite of the hexagonite variety, occur in considerable quantity at the old Loomis Talc Mine located on Highway 58, just northwest of Fowler, St. Lawrence County. The spectacular specimens consist of multitudes of rounded crystals of transparent hexagonite so loosely held together that individual fragments can be detached with the fingers. The grains are mainly small, less than ⅛ inch, but at times, slender individuals up to ½ inch or more in length are available. If clear and flawless, these can be faceted into small gems of pleasing color and considerable brilliance.

SCAPOLITE

Transparent scapolite suitable for faceting gems is rarely found in North America and then only in sizes sufficient for very small stones. A useful variety which has some merit for cutting is a translucent grayish material which can be cut into fairly distinct catseyes. This kind has been found in the Grenville metamorphic limestones of Ontario and Quebec. The name scapolite has been derived from the Greek word for "rod" in allusion to the squarish prismatic crystals which characterize the usual habit.

Scapolite is the group name for a series of closely-related Tetragonal aluminum silicates which also contain calcium and sodium and differ from each other in respect to the content of the latter two elements. The calcium-rich end member is called *meionite*, and is followed by *wernerite* and *mizzonite*, while the sodium-rich end member, *marialite* completes the series. The relationships of the Scapolite Group are shown in these formulas: meionite $Ca_4Al_3(Al,Si)_3Si_6O_{24}(Cl,CO_3,SO_4)$, to wernerite, to mizzonite, to marialite $Na_4Al_3(Al,Si)_3Si_6O_{24}(Cl,CO_3SO_4)$.

Scapolite species form characteristic stubby crystal prisms of square cross section, terminated at each end by low four-faced pyramids. Crystals are rarely smooth and glistening, most of those found in Canada being rather crude, without sharp corners, and dull to greasy in luster. Numerous minute cleavage splits and cracks parallel to each of the four prism faces in Canadian crystals cause the catseye effects mentioned above; in addition, many narrow rodlike inclusions of a dark mineral are also seen oriented in the same directions. Hardness within the group varies from about 5½ to 6. Specific gravity varies from 2.70 to 2.74. Refractive indices are variable according to composition but may fall within these ranges:

	REFRACTIVE INDICES		BIREFRINGENCE
	ω	ε	
Meionite	1.58 — 1.60	1.55 — 1.56	0.03 — 0.04
Wernerite	1.56 — 1.58	1.54 — 1.55	0.02 — 0.03
Mizzonite	1.53 — 1.56	1.52 — 1.54	0.01 — 0.02
Marialite	1.539	1.537	0.002

All of the members of the group are uniaxial and optically negative. Scapolite is found in white, milky or gray translucent crystals; also in yellow, pink, blue and violet.

LOCALITIES

Greenland. In the Umanak District, transparent colorless or faintly yellow crystals up to ¾ inch are found on the mountain of Kangeq at Niaqornat.

Quebec. Good lemon-yellow scapolite, sometimes clear enough to facet small gems, is found near Grenville, Argenteuil County. In Hull County, the King Edward Mine in the northern part of Templeton Township on Lot 8 on Gore Mountain, has produced glassy blue scapolite of cuttable quality. This mine is near the west shore of Rheaume Lake. The Wallingford Mine in the west half of Lot 16, Range VIII, in the same township, is located about 1½ miles west of Perkins Mill village and has produced fibrous forms of scapolite altered into lilac *pinite*, locally called *wilsonite*. Some of this material works into attractive cabochons of silky luster. In Gatineau County, the Nellie and Blanche Mine on Lot 10, Range X, Hull Township, has yielded exceptional scapolite crystals up to 8 inches in length; refractive indices on this mineral give: $\omega = 1.574$, $\varepsilon = 1.550$; birefringence 0.024. The latter locality is about 2 miles southwest of Cantley. Small faceted gems have been cut from the crystals but they have been found most useful for making catseyes. Similar material has come from the Dacey Mine in the same county, located 1½ miles southwest of Wilson's Corners on Lot 12A, Range XV, Hull Township.

Ontario. The same metamorphic limestones of the Grenville Series which produce scapolite in Quebec also furnish attractive material in this province. In Haliburton County, exceptionally large crystals up to 3 inches by 3 inches have been obtained from shallow pits dug by mineral collectors in the hills near the shore of Loon Lake about halfway between Drag Lake Lodge and Essonville, Monmouth Township. Very small gems of only ¼ carat but clear and beautiful yellow, have been cut from material found near

Drag Lake, Dudley Township. In Renfrew County, unevenly colored pale green facet grade scapolite has been found in the old Spain Mine on Lot 31, Concession IV, just south of Highway 41 and 6 miles northeast of Griffith Bridge, Griffith Township. A gem of 1.75 carats was cut from some of the transparent material. Large rude crystals of scapolite also occur in the vicinity of Eganville.

Massachusetts. Massive pink chatoyant scapolite is found in metamorphic limestone in a quarry 2 miles directly east of Bolton, Worcester County, and several hundred feet north of Highway 117. Large crystal aggregates from 6 to 24 inches across and firm enough for polishing are found here. The color is beautiful pinkish-lilac, paling to lighter shades toward crystal borders. Some of the individual crystals show clear glassy centers. The American Museum of Natural History collections include a polished slab measuring 3 by 4 inches as well as a cabochon of $1\frac{1}{4}$ by $1\frac{1}{2}$ inches.

DANBURITE

This rare relative of common topaz is sometimes found in crystals large enough to afford small colorless faceted gems. Although named for its occurrence in the city of Danbury, Connecticut, it has been found in gem quality in North America only in the state of San Luis Potosi, Mexico. Danburite has little to commend it as a gemstone since it seldom occurs in colored varieties or distinguishes itself in any way from a host of other colorless species. Being rare, it is prized only by collectors and museums.

Danburite is calcium borosilicate with the formula: $CaB_2Si_2O_8$. It is found in high-temperature veins and at contacts between metamorphosed rock masses. Crystals are usually slender four-sided prisms, several times as long as they are thick, smoothly-faced, and often quite transparent and flawless. Crystallizing in the Orthorhombic System like its relative, topaz, there is considerable resemblance between crystals of both species except that the pronounced and perfect cleavage of topaz is absent. Danburite is fairly hard, about 7 or slightly more; the specific gravity ranges between 2.97 and 3.02. Refractive indices are as follows: $a = 1.630$, $\beta = 1.633$, $\gamma = 1.636$. The birefringence is only 0.006 and the dispersion 0.016. Danburite is biaxial and optically negative. Mexican material is colorless but clear yellow crystals are known from Burma.

LOCALITY

San Luis Potosi. The exact locality for danburite is not stated in any literature except as from Charcas, San Luis Potosi. Specimens brought back to the United States proved to be groups of crystals covered almost entirely by encrustations of calcite which it was necessary to remove with acid in order to expose the crystals. Groups ranged in size from 3 by 6 inches to as much as 5 by 17 inches while individual crystals measured from 1½ to 3 inches in length. About 60 per cent were estimated to be clear enough to facet into flawless emerald-cut gems of from 2 to 5 carats weight. Aside from calcite, pyrite is the only other mineral associated with the danburite upon the groups examined.

CHONDRODITE

An extremely rare garnet-red gem is sometimes cut from transparent chondrodite found in only one locality in North America: the long-abandoned Tilly Foster Iron Mine on Highway 6, 6 miles northwest of Brewster, Putnam County, New York. Although chondrodite occurs in many places in the Middle Atlantic States, in fact wherever metamorphic dolomitic limestone is found, it generally appears as formless blobs or irregular grains only slightly translucent and totally unfit for cutting. At the Tilly Foster locality however, it was found in beautiful, sharp, shiny crystals associated with a peculiar soft asbestos-like serpentine in crack and fissure fillings next to the contact between the great magnetite body and metamorphosed limestone. Many of these outstanding crystals proved to be perfectly transparent and afforded small but unique gems.

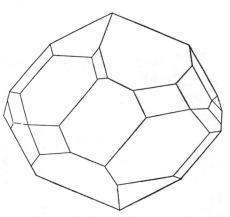

FIGURE 137. Chondrodite crystal from the Tilly Foster Mine, Brewster, New York.

Chondrodite is a member of the Humite Group of minerals, each of which is a fluosilicate of magnesium differing only slightly in chemical composition and in physical and optical properties. The assumed composition for chondrodite is: $2Mg_2SiO_4 \cdot Mg(OH,F)_2$. Crystals belong to the Monoclinic System and are often wonderfully rich in faces as shown in Figure 137. In size, they vary from minute individuals to those up to ¾ inch across and superficially resemble almandine garnet crystals but are less spherical in general form. Hardness is quite low, less than 6, while traces of cleavage can be noted in several directions upon the irregular fracture surfaces. Chondrodite is easily fractured and care must be exerted in cutting to prevent inadvertent breakage. The gravity varies from 3.1 to 3.2. Textbook values for refractive indices show: $\alpha = 1.59\text{-}1.60$, $\beta = 1.60\text{-}1.62$, $\gamma = 1.62\text{-}1.64$. Two cut specimens in the author's collection showed the following: $a = 1.608$, $\gamma = 1.640$ and $a = 1.616$, $\gamma = 1.648$; birefringence is 0.032, biaxial, positive. Gem quality specimens are invariably a rich brownish-red shade very similar to some varieties of almandine garnet. Trichroism is barely distinct, varying from dark brownish-red to dark orange-red.

The period during which the best chondrodite crystals were found at the locality extended from 1891 to 1892 when the particular zone in which they occurred was being actively mined, however, occasional specimens are still found on the dumps. A splendid specimen of rough is in the American Museum of Natural History, comprising a piece of magnetite matrix about 2 inches by 3 inches in size with crystals of gem quality up to $\frac{1}{2}$ inch and $\frac{3}{4}$ inch perched on top. In this same museum are two brilliant cut specimens, one $\frac{1}{8}$ inch and the other $\frac{1}{4}$ inch in diameter. Kunz records a cut example measuring $\frac{1}{4}$ inch by $\frac{1}{2}$ inch in size. The largest of the author's stones is a coffin-shaped stepcut gem about 5/16 inch in length and weighing .85 carat.

FIGURE 138. A small but fine matrix specimen of benitoite showing several medium size crystals in the center of the specimen along with black neptunite crystals on the right. The matrix is bluish-gray serpentine partly covered with snow white massive natrolite. Specimen size, about 6 inches in length.

BENITOITE

In their studies of the mathematics of crystals, mineralogists found it possible to group all crystals into six broad systems, further subdivided into 32 classes according to the symmetry or lack of symmetry in the arrangement of crystal faces. Thus, the Hexagonal System was theorized to have no less than 12 of these classes within it. Although 10 of the 12 were soon found to have actual examples in nature, two remained represented by nothing more than theory. It was with considerable gratification therefore that a relative newcomer to the ranks of gemstones, benitoite, was found to fit one of the missing classes. A further distinction of this beautiful blue mineral is the fact that in all the world, it is found only in a limited area in San Benito County, California from which locality it receives its name. Benitoite crystals are wonderfully transparent, rich blue in color, and though soft, provide gems as lovely as the finest sapphires.

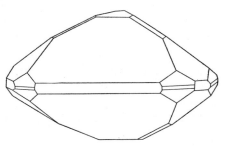

FIGURE 139. A crystal of benitoite from California as viewed from the side. When viewed from above, the crystal would appear like a triangle with the sharp corners slightly beveled.

Benitoite is a barium titano-silicate, crystallizing in the ditrigonal-dipyramidal class of the Hexagonal System; its formula is $BaTiSi_3O_9$. Figure 138 illustrates a typical specimen showing a mass of serpentine sprinkled by benitoite and black neptunite crystals; Figure 139 illustrates the crystal form. Specific gravity ranges from 3.65 to 3.69 and the hardness is stated to be 6½ although in lapidary work it seems closer to 5. Benitoite has no cleavage planes but fractures easily, producing shining conchoidal to irregular fracture surfaces. Refractive indices are high: $\omega = 1.757$, $\epsilon = 1.804$; birefringence is 0.047; uniaxial, positive. The large double refraction is easily noted when faceted gems are examined under a loupe. The color dispersion is also large: 0.039 for the ordinary ray and 0.046 for the extraordinary ray. Dispersive effects are easily noted in cut gems, reddish reflections being commonly observed.

The color of benitoite is one of its most attractive qualities, the usual shade being fairly intense blue often verging on purplish-blue. However, absolutely colorless specimens are also found as well as a variety of intermediate shades. In some crystals, coloration is arranged in zones, being most intense toward the edges of the flattened triangular crystals and pale or even colorless in the centers. As may be expected, colored specimens are strongly dichroic showing a rich blue in one window of the dichroscope and colorless in the other. Examination of crystals shows that the last is seen when looking down upon the tabular portion and the dark blue color is observed laterally through the edges. The depth of hue in a finished gem depends upon how carefully the cutter takes this into consideration when orienting the rough.

LOCALITY

California. Benitoite was discovered in the fall of 1906 by a prospector named J. M. Couch who brought out some crystals from the now well-known locality in San Benito County. Various local experts called the stones sapphire but others said they were "volcanic glass." It was not until 1907 when samples were turned over to Dr. G. D. Louderback of the University of California that the existence of a new mineral (and gem) was confirmed. Contrary to what has been stated above, Dr. Louderback's own account of benitoite states that the discoverers of the new mineral were Mr. T. E. Sanders and a Mr. Hawkins who found the deposit while prospecting in the southern part of the San Diablo Range near the San Benito-Fresno county line. The stones were brought to Dr. Louderback's attention by the jewelry firm of Shreve & Co., who had not been able to identify them.

In any case, the announcement of the existence of benitoite created a stir in the gem world and it was not long before a supply of rough was placed upon the market. Prices of cut gems were held at high levels and even today, flawless gems over one carat in size command as much as $100 per carat. Unfortunately, most crystals are so small that cut stones of over one carat are uncommon and those of over three carats are counted as rare. The largest cut gem in existence is only 7.5 carats in weight and is on exhibit in the U.S. National Museum. An emerald-cut gem of 3.57 carats is in the American Museum of Natural History while smaller examples are sprinkled throughout numerous private collections.

The benitoite deposit lies in a wild and generally impassable region of San Benito County about 25 miles north of Coalinga near the headwaters of the San Benito River. The mine is accessible by a tortuous dirt road from either Hernandez or New Idria, which climbs through rugged terrain until it terminates at the workings at an elevation of 4500 feet above sea level. In this region, serpentinous rocks predominate, outcropping over an area of three by fifteen miles, and it is in serpentine that the benitoite-bearing veins are emplaced. Forming roughly parallel swarms, each of the veins is filled almost completely with porous snow-white fibrous natrolite. The serpentine some distance away is greenish in color but next to the natrolite veins it is pale blue-gray, soft and chalky in texture, and at times displaying a silky sheen. The natrolite forms very small spherical masses consisting of numerous minute radiating crystal prisms. The thickness of the veins varies from paper-thin to 2 inches or more. Benitoite in groups of various sized-crystals, occurs principally in the thicker portions of the veins and is generally completely enclosed by natrolite. When the latter mineral is removed by dissolution in hydrochloric acid, it is seen that most of the benitoite crystals are grown upon the serpentine walls along with jet-black crystals of neptunite and very deep red, almost black crystals of joaquinite. One pocket however, produced a number of loose, perfectly formed crystals of benitoite. Ordinary specimens often show benitoite crystals attached by one of the narrow edges but others are also found lying flat. In size, crystals vary from minute triangular wafers to stout individuals as much as two inches across. In the American Museum of Natural History a magnificent matrix specimen is on view showing crystals up to 2 by 2 inches on a slab of serpentine 1 by 1½ feet in size. Some of the finest specimens are those in which the customary dissolution of the natrolite by acid has been arrested at a point where the blue benitoite, shiny black neptunite, and the minute joaquinite crystals are set off against a perfectly white field of massive natrolite.

It is interesting to note that in 1956, a second locality was announced for benitoite-bearing natrolite, very much like the original and only a short distance away. Up to this time, the original discovery remained the only place where benitoite occurred.

IOLITE
(*Cordierite*)

Among the less common gemstones, iolite enjoys the distinction of exhibiting an extremely strong and contrasting trichroism. In clear specimens, two shades of blue and an incongruous straw yellow are seen in the same piece. The blue and yellow colors are so marked that they can be observed readily even in rough fragments and have given rise to another name for this species, *dichroite*. Other names are "water sapphire" and "lynx sapphire," sometimes used in Ceylon for pale and dark colored varieties respectively. Since both of these names are misleading, their use is discouraged. Some authors use the name cordierite instead of iolite but since the latter name was coined at an earlier date it should have preference. The name iolite is derived from the Greek word for violet while cordierite is named after the mineralogist who described the species.

Iolite is an Orthorhombic hydrous magnesium aluminum silicate but iron frequently replaces part of the magnesium. A recent mineralogical work gives the following formula: $(Mg,Fe)_2Mg_2Al_4Si_5O_{18}$. It is characteristically a mineral of metamorphic rocks such as schists and gneisses, and is regarded as indicative of high formative temperatures and pressures. Gem quality material is seldom found in crystals with good faces, most specimens being nothing more than angular fragments broken from formless nodules or lenses completely enclosed in rock. Hardness varies between 7 and 7½ but this difference is seldom apparent in cutting gems where it seems to be about the same hardness as quartz (7). Iolite is brittle but does not fracture easily; fracture surfaces are irregular to conchoidal in character and glassy to greasy in luster. There is one distinct but difficultly developed cleavage. The specific gravity varies considerably because of numerous inclusions; gem material generally ranges between 2.58 and 2.60. Refractive indices are variable, the following ranges may be encountered in gemstones: $a = 1.53$-1.54, $\gamma = 1.54$-1.55; birefringence 0.010, biaxial, negative. With such low refractive powers, difficulties are encountered in cutting satisfactory gems since the beautiful blue colors are ordinarily so intense that a gem cut deeply for adequate reflection of light is apt to be much too dark. Conversely, if cut too thin, brilliance is lost and the gem appears lifeless. Although absorption of light is much less along the direction of the crystal in which the yellow color is observed, gems cut with this color "face up" appear dingy and unattractive. For these reasons, iolites over a carat or two in weight can be cut successfully only from exceptionally clear material which is not too dark. In the dichroscope, the colors most commonly observed are intense purplish-blue, a somewhat paler and less purplish-blue, and straw yellow. In stones of lighter color, the second shade of blue is apt to be pale bluish-gray.

LOCALITIES

Greenland. Iolite in clear fragments occurs in the rocks of Uiordlersuak Island on the west coast north of Upernivik near 73 degrees north. Pieces as large as 1½ inches of grayish-violet color have been observed in pegmatites on Upernivik and Langoe islands, approximately 72 degrees, 47 minutes north latitude. Further south in the Godthaab District, iolite occurs associated with gem garnet and hypersthene in the region between the eastern extremity of Ameralik Fjord (Ameragdla) and the glaciers directly east and distant ten miles.

North West Territories. Material of deep blue color and sufficiently clear for faceted gems has been picked up upon Garnet Island, Baffinland. The fragments are found associated with white feldspar, and range up to 2 inches in diameter. They are thought to have weathered from schist. In recent years, considerable iolite has been found at a number of localities in the Great Slave Lake Region. The most prominent locality is 7 miles south of

Ghost Lake upon the 115th meridian where crystals up to 4 inches in length have been found in pegmatites penetrating garnet sillimanite schist. Ghost Lake is about 90 miles slightly west of north of Yellowknife. The largest crystals measured 4 inches by 2 inches but most were less. Irregular masses devoid of crystal form were also found. All specimens were invariably fractured, preventing the cutting of large gems. It has been reported that in 1947, a shipment of about 200 pounds of iolite was made from this deposit, of which some 200 carats proved cuttable, being worth perhaps $10 per carat after finishing. So far as is known, no flawless gems of over two carats have been cut from this material. Between Ghost Lake and Ranji Lake, other iolite occurrences are found; also at a point 3 miles northwest of the west end of Ghost Lake.

Connecticut. Another locality for facet grade material is at Hungry Horse Hill in Guilford Township, New Haven County. Here irregular masses of fine blue material are found enclosed in a fine-grained quartz-feldspar-biotite rock, probably gneiss, outcropping upon farmland. Some masses reach as much as 2½ inches in diameter. The American Museum of Natural History has on display a deep blue ⅛ inch faceted gem and a ⅜ inch brilliant cut from this material.

Wyoming. Iolite is a widespread constituent of schistose and gneissic rocks in the Laramie Range of Albany County. One estimate has placed the quantity available at thousands of tons. Specimens from this locality examined by the author are glassy broken fragments of rather light blue color, verging toward grayish; small sections are clear and suitable for faceted gems. It is entirely possible that important amounts of gem quality material will be produced from this area in the future.

ANDALUSITE
(*Chiastolite*)

In nature, andalusite appears in two radically different forms, the first—clear, hard, and tough crystals eminently suitable for faceted gems of fine color and brilliance; and the second—dull, earthy crystals which are attractive only because interesting cross-like patterns are seen in cross-section. The latter type will be discussed here because of its frequent employment for gem purposes and its relative abundance in North America. The clear form, far more valuable and attractive, has not yet been found on this continent. The earthy variety is known as *chiastolite*, and derives its name from the Greek word for "arranged crosswise" in allusion to the dark inclusions which often form cross-like patterns within the crystals. The species name is derived from the occurrence of this mineral in the Province of Andalusia in Spain. Chiastolite patterns are obtained by slicing the crystals across like a loaf of bread and polishing the slices. Typical patterns are illustrated in Figure 140.

Pure andalusite has the formula: Al_2SiO_5 but in chiastolite, the black crosses are believed to be carbonaceous impurities which have been forced into regular patterns by the atomic structure of the crystal and hence render the above formula only approximate. Crystallizing in the Orthorhombic System, crystals of andalusite and chiastolite assume long prismatic forms, chiastolite especially producing elongated crystals of rough exterior without trace of crystal faces.

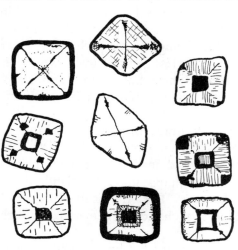

Chiastolite is very soft, about $3\frac{1}{2}$ to $4\frac{1}{2}$, a striking contrast to the pure mineral which has a hardness of $7\frac{1}{2}$. The specific gravity of pure andalusite varies from 3.10 to 3.20 but is less in chiastolite. Refractive indices for facet-grade material from

FIGURE 140. Some of the patterns shown by cross-sections of chiastolite crystals.

Brazil and Ceylon range from $\alpha = 1.633$ to $\gamma = 1.644$; birefringence 0.011; another authority fixes the range as $\alpha = 1.627$-1.640, $\gamma = 1.641$-1.648; birefringence variable, 0.007-0.013. Andalusite is biaxial, negative. The color of clear material ranges from olive-green to pale reddish-brown, showing a strong brownish-red in one crystal direction. In chiastolite, the color ranges from various shades of creamy-white, gray or yellow for the pale sectors of the internal pattern to deep brown or black for the carbonaceous inclusions.

As found in North America, chiastolite crystals vary in size from $\frac{1}{2}$ inch to some as much as 7 inches in length and $1\frac{1}{2}$ inches in diameter. The exterior is always rude, pitted, and frequently covered with flakes of mica from the schistose metamorphic rocks from which crystals are removed. Being more resistant to decay, they are often found loose in the soil. Sometimes the rock studded with embedded crystals is sliced across and polished to show both the crystals and their peculiar cross-sectional patterns. Ordinarily however, individual crystals are sawn into thin sections, polished and then mounted on glass to show the progressive change in patterns. In jewelry, small quantities have been used as cabochons or set in cheap mountings as novelties. Finished stones are not beautiful in the accepted sense of the word but have a certain measure of attractiveness on account of their patterns.

LOCALITIES

North West Territories. Pink and pale violet crystals up to several inches in length are not uncommon in pegmatite and quartz veins in the MacKenzie District. Some of these crystals have been reported as having slight gem value but unfortunately further details are lacking. Finely-patterned chiastolite crystals are found in a number of places in the Great Slave Lake region near Quyta Lake, 20 miles north of Yellowknife. Inclusions vary from brown to black in color and the contrast between light and dark areas is very strong. Crystals range in size from ¼ inch diameter upwards.

British Columbia. Chiastolite is common in the black schists of the hills west of Armstrong in the Vernon Mining District.

Quebec. A number of chiastolite localities are recorded in the townships of Compton, Eaton, Emberton, Hampden and Marsden in Compton County; also in micaceous argillite on Lake St. Francis in Frontenac County; at Stanstead, Hatley and Barbstone in Stanstead County.

New Brunswick. Chiastolite occurs in fine-grained micaceous schist at Moore's Mills, Charlotte County.

Nova Scotia. Chiastolite is found at Geizer's Hill west of Halifax.

Massachusetts. Excellent chiastolite crystals occur in rock at Lancaster in Worcester County and at Westford in Middlesex County. The Lancaster locality is noted for firm matrix rock which can be sliced across and polished to show the embedded crystals and their patterns.

California. Many fine crystals of chiastolite have come from several localities in Madera County. A very old locality is along the Chowchilla River, especially from near Chowchilla Crossing on the old Fort Miller Road. In this region are found dull black to gray micaceous schists belonging to the Mariposa series and containing much chiastolite. The average crystal size is ⅜ inch diameter with many up to ¾ inch diameter or, very rarely, up to 7 inches in length and 1½ inches across. Patterns usually consist of thin black diagonal lines which connect opposite edges of crystal prisms and swell to a black square in the center. In adjoining sections, this central square expands to form rectangular figures which eventually reach the sides of the prisms. A very large specimen recorded from this area measured 2 by 3 by 3 inches and exhibited excellent markings. In this same county, many loose crystals are found in soil in an area about ½ mile west of Daulton on top and along the sides of a low hill at the old Daulton Copper Mine. Rough prisms reach sizes ranging from ⅛ to ⅜ inch thick and up to 3 inches in length. The interiors show usual cruciform patterns against gray, brown, green, and dark yellow backgrounds. In Mariposa County, chiastolite is reported from rocks near Moore's Flats; also from slates at

Hornitos and at a point 12 miles south of Mariposa. Crystals of fair to good internal marking occur in schists along Walker's Creek southeast of Bakersfield, Kern County. Specimens up to ½ inch in diameter occur in the cordierite slates at the junction of Franklin and Coldwater canyons in the Santa Monica Mountains of Los Angeles County.

Sonora. Chiastolite crystals are found in the Arroyo Escondido near San Marcial, in the Guaymas District.

Mexico. Chiastolite is found in the Valle de Bravo District at Ixtapan del Oro.

KYANITE

One of the most unique of all gemstones is kyanite. This fractious blue or green mineral has the distinction of showing tremendous differences in hardness along its principal cleavage plane and scratch tests performed upon its surface are sure to excite the wonder of spectators. A small steel point stroked across the short way of the crystal slides along without scratching, but when stroked the other way, promptly cuts a deep groove filled with whitish powder. This experiment is most instructive to students of mineralogy but leaves gem cutters on the verge of tears because the slightest inattention to cutting a kyanite crystal may result in its shattering into useless splinters. The enormous difficulties attendant to lapidary treatment cause kyanite to be esteemed as a rarity since so few gem-quality specimens manage to survive to the finished state.

Kyanite often makes a most beautiful faceted gem, blue specimens sometimes resembling sapphire, while crystals in green, pale blue, or mixtures of both colors afford pleasing and interesting contrasts. The name of the species acknowledges the predominance of blue shades since it has been formed from the Greek word for blue; an earlier way of spelling the name, *cyanite*, has now gone out of use. Kyanite has also been called *disthene*, a word derived from the Greek words for "two" and "hard" in allusion to the differences of hardness remarked upon above.

The formula of kyanite is exactly like that of andalusite and sillimanite, Al_2SiO_5, but the differences in atomic arrangement cause marked differences in all properties. Kyanite crystallizes in the Triclinic System but is seldom seen in any form except flat blades displaying prominently the smooth broad cleavage plane referred to above, plus deep striations along the sides and ends. This habit of crystallization is so distinctive that no other mineral can be readily mistaken for it. A typical crystal is illustrated in Figure 141. Upon the principal cleavage plane, the hardness in the soft direction is only 5, while at right angles it is 7. The luster on this plane is glassy to pearly but elsewhere it is inclined to be dull. The specific gravity is high: 3.55 to 3.67; Yancey County, North Carolina, material of a bluish-green color registers 3.64. The refractive indices of kyanite are variable; one authority gives: $\alpha = 1.712$, $\gamma = 1.728$; birefringence 0.016. An examination of a bluish-green faceted gem from Yancey County gave: $\alpha = 1.714$, $\gamma = 1.731$; birefringence 0.017. Kyanite is biaxial, negative. In color, kyanite is seldom uniform in shade, mixtures or patches of blue, green, and colorless may be seen in a single specimen. Kyanite is trichroic; blue specimens generally exhibit shades of pale, almost colorless blue, medium blue, and dark blue. Greenish material from Yancey County gives very pale, almost colorless green, pale greenish-yellow and green.

FIGURE 141. Blue kyanite in quartz from Hurricane Mountain, North Carolina. The bladed crystal is typical of this mineral; the upper surface is that along which the principal cleavage plane occurs. Courtesy Smithsonian Institution.

LOCALITIES

North Carolina. Colorless to deep blue crystals occur in typical bladed individuals in a milky quartz vein near the summit of Yellow Mountain, 4 miles southeast of Bakersville on the road to Ledger in Yancey County. Crystals range in size from 1 to 2 inches in length and about ½ inch in width or slightly more. Figure 141 shows a fine example embedded in quartz. In another part of Yancey County, beautiful pale green crystals, wonderfully clear and often largely flawless, were found loose in the soil of what was formerly known as the Tiel Young Farm near the North Toe River, a few miles from Spruce Pine. George English of New York City, an early mineral dealer, worked this deposit for some time, and it was through his efforts that much fine material was collected. Some exceptionally large crystals were uncovered in 1896. Digging in the field where the crystals were found, showed them to have originated in a much decomposed mica schist which appeared to be the bedrock. Single crystals and several joined together were found, some groups reaching fist-size. The majority were a lovely uniform bluish-green color, very much like certain Brazilian aquamarines; others had blue centers. Single crystals reached dimensions of from ½ inch in length to as much as 1¼ inches by 2¼ inches. The author has a fine, almost flawless stepcut faceted gem of this kyanite which measures about ⅜ inch by ½ inch and weighs 6.57 carats.

EPIDOTE AND PIEDMONTITE

Ordinarily a very dark brownish-green, epidote is seldom used in faceted gemstones because the absorption of light even in very small specimens causes gems to appear quite black. However, its unusual nature and rarity provide some appeal to collectors and suitable crystals are cut from time to time to satisfy their modest demands. Massive epidote, and its reddish cousin, piedmontite, are sometimes cut in cabochons, providing in many cases very attractive gems. The name epidote has been derived from the Greek word for "increase" in allusion to the tendency for its crystals to grow with one face longer than others. Piedmontite owes its name to the occurrence of this species in the Piedmont region of Italy.

Epidote is calcium aluminum-iron silicate with water while piedmontite varies slightly in that part or all of the iron is replaced by manganese. These relationships are: epidote, $Ca_2(Al,Fe)_3(SiO_4)_3(OH)$; and piedmontite, $Ca_2(Al,Mn)_3(SiO_4)_3(OH)$.

Slight substitutions of elements for those listed above often result in drastic changes in appearance and properties. In the case of epidote, the presence of iron causes the exceedingly deep and dingy colors noted in the ordinary material and it is not until it is partially or completely replaced that colors lighten. Both minerals are common in metamorphic rocks and in altered igneous rocks, but epidote also occurs in fine crystals in quartz veins and pegmatites. Although piedmontite crystals are exceedingly small as a rule, forming dense felted masses similar in texture to zoisite, epidote frequently forms rather large splendant crystals much prized by mineral collectors for their beauty and perfection. Figure 142 illustrating a fine crystal cluster from a noted Alaskan locality gives some idea of their beauty. Both species crystallize in the Monoclinic System, forming rather narrow prismatic crystals rich in faces. Massive forms occur as irregular grains or patches in rock, and, as in the case of UNAKITE, add considerable attractiveness. Epidote and piedmontite possess a single perfect cleavage which appears parallel to the longest sides of crystals but this cleavage is developed with difficulty. The luster is glassy to somewhat greasy, the fracture conchoidal. Hardness varies in crystals from 6 to 7 but is noticeably lower in fibrous massive varieties. Specific gravity ranges from 3.25 to 3.50 in both minerals. Refractive indices are very variable, depending on composition, however, a standard set of values for epidote is: $\alpha = 1.729$, $\beta = 1.754$, $\gamma = 1.768$; birefringence 0.039; biaxial, negative. In piedmontite, the optic sign is positive.

In color, epidote has been found in many hues including black, gray, and even white, however, the vast majority of specimens exhibit some shade of the peculiar yellow-green, slightly brownish in cast, known as "pistachio green." This hue is so distinctive in character that it serves as a means of instantly identifying most epidote in the field, in fact, an alternate but rarely used name for epidote is *pistacite* in allusion to this peculiar hue. Piedmontite, on the other hand, is found in very different colors on account of its manganese content, varying from pale to very dark brownish and purplish reds. Pleiochroism in epidote is very strong, showing generally green, brown and yellow; piedmontite shows red, violet and yellow.

FIGURE 142. A magnificent group of bladed epidote crystals with small quartz crystals from the mines on Copper Mountain near Sulzer, Prince of Wales Island, Southeastern Alaska. The specimen has been lightly "smoked" with ammonium chloride to emphasize the forms. Courtesy Smithsonian Institution.

LOCALITIES

Alaska. Magnificent crystals of epidote (see Figure 142) occur in the Green Monster Copper Mine near Sulzer on Prince of Wales Island in Southeastern Alaska. The workings are located at the northern end of a narrow inlet which begins near the southwestern corner of the island. Epidote is found in a contact zone next to metamorphic limestone associated with rock crystal, chalcopyrite, grossularite garnet and other minerals. Many of the epidote crystals are enormous, some reaching dimensions of 4 inches in length, but only the smallest furnish clear material from near their tips.

Pennsylvania. Some very compact cuttable piedmontite-bearing altered rhyolite is found next to basalt at two places on the west side of Buchanan

Valley and at another place on the west side of Piney Mountain in Adams Co. The fine-grained rhyolite is handsomely mottled and colored by streaks of minute needle-like crystals of piedmontite growing in radiate fashion. Considerable quantities of bright green massive epidote occur associated with cuprite and native copper in rhyolite elsewhere in Adams County; localities are described fully under COPPER RHYOLITE.

California. Crystals of dark brown epidote, sometimes quite clear and then suitable for faceted gems, are found associated with quartz and scheelite at the Huckaby and Little Acorn mines in the Greenhorn Mountains of Kern County (see SCHEELITE). Prisms of epidote up to ½ inch in diameter and several inches in length have been found here while small needles often penetrate rock crystal and provide still another useful gem material.

Numerous clear epidote crystals of typical pistachio color occur associated with grossularite garnet at the McFall Mine located 7½ miles southeast of Ramona, San Diego County.

North Carolina. Large numbers of splendid, doubly-terminated epidote crystals of dark greenish-brown color have been found recently upon the Clarence Wilson Farm about 3 miles northeast of Bakersville, Mitchell Co. The largest crystals reached lengths of 6 inches but the clearest examples were considerably less and also much more slender. The occurrence is in an albite vein in which cavities are lined with albite and epidote crystals although the best epidote specimens have been removed from a brownish greasy clay in which they were found loose.

STAUROLITE

On account of its habit of growing twin crystals which resemble crosses, staurolite is frequently used in the form of charms and amulets, retaining even in this enlightened era some supposedly beneficial value. Crystals of this type are popularly known as "fairy crosses," "fairy stones," etc., and indeed the well-known tendency of this mineral to twin in this fashion has given it its species name from the Greek word meaning "cross." Twins of staurolite are, in the rough state, generally most unattractive except for their curious geometry which has excited the wonder and superstitious instincts of people for centuries. It is said that the Swiss still use crosses of staurolite as amulets at baptisms in Basel. In the United States, many are sold as curios in several areas, notably in the southeastern states where large numbers are found eroding from the schistose rocks in which they occur. The following text from a sales pamphlet published many years ago, earnest if amusing, extols the virtues of staurolite crosses:

Fairy Stones
Curious Natural Crosses

The stones, found in Patrick County, Virginia, were pronounced by Professor McCreath, Ginth Duna, and other Scientists, as heretofore unknown to the Mineral World. These stones, which range in size from one-fourth to three-fourths inch, are all in the form of crosses, some plain Roman, and others perfect Maltese crosses, but no two alike. They were brought to notice by traveling Mineralogists, who were struck by them while passing over a little knoll where they are found. They make very unique and pretty watch charms, scarf pins, cuff buttons, and other ornaments.

The secret of this discovery was not generally made known until the years 1893 and 1894, since which time they have been much sought for in all parts of the world. President Cleveland was sent one when he got his second nomination. They were considered by the old natives, years ago in this section, as lucky stones.

These stones contain Titanite, Tourmaline, Garnet, Aluminum, and Steatite. Titanite being the principal material. They are dark brown, of several hues, and some black.

Their value may be estimated according to their size. They may be ordered from —————, —————, Winston, N.C.

The two types of right-angle crosses referred to in this sales brochure are found in nature it is true, but the overwhelming majority are uncooperative and twin at oblique angles! Because of this unfortunate tendency on the part of staurolite, and in view of the greater popularity of right-angle crosses at roadside stands, it is necessary to augment nature in some way. This is done by using a grayish talcose schist, not at all related to staurolite, and forming the desired crosses by sawing and filing into shape. These are then soaked in linseed oil to give them the desired dark brown color. The versatility of this material often leads to some amusing results, the carvers turning out crosses which are not only twinned once but again and again on each limb in utterly fantastic combinations. Even natural crosses which mostly are dull and earthy on their exteriors, are "helped" by judicious filing and soaking in oil.

Mineralogically, staurolite is an iron aluminum silicate corresponding to the formula: $FeAl_4Si_2O_{10}(OH)_2$. When untwinned, crystal prisms show the membership of this mineral in the Orthorhombic System since the ends are flat planes at right angles to the sides of the prism, while the faces on this portion are simple rectangles but inclined to each other so that a beveled appearance is given. Twins cross each other almost at right angles but as mentioned before, most commonly at approximately 60°. There are many variations of course, sometimes the individuals being of different sizes, sometimes as many as three or four are twinned together. A typical twin crystal is delineated in Figure 143. Crystals range in size from less than ½ inch in

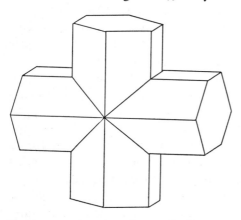

length to some which are several inches long. Typical crystals from near Taos, New Mexico are illustrated in Figure 144. Staurolite is almost wholly confined to crystalline schists and gneisses but is also found in areas of contact metamorphism. It is frequently associated with garnet, kyanite, sillimanite, and tourmaline. In Virginia, minute crudely spherical garnets, scarcely as large as the head of a pin are often enclosed in the crystals and on account of their greater hardness, prevent them from being filed to improve their form.

FIGURE 143. A twinned crystal of staurolite showing the cruciform shape.

Many such crystals are deeply altered to a talcose mixture, far softer than the fresh mineral. When unaltered, staurolite possesses a hardness of 7 to 7½ and forms sharp crystals with bright smooth faces. Fresh specimens sometimes show traces of cleavage with conchoidal fracture surfaces of glassy luster but altered types are completely dull. The specific gravity of unaltered staurolite ranges between 3.65 to 3.77, however, altered types can be expected to be considerably less. Refractive indices are: $a = 1.74\text{-}7.75$; $\gamma = 1.75\text{-}1.76$; birefringence 0.01; biaxial, positive. In clear material of brown color the trichroism is some shade of deep brownish-red, orange-red, and pale yellow.

LOCALITIES

Nova Scotia. Staurolite crystals are abundant on the Jordan and Sable rivers in Shelburne County.

Maine. The mica slate at Windham, Cumberland County is filled with large crystals but few are good twins.

New Hampshire. Simple large brown crystals occur in mica slate near the old Franconia Iron Mine south of the summit of Ore Hill, also 1½ miles south of Sugar Hill, on the shores of Mink Pond in loose crystals and at Lisbon in Grafton County. In the above occurrences good dark brown unaltered crystals occur up to 4 inches in length; some are fine right angle twins. Good crystals also occur near Grantham and Claremont in Sullivan County.

Vermont. Good brown crystals occur at Cabot, Washington County.

Massachusetts. Fine crystals are found in Chesterfield Township, Hampshire County.

Connecticut. Staurolite is common in mica schists in Litchfield County and in the Bolton schists of Middlesex County; it is found abundantly at Bolton, Tolland, Vernon, and Stafford in Tolland County and at Southbury and Litchfield in Litchfield County.

Virginia. The famous staurolite crystals of this state have been commemorated by the creation of Fairystone State Park near the area in which they occur. Actually very few are obtainable from within the park, the selection of its site being guided more by practical than geological considerations. In the southern part of the state are found two belts of staurolite-bearing rocks, both roughly parallel. The first belt begins 4 miles southwest of Stuart in Patrick County and continues 19 miles northeast of Stuart. The second belt is offset ½ mile to the southeast from the first, and begins about 9 miles northeast of Stuart, continuing northeast and crossing the northwest corner of Henry County, finally ending beyond the Franklin County line. Crystals occur in biotite-chlorite schist, in sericite-staurolite schist, and in an iron-stained quartz-mica schist, all of which belong to the Wissahickon formation. A count of a large sample of twin crystals from this area shows that 75 per cent cross at angles of 35° and 60° while less than 5 per cent form excellent 90° crosses. Most of the crystals are found lying loose in the topsoil. A brisk business in crystals is done by roadside dealers near Fairystone State Park.

North Carolina. Very large brownish-red crystals 2½ to 3 inches long and 1 inch to 1½ inches in width, occur in singles and twins at the Parker Mine, also at Unaka, Marble, and in Moss Creek in the Snow Bird Mountains. There are numerous other localities in both Cherokee County and in Mason County where crystals occur abundantly in clayey and talcose slates as at Persimmon Creek and Hanging Dog Creek; also at Bear Creek in Madison County; on Tusquitee Creek near Hayesville and about one mile east of Brasstown in Clay County.

Georgia. Staurolite crystals are found mostly in the north in Cherokee, Pickens, Gilmer, and Fannin counties. They are found lying loose in the topsoil, in the gravels of creeks, and also partly or fully enclosed in the schistose rocks in which they occur. Many crystals, often twinned, come from areas south and west of Ball Ground in Cherokee County; fine specimens have been found along the east side of Sharp Mountain Creek one mile west of Fairview Church; a famous locality, still productive after many years of collecting, is on the north side of Bluff Creek on the J. M. Spear Farm along Route 1, 4½ miles west of Ball Ground. The best crystals from this locality are generally under ½ inch in size. Exceptional crystals occur in Fannin County; from here come perfect, shiny crystals of black color, predominantly twinned at oblique angles but only rarely at the desired 90 degrees. Good collecting places are on the property of J. F. Hackney near Blue Ridge, from a point immediately west of Cole's Crossing in very fine specimens, upon Windy Bluff several miles northwest of Mineral Bluff, and in railroad cuts near Blue Ridge.

Minnesota. Unaltered dark brown crystals occur in schists along the banks of the Mississippi River about three miles from Royalton, Morrison Co. At Blanchard Dam nearby, many fine crystals are recovered by screening gravels either below the outcropping schists or below the dam. Many crystals

FIGURE 144. Staurolite crystals or "Fairy Crosses" showing the twinning which gives rise to the cross form. The center specimen is still partly covered by the micaceous schist in which these crystals are found imbedded. The bottom specimen has been filed and impregnated with oil. Although these specimens come from Taos, New Mexico they are typical of those found elsewhere as in Georgia and Virginia. Courtesy Department of the Interior, National Park Service.

are twinned at right angles but few are over an inch in size. Good crystals are also found in the gravels of Elk Creek near Little Falls in the same county.

Idaho. Rather crude crystals up to 4 inches in length are found in the vicinity of Bathtub Mountain in Shoshone County; also in twins and singles loose in soil or still in place in schists south of Avery.

New Mexico. The Spanish-Americans of Taos County often carry staurolite twins as good luck charms, obtaining them from among the thousands which occur in schists in the Glenwoody and Picuris districts. Twins are sold by the Indians and curio dealers as "luck" stones, the standard price being about ten to fifteen cents. The large masses of schist and quartzite which outcrop for many miles in Taos County between Velarde and Pilar on Highway 64 between Santa Fe and Taos, provide many good collecting places. Crosses are abundant in the numerous washes just north of Pilar and to the east in the low hills which consist partly of staurolite-bearing schists; the northwest portion of these hills is especially recommended. Staurolite crystals are also common in the schists of the Manzano Mountains of Torrance Co.

COLEMANITE

Sometimes cut as a curiosity, transparent colemanite provides interesting faceted gems. It is a boron mineral, surprisingly rare except in the desert regions of Southern California where it occurs abundantly in the Tertiary sediments of Inyo, Kern, San Bernardino, Los Angeles, and Ventura counties. At one time it was the most important source of borax until another borate, kernite, was discovered and found to be a more suitable ore.

Colemanite is a hydrous calcium borate: $Ca_2B_6O_{11} \cdot 5H_2O$, crystallizing in the Monoclinic System and forming crystals which frequently resemble rhombohedrons in general form. Faces are smooth and glassy in luster, causing sections of matrix to sparkle brilliantly under good illumination. The best crystals, varying in size from minute to as much as several inches across, occur in geodes and vugs embedded in soft clayey sediments. The hardness is stated to be $4\frac{1}{2}$ but in its preparation into gems, it seems closer to 5. It is brittle, showing an irregular to subconchoidal fracture and with a very perfect easily developed cleavage. A pearly luster is frequently seen on the face which coincides with the cleavage plane. The specific gravity is low and varies but little from 2.423. The refractive indices are: $\alpha = 1.5863$, $\beta = 1.5920$, $\gamma = 1.6140$; birefringence 0.0277; biaxial, positive. In color, colemanite varies from pure white in clouded specimens to colorless or faintly straw yellow in clear crystals.

California. In Inyo County, fine material has come from the borax mines in Furnace Creek Wash where a narrow belt of Tertiary lake deposits on the south side near the floor of Death Valley have been mined extensively for borate minerals. Doubly-terminated crystals up to 2 inches across have been found in Gower Gulch. In the Ryan District, just outside Death Valley National Monument, similar specimens have been found. The Russell Mine at the northern end of the Black Hills produced exceptionally large crystals. In San Bernardino County, beautiful crystals in geodes associated with celestite crystals occur in the Calico District at Borate near Yermo.

BARITE

As a mineral, barite is among the most common of all, good specimens being found in almost every comprehensive collection. Transparent and flawless crystals are equally common but because of their softness, extreme sensitivity to heat, and no less than three easily-developed cleavages, are seldom successfully cut into gems. Needless to say, there can be no commercial application of such fragile gems but a small number are cut as curiosities for private collectors. Massive, finely fibrous material is also known and

FIGURE 145. Clear golden brown barite crystals perched on yellow calcite. This specimen is from the noted locality on Elk River, Meade County, South Dakota, and measures about 3 inches across the face while the largest crystal is about ¾ inch in length.

has been cut and polished into ornamental items, particularly in England where it occurs in concretionary masses in clay near Youlgreave, Derbyshire. Similar material also occurs in the State of New York but has seen little use up to now.

Barite is a sulfate of barium with the formula: $BaSO_4$, and is found most frequently in sedimentary formations and in metallic ore veins. Crystallizing in the Orthorhombic System, it forms tubular crystals and prisms of rectangular or square cross section. Typical crystals from South Dakota are shown in Figures 145 and 146. The hardness is very low, ranging from 3 to $3\frac{1}{2}$. Of the three cleavages mentioned, two cross each other almost at right angles and the third passes through both. Where cleavage separations are numerous, the luster inclines toward pearly but elsewhere the luster is glassy to slightly greasy. Ordinary fracture surfaces vary from irregular to conchoidal. The specific gravity of barite is unusually

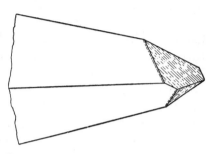

FIGURE 146. An idealized representation of the barite crystals shown on matrix in Figure 142. In the actual crystals, broad faces are gently curved.

high, 4.5, and serves as a valuable means of identification in the field for few minerals of similar appearance weigh so heavily in the hand. This outstanding property has given it its name, being derived from the Greek word for "heavy." Refractive indices are: $\alpha = 1.6362$, $\beta = 1.6373$, $\gamma = 1.6482$; birefringence 0.012; biaxial, positive. Brown material from South Dakota and blue material from Colorado average: $\alpha = 1.634$, $\gamma = 1.647$; birefringence 0.013. Trichroism is very weak; in the dichroscope, Colorado material gives scarcely perceptible blue, pale blue and colorless while South Dakota barite reveals only a slight change in intensity in the basic golden brown hue.

LOCALITIES

Ontario. Transparent, well-formed crystals of colorless barite up to $1\frac{1}{2}$ inches in diameter, have been found in the Beaver Junior Mine near the southeast corner of O'Connor Township in the Thunder Bay District. This locality is about 3 miles north of Hymer's Station on the Canadian Pacific Railroad. Also in the same vicinity, fine transparent pale brown crystals have been found in the Hidden Treasure Mine in the south half of Lot 16, Concession IV, Pearson Township.

British Columbia. Fine large crystals, sometimes up to 4 inches in length, pale yellow in color and perfectly transparent, occur in pockets in a vein of fluorite at the Rock Candy Mine on Kennedy Creek, about 15 miles north of Grand Forks. Crystals are relatively strong and only one cleavage is easily developed.

New York. Massive barite of good quality and capable of a beautiful polish, has been reported from Pillar Point opposite Sackett's Harbor in Jefferson County.

Colorado. Pale blue tabular crystals of rectangular outline and beveled edges occur in large quantities in an altered volcanic ash deposit in Weld County. This locality is often given as "Sterling" but in reality this town is further removed from the deposit than Stoneham which is only 3 miles away. The white calcereous ash deposits are exposed in a series of gullies 3 miles northeast of Stoneham and may be reached by automobile from a point on Highway 14 about ½ mile east of the town. Locally, the whitish bluffs are called "The Chalk Cliffs." Because of the crumbly nature of the enclosing material, numerous crystals were originally found lying loose upon the slopes but in recent years, the best have been obtained by digging. Crystals range in size from ½ inch to 1 inch in width to several inches in length.

South Dakota. Large quantities of massive dark brown barite in the form of irregular geodes occur in the Pierre shales of Meade County and are exposed in the bed and along the banks of Elk Creek north of Wasta. Geode cavities are lined with small yellow calcite crystals upon which are perched single crystals or groups of beautiful transparent golden brown barite (see Figure 145). The common form is a squarish tapering prism topped by a simple chisel-like point (see Figure 146). Most crystals are less than 1 inch or 2 inches in length but of superb quality, while larger specimens are inclined to be less clear and rougher surfaced. An enormous crystal as thick as a man's wrist and about one foot in length has been recorded from this deposit. Crystals vary in color from pale yellow through amber and sherry, to a rich golden brown. Barite from this locality has been more successfully cut than from other places, the crystals seeming to be far less inclined to split. A magnificent matrix specimen measuring 12 inches by 10 inches with a dozen fine crystals perched upon yellow calcite is on view in the U.S. National Museum.

CELESTITE

Far too soft to be considered for jewelry purposes, celestite is only cut as a cabinet curiosity. This mineral occurs mainly in the form of translucent fibrous or platey masses but sometimes good crystals clear enough to facet are found. Being extremely soft and sensitive to heat and shock, the mere act of cutting celestite is an unusually severe test of lapidary skill. The name of the species has been derived from the word *coelestis*, meaning "heavenly" in allusion to the bright sky-blue color in which this mineral is frequently found. It is interesting to note that the blue color of some varieties has been attributed to the presence of minute quantities of gold.

Celestite is strontium sulfate, with the formula $SrSO_4$ and like other sulfates, occurs almost exclusively in sedimentary rocks. It crystallizes in the Orthorhombic System, commonly as thick tablets or squat prisms of diamond-shaped cross section. The hardness is very low, 3 to $3\frac{1}{2}$, while several cleavages, one perfectly and easily developed, further contribute to its fragility. Celestite varies from 3.96 to 3.98 in specific gravity. Refractive indices are moderate: $a = 1.6215$, $\beta = 1.6237$, $\gamma = 1.6308$; birefringence 0.093; biaxial, positive. Celestite is ordinarily either colorless or blue but frequently the latter is found as zones in colorless individuals. Reddish, brownish, and greenish tints have also been noted. A blue and colorless zoned type from Texas shows in the dichroscope: rich purplish-blue, pale bluish-green, and colorless. In contrast, bright orange material from Canada shows no perceptible change.

LOCALITIES

Ontario. Bright orange crystals in bladed aggregates occur in grayish limestone at the Forks of Credit, Caledon Township, Peel County. The striking color contrast affords fine mineral specimens but the individual crystal blades are seldom thick enough to yield gems over $\frac{1}{8}$ inch in diameter.

Texas. Localities for fine crystallized celestite occur in poorly consolidated Cretaceous and Permian age sediments. Crystals are found filling perfectly round geodes, and if space exists in the centers, grow to perfection in stubby squarish prismatic crystals. The tips of crystals are fine blue in color but the bases and the roots in the walls of the geodes are colorless or white. Geodes reach several inches in diameter with individual crystals ranging from $\frac{1}{2}$ inch to 1 inch in thickness. Material of this kind is found at the noted Mount Bonnell locality about 5 miles west of Austin in Travis County; also on Little Lucy Creek, 6 miles north of Lampasas in Lampasas County.

TEKTITES

In certain parts of the world, small rounded vitreous objects found in the soil or resting upon the ground have long excited curiosity; in respect to appearance, fracture and color, they looked like nothing more than congealed drops of ordinary glass, somewhat the worse for wear after long burial. When found in civilized lands, it was assumed that they represented waterworn and decomposed remnants of some ancient glass-making enterprise but it was not until the history of glass-making was traced back to its earliest beginnings that the suspicion grew that perhaps these were not man-made glasses after all. In some areas where these strange objects were most abundant, history showed beyond doubt that no civilization capable of making glass had ever existed there. Furthermore, scientific advancements permitted more accurate examinations of physical and chemical properties and proved conclusively their dissimilarity to any man-made glass. Since "swirl" marks inside these objects indicated a former partially fluid state, they were collectively labeled tektites after the Greek word for "molten." For many years a controversy has raged about their true origin, the latest students of the problem believing them to be descended to earth from outer space.

The earliest record of tektites concern those from Bohemia called *moldavites* after the Moldau River region in which they occur in some abundance as weathered nodules of deep bottle green color. Excavations of paleolithic sites show splinters and fragments of moldavite among rubbish and indicates their use as far back as 25,000 years. Millions of tektites have been found in Bohemia and elsewhere as in Australia (*australites*), in the Philippines (*rizalites*), in Borneo (*billitonites*), and even in the United States in Texas (*bediasites*) and in Georgia. When clear and of suitable color, tektites have been used for cutting into inexpensive gems.

The composition of tektites does not resemble any known rock from which they could have formed, nor any volcanic glass such as obsidian, or any kind of glass produced by man. The temperature needed to melt tektites is almost 200°C higher than that required to fuse Pyrex glass. Many tektites are found to be curiously formed with grooves and channels on the outside suggesting melting from friction generated by passing through the atmosphere at tremendous speeds, while the narrow areas on the earth in which they are found indicate that perhaps a single very large mass entered the atmosphere, breaking up into smaller and smaller pieces under the strains developed by frictional heat. The only verified tektites from all of North America are the Texas bediasites which were given their curious name after an Indian tribe formerly inhabiting the region, and a few examples recently found in Georgia.

Bediasites show specific gravities ranging from 2.433 to 2.334, averaging 2.374. This compares to 2.3-2.5 for moldavite. The refractive index varies from 1.488 to 1.512, averaging 1.4971, and of course is always single since the material shows no trace of crystal structure. These values compare with 1.49-1.50 for moldavite. A set of values recently determined on a tektite from the L. J. Allen Farm in Dodge County, Georgia, are $2.272 \pm .002$ for specific gravity and $1.491 \pm .002$ for refractive index. Bediasites seem black but thin sections show that the color is actually dark brown with a greenish cast. The resistance of these tektites to heat is remarkable; when very thin sections are fired to white heat and plunged into cold water they do not shatter as any ordinary glass would but merely develop small check marks along the edges. The composition of bediasite shows 77.76% silica, 13.30% alumina, 3.36% iron oxide, and lesser amounts of magnesium, sodium, potassium oxide, and much smaller amounts of manganese, calcium, and titanium oxides. Bediasites break with considerable difficulty and show the conchoidal fracture typical of all glass-like materials; the hardness is between 5 and 6. Georgia tektites also appear dark but when held up to the light, a greenish color reminiscent of that observed in moldavite is transmitted.

In Texas, numerous specimens of bediasite have been sent off by local residents to be cut into gems of considerable interest but of little real value. Because of their rarity and great scientific value, the cutting of bediasite is to be deplored, especially when finished gems offer so little beauty. Locally it is called "black diamond" or sometimes "volcanic glass" because of its resemblance to obsidian. Although recognized as true tektites as late

FIGURE 147. Bediasite from Texas. The left hand specimen is weathered and worn but the right hand one shows fresh surfaces due to peeling. The larger bediasite is about 2 inches in length. Courtesy Smithsonian Institution.

as 1936, residents claim knowledge of bediasites for perhaps 50 years before. Intensive inquiry by investigators interested in the tektite problem uncovered about 500 specimens in the hands of local inhabitants and since that time (1940) probably many more have been found. Of almost 80 specimens examined, the smallest weighed 0.5 grams, the largest 59.4 grams, and the average was 15.57 grams. In respect to shape, bediasite appears in highly irregular forms, some are disc- or bean-shaped, while others are almost spherical. The textures of the surfaces vary from smooth to rough, some showing deep furrows. Figure 147 illustrates several typical bediasite nodules. Very few Georgia tektites have been found to date but vigorous publicity, like that which proved successful in the bediasite area, is being given to the discoveries recently made, and more finds are expected to appear. Up to January 1959, nine examples have been verified as true tektites.

LOCALITIES

Georgia. The first recorded finds of tektites in this state were made by Dewey Horne upon farmland near Dubois, a small community in Dodge County 2½ miles southwest of Empire and close to the border of Bleckley Co. Mr. Horne found four specimens some time before 1939 for in that year three were sent to the Smithsonian Institution for examination, one of which was furnished some time later to Dr. Virgil E. Barnes of the University of Texas whose careful investigations of the Texas tektites are well known to geologists all over the world. In 1950, Dr. A. S. Furcron of the Georgia Geological Survey received a single specimen from a Mr. Crosby who found it upon the Hall Farm 3 miles east of Empire in Dodge County. Although the precise limits of the Georgia tektite field have not been established, it is believed that the largest number will be found in Dodge and Irwin counties in exposed soils of Miocene age. Investigations in the field by Dr. Barnes and George A. Bruce of Atlanta in 1958, brought to light several specimens in the hands of local residents, one belonging to Ellis Owens being especially noteworthy. This example, a fine disc-shaped tektite measuring 2 inches by ¼ inch, was found upon the farm of Mrs. Shad Brown at Roddy, several miles east of Dubois. Another specimen examined was an oval disc measuring 2 inches by 1½ inches by ¼ inch, and like the other, was superficially black but showed olive green in transmitted light. A fine specimen has also been found recently by Hardy Scott in an area about four miles southwest of Osierfield; this tektite has been presented to the Georgia Geological Survey. In general, all Georgia specimens are discoid in form, dark olive-green in color, translucent, and extensively pitted with small circular depressions. The name "empirite" for these tektites has been proposed in honor of the nearest principal community.

Alabama. "Dark green to dark blue celestial glasses" were once reported from near Centre in Cherokee Co. They were said to be associated with iron meteorites in an oval area heavily sprinkled with rock fragments.

Oklahoma. Tektites have been reported from near Delhi, Beckhan Co.

Texas. Authentic finds of bediasite center about a rather small area in Grimes County although a few have been reported from near Sandies Creek about 9 miles northwest of Cuero in De Witt County, and also from Lee and Lafayette counties. All localities are aligned from northeast to southwest spanning a distance of 130 miles and indicating a more or less continuous belt of tektite falls. In Grimes County, all finds have been made within an oval area beginning next to the Brazos River at the western extremity of the county about 2 miles southwest of Lamb Springs and extending northeast to about 2 miles northeast of Keith, the latter representing the narrow part of the oval. The heaviest concentrations occurred in the immediate vicinity of Lamb Springs, Greenwood, Keith and Carlos. Many have been picked up in the gravels of Jarvis, Elm, Alum, Dinner and Lake creeks, also around the headwaters of Gibbons Creek. In all of these localities, bediasite pebbles appear associated with Uvalde gravels of Pleistocene age.

CHAPTER VI

Massive and Decorative Gemstones

BOTH massive gemstones and a number of rocks suitable for lapidary treatment are discussed in this chapter. In general, few are suited for the delicate treatment ordinarily accorded to material destined for use in jewelry.

FROM GRANITES AND PEGMATITES:

Granite
Graphic Granite
Unakite
Quartz Porphyry (Leopardite)
Orbicular Gabbro-Diorite
Lepidolite and Muscovite Mica

FROM VOLCANIC ROCKS:

Obsidian
Banded Rhyolite

FROM CAVITIES IN LAVA:

Pectolite
Datolite
Prehnite
Chlorastrolite
Mordenite
Natrolite and Mesolite
Thomsonite

FROM VEIN DEPOSITS:

Fluorite
Smithsonite

FROM OXIDIZED ZONES IN COPPER DEPOSITS:

Malachite and Azurite
Shattuckite

FROM METAMORPHIC DEPOSITS:

Wollastonite
Lapis Lazuli
Fibrolite (Sillimanite)
Zoisite and Clinozoisite
Serpentine
Copper Rhyolite
Red Corundum in Amphibolite

FROM SEDIMENTARY ROCKS:

Pyrite
Calcite
Howlite
Ulexite
Gypsum
Catlinite
Argillite
Bauxite

496

GRANITE

Granite is seldom thought of as being suitable for anything but buildings, monuments, and other massive applications demanding huge blocks of stone capable of taking a high polish. Nevertheless, several varieties have been employed for smaller objects of ornament such as spheres, book ends, paper weights, etc., and even to a very limited extent, in cabochons for use in jewelry. Essentially, granite consists of quartz, feldspar, and mica, each forming irregular grains evenly distributed in "salt and pepper" fashion throughout the mass of the rock. However, some varieties may contain only two of these minerals, or perhaps, another in place of one of the ordinary constituents. In any case, slight variations are commonly lumped together under the general term "granite" although they may be named otherwise if technical classifications were followed.

LOCALITIES

Minnesota. Throughout western St. Cloud Township in Stearns County, is found a rich red granite which owes its coloration to an abundance of bright red feldspar granules. In the trade it is called "St. Cloud Red" and furnishes a very handsome stone capable of receiving a fine glassy polish.

Wisconsin. Several handsome granites are especially suited to the needs of the lapidary, providing tough compact material of rich coloration. An exceptionally colorful kind is known as "Red Waupaca" and is quarried about 5 miles north of the city of Waupaca, Waupaca County. The grain size is coarser than in most granites but the unusual contrast of large bright red feldspar grains cemented together by green epidote and minor quantities of black hornblende more than offset this slight defect. In Marathon County, a handsome uniform red granite has been extensively quarried about 10 miles north of Wausau and is known in the trade as "Wausau Red." It is characterized by dark red grains of feldspar in white to grayish-white quartz; the grain size is small.

GRAPHIC GRANITE

In many pegmatites, certain zones contain masses of feldspar penetrated in regular geometric fashion by numerous parallel slivers or "rods" of grayish, whitish, or smoky quartz. The arrangement of the quartz is such that a specimen cut across their ends displays a curious pattern reminiscent of cuneiform or Hebraic writing. The similarity to writing led to the present name of this interesting material. Graphic granite varies from a very coarse texture to some which is so fine that close examination is needed to see the pattern. Good specimens, showing a strong contrast in color between the quartz and feldspar, are comparatively scarce but make handsome ornaments. Graphic granite parts readily along the contacts of quartz with feldspar, while the latter, with its easily developed cleavages, also contributes to fragility, consequently considerable care is needed in working this material to avoid crumbling. A fine polished slab of graphic granite is shown in Figure 148. Graphic granite is common wherever granitic pegmatites occur. It is found in numerous feldspar and gemstone deposits in Maine, Connecticut, and other places in New England; also in tremendous quantities in the pegmatites of the Pala District, San Diego County, California (see TOURMALINE).

FIGURE 148. Polished slab of graphic granite from Hybla, Ontario, measuring 15 inches by 11 inches. The rock consists entirely of flesh-pink feldspar penetrated by angular inclusions of smoky quartz. Courtesy Smithsonian Institution.

UNAKITE

The predominance of a bright red to pink feldspar mixed in even proportions with light green epidote, gives unakite a high degree of attractiveness and a lasting popularity among amateur cutters. This granite-like rock occurs as seams and veins enclosed in larger masses of ordinary granite in several localities in the Appalachian Mountains of Eastern United States. It derives its name from the first place in which it was found, the Unaka Mountains between North Carolina and Tennessee. Figure 149 illustrates a cabochon of polished unakite and gives some idea of the granular structure although nothing whatever of the handsome coloration.

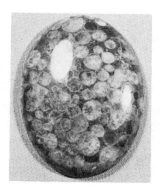 

FIGURE 149. Unakite and epidote from **Rose River**, Virginia. The left hand cabochon is handsome orbicular epidote of pistachio green color in a groundmass of dark purplish-red jaspery material. The right hand cabochon is unakite showing patches of pink feldspar and pale green epidote with small dark spots of smoky quartz. Each cabochon is about 1¾ inches in length.

LOCALITIES

Virginia. Two deposits exist in this state, both productive of good material. The first is a large vein of unakite which outcrops on either side of the steep ridge at Fisher's Gap in the Blue Ridge and is accessible from the Skyline Drive which traverses the crest of the ridge. The locality on the east side of the ridge is about .8 miles almost directly south of Fisher's Gap and about 1½ miles by dim narrow dirt road which departs the Drive at the Gap and descends into the valley of the upper Rose River in Madison County. The second or western outcrop is also below the Drive, and crosses the road leading from the Gap to Marksville in Page County. The exact point is near the 2000 foot level where the road makes a series of switchbacks. The valleys and streambeds below both outcrops often produce rounded boulders of unakite eroded from the outcrops above. On the eastern side in Madison County, stray boulders have been noted in the bed of the Rose River as far as Syria and even further downstream.

The second major occurrence of unakite in Virginia is considerably further south in the vicinity of Vesuvius in Rockbridge County. The deposit is located immediately east of Vesuvius on the road between that community and Montebello (State Highway 56) and just west of the border of the George Washington National Forest. Unakite occurs over a fairly extensive area which runs north and south of the road. In quality, Vesuvius unakite is said to be superior to that found at Fisher's Gap.

North Carolina. Unakite occurs extensively over a wide area centered about 5 miles southwest of Hot Springs in Madison County, very close to the border of Tennessee. The countryside is rugged and elevations are generally between 2500 and 4500 feet above sea level. Unakite is well exposed along Roaring Fork, a short distance above its confluence with Meadow Fork. Other localities are almost too numerous to mention but specimens have been found in the broad area between Cocke County, Tennessee, and Madison County, North Carolina at the following places: the Bluff, Walnut Mountain, along Bald Creek near Beelog, also at Max's Patch. Some unakite has also been found in Sevier and Yancey counties in Tennessee and North Carolina respectively. All of the occurrences are upon the high ridge marking the boundary between the two states mentioned.

QUARTZ PORPHYRY
(*Leopardite*)

A handsome black-spotted rock locally known as "leopardite," is found exposed in several outcrops at Belmont Springs, about 1½ miles east of Charlotte in Mecklenburg County, North Carolina. The basic rock is granular quartz and feldspar, almost pure white in color, with black dendritic markings caused by infiltrated manganese oxides. From the side, the markings resemble long plumes, but when the rock is cut across, a series of circular black spots is revealed which are vaguely similar to the black spots seen on the pelts of leopards. Although too coarse for jewelry, this material is suited for small ornamental objects.

ORBICULAR GABBRO-DIORITE

Also in North Carolina is found an interesting rock which seems suited for coarse ornamental items. Principally composed of white feldspar of a compact nature, inclusions of perfectly circular spherules of dark green hornblende provide a strong and pleasing contrast, each of the spherules being about the size of a pea and firmly embedded in the feldspar matrix. This rock occurs in the form of large boulders in a limited area about 1 mile west of the old Oaks Ferry on the Yadkin River in Davie County.

LEPIDOLITE AND MUSCOVITE MICA

Although readers are undoubtedly most familiar with mica in large sheets such as is commonly employed in electrical devices, several species of the Mica Group occur in fine-grained compact masses suitable for carving or preparation into objects of ornament. Among these are lepidolite or *lithium mica*, and pink muscovite. Lepidolite is very common in lithium-bearing pegmatite bodies and at one time served as one of the principal ores of this metal. On the other hand, although similar in form and appearance, pink muscovite is very rare and has been noted in good lapidary material only in the New Mexican localities described below. Both species are attractive in color, ranging from pale pink to pale lilac, sometimes deep lilac in shade, and are easily worked with ordinary steel tools if free of quartz and other hard minerals. Because of their porous nature, however, it is difficult to impart a good polish and most attempts stop at a high glossy finish. Many amateurs use massive lepidolite for book ends, ash trays, or as spheres while pink muscovite from New Mexico has been additionally employed in gems for jewelry.

Muscovite mica has been known for thousands of years, and not too long ago was popularly referred to as *Muscovy glass* since it was found in exceptionally large sheets in Muscovy (Russia). Lepidolite was named *Schuppenstein* or "scale stone" by the early German miners and from this arose the idea of using the Greek word for *scale* to form the present name. Although muscovite is extremely common in many kinds of rock, it reaches its greatest perfection in pegmatites where it sometimes forms foliated crystals or "books" as much as several feet in diameter. The rose-colored type described below is most unusual both because of the color and the very small size of the crystals. Lepidolite, on the other hand, is commonly found in pegmatite bodies in crystals which may be too small to see or in broad books several inches across.

The Mica Group to which both species belong, consists of related silicates of complex formula which all crystallize in the Monoclinic System although the six-sided outline of books would lead one to believe they belonged to the Hexagonal System. The formula for muscovite is $KAl_3Si_3O_{10}(OH)_2$; that of lepidolite reflects the lithium content: $K_2Li_3Al_4Si_7O_{21}(OH,F)_2$. In pegmatites, both are frequently seen together, in some cases the purplish lepidolite forming beautiful scalloped fringes on pale silvery green muscovite books. The hardness of both varies from about

2½ to 4 in solid crystals but massive granular forms appear about 3. The cleavage surface of mica is too well known to discuss here but of course is far less obvious in fine-grained massive types; in these, fresh broken surfaces show cleavages only as minute twinkling reflections. The specific gravity of muscovite ranges from 2.8 to 3.0; lepidolite is slightly higher, from 2.8 to 3.3. However, porous massive forms may be expected to test at the lower values given. Refractive indices for muscovites are: $\alpha = 1.552$, $\beta = 1.582$, $\gamma = 1.588$; birefringence 0.036. For lepidolite: $\alpha = 1.530$, $\beta = 1.553$, $\gamma = 1.556$; birefringence 0.026. Both are biaxial and optically negative. Ordinary muscovite is silvery, gray, greenish, brown, yellow, and more rarely, pink or red; lepidolite may be white, yellowish, grayish, pink, red, purple or lilac.

LOCALITIES

Maine. Lepidolite is found in many pegmatites in Oxford and Androscoggin counties. Exceptionally fine-grained material has come from the Black Mountain Mica Mine in Rumford Township and a deep reddish-purple kind from Mount Apatite near Auburn, Androscoggin County. Huge masses are sometimes encountered as at Black Mountain where a solid mass was exposed during quarrying measuring 12 by 18 feet across the face.

Connecticut. Some good lepidolite has been found from time to time in the various pegmatite quarries surrounding Middletown, Middlesex County.

New Mexico. A purplish muscovite, strikingly like lepidolite in color and form, and often mistaken for that mineral, occurs in considerable quantity in pegmatite dikes near the Harding Mine in southwest Taos Co., located 16 miles south-southwest of Taos and 9½ miles due east of Embudo. The muscovite locality is about 3 miles northwest of the mine near the summit of the south bank of the Rio Grande River and a mile or so southwest of Pilar (Cieneguilla). Muscovite occurs as extremely fine-grained masses associated with spodumene, quartz, albite, and microcline in the core unit of a large pegmatite. Masses sometimes reach as much as a foot in diameter but most are only several inches across and highly irregular in form. Color ranges from gray to pink, wine-red, ruby-red, and deep lilac although the predominant shade is a peculiar grayish-pink. This material enjoyed some vogue as cabochon and ornamental stone and was once sent East in quantity for possible employment in jewelry but this venture did not succeed because the mica proved too soft and too difficult to cut and polish. At the Harding Mine, both muscovite and ordinary lepidolite are also found, the latter formerly quarried and shipped as an ore of lithium.

California. Numerous localities for lepidolite occur where pegmatites have been opened for gemstones, among them are the Anita Mine near Sage in Riverside Co., the mines on top and on the flank of Tourmaline Queen Mountain at Pala, San Diego Co., also the mines on Hiriart Hill nearby. The outstanding producer of lepidolite was the Stewart Lithia Mine at Pala which at one time supplied virtually all of the world's lithium ore. Tremendous quantities of fine-grained lepidolite may still be seen scattered about the workings and in the old open cuts on the eastern side. This locality also produced the well-known compact lepidolite shot through with sprays and sunbursts of pink tourmaline, which were once standard specimens in every mineral collection of consequence. The color of the massive material varies considerably, a grayish-lilac being most common while decided pinks or purplish-pinks are less frequently met with. Pink tourmaline in the form of fine needles to pencils as much as 3/16 inch diameter is abundant and by virtue of its much greater hardness, makes lapidary treatment more difficult than for ordinary pure lepidolite. Much of this material is also penetrated by white blades of cleavelandite and sometimes grayish quartz. In time, the lepidolite from this mine fades to pale, slightly-purplish gray. For more detailed information on this and other localities in California and Maine where lepidolite occurs, consult TOURMALINE.

OBSIDIAN

A popular cutting material among amateurs is a widely-distributed glass-like lava of many colors called obsidian. It derives its name, according to Pliny, the ancient Roman naturalist, from a certain Obsius who found it in Ethiopia. Originally named *obsianus* the spelling changed over the centuries until it evolved into its modern form. This material is interesting in many ways; for all practical purposes it is a true glass since it represents a quickly congealed mass of molten rock, which, had it time to cool in a more leisurely fashion, would have crystallized into a rock corresponding to granite or rhyolite. Next, like glass, it shows no trace of crystalline structure nor possesses an established composition and must therefore be considered a rock rather than a mineral. Finally, it is exceedingly brittle and breaks easily with shiny conchoidal fractures, a feature so perfectly developed that it suffices to identify obsidian wherever it is found in the field.

Obsidian occurs in huge masses, sometimes in deposits which contain millions of tons though not all of gem quality by any means. Unflawed blocks up to a foot or so across are common. An interesting mode of formation is represented by small nodules of obsidian popularly called "Apache tears." These are found in profusion in a number of the western United States and have a curious geological history. It seems that some obsidian flows are susceptible to alteration which proceeds rapidly along cracks and

FIGURE 150. Two common forms of obsidian. On the left is ordinary black material from Mono Craters, California, showing the characteristic conchoidal fracture. On the right is a mass of perlite from near Superior, Arizona, enclosing small gray transparent nodules or "Apache tears." Courtesy Smithsonian Institution.

fissures until the entire mass may, in time, be reduced to a puffy porous rock called *perlite*. Because of the entrapped air, it is much used for making light concretes and is also used as an insulating material. In perlite, places are often found where alteration has not reached everywhere and consequently small transparent glassy nodules are discovered nestled in layers of the whitish porous perlite. Wherever this rock has eroded, such nodules are found scattered profusely upon the surface of the ground. Specimens of massive obsidian and Apache tears in perlite are shown in Figure 150.

Obsidian occurs in many colors but black is by far the most common; brown, red, and even green, are also known. A unique and beautiful variety is called *snowflake* or *flowering obsidian* in allusion to the light bluish-gray spots, like snowflakes or flowers, which are sprinkled throughout perfectly black material, affording handsome and striking contrasts when cut and polished. Other types show iridescence reflected from many minute inclusions arranged in layers, furnishing the material known as *rainbow obsidian*. In still other kinds, silvery or gold inclusions, strongly metallic in luster, provide beautiful spangled gems. Perhaps the best is a variety from Mexico in which the golden inclusions are fairly coarse and highly reflective. A variety in which both black and brown obsidian occur mixed in streaks and swirls is known as *double-flow obsidian,* and if the brown is decidedly reddish in cast, as *mahogany obsidian* or *marekanite.* If cut at right angles to the layering, red-spangled obsidian is called *gold sheen obsidian;* if the inclusions are grayish-silver in color, it is called *silver sheen.* Still another variety of obsidian shows black angular brecciated fragments cemented together with red material in beautiful patterns, however, this variety bears no special name.

The applications of the many varieties of obsidian to jewelry and ornament are legion; it is cut as cabochons, and very attractive ones too, or faceted into gems if sufficiently light in color and transparent. This method is applied frequently to Apache tears since these are often quite clear and not too dark. Recently, much obsidian has been employed in tumbled gems, especially the snowflake types. In Mexico, a thriving industry turns out very attractive small carvings which are set in bracelets, rings, and other forms of silver jewelry. Pure black is most frequently used since it provides a striking contrast to the bright luster of the polished silver.

The usefulness of obsidian was fully appreciated by American Indians who dug, bartered, and worked obsidian from many places. Its perfect texture and easy fracture made it much prized both for chipping into small arrowheads and for making large ceremonial sword or spear blades. In California, blades of worked obsidian were used as currency, the larger being equivalent to $20 in value. Black blades used by the Huroks of the northern part of the state, brought about $1 per inch of length but red blades were scarcer and hence more valuable. Blades about 33 inches in length were considered almost priceless. In this state, ten localities for digging obsidian were known to the Indians; in Oregon, the Indian name for the river now known as the John Day was their equivalent for obsidian. Glass objects were made by the Mandan Indians of the Great Plains who are said to have learned how to smelt obsidian from the Snake Indians of Idaho. Even so far east as Ohio, the Mound Builders were found to use obsidian extensively, undoubtedly bartering their supplies from tribes farther west since this rock is not known to occur east of the Mississippi. One grave in Ohio yielded a beautifully executed knife blade 18 inches in length.

Perhaps nowhere did the art of obsidian working reach such a high degree of perfection as in Mexico. The prehistoric inhabitants, richly supplied by an abundance of flawless material, turned out remarkable carvings, ceremonial blades, and even mirrors. In the American Museum of Natural History are three fine obsidian mirrors, one is oblong and measures 17¼ by 12 inches, another is 12 by 9½ inches, and the third, a round mirror, is

10½ inches in diameter. The Aztecs called obsidian "iztli," surnamed "teo-tetl" or "divine stone" because of its great usefulness. One of their gods was named Itzpoppalotl, meaning "obsidian butterfly." This aboriginal esteem for obsidian was evidenced wherever this rock occurred in North America, and, as shown by its wide modern employment in the lapidary arts, it enjoys almost as much regard today.

As remarked before, the chemistry of obsidian is not fixed by any means, but in general, analyses show it to be composed of silica in percentages varying from about 66 to 77 per cent, with the next major constituent, alumina, varying from 13 to 18 per cent. Small amounts of iron oxide, potassium oxide, sodium oxide, lime, and magnesia are also found. Obsidian is amorphous but sometimes minute, partly-crystallized inclusions of other minerals can be seen suspended in otherwise uniform material. Spherulites of quartz of grayish color are frequent, especially in the obsidian of Yellowstone Park, Wyoming, where they often appear as hollow cavities of considerable size. Similar inclusions but more solid and not affecting the process of polishing, are found in the snowflake obsidian of Utah. Other inclusions in the form of exceedingly thin flakes give rise to the sheen obsidians as well as to those which are colored or iridescent. Flow marks or striae are noticeable in all material. Obsidian is not very hard, about 5 on the Mohs Scale, however, it is very brittle and requires much care in handling to prevent inadvertent breakage. The fracture is perfectly conchoidal showing a shining glassy luster on fresh surfaces (see Figure 150). In the field, obsidian is easily attacked by weathering and sandblasting and specimens are mostly frosted or dull on their exteriors. Specific gravity ranges from about 2.33 to 2.47 but is sometimes higher. The refraction of obsidian is single and invariably very low; typical values are $n = 1.48\text{-}1.51$; on this account and no matter how clear or how pale in color, transparent specimens cannot produce brilliant faceted gems because so much light is lost through leakage.

LOCALITIES

Alaska. Obsidian occurs in several places along the Aleutian Islands, one of the most noted being in the vicinity of the extinct volcano known as Mt. Makushin near the entrance to Dutch Harbor on Unalaska Island.

British Columbia. Black obsidian in small to large sizes occurs in considerable quantity on the higher eastern slopes of the Ilgachuz Mountains, 20 miles north of Anahim Lake near Tweedsmuir Provincial Park. Better material is found on Anahim Peak between the Ilgachuz Mountains and the Tsitsutl Mountains. Obsidian of unspecified quality occurs at Tsookatli, a small islet northeast of Taskaiguns in the upper part of Massett Inlet on the Queen Charlotte Islands of the Pacific Coast of this province.

Colorado. Apache tears are abundant in perlite outcropping at the base along the north and southeast sides of Ruby Mountain, Chaffee County. Massive obsidian is found near the summit crater of Specimen Mountain in Rocky Mountain National Park, 18 miles northwest of Estes Park in Larimer County.

Utah. The source of flowering or snowflake obsidian is in Millard County where much material has been removed from a large deposit near Black Rock in the southern part of the county. The locality is about 30 miles north of Milford, near Coyote Springs and Fort Cove. Black material also occurs at White Mountain nearby. This unique obsidian was discovered only in 1942 and illustrates how recently some gemstone finds have been made in North America. The obsidian from this deposit also includes red and black types as well as mixtures of both. Obsidian has also been obtained from Promontory Point on Great Salt Lake near Willard, Box Elder County.

New Mexico. Transparent to jet-black obsidian pebbles are plentiful on the desert road south of Las Cruces, Dona Ana County and also found 5 miles west on the road leading from Mesilla.

Arizona. Apache tears are abundant in several places in Maricopa County. Beautifully transparent nodules, frequently cut as faceted gems, are found in a wash a short distance west of Aguila on Highway 60-70 in the northwestern part of the county. Numerous specimens are found several miles south of the old Vulture Mine in the Vulture Mountains. Similar nodules are found on low mesas south of Wickenburg in the same range. In Pinal County, many Apache tears are obtained incidental to the commercial mining of extensive beds of perlite located several miles to the south and southwest of Superior. These nodules still show curved scales of white perlite adhering to their surfaces; many are sold every year for lapidary and specimen purposes (see Figure 150).

Wyoming. One of the most famous localities for obsidian, but productive of rather mediocre material only, is Obsidian Cliff in Yellowstone National Park in the northwest corner of the state. Obsidian Cliff is located directly upon and towers over the Central Loop Road at the northern end of Beaver Lake, 11 miles south of Mammoth. The cliff is part of an enormous flow which stretches for 2½ miles eastward into the forests; at the road it rises from 100 to 200 feet and consists primarily of black obsidian and lesser amounts of brown and brown and black double flow obsidian. Other colors are purplish-brown, greenish, and many combinations of all hues mentioned, including sheens.

Oregon. Perhaps the most important single locality in the continent is the enormous mass of obsidian known as the Glass Buttes. This prominence is about 12 miles southeast of Hampton in the northeast corner of Lake County, just below the border of Deschutes County and easily reached by

Highway 20. Such a large area is covered by broken blocks and masses detached from the mountain that excellent specimens may be obtained only a few feet from the highway. Blocks range in size from 2 to 20 pounds but much larger masses are also available. Varieties are almost numberless; solid colors in black and red are common but beautiful spiderweb brecciated types in these colors also occur; also silver and gold sheens, and banded kinds showing strong iridescence in many colors (*rainbow obsidian*). The latter are highly interesting because of their very sharp banding and the presence of inclusions which give rise to iridescent colors. If cut in cross section, the color is lost but curious swirls of contrasting opaque and transparent material are then revealed. Cut the other way, a solid sheet of color is exposed, or, if cut at an angle, a series of chevrons corresponding to several colored layers. Layers range from 1/32 inch to ½ inch in thickness and may number in the hundreds in a block of about 12 inches in thickness. The principal colors are blue, purple, red, green, pink, copper, and gold.

Another Oregon locality of some importance is in Deschutes County about 30 miles south of Bend along the road between Paulina Lake and East Lake; much material of all types occurs here.

Nevada. Beautifully banded and swirled material showing jet-black figures against a grayish translucent to transparent background is found at a popular collecting place on Queen Mountain at Montgomery Pass on Highway 6 in Mineral County. In Esmeralda County, translucent Apache tears are abundant on the western shores of Fish Lake about 10 miles slightly west of south of Coaldale. In Washoe County, nodules up to fist-size are found over a broad area near the headwaters of the Little High Rock Creek in High Rock Canyon, between highways 81 and 34 and at the place where the canyon is crossed by the Lost Creek Canyon Road.

California. Obsidian is widespread over a productive area 80 acres in extent centered about Glass Mountain (or Buttes) near the border of Siskiyou and Modoc counties. The principal locality is upon the slopes of Sugarloaf Mountain 5 miles east of Davis Creek Ranger Station where beautiful material of the following types is found: gold, silver, and rainbow sheens, dark reddish-rose, blue, dark green, and black; also double-flow. Some is transparent and shows alternate stripes of grayish clear material and opaque black. Flawless pieces up to 150 pounds weight have been obtained here as well as huge blocks up to 500 pounds. As in Oregon localities, much of this material has been mined commercially. In Lake County, quantities of common obsidian are found at Clear Lake and Lower Clear Lake while a better grade, formerly used by the local Indians, is found on Cole Creek. In Tulare County, good material is found in the Coso Mountains east of Little Lake on Highway 35 near Coso Hot Springs. Obsidian is also found on Mount Kanaktai in Sonoma County. Much material has been obtained from the

Mono Craters, a series of recent volcanoes aligned in a row south of Mono Lake in Mono County, a few miles east of Highway 395. The largest cone is 9000 feet above sea level. At the northern end of this area is found very good black, beautiful gold and silver sheen, and rainbow types, some beautifully banded. The best material comes from the vicinity of Panum Crater close to the south shore of Mono Lake.

Hidalgo. Obsidian is widely distributed throughout Mexico from its northern border to Guatemala but the most famous locality is a series of ancient Aztec quarries at the Sierra (or Serro) de La Navajas (Hill of Knives), 10 miles east of Pachuca near Antotonilco in the State of Hidalgo. Obsidian is found here over hundreds of acres within an area 1½ miles in length and averaging ½ mile in width. Heaps of discarded chips and blocks are everywhere and must contain hundreds of tons of good cutting grade material. Most is the ordinary black kind but some very fine golden sheen also occurs as well as reddish kinds and red and black mixtures. Obsidian also occurs at Zacaultipan, a locality 15 miles south of Tulancingo.

Jalisco. Good material is found at Teuchitlan, Ixtlan de los Buenos Aires, Cerro Tepayo and at Etzatlan.

Vera Cruz. Obsidian is found upon Pica de Orizaba.

Michoacan. Good material occurs near Zinapecuaro.

Puebla. Black obsidian is found at San Juan de Los Llanos.

Queretaro. Much black obsidian occurs sprinkled over the surface of hills and valleys along the highway from Queretaro to San Juan del Rio; also at a point 8 miles east of Queretaro.

Mexico, D. F. Magnificent golden sheen obsidian with beautiful, strongly reflective spangles in a background of dark brownish-black is found in a large deposit within the Federal District.

Guatemala. Extensive ancient obsidian quarries worked by the Mayans are located at La Joya, 18 miles east of Guatemala City; others are known at Fiscal on the railroad from Guatemala City to Zacapa; also near Antigua.

BANDED RHYOLITE

The term rhyolite is commonly used to designate a very fine-grained volcanic rock in which the individual mineral particles are too small to be clearly seen with the naked eye. Rhyolites are extremely common in the Western United States where they form large flows of pale red, cream or whitish rocks of almost chalky texture. Microscopic examination shows them to consist primarily of grains of orthoclase and quartz, with lesser amounts of biotite, hornblende and pyroxene cemented together with glassy material similar to obsidian in composition. Many rhyolites are porous, and in favorable situations, absorb water solutions containing oxides of iron and manganese which infiltrate into the cores of large blocks. Successive waves of infiltration produce banded patterns, roughly parallel to the exterior planes of the blocks but gradually becoming more curved toward the interior. Rhyolite of this sort, when broken open, shows beautiful banding in strongly contrasting colors and then furnishes the material popularly known as *wonderstone*.

It is quite probable that infiltrating solutions are accompanied by a certain amount of dissolved silica since specimens in which the colors seem most bright also seem to be the most compact and easily polished. Ordinary rhyolite and poorer grades of wonderstone are so porous that the best finish obtainable is no more than a gloss. The colors of wonderstone generally confine themselves to shades and tints of cream, pale brown, red, yellow, and, more rarely, orange. Solutions apparently enter along crevices in larger masses of rhyolite which have become cracked and jointed either through cooling contractions or through weathering.

Wonderstone is used in considerable quantity for coarse ornaments but only a small amount of the best material is suitable for cabochon work. Much is too porous to take a good polish and this discourages more extensive employment.

LOCALITIES

Montana. Literally thousands of tons of wonderstone are found scattered over the ground and partly embedded in the soil in an area 37 miles east of Dillon along the Sweet Water Road from the city to the valley of the Ruby River in Madison County. Material is found in chunks ranging from several inches in diameter to those which are too large to carry off. Concentric bandings follow closely the angular outline of blocks but rapidly pull away as the center is approached, forming oval and circular patterns of striking grace and color. Bandings are generally several shades of brown, red, cream, gray, yellow, purplish-red, etc. This material takes a fair to good polish. Silicified rhyolite, locally termed "onyx," occurs in the Gravelly Range south of Butte, Silverbow Co.

Nevada. Large quantities of wonderstone occur near the old silver mines at Tuscarora in the western part of Elko County and at Little Antelope Summit (elev. 7433 ft.) on Highway 50 about 40 miles west of Ely in White Pine County. A locality of lesser importance is situated about 14 miles from Fallon in Churchill County. One of the earliest occurrences to be developed commercially is located north of Tonopah in Mineral County.

Utah. Boulders of good quality wonderstone along with agate and petrified wood are found in the upper reaches of Beaver Dam Wash northwest of Castle Cliff Station in Washington County.

New Mexico. A beautiful silica gemstone essentially identical in appearance to wonderstone is found near the hot springs of Truth Or Consequences, Sierra County. It is hard, compact, sharply and colorfully banded, and takes a polish far superior to ordinary banded rhyolite. Locally the rather fanciful name of *elixirite* has been appended to it in allusion to its supposed hot springs origin. This material occurs in seams several inches wide embedded in sandstone and is stated to be an alteration product of the sandstone due to infiltration by mineralized waters from ancient springs located about 100 yards above the deposit. It is beautifully patterned in purplish-brown, brown, yellow-brown, yellow, and orange-yellow. The hardness is said to be about 6½ and the specific gravity about 2.8.

California. Small rounded nodules of colorful wonderstone occur scattered over the sands of Pinto Wash and its tributary washes in the extreme southern part of San Diego County, south of Highway 80. Pinto Wash is located at the foot of the steep-walled mountains which rise abruptly from the floor of the Imperial Valley along its western side.

PECTOLITE

When sufficiently compact, massive pectolite provides both an unusual and beautiful chatoyant cabochon material. An especially solid type of almost jade-like consistency occurs in Arctic Canada and Alaska and at one time saw extensive use among the Eskimos for adzes, hammers, and other implements subjected to severe treatment. Ordinarily, pectolite occurs as perfectly spherical crystal aggregates lining gas cavities in volcanic rocks. Cutting into one of these ball-like growths reveals a multitude of minute fibrous crystals radiating outward from a common center and displaying silky reflections along the sides. Large growths split readily and are of little use in lapidary work, however, when radiate masses are small and fill cavities completely, the resulting material is sufficiently strong to withstand cutting. The name of pectolite is derived from a Greek word meaning "compact" in reference to its structure.

Crystallizing in the Monoclinic System, pectolite is a hydrous calcium sodium silicate with the formula: $Ca_2NaSi_3O_8(OH)$; it is most frequently found associated with zeolites such as natrolite, stilbite, heulandite, etc., but distinct crystals are very rare. Two perfect prismatic cleavages promote easy splitting along radial directions, often resulting in development of splinters capable of penetrating the skin if specimens are handled roughly. In size, individual masses range from about 1 to 3 inches in thickness. The specific gravity is low, ranging from 2.74 to 2.88. Refractive indices are: $\alpha = 1.595$, $\beta = 1.606$, $\gamma = 1.633$; birefringence 0.038; biaxial, positive. The color seems pure white when fibers are viewed from the side, but when specimens are cut and polished across the ends, the color is seen to be grayish or greenish or sometimes brown due to staining by iron oxides. There is no commercial use for pectolite but very compact pieces are occasionally cut into fine chatoyant cabochons for collectors (see Figure 151).

LOCALITIES

Alaska. Pale bluish, greenish, and grayish translucent pectolite of extremely fine texture and remarkable toughness has been recognized in many Eskimo artifacts. Early explorers of the Arctic were told that the material occurred in a number of places in a mountain chain which parallels the northwest coast between Kotzebue Sound and Point Barrow; also in places along the north coast of the Yukon Territory of Canada. One locality is stated to be 25 miles up the Yukon River from Nulato. Because of its tough nature, the Eskimos called pectolite "kaudlo," the same term used to designate the Kobuk nephrite, and it is noteworthy that implements made of pectolite have long been mistaken for nephrite.

FIGURE 151. Polished specimens of silky white pectolite from Alps Road, Passaic County, New Jersey. The largest cabochon is about ¾ inch in diameter.

New Jersey. Pectolite has long been obtained from the traprock quarries of northern New Jersey in the form of perfectly spherical masses lining gas cavities in lava. Unusually compact nodules consisting of solid spherical intergrowths occur in traprock in a small abandoned quarry along Alps Road above Packanack Lake, Passaic County. Though seldom over an inch in size, the nodules take a very fine polish and display an interesting mottled pattern in pure white and greenish-gray chatoyant areas as shown in Figure 151.

California. Excellent cutting material in the form of narrow seams occurs in serpentine in a road cut 1½ miles east of Middletown on the highway to Lower Lake in Lake County. Seams are about ½ to 1 inch thick and consist of white pectolite in numerous individual radiated groups filling the vein space solidly. This material cuts and polishes readily and makes fine chatoyant cabochons.

DATOLITE

Among the gemstones unique to North America is the peculiar porcelainous massive form of datolite found only in the copper mines of the Lake Superior region. Here occur nodules ranging in size from a fraction of an inch to as much as 6 inches in diameter, mostly white in color but also attractively stained by inclusions of metallic copper. Clear datolite is also found in several places which will be described below; from suitable material, small faceted gems can be cut of little commercial value but of considerable interest to collectors. The name datolite has been derived from the Greek word meaning "to divide" in reference to the crumbly nature of crystalline aggregates.

In composition, datolite is allied to danburite and is a basic calcium borosilicate of the formula: Ca_2B_2 $(SiO_4)_2(OH)$. It forms beautiful sharp glassy crystals belonging to the Monoclinic System which are noted for the variety and complexity of their faces (see Figure 152). The finest specimens are obtained from cavities in pillow basalt where they may appear singly, in groups, or as tightly-packed aggregates of crystals with only the transparent points protruding into the openings. Individuals may vary in size from less than $\frac{1}{8}$ inch to some as at Westfield, Massachusetts, which frequently exceed 2 inches across. Common associated minerals are prehnite, babingtonite,

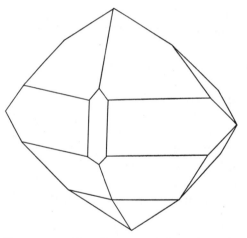

FIGURE 152. Datolite crystal from Bergen Hill, New Jersey.

calcite and several zeolites. Datolite is from 5 to 5½ in hardness, without cleavage planes, but rather brittle except in the case of massive material which is very tough. Fracture surfaces on crystals vary from irregular to conchoidal; the luster is glassy to slightly oily. Specific gravity ranges from 2.8 to 3.0 but massive material is somewhat lower. Refractive indices are: $a = 1.626$, $\beta = 1.654$, $\gamma = 1.670$. The birefringence is 0.044 and large enough to cause easily visible doubling of facet junctions as observed in cut specimens. Datolite is biaxial, negative. There is very little dispersion and faceted gems are attractive only because of their curious faintly greenish color: no trichroism can be detected. Crystals are always some delicate shade of yellowish-green. Nodular forms are highly interesting because of the considerable quantity of finely divided native copper which is sprinkled densely through outer zones. Toward the center, copper granules become smaller in size and diminish in number until the cores remain snow-white. Granules are so small as to require a hand lens to see clearly. The exterior of nodules is coarse and rough and gives little hint of the material within. White is by far the most common color of massive datolite but reddish, brownish, and even tints of purple are encountered. In some nodules, other coloring agents impart shades of pink, light red, gray, yellow, orange, green and purplish-gray. Bright-colored specimens are highly prized but seldom cut except as polished nodule halves. Several nodules are illustrated in Figure 153.

LOCALITIES

Massachusetts. The most notable locality for fine large crystals of facet grade is the Lane Quarry and other openings in the diabase sill known as the Holyoke Range which appears intruded into Triassic sandstone between Springfield and Westfield in Hampden County. The quarries are about midway between the communities mentioned. The diabase is fine-grained material of dark greenish-gray color containing numerous shear zones in which datolite, calcite, quartz, and other minerals occur lining cavities. A sheet covered by large datolite crystals is in the U.S. National Museum and measures about 12 inches square. One of the largest crystals on record measures 2¾ by 2¼ by 2 inches. Insofar as facet material is concerned, the best crystals have been found loosely embedded in friable chlorite in pocket or seams next to large openings in the diabase. A cut gem of Westfield datolite ⅜ inch across is in the American Museum of Natural History; another is in the U.S. National Museum; the author owns one of ½ inch diameter which weighs 2.18 carats.

Connecticut. In 1958, the Roncari Quarry at East Granby, Hartford County, yielded considerable quantities of excellent datolite similar in all respects to that found at Westfield, Mass. Splendid large pale greenish crystals are found lining cavities in pillow basalt and at times are associated with calcite, milky quartz, and amethyst crystals. The latter are very pale however, and of no interest except for specimens. Datolite crystals from this quarry are stated to reach as much as 2 inches in diameter.

New Jersey. Datolite crystals similar to those of Westfield but much smaller in size, have been found in the lava sills of the northeastern part of the state, particularly in Passaic and Bergen counties.

Michigan. The old Quincy Mine has been the most prolific source of datolite nodules in the copper region of Keeweenaw Peninsula. The extensive dumps from which some material is gleaned even today, are located across the narrow arm of Portage Lake from Houghton in Houghton

FIGURE 153. Datolite nodules from Keeweenaw Peninsula, Michigan. The larger specimen measures 2¼ inches across; both nodules are basically white massive datolite stained with minute specks of native copper.

County. Splendid material has also come from the Iroquois Mine and others north of Houghton; also from the Clark Mine about 2 miles east of Copper Harbor near the tip of the peninsula in Keeweenaw County, and from the Delaware Mine near Delaware on Highway 41 in the same county; additionally from the Mass Mine near Mass on Highway 26 in Ontonagon Co. Massive translucent datolite was once found comprising almost the entire filling of a copper-bearing vein upon Isle Royale as at an old working near the Epidote Mining Claim. During mining, openings were found in which very fine crystals of datolite lined the walls. Massive material is generally white except where stained by disseminated copper. Another occurrence upon this island is at Thomsonite Beach where small nodules are sometimes found.

PREHNITE

Interesting cabochons and faceted gems are frequently cut from suitable masses of green prehnite. Exceptionally translucent specimens can be prepared into faceted stones which though lacking the sharp sparkle of perfectly clear gems, glow with a not unpleasant greenish or yellowish light. Prehnite commonly occurs in volcanic rocks, especially those dark colored basalts known to quarrymen as "trap rocks," and are found covering thousands of square miles of the earth's surface in Eastern Canada, the Northeastern United States and elsewhere. In these rocks, cavities are frequently found in which prehnite forms rounded masses lining the walls and associated with calcite, apophyllite, datolite, etc. Such combinations are often spectacularly beautiful and much prized for mineral collections but unfortunately, little of the prehnite is suitable for lapidary work, being either too thin or too porous to take a flawless polish. Close examination shows massive prehnite to be composed of many exceedingly fine fibrous crystals growing in radial fashion from focal points on cavity walls. When cut across the fibers, a certain chatoyancy is induced in finished gems, while cuts taken across the tops of fibers yield gems which are uniform in texture and deeper in color since no light is reflected from the internal junctions between crystals. Prehnite receives its name from Colonel von Prehn who first brought this mineral to Europe from the Cape of Good Hope.

Prehnite is a hydrous calcium aluminum silicate, $Ca_2Al_2Si_3O_{10}(OH)_2$, and crystallizes in the Orthorhombic System. Individual, well-formed crystals are very rare, the usual growth habit being that described above. Its fibrous structure imparts a surprising degree of toughness although the hardness is only 6 to $6\frac{1}{2}$. Fracture surfaces show a silky to pearly luster caused by reflection of light from the numerous slender crystals. The specific gravity ranges from 2.80 to 2.95, a variation no doubt due to the numerous minute cavities which are frequently seen in massive material. Refractive indices are: $\alpha = 1.616$, $\beta = 1.626$, $\gamma = 1.649$; birefringence 0.003; biaxial positive. The color is generally some shade of yellowish-green but is apt to fade to greenish-yellow if long exposed to sunlight. Some greens and yellows are very faint, almost colorless. Very dark green colors are frequently due to inclusions of byssolite (amphibole). Specimens do not show perceptible trichroism.

LOCALITIES

Greenland. Wide botryoidal sheets over 1 inch thick and of fine color are found on the beach at Qeqertarssuaq between Naujat and Tuperssuarta in the Umanak District.

North West Territories. Fine green material has been found with calcite and quartz in veins traversing the lavas of Adams Sound, Admiralty Inlet, Baffinland.

Nova Scotia. Prehnite of good quality is common at Clark Head, Cumberland County, at Clifton in Hants County, and at Black Rock in Kings County.

New Brunswick. Prehnite occurs in basalt at Dalhousie, Restigouche County.

Ontario. In addition to amethyst and agate, the extensive basalt sheets of the north shore of Lake Superior in the Thunder Bay District provide prehnite as at Saint Ignace and Simpson Islands, also upon the Slate River and the Kaministikwa River.

British Columbia. Fine material has been found in the LeRoi Mine at Rossland, a small town several miles west of Trail in the extreme southern part of this province in the Kootenay District.

Massachusetts and Connecticut. Beautiful masses occur in cavities in several basalt sills which traverse these states from north to south along the Connecticut River Basin. The quarries at Westfield, Hampden County, and the Cheapside Quarry in East Deerfield, Franklin County, Massachusetts, have been productive in the past.

FIGURE 154. Massive prehnite covering a slab of altered volcanic rock, West Paterson, New Jersey. The cabochon in the foreground was cut from prehnite found at Centreville, Virginia. The rough specimen measures about 8 inches from tip to tip.

New Jersey. Undoubtedly the finest colored prehnite in North America and possibly in the world, has come from the lower New Street Quarry in West Paterson, Passaic County. Crusts up to one inch thick were found lining cavities of small to large size in a grayish-green pillow basalt in this quarry. Many other minerals associated with the prehnite formed outstanding specimens prized by mineral collectors everywhere. Masses of bright green material up to 8 by 8 inches were common, while smaller pieces were obtained by the pound. A typical specimen is illustrated in Figure 154. Unfortunately, work ceased at this quarry many years ago and unless blasting is resumed, there is little hope of finding more material. Very fine prehnite has also come from a host of places in this state and only the most important localities can be mentioned, viz., Passaic County: Francisco Bros. Quarry at Great Notch; Prospect Park Quarry on Planten Avenue, Paterson; Braen's Quarry in Hawthorne. Essex County: Upper Montclair; Short Hills. Morris County: Millington. Somerset County: Bound Brook; Rocky Hill; Somerville. Union County: Summit. Mercer County: Princeton; Hopewell. Union & Somerset Counties: Plainfield and North Plainfield. All of the quarries in which prehnite occurs are carved from the steep-walled basaltic sills which cross the northern part of New Jersey in a southwesterly direction from its northern boundary to the Delaware River.

Virginia. In the early 1950's, splendid masses of green prehnite frequently associated with tufts of grayish-green byssolite and large pearly crystals of white apophyllite, were found lining seams and cavities in the Centreville Quarry a short distance west of the town of the same name. The quarry lies on the south side of Highway 29-211 and exploits a large mass of coarsely granular diorite quite unlike ordinary basalts in which prehnite usually occurs. Masses up to 24 by 18 inches in size have been removed from one giant crevice near the floor of the quarry. All sections of prehnite from this quarry are unusual in another respect: their thickness varies from several inches to as much as 4 or 5 inches and all solid prehnite! Unfortunately, not much is suited for cutting because of the presence of numerous minute vugs which, upon cutting, trap polishing powder and cause disfigurement of finished stones. An interesting chatoyant, snow-white thaumasite was found associated with prehnite at this quarry and some was sent to Germany by a collector to be cut into beads.

Michigan. Cuttable prehnite of good color and translucency occurs in a number of the copper deposits on the Keeweenaw Peninsula of Northern Michigan, as upon the dumps of the mines near Phoenix, Keeweenaw County, the Isle Royale Mine and the Huron Mine near Atlantic, Houghton County.

CHLORASTROLITE

Around Lake Superior, a unique gem called *greenstone* in allusion to its dark grayish-green color, is highly prized by the residents. To science, this gemstone is known as chlorastrolite, a title which is far more descriptive since its Greek derivation means "green star." Upon viewing a polished specimen, the first impression is of a beautifully regular pattern of miniature polygons fitted together like the segments of a turtle's back. Then as the gem is tilted under the light, one is suddenly aware that the mottled pale and dark green patches shift with the slightest movement. A magnifying glass shows that each segment consists of thousands of minute needles radiating outward from a common point in the center. As the gem is tilted, some needles are turned broadside reflecting a strong silky luster, while others turned on edge become dark. Another slight movement will cause the patterns of light and dark to reverse themselves. The name "green star" is now seen to be most appropriate because the reflections within each segment are like miniature star beams flashing and twinkling from an infinitely small central point. The drawing in Figure 155 illustrates a typical cabochon gem.

Chlorastrolite is somewhat of a mineralogical puzzle; some investigators believe it to be a separate mineral species allied to zeolites while others say it is merely a variety of prehnite. Very few technical references exist on the subject and apparently no one has taken the trouble to positively determine its true identity. Chlorastrolite forms within small gas bubble spaces in lava where it is found alone or in association with calcite, spongy growths of greasy greenish chlorite sometimes permeated with a reddish clay, and small specks of native copper. Occasionally radiated masses of white to pink thomsonite are found in the same cavity. Each nodule is completely encased by an envelope of the green chlorite referred to above, which

FIGURE 155. A polished chlorastrolite cabochon.

is soft enough to permit the separation of nodules from enclosing rocks without breakage. Chlorastrolite is variable in hardness but generally lies somewhere between 5 and 6. The specific gravity is also inconstant but averages 3.2 in good compact specimens.

There is only one significant locality for this gemstone: upon Isle Royale National Park, a large rocky densely-wooded island in the northern part of Lake Superior and politically part of Michigan. Almost solid rock, Isle Royale is ribbed and ridged along its entire length presenting steep rough shorelines indented by numerous coves. Some idea of the terrain is given in the photograph in Figure 156. Rocks are principally ancient lavas but a conglomerate mass extends along the north shore of Siskowit Bay and is well exposed in Conglomerate Bay. Both rock types yield a variety of gemstones although chlorastrolite occurs only in the lavas. Chlorastrolite was first mentioned from this island by Dr. Charles T. Jackson in a geological report published in 1849 and it was he who suggested its present name.

Good specimens of chlorastrolite occur both free and in matrix upon the beaches of Mott and Smithwick islands on the southern coast of the northeast end of the main island; other places are near Old Light and along the south shore of Siskowit Lake; also from near Todd Harbor on the north shore of the main island; Scoville Point near the extreme eastern end and various places in the interior between Rock Harbor and Siskowit Lake are also fruitful hunting grounds.

FIGURE 156. A scenic view of the rocky shoreline of Isle Royale, Michigan, the only locality of importance for chlorastrolite. Courtesy Isle Royale National Park.

Chlorastrolite nodules are never large and the average finished gem rarely exceeds ½ inch in diameter although exceptional specimens may provide gems up to 1 inch across. Perhaps the largest examples ever found did not exceed 1½ to 2 inches in length; a fine specimen of about this size is in the collection of the Chicago Natural History Museum and is one of the largest in the country. In cutting, high rounded cabochons conforming as much as possible to the outline of the original pebbles are preferred. The "stars" of individual fiber groups are most beautiful just beneath the rind and if grinding is carried on carelessly, an otherwise excellent pebble can be ruined. Good quality material takes a fine glassy polish which brings out the chatoyancy of the fibers to the highest degree. High grade specimens are relatively rare and an annoying number of defects are found in most pebbles which ruins them for gems. In this connection, some local residents make a practice of bleaching finished gems by exposing them to sunlight in the belief that paler gems display their chatoyancy better than the darker kinds. Whether this treatment is effective or not is debatable, it being very possible that the paling in color, if any, comes about from evaporation of water trapped between the fibers rather than an actual reduction in color intensity in the chlorastrolite itself. It is claimed that bleaching is complete within from 3 to 30 days after exposure and some authorities state that if the color has not changed by that time, it never will.

MORDENITE

Named after its occurrence near Morden, Nova Scotia, mordenite is a member of the Zeolite Family of minerals and is most closely related to heulandite. At Morden it has been found in small nodules of white to cream color displaying radiated internal structure, and, when cut, a handsome silky luster. Most of the nodules are less than an inch in diameter and without commercial significance, however, a few have been polished into cabochons and beads.

Nodules are found at the base of a towering cliff along the shores of the Bay of Fundy near the small community of Morden in Kings County, Nova Scotia. The source of the material is a vein in the basalt of which the cliff is composed.

NATROLITE AND MESOLITE

Natrolite and mesolite are closely related minerals belonging to the Zeolites, and, like other members of this important Family, are found almost exclusively in cavities in volcanic rocks. Both species start their growth upon the walls of such cavities, beginning with a vanishingly small nucleus from which thousands of minute needle-like crystals radiate outward until the entire cavity is filled or nourishing solutions exhausted. The resultant fibrous masses are perfectly white and beautifully chatoyant, displaying a strong silky luster reflected from many minute prisms.

Some natrolite is found in which the individual prisms are large enough to cut into faceted gems of a fraction of a carat in weight and a few of this size have been cut from time to time for collectors of the unusual.

Natrolite receives its name from the sodium in its content, an older name for this element, *natrium*, providing the necessary prefix. Mesolite is derived from the Greek word for "middle" since this species is intermediate in composition between natrolite and scolecite. Like other Zeolites, both minerals are noted for a curious atomic structure in which water is held so loosely that it can be driven off by application of heat without destroying the mineral in the process. Another property which is also distinctive, and, incidentally, of great interest to the housewife, is the ability of these minerals to absorb from "hard" water those elements which cause it to be so inefficient in its cleansing action. Indeed, so effective are these minerals in this respect that an enormous water-softening industry depending upon artificial zeolites has sprung up in the United States, catering to those sections where only hard water is available.

Chemically, both species are very similar, natrolite being hydrous sodium aluminum silicate while mesolite differs only slightly in that some calcium replaces part of the sodium. However, this small difference is still sufficient to cause important changes in crystallization as shown by the fact that natrolite is Orthorhombic while mesolite crystallizes in the Monoclinic System. Their formulas are: natrolite $Na_2Al_2Si_3O_{10} \cdot 2H_2O$, and mesolite $(Na,Ca)_2Al_2Si_3O_{10} \cdot 3H_2O$.

Both minerals are only 5 in hardness and display perfect prismatic cleavages which render single crystals remarkably fragile, however, compact masses are sufficiently tough to satisfactorily withstand lapidary treatment. Specific gravities are modest in value, ranging from 2.20 to 2.25 for natrolite and about 2.29 for mesolite. Refractive indices are very low: natrolite $\alpha = 1.480$, $\beta = 1.482$, $\gamma = 1.483$, birefringence 0.003; mesolite $\alpha = 1.505$, $\beta = 1.505$, $\gamma = 1.506$, birefringence 0.001. Both species are biaxial, positive. Ordinarily, natrolite and mesolite are colorless in clear crystals, or snow white in massive form, however, cream, red, green and yellow specimens are also known.

LOCALITIES

Nova Scotia. Handsome specimens of natrolite in massive form, often suitable for cutting, occur at Cape d'Or, Five Islands, Horse Shoe Cove, Swan Creek, and Two Islands in Cumberland County. Eroded masses of natrolite or mesolite occur on the beach below Cape Blomidon in Kings County; also at North Mountain and Port George in Annapolis County. Some of the Nova Scotian material is ivory-white grading into yellowish- or greenish-white. In times past it has enjoyed some use as cabochons and beads. All of these occurrences are derived from volcanic rocks (traps) which occur extensively over much of northwestern Nova Scotia.

New Jersey. Natrolite in splendid radiate groups of transparent needles occurs in numerous traprock quarries in the northern part of the state, especially from those in Passaic and Bergen Counties, but solid material suitable for cutting is rare.

Montana. Large prisms of colorless natrolite, square in cross section, occur in an undefined locality in Park County. Some of the crystals are just thick enough to afford very small faceted gems of a fraction of a carat in weight.

Oregon. Fine compact silky masses of mesolite occur in some abundance in cavities in the volcanic rocks of Mount Pisgah, 3 miles east of Goshen in Lane County where mesolite occurs in association with calcite, heulandite, agate, and quartz. The color is snow-white and a smooth lustrous polish is easily obtained. Large compact masses of natrolite have been reported from basalts near McLeod in Jackson County.

California. Some natrolite, hard and compact enough for polishing, has been reported from the basalts surrounding Calabasas on Route 101 about 8 miles north of Malibu Beach in Los Angeles County.

THOMSONITE

Thomsonite is a zeolite mineral rarely occurring in distinct crystals. It is usually found as spherical aggregations of exceedingly fine needles forming dense compact masses. When pure, it is dead-white in color but infiltrations of foreign minerals during growth often cause spherules to show distinct and colorful banding. When polished, specimens of this sort show beautiful concentric markings in cream, green, black, red, and paler shades of these colors. A radically different form of thomsonite has been given the varietal name of lintonite and for some time it was thought to be a distinct mineral species. This variety is so extremely compact that no trace of individual crystals can be seen and the small pebbles and masses

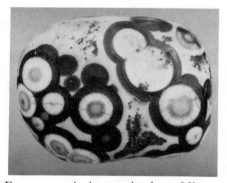

FIGURE 157. A thomsonite from Minnesota showing the radiate structure and the contrasting colored rings. Courtesy Smithsonian Institute.

in which it is found show a high degree of translucency. At a casual glance, it appears very much like certain olive-green translucent Burmese jadeite. Lintonite is named after Laura A. Linton, who analyzed it, while thomsonite is named after a Scotch chemist, Dr. T. Thomson.

Thomsonite is an Orthorhombic complex hydrous calcium, sodium, aluminum silicate with the following formula: $(Ca,Na_2)Al_2Si_2O_8 \cdot 2\frac{1}{2}H_2O$. Ordinary fibrous types are about 5 in. hardness but lintonite is closer to $5\frac{1}{2}$. Specific gravity ranges from 2.3 to 2.4. Refractive indices are: $\alpha = 1.514$, $\beta = 1.520$, $\gamma = 1.542$; birefringence 0.028; biaxial, positive. Due to its fibrous nature, indices are difficult to measure. Thomsonite and its principal variety lintonite, are found exclusively in volcanic rocks where they occur as seam or gas cavity fillings, the latter characterized by roughly spherical shapes. The vast majority of nodules range from ⅛ inch to about ⅝ inch in diameter; specimens over 1 inch are highly prized if otherwise suitable for cutting.

LOCALITIES

Ontario. Thomsonites of reddish and brownish tints and almost identical to those from Minnesota are found upon the beaches of Michipicoten Island in the northeastern part of Lake Superior.

FIGURE 158. Thomsonite from Minnesota and New Mexico. Large oval cabochons at the bottom have been cut and polished from massive seam thomsonite found in New Mexico while smaller specimens are from the noted locality in Cook County, Minnesota.

Michigan. Thomsonite and lintonite are found on nearly every pebbly beach of Isle Royale. The principal localities are on the north shore where volcanic rocks are most abundant as for example in Duncan Bay in the northeast end of the island, at a place appropriately named Thomsonite Beach. Another beach bearing the same name is in Todd Cove. Many nodules embedded in rock can be seen opposite Hawk Island near McCargo Cove. Numerous small nodules occur on the beaches of the small island southwest of Smithwick Island. Lintonite, sometimes in specimens up to 1½ inches long, has been found along the shores of Stockly Bay.

Minnesota. The principal North American locality for thomsonite is Thomsonite Beach, a shallow indentation on the north shore of Lake Superior, Cook County. The beach is a short distance from Highway 61, about 5½ miles southwest of the town of Grand Marais. On the beach, which extends about ¼ mile southwest of Terrace Point, rounded pebbles of thomsonite are found mixed with other minerals which have eroded from the Keeweenawan basalts and other rocks in the immediate vicinity. The basalt is weathered rather extensively next to the beach and many nodules have been obtained by prying blocks loose and breaking them up. Underneath, where the rock is fresher, the nodules are firmly encased and it is seldom possible to remove them without fracturing.

This locality has provided bushels of thomsonite nodules in years past and even today, especially in spring or after severe storms, it is possible to go to the beach and find more. Most specimens are coated with an opaque dark green skin which gives little indication of the quality within, and indeed makes identification a matter requiring some little experience. The pebbles are generally spherical in shape, sometimes flattened, and at other times, quite irregular in form. Coloration is most intense and most contrasting in the layers immediately beneath the skin. In general, dark green and black appear next to the skin while pink and yellowish-pink are met in the interior. Often a number of separate radiated masses occur within one nodule and it is from such pebbles that the best "eyes" of contrasting color are obtained. Typical specimens are shown in Figures 157 and 158. Basalt containing thomsonite occurs in a very restricted area and one authority estimates this to be only 65 feet across the outcrop. Lintonite in small dark olive-green pebbles is found at this locality also.

FLUORITE

Though soft, brittle, easily cleaved and remarkably low in refractive power, fluorite is so beautifully colored and often so clear, that it is used for many ornamental purposes in spite of its drawbacks. In China, large pieces of transparent green material are frequently used in carving and invariably mislabeled "green quartz." In England, a lovely purple, blue, and white banded kind, known as *blue john* was once extensively turned into handsome bowls, cups, saucers, and other items, remarkable for their delicacy and display of pleasing patterns in contrasting colors. A number of North American localities provide suitable material which has also enjoyed some use for ornamental purposes. Faceted gems are frequently cut but as collector's items only since they are far too fragile and soft to stand wear in jewelry. Fluorite receives its name from the Latin word *fluere*, to flow, in allusion to its easy melting. It is alternatively spelled fluor or fluorspar.

The chemistry of fluorite is simple, it is calcium fluoride with the formula: CaF_2. Occurring in a wide variety of situations, it frequently fills veins in which it is the principal mineral and commonly forms the gangue of lead and silver ores. It also occurs in sedimentary rocks such as dolomite and limestone, often forming fine crystal groups lining walls of cavities and crevices. Crystallizing in the Isometric System, fluorite is most commonly observed in simple cubes although crystals frequently show each corner cut off by partial development of octahedral faces. An example of twinned crystals is shown in Figure 159. Only 4 in hardness, fluorite is far too soft to be durable while four easily-developed cleavages parallel to each of the faces of the octahedron, further contribute fragility. Cleavage surfaces though easily produced, are seldom perfectly smooth, exhibiting a texture like that seen on glass when it is frosted over with ice.

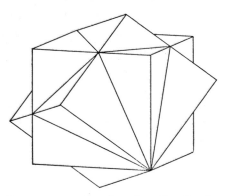

FIGURE 159. A pair of cubic fluorite crystals twinned in the peculiar fashion characteristic of this mineral.

In respect to specific gravity, values range from 3.17 to 3.19 depending upon purity. Compared to other gemstones, the gravity is high and affords a simple means of distinguishing fluorite from other gems of similar appearance. In the case of the Chinese "green quartz" for example, if one were to weigh a carving of genuine quartz of about the same size in one hand and the fluorite in the other, the difference would be immediately noticeable. Being Isometric, only one index of refraction is noted: $n = 1.434$. Fluorite is colorless and clear when pure but ordinarily is some decided shade of purple, blue, gray, green, yellow, brown, and far more rarely, pink to red. Purple shades are often so dark they appear black. Coloration is commonly zoned parallel to crystal faces in sharp bands of varying thickness. Crystals often contain inclusions of gas and liquid, also various ore minerals such as galena and marcasite which are sometimes profusely distributed in zones much like coloring bands.

Fluorite is a favorite of mineral collectors who specialize in observing the glow excited in certain minerals when irradiated by ultraviolet light. In fact, this property is called *fluorescence* because it is shown so well by this species. Some specimens glow perceptibly in the Ultraviolet-rich rays of sunlight. Fluorescence is mostly blue and purple although sometimes red is observed. Another peculiar property of some fluorite varieties is a weird greenish glow which may be observed in a darkened room when pieces are strongly heated. This property is called *thermoluminescence* and those fluorites showing this behavior are called *chlorophanes*.

In connection with the cleavages characteristic of this mineral, some persons in the mining district of Illinois and Kentucky take rough specimens and form beautiful octahedrons by cleverly splitting off sections of the rough until the desired degree of geometric perfection is obtained. These make interesting and colorful additions to any collection and many are sold each year. Since color bands follow the original cubic form, the tips of octahedral cleavages may be purple while the center portion remains yellow.

A cleavage octahedron of this type is illustrated in Figure 160. Small numbers of faceted gems are also sold through mineral dealers while many more are cut by amateurs.

FIGURE 160. Two pieces of fluorite showing the octahedral cleavage plans so prominently displayed by this mineral. The specimen on the left has been deliberately cleaved to as nearly perfect form as possible. The large faceted gem in the foreground was cut from Westmoreland, New Hampshire material and shows the rather low degree of brilliance characteristic of fluorite; its weight is 124 carats and it measures 1 5/16 inches in length and ¾ inch in width.

LOCALITIES

Ontario. Crystallized specimens suitable for faceted gems, are found in especial perfection in Madoc and Huntington townships, Hastings County. Altogether, about 30 mines and prospects exploit numerous veins of fluorite about the north shore of the west arm of Moira Lake, a body of water several miles southwest of the town of Madoc. Another group of mines extends in a southerly direction for several miles south of Jarvis Lake, about 4 miles west of Madoc. A third group is 2 miles west of this same town. Fluorite from this district shows a refractive index of $n = 1.4340$. Colors are mostly gray, green, and colorless, but honey-yellow, blue, purple, rose, and red are also found. The crystals are often bright and clear and most attractively arranged in groups upon matrix, exceptionally fine crystals coming from the Keen Vein and the Perry Mine. The Keen Vein is almost on the northern shore of the west arm of Moira Lake and has produced crystals up to 4 to 5 inches in diameter as well as optical quality crystals occurring as inclusions in gray fibrous celestite. The Perry Mine is located very close to the junction of the west and east arms of the same lake along the northern shore, several miles south of Madoc and is noted for its well-developed crystals of yellow, pale green, and colorless fluorite. A peculiarity common to these deposits is the occurrence of fluorite crystals in celestite; when completely embedded, crystals show brilliantly smooth faces, but when exposed as in a cavity, show only frosted and dull faces. The largest crystals found in this region have measured 18 inches across.

Too numerous to list here, deep purple massive fluorite capable of taking a fine polish and suitable for ornamental objects is found at many of the apatite deposits of this province (see APATITE).

British Columbia. Very fine crystals occur in the Rock Candy Mine, a working devoted to the extraction of fluorite from veins in syenite on Kennedy Creek about 15 miles north of Grand Forks. Crystals are found lining large cavities in seams of massive fluorite, some of the openings reaching as much as 3 to 4 feet across. The color is usually green but colorless and purple varieties also occur.

New Hampshire. Startlingly beautiful masses of green transparent fluorite have been mined from a series of veins in gneissic rocks in Westmoreland and Chesterfield townships, in Cheshire County. The color is exceptionally pure and rich, and is reminiscent of the hue of emerald. The beauty of this material has no peer in North America and is rarely excelled elsewhere. The mines are located in a small area several miles northwest of Spofford Lake and are easily reached by hiking from a small country road which runs roughly parallel to Highway 63 a short distance to the west. One mine is located immediately west of the old Leonard Farm on the northeast flank of Bald Hill. Mainly vivid green, some fluorite is paler with a suggestion of blue but deep purple, colorless, and blue also occur. Cleavage octahedrons up to 9 inches on edge have been obtained from some of the veins while virtually flawless gems up to 100 carats weight have been cut from clear places. The percentage of clear material is high. A large faceted gem is shown in Figure 160 while an etched crystal is shown in Figure 161.

New York. Large cubic crystals of pale green fluorite were taken many years ago from a deposit in sedimentary rock on the northeastern shore of Muskalonge Lake in Jefferson County, the largest crystal on record measured about 5 inches on edge. Similar material was found at Macomb in St. Lawrence County.

Kentucky-Illinois. The most important deposits of fluorite in the United States occur in a small area in Hardin and Pope counties in Illinois and in the adjacent portions of Crittenden County in Kentucky across the Ohio River. In Illinois, mines are principally concentrated near Rosiclare between Big Grand Pierre Creek just west of Shetlerville and Big Creek just east of Rosiclare. Important mines are also located near Cave-In-Rock and 4½ miles to the northwest. At these localities fluorite is found in veins emplaced

FIGURE 161. A virtually flawless etched crystal of fluorite from Westmoreland, New Hampshire. This photograph fails to convey to the reader the intense emerald-green color. Its measurements are 7½ inches by 5 inches by 3 inches. Courtesy Smithsonian Institution.

along fault fissures in Mississippian limestone and sometimes in sandstone. Most veins are filled solidly with fluorite but cavities occur frequently and from these come the splendid crystallizations for which this district is famous. A large variety of hues and shades is found, from colorless to yellow, amber, light green, blue, and purple, in many instances zoned parallel to crystal faces. At Cave-In-Rock the most common coloration scheme is light yellow with a thin surface layer of purple, a very striking and lovely combination. At Rosiclare, crystals are often pale blue with a few thin bands of purple. A mine in Kentucky furnishes colorless cubes with thin purple or rose bands. Many crystals show zones in which numerous minute marcasite crystals suspended in clear fluorite appear to be standing on edge like small spears or miniature fir trees. Large crystals are common at the several localities, often reaching 4 inches or more on edge. Highly translucent to perfectly transparent crystals and masses are often split into cleavage octahedrons and find a steady sale as mineral specimens and as curios. A splendid group of crystals up to 12 inches across on a slab measuring 18 inches by 18 inches from Cave-In-Rock is on view in the American Museum of Natural History.

New Mexico. In Bernalillo County fluorite is found in the Tijeras Canyon District; in the Mogollon, Taylor Creek, and Wilcox districts in Catron

County; at many places in Dona Ana County; abundant in the Burro Mountains of Grant County. Several mines and prospects are located in Hidalgo and Lincoln counties as well as in Luna County. In Rio Arriba County, large quantities have been mined in the Bromide and Petaca districts. Excellent specimens occur in Grandview Canyon and at Hansonburg in Socorro County; also from the Caballos Mountains of Sierra County and in the Red River District of Taos County.

California. Transparent crystals of optical grade fluorite were once taken from the Floyd Brown Mine near Blythe, Riverside County.

SMITHSONITE

Although common in many ore bodies, smithsonite is surprisingly rare in good gem quality. Used primarily for cabochons, some massive types are also cut effectively into small faceted gems if sufficiently translucent. Like other carbonates, malachite and azurite being good examples, smithsonite is found in the uppermost portions of ore bodies where it forms at the expense of other minerals which have been attacked by surface waters bearing carbon dioxide in solution. In the process, smithsonite is created and deposited by solutions as thick rounded crusts along crevices and fissures. Such crusts may be several inches thick and composed of millions of tiny crystals standing shoulder to shoulder and radiating outward into the openings. The scarcity of good material is due to the fact that ore zones in which this mode of formation takes place are seldom deep and quickly mined out. If pure, smithsonite would be colorless and uninteresting but fortunately in some deposits, metallic impurities impart bright colors and cause it to be prized for gem purposes. Smithsonite was given its name in honor of James L. M. Smithson.

Pure smithsonite is zinc carbonate, $ZnCO_3$, but is rarely found in this form, most examples showing some replacement of zinc by minor quantities of iron, calcium, copper or manganese. Copper causes beautiful bluish or greenish shades, cobalt colors smithsonite pink, while the bright yellow of "turkey fat" ore from Arkansas is caused by the admixture of greenockite, a cadmium sulfide. Although crystallizing in the Hexagonal System and forming rhombohedral crystals similar to calcite, single, easily-visible individuals are seldom found, by far the largest quantity of smithsonite appearing as massive material composed of many minute crystals. The close-grained structure imparts a surprising degree of toughness in spite of the modest hardness which measures only 4 to 4½. The fibrous structure is revealed when a massive specimen is broken, showing a slight silky luster from numerous cleavage surfaces of individual crystals. When fractured across the fibers, the surface is finely-granular and somewhat greasy in luster. Specific gravity is high, ranging between 4.3 and 4.45. Refractive indices reflect the very high degree of birefringence noted in all carbonates, in this case, the difference between the rays $\omega = 1.848$ and $\epsilon = 1.621$, being 0.227. Smithsonite is uniaxial, negative.

In spite of the strong colors of some varieties, dichroism is seldom distinct and in most instances is imperceptible. Gem varieties of smithsonite generally include highly translucent blue and green material but yellow, brown, and other colors are also known and sometimes used for ornamental objects if not for gems. Coloring is seldom uniform, examination across layers of massive material showing thin, intensely-colored bands alternating with colorless bands or those of lighter color.

LOCALITIES

Arkansas. Bright yellow smithsonite known as "turkey fat" ore is found in some abundance in the lead and zinc mines of Marion County, especially at the Morning Star Mine near Yellville. This is a typical limestone deposit in which ores occur as disseminated granules and masses replacing limestone. The turkey fat ore is found lining open cavities, fissures, and filling spaces between brecciated fragments of rock. Not many specimens show thick uniformly colored coatings of smithsonite however, in most cases layers next to the limestone being virtually colorless with only a few thin bands of yellow.

Washington. Fine quality smithsonite has been found in the Josephine Mine near Metaline Falls in Pend Oreille County.

California. Pale greenish-blue material said to be similar to that from the Kelly Mine in New Mexico, once came from the Cerro Gordo District of Inyo County. Here it occurred in copper prospects and mines associated with copper carbonates, linarite, brochantite, caledonite, etc. The Cerro Gordo mines are about 6 miles northeast of Keeler.

New Mexico. Beautiful compact smithsonite occurs in some abundance in the Magdalena District of Socorro County, especially at the Kelly Mine which lies at the western base of the Magdalena Mountains about 3 miles northeast of Magdalena. Botryoidal encrustations are found from ¼ inch to several inches thick lining cavities in zinc ore veins. Colors range from pale bluish to blue, bluish-green, apple-green, also white, brown, and yellow, the latter due to inclusions of greenockite. Some stalactitic growths draped from the roofs or pockets show bright yellow rings in a blue background and provide exceptionally handsome mineral specimens when cut across and polished. Purple rings have also been observed and are thought to be due to inclusions of native copper. An enormous cavity was found many years ago in the Kelly Mine which provided hundreds of pounds of excellent material.

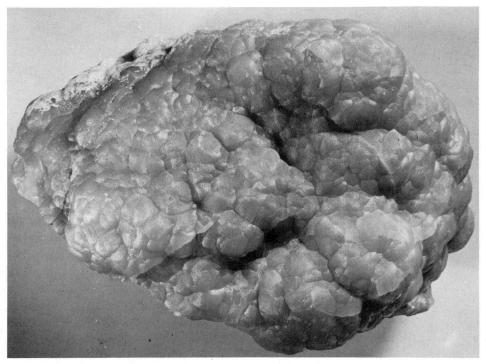

FIGURE 162. A magnificent rounded mass of translucent pale blue smithsonite from the Kelly Mine, Magdalena, New Mexico; size: 11 inches by 8 inches. Courtesy Smithsonian Institution.

This opening measured several feet across and plunged along the orebody to a depth of 25 feet. The country rock at Kelly is fossiliferous limestone and some curious specimens have been found in which crinoid stems and shells of mollusks have been faithfully replaced by smithsonite. Encrustations sometimes take curious forms; one writer describing the deposit mentioned a rounded mass the size and shape of a human head. Utilization of Kelly Mine material for commercial purposes took place about 1907 when the workings were operated by the Tri-Bullion Smelting & Development Company. Smithsonite was separated from other ores and sold at the mine for from $2 to $5 per pound. Much of it was acquired by the Goodfriend Brothers of New York City who advertised it under the name of "bonamite," a term derived from the French words for "good friends"—*bon ami*. However, commercial success was limited and since then, Kelly material has not been consistently marketed by any gemstone dealer but rough specimens suitable for mineral collections still appear upon the market from time to time. Magnificent examples are included in almost every museum collection in the United States, for example, a botryoidal mass measuring 10 by

18 inches across is exhibited by the American Museum of Natural History in New York. A fine specimen in the U.S. National Museum is illustrated in Figure 162.

MALACHITE AND AZURITE

In favored places, copper deposits near the surface of the earth are influenced by the action of downward percolating waters which cause massive copper sulfides and accessory minerals to be converted into a variety of new species. Formed in this manner by water charged with carbon dioxide, are malachite and azurite, two closely-related basic carbonates of copper. These are among the most colorful of all massive gemstones and have been known and used in jewelry and ornamentation for thousands of years. Malachite is named after the Greek word for mallow in allusion to the bright green color of the leaves of this plant; similarly, azurite is named after the color azure-blue.

Both malachite and azurite are prized almost solely for their beautifully banded massive forms although crystals of azurite are sometimes cut as curious faceted gems.

FIGURE 163. Malachite from Clifton, Arizona. Courtesy Smithsonian Institution.

Malachite crystals are far too small to be of any value singly although in aggregate, they form fibrous tough masses particularly well-adapted for a number of lapidary applications. Figure 163 illustrates a fine polished specimen of malachite from Arizona. Occasionally both minerals occur together in alternating bands, providing a most handsome contrast in hue when cut and polished. This type of material is sometimes called *azurmalachite;* an example is shown in Figure 164. Although substantial quantities of excellent malachite have been found in North America, the record for large masses of gem material must go to the deposits of Nizhne-Tagilsk in Siberia where enormous blocks, sometimes a number of *tons* in weight were recovered and extensively employed in ornament by the Czarist lapidaries of Ekaterinburg. It is probable that the most important deposits of this mineral in North

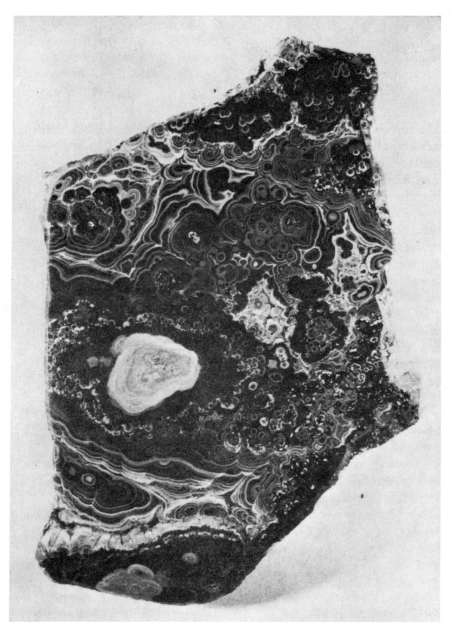

FIGURE 164. An 8 inch by 6 inch polished slab of azurite and malachite from Bisbee, Arizona showing the fine circular bandings typical of these brilliantly-hued copper minerals. The darker rings are deep blue azurite while the lighter areas are green malachite. Courtesy Smithsonian Institution.

America seldom produced masses over 100 pounds in weight of good quality throughout.

Although both malachite and azurite are basic carbonates of copper, they differ slightly in chemical composition and in atomic structure, and therefore differ appreciably in properties as well as in color. Malachite is assigned the formula: $Cu_2CO_3(OH)_2$ and azurite: $Cu_3(OH)_2(CO_3)_2$. Malachite crystals are exceedingly fine and needlelike while azurite, on the other hand, often grows in rather large splendant wedge-shaped crystals in druses in cavities, sometimes partly altered into malachite. Both species crystallize in the Monoclinic System. Massive forms of malachite show beautiful and intricate bandings in various shades of green, the lighter colors representing less compact material and the darker, the more solid. Bandings are caused by successive deposits upon walls of cavities and may range in thickness from paperthin to masses as much as foot or more in depth. In North America, thick masses are seldom found, the usual depth being from ½ inch to 1 inch or slightly more. Azurite in massive form seldom shows the pronounced banding of its close relative, the several stages of deposition marked only by a gradual shading in the normally very dark and intense blue. Where grown together, both minerals may show bands parallel to the walls of the cavity, or, as in the early finds at Bisbee, Arizona, in concentric rings surrounding a small open hole in stalactites. The latter formations provided some of the most colorful material known from any locality in the world.

The hardness of both species is low, varying from 3½ to 4 with the higher value being approximately correct for the most compact of massive forms. Fracture surfaces are irregular to splintery, and, in the case of malachite, somewhat silky in luster due to the numerous fibers. Both are rather tough in spite of their low hardnesses. Specific gravities differ markedly, malachite ranging from 3.60 for massive kinds upwards to 4.07 for crystals; azurite ranges between 3.770 and 3.776 in crystals but there is no established value for massive material. Refractive indices for malachite are: $\alpha = 1.655$, $\beta = 1.875$, $\gamma = 1.909$; birefringence 0.054; biaxial negative. Azurite indices are: $\alpha = 1.730$, $\beta = 1.758$, $\gamma = 1.838$; birefringence 0.108; biaxial positive.

LOCALITIES

Arizona. Enormous quantities of malachite and azurite in all forms were produced from a series of copper deposits in the vicinity of Bisbee, Cochise County. The Copper Queen Mine was especially noted for large and thick masses of cuttable malachite, one observer stating that in a short period of time during mining in the upper levels, over 1½ tons of material was extracted. Representative of size is the specimen in the American Museum of Natural History, a polished slab measuring 12 inches by 12 inches. In

Greenlee County, the Detroit and Manganese Blue mines at Morenci also produced magnificent material, especially stalactites of alternating malachite and azurite, often several inches thick. These mines produced heavily about the turn of the century but after exhausting their surface deposits in 1904, turned downward to exploit the valuable but uninteresting sulfide ores of greater depth.

Utah. Some excellent malachite of gem grade was obtained in 1943 from the Dixie Apex Mine near St. George, Washington County.

SHATTUCKITE

Shattuckite is a rare copper mineral occurring in massive form in several copper deposits in the state of Arizona. So far as is known, this is the only area in North America where appreciable quantities have been found. Attractive deep blue in color, shattuckite closely resembles azurite, and, in good specimens, has been put to the same lapidary uses. The name is derived from its original locality, the Shattuck Mine at Bisbee, Cochise County, Arizona.

Shattuckite is a hydrous silicate of copper crystallizing in the Monoclinic System and in accordance with the formula: $2CuSiO_3 \cdot H_2O$. Distinct crystals are rare, the usual mode of occurrence being irregular masses of many small spherules, each of which is seen to consist of minute fibrous crystals radiating from a common center. This mode of growth is distinctive and serves to distinguish shattuckite from azurite with which it can be easily confused. The hardness is low, about 3.5 to 4.0, and consequently it is in the same class as azurite and malachite insofar as durability is concerned. The specific gravity for pure material is 3.8 but this value may vary considerably since so little material is actually pure. Refractive indices determined upon pure material are as follows: $\alpha = 1.752$, $\beta = 1.782$, $\gamma = 1.815$; birefringence 0.063; biaxial, positive. Thin slivers show distinct pleiochroism varying from light to dark blue.

The copper mines of the Ajo District of Pima County, Arizona, yield considerable quantities of cutting and specimen material from time to time. It is reported as most abundant in the New Cornelia open pit in this district where it is found associated with azurite, malachite, and chrysocolla. A polished mass of 4 by 6 inches from Ajo is in the American Museum of Natural History, as well as a cabochon of 1 by 1½ inches prepared from material coming from Jerome, Yavapai County.

WOLLASTONITE

This calcium silicate is sometimes found in fibrous masses sufficiently compact to receive a polish and has been cut from time to time as a curiosity. It was named many years ago after the English chemist and physicist, W. H. Wollaston. Mainly found in contact metamorphosed limestone bodies, wollastonite most commonly appears as coarse bladed masses rarely showing good crystal form. When pure, it is simple calcium silicate with the formula: $CaSiO_3$ and crystallizes in the Monoclinic System. The hardness varies from $4\frac{1}{2}$ to 5; specific gravity from 2.8 to 2.9. Refractive indices are: $\alpha = 1.616$, $\beta = 1.629$, $\gamma = 1.631$; birefringence 0.015; biaxial, negative. Massive forms vary in color from pure white to gray, also red, yellow, brown.

LOCALITIES

New York. A white cabochon measuring 1 inch by $1\frac{1}{4}$ inches is in the collection of the American Museum of Natural History and was cut from material originating from near Lake Bonaparte in the northern end of Lewis County.

Michigan. During the working of the Cliff Mine on the Keeweenaw Peninsula for copper, compact wollastonite suitable for cutting was occasionally found. The material was pale flesh-red in color, extremely fine-textured, and remarkably tough. It was stated to be easily and perfectly polished. Similar massive wollastonite has been reported from near Scoville Point on Isle Royale.

Morelos. White massive wollastonite accompanies the pink grossularite garnets found near Xalostoc and is cut and polished with them in slabs (see GARNET).

LAPIS LAZULI

Prized for thousands of years for its intense pure blue color, lapis lazuli is in reality not one but a combination of several distinct minerals. Properly, it should be called a *rock*—but certainly a most lovely and unusual one! Perhaps the most striking feature of lapis, aside from the intense color, is the presence of numerous grains of bright brass-yellow iron pyrite. This association is so unvarying that it serves as a valuable means of distinguishing lapis from other minerals of the same color. Close examination of typical specimens shows lapis to be far from uniform; gray to white patches betray the presence of calcite, black spots may be either mica or diopside, while variations in the blue color itself, show that even this is not uniform. Actually, several bright blue mineral species contribute their color, the principal being *lazurite*, a sodium aluminum silicate with sulfur, and *hauynite*, also a sodium aluminum silicate but with calcium in addition to sulfur. Both are closely related chemically and it is believed that scarcely any lapis is really all one or the other, but rather a mixture of both.

Lapis lazuli is a product of contact metamorphism, occurring in limestones near their contact with igneous rocks, or in schists in which some lime has been introduced. Except for the classic localities in Afghanistan and Turkestan, lapis is not common elsewhere. Some good material is found in quantity in Chile but most is pale blue rather than dark blue. In North America, only a few localities are important.

It is almost impossible to say anything exact about the properties of such an inexact mixture as lapis lazuli, however, specific gravity determinations have shown the usual range to lie between 2.75 and 2.90, but pieces in which the content of pyrite (sg = 4.94) and calcite (sg = 2.72) vary considerably may show extreme values of 2.45 to 2.94. The hardness is about 6, but again appears to vary according to the quantity of soft calcite and hard pyrite. In color, lapis lazuli ranges from a greenish blue to pure deep blue and thence to a blue of purplish cast.

LOCALITIES

North West Territories. Splotchy blue and gray material with specks of iron pyrite is reported from an unspecified locality on Baffinland.

Colorado. The most important locality in North America is that on the west slope of Italian Mountain, Gunnison County. Here at an altitude of 12,500 feet, three stringers of lapis lazuli, some up to 7 and 8 inches in thickness, occur in Paleozoic metamorphic limestone locally intruded by diorite. The color of this material is excellent but patches of pure hue are never very large, probably not over 1 inch across. Pyrite specks within the lapis itself are extremely minute, requiring the use of a loupe to see clearly, but near the edges of the lapis veins are coarser aggregations which trail through the enclosing grayish and white rock like irregular veils and streaks. The grain size of the lapis and its enclosing minerals is extremely fine. As a whole, the color is every bit as good as fine quality Afghanistan material.

California. An interesting but commercially unimportant deposit of lapis lazuli occurs on the north slope of the south fork of Cascade Canyon, about 12 miles from the city of Upland, San Bernardino County, and about 5 miles by trail from the mouth of San Antonio Canyon where the nearest approach by road is possible. At the locality, the lapis occurs in very thin sheets interbedded with diopside, quartz, mica, and other minerals in a highly metamorphosed schist. Since the flat seams are only a fraction of an inch thick, care must be exercised in cutting lest good colored material be inadvertently ground away. Boulders containing lapis have been found in the canyon for some distance below the mine. One mineralogist who has examined the material states that hauynite rather than lazurite is the principal blue mineral. A specimen in the author's collection from this locality shows dark to pale blue lapis with many very small specks of iron pyrite disseminated throughout the mass. The layers are very flat and parallel; good dark blue material occurs only in a thin streak which rapidly fades to disagreeable grayish or greenish colors on either side.

FIBROLITE
(*Sillimanite*)

In 1956 and 1957, considerable publicity was given to a massive form of fibrolite suitable for cabochon gems which had been found in pebbles in the gravels of the Clearwater River in Idaho. As its name implies, fibrolite occurs mainly in compact masses consisting of many minute fibrous crystals. The toughness of such material is attested to by the American Indians who frequently used fibrolite pebbles to fashion hammers and other pounding tools. Examinations of polished Idaho material show it to display a certain chatoyancy, however, it still seems more suited for the uses to which it was put by the Indians. To gemologists, fibrolite is best known as the pale powder-blue tabular crystal fragments which are found in the gem gravels of Ceylon and Burma and faceted from time to time into small gems. Although advertisements of Idaho material claimed it to be "gem" sillimanite, by custom this appellation has been hitherto accorded only to the transparent material just described. Sillimanite, incidentally, is the alternate name for fibrolite and honors the noted early American mineralogist, Benjamin Silliman.

Rounded pebbles of fibrolite have been found in the gravels of the Clearwater River from Lewiston, Idaho, to almost 100 miles upstream, an especially prolific stretch lying between Lewiston and Myrtle where gravel bars are searched during periods of low water.

ZOISITE AND CLINOZOISITE

Zoisite and clinozoisite are members of the Epidote Group, and, though related to epidote, bear important differences. Zoisite is useful in lapidary work only in the bright pink massive form known as *thulite*, a name given to this variety because of its occurrence in the Telemark District of Norway, anciently known as Thule. The basic name of the species, zoisite, honors Baron Zois. Clinozoisite is, by custom, the name awarded to zoisites which contain *some* iron, but less than 10%, and thus tend to grade into epidote.

The only material of gem interest is furnished by clear brown crystals which can be faceted into small gems.

Zoisite is a hydrous calcium aluminum silicate with the formula: Ca_2Al_3 $(SiO_4)_3(OH)$; when some of the aluminum is replaced by iron, the variety becomes clinozoisite and is marked by striking differences in all important physical and optical properties. Zoisite belongs to the Orthorhombic System and commonly occurs in prismatic crystals, often exceedingly thin and felted together in random fashion as in thulite. On the other hand, clinozoisite crystallizes in the Monoclinic System like epidote, and like that mineral, tends to develop thick prismatic crystals showing one perfect and one imperfect cleavage. The hardness of individual crystals is about 6 but in finely fibrous forms of zoisite, it seems very soft perhaps 5 or less. Specific gravity of zoisite is 3.25 to 3.37; thulite is much lower, about 3.12. Clinozoisite shows specific gravities which are closer to epidote, viz: 3.25 to 3.5. Refractive indices of zoisite are: $a = 1.700$, $\beta = 1.703$, $\gamma = 1.706$; birefringence 0.006; biaxial, positive. Clinozoisite gives: $a = 1.724$, $\beta = 1.729$, $\gamma = 1.734$; birefringence 0.010; biaxial, positive. The color of zoisite varies from gray, grayish-brown, yellowish, greenish, and pink, but only the latter is of interest in gemstones. Clinozoisite crystals are brown to olive-green in color. *Pink* zoisite varies in color from pale pink to rich pink and to brownish-red, often mottled within the same piece. Zoisite (thulite) is strongly pleiochroic showing: light rose, deep rose, and yellow; clinozoisite shows: dark brown, pale warm brown, and rich brownish-green.

Although thulite is utilized in its massive form for ornamentation, few persons realize that it is the milky to colorless quartz accompanying the exceedingly minute needles of thulite which lends them the necessary strength and hardness to receive a polish. Without quartz, attempts at polishing would merely result in crumbling away of the thulite. The finest material from the standpoint of lapidary work, is that in which the quartz is evenly dispersed and partly filled by needles of thulite.

LOCALITIES

Greenland. In East Greenland, very beautiful rose thulite resembling that of the famous locality in Norway, is found in lenses in quartz veins which penetrate gneiss on the vertical walls of Franz Joseph's Fjord. The locality is on the north side of the fjord near its head, about 200 meters from the margin of Nordenskiold's Glacier.

North Carolina. Thulite occurs at the Putnam Mine, 5 miles northwest of Spruce Pine, also in the Deer Flat Mine and Pine Mountain Mine nearby, all in Mitchell County. Masses almost an inch thick occur in oligoclase feldspar but are coarse-grained and not well suited for cutting. In this same county, the Hawk Mica Mine, 1 mile north of Hawk Post Office occasionally furnishes oligoclase, colored pink by inclusions of very minute needles of thulite. In Yancey County, thulite occurs in fine-grained masses of small size at the Spider Mine on the Blue Rock Road. All of the above material has been used for cabochons.

Washington. Thulite in quartz veins is found in hornblende schists along the sides of a small creek which enters Tunk Creek from its north side in Tunk Creek Canyon, Okanogan County. Tunk Creek enters the Okanogan River about 7 miles northeast of Riverside or about 15 miles northeast of Omak by road. A few boulders containing thulite have also been found in the bed of the creek.

Nevada. Thulite is found in three places in this state, each occurrence being adjacent to the contacts of metamorphosed limestones or dolomites with granite. The first locality is the southern part of the Pine Nut Mountains at Lat. 38°-46′N. and 118°-18′W. in Douglas County. The next is in the Singatse Range, about ¾ mile east of the ghost town of Ludwig in the Yerington Mining District, Lyon County. The last locality is in Ryan Canyon, about 5 miles southeast of Thorne, Mineral County.

New Mexico. Rose-red to geranium-pink thulite is found in quartz in a pegmatite dike traversing schist just south of Pilar Post Office (formerly known as Cieneguilla) on the east bank of the Rio Grande River and high above the Taos-Santa Fe Highway. Some of this material has been very successfully used for gems and in ornamental objects. In places, the quartz and thulite occur as patches of about ½ inch in diameter, evenly distributed throughout the rock.

Baja California Norte. Fine clear crystals of brown clinozoisite occur in a quartz vein near the scheelite mines at Gavilanes, south of Tecate and northeast of Ensenada. Crystals range in size from narrow prisms of less than ⅛ inch to some which are several inches thick and perhaps 4 to 5 inches in length. The quartz in which these crystals grow varies from milky to clear, the best material being found in the latter or in pockets within the vein. The clinozoisite is very brittle and weak due to frequent development of cleavages but clear pieces of facet grade have been found from which gems of several carats may be cut. Colors vary from pale brownish-yellow to very deep rich brown but the latter is the predominant hue. Crystals resemble epidote in respect to form but are inclined to be less perfectly developed.

SERPENTINE

Serpentine is an abundant and widespread rock-forming mineral which underlies many square miles of the North American continent. Despite its abundance, solid crack-free types of considerable translucency useful for ornamental purposes, are relatively rare. There are numerous varieties of serpentine but only several are of interest here. *Retinalite*, named after its resinous luster, is a waxy translucent serpentine found in bright yellow or green-yellow colors, and, along with *bowenite* and *williamsite*, furnishes the material known collectively as *noble* or *precious* serpentine. Bowenite receives its name after G. T. Bowen who first described this variety, while williamsite is named after L. W. Williams from whom the first specimens were received for identification. The species name is of less certain derivation, some believing it so named from a fancied resemblance to mottlings and markings seen on the backs of snakes. Very impure or barely translucent varieties capable of taking a polish are used extensively in building decoration, one of the most popular being *verde antique,* or literally, "ancient green," in allusion to its color and extensive use over the centuries. A fine-grained serpentine occurring in curious colored bands is known as *ricolite* after its occurrence near the community of Rico in New Mexico.

Aside from extensive use of impure serpentine in statuary and buildings, this mineral in its translucent forms has seen much employment in carving, in jewelry, and in numerous small objects of ornamentation. Bowenite, the compact granular variety of high translucency, strongly resembles certain types of jadeite and in China, has been used extensively for carvings sold as "Soochow jade" or "new jade." The lovely green williamsite provides very handsome cabochon gems and has seen some use in jewelry, particularly in the form of beads. Since serpentine is not a hard mineral, its use is confined to those objects of ornamentation which will not be subject to hard wear.

As a mineral, serpentine remains somewhat a mystery in spite of its having been known to man for thousands of years. It never forms distinct crystals for example, unless individual fibers are taken to be distinct crystals. Many kinds are so finely-granular or minutely fibrous that the strongest optical microscopes give no information on structure. X-ray studies and recent investigations using electron microscopes, however, show that serpentine is Monoclinic but several differing crystal structures occur. Both plate-like and tube-like structures have been identified. In respect to origin, serpentine is regarded as an alteration product of magnesium silicate minerals and by taking up water during the process of formation, becomes itself a hydrous magnesium silicate bearing the formula: $Mg_3Si_2O_5(OH)_4$. It is often present wherever dark colored magnesium silicate rocks occur and is also found in magnesian or dolomitic limestones which have been metamorphosed by the intrusion of volcanic rocks. The hardness varies from $2\frac{1}{2}$ to 5, with the last value typical of varieties useful for gems. Specific gravity varies considerably also, ranging from 2.2 to 2.6. Refractive indices taken from gem specimens are only average values because of the felted structure; they range from as low as 1.490 to as high as 1.571. The refraction is biaxial, negative.

The luster of serpentine varies from dull to greasy depending upon whether the structure is granular or fibrous. Exceptionally compact types such as retinalite, display conchoidal fractures with a glistening waxy or greasy appearance. Coarse-grained kinds, such as williamsite and bowenite, appear rough and break with dull, irregular surfaces. Toughness varies with structure also, fine-grained types tending to be somewhat brittle and heat sensitive while coarser types are exceedingly tough like jade and consequently almost impervious to shock. Serpentine occurs in a bewildering variety of colors, ranging from pure white to black although the latter is usually seen to be very dark green in thin splinters. The predominant color is green, from yellow to olive in cast to bright green suggestive of the hue of emerald (williamsite). Yellow, orange, red, brown, and combinations are also common.

LOCALITIES

Greenland. Yellowish-green noble serpentine occurs in several places on the west coast, notably in Godthaab Fjord, upon the island of Bjorne near its southern end. It is also reported from near Tindingen, 32 miles southwest of Ivigtut in the Frederikshaab District, where it occurs associated with talc and actinolite in veins penetrating granite. Early mineralogical reports indicate the presence of a number of nephrite jade deposits in Greenland, however, these may consist of serpentine since this mineral has often been mistaken for jade (see JADE).

Alaska. Good serpentine associated with talc and chromite, occurs at Red Bluff Bay, Baranof Island, Southeastern Alaska.

Quebec. Good noble serpentine occurs in Megantic County associated with chromite in the pits of the Megantic Mine near Black Lake, Coleraine Township. The very rare and beautiful pale purple chrome mineral, stichtite, is sometimes found as thin seams in the serpentine. Williamsite occurs at the Montreal Chrome Pit, 1 mile southeast of the south end of Little St. Francis Lake in Coleraine Township. In Argenteuil County, yellow to dark yellow-green material occurs in the underground workings of the Canadian Refractories, Ltd., mines at Kilmar. Noble serpentine, pale brownish-yellow, yellow, yellowish-green, and rarely, bright blood-red, occurs in seams associated with magnesium minerals and metamorphic limestone at the Canadian Aluminium Company quarry, 2 miles southeast of Wakefield, Gatineau County, almost on the border of Gatineau County.

Maine. Fine quality green serpentine embedded in common serpentine occurs on Little Deer Isle, Hancock County.

Vermont. Enormous quantities of verde antique have been quarried from a number of places in the central part of the state, notably from Windham, Rochester, and Warren valleys. Noble material occurs at times in seams in the darker commercial stone.

Massachusetts. Fine quality green and yellow material has been obtained for many years as small patches in metamorphic limestone in several quarries about 2 miles south of Newburyport in Newbury Township, Essex County. Locally, the long-abandoned pits are known as "Devil's Den" and "Devil's Basin." The majority of the serpentine here is of the verde antique type but noble material is also present.

Rhode Island. Translucent and tough, the jade-like variety bowenite comes from a classic locality in the northern part of this state. Some question exists as to the exact locality of the first discovery since it appears that the "Smithfield" (township) occurrence mentioned in old mineralogical text-books, is probably the same as the Dexter Lime Quarry which is now in Lincoln Township. In the same general vicinity where metamorphic lime-stones are quarried for making lime, other quarries also produce bowenite, notably the Harris and Conklin quarries which span opposite sides of Highway 146 near Limerock, about 5 miles north of North Providence. In these pits bowenite occurs as pale yellow, yellowish-green and pale pure green masses in dolomitic limestone.

New York. In St. Lawrence County, locally-produced mottled serpentine was employed many years ago for the production of small objects of ornamentation. Outcrops of translucent to opaque material occur along the Oswegatchie River in the town of Gouverneur and at other places in the vicinity. Colors are generally green, pale green, blue-green, and a peculiar dull gray opaque kind called "London smoke." A favorite ornament carved by local residents many years ago, resembled an ordinary egg, nicely shaped and polished from material in a variety of colors. In Lewis County, suitable material has been found in a talc-serpentine quarry about 3 miles northeast of Natural Bridge. To the south, in a belt extending from Rockland County to Dutchess County, occasional occurrences of noble serpentine are noted in road cuts, quarries and other excavations, forming seams in gneissic rocks. Beautiful red, green, and white serpentine has been quarried from a deposit located near Portchester, on Long Island Sound in Westchester County and is said to take a beautiful polish. Many years ago dark green serpentine was quarried on Staten Island in the Borough of Richmond, New York City.

New Jersey. A famed locality for precious serpentine is found several miles north of Montville in Morris County. Here on the summit of a low spur of Turkey Mountain overlooking the west shore of Lake Valhalla, lies an abandoned quarry for magnesian metamorphic limestone used many years ago for burning into agricultural lime. The locality is reached by a dim oxcart trail ascending from the lakeside road at a place near the northwest corner of the lake where a small creek enters. This trail rises and curves toward the south and covers a distance of about ¾ mile. In the much overgrown pits are found boulders of diopside, marble, large sections of dark green serpentine and other minerals. The best serpentine, a highly translucent yellow material, forms sheaths surrounding large nodules and masses of grayish to white granular diopside. Further from the diopside cores the serpentine becomes darker in color and less translucent until a far less attractive grayish-green material is found. The best grades, unfortunately, are relatively brittle and seldom show crack-free areas larger than an inch across. At another locality in northern New Jersey, a peculiar brownish manganiferous serpentine occurs in association with zinc minerals in the workings of the New Jersey Zinc Company at Mine Hill, Franklin, Sussex County, and was once polished in slabs and sold under the false name of "smithsonite." Refractive indices of this material are stated to be: $\alpha = 1.561$, $\beta = 1.567$, $\gamma = 1.568$.

Pennsylvania. Upon Chestnut Hill, north of Easton in Forks Township, Northhampton County, are a number of large pits from which much serpentine has been quarried. The principal working is known as the Verdolite Quarry and is located on River Road 1 mile north of Easton. Other quarries are in the immediate vicinity and also about 2 miles to the southwest just east of Bushkill Creek. The rocks found in this area are an interesting and complicated mixture of gneisses, metamorphosed limestones, and pegmatites. Occurring mainly in the limestone, precious serpentine forms pale yellowish and greenish irregular masses. Gemmy pieces are not common, and occur only as small nodules, lenses or seams. In appearance Easton serpentine is similar in quality to Montville, New Jersey material. Proceeding southward from Easton, some fine green serpentine was once obtained from Brinton's Quarry, 3 miles south of West Chester, Westtown Township, Chester County. Massive serpentine was once produced in which narrow seams and veins of noble materials, approaching williamsite in quality and color, was found along with a variety of other interesting minerals. At one time slabs showing these associations were cut and polished and disposed of as mineral specimens. Bronzite with pronounced metallic luster occurs also in the form of small grains. In this same county, at Corundum Hill, 2 miles northeast of Unionville in Newlin Township, noble serpentine is found in minor quantities.

Maryland. The finest serpentine in all the world has come from the chromite mines near Rock Springs, Maryland. This is the classical locality for the williamsite variety which here reaches perfection. Although a considerable number of mines and prospects occur in the general area, only the Line Pits, located precisely upon the state boundary between Lancaster County,

Pennsylvania, and Cecil County, Maryland, have furnished the best grades in important quantities. Known and worked over a hundred years ago as a source of chromium ores, these mines were last worked in 1918 and again in 1920, but in each case, only briefly. Today nothing remains except water-filled open shafts amid scrub oaks and underbrush typical of the "serpentine barrens." The workings and dumps are reached by dirt road from Rock Springs crossroads and bear ¾ mile northwest from the crossroads. The cylindrical chromite ore body, averaging about 6 feet in diameter, plunged at an angle of 60 degrees, and, when last mined, attained a depth of several hundred feet. The ore body was emplaced in a dirty greenish-brown common serpentine country rock but separated therefrom by a sheath of purer material plus an assemblage of interesting minerals such as purple kammererite, transparent to white brucite, magnesite, etc. Wherever the serpentine contacted the chromite, it became much clearer and took on the "emerald green" color which is so distinctive in this variety. The best material is invariably associated with chromite and when completely enclosed by this mineral, is entirely free of the brownish tinge which causes ordinary serpentine to be dingy and dull. Chromium, probably substituting for part of the magnesium in the serpentine, is believed responsible for the unique color. Although fine large masses a number of pounds in weight have been obtained from this locality, most specimens are seldom free of cracks and fissures filled with white magnesite, and for this reason, clear gemmy pieces seldom exceed several inches in diameter. In addition to the williamsite (an unusually compact and fine-grained material it may be added) another easily-split kind showing a platy to fibrous structure is also found. Some of this is remarkably translucent, in fact, almost transparent and, if cut with care yields beautiful cat's eye gems with a weak but distinct "eye." Still another kind useful for cutting is noted here: a grayish-green opaque material of silky texture occurring as narrow seams in the coarse country rock. The latter is similar to California *satelite*, a variety which will be described later.

Arizona. The noted commercial deposits of serpentine asbestos (chrysotile) in this state are located in the cliffs of the Salt River in Gila County, about 10 miles southeast of Young Post Office, and about 3 to 4 miles west of the Apache Indian Reservation. Translucent to opaque serpentine in fair cutting grade is found here in some abundance but though extremely compact, its colors are dull shades of olive-green and yellowish-green. The deposits are embedded in grayish-blue limestone which has been locally metamorphosed by intrusions of volcanic rocks. The serpentine area is about 10 to 12 miles in length and stretches from the foot of Sierra Ancha to Canyon Creek.

New Mexico. One of the best known American serpentine varieties is the sharply-banded greenish material called *ricolite*. It occurs in great quantity in Ricolite Gulch, a small declivity tributary to the Gila River and located about 6 miles northeast of Red Rock, Grant County, on the west bank of the river. The material from the main deposit is obtainable in large blocks and at one time was quarried as building stone for interior decoration. As at the Salt River deposits in Arizona, the formation of serpentine is due to the intrusion of volcanic rocks into magnesian limestones. The characteristics of ricolite are distinctive: it is opaque to barely translucent, usually some shade of grayish-green, and strikingly banded in a variety of colors from dark to light green, yellow, white, etc. Although remarkably uniform in texture, it is somewhat porous and does not polish readily nor to a high finish. It is so soft and so free of hard impurities that it can be easily worked with steel tools.

California. A fibrous grayish to greenish-blue variety of serpentine, possessing a unique if not outstanding beauty, is found in narrow seams enclosed in common serpentine and steatite in Tulare County. At one time it was utilized commercially as a gemstone and was given the name *satelite*. In spite of its fibrous nature, it polishes to a high luster and produces a fairly strong chatoyant band when cut in cabochon form. The exact location is upon the south end of Venice Hill, 8 miles east of Visalia and near the famous chrysoprase deposits. In the north of the state, williamsite has been reported from near Indian Creek, north of Happy Camp, Siskiyou County. This locality is close to the californite (IDOCRASE) locality.

Cuba. Very pretty translucent noble serpentine has been reported from a strip mine 15 kilometers east of Matanzas in the province of the same name.

COPPER RHYOLITE

A handsome ornamental material useful in many lapidary projects and locally (and inaccurately) called *cuprite*, occurs in places in the altered rhyolites of South Mountain, Adams County, Pennsylvania. These rocks are found over considerable areas in Hamiltonban and Washington townships and have been mined from time to time for the sake of their copper content. Abandoned opencuts provide most of the cutting material which is broken out of the exceedingly tough rock by means of sledge hammers.

Technically, the rocks are basalts, rhyolites, and rhyolite-porphyries which have undergone extensive alteration due to infiltration by silica- and copper-bearing solutions. Original rock textures have been all but obliterated by this metamorphic action. Essentially, the rocks consist of quartz with appreciable amounts of green epidote and very small quantities of metallic copper, cuprite, azurite, and malachite. The necessary beauty is provided by the pleasing combination of bright green epidote with patches or spots of vivid red and orange cuprite. The latter seldom occurs in solid form but acts mostly as a staining agent in quartz, forming haloes or patches surrounding wires or nodules of native copper. Much of the rock is orbicular, consisting of small oval or tear-drop amygdules of clear quartz, epidote, and cuprite with copper cores. The orbicular pattern adds considerable interest to specimens even when colors are not as vivid as desired.

As a cutting material, the rhyolites of South Mountain are suitable for both large and small objects of ornamentation, however, the mixture of minerals requires considerable care in polishing in order to achieve a satisfactory finish. In general, the same techniques applicable to the treatment of jade are successful with this material. Only a small amount of the rhyolite is produced each year by amateur cutters and consequently its employement in the lapidary arts is mainly local although it deserves wider recognition. A series of cabochons of this material is illustrated in Fig. 165.

FIGURE 165. Cabochons of copper-bearing rhyolite from Adams County, Pennsylvania. The primary colors are pale green and orange from included epidote and cuprite. Small circular spots are quartz stained with malachite or cuprite. The largest gem is almost 2 inches long.

Copper-bearing rhyolites occur along densely-wooded slopes in rugged terrain west and northwest of Maria Furnace in Adams County. One of the best places is the Bingham Mine, located low on the east slope of Pine Mountain, 2½ miles west-southwest of Maria Furnace, and about 1 mile north-northeast of Gladhill. Several pits are located directly south of the junction of Copper Run with Toms Creek and distant .6 mile, atop a steep ridge. Another mine is located near the fork of Copper Run about 1.1 miles north of its junction with Toms Creek. One-half mile north of this locality is still another prospect atop a steep mountain. Two prospects are located about .6 mile north-northeast of Mount Hope on the east slope of a small conical hill. Several prospects are on the east slope of Jacks Mountain near its base. The Virgin Copper Mine is ¾ mile northeast of Beartown Church in Washington Township. The Eagle Metallic Mine is at the head of Miney Run about ½ mile east of Charmian. A beautiful breccia consisting of angular fragments of dark red siliceous material in paler rock is obtainable from a rhyolite body near its contact with basalt at a point 2 miles east of the South Mountain Sanatorium. Aside from the Virgin Copper Mine, all localities mentioned are in Hamiltonban Township.

RED CORUNDUM IN AMPHIBOLITE

During corundum mining at Buck Creek in Clay County, North Carolina many years ago, the attention of gem collectors was drawn to a bright emerald-green schistose amphibolite rock enlivened by a sprinkling of ruby-red corundum nodules. The beauty of the material naturally aroused speculation as to possible uses in the lapidary arts, however it was found that the wide variation in hardness between the amphibole and the corundum made polishing a difficult feat. Years ago the green amphibolite from this locality was called *smaragdite* from the German word "smaragd" meaning emerald, in allusion to its emerald-green color. It is interesting to note that the coloration of the amphibole and that of the ruby-red corundum included within are both due to the presence of chromium; in one it imparts a bright green color, in the other a deep vivid red. The amphibolite is laminated in structure, bright green in color, and glistens from countless minute cleavage and parting plane reflections, while red corundum is sprinkled evenly throughout in rounded masses from pea to hazel nut size. In places red corundum is replaced by blue with a corresponding paling of color of the enclosing amphibole. Neither the red nor the blue corundum show any degree of transparency and hence in themselves are unsuited for gems.

The principal locality for this material in the Buck Creek area is in the Maney Cut; similar material has also been reported from Shooting Creek near Elf in the same county.

PYRITE

Brassy yellow common pyrite or fool's gold as it has been known to those who mistook it for the far more valuable mineral, is extremely widespread and abundant. It occurs in masses and splendid shining crystals in thousands of localities and in almost all kinds of rocks. Perhaps it is its very abundance which prevents its more extensive use in jewelry for it cuts well, is easy to find in suitable pieces, and possesses a beautiful luster when polished. Much of the so-called jewelry "marcasite" was once prepared from pyrite but even this cheap material has now been superseded by stainless steel and the glistening gems of small size that one sees nowadays in "marcasite" jewelry are in reality nothing more than that metal. Pyrite receives its name from the Greek word meaning "of fire" in allusion to its ability to emit sparks when struck against hard steel.

Pyrite is a simple Isometric sulfide of iron, FeS_2, commonly found in ore bodies and also in a variety of other occurrences such as in coal veins and sedimentary deposits. It is fairly hard, 6-6½, breaking with a lustrous conchoidal fracture, however it is exceedingly brittle. The color is generally pale brass-yellow of perfect metallic luster but many crystals are found tarnished or stained. The most common crystal forms are the cube and the pyritohedron, the former often striated with minute parallel grooves, and the latter recognizable for its unique five-sided faces.

Jewelry containing pyrite is now rarely seen but around 1900, and earlier, a considerable amount of pyrite in the form of thin sheets covered with minute sparkling crystals was employed for sets in inexpensive brooches. The material used was obtained in the coal mines of Pennsylvania where pyrite was found encrusting narrow crevices in slate and anthracite, forming compact groupings of small crystals of great regularity and brilliance. Slabs of crystals no more than ¼ inch thick, needed only flatting on the back and trimming to proper outline to fit into brooch, stickpin, button, and cufflink mountings. The best material came from the Raven Run Mine and others in the vicinity of Mahonoy City and Pottsville in Schuylkill County but fine quality specimens also were found in the mines around Hazleton and West Pittston in Luzerne Co.

CALCITE

In nature, calcite occurs in enormous quantities as the principal constituent of limestones and marbles. Entire mountain ranges consist of impure calcite while thousands of cubic miles underlie many parts of North America, especially beneath the more level portions of the United States. Compact evenly-textured types of suitable coloration are used extensively for buildings and in ornaments; a special type of limestone deposited from cold water solutions and popularly known as *onyx*, or *onyx marble*, is used for table tops, counters, bookends, penstands, and many other decorative purposes. Calcite frequently occurs in beautiful clear crystals, often of large size, but of little value for gems because of softness and easy cleavability. The name calcite is derived from the Greek word *calx*, meaning burnt lime, while the term "onyx" is appropriated from true onyx which is a type of chalcedony showing strongly contrasting straight color bands and much used for cutting cameos and intaglios. Some confusion also exists in respect to *alabaster*, a term sometimes improperly applied to calcite onyx because of its resemblance to true alabaster which is in reality a fine-grained translucent gypsum. A fibrous variety of calcite, *satin spar*, is also confused with gypsum satin spar but in this case, there seems to be no priority of use to establish the right of either species to be called this name alone. Perhaps it would be better to be slightly more technical and call fibrous varieties of both, *chatoyant calcite* or *chatoyant gypsum*, as the case may be.

Chemically, calcite is calcium carbonate with the formula $CaCO_3$. In crystallized form it is mostly found pure but in some instances the substitution of certain elements for calcium provides a series whose end-members lead to entirely different minerals. For example, if manganese is gradually substituted for calcium, a mineral more and more closely resembling rhodochrosite ($MnCO_3$) results until it becomes difficult to tell which is which without a careful chemical analysis. Crystals of calcite occur in bewildering variety and complexity and vary from scarcely visible individuals to those several feet across. As a rule, crystals characteristically form sharp-pointed or "dog tooth" individuals whose tapering sides show faces and angles derived from the threefold symmetry of the Hexagonal System to which this mineral belongs (see Figure 166). Calcite possesses three evenly-spaced

FIGURE 166. Facet grade calcite of rich brown color from near Rosarito Beach, Baja California Norte. The cut gems weigh from left to right, 23.45 carats and 40.76 carats. The crystal on the right is about 3 inches tall. Normally these crystals are coated with a white mineral which disguises the color and the specimens shown here have been cleaned with dilute acid.

cleavages which are so easily developed that it is next to impossible to break a specimen in a direction other than along a cleavage plane. If a crystal is carefully split along these planes, a rhombohedron, all of whose six sides are cleavage planes, will result (see Figure 4). For this reason, the cleavage of calcite and other carbonates in the same class, is said to be rhombohedral. With a hardness of only 3, along with easy cleavage, calcite proves to be an unusually fragile mineral and the only saving grace which makes it at all suitable for structural or ornamental purposes is its tendency to form fine-grained masses of acceptable toughness. Massive calcite varies from very coarse types noted in metamorphic limestones in which individual crystal grains are several inches across, to very fine kinds as in some statuary marbles. As the grain size decreases, greater toughness is imparted but if the grains become coarse, the material is easily shattered. The luster of crystals is generally glassy but may be pearly upon cleavage surfaces; in massive material the luster is sugary to somewhat greasy depending on the size of individual crystal grains. Fibrous chatoyant types frequently show strong and beautiful silky luster. Because onyx types form by the aggregation of numerous elongated crystal prisms, the luster may be decidedly pearly or silky, depending on which way the specimen is viewed. More will be said later about their structure and formation.

The specific gravity of pure calcite seldom varies from the standard value of 2.710 but considerable variation is noted in onyxes because of their porous structure and the frequent presence of impurities, i.e., from 2.67 to 2.87. Refractive indices of crystalline material vary according to purity, ordinary calcite giving $\omega = 1.658$, $\epsilon = 1.486$, birefringence 0.172, while the addition of manganese or other replacement elements causes both indices to rise and increases birefringence. The optical character is uniaxial negative. The enormous double refraction of calcite has led to its wide use in optical instruments, gemologists employing a small prism in dichroscopes to separate dichroic colors, while mineralogists use several special prisms called *nicols* in petrographic microscopes to determine optical properties of unknown minerals. The double refraction of calcite is strikingly shown in Figure 4.

Pure calcite is completely colorless but crystals and massive types often exhibit color according to the presence of impurities. In crystals, yellow and brown are common hues while in onyx, basic colors are most frequently some off-shade of white frequently varying in intensity or in hue from layer to layer. Fissures or cracks in onyx also introduce various metallic salts which stain adjacent material by infiltration and produce very beautiful and interesting patterns.

A few words about the exact nature of onyx marbles may be appropriate at this point to give the reader a clear picture of their origin and nature. Two forms of water-deposited calcite are known, the first being laid down by hot springs and called *travertine,* and the second being deposited by cold springs and called *onyx.* The separate modes of formation cause striking differences in properties: travertine is soft and very porous due to numerous cavities, some of which are large enough to insert a finger, and naturally it takes a poor polish; it is also much less dense; in onyx on the other hand, the very slow rate of deposition causes a translucent form of calcite to deposit, consisting of millions of minute fibrous crystals growing at right angles to the layers. Onyx is very much more dense, furthermore, and on this account takes a superb polish which rivals that seen on well-prepared specimens of agate. Good examples of travertine may be seen in Yellowstone National Park at the Mammoth Hot Springs where new outbursts of hot mineralized water actively deposit travertine before the very eyes of spectators. The easy solution of calcite in water is accounted for by the carbon dioxide which is absorbed from the atmosphere and when present in water acts like an acid. Underground water thus dissolves calcite in one place and deposits it elsewhere, sometimes far removed from the original point of solution. Many caverns in limestone regions have been formed this way as well as unusually compact types of limestone which were originally porous and not fit for polishing until their structures had been consolidated by addition of calcite brought in by solutions. Much material of this sort is quarried for interior decoration and often contains a host of fossil shells and other marine organisms whose minutest detail has been faithfully preserved. A coral limestone found in Michigan and locally called "Petoskey Agate," is popular among amateur cutters because of the interesting effects provided by the coralline structure. An example is illustrated in Figure 167.

LOCALITIES

British Columbia. A large deposit of onyx is reported adjacent to mineral springs near Hudson Hope in the Peace River Mining Division.

Alberta. Pale brown onyx occurs ¼ mile west of Brule Lake, Jasper Park.

Ontario. Calcified corals similar to the "Petoskey Agates" of Michigan have been found in the limestones of Kettle Point on the shore of Lake Huron, 35 miles east of Sarnia.

New York. Lower Devonian limestone once quarried for building purposes and containing a multitude of fossil organisms, outcrops 2½ miles east of Buffalo in Erie County at the old Fogelsanger Quarry and provides polishing material similar to the "Petoskey Agates" of Michigan. Corals are the principal organism petrified, especially the *Favosites* or "honeycomb corals."

West Virginia. Greenish-white translucent onyx, said to be similar to Mexican, was once quarried from a deposit near Willowton, Mercer County.

Caverns of the United States. It would serve little purpose to list all of the caves or cavern regions of the United States in which brownish banded cave onyxes are found since there are so many, however, most caverns of note are found in the East, especially in limestones underlying much of Virginia, West Virginia, Tennessee, Kentucky, etc. Caverns form as a result of carbon dioxide charged water entering cracks and dissolving the limestone. Most of the calcite in solution is carried away but some is redeposited upon walls, floors, and from ceilings in the form of stalactites and stalagmites. Although the preponderant hue is brown, fairly colorful pale brown and yellow shades occur in some places. Being formed slowly, cave onyx is identical in all major respects to onyx externally deposited by cold springs, however, brown is not a popular color and for this reason the vast quantities of cave onyx readily available in numerous places in the cavern regions have had little utilization. A small quantity is cut and polished into a variety of souvenirs for the tourist trade, the raw material being locally quarried from "sinks" or steep-walled pits or gorges where the roofs of caverns have fallen in. Although stalactites and stalagmites form interesting circular patterns when cut through, the best cave onyx is generally found in floor deposits which may reach depths of several feet. The recent staining techniques adopted in the onyx industry of Mexico (Puebla), may, if intelligently applied to domestic cave onyxes, overcome some of the objection to lack of suitable colors.

Kentucky. The petrified skeleton of a small, long-extinct crustacean, the *trilobite*, was once worn for ornamental purposes in the region about Covington and Cincinnati. It seems that in some of the local limestones, the remains of this animal had been faithfully preserved in calcite and when found loose in the ground or extracted from cavities in the rock, aroused the interest of some of the residents, one of whom hit upon the idea of mounting them in stickpins or scarfpins. Trilobite fossils found here are the species *Calymene senaria* and are found curled up in neat spirals showing deep and regular grooves where their armor plates overlap. Varying from ¼ inch to 2 inches in diameter, they once sold for from $.25 to $5 each, depending on size and perfection. The exteriors were often covered with minute clear calcite crystals which added further interest to an already absorbing curiosity.

Michigan. The complete replacement of coral structure by calcite is typical of certain limestones in this state where nodules corresponding to individual colonies of coral organisms have been picked up as waterworn pebbles scattered over wide areas and also obtained in place in a number of quarries in the Traverse limestones of this state. Locally they are called "Petoskey Agates" after their abundance near the town of Petoskey in Emmet County where many were cut and polished as souvenirs years ago. Some are still processed in communities near tourist resorts but the volume of business is probably much less than it used to be. The use of the term "agate" in the popular name is unfortunate for there is not the slightest resemblance chemically or physically between these corals and chalcedony, however, corals are sometimes petrified by silica and this may have led to the adoption of the misleading term. A better title would be Petoskey Stones, one that is at least as popular and certainly less controversial.

The species of coral commonly seen in the Traverse formation limestones is *Hexagonaria*, variety *Prismatophyilum percarnatum*, with a general pattern like a series of tiles of hexagonal outline fitted closely together. In the center of each are many thin webs which radiate outward to meet the exterior wall. The size of individual segments varies from about ¼ to ¾ inch in diameter (see Figure 167). Many individual segments are found joined together in "colonies" forming rounded masses of from several inches to as much as 8 inches or 10 inches across and weighing up to 50 pounds. In addition to the *Hexagonaria*, another species, *Favosites*, is also found and also forms colonial masses showing a "honeycomb" pattern when polished. These are especially abundant in the Alpena area. Solitary coral organisms such as the "cup" and "horn" corals also make interesting cutting and polishing material and are found in many Traverse formation outcrops especially at the old Rockport Quarry (see below). Other calcified fossils which sometimes make good lapidary material are massive *bryozoans* and *stromatoporoids* (extinct coral-like organisms).

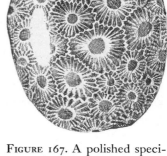

FIGURE 167. A polished specimen of coral replaced by calcite, the so-called Petoskey stone; Michigan.

Localities for petoskey stones and other calcified fossils are numerous within the tier of northern counties including Antrim, Alpena, Charlevoix, Cheboygan, Emmet, and Presque Isle. Especially prolific sources are from Charlevoix to Harbor Springs and Petoskey and elsewhere along the south shore of Little Traverse Bay in Emmet County, at Stony Point and near Charlevoix in Charlevoix County, along the shores of Burt Lake and near Columbus Beach at Indian River in Cheboygan County, and along the shores of Torch Lake about halfway between Traverse City and Petoskey in the western end of Antrim County. Unweathered specimens can be collected from the old limestone quarries along the shore bluff of Little Traverse Bay from Petoskey west to Charlevoix; also in quarries in Alpena County and in the Afton-Onaway area in Cheboygan and Presque Isle counties. One of the best places is in the dumps of the old Rockport Quarry, located about 11 miles northeast of Alpena, just south of the Presque Isle County line along Lake Huron. Michigan corals have been widely distributed as alluvium, and specimens have been picked up as far away as the Maumee River in Allen County, Indiana.

Iowa. Corals very similar to those of Michigan but of smaller pattern (*favosites*) are found in gravels and in low bluffs along streams in Linn County. Splendid specimens occur in the vicinity of Coralville and Iowa City in Johnson County, and, like those found in Michigan, have also been cut into ornamental items.

Montana. A vein of onyx, attractively patterned and banded, and taking a fine polish, has been quarried commercially by a St. Paul firm 5 miles northwest of Manhattan in Gallatin County. The deposit is said to be 65 feet wide; material from this place has been sold as "Montana onyx."

Wyoming. In 1939 an onyx deposit was opened near Jay Em in Goshen County; the reported use was for mantels. Attractive material taking a good polish occurs north of Guernsey in Platte County.

Utah. Dark and light amber onyx has been quarried to some extent from a locality near Pelican Point, Utah County. Near Lehi in the same county, occurs a beautiful highly translucent type noted for its lemon-yellow, orange, dark buff, chrome-yellow, and pure white colors, whose translucency and coloration are so unusual for onyx that some persons have been led to believe it to be artificial. The specific gravity of pure material is 2.72. The deposit is a vein about 4 feet in thickness in limestone. In Tooele County, some onyx has been quarried near Grantsville, a large quantity being used for terrazzo work, chicken grit, stucco, etc., but some exceptional blocks were sold for ornamental purposes. Considerable quantities also occur in this county about 4 miles due south of Low in the Cedar Mountains where it was once quarried from veins reaching lengths of as much as 4500 feet. Colors range from white through cream, also pink, lavender, and yellow shaded with brown; all tend to be light in tone.

In southwestern Utah, attractive translucent green onyx occurs at Hatch in the southwestern part of Garfield County; another large deposit occurs 1½ miles south of Hatch upon Mammoth Creek. The latter place is said to furnish large flawless blocks.

New Mexico. Faintly greenish onyx is said to be found in caves in the Organ District of Dona Ana County. Brown banded cave onyx is abundant in the Carlsbad Caverns of Eddy County and in caverns of lesser size in the surrounding area underlain by similar limestones. Delicately banded onyx comes from the Central District of Grant County also in the White Oaks District of Lincoln County. Cave onyx occurs in caverns of the Placitas District in Sandoval County, also near Las Vegas in San Miguel County. Beautiful onyx of commercial grade occurs about 4 miles west of Columbus in the foothills of the Tres Hermanas Range in Luna County, at a point about 4 miles north of the Mexican border. The onyx seams vary from 6 inches to about 16 inches in thickness and contain extremely compact material of considerable translucency, basically creamy white in color with a slightly pinkish cast. Bands of opaque white alternate with translucent areas.

Arizona. The most important deposit of onyx in this state is located at Mayer in Yavapai County, just to the west of this town across Big Bug Creek. Mayer is on Highway 69, 27 miles southeast of Prescott by road. This locality has been known for many years and considerable material has been removed from the extensive deposits which range from 1 to 25 feet in thickness and cover over 200 acres. The country rock is schist turned on edge and intruded by volcanic dikes. Onyx occurs interbedded with blocks of broken country rock or forming solid masses frequently very thick but seldom free of flaws. Colors are extremely varied and include amber, white, yellow, brown, deep brownish-red, and sometimes a lovely green. Mottled types locally called "paisley shawl" are much prized. The specific gravity of brown material is 2.67 while that of green onyx is 2.75. At one time Mayer onyx was shipped to Omaha, Nebraska for finishing into a variety of ornamental items.

Another important deposit of onyx occurs near Cave Creek in Maricopa County about 3 miles north of Seven Springs and almost on the border between Maricopa and Yavapai counties and is reached by road from Cave Creek. The country rock at this deposit is slaty schist intruded by dikes of quartz porphyry and diorite, overlain in places by basalt sheets. The main locality is on the western slope of a low hill capped by basalt where the onyx bed reaches a maximum thickness of ten feet but the largest blocks recovered so far have not been over four feet thick. Prevailing colors are green and yellow with veinlets of brown and red. Considerable quantities have found ready sale to manufacturers in Arizona who used it for novelties and ornaments but compared to the Mayer deposit, the Cave Creek bed is considerably less in extent and in volume.

A small deposit of onyx near Flagstaff in Coconino County was once worked under the name of the Brown Onyx Quarry. Another locality for good onyx is given as 12 miles north of Wikieup along the Big Sandy River in Mohave County.

Washington. White translucent onyx, said to be abundant, has been reported from Number One Canyon just outside of Wenatchee in Chelan County.

California. Onyx has been quarried from a point 6 miles south of Berryvale in Siskiyou County; also near Healdsburg in Sonoma County. In Napa County, brown banded onyx occurs at the Manhattan Quicksilver Mine. A small deposit of brown onyx consisting of two veins each about 5 inches thick is located on Sulphur Creek in Colusa County.

Between Fairfield (Suisun) and Vacaville in Solano County are located two deposits of onyx which have been extensively quarried in years past. The first locality, often labeled "Suisun," is about one mile from Highway 40 on top of a small hill. In this deposit is found a beautiful rich reddish-

brown onyx which was quarried as early as 1884 and much used for ornamental purposes. The brown coloration varies from amber to deep brown,
although red and orange are also said to be found from time to time. The
other quarry is located on the opposite side of Highway 40 about two miles
away and yielded large flawless blocks of compact pure white onyx which
was sent to France for manufacture into clock cases and other objects. This
material is layered with fine wavy whitish lines which lend much interest
to otherwise plain material. Both onyxes from these localities are capable of
taking fine polishes. The specific gravity is 2.70.

Important deposits of onyx occur in the Santa Lucia Range of San Luis
Obispo County about 5 miles south of Pozo near Salt Creek. This is the
same locality variously pinpointed as "near Musick" or "near Arroyo
Grande." It may be reached by road from Routzahn County Park, distance
9.7 miles, thence by trail to the east about 1 mile from the road. Original
quarrying operations began here in 1890 when two openings were made in
onyx seams located about ½ mile apart on an east-west line on either side
of a small hill. The onyx veins are enclosed in slatey limestone and appear
as layers from 1 to 10 inches thick which in places swell to as much as
30 inches. At one time flawless blocks were quarried up to 3 to 6 feet square.
Colors are various but white prevails; others are pink, purple, orange, blue,
red, and olive, each tinging the basic white material. The onyx is translucent,
takes a good polish, and is much used by amateurs of California for working
into bookends, spheres, and other ornamental objects.

In San Bernardino County several commercially unimportant deposits
have been found at widely separated points but like the preceding deposit,
furnish good material for amateur lapidary work. The first is a narrow seam
of white material stained various colors outcropping on the western flank of
Pyramid Peak about several hundred yards east of Highway 190 and about
¼ mile southeast of where that road enters the eastern side of Death Valley
National Monument. So-called "silver" onyx is obtained from seams on the
west side of the entrance to Mule Canyon about 2½ miles from the ghost
town of Calico. Some good material in various colors occurs at an old quarry
one mile above Pipes Canyon Public Camp ground in Pipes Canyon about
15 miles by road northwest of Yucca Valley. Brown-banded material is occasionally found in the limestone quarries near Colton not far from Riverside.

Baja California Norte. One of the most important sources for commercial onyx in the entire continent lies almost 300 miles southeast of San Diego,
California, in the middle of the arid and desolate interior of this Mexican
state. The quarries are located at the end of a side road which diverts eastward from San Augustin, a cattle ranch 222½ miles south of Ensenada along
the main north-south peninsular highway. The side road extends slightly
over 10 miles at which point the large openings from which the onyx is

removed are visible. The small community near the deposits is called El Marmol, the Spanish name for "marble," and boasts the world's only school-house made completely of onyx.

The principal deposit at El Marmol is exposed in the Pedrara Quarry, and consists of three distinct horizons of onyx outcropping over a vertical distance of 40 feet and 1200 feet laterally while the length of the deposit is estimated at 3,000 feet. The upper layer is thin but highly colored and furnishes small masses suitable for spheres, pen bases, and other items. The second layer varies in thickness from 1 to 2 feet and is suitable for quarrying into large blocks. The third layer is the thickest of all, supplying blocks which range from 1 to 4 feet in thickness and often as much as 6 feet on edge. The prevailing country rock is a friable sandstone with alternating layers of calcareous conglomerate and onyx. All material is very fine quality both in respect to freedom from flaws, useful size, translucency, and coloration. The prevailing color is white or some slight tint thereof, however, delicate rose and light green are also common. Wherever cracks have appeared, sharp veinlets of red, brownish-red, and other hues occur due to the infiltration of iron-bearing solutions. Specific gravity ranges from 2.77 to 2.79.

At the quarries, explosives are used only to strip off the overburden while the actual dislodgment of

FIGURE 168. Quarrying calcite at the Pedrara Quarry near El Marmol in Baja California Norte. The large block in the foreground upon which the men are standing shows banding of onyx layers. Courtesy Southwest Onyx & Marble Company.

onyx slabs is accomplished by drilling a series of holes through the layers and driving wedges in them to cause the block to art from the remainder of the ledge. Figure 168 shows workmen at the quarry employing this method, the so-called "plug and feather" system. After blocks are dislodged, they are carefully hand-trimmed, marked, and hoisted aboard trucks which deliver them to the Southwest Onyx & Marble Company of San Diego, California, owners and operators of the onyx deposits.

The processing of the onyx in the company plant in San Diego was observed by the author through the courtesy of John Y. Mills, the proprietor. Because of its softness, the most practical and least wasteful method of reducing blocks to size is by sawing with "gang saws" which consist of nothing more than steel bands stroked continually across the blocks until they are separated into slabs. The actual cutting is done by quartz sand which is fed to the blades with a copious supply of water. Onyx blocks may be sawed across the grain or parallel to the grain, each giving completely different effects. Cutting across shows a variety of sharp bandings of contrasting tints along with colored stainings in healed fissures and cracks but cannot yield large slabs. On the other hand, although large slabs can be had by sawing blocks parallel to the bedding planes, the patterns and coloration are not so striking and beautiful as the other way. After slabs leave the sawing dollys, they are further sectioned by diamond saws into blocks, circles, etc.—whatever is needed for the objects being made. Penstands are made by stacking many sawn blocks on edge and lapping to size on a huge horizontal wheel charged with sand and water. This process is repeated for all edges until every piece is uniform. The pieces are then embedded in a tray and polished by a whirling overhead buff charged with tin oxide.

Across the Peninsular Divide to the east of El Marmol is another large deposit of onyx which appears similar in all important respects. This deposit lies in a deep canyon called Tule Arroyo and has formed upon dark mica schists and bluish-gray silicified limestones and quartzites. There are two distinct horizons in this deposit showing spring activity taking place at widely separated times. Another quarry south of El Marmol but not now working, is reached by turning due south from the main peninsular highway at a point about 12 miles south of San Augustin. The distance from this intersection to Cerro Blanco, the site of the quarry, is 22 miles. Much further south is another onyx quarry at a place called El Marmolito in allusion to its lesser importance. These workings are reached by turning east on a 7½ mile road leading from a place called Rosarito, a collection of ranches opposite the Bahia Santa Rosalia on the Pacific coast. The distance from El Marmolito to Ensenada is approximately 348 miles. The last locality is said to have been worked by a company who imported Yaqui Indians from Mexico as laborers and accordingly sold the stone under the trade name of "Yaqui Onyx."

Some years ago in northern Baja California not far from Rosarito Beach, magnificent crystallized calcite crystals were uncovered from cavities within an amygdaloidal volcanic rock upon the Viasteros Ranch, a mile or two directly inland from this seacoast town. The locality is on the southeast slope of rounded hill about ¼ mile east of the Viasteros farmhouse. An enormous opening was uncovered which proved to be lined with sheets of calcite crystals of beautiful rich brown color, somewhat orange to reddish in tone.

In size, individual crystals ranged from ½ inch to as much as 4 inches tall and several inches thick, consisting of simple rhombohedrons with curved faces. All were coated with fluffy white deposits of calcite which were readily dissolved with acid to uncover the crystals. Many are clear and flawless and afford exceptional faceted gems as for example a specimen in the U.S. National Museum which weighs 45 carats. The author has in his collection, a flawless gem of deep brown color cut in step fashion and weighing 40.76 carats (see Figure 166). This locality has not been exhausted but explosives would be required to obtain more specimens.

Coahuila. Onyx deposits have been worked to some extent at Jimulco,

Puebla. The principal deposits of the well known "Mexican Onyx" are located southeast of the city of Puebla between Tecali, Tzicatlacoya, and Tepene. The most noted quarry, La Pedrara, is about 21 miles from Puebla in the Tecali district. The deposit covers about 3 acres and has been mined along its edge to a depth of 7 feet. Fine green material sprinkled with dashes of red or pink and of excellent texture is produced. The Antigua Salines deposit in the Tehuacan district ranks next in importance, consisting of a deposit of 2 acres extent in the side of a hill. The third ranking district is La Sopresa, covering about 5 acres, located 35 miles west of Antigua Salines. The onyx is generally translucent white but some green is also found. Four miles east of Sopresa is the La Mesa deposit covering almost 30 acres atop a flat hill and hence the largest of the group. Despite its size, the blocks obtained from the beds are generally small. Other quarries in Puebla are: El Mogote, Lajas, Agua Esconda, Desampero, Mehuantepec, Tepeyac, Tecoluco, La Paoma, and La Reforma. In all of the onyx district, the underlying rocks are principally limestones intruded or covered by lavas.

In 1940, Mexican workers in onyx discovered that aniline dyes could be used to stain the slightly porous material into almost any color of the rainbow and proceeded at once to turn out thousands of ornamental objects including gems for jewelry. What had been rather drab material now could be given dazzling hues and a lively industry in this phase of onyx work soon sprang up. In the processing of onyx, blocks of rough are first sawed with ordinary steel saws until pieces of the desired size are obtained. Carving, if necessary, is done with steel tools and surfaces smoothed with ordinary sandpaper. Objects are then placed in water solutions of organic dyes which are warmed gradually to prevent cracking of the onyx; only a few minutes are necessary for the dye to penetrate. The final polish is applied by cloth buffs and polishing powder. Large numbers of dyed onyx stones are set in inexpensive silver jewelry but sometimes customers are far from pleased when colors begin to fade, which, unfortunately, happens in a short time. In 1943 a campaign was launched to sell bright green-dyed onyx as "Mexican jade." This misnomer, made all the more misleading because true jade in carved form has been found in ancient Indian sites, was so vigorously opposed that advertising using the term was forced to cease.

Cuba. Large masses of banded onyx of fine quality are obtained from the Santa Barbara Quarries on the Central Highway just east of Havana. The material is said to be very handsome and accepts a fine polish.

HOWLITE

Popular in the western United States for many lapidary purposes, howlite is virtually unknown elsewhere. Occurring in relatively large cauliflower-like masses of snow white material, delicately and handsomely veined in black, it is in demand for making book ends, spheres, ash trays, and even for cutting cabochons for jewelry. A photograph of a typical nodule from the Tick Canyon locality in California is shown in Figure 169. Howlite is very soft and easily worked, however, it is porous and does not polish easily nor to a very high gloss. This interesting mineral is named after Professor H. How of Nova Scotia.

FIGURE 169. A "cauliflower" nodule of white howlite delicately veined with black. Tick Canyon, California. Size: about 3 inches in length.

Howlite is a hydrated silicoborate of calcium with the formula: $Ca_2SiB_5O_9(OH)_5$. Although crystallizing in the Monoclinic System, it is rarely found in distinct crystals, the vast majority of occurrences furnishing only compact massive material of smooth, somewhat sugary texture. Nodules occur as concretionary growths from an inch or so in diameter to some which exceed 12 inches; exceptional nodules up to 100 pounds have been recorded. It is found chiefly in sedimentary beds either with gypsum and anhydrite as in Nova Scotia, or with other boron minerals as in the California deposits. The hardness is very low, about $3\frac{1}{2}$ or even less. The specific gravity is also low, ranging from 2.53 to 2.59. Refractive indices are as follows: Windsor, Nova Scotia, $\alpha = 1.586$, $\beta = 1.598$, $\gamma = 1.605$; Ryan, California, $\alpha = 1.583$, $\beta = 1.596$, $\gamma = 1.605$. The birefringence is 0.019 and 0.022 respectively; biaxial, negative. The only color in which howlite has been noted is pure white although this may be modified at times by veinings of black or tinges of brown, due, in each case, to the presence of foreign matter. Howlite is easily soluble in dilute acids and for this reason polished specimens will lose their gloss if handled excessively.

LOCALITIES

Nova Scotia. Originally found and described from deposits in Hants County, howlite occurs as nodules ranging from 1 to 8 inches in diameter embedded in anhydrite and gypsum near Windsor, at Brookville, and at Wentworth (formerly called Winkworth), Newport Station, Noel, etc.

California. The most productive locality for howlite is in the famous borate deposit of the Sterling Borax Mine in Tick Canyon, Los Angeles County. Tick Canyon is a side canyon of Mint Canyon and is easily reached by automobile from Saugus. The deposit in which the nodules occur consists of gray clay and shale beds of about 10 feet in thickness and capped by sandstone. Carbonaceous matter is present and is probably the cause of the delicate black veinings which lend so much attractiveness in polished specimens. Very large nodules have come from this mine: the usual size varies from 3 to 4 inches in diameter but larger specimens reach 8 to 12 inches diameter.

Other localities producing small amounts of howlite are in the borate beds of Calico, San Bernardino County, and at Russell and other borate Mines near Frazier Mountain, north of Lockwood Valley in the northeast corner of Ventura County.

ULEXITE

Far too soft to be of any practical gem value, this rather rare borate nevertheless provides some of the finest quality cat's eyes known to any species in the Mineral Kingdom. These are cut from the fibrous material which is found filling seams in the famous borate deposits of the Southern California desert regions. Finished stones are perfectly white and dazzling in brilliance. Close examination of massive fibrous material shows it to be composed of innumerable slender crystals, packed closely together and standing on end in relation to the walls of the seams in which it occurs. Another effect, scarcely less startling than the first, is obtained when a section is polished across the ends of the fibers. Such a piece placed upon a sheet of newspaper will show the newsprint reflected faithfully and mysteriously upon its upper side. This unique property caused one mineral dealer to dub ulexite "television stone," a not inappropriate title and certainly an amusing one. This effect is easily noticeable in seam sections as much as 4 inches thick but naturally only clean material without cavities or inclusions must be used. This species received its name after G. L. Ulex, who first described it.

Ulexite is a Triclinic hydrated borate of sodium and calcium, with the formula: $NaCaB_5O_9 \cdot 8H_2O$; it is very fragile and weak, and occurs in a variety of forms including the so-called "cotton balls" and "sheet cotton" which are fluffy masses of extremely minute crystals arranged in random fashion. The only useful form in lapidary work is the fibrous type already described. The hardness is low, about 2 to 2½ and causes considerable difficulty in forming stones without breaking them. Additionally, it is very heat-sensitive. The specific gravity is 1.955. Refractive indices are: $a = 1.492$, $\beta = 1.506$, $\gamma = 1.530$; birefringence 0.038; biaxial, positive.

Ulexite is invariably pure white or silvery white in fibrous kinds when viewed through the sides of the seams; through the ends of the fibers, however, it appears colorless or sometimes greenish because of clay inclusions. The "television effect" is due solely to the remarkable transparency along this direction, each minute cylindrical crystal receiving light rays at one end then reflecting them along the sides until they appear again at the other end. Catseyes are cut across the fibers of seam sections and may be obtained as much as an inch across. The author has seen a beautiful sphere of ulexite measuring 1¼ inches diameter, cut from a pure seam section. Unfortunately, ulexite is not a very stable mineral and several cabochons in the author's collection show an appreciable loss of polish due to decomposition of surface material. Close examination shows a thin film of powdery material which presumably is an alteration product or perhaps a water soluble mineral present with the ulexite.

LOCALITIES

Nevada. Fibrous ulexite masses up to 3 inches thick occur in White Basin, Clark County.

California. Ulexite is found in the Mount Blanco District of Inyo County, especially in the several tunnels excavated for borax minerals in the clay hills on the northern flanks of the Black Mountains in the southeast section of Death Valley. The best material has come from the Kramer District in southeastern Kern County, an area about 35 miles southeast of Mojave, midway between Mojave and Barstow and immediately north of Boron, a station on the Santa Fe Railroad. Here it occurs in outstanding specimens in the Suckow Mine in veins varying from paperthin to as much as 4 inches thick in bluish-gray or greenish-gray clays.

GYPSUM

Gypsum is an extremely versatile commercial mineral, large quantities being burned each year to make plaster, a substance which is familiar to everyone as the material from which wall boarding is made. In fact, the name by which we know this mineral is derived from the ancient Greek word for "plaster." An unusually compact finely-fibrous form of considerable translucency known as *alabaster* has been used for centuries for carvings and is still extensively used for various ornamental objects, many of which are now imported from Italy. It occurs in important deposits in North America also, and will be mentioned later under the proper places. Somewhat less common in good quality is another translucent form known as *satin spar*, a form of gypsum in which multitudes of very fine transparent parallel fibrous crystals fill seams in ordinary gypsum. Excellent cat's eyes can be cut from this material but it has been used most extensively as beads in necklaces, showing in direct light, a fine silky chatoyancy. Many satin spar ornaments and jewelry items are made in England from exceptional material. Unfortunately, gypsum in all its forms is extremely soft, causing all ornaments made from it to lack the important quality of durability.

Gypsum is calcium sulfate dihydrate with the formula: $Ca(SO_4) \cdot 2H_2O$. As the formula shows, water is present and it is this which makes gypsum convertible into plaster. Upon heating to several hundred degrees, the water is partly driven off, and the gypsum converted into a white powder. The process is reversed by adding water, the powder "setting up" into the familiar solid material seen in wall board, in statuettes, etc. Gypsum crystallizes in the Monoclinic System, forming in many sedimentary deposits, splendid transparent crystals of the variety known as *selenite*. Although seemingly suited for cutting into gems, these crystals are far too soft since they can be scratched easily with a finger nail. Gypsum is only 2 in hardness and of all minerals, only talc proves to be softer. However, because of its softness, both its varieties, alabaster and satin spar, are easily worked with ordinary steel tools. The specific gravity of pure gypsum is close to 2.317 but the porous nature of massive kinds lowers this value to about 2.20. Refractive indices are low: $a = 1.5207$, $\beta = 1.5230$, $\gamma = 1.5299$; birefringence 0.092; biaxial, positive. When pure, gypsum is colorless, or, in satin spar, silvery white; pale pink and cream are noted commonly in alabaster.

LOCALITIES

Alaska. Fine alabaster occurs along Iyoukeen Cove on Chichagof Island, Southeastern Alaska.

New Brunswick. Very beautiful snow-white alabaster has been obtained in the gypsum quarries at Hillsborough in Albert County.

New York. Although satin spar has been found in narrow seams in limestone in the region around Niagara Falls, most, if not all of the material sold at the souvenir stands and stores, comes from England.

Michigan. Commercial alabaster occurs at several places in this state. Fine pink material is found in the gypsum quarries at Grandville near Grand Rapids, Kent County; it takes a beautiful polish and has been extensively used for manufacture into a wide variety of ornaments. A series of gypsum quarries near National City and Alabaster in the southern part of Iosco County have provided much good carving grade alabaster from which bowls, screens, trays, etc., have been prepared. The town of Alabaster is on the shore of Saginaw Bay, Lake Huron, while National City is about 15 miles to the northwest. Satin spar occurs at Pointe Aux Chenes, about 10 miles west of St. Ignace, Mackinac County.

Oklahoma. Gray and pink alabasters are found in many places in the gypsum deposits of Precambrian age in the western part of the state; deposits are most abundant in Beckham, Blaine, Greer, Harper, Jackson, and Major counties.

South Dakota. Alabaster occurs in the Spearfish "red beds" of the Black Hills and was formerly used by the Indian inhabitants for carvings. The color varies from pure white to gray, sometimes stained and mottled by iron oxides.

Wyoming. Alabaster has been locally produced and carved in Casper, Natrona County, and in Thermopolis, Hot Springs County.

Colorado. Exquisite pink satin spar is found in seams in massive gypsum in Perry Park in the foothills of the Front Range, about 10 miles northwest of Palmer Lake in Douglas County. Some is perfectly white and all shows good chatoyancy. The associated compact gypsum grades into alabaster. In Owl Canyon, Larimer County, alabaster is found in seams 3 to 4 feet thick at a point about 2 miles northeast of Owl Canyon Store. Articles fashioned from this handsome pink-veined and mottled material have been shipped to many points in the United States. In Jefferson County, alabaster occurs near Bear Creek between Golden and Ralston.

New Mexico. Yellowish-white alabaster, locally known as "Mexican onyx," occurs in the Tularosa District, 1½ miles south of Bent, Otero County. Satin spar is reported from an area about 4 miles northwest of Socorro and east of Strawberry Peak in Socorro County.

Oregon. Fine satin spar is often found in a commercial gypsum quarry located 2 miles north of Durkee, Baker County.

Chihuahua. Alabaster is found in the Cerro del Marmol in the Sierra de Carrizo, near Moqui in the Camargo District.

Guerrero. Alabaster is found in the Mina la Cruz and other mines at Huitzuco in the Hidalgo District.

Puebla. Alabaster occurs near Pueblo San Miguel Ayotla and Lomas del Calvario in the Matamoros Izucar District.

Tamaulipas. Alabaster is found near Cruillas in the Distrito Norte.

Jamaica. Much alabaster occurs as layers in massive gypsum in the abandoned quarry near Beito.

Puerto Rico. Satin spar and alabaster are found several miles northeast of Ponce in the southern part of the island.

CATLINITE
(*Pipestone*)

When early explorers penetrated the interior of North America, particularly into the Great Lakes Region, they found the Indians employing ceremonial tobacco pipes or *calumets*, made from a highly-prized soft reddish stone. The eminent artist, George Catlin, who traveled among the American

FIGURE 170. A view in Pipestone National Monument showing piles of rubbish discarded from the catlinite quarries which mark the outcrop of the bed. Courtesy Pipestone National Monument.

Indians making numerous sketches and paintings, arrived at the sacred pipe-stone quarry in 1836 after some trouble with a band of Indians who sought to bar his passage there. He found that the grounds surrounding the quarry were held so inviolate that normally belligerent tribes came to a truce in order that each could obtain its annual supply of this treasured commodity. In honor of Catlin, this material now enjoys its present name. Aside from its intriguing historical background which deserves recognition here, catlinite holds no interest for jewelry although a considerable quantity is carved each year into a variety of trinkets and objects.

Catlinite is evidently a partially metamorphosed clay, very fine-grained and compact. It is smooth in texture and cuts easily with steel, leaving a glossy surface under the blade. Analysis of typical material from the Minnesota locality, shows it to consist of sericite, partly replaced by pyrophyllite, and stained by hematite. Also present are diaspore, pyrite, and the micaceous form of hematite known as specularite. It usually occurs interlaminated in Sioux quartzite and is believed to be consolidated ancient marine sediment of Cambrian age. In the Minnesota locality which is the principal one, it occurs in a bed 15 to 18 inches thick, overlaid by quartzite. The method of extraction used by the Indians involves stripping off the overburden and splitting out the catlinite in slabs ranging from 1 to 4 inches thick. These pieces form convenient working sizes for shaping into pipes and other objects.

LOCALITIES

Minnesota. The principal occurrence of catlinite is preserved in the Pipestone National Monument, a plot of land embracing the catlinite quarries and certain historical shrines located immediately north of the city limits of Pipestone, in Pipestone County. Catlinite beds occur beneath a ridge of quartzite which rises as a shallow escarpment from the prairie, reaching heights of from 25 to 30 feet and encompassing a series of quarries extending ½ mile along the outcrop. The material is bright red in color. A general view of the main quarry system extending in north-south direction is shown in Figure 170. The method of quarrying is well illustrated in Figure 171 where the quartzite overburden appears as a steep face on one side of the trench and the rubble blocks on the other. The carving of catlinite is a simple though time-consuming process, involving the use of steel carving tools, files, and other devices for finishing the surface and boring holes in smoking pipes. Under the aegis of the Pipestone Indian Shrine Association, quarrying and working catlinite is encouraged, and a shop for disposing of the worked items is maintained in the Museum at the Monument. Several years ago, catlinite was advertised briefly in amateur lapidary magazines as a carving material but responses to this appeal are not known.

Wisconsin. Catlinite occurs near Devil's Lake, also near Rice Lake in Barron County. There are at least five quarries in this county and another in Chippewa County.

Other Localities. Minor quarries for catlinite are recorded near Sioux Falls, South Dakota; also from an indefinite locality in Scioto County, Ohio. Vague references state that the "oldest" catlinite quarry in North America

FIGURE 171. A close-up of one of the quarries along the catlinite outcrop. One of the local Indians authorized to dig catlinite is holding several thin slabs which have been dug from the floor after the overlying quartzite has been removed. Courtesy U.S. Geological Survey.

is located in Arizona. Specimens of catlinite have also been found in glacial drift of the upper Mississippi Valley.

ARGILLITE
(*Haida Slate*)

Among the raw materials used by the artisans of the Indian tribes inhabiting the shores of British Columbia and Southeastern Alaska, is the easily carved claystone called "Haida slate" found only in one deposit in the

FIGURE 172. Haida argillite carvings. The carving at the left measures 13¾ inches long, 9¼ inches wide and 2 inches thick at the ends, and represents a sculpin with three human heads along its back. The carving on the right measures 23½ inches long, 14 inches wide, and 2¼ inches thick. The human figures at each end are shamans while in the center, a raven is emerging from a halibut; the side figures carved in low relief appear to be head-on views of killer whales. Both specimens are on exhibit in the Southwest Museum in Highland Park, Los Angeles, California. Courtesy Southwest Museum.

Queen Charlotte Islands, British Columbia. Technically, the rock used by the carvers is a dark gray argillitic shale which occurs in sharply layered beds and consists mainly of consolidated carbonaceous clay. The first examples of art work prepared from this rock appear to have been made about 1820 since it seems that the deposit was not recognized before this time. The best known carvings are miniature totem poles or "family trees," a form of sculpture brought to its greatest perfection in North America only among the Thlingits and Haidas of the area mentioned. Other objects took the form of boxes, food utensils and containers, and a variety of purely decorative items (see Figure 172). Since Haida Slate is soft and works easily with steel tools, designs are deeply incised if not carved altogether in the round.

As in their woodcarvings, the Haida and Thlingit artisans employed the fluid graceful lines and curves which characterizes their art, sometimes using mother of pearl from the abalone to emphasize points of design. It is much to be regretted that this form of native art has now virtually died out. An account of a visit to some of the villages of this region a few years ago indicated that the last truly skilled carver was advanced in years and may now be deceased.

The argillite used for these carvings is obtained halfway up the slope of Slatechuck Mountain on Slatechuck Creek at the foot of Skidegate Inlet about 8 miles west of Skidegate Village, Graham Island, in the Queen Charlotte Islands. It occurs as a soft grayish rock separated by pronounced bedding planes and easily broken out by ordinary steel tools. The intensely black color of finished pieces is not natural, being obtained only after staining with a black dye or as in recent years, with graphite stove polish.

BAUXITE

Ordinarily, bauxite is soft and porous, and completely unsuited for any purpose except as an ore of aluminum, however, at times, it has been found hard enough to polish. Such material occurs near the town of Bauxite in Saline County, Arkansas, where it receives locally the name "heliotrope bauxite" in allusion to its spotted deep red and green coloration. The town of Bauxite, known for its mines of that mineral, is located about 30 miles southwest of Little Rock. As an ornamental gemstone bauxite from this locality is neither sufficiently beautiful nor outstanding in other ways to be regarded as more than a lapidary curiosity.

CHAPTER VII

Organic Gemstones

THOSE materials found naturally in the earth's crust but derived from the remains or the products of living creation; included are pearl and shell as well as coral, materials which by custom have been classed with mineral gemstones.

PEARLS AND SHELL

Among the thousands of members of the Animal Kingdom, few are so strange as those belonging to the great class (or phylum) of *mollusca*, or shellfish as these animals are more popularly known. The mollusca include snails, mussels, oysters, whelks, limpets, squids, etc., many of which are familiar to readers as essential items of food. Mollusca are widely distributed both in fresh and salt waters and some, such as certain snails and slugs, even live entirely on land. The mollusca are subdivided into five large classes of which three, the *Pelecypoda*, the *Gastropoda*, and the *Cephalopoda*, provide the beautifully iridescent material known as *nacre* or *mother of pearl*, and concretions of this same substance known as *pearls*.

The Pelecypoda include several families of special interest since the vast majority of pearls and nacre are provided by their genera, for example, the precious pearl of the gem trade is found in shells of the saltwater genera *Pinctada* and *Avicula* while freshwater pearls and nacre are provided by members of the genera *Anodonta, Lampsilis*, etc. The Gastropoda are much less important, providing pearls of pretty color but totally lacking iridescence from the genus *Strombus*, also some shell useful for carving into cameos from members of this genus and others such as *Cassis*. Both genera owe their usefulness for cameo carving to the fact that shells of their members consist of several layers of which the outer are light in color and the inner are darker. By skillful carving away of outer layers, it is possible to create cameos showing a white pattern or figure in bas relief upon a darker ground. The Gastropoda also provide beautiful pearls and magnificently colored iridescent mother of pearl from the familiar abalones or species belonging to the genus *Haliotis*. The Cephalopoda include only one shellfish of interest in the lapidary or jewelry arts, namely, the pearly nautilus (*N. pompilius*), from the shell of which some excellent mother of pearl is obtained, however, this animal is not found in North American waters and is therefore of no further interest in this discussion.

The majority of mollusks protect their soft bodies by creating hard coverings consisting of minute crystals of calcium carbonate arranged in exceedingly thin layers and cemented firmly together by deposits of an organic albuminoid substance known as *conchiolin*. In saltwater species, the calcium carbonate is identical to the Orthorhombic mineral *aragonite*, while in freshwater species, the Hexagonal equivalent, *calcite*, is also found in the shells. Analyses of pearly shells show them to consist of 2 to 4 per cent water, 10 to 14 per cent conchiolin, and the rest calcium carbonate. Though comprising only a modest amount of the whole, conchiolin imparts great toughness because of the unique method by which it cements together the mineral substance of the shell. Microscopic examination of pearls and nacre show the existence of numerous thin layers of aragonite or calcite crystals, each individual crystal standing on end and embedded and cushioned in films of flexible conchiolin. Apparently the sheets of crystals are not continuous but are applied by the animal in numerous miniscule patches which overlap each other like a host of silvery leaves. The fit between patches is very exact and scarcely any unused space remains, resulting in the pearly matter approximating closely the specific gravity of the mineral of which it is chiefly composed. Thus in a typical saltwater pearl, the density is only slightly less than that of aragonite (s.g. = 2.93), the lower value being caused by the lesser densities of conchiolin (s.g. = 1.34) and water (s.g. = 1.00). The total range of densities is from 2.60 to 2.80 with the higher values belonging to pearls and shell from conches.

The arrangement and depth of aragonite or calcite crystals has much to do with the presence of absence of iridescence or *orient*, as this effect is called in the pearl trade. If extremely fine crystals are formed through the secretions of the mollusks, and their arrangement is haphazard, the resulting shell is barely translucent at best and looks for all the world like nothing more than ordinary porcelain. This type of formation is characteristic of edible clams and oysters, and of course results in shells and pearls of no decorative value whatsoever. On the other hand, in those in which the minute prisms of mineral matter are relatively large, clear, and arranged in the regular order mentioned previously, the passage of light is made far more easy and the substance of the shell and associated pearls is more translucent. The iridescence of nacre whether it be upon inner faces of shells or upon pearls, is due to the diffraction of light along the irregular edges of the overlapping patches of nacreous matter and the interference of light at the junctions of the layers. The satiny sheen of pearl is strikingly similar to that observed in some opaque feldspar moonstones.

During their lifetimes, few mollusks are afforded the opportunity to live out their allotted spans without being attacked by enemies. Anyone who has examined an abalone for example, is struck by the numerous channels and tunnels cut into the shell by boring worms. In places, the worms break through the shell but before they can cause serious damage to the soft-bodied abalone, the latter seals off the break by depositing additional nacre in a rounded bulging extension of the inner wall. Other irritants such as grains of sand, small fragments of vegetable or mineral matter, small crabs, and other more strange objects which have somehow forced their way into the private inner chamber of the mollusk are similarly dealt with. Bulges of this sort are common in many other mollusks besides the abalones, and from their most ordinary shape are called *blister pearls*. If the form is symmetrical and the coating sufficiently beautiful, they may be carefully cut away from the shell and effectively mounted in jewelry as if they were solid pearls sawn in two. However, the classic pearls of jewelry, characterized by spherical or approximately spherical forms, owe their origin to another cause since they grow entirely encased within the soft fleshy body of the mollusk and thus become covered on all sides by nacre. Pearls of this kind begin with the entry within the shell of minute wriggling parasites known as trematodes and cestodes. Unlike inanimate matter which comes to rest somewhere between the shell and the body of the mollusks and can be leisurely covered with nacre, these parasitic worms move about vigorously and defy attempts to pin them against the inner wall. The mollusk combats this activity by developing a recess in its outer nacre-depositing skin or *mantle*, in which the worm is trapped. Eventually this recess closes over and seals the minute offender in a sac or cyst whose inner surface is lined with tissue identical to that which produced nacre. When this happens, the worm is covered repeatedly until it is entombed within a pearl. The deposition of nacre continues over the years and apparently does not cease until the mollusk dies although Japanese cultured pearl experts indicate that covering growth on artificially-implanted nuclei continues rapidly only for about 4 years, after which time it tapers off sharply. Not all loose or *free* pearls are caused by parasitic organisms by any means, many other foreign substances having been found at the cores of dissected pearls, but it is necessary in all cases that the encysting process described take place if an unattached pearl is to result.

Pearls found within the fleshy parts of mollusks are often far from ideal in form, a truly spherical specimen being especially rare. In some cases, the partly-formed free pearl is released by the animal or works its way loose and becomes attached to the shell. In other instances, several impurities or irritating particles present at the same time, grow together to form odd-shaped pearls known as *baroques*. The extreme in oddity is found in the pearls from freshwater mussels of North America which, when wildly fantastic in form, are collectively called *slugs* but earn other more descriptive names depending on their likeness to familiar objects. (Figure 173.) Among the fishermen

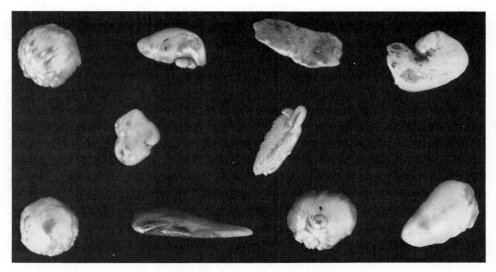

FIGURE 173. Freshwater baroque and slug pearls. The round specimens are about 3/8 inch in diameter. Courtesy Smithsonian Institution.

for pearly freshwater mussels, slugs may be called "spikes" or "points," "wings" or "angel-wings," "nuggets," "chunks," "dog teeth," and other colorful names. The term "hinge" pearl is used to designate those of extremely irregular form found in the deep recesses within the shell next to the hinge of the mussel. Most of the pointed, flat, or elongated specimens, often very sharp-edged, are removed from this section. Naturally the pearls most highly prized for jewelry are those of greatest perfection of form, ignoring other considerations for the moment, but they are also the most rare. Free pearls of good form are sold by the *grain*, a traditional measure of pearl weight equivalent to one-fourth of a carat. On the other hand, slugs and *seed* pearls are sold by the ounce.

Within a single mollusk may be found as many as a hundred small seed pearls, some of which are almost too small to see, or there may be only one pearl of small to large size, or, as is overwhelmingly the case—nothing at all! Carefully-kept records on the freshwater mussel fisheries of the Mississippi River basin have shown that only ½ ounce of slugs can be expected from every *ton* of shell while pearls of good form are even less frequently encountered. Like all other gems, the value of pearls is influenced in no small measure by their rarity. Freshwater seed pearls sold in 1925 for about $.50 per ounce but single pearls of perhaps 10 grains or so, sold for several hundred dollars. A fine pearl of 64 grains (16 carats) found in Peoria Lake many years ago sold for $2500. The demand for freshwater pearls has declined over the years, not so much on account of their lessened value, but because of the marked drop in the production of the shell by the mussel-fishery of the United States whose whole economy depends on the button-making value of mother of pearl and not that of the pearls themselves which are nothing more than a byproduct. Another cause for decline is the depletion of the shellfish brought about by years of over-fishing plus pollution of formerly clean streams and the creation of stagnant waters unsuited to the requirements of the mollusk by the building of 'flood control" and "navigation" dams. The installation of such dams in the Mississippi River, according to local fishermen, has done more to destroy the mussel population than any other single factor. However, in streams in which conditions are essentially unchanged, only several years of reduced or regulated fishing are needed to allow the shellfish to reestablish themselves in large numbers. Recent investigations of the natural history of freshwater pearl mussels has shown that the "comeback" of an overfished stream is not always along the lines desired since the largest and finest species often require up to ten years to mature while the smallest species, some only two or three inches in length and of little economic value, return in droves and dominate the stream population.

The life cycle of the freshwater mussel is furthermore peculiarly dependent upon the fish population of the waters in which it is found, and as the abundance of fish varies, so does the abundance of mussels. The reason for this strange state of affairs is easy to understand when it is realized that each mussel passes through a larval stage during which time it must find a suitable fish host and adhere to its fins or gills until the larval stage is over. This is but another example of the wonderful and all too often unrealized interdependencies to which life forms in nature owe their very existences. Thus, the yellow sand shell (*Lampsilis anodontoides*), one of the largest and most beautiful of all freshwater mussels in the Mississippi River drainage, depends upon the garfish or gar pike as its host. Yet this fish is strongly detested by sport fishermen who claim it to be destructive to other fish and even to birds and never lose an opportunity to kill off this aquatic "varmint." By their zealous and altogether too successful attempts, the garfish is now much more rare than before and so too is the yellow sand shell. Less tragic is the mutual reliance of the common Mississippi River sheepshead or fresh-water drumfish and a number of mussels. This stout-jawed fish is specially fitted by nature with rounded plates within its jaws and throat designed to crush the mussels and free their flesh for ingestion. However, this is not all a one-way street for as the mussels are shattered by the powerful jaws of the sheepshead, thousands of larvae are released which promptly fasten themselves to the gill-rakers of the fish and stay there until they have converted themselves into the final stage in which they will spend the remainder of their lives.

SALTWATER PEARLS AND SHELL

Some of the finest pearls in all the world are found in Caribbean waters and in the bays along the Pacific Coasts of Mexico and Central America. The Gulf of California is especially noted for its steely-gray specimens which, known as *black* pearls, are often exceptionally large and fine. All commercially valuable pearls are obtained from the species belonging to the genera *Avicula* and *Pinctada* of the family *Aviculidae*. The Pinctadas provide the major portion of pearls and shell while only a single species of the Aviculas, *A. vinesi*, has provided some pearls from a series of shell beds located in the northern reaches of the Gulf of California near the outlet of the Colorado River.

The pearl-bearing shellfish included in the Aviculas and Pinctadas are commonly called "oysters" although they are not in any way related to the common edible oysters of cooler waters of both the Atlantic Coast (*Ostrea virginica* & *O. borealis*) and the Pacific Coast (*Ostrea lurida*). Although edible species occasionally produce pearls, one glance at either their drab shells or their equally drab pearls is sufficient to dispel any notion that they are related. A further distinction is apparent in the size and shape of the shell pairs which in the edible oysters are extremely uneven in general form and one valve is always considerably larger than the other. In the pearly oysters, both valves are regular in form, sometimes even beautifully symmetrical, and almost exactly alike in size. Furthermore, pearly oysters shortly after a free-swimming phase following spawning, attach themselves to the ocean bottom by means of hairlike fibers growing from near the hinge known as the *byssus* and thus proclaim their near relationship to the common edible saltwater mussel (*Mytilus edulis*) which does likewise. The greatest difference of course, is the typical pearly nature of one as compared to the other.

In the waters of the Caribbean Sea and the Gulf of Mexico, only one important pearl-bearing species, the *Pinctada radiata*, is found in any quantity although a very small and useless Avicula is also known. The northern-

most *radiatas* are found in beds along the Mexican coasts of Campeche Bay
near Coatzocalcos. A bed ten miles in length near Punta San Cristobal was
worked by private enterprise under license from the Mexican Government
in 1910, producing, it is said, some very fine pearls including black pearls.
Further east, some excellent pearls have been recovered from *radiata* beds
fished from waters along the north coast of Haiti. As a genus, the Pinctadas
are noted for the thinness of their shells, frequently so thin as to be quite
translucent. The exterior is very gnarled and rough although the shell itself
is gracefully formed. The hinge is wide and forms "wings" which reach a
total width almost that of the shell diameter. The Caribbean species ranges
from 1 ½ to 3 inches in diameter, averaging about 2 inches and is found predominantly in shallow water attached to rocks. Although the fragile shells
are completely valueless, the pearls are of topnotch quality and much in
demand. It is interesting to note that a close relative, the *Pinctada martensi,*
provides the cultured pearls of Japan. Records show that in 1869, British
firms imported West Indian pearls valued at $214,000 from fisheries sur-
rounding the islands of St. Thomas, now a United States possession, and
Grenada. St. Thomas is a small island of the Virgin Island Group lying just
east of Puerto Rico while Grenada is the southernmost of the Lesser Antilles
in the chain known as the Windward Islands and not far removed from the
famous pearl-fishing grounds around Isla de Margarita (Island of Pearl), a
possession of Venezuela, and for many years, one of the world's most important sources of fine pearls. Productive shells beds are found wherever currents and suitable bottom conditions exist within the Caribbean Sea and
include places along the north coast of South America, on the east coasts of
Costa Rica and Nicaragua but not along much of the coasts of Panama where
the sea waters are inclined to be stagnant and lacking the steadiness of water
flow which the pearl-bearing shellfish require. In Nicaragua, a few fine pearls
have been recovered from beds on the east coast near San Juan del Norte.
Radiata pearls are noted for their white or near-white body color, often
decidedly tinged with gold or yellow. They enjoy a fine reputation in the
trade both on account of their beautiful translucent orient and their perfect
form. Their specific gravity ranges from 2.65 to 2.75.

The narrow strip of land comprising the Isthmus of Darien in the
Republic of Panama and separating the waters of the Atlantic from those of
the Pacific, marks an enormous difference between the types of pearl-bearing
oysters for those on the Pacific side, perhaps geographically only 50 miles
or so removed from Atlantic species, are much larger and thicker while their
pearls tend strongly to deeper colors, especially in steel-gray and blue-gray
(black pearls). The principal species found in Panamanian waters is one and
the same as that which is fished from the 3000 mile stretch of water terminating in the Gulf of California in northwestern Mexico and is known as

Pinctada margaritifera mazatlanica, a compound name signifying the genus, the species, in this case *margaritifera* showing its alliance to the true pearly oyster found elsewhere in the Pacific and Indian Oceans, and in *mazatlanica*, the varietal name after its occurrence near Mazatlan on the Pacific coast of mainland Mexico. The *mazatlanica* produces shells of excellent commercial quality, combining an average size of 6 inches to some which are 8 inches in diameter, good thickness of shell, and fine bright silvery nacre. The lips of the valves are tinged dark green while the exteriors are colored pale yellow or pale brown but the latter is often effectively disguised by a multitude of sea growths which attach themselves during the lifetime of the oyster. The varieties obtained in the Bay of Panama where formerly the foremost fisheries were located, as well as those found further north, are known as "Panama shell" and enjoy a fine reputation among users of mother of pearl. The greatest part of the nacre is beautiful silvery white, tinges of other colors, especially green and black appearing along the lips, however, the pearls themselves frequently deviate from this character, often appearing in greenish tinges, in greenish-gray and various shades of steely-gray or bluish-gray. In years past the major source of revenue has been in the sale of the shells with pearls reckoned only as a welcome sideline, however, the development of extensive oyster fisheries along the coasts of Australia where similar *margaritiferas* thrive and produce magnificent large shells often reaching 10 inches or more in diameter, has caused the eclipse of the Panamanian and Central American fisheries which presently lie dormant.

Locally the best pearl beds surround the Islas de las Perlas or Pearl Islands, situated about 40 miles south of Panama City. The finest shells and pearls have been fished from the waters in the immediate vicinity of Isla San Jose.

As mentioned before, suitable bottom conditions, currents, and other factors, influencing the growth of pearl oysters cause a succession of beds to appear all along the Pacific coast of Central America to as far north as the Gulf of California where exceptionally important beds which will be described shortly, provide a supply of shells. West of the Bay of Panama, fine shells and pearls have been fished from the waters of the coast and from the islands of Contreras, Secas, Jicaron, Coibita, and Coiba. Reefs in the Chiriqui Lagoon or Golfo de Chiriqui have also been productive as well as scattered beds along the south coasts of the Panamanian provinces of Panama, Chiriqui, and Veraguas. From Punta Burica in Panama, rich beds occur northwestward to connect with prolific fishing grounds along the shores of Golfo Dulce in the southwestern corner of Costa Rica. Further northwest along the coast, well-populated beds appear from near Ocos in Mexico close to the border of Guatemala, and extend as far as Mazatlan in Mexico. Quantities of pearl oysters again appear in the waters of the Gulf of California along both the

FIGURE 174. A recent photograph taken at the San Francisquito Bay pearling grounds of Baja California, Mexico, showing John D. Craig of Los Angeles examining several pearls which have just been extracted from *Pinctadas*. Note the shell in the foreground showing the typical "hourglass" or "winged" outline of the *Pinctada*. Courtesy John D. Craig.

mainland coast and the east coast of Baja California as well as upon the reefs surrounding the islands within the Gulf and even as far north as the outlet of the Colorado River.

Although known to local Indians for hundreds of years before, the astonishing pearl resources of the Gulf of California were first revealed to white men in 1535 when Hernando Cortez' expedition landed upon the island formerly known as Isla Santiago and now named Isla Cerralvo, the southernmost island in the gulf. The beds were worked more or less vigorously up to 1941, a period of over 400 years, but in the latter year a peculiar blight struck the beds and virtually exterminated the oyster population. However, members of the Pearling Guild, the modern organization which for many years has been established in Baja California to regulate pearl fishing, discovered a few beds in which the oysters were untouched by the disease or had developed a resistance to its ravages. Breeding oysters were removed from these beds and distributed to other reefs known to provide

FIGURE 175. At the San Francisquito Bay pearling grounds of Baja California Mexico, several Mexican "skin divers" are bringing up the shells of the pearl-bearing *Pinctada margaritifera mazatlanica* while the boatman is keeping position over the well-populated bed. The light-skinned lad is a member of John D. Craig's party who explored the pearling grounds recently and filmed interesting views and scenes of pearling life. Courtesy John D. Craig, Los Angeles, California.

favorable growth conditions. The transplanting operations were successful and in recent years, as shown in Figures 174 and 175 profitable pearling on a modest scale has been resumed.

Until 1874, all fishing had been carried on by the use of native divers who descended to a maximum depth of about 35 feet in their search for oysters. However, in that year, diving suits were introduced which enabled attainment of depths of 180 feet as well as permitting divers to spend several hours at a time on the bottom. Today's fishing techniques are very simple and merely call for the use of small boats large enough to hold the daily catch, a crude air-pumping apparatus, and several crew members in addition to the diver. The latter, when lowered to the bottom, collects oysters which he places in a wire basket. When full, he tugs on the line and the basket is hauled up and emptied. In this way fishing proceeds until the daily stint is done. Because of currents and dangerously rough waters stirred by the late afternoon winds, as well as the heat of the day, fishing is carried on in the morning only between the hours of 9 and 12 while the afternoon is devoted to cleaning the catch and repairing the gear. After the morning's fishing, each crew returns to the beach where the oysters are piled up in the shade of a tarpaulin and, as shown in Figure 174 the opening ceremony is done by all hands facing each other with a shell half set in their midst to receive the pearls. This routine is followed each day until the season is closed and at this time, the take is divided as follows: for the diver—70 per cent, for the line tender—20 per cent, for the remainder of the crew—10 per cent to be split among them. The fishing season today is carefully regulated by the rather secretive Pearling Guild which permits only a two-months season each year. In this relatively short period, each crew will beach about 20,000 oysters. Fishing is done first next to shore in waters seldom over 35 feet deep and without the benefit of diving suits; as these beds are exhausted, the boats move out into waters to 70 feet in depth but are forced to use their rather crude but effective diving gear. Shallow water fishing is less bothersome without such gear and consequently, as shown in Figure 175, all shells are brought up by the divers unencumbered by swimming fins or goggles. The waters of the Gulf are exceedingly clear enabling the divers to see exactly what they are looking for. Modern fishing is confined to the vicinity of La Paz and Tiburon (shark) Island. Some corals are also collected for specimen purposes. In the Gulf of California, the tidal range is about 20 feet and consequently the currents are swift during high and low water slacks. Formerly the fishing season lasted from June to December and 3 hours of active fishing were engaged in each day during slack water. A good day's work for the average diver in the days when diving gear was not available produced about 120 shellfish although the best men averaged about 180.

The principal species in the Gulf of California, the *Pinctada margaritifera mazatlanica*, locally known as the "concha de perla fina," generally exhibits pure silvery-white nacre striped with vague bluish-gray or yellow bands and rimmed at the lips with dark green bands, and resembles closely its near-relative, the black-lip oyster of Australia. In size, they range from 2 to 8 inches in diameter, averaging about 5 inches. They are mostly found on rocky bottoms where they attach themselves tenaciously by the byssus. Their position is vertical and the grip of the byssus is often so strong that it is necessary for the diver to cut it through although most can be detached with a firm twist. The pearls themselves are found encased in a black jelly-like transparent membrane (mantle) which provides the outermost covering of the animal. The shells are usually completely disguised by dense growths of seaweed and marine organisms. In weight, mazatlanicas average 7000 to the ton. The pearls are noted for their wide variety of color of which the steely-gray or bluish-gray "black" pearls are by far the best known. Some of these are truly magnificent and deserve their lasting fame as objects of beauty. Other hues are also known, namely: greenish, brownish, numerous shades of gray and blue gray, and of course, all shades of white. Fine blacks are valued considerably over pure whites. Large pearls are fairly common. The forms are variable, ranging from perfect spheres to pear-shaped, egg-shaped, or flattened "button" pearls. Many are found attached to the shells and of course are far less valuable than free specimens. In years past, virtually all pearls were exported straight to London or Paris. The present trade channels are not known to the author.

The largest Gulf pearl of record is ¾ inch in diameter and originally sold in Paris to a representative of the Emperor of Austria for $10,000. Another enormous pearl of about 400 grains was found near Loreto and dispatched to Spain to become part of the royal regalia. The Bay of Mulege on the east coast of Baja California once yielded a specimen the size of small bird's egg which also weighed about 400 grains. During 1883, a light brown pearl speckled by darker shades of this color and weighing 260 grains was recovered from the Gulf and was valued at $8,000. Another, a pear-shaped gem, white in color and speckled with dark tints, weighed 176 grains and was valued at $7,500. In 1881, a black pearl of 162 grains fetched $10,000 in Paris.

The range of *P. margaritifera mazatlanica* is throughout the entire Gulf although the most heavily populated beds are concentrated along the east coast of Baja California in the 300 mile stretch from Cape San Lucas to the Bay of Mulege. The best beds skirt the shores of the numerous islands which form a chain some 200 miles in length from Punta de la Ventana to the Bay of Mulege. The islands which have been most productive are Cerralvo, Espiritu Santo, Carmen, Tiburon, and San Jose whose waters range from 12 to 150 feet in depth for some distance offshore. In addition, excellent beds formerly existed near Loreto, in the vicinity of Punta Lorenzo just north of La Paz, in the harbor of La Paz and in that of Picheluigo.

In the extreme northern section of the Gulf, the second pearl-bearing species found in these waters, the *Avicula vinesi*, formerly was abundant in beds very near the mouth of the Colorado River but like the Pinctadas has also markedly declined in population. Its shell is as thin as its cousin in the Atlantic and is useless as mother of pearl but early fishermen stated that its pearls were unusually common and often of excellent quality.

Next in rank to the conventional pearl-bearing shellfish just noted are the several species of abalone or *Haliotidae*. Commercially, their pearls and shell are far less valuable than those obtained from the pearl oysters of the gem trade but the fishery is large and economically important in California and Mexico. The principal product of the abalone fishery is the tough but tasty meat which comprises the huge central muscle used by the abalones for moving about upon reefs and for clamping down their shells when disturbed. Much of the gorgeously colored iridescent shell is also used decoratively including numerous applications in inexpensive jewelry, but pearls are a decided rarity and seldom offered for sale.

Within the mollusca, abalones are included under the *gastropoda*, a name which literally means "stomach walker" from the fact that the shellfish of this class move about on a single muscular appendage or "foot" which is continuous with the remainder of the body, including the intestinal tract. The genus *Haliotis* is represented with useful species only along the Pacific shorelines of North America as follows:

COMMON NAME	SPECIES NAME	SIZE	HABITAT
Red abalone	*H. rufescens*	10″-12″	N. California to Mex.
Green abalone	*H. fulgens*	7″-8″	Calif. to Mexico
Pink abalone	*H. corrugata*	5″-7″	Monterey, Calif. to Mex.
Threaded abalone	*H. assimilis*	4″-5″	California
Japanese abalone	*H. kamtschatkana*	4″-6″	S. Alaska to N. Calif.
Black abalone	*H. cracherodi*	4″-6″	California to Mexico

The form of the abalone is very characteristic and unlike that of most of the snails which belong among the gastropoda. The coiled spire in the abalone is very flat and really consists of only one large whorl whose opening is the mouth of the shell. Even more characteristic is the row of holes which proceeds in a gentle curve from near the lip crossing over the arch of the shell somewhat to one side of the crown. These holes are located over a slit in the mantle fold which leads to the gill cavity and provides the exit for waste products. The holes range in size from ⅛ to ⅜ inch in diameter and number about three or four. These follow the spiral pattern of the shell and as the animal attains maturity, the earlier smaller vents are fused shut by deposits of nacre. As the animal grows in size, burrowing creatures, especially the boring *Pholididea parva* mollusk, raise havoc with the shell and frequently penetrate to the interior where further access is denied by the creation of a blister. However, out of about 1000 abalones, only one shows such a blister pearl due to this cause.

Abalones prefer depths of water from about 6 to 60 feet along rocky shore-lines. By suitable movements of its foot, the abalone is able to move about fairly rapidly, preferring in all cases, to proceed along smooth rocks where it can clamp down its shell by arching the central muscle and thus creating an enormous suction. The force of suction developed is almost incredible; a flat iron thrust carelessly under the edge of the shell will, if left there, cause the animal to fasten itself so tenaciously that the shell will be shattered by attempts to dislodge it before the muscle will relax its tension. Gathering abalones accordingly calls for precise and quick movements on the part of the fisherman who must insert his iron tool under the edge of the shell and pry upward before the animal is aware that he is being disturbed. Tales are told along the California coast of luckless divers who drowned when they rashly attempted to pry an abalone loose with their fingers and were caught in a vise-like grip from which there was no escape. Fishing for abalones has been carried on for many years by the Indians of the Pacific Coast and the pursuit of this shellfish was taken up by the white man when he arrived upon the scene and in later years by the Chinese and Japanese to whom the meat of the abalone is a highly prized article of the diet. Today much meat is consumed locally either ground up for chowder or for patties, or the entire muscle beaten with a mallet to make it more tender for frying.

The utilization of the shell for ornamental purposes is also of long standing, and dates back to an indefinite time in the past when the Indians learned to make fish hooks, needles, and other objects of utility as well as shaping exceptionally fine pieces into pendants and other items of ornament. Even today the Indian silversmiths of the Southwestern United States employ abalone shell for inlay in silver jewelry along with coral and turquois (see TURQUOIS). The black and green abalones are particularly vivid in coloration, the latter shell aptly being described as like a peacock's tailfeathers in appearance. Although all of the shell is useful for ornamental purposes, the brightest colors and most intricate patterns are found within a small patch just under the dome of the shell corresponding to the place where the large central muscle is attached. Abalone shells are frequently polished whole for objects of decoration or for ashtrays. The exterior is first given a rough grinding on silicon carbide wheels fed with water and then sanded on a felt wheel to which loose silicon carbide grit has been applied. The final lustrous polish is applied with a felt polishing buff impregnated with tripoli. When cut into ornaments, as many as 15 pieces can be removed from the shell including a curved section of the lip which can be fashioned into a miniature paper knife. Flatter pieces may be sawed into animal or bird representations and used as pendants, or if flat enough, inlaid into wooden boxes.

In respect to pearls, both blister and free pearls are found although the latter are naturally much more rare than the first. Blister pearls have been known to form about an astounding variety of objects which have found their way into the space between the mantle and the shell. Rarely, a small crab is the cause of a blister pearl and one instance has been known where a blister reproduced perfectly the outlines of such an unwelcome guest. Blister pearls also form over fragments of sea urchin spines, chiton shells, razor clam shell fragments, and pebbles. Good examples of blisters are in demand for use in artistic jewelry, particularly pieces created in the modern "free form" style. Pearls are generally green, blue-green, or yellow to pink in color and always intensely hued. Their surface texture is far more coarse and scaly than that noted in pearls taken from members of the Pelecypoda. Seldom spherical in form, most examples are elongated masses of approximately circular outline, sometimes button shaped, or simply irregular. Small examples have sold for as little as $1 but finer pearls of good size may bring as much as $100 and sales of exceptionally large specimens have been known to bring as much as $500 to $1000. The maximum size of abalone pearls is about 80 grains although baroques may reach as much as 240 grains.

The distribution of abalones along the Pacific Coast of North America is fairly well defined in the southern stretches but the distribution of the Japanese abalone in Alaska is not so clearly established. However, this species is known to be abundant along the shores of Prince of Wales Island and also Baranof Island. In British Columbia, extensive beds are found along the ocean shores of the Queen Charlotte Islands. In California, the principal beds are along the reefs of Catalina, Santa Rosa, and other Channel Islands located offshore of Los Angeles. In the San Francisco Bay region, abalones have been fished for many years from the vicinity of Halfmoon Bay and along the shores of Mendocino County. The rocky shores of Point Loma near San Diego have been especially productive. Similar rocky shores extend southward from San Diego all along the Mexican states of Baja California Norte and Baja California Sud.

In another division of the great class of Gastropoda are found several interesting and beautiful shellfish whose calcareous shells sometimes lend themselves to uses in the lapidary arts as well as providing from one of the families involved a modest quantity of pearls. The best known of these shellfish inhabit the warm waters of the West Indies and parts of Florida and comprise members of the families *Strombidae* and *Cassididae*, the former including the well-known *Strombus Gigas*, or giant conch, and the second including the *Cassis madagascarensis*, the helmet shell.

Conches, like other Gastropoda, are actually snails and exhibit a similar shell form consisting of a tapered tube coiled into a spire with a large flaring mouth from which issues the animal. All conches thrive on the flat-topped coral reefs which abound in the West Indies and the Florida Keys. When alarmed, the animal promptly withdraws into the inner recesses of the shell and it is impossible to extract him unless the shell is cooked or the tip knocked off to release the suction which he is capable of applying against the smooth inner sides. Giant conches often reach very large sizes, some attaining heights of at least 10 inches but the average is perhaps 6 to 8 inches. The cameo conches are generally smaller by several inches.

Conch pearls are not iridescent like the precious pearls of the gem trade but do possess an attractive shimmering luster which with the lovely pink color makes them sought after. The pearls are seldom exactly round, almost every one being somewhat elongated like a watermelon. Colors are chiefly some shade of pink, with or without patches or zones of white, but salmon pink, yellow, and even purplish-black specimens have been found. In time, like the pink inner lining of the shell itself, conch pearls fade and it is this which has caused them to lose favor in the jewelry trade. Prior to 1900, the vogue for pearls was largely satisfied by specimens captured on the reefs of Eleuthera and Exuma Islands in the Bahamas and the pearls marketed primarily in Nassau. In 1930, a pure white conch pearl weighing 16 grains was brought in to Key West and was said to have sold for $1500. In 1931, a fine small pearl of 8 grains was found at the Dry Tortugas and $50 was offered for it.

FIGURE 176. A cameo figure representing Columbus cut in a helmet shell. Although the specimen illustrated is probably from the Red Sea or perhaps from waters surrounding Madagascar, the form of the shell and the contrasting colored layers are very similar to helmet shells from the West Indies. Courtesy Fish & Wildlife Service.

The several members of the genus Cassis, although occasionally furnishing curious if not beautiful pearls, are prized chiefly for the layered shells which can be cut into cameos. In fact, one of the species, *Cassis cameo*, obviously receives its name from this feature of its structure. The range of the Cassidae corresponds roughly to that of the Strombidae and since members of both families are very similar, species of each may be found on the same reefs. Although cameos have been carved chiefly from the Cassidae because of the much stronger contrast in hue between the exterior white or cream-colored layers and inner brown layers, the giant conch has also been extensively employed for this purpose although the gradation in color between the white and pink is less strong and requires bolder carving treatment to provide an effective contrast. Practically all shell cameos now appearing upon the market are carved in Italy at Torre del Greco a few miles from Naples from raw shell obtained from African or Eastern waters. An attractive cameo cut into a helmet shell is illustrated in Figure 176.

Fairly attractive small pearls are also furnished by the ordinary edible sea mussel (*Mytilus edulis*) whose densely-packed colonies adhere to sea walls and piles along the colder waters of both the Pacific and Atlantic coasts of North America. The interior of these black-skinned mussels is grayish-purple in color and possesses a feeble iridescence which is reflected in the pearls. The latter may be an attractive pink, purple, bronze, or yellow but are seldom very large. In Alaskan waters near Baranof on Baranof Island in Southeastern Alaska, mussels are abundant and Fred Bahovec informs the author that he has collected many small pearls which he believes were ultimately disposed of to Japan for use as nuclei in the growth of cultured pearls. Mr. Bahovec states that the pearls range in size from less than 1/16 inch to as much as ⅜ inch in diameter with the larger specimens tending to be irregular in form. The colors found ranged from white, pale blue, orchid, dark blue, greenish-blue, to black. One noteworthy exception was a pearl of gold color but this was very small in size. Another type was shaped like a button with an "eye" of contrasting color; still another type was like a flattened round biscuit.

The hard clam, quohog, or *Venus mercenaria* of the East Coast of the United States and Canada has also produced pearls but of course, these cannot be of great value since the calcareous shell matter of this animal is no more beautiful than a piece of ordinary white china. However, they do occur and sometimes arouse hopes in their finders that they have a "pearl beyond price." A fine specimen was found about 1941 in a deformed clam taken from a mud flat in the Indian River, a tributary to Milford Harbor in Connecticut. The pearl was ovoid, symmetrically formed, pale pink in color, and measured approximately ½ inch in length and weighed 15½ carats. The shell in which it was found was curiously deformed, and, as other observers have noted, often indicates that a large pearl is within.

Lackluster pearls are also found from time to time in the several edible oysters of the Pacific and Atlantic coasts of North America but have nothing to commend them except their curiosity value. It is often said that such pearls would be fine in quality were they not heated excessively during cooking, however, this is not the case since those which have been extracted from the raw mollusks are soft and dull and their appearance is neither improved nor detracted from by cooking.

FRESHWATER PEARLS AND SHELL

It is not popularly appreciated that in the freshwaters of North America are found enormous numbers of mollusks whose shells are beautifully iridescent and sufficiently thick to be useful for a variety of ornamental purposes while the pearls found within them are often fully as fine as those recovered from comparable saltwater species. Nacreous "clams" or "mussels," as they are popularly called, are found in virtually every watershed of North and Central America from the Arctic Regions through Canada, the United States, Mexico, and abundantly even in the torrid tropical regions of Panama. The family of bivalve mollusca to which these species belong is the *Unionidae* with the several hundred species being spread among over forty genera. Freshwater mussels have been most extensively utilized in the United States whose waters contain the largest number of species of any comparable region in the entire world and whose shells are without peer in respect to quality and size. The following species are the most important and have been utilized mainly for mother of pearl for making buttons or as sources of beautiful, deeply-hued pearls of considerable value:

In appearance, the Unionidae are characterized by two valves of equal size and shape covered by a thin conchiolin membrane which varies from pale olive-green through black. The general profile is oval although the Quadrulas are inclined to be squarish or rectangular in outline with rounded corners. Some species are very elongate and form thin graceful ovals as in the Alasmodons. The thickness is also variable; some species are exceedingly thin in cross-section while others are as plump as the common saltwater clam and probably from the similarity, gave rise to the name "clam" for certain of the freshwater Unionidae. Aside from the Alasmodons, Anodontas, and the Elliptios which inhabit in large numbers many watersheds flowing into the Atlantic Ocean, almost all other genera are found in the great central watershed of the Mississippi River. The relatives of the Anodontas are furthermore characterized by graceful elongated oval outlines and thin shells which are frequently so translucent that it is possible to hold the shellfish up to the light and observe the faint outlines of the viscera. Unlike other genera, they also prefer quiet waters, lake bottoms, and even silty or muddy bottoms so long as the silt is not frequently disturbed. In contrast, the species of the Mississippi watershed prefer rather swift-flowing clear streams with naturally sandy or gravelly bottoms. However, other species in this watershed survive well on bottoms which are silty or in waters which are decidedly muddy. The depth of water generally seems unimportant and good shells may be gathered from waters which are only ankle-deep or over a man's head. The

GENUS	SPECIES	POPULAR NAME	REMARKS
Actinonaias	*A. carinata*	Mucket. Especially valuable for buttons.	
Anodonta	several	Mussel. Thin-shelled; common in the Atlantic drainage of the N.E. United States & Canada.	
Crenodonta	*C. plicata*	Three ridge or bluepoint. Noted for large numbers of pearls.	
Ellipsaria	*E. lineolata*	Butterfly.	
Elliptio	*E. complanata*	Mussel. Common in the Atlantic drainage of the Eastern United States.	
Fusconaia	*F. ebena*	Niggerhead. Excellent button shell.	
Lampsilis	*L. anodontoides*	Yellow sand shell. Often provides the most valuable pearls and the longest pieces of mother of pearl useful for such purposes as knife handles.	
	L. siliquoidea	Fat mucket.	
	L. ventricosus	Pocketbook.	
Lasmigona	*L. complanata*	Hackleback or white heel-splitter.	
Margaritifera	*M. margaritifera*	Pearl mussel. Thin-shelled; found in Atlantic drainage of N.E. United States and Canada. A subspecies with purplish nacre and sometimes producing beautiful colored pearls is common in the waters of the Northwestern United States and Western Canada.	
Megalonaias	*M. gigantea*	Washboard; up to 10″ in length.	
Plethobasus	*P. cyphyus*	Bullhead.	
Potamilus	*P. alatus*	Purple heel-splitter.	
Quadrula	*Q. pustulosa*	Warty back.	
	Q. quadrula	Mapleleaf.	
Tritigonia	*T. verrucosa*	Buckhorn.	

depth of water is important in one respect and that is, it must be constant and not subject to drastic changes in level. Not all species develop iridescent nacre, some grow only a white material which is feebly pearly at best but others develop mother-of-pearl which shines and glows with many pastel tints ranging from pink, brown, lavender, green, etc. Many species, especially among those of the Mississippi watershed, provide pure silvery white nacre with only the slightest trace of color. The size of shells is variable but as a general rule they vary from several inches to as much as 10 inches in length. The thickness of the shells, an important consideration in the manufacture of buttons, may be as much as ¾ inch although the average is probably about ½ inch in the thickest parts. Like the saltwater pearl-bearing oysters, the animal is fitted with a thin transparent enveloping membrane, the mantle, which sheaths the organs and provides the mechanism for the deposit of nacre upon the walls of the valves.

The habitat of the Unionidae is always upon the bottom in which they burrow and permit only the lips of the valves to protrude above. When undisturbed, these lips can be seen separated by a gap of perhaps ⅛ inch to ¼ inch lined with the waving edges of the mantle. If a wedge-shaped twig is inserted, the animal contracts the valve-closing muscle with such force that the entire shellfish can be wrenched from the bed with the twig alone. In the waters of the Mississippi, this is taken advantage of in fishing by dragging a pole along the bottom from which are suspended a number of lines equipped with steel treble-hooks without barbs. As this "crowfoot bar," as it is called, is towed along the bottom, any mussel unfortunate enough to feel one of the hook prongs enter the shell opening, clamps down upon it and is forthwith dragged from his bed. Involuntarily, the animal retains his grip so long as the obstruction is felt and thus is easily hauled up after the fisherman completes a run along a selected stretch of the river or lake. Other "clammers" use tongs to feel along the bottom and dislodge the shellfish while still others walk along the bottom and when a shellfish is felt with their bare feet, reach down and collect the animal. In clear waters, a number are also recovered by diving.

Although the Unionidae often produce finely-formed pearls of beautiful luster and color, they are perhaps unique among shellfish for the quantity of baroque and "slug" pearls found within them. One authority believes that their life in swiftly-flowing streams, subject to spring floods and the washing down of much debris, greatly enhances the likelihood that foreign matter will force its way into the inner recesses of the shell where pearls will eventually be formed. Those shells which produce pearls of substantial size seem often deformed in shape, bulging or bent, or otherwise lacking the smooth contours characteristic of a healthy shellfish. On the other hand, perfectly symmetrical shells indicate completely normal growth and the absence of any accidents which may have forced foreign particles into the recesses of the shell. In such examples, only fine mother of pearl is found but seldom any pearls of consequence. After a fisherman accumulates a boatload of shells, he takes them ashore and dumps them into a vat filled with water brought to a simmer by a wood fire built beneath. In a few minutes of steaming, the mussels die and the shells gape open. The shellfish are then cleaned of the viscera which are carefully felt through to detect any pearls. It is popularly believed in some gemological circles that steaming destroys the orient of freshwater pearls but this is actually not the case. The vast majority of pearls of all forms destined for the gem market have been removed from mussels which were processed in the manner just described. Although simmering does not destroy the orient of freshwater pearls, there is reason to believe that saltwater are seriously damaged if subjected to this treatment. Pearls and slugs which have been collected by the individual fishermen are kept in small lots and sold to buyers who frequent the fishing grounds. Most are local residents, perhaps members of jewelry firms of nearby towns, and they in turn also save the pearls in larger lots until buyers from New York or other large cities arrive on their annual rounds to buy large quantities for disposal through normal wholesale gem-trade channels. The shells which are the major source of income to the fishermen, are collected and shipped to pearl button manufacturers.

Since the turn of the Century, the production of mussels has remained at an impressive figure but has suffered a decline in the last decade or so. Figures collected by the U.S. Fish Commission indicate that for 1903, the value of shell was $316,647 while the value of pearls and slugs was $213,451. In 1906, various rivers of the Mississippi watershed produced pearls and slugs valued at $381,000 as well as 43,500 tons of shells valued at $348,000. In that year the production from the Wabash River alone was estimated at from $100,000 to $150,000. At this time, pearls sold for from $1 to $2000 each while slugs received from $1.50 to $60 per ounce. Some interesting statistics gathered in 1906 indicated that most pearls sold were either white or cream with lesser quantities of pink, purple, blue, and rarely, steel-gray. The occurrence of various shapes was as follows: irregular—40%; button—25%; round—15%; oval—10%; pear—5%; drop—5%. In 1910, an estimated $100,000 worth of pearls were produced from Illinois of which $10,000 was credited to the Fox River and the remainder from the Illinois River. In that year shells for making buttons sold for from $15 to $25 a ton. In 1953, fishermen on the Mississippi River near McGregor, Iowa, found several large pearls one of which was sold for $400 and the smaller of the two for $250. In 1955, the production of shell and pearls (and slugs) from rivers of the Mississippi drainage amounted to 32,366,000 pounds valued at $684,000 with an additional value of $64,000 for pearls and slugs. The production by states and watersheds are shown in the table on the next page.

From this it can be seen that the major production of pearls and slugs is presently obtained from the Tennessee, Alabama, and White Rivers.

LOCALITIES

It would be almost impossible to name every stream within the North American continent wherein Unionidae have been found and the best that can be done is to list briefly a few streams and other bodies of water in which those interested may hunt for shellfish.

Alaska and Canada. Only several species of importance are known from Alaska and Northern Canada but pearls of fine quality are sometimes found in them. Good pearls have been found in mussels of the Ungava Region of Labrador and Quebec, in the Nelson River drainage of Manitoba, and in

1955 PRODUCTION BY STATES

STATE	SHELL (LBS.)	VALUE	VALUE PEARLS & SLUGS
Alabama	13,564,000	$271,000	$25,000
Arkansas	5,532,000	136,000	13,000
Illinois	18,000	—	—
Indiana	1,004,000	19,000	2,000
Kentucky	4,348,000	98,000	9,000
Tennessee	7,900,000	160,000	15,000

1955 PRODUCTION BY RIVERS

Mississippi	1,106,000	27,000	2,000
Ohio	2,934,000	66,000	7,000
Tennessee & Alabama	22,878,000	463,000	43,000
Wabash	928,000	17,000	1,000
White	4,520,000	111,000	11,000

Data from Fish & Wildlife Service Fishery Statistics of the United States, 1955.

numerous streams in Ontario, Quebec, and the Maritime Provinces; also Newfoundland. The Mackenzie River drainage of the North West Territories, the Saskatchewan River drainage of Saskatchewan, and Lake Winnipeg in Manitoba also provide occasional pearls and slugs from native species.

Maine. Streams in the western part of the state as well as those near Moosehead Lake have provided a few fine pearls.

Massachusetts. Mussels producing fine but small pearls occur in many ponds and rivers; the Nonesuch Pond in Middlesex County, has produced a few from the *Elliptio complanata*. Ponds in Greenwich and Pelham townships in Hampshire County have also furnished some fine pearls said to be the best found in the state. The Sudbury River above Concord and the Connecticut River have also been productive.

Connecticut. From the headwaters of the Mystic River; also in the Shepaug River and in lakes and streams in Litchfield County.

New York. In many streams of the northern part of the state draining into the St. Lawrence River; specifically from the Grass River; in the upper reaches of the Hudson River and tributaries; in the Pearl River and others in Rockland and other southern counties.

New Jersey. In virtually all streams and lakes of the northern part of the state, particularly such lakes as Greenwood Lake, Lake Hopatcong, Green Pond, etc.

Pennsylvania. Headwaters of the Schuylkill River near Tamaqua, Quakake, and Mahonoy City, also such tributaries as Lewiston, Nipert, Still, Locust, and Hecla creeks. Some fine and large pearls have been obtained in blue, lavender, pink, and cream or white colors.

Maryland. From brooks at the head of Chesapeake Bay in Kent and Cecil counties; all colors but small in size.

Virginia. In the Clinch River, James River, and tributaries; in Powell River.

North Carolina. Sometimes in large quantity in the Neuse River, Yadkin River, Cape Fear River, Catawba River, Roanoke River, Irwins Creek; Long Creek, Livingstons Creek, etc.

South Carolina. Cooper River, Congaree River, and Santee Canal; also many other streams and tributaries to the large rivers mentioned.

Florida. Freshwater pearly mussels are extremely widespread, almost every one of the slow-moving streams and shallow lakes being abundantly stocked. Pearls are rare but have been found in mussels from the Ocklockonee River and the Sopchoppy, a tributary; also from Lake George and Lake Monroe in Seminole County; Lake Griffin in Lake County, and Lake Okeechobee. Other mussel streams and lakes are: St. Mary's River, Small Creek, Orange Springs, Withlacoochee River, Appalachicola River, Suwanee River, Escambia River, Lake Ashby, and Lake Beresford.

Georgia. Mussels are abundant; many pearls from those in the Etowah and Oostanaula Rivers near Rome; also from Johns Creek a tributary of the latter. Sometimes fine pearls are found in the mussels of Flint River, Ocmulgee River and Ocanee River. The Ogeechee River in Bryan County has produced fine shell and pearls; also from streams in Montgomery and Wheeler counties. A few pearls have been found in Bulltown and Altamaha swamps in Liberty County. Other streams are: Connasauga River, Othcalooga Creek, Swamp Creek, Chattanooga River, Chattahoochee River, Spanish Creek, Appalachicola River, Spring Creek, and Stump Creek.

Alabama. Shell production important; pearls are common. The following streams contain important species: Alabama River, Tennessee River, Tombigbee River, Black Warrior River, Coosa River, Cahawba River, Patsaliga and Little Patsaliga creeks, Big Prairie Creek, Village Creek, Uphaupee Creek, Swamp Creek, and North River.

Tennessee. Large quantities from a number of streams (see text) especially the Cumberland, Tennessee, and Clinch rivers; also from Stone River, Harpeth River, Holston River, Duck Creek, Calf Killer Creek, Watauga River, Big Pigeon River, French Broad River, Hiawassee River, Tellico River, Caney Fork, Powell River, and Elk River.

Kentucky. Green River; also Tennessee River (see text).

Ohio. Ohio River, Scioto River, and many other streams; fine pink pearls have been obtained from the Little Miami River in Warren County near Waynesville and from the Miami Canal.

Indiana and Illinois. The Wabash River has produced and still produces fine pearls from mussels fished for over 150 miles from Lafayette downstream to Vincennes. Good pearls have been taken from streams in Woodford, Tazewell and McLean counties in Illinois.

Iowa. Swift-flowing stretches of the Mississippi River are still productive.

Michigan. Detroit River, Cass River, Rouge River; also many others including those on the Keeweenaw Peninsula.

Wisconsin. Many intensely-colored pearls of fine quality have been found in Lafayette County, especially in the Pecatonica River between Darlington and Gratiot; also from the Sugar River near Brodhead and Albany in Green County; Grant River near Potosi and the Wisconsin River near Boscobel in Grant County; the Mississippi River between Prairie du Chien and Lynxville in Crawford County; generally in streams in Calumet and Manitowoc counties; also in the Rock River and Apple River.

Arkansas. Many fine pearls from virtually every suitable stream in the state; in the Arkansas River, White River, Ouachita River, Black River, Cache River, St. Francis River, Current River, Little Red River, and Saline River.

Minnesota. Lake of the Woods; St. Peters River; also many others.

Kansas. Spring River; Verdigris River.

Missouri. Jack's Ford; Current River.

Texas. Sabine River, Brazos River, Guadalupe River, Colorado River, Llanos River, Rio Grande River, Trinity River, Concho River, and Caddo Lake.

Washington. Mussels from Tacoma Creek in Pend Oreille County are said to have yielded 27 well-formed pearls of lavender color.

Mexico. Numerous species are found in both the Gulf of Mexico drainages and streams draining toward the Pacific Ocean on the western side; Oaxaca; Jalisco—Lake Chapala; Chiapas—Rio Michel; Yucatan; Nueva Leon—Rio Salado; Vera Cruz—Sapotal River and Medellin River, etc.

Guatemala. Rio Usumasinta, Lake Yzabel, Rio de Salinas.

Nicaragua. Lake Nicaragua.

Honduras. Goascoran River, Patook River.

Also in Costa Rica, Panama, and Cuba.

CORAL

The only North American coral useful for jewelry purposes is a bright red branched *Gorgon* found in the deep waters off the coast and in the channels of Southeastern Alaska. The group to which this coral belongs is the *Alcyonaria*, the specific member found in Alaska being *Primnoa Resedaformis*. All members of this group are related to the sea fans and sea pens and are characterized externally by a single axis with numerous branches spreading outward in a complicated network. The skeletons differ from those of ordinary corals in that they lack a stony calcareous central support member, being instead, flexible and broken only with difficulty. Although bright red in color externally, it is the horny skeleton which is used for gem purposes. The color is dead-black banded with yellow rings and when polished, sometimes shows a faint chatoyancy from the fibrous structure. Deep fishing in Alaskan waters often brings up specimens from as much as 1000 feet below the surface. Recently a Western Atlantic relative of the precious coral of the Mediterranean and the Azores has been found in the West Indies but it is very scarce and only a few specimens for scientific purposes have been obtained.

AMBER

Amber is a familiar substance to many persons, but without special knowledge of its origin, most would not guess that it actually occurs in the earth's crust buried under many layers of sand, clay and gravel, and represents the hardened gummy exudations of long extinct trees. Amber was well known to the ancients for its name comes from the Arabic word *anbar*, later Latinized into *ambar* and thence altered by the French into the modern spelling *ambre* from whence we obtain *amber*. The mineralogical name is *succinite*, derived from the old Latin alternate name: *succinum*. The latter also forms the root for the word describing the principal constituent of amber, *succinic acid*.

Although the ancient amber-producing trees are extinct it is believed that an evergreen very much like our American *Thuja occidentalis*, more familiarly known as Arborvitae or white cedar, was mainly responsible for the production of the resins which ultimately hardened into amber. In the beginning, the Amber Forest covered much of the Northern Hemisphere with vast carpets reaching into what are now Asia and North America. Gigantic upheavals caused extensive areas of this ancient land to be submerged by water while higher parts lost most of their forest covering through destructive erosion. Of this enormous ancient woodland, only small fossil remnants are found here and there, including a few in North America among other places. It is from such sedimentary deposits that amber is obtained whether accidentally through erosion or by purposeful mining. None of the North American deposits yield the profusion of large high quality specimens typical of European sources, but, as described below, some localities are important and others at least interesting.

Amber is found only in weakly-compacted sediments since compression and subjection to more than moderate heat as would occur if the sediments were metamorphosed, would surely have destroyed all traces of its existence.

Amber is a very fragile substance really, and accordingly it is seldom seen in coal harder than lignite, occurring most frequently in loose sands and clays, or sometimes in peat. Being loosely imbedded and light in weight, it is readily detached by erosion, often being carried many miles from its point of origin.

Amber consists almost entirely of carbon (79%), hydrogen (10.5%), and oxygen (10.5%), with slight traces of sulfur and yielding but a fraction of one per cent of ash when fully consumed after burning. As may be expected of its organic origin, it yields readily to heat, softening at 150°C, and melting between 250°C and 325°C. When set afire it burns with a yellowish sooty flame, giving off a typical "piney" aroma. Amber is not a single chemical compound but is a mixture of hydrocarbons, the principal constituent being succinic acid, $COOH(CH_2)_2COOH$, a white crystalline substance which is also found in certain living trees and shrubs. The hardness varies from 2 to 2½; it is fairly tough, and can be carved readily with steel tools into delicate objects. It breaks with a conchoidal fracture leaving smooth glistening surfaces somewhat oily in luster. Because of considerable variation in composition, amber shows specific gravities ranging from 1.05 to 1.10, although some has been found as low as 1.031 and as high as 1.168. Refractive indices are less variable, averaging 1.54. Being a solidified fluid, amber is without crystal structure and therefore shows only one refractive index, however, slight variations in different areas in a single specimen may be noted because it may be made up of more than one flow of sap. In such cases, the interior mass exhibits the same kind of wavy or curved lines seen in water in which sugar syrup has been poured. Much amber is perfectly transparent and without flaw, but minute bubbles or impurities trapped during solidification may render some specimens virtually opaque. Insects often form interesting (and valuable) inclusions since they are perfectly preserved fossils of long extinct species. Good examples command a far higher price than ordinary flawless material. In color, amber varies from pale yellow to reddish- or brownish-yellow to yellowish-brown. When freshly dug, nodules often appear opaque because external layers are filled with sand, soil, or vegetable debris. If found detached from deposits, nodules may be frosted from abrasion or cracked and roughened due to slight surface alteration; in form, they may vary from small droplets to roughly spherical masses, or flattened as if solidified from a puddle of resin. Individual pieces range from minute beads of less than ⅛ inch in diameter to specimens a number of pounds in weight.

LOCALITIES

Greenland. A prolific locality for amber is that at Kudlisat near the southeast tip of Hare Island, a small land mass several miles northwest of the northern extremity of Disko Island on the west coast of Greenland. Here it is found as honey-yellow, brown, or almost black nodules up to ¾ inch in diameter in beds of brown lignite and cannel coal. The harder of these beds pass by degrees into a remarkable soft bituminous wood which still retains much of its original structure. Numerous bits of amber occur associated with the wood and distributed parallel to the bedding. The specific gravity is 1.091. In the Ritenbenk District, clear brown nodules of amber up to ⅜ inch in diameter occur abundantly in coal-bearing clay at Atanikerdluk and Arsarak; masses of golden brown color up to 1¼ inches diameter are found in a schistose sandstone at Unartuarssuk and at Ujaragsugssuk. This material is exceptionally clear; the specific gravity is 1.055.

Manitoba. Beautiful amber called *chemawinite* or *cedarite*, has been found in quantity among the sands and gravels of the southwest margin of Cedar Lake in west central Manitoba. The deposit is believed to be ancient delta material brought down by the Saskatchewan River which enters the lake nearby. Decayed wood fragments are found in profusion along the amber-bearing portion of the beach wherever it has been tested by shallow pits to determine its extent. Amber occurs as water worn nodules up to 1½ inches diameter in a belt from 80 to 120 feet in width extending about one mile along the shore. Many fragments take the form of stalactites and show distinct flow markings. Insects are common in some pieces but are seldom over 1/16 inch in size. The specific gravity averages 1.536; refractive indices lie between 1.035 and 1.051. Cedar Lake amber ranges from pale honey-yellow to dark brown in color, mainly transparent but sometimes heavily spotted with inclusions. Very attractive cabochons up to ¾ inch across have been cut from this material, and, over the years, a considerable quantity has been removed from the deposit but apparently never commercially or in systematic fashion.

British Columbia. Amber occurs associated with coal in many places in this province. In the Nanaimo Mining Division it is found as small grains along the Nechako River south of Fort Fraser, in nodules embedded in shaly sandstone of the Gething formation of Lower Cretaceous age along the Peace River Canyon in the northeastern part of the province, and in small spots and drops on the south bank of the Quesnel River in the Quesnel Mining Division; also in sizeable nodules in the Haida formation of Tertiary and Cretaceous age on Graham Island of the Queen Charlotte Islands off the Pacific coast, and elsewhere.

Alaska. The most northerly cape of this state, Point Barrow, is noted among the Eskimos for amber found in beach gravels and sands. The exact source is not known but it frequently occurs in ¼ inch and larger water-worn fragments between Harrison Bay and Smith Bay. The local Eskimo name for amber is "auma" or "live coal." Further south, fragments have been found in the alluvium of the Yukon River Delta. In the Port Clarence District of northwestern Alaska, pockets of amber were frequently encountered in the Chicago Creek Coal Mine on Chicago Creek, a tributary of the Kugruk River. Coal beds outcrop on certain of the easterly Aleutian Islands as well as on the adjacent portions of the Alaska Peninsula and release amber which finds its way to the beaches of Aliaka, Unalaska, Ookamak, and Umnak Islands of the Fox Island Group. Amber beads have been uncovered in ancient graves on Unalaska Island. Lignite coal beds of the southern coast of the Alaska Peninsula yield a considerable quantity of amber but never in very large pieces. One of the bays of this coast has been named Amber Bay in allusion to its occurrence.

Massachusetts. Tertiary greensand and marl formations of Nantucket Island yield occasional fragments of yellow amber, the largest on record being an unusual specimen weighing 12 ounces and found some years before 1883. Similar sediments outcropping on the steep bluffs of Gay Head on the western tip of Martha's Vineyard also yield small nodules which are picked up from time to time on the beaches below.

New York. Considerable amber was found many years ago in the Androvette Clay Pits near Kreischerville on the shore of Arthur Kill at the southwest tip of Staten Island, Borough of Richmond, New York City. Tears and drops up to ¾ inch occurred in various shades of yellow and reddish yellow; opaque grayish white specimens were also found.

New Jersey. The largest quantity of amber in North America has been produced from a tier of New Jersey counties extending from Middlesex County in the north to Salem County in the south, coinciding with the amber-bearing Cretaceous formations which progress in a broad belt parallel to the sea coast but some miles removed inland. Most was produced incidental to the digging of calcareous sands known as marls, and others bearing glauconite, a hydrous silicate of iron and potassium of some value as a fertilizer on account of its potassium content. Small quantities of amber have also been produced from sand and clay pits. At one time, excellent specimens of amber were relatively common, so common in fact that workmen would often burn pieces to amuse themselves. In 1886 an unusually rich section of a marl bed near Shark River produced a full barrel of amber but this was a freakish occurrence since further excavation of hundreds of tons of marl failed to deliver another specimen. The demand for marls ceased as a result of the introduction of superior fertilizers and brought to a standstill the only significant production of amber in North America. Today very little is found except an occasional specimen washed from a creek bank or exposed in clay, sand, or gravel pits.

Some differences in New Jersey amber as compared to Baltic material were discovered when Burlington County specimens were subjected to a variety of tests. It was found that the local amber averaged slightly higher in specific gravity, and unlike Baltic amber which fused into a sluggish liquid, it melted readily into a mobile liquid. It was also found to take fire quickly, burning rapidly with a yellowish smoky flame and leaving behind a small quantity of dark-colored ash. The amber dissolved freely in chloroform, carbon disulfide, and in turpentine; it proved only slightly soluble in alcohol and ether, and was partially decomposed by potassium hydroxide. When partly dissolved in concentrated sulfuric acid, the solution turned red. This behavior corresponds in most essentials to that noted in Baltic amber.

Special localities for New Jersey amber are as follows: four miles southeast of Trenton from the bed of Crosswicks Creek which serves as the common border between Mercer and Burlington counties, as yellow to whitish grains, seldom over one inch in size, resting on lignite and sometimes associated with iron pyrites; from near Vincentown in Burlington County; small grains from the southwest branch of Mantua Creek near Sewell in Gloucester County. The largest specimen of amber from New Jersey, and possibly from all of North America, was found in a marl pit close by Oldmans Creek near Harrisonville, Gloucester County, where a huge mass weighing 64 ounces was uncovered, measuring 20 inches in length, 6 inches wide, and about 1 inch thick. This phenomenal specimen was pale grayish yellow in color but far from clear because of numerous inclusions of glauconite. The specific gravity was determined to be 1.061.

Maryland. An old locality frequently mentioned in literature is that of "Cape Sable" on the Magothy River. The name is now North Ferry Point and is so indicated on all modern maps. Considerable amber has been found at the base of steep undercut bluffs where a bed of amber-bearing lignite about 4 feet thick is exposed. A recent examination of the beds failed to uncover more than very small beads of clear brownish amber occurring in the lignite. The latter is so poorly consolidated that it looks like recently decayed vegetable matter. Old records indicate that specimens up to 4 to 5 inches in diameter were found but questioning of some of the local inhabitants living nearby, indicates that almost no amber of any size has been picked up from the beach in recent years. Not too far from the Magothy River is another amber locality where small specimens have been found occasionally, namely, Sullivan Cove on the Severn River. This cove is on the north shore of the river, immediately southwest of Severna Park.

North Carolina. Lumps of several ounces weight occur in the Tertiary marl beds of Pitt County and elsewhere in the eastern part of the state.

Tennessee. Small pieces of amber of Cretaceous age have been found in the sands of Coffee Bluff on the Tennessee River in northern Hardin County.

Mississippi. A soft, brittle, grayish to yellowish opaque amber-like resin occurs in clays of the Tuscaloosa formation near Paden in Tishomingo County, and near Charleston, Tallahatchie County in the northeast portion of the state.

Arkansas. Amber pieces up to 3 by 3 by 1 inch have been found in lignite clay in a railroad cut on the Missouri Pacific Railroad near Gifford, Hot Springs County.

Kansas. Small quantities of very dark-colored Cretaceous amber were found in lignite beds along the banks of the Smoky Hill River, about 5 miles south of Carneiro in Ellsworth County. This locality is now submerged beneath the waters behind Kanopolis Dam but other exposures of this formation may yield specimens. Pieces ranging from the size of a pea up to 4 inches across were recovered. It is cloudy to translucent, yellowish or brownish in color, and only slightly heavier than water; it burns readily with a smoky flame. The luster is waxy to resinous and the fracture conchoidal. Locally it has been named *jelinite* in honor of its discoverer, George Jelinek of Ellsworth.

Texas. Small rich-brown nodules occur in Cretaceous coal at Eagle Pass and on Terlingua Creek in Brewster County. Though abundant, the largest pieces average only a fraction of an inch across.

South Dakota. Lignite beds along the western border of the Black Hills yield small rounded or disk-shaped masses of an amber-like resin. The color is yellow to brownish-yellow, the hardness 3.0 while the specific gravity is slightly above that of water. This resin burns readily with a long smoky flame producing a pitchy odor.

Colorado. Amber occurs infrequently as small grains in the coal of the Laramie formation in Boulder County and adjacent counties.

Wyoming. Thin seams of an amber-like resin occur in the Fort Union coal beds of the Powder River coalfield in Converse County.

New Mexico. Amber is abundant as large lumps and streaks in the Sugarite Mine and in the Yankee Coal Bed in the Raton coalfield in Colfax County. Amber-like resins have been found as irregular lumps in the coal of the Gallup-Zuni coalbeds of McKinley County, also abundantly in the coal south of Devil's Pass, 12 miles northeast of Thoreau and elsewhere in the same vicinity in McKinley County. Much of this resin may be *wheelerite*, a name applied to a fossil resin found in northwestern New Mexico and noted for its easy solubility in alcohol, in which respect it differs markedly from true amber. Wheelerite is abundant in the coal of the Upper Cretaceous in the Rio Puerco field of Sandoval County; also in the Durango-Gallup field of San Juan County; also in McKinley County.

California. True amber is found as small flecks in lignitic wood enclosed in Eocene rocks of Simi Valley, Ventura County. The rock consists of poorly consolidated shales of dark gray color derived from clay wherein the amber is found associated with wood and other plant remains.

Oaxaca. Amber has been found in the Cuesta de Tlanjuapan on the Isthmus of Tehuantepec.

Chiapas. Large pieces of amber in various shades of red to yellow, also black, occur abundantly in the alluvium near the Huitapan River in the Simojovel district, along the slopes of a heavily forested mountain which overlooks the river. Heavy rains wash out further supplies from gorges and gullies.

Dominican Republic. The amber of this Caribbean republic apparently provided Christopher Columbus with his earliest experience with American gemstones since in the account of his Second Voyage to the New World, he mentions amber as being found on the island of Hispaniola of which the Dominican Republic is now the eastern half. This locality ranks among the first in productivity in North America, having yielded many specimens since the time of its discovery and still producing specimen material. Amber occurs embedded in very friable sandstone impregnated with lignite on a hill known as the Palo Quemado in the Province of Santiago. This prominence reaches an elevation of 1800 feet and is at the headwaters of the Licey River next to a small branch known as the Miguel Sanchez. It is about 30 miles south of the north coast of the island, about 10 miles northwest of Tamboril and 7 miles north of the city of Santiago. The Monte Cristi Range which forms the northern border of the large central plain called the Vega Real, consists chiefly of Tertiary sandstones, shales, and conglomerates, the latter being rather soft and extensively eroded. Amber occurs in a number of places in this range wherever the sandstones contain carbonaceous matter and lignite, however, the principal producing area is that northwest of Tamboril. In places the amber-bearing sandstone is hard and unprofitable to work because the amber nodules would be shattered during removal. In certain sections the sandstone turns to conglomerate which contains white quartz pebbles several inches in diameter as well as numbers of small bright red jasper pebbles. Fossil plant leaves are found in the sandstones associated with woody remains characteristic of lignite. Amber occurs in oval masses ranging from an inch or two up to the size of a man's fist. Exceptional specimens of several pounds weight have also been found. Nodule exteriors are dirty and dull and covered with a brown crust which must be scraped off to reveal the character of the material within. The specific gravity is 1.048. In color, Dominican amber varies from yellow to red to brown with brownish colors perhaps being more common. The red color is said to bleach to yellow or brown after a few hours exposure to the sun. A specimen in the author's collection, several inches long, and showing good transparency is impure in places due to numerous inclusions of organic matter. Dominican amber polishes beautifully.

Puerto Rico. Eastward from the Island of Hispaniola, amber occurs in the Tertiary deposits of Puerto Rico. Pieces are small in size, seldom as large as a walnut, but distributed over a wide area. One productive locality is in the northwest corner of the island about 2½ miles southeast of Aguadilla and near the village of Moca. A better known occurrence is that in the eastern part of the island in the Barrio (township) Mariana of Humacao. Here it is found in several fields about 5 miles due west of Humacao as small nodules considerably altered on the outside but invariably clear in their centers. Considerable quantities have been collected over the years and local residents claim it was once burned as incense in their church.

Anguilla. Small clear nodules of amber associated with lignite occur in a submerged bed off the beach of Crows Bay and are occasionally washed up on shore.

JET

During the Victorian Era, the use of black gems in elegant mourning jewelry was a widespread custom, for the gay people of that day liked a show of finery even under somber circumstances. Of all funereal gemstones, none was so well liked as jet. Velvety-black in color, warm to the touch, and featherlight in weight, it could be worn in festoons, literally, and indeed sometimes was. Perhaps this preoccupation with jet seems silly in these enlightened days, especially since this prized material is nothing more than coal, yet it is interesting to note the recent return to favor of antique jewelry in the Victorian mode. Perhaps the now defunct jet industry will revive and this once popular gemstone will again be mined. The extent of jet manufacture in bygone days is not popularly appreciated. For example, the entire town of Whitby in England was devoted entirely to the production of a tremendous variety of gems for jewelry, cameos, cups and goblets, carvings, in fact almost anything one could care to mention, providing it fitted within the size limitations of the raw material. The carving of jet is unfortunately almost a lost art even though considerable quantities of raw material remain in the ground at many localities, including some in North America. The name of jet has been derived through a series of steps from the original Greek name for a place or part of an ancient region in Asia Minor, where presumably jet was mined. The Greek name resulted in the Latin *gagates*, which in turn became *jaiet* in French and by an easy transition into our *jet*.

Although it is true that jet is a type of coal, it is a special kind which owes its characteristics to its mode of formation. Whereas ordinary coals have been subjected to sufficient heat, pressure, and chemical alteration to destroy completely all traces of the vegetable life from which they were originally formed, jet has not and consequently retains much of its woody structure. In fact, when found in place, usually embedded along layers in poorly consolidated shales, clays, or sands, jet occurs in the form of recognizable logs and limbs, much flattened and compressed, but unmistakably woody in nature. The general class of coal in which this partial change is a characteristic feature, embraces all brown coals and lignites with the latter term being more or less reserved for those in which the woody structure is distinct. Thus jet can be considered a variety of *lignite*. It is the retention of this woody structure which gives jet a certain degree of toughness and permits it to be cut and carved without fear of crumbling to powder. Jet takes a beautiful lustrous polish but since it is not as dense as inorganic gemstones, the polish is less harshly brilliant.

There is scarcely any mineral matter in jet and analyses show carbon to be the principal constituent with appreciable quantities of hydrogen and oxygen which have combined with carbon to form a variety of organic compounds. Like other soft coals, jet burns with a smoky yellow flame but does not "cake" or coke. When scratched, a characteristic brown streak is left behind which serves at once to distinguish jet from other coals or even from plastics which may look like jet. Another point of identification is the many slightly dull places on broad polished surfaces which show distinct fibrous structure under high magnification. The specific gravity of jet is very low, not much above that of water: 1.30 to 1.35. The hardness is low also, ranging broadly from 3 to 4. In color, jet is usually dull black when very compact but inclines toward brownish when more porous.

LOCALITIES

Nova Scotia. Fine pieces of jet have been found in the coal beds of Nova Scotia, especially from near Pictou in Pictou County. Some of this has been used for ornamental purposes.

Maryland. Lignite of sufficient hardness and compactness to be called jet has been reported from two localities in this state, both in Anne Arundel County. The first locality is in the old limonite iron ore pits at Loper Hall where jet was found in seams in sedimentary formations containing much woody debris. The second locality is at Fort Dorsey. Examination of the vegetable debris indicates it is derived from coniferous trees.

Colorado. Jet has been found in a number of places in the coalbearing formations of this state, and, if old accounts are to be trusted, in considerable quantity. It is said to occur in the coal seams of Wet Mountain Valley at Trinchera Mesa, Las Animas County. Trinchera Mesa is near the border of

Colorado and New Mexico and about 34 miles southeast of Trinidad. In El Paso County, masses of jet up to 12 inches in length and 4 to 5 inches in width have been dug from the coal deposits.

New Mexico. Jet occurs in the vicinity of Santa Rosa in Guadelupe County. Excavation of ancient Indian sites in Chaco Canyon in San Juan County revealed the use of jet in ornaments and ceremonial objects by the early Indian inhabitants and since coal seams occur in this canyon it is surmised that the jet used by the Indians came from this source. In Valencia County, seams of cannel coal are found up to 20 inches thick and also appear to have been used as sources of jet by the early Indians of this area.

Texas. Jet occurs as flattened tree trunks in a thin layer of lignite which occurs 100 to 200 feet below the San Carlos Coal Bed in Presidio County.

Utah. The outstanding source for jet in North America lies in a barren desolate waste in Wayne County where it occurs in a narrow coal seam in Coaly Basin, a small depression along Coaly Wash, about 5 miles due west of Fairview Ranch. The latter place is located about 10 miles south of Hanksville. Coaly Basin, along whose precipitous sides the jet-seam outcrops, is almost on the boundary between Garfield and Wayne Counties, and upon the northwest flank of Mt. Ellen in the Henry Mountains. In the basin, jet is found only in the upper of two exposed seams where it occurs as disk-like inclusions in the seam, each mass representing a severely compressed tree trunk. Jet found near the surface is badly checked but that found deeper is of much better quality. Pieces range in size from small slabs to those up to 10 by 10 by 2 or 3 inches thick. The exterior is ribbed and grooved and shows traces of the grayish clay which is locally abundant. This deposit has been known for many years but earliest records indicate that commercial production first took place in 1919 when a considerable quantity was mined. In 1925 a mineral dealer removed about a ton of jet for disposal as specimen and lapidary material. As late as 1956, at least one dealer in California had specimens for sale from this locality pointing to even more recent visits. The jet from this locality takes a fine lustrous polish but is not as hard or dense as that from England.

ANTHRACITE COAL

Of all minerals, coal is least likely to be thought of as a "gemstone" or even as an ornamental stone. Nevertheless, for many years, a surprising quantity of exceptionally pure and compact anthracite or "hard" coal was employed for just these purposes. In this connection, it is interesting to note that as recently as 1957, anthracite baroques for setting into inexpensive jewelry were advertised in some of the amateur lapidary journals.

The use of anthracite in jewelry is not as ridiculous as it seems in spite of the fact that the enormous quantities available cause all objects made from it to be worth scarcely more than the labor expended on them. Good material is sufficiently resistant to abrasion so that it does not smudge or rub off upon clothing. Though not as tough as jet, it takes a brilliant polish and could still be used today for a number of ornamental purposes.

However all this seems to be a thing of the past, for in the days when hard coal was being carved into a variety of ornamental objects such as small vases, blocks with scenes, ashtrays, and many other items, examples could be seen in almost every home in the coal-mining districts of the eastern United States. Many readers from this section will surely remember the impressive monuments of anthracite which adorned the front steps of coalyard offices or occupied a pedestal inside the door. Not a small amount of art and skill were expended upon their carving. The faces of blocks were often chiseled into bas-relief, showing the colliery from whence came the coal, embraced by polished raised lettering giving the motto and the name of the company.

Although coal proved easy to work, not everyone possessed the requisite manual and artistic skill, and for this reason qualified artisans were few in number. Most were recent immigrants from various European countries who had found employment in the vast network of mines in Pennsylvania. With them, they brought their native skills including the ability to carve. Needless to say, the art of sculpturing coal is rapidly dying out, and, in time, carved objects may become collector's items like so many other Victorian ornaments.

Coal carving was concentrated in towns of the hard coal region of eastern Pennsylvania, a notable center being Mountain Top near Glen Summit, Luzerne County. The Franklin Mine at Ashley, the Spring Tunnel Mine at Summit Hill, and the mines at Nanticoke all provided top-quality raw material. Articles were retailed extensively in Scranton, Wilkes Barre, Pittston, and Mauch Chunk.

APPENDIX 1

Bibliography

GEMOLOGICAL AND MINERALOGICAL:

ANDERSON, B. W.—*Gem Testing*. Emerson, New York, 1948. Good discussion of gemology leading toward practical testing of gemstones.

BALL, S. H.—"The Mining of Gems and Ornamental Stones by American Indians." *Bureau of American Ethnology, Anthropological Papers, No. 13, Bureau Ethnology Bulletin 128*, 1941.

BROWN, R. W.—"Plantlike Features in Thundereggs and Geodes." The *Smithsonian Report for 1956*, pp. 329-339, 1957. Discusses growth and formation of mossy, dendritic, and other forms of inclusions in chalcedony.

CHESTER, A. H.—*A Dictionary of the Names of Minerals including Their History and Etymology*. John Wiley & Sons, New York, 1896.

DAKE, H. C., F. L. FLEENER & B. H. WILSON—*Quartz Family Minerals*. Whittlesey House, McGraw-Hill Book Company, Inc., New York, 1938. A popular book on the many members of the quartz family.

FEUCHTWANGER, L.—*A Popular Treatise on Gems*. D. Appleton & Company, New York, 1859. Deals briefly with some North American localities but is mainly of interest for historical reasons.

FISCHER, W.—"Zum Problem der Achatgenese." *Neues Jahrbuch für Mineralogie, Abhandlungen*, Band 86, pp. 367-392. July, 1954. A review of the theories concerning the genesis of agate.

FORD, W. E.—*A Textbook of Mineralogy*. John Wiley and Sons, Inc., 4th Edition, New York, New York, 1932. Exceptionally thorough book but not for beginners.

HOWELL, J. V.—*Glossary of Geology and Related Sciences*. American Geological Institute, Washington, D.C., 1957. A comprehensive glossary compiled by the A.G.I. and member societies.

HURLBUT, C. S.—*Minerals and How To Study Them.* John Wiley and Sons, Inc., New York, New York, 1952. A good beginning text.

KRAUS, E. H. & C. B. SLAWSON—*Gems and Gem Materials.* 5th Edit. McGraw-Hill Book Company, Inc., New York, 1947. A popular gemological book.

LIDDICOAT, R. T., JR.—*Handbook of Gem Identification.* Gemological Institute of America, Los Angeles, California, 1948. An easily understood textbook.

MERRILL, G. P.—*Handbook and Descriptive Catalogue of the Collections of Gems and Precious Stones in the United States National Museum.* Smithsonian Institution, U.S. National Museum Bulletin 118, 1922.

PALACHE, C., H. BERMAN & C. FRONDEL—*Dana's System of Mineralogy,* John Wiley and Sons, Inc., New York, New York; Vol. I, 1944; Vol. II, 1951. Highly technical treatment of mineralogy in an up-to-date revision of an old classic.

POUGH, F. H.—*A Field Guide to Rocks and Minerals.* Houghton Mifflin Company, Boston, Mass., 1953. A particularly competent guide.

POUGH, F. H., J. J. BOWMAN & C. M. HOKE—*The Jeweler's Dictionary.* Jeweler's Circular-Keystone, New York, New York, 1945.

RICE, C. M.—*Dictionary of Geological Terms.* Published by the author at Princeton, New Jersey, 1951.

SHIPLEY, R. M.—*Dictionary of Gems and Gemology.* Gemological Institute of America, Los Angeles, California. Useful compendium on gemology.

SMITH, G. F. H.—*Gemstones.* Revised by F. C. Phillips, Methuen & Co. Ltd., London. 13th Ed., 1958. The best general treatment of the subject of gemology in the English language.

WEBSTER, R.—*The Gemologist's Compendium.* N. A. G. Press, Ltd., London. Excellent compilation of an enormous variety of useful facts.

GUIDEBOOKS:

BITNER'S—*Arizona Rock Trails.* Bitner's, Scottsdale, Arizona, 1957. A series of 20 small charts on which are shown 60 locations for gemstones and minerals in Arizona.

DAKE, H. C.—*Northwest Gem Trails.* Mineralogist Publishing Company, Portland, Oregon, 1950. Locality information on Oregon, Washington, Idaho, Montana, and Wyoming.

DUKE, A.—*Arizona Gem Fields.* Alton Duke, Yuma, Arizona, 1957. Guide to mineral and gemstone localities.

GERHARD, P. & H. E. GULICK—*Lower California Guidebook.* Arthur H. Clark Company, Glendale, California, 1956. Mentions calcite onyx quarries, turquois mines, and pearling in the Gulf of California.

HENRY, D. J.—*Gem Trail Journal.* Gordon's, Long Beach, California, 1952. Good locality information on the Western United States.

————*California Gem Trails.* Gordon's, Long Beach, California. 3rd Edition, Revised. Locality information on California, especially in its southern part.

————*The Rock Collector's Nevada and Idaho.* Gordon's, Long Beach, California, 1953. Details on how to reach localities in these states and what to find there.

QUICK, L.—*The Rockhound Buyers Guide.* Lapidary Journal, Del Mar, California. Various issues commencing in 1953; much field trip information is included.

RANSOM, J. E.—*Arizona Gem Trails and the Colorado Desert of California.* Mineralogist Publishing Company, Portland, Oregon, 1955.

————*Petrified Forest Trails.* Mineralogist Publishing Company, Portland, Oregon, 1956. Describes petrified forests of the United States and gives locality information.

SIMPSON, B. W.—*Gem Trails of Texas.* Gem Trails of Texas, Granbury, Texas, 1958.

ZEITNER, J. C.—*Midwest Gem Trails.* Mineralogist Publishing Company, Portland, Oregon, 1956.

MAGAZINES AND PERIODICALS:

American Mineralogist—Journal of the Mineralogical Society of America. Editor, Lewis S. Ramsdell, Department of Mineralogy, University of Michigan, Ann Arbor, Michigan. Highly technical.

Earth Science—Box 1357, Chicago 90, Illinois. A magazine which covers all aspects of the earth sciences.

Gems & Gemology—Gemological Institute of America, 11940 San Vicente Blvd., Los Angeles 49, California. Often contains articles on American gemstones.

Gems & Minerals—Box 687, Mentone, California. Popular magazine covering all aspects of the earth sciences.

Lapidary Journal—P. O. Box 518, Del Mar, California (street address, 241 Twelfth St.). Widely-read magazine covering the lapidary arts.

Mineralogist—329 Southeast 32nd Avenue, Portland 15, Oregon. Another popular magazine covering all aspects of the earth sciences.

Rocks & Minerals—Box 29, Peekskill, New York. Along with the other popular magazines mentioned, covers the field of earth sciences.

PEARLS:

BAKER, F. C.—"*The Freshwater Mollusca of Wisconsin.*" Wisconsin Academy of Sciences, Arts, and Letters, Madison, Wisconsin, 1928. *Part II, the Pelecypoda.* Also published as Bulletin 70 of the Wisconsin Geological & Natural History Survey.

BRANN, W. P.—"Fresh-water Mussel Shells, the Basis for an Arkansas Industry." *University of Arkansas Bulletin,* Vol. 40, No. 20, Dec. 1, 1946.

GALTSOFF, P. S.—"The Pearl Oyster Resources of Panama." *Special Scientific Report; Fisheries No. 28,* U.S. Department of the Interior, Fish and Wildlife Service, 1950.

KUNZ, G. F.—"The Freshwater Pearls and Pearl Fisheries of the United States." *Bulletin of the U.S. Fisheries Commission.* Vol. XVII, pp. 373-426, 1898.

KUNZ, G. F., & C. H. STEVENSON—*Book of the Pearl*, The Century Co., New York, New York, 1908. Exhaustive and still authoritative; includes freshwater pearls.

DEPOSITS AND LOCALITIES:

ADAMS, F. & A. BARLOW—"Geology of the Haliburton-Bancroft Area." *Geological Survey of Canada Memoir 6*, 1910.

ADAMS, J. W.—"Beryllium Deposits of the Mount Antero Region, Chaffee County, Colorado." *U.S. Geological Survey Bulletin 982-D*, 1953.

ANDERSON, E.—"Asbestos and Jade Occurrences in the Kobuk River Region, Alaska." *Territory of Alaska Department of Mines Pamphlet No. 3-R*, May 1945, revised to Dec. 1945.

BANNERMAN, H. M.—"The Fluorite Deposits of Cheshire County, New Hampshire." *New Hampshire Mineral Resources Survey, Part V. N.D.*

BARLOW, A. E.—"Corundum, Its Occurrence, Distribution, Exploration and Uses." *Canada Department of Mines, Geological Survey Memoir 57*, 1915.

BARNES, V. E.—"North American Tektites." *University of Texas Publication 3945*, pp. 477-582, June 1940. An exhaustive treatise on the subject with much background material on tektites from other countries. An extensive bibliography is included

BASTIN, E. S.—"Economic Geology of the Feldspar Deposits of the United States." *U.S. Geological Survey Bulletin 420*, 1910. Describes many pegmatites containing gemstones.

————"Geology of the Pegmatites and Associated Rocks of Maine." *U.S. Geological Survey Bulletin 445*, 1911. Detailed descriptions of famous gemstone deposits.

BERG, E. L.—"Notes on Catlinite and the Sioux Quarries." *American Mineralogist*, Vol. 23, No. 4, April 1938.

BILLINGS, M. P.—"Topaz and Phenacite from Baldface Mountain, Chatham, New Hampshire." *American Mineralogist*, Vol. 12, No. 4, April 1927.

BLANK, E. W.—"Diamond Finds in the United States." *Rocks & Minerals Magazine*, Vol. 9, Nos. 10, 11, 12; Vol. 10, No. 1, 1934-1935.

BOGGILD, O. B.—*The Mineralogy of Greenland*. C. A. Reitzel, Copenhagen, 1953. Contains much locality information.

BRESSLER, C. T.—"Garnet Deposits near Wrangell, Southeastern Alaska." *U.S. Geological Survey Bulletin 963-C*, 1950.

BRETON, A.—"Some Obsidian Workings in Mexico." *Proceedings of the International Congress of Americanistes*, 13th Session, New York, pp. 265-268, 1902.

BROMFIELD, C. S. & A. F. SHRIDE—"Mineral Resources of the San Carlos Indian Reservation, Arizona." *U.S. Geological Survey Bulletin 1027-N*, 1956. Describes the peridot field.

BROWN, A. P.—"Notes on the Geology of the Island of Antigua." *Proceedings of the Academy of Natural Sciences of Philadelphia* (Pa.), pp. 584-616, Nov. 1913. Describes occurrence of silicified wood.

CAMERON, E. N., D. M. LARRABEE, MCNAIR, A. H., PAGE, J. J., STEWART, G. W., & SHAININ, V. E.,—"Pegmatite Investigations, 1942-1945, New England." *U.S. Geological Survey Professional Paper 255*, 1954. Describes many pegmatites yielding gemstones.

CAMERON, E. N., R. H. JAHNS, A. H. MCNAIR & L. R. PAGE—"Internal Structure of Granitic Pegmatites." *Monograph 2*, Economic Geology Publishing Company, Urbana, Illinois, 1949. Excellent though technical discussion of pegmatite bodies.

CHESTERMAN, C. W.—"Nephrite in Marin County, California." *California State Division of Mines Special Report 10-B*, 1951.

CLABAUGH, S. E.—"Corundum Deposits of Montana." *U.S. Geological Survey Bulletin 983*, 1952. Exceptionally detailed and thorough treatment of sapphire deposits.

COLEMAN, R. G.—"Jadeite from San Benito County, California." *Gems & Gemology*, Vol. VIII, No. 11, Fall 1956. Chemical and physical properties of the jadeite are given as well as a general discussion of the deposits.

CRAWFORD, P., and F. JOHNSON—"Turquoise Deposits of Courtland, Arizona." *Economic Geology*, Vol. 32, pp. 511-523.

CRIPPEN, R. A., JR.—"Nephrite Jade and Associated Rocks of the Cape San Martin Region, Monterey County, California." *California State Division of Mines Special Report 10-A*, 1951.

deSCHMID, H. S.—"Feldspar in Canada." *Canadian Department of Mines Report No. 401*, 1916. Some gemstone localities are described.

DIETRICH, R. V.—"Virginia Mineral Localities." *Bulletin of the Virginia Polytechnic Institute, Engineering Experimental Station Series No. 88*, Vol. XLVI, No. 11, 1953.

DUSTIN, F.—"The Gems of Isle Royale, Michigan." In: *Vol. XVI of Papers of the Michigan Academy of Science, Arts and Letters*, Ann Arbor, Michigan, 1932.

ELLSWORTH, H. V. & F. JOLLIFFE—"Some Recently Discovered Minerals of the Great Slave Lake Area, Northwest Territories." *University of Toronto Studies, Geological Series, No. 40: Contributions to Canadian Mineralogy, 1936-1937*. Briefly discusses iolite occurrences.

EMMONS, G. T.—"Jade in British Columbia and Alaska and Its Use by the Natives." *New York Museum of the American Indian, Heye Foundation, Indian Notes and Monographs, No. 35*, 1923.

ENGEL, A. E. J.—"Quartz Crystal Deposits of Western Arkansas." *U.S. Geological Survey Bulletin No. 973-E*, 1951.

ERD, R. C. & M. D. FOSTER—"Faustite, a New Mineral, the Zinc Analogue of Turquois." *American Mineralogist*, Vol. 38, Nov.-Dec., 1953, Nos. 11 & 12, pp. 964-972.

FOSHAG, W. F.—"Mexican Opal." *Gems & Gemology*, Vol. 7, No. 9, Spring 1953, pp. 278-282. An excellent article based on personal observations of the late author.

————"Mineralogy and Geology of Cerro Mercado, Durango, Mexico." *Proceedings of the U.S. National Museum, Vol. 74, Article 23,* pp. 1-27, 1928. Describes apatite occurrences.

————"Mineralogical Studies on Guatemalan Jade." *Smithsonian Miscellaneous Collections, Vol. 135, No. 5, Publication 4307,* Dec. 3, 1957. This is the translation of the work originally prepared in Spanish for Guatemala in 1954.

FREEMAN, B. C.—"Mineral Deposits in Renfrew County and Vicinity." *Canada Department of Mines, Geological Survey Memoir 195,* 1936.

FRONDEL, C. & M. L. LINDBERG—"Second Occurrence of Brazilianite." *American Mineralogist,* Vol. 33, Nos. 3 & 4, Mar.-Apr., 1948.

FURCRON, A. S.—"Staurolite and Its Occurrence in Georgia." *Earth Science Digest,* Vol. 3, No. 7, pp. 7-12, Feb. 1947.

GALBRAITH, F. M.—"Minerals of Arizona." *Arizona Bureau of Mines Bulletin 149,* revised as Bulletin 153, 1947.

GIANELLA, V. P.—"Nevada's Common Minerals." *University of Nevada Bulletin Geological & Mining Series No. 36,* 1941.

GILLULY, J.—"Geology and Ore Deposits of the Stockton and Fairfield Quadrangles, Utah." *U.S. Geological Survey Professional Paper 173,* 1932. Describes variscite deposits.

GLASS, J. J.—"The Pegmatite Minerals from Near Amelia, Virginia." *American Mineralogist,* Vol. 20, No. 11, Nov. 1935.

GORDON, S. G.—"The Mineralogy of Pennsylvania." *Special Publication No. 1 of the Academy of Natural Sciences of Philadelphia,* 1922.

GREGORY, H. E.—"Geology of the Navajo Country." *U.S. Geological Survey Professional Paper 93,* 1917. Deals with geology and mineralogy of garnet, peridot, and petrified wood deposits.

GRIFFITTS, W. R., R. H. JAHNS & R. W. LEMKE—"Mica Deposits of the Southeastern Piedmont, Part 3, Ridgeway-Sandy Ridge District, Virginia and North Carolina, with Part 4, Outlying Deposits in Virginia." *U.S. Geological Survey Professional Paper 284-C,* 1953.

GRIFFITTS, W. R. & J. C. OLSON—"Mica Deposits of the Southeastern Piedmont, Part 5, Shelby-Hickory District, North Carolina, with Part 6, Outlying Deposits in North Carolina." *U.S. Geological Survey Professional Paper 248-D,* 1953.

————"Mica Deposits of the Southeastern Piedmont, Part 7, Hartwell District, Georgia and South Carolina with Part 8, Outlying Deposits in South Carolina." *U.S. Geological Survey Professional Paper 248-E,* 1953. Above papers describe some pegmatites furnishing gemstones.

HADLEY, J. B.—"Preliminary Report on Corundum Deposits in the Buck Creek Peridotite, Clay County, North Carolina." *U.S. Geological Survey Bulletin No. 948-E,* 1949.

HAMLIN, A. C.—"*The History of Mount Mica.*" Published by the author, Bangor, Maine, 1895. Authoritative account of early mining for tourmalines.

HANLEY, F. B.—"Minnesota's Thomsonite Beach." *Rocks & Minerals Magazine,* Vol. 14, No. 12, Dec. 1939.

HANLEY, J. B.—"Economic Geology of the Rincon Pegmatites, San Diego County, California." *California Division of Mines Special Report 7-B, 1951.*

HARRISON, J. M. & Y. O. FORTIER—"Occurrences of Quartz Crystals. Leeds County, Southeastern Ontario (Report & Map)." *Canada Department of Mines & Resources, Mines & Geology Branch, Geological Survey Paper 44-8, 1944.*

HASTIE, R.—"My Trip to Jade Mountain in Alaska." *Lapidary Journal,* Vol. 9, No. 4, Oct. 1955. Interesting and informative account of a recent visit.

HEINRICH, E. W.—"Pegmatites of Eight-Mile Park, Fremont County, Colorado." *American Mineralogist,* Vol. 33, July-August, Sept.-October, 1948.

————"Pegmatites of Montana." *Economic Geology,* Vol. 44, No. 4, June-July, 1949. Briefly describes the amethyst-bearing Pohndorf pegmatite.

HEINRICH, E. W., & J. C. OLSON—"Mica Deposits of the Southeastern Piedmont, art 11, Alabama District." *U.S. Geological Survey Professional Paper 248-G,* 1953. Some gemstone localities are included.

HEINRICH, E. W., M. R. KLEPPER & R. H. JAHNS—"Mica Deposits of the Southeastern Piedmont, Part 9, Thomaston-Barnesville District, Georgia with Part 10, Outlying Deposits in Georgia." *U.S. Geological Survey Professional Paper 248-F, 1953.*

HIDDEN, W. E. & J. H. PRATT—"On Rhodolite, a New Variety of Garnet." *American Journal of Science,* Vol. V, Apr. 1898. North Carolina garnet.

HOBBS, W. H.—"The Diamond Fields of the Great Lakes." *Journal of Geology,* Vol. VII, No. 4, May-June 1899.

HODSON, G. K. & H. C. DAKE—"Opal Mines and Mining in Nevada." *Mineralogist Magazine,* Vol. 18, No. 4, Apr. 1950, pp. 171-179, 198, 200, 202, 204. An exhaustive article on the Virgin Valley deposits.

HOLDEN, R. J.—"The 'Punch' Jones and Other Appalachian Diamonds." *Bulletin of Virginia Polytechnic Institute Engineering Experiment Station, Series 56,* 1944.

HOLMES, W. H.—Amber. An article in: "The Handbook of American Indians North of Mexico." *Bureau of American Ethnology,* Bulletin 30. Part I, p. 48, 1907.

————"The Obsidian Mines of Hidalgo, Mexico." *American Anthropology,* Vol. 2, pp. 405-416, 1900.

IVES, R. L.—"Topaz Areas of the Thomas Range, Utah." *Rocks and Minerals Magazine,* Vol. 22, No. 11, 1947. Maps, photos, and detailed directions for reaching localities.

JAHNS, R. H.—"Mica Deposits of the Petaca District, Rio Arriba County, New Mexico." *New Mexico Bureau of Mines and Mineral Resources Bulletin 25,* 1946. Mentions several gemstone localities.

JAHNS, R. H. & L. A. WRIGHT—"Gem and Lithium-Bearing Pegmatites of the Pala District, San Diego County, California." *California Division of Mines Special Report 7-A, 1951.*

JOHNSON, D. W.—"The Geology of the Cerrillos Hills, New Mexico." *School of Mines Quarterly,* Vol. 24, 1903, pp. 493-499 *(areal geology)*; Vol. 25, 1903, pp. 69-98 (*petrography*). Good account of mineralogy and geology of the Cerrillos deposits.

JOHNSTON, R. A. A.—"A List of Canadian Mineral Occurrences." *Canada Department of Mines, Geological Survey, Memoir 74,* 1915. Exhaustive list of localities but now out of print.

JULIHN, C. E. & F. W. HORTON—"Mines of the Southern Mother Lode Region; Part I—Calaveras County (California)," *U.S. Department of the Interior, Mineral Industries Survey of the United States, Bulletin 412,* Washington, D.C., 1938. Describes the quartz crystal localities near Mokelumne Hill.

KELLY, C.—"Gem Stones Found in Veins of Coal." *Desert Magazine,* Nov. 1942. Utah jet locality described.

KIERSCH, G. A.—"Mineral Resources, Navajo-Hopi Indian Reservations, Arizona-Utah." Vol. II, *Nonmetallic Minerals.* University of Arizona, 1955. Latest account of pyrope and peridot occurrences.

KUNZ, G. F.—"Gems and Precious Stones of North America." *Scientific Publishing Company,* N.Y., 1890, 2nd Edition, 1892. The first systematic treatise on North American gemstone localities.

————"History of the Gems Found in North Carolina." *North Carolina Geological and Economic Survey, Bulletin 12,* 1907.

————"Gems, Jeweler's Materials, and Ornamental Stones of California." *California State Mining Bureau, Bulletin 37,* 1905.

————"Gems and Precious Stones of Mexico." *Secretaria de Fomento, Mexico,* D. F., 1907.

LANDES, K. K.—"Origin of the Quebec Phlogopite-Apatite Deposits." *American Mineralogist,* Vol. 23, No. 6, June 1938. Mineralogy of the apatite deposits.

LARSEN, E. S., III—"The Mineralogy and Paragenesis of the Variscite Nodules from Near Fairfield, Utah." *American Mineralogist,* Vol. 27, Nos. 4, 5, 6, 1942.

LARSEN, E. S. & E. V. SHANNON—"The Minerals of the Phosphate Nodules from Near Fairfield, Utah." *American Mineralogist,* Vol. 15, No. 8, pp. 307-337, 1930. An excellent description of the many rare phosphates which occur along with variscite; characters are briefly described.

LAUSEN, C.—"Occurrence of Olivine Bombs near Globe, Arizona." *American Journal of Science,* 5th Series, Vol. 14, pp. 293-306, 1927. On peridot.

LEIPER, H.—"Spectacular Find of Sphene Made In Mexico." *Lapidary Journal,* Vol. 12, No. 4, Oct. 1958.

LEMKE, R. W., R. H. JAHNS & W. R. GRIFFITTS—"Mica Deposits of the Southeastern Piedmont, Part 2, The Amelia District, Virginia." *U.S. Geological Survey Bulletin* 248-B, 1952. Famous gemstone pegmatites thoroughly described.

LEMMON, D. M.—"Augelite from Mono County, California." *American Mineralogist,* Vol. 20, No. s9, Sept. 1935.

LOTHROP, S. K., W. F. FOSHAG & J. MAHLER—"*Pre-Columbian Art.*" Phaidon Press, Ltd., London, England, 1957. Magnificent color plates of the Robert Woods Bliss collection including many examples of jadeite.

LOUDERBACK, G. D.—"Benitoite, A New California Gem Mineral." *Bulletin of the Department of Geology, University of California*, Vol. 5, No. 9, 1907.

MAINE GEOLOGICAL SURVEY—"Maine Pegmatite Mines and Prospects and Associated Minerals." *Minerals Resources Index No. 1*. Department of Development of Industry and Commerce, Augusta, Mar. 1, 1957. Excellent mapped guide to localities.

MANCHESTER, J. G.—"Collecting Semi-Precious Stones in Florida." *Rocks & Minerals Magazine*, Vol. 16, No. 12, Dec. 1941. Excellent article on the silicified corals of Tampa Bay.

————"The Minerals of New York City and its Environs." *Bulletin of the New York Mineralogical Club*, Vol. 3, No. 1, Jan. 1931.

MARTIN, J. G. M.—"Historical Himalaya Tourmaline Mine Resumes Production." *Gems & Gemology*, Vol. IX, No. 6, Summer 1958. Thorough description of recent work along with excellent photographs of the mine, pockets and crystals.

McCONNELL, D.—"Garnets from Sierra Tlayacac, Morelos, Mexico." *American Mineralogist*, Vol. 18, pp. 25-29, 1933. Describes grossularites from Xalostoc.

McLAUGHLIN, T. G.—"Pegmatite Dikes of the Bridger Mountains, Wyoming." *American Mineralogist*, Vol. 25, Jan. 1940, pp. 46-68. Mentions gem beryl.

MEEN, V. B. & D. H. GORMAN—"Mineral Occurrences of Wilberforce, Bancroft, and Craigmont-Lake Clear Areas, Southeastern Ontario." *Guide Book for Field Trip No. 2*, Geological Society of America and Geological Association of Canada, 1953.

MERRILL, G. P.—"On the Serpentine of Montville, New Jersey." *Proceedings of the United States National Museum*, 1888.

————"*Stones for Building and Decoration*." John Wiley & Sons, New York, New York, 2nd Edition, 1897. Contains much information on serpentine and other decorative stones.

————"The Onyx Marbles: Their Origin, Composition, and Uses, Both Ancient and Modern." *Report of the U.S. National Museum* for 1893, 1895.

MILLER, W. J.—"The Garnet Deposits of Warren County, N.Y." *Economic Geology*, Vol. VII, No. 5, Aug. 1912.

MISER, H. D. & C. S. ROSS—"Diamond-Bearing Peridotite in Pike County, Arkansas." *Economic Geologist*, Vol. XVII, No. 8, Dec. 1822. Excellent review of history; maps.

MOORE, C. H., JR.—The "Staurolite Area of Patrick and Henry Counties, Virginia." *American Mineralogist*, Vol. 22, No. 9, Sept. 1937.

MURDOCH, J. & R. W. WEBB—"Minerals of California." *Division of Mines, Bulletin 173*. San Francisco, California, 1956. Locality information on all of California.

NASON, F. L.—"Newcomb Tourmalines." In: Some New York Minerals and Their Localities. *New York State Museum Bulletin*, No. 4, August, 1888.

NORTHROP, S. A.—"The Minerals of New Mexico." *University of New Mexico Bulletin, Geological Series*, Vol. 6, No. 1, 1942. Much valuable locality information.

————"Thulite in New Mexico." *American Mineralogist,* Vol. 20, No. 11, Nov. 1935.

OLSON, E. E.—"History of Diamonds Found in Wisconsin." *Gems & Gemology,* Spring 1953.

OLSON, J. C.—"Economic Geology of the Spruce Pine Pegmatite District, North Carolina." *North Carolina Department of Conservation & Development, Division of Mineral Resources Bulletin 43,* 1944.

OSTRANDER, C. W. & W. E. PRICE, JR.—"Minerals of Maryland." *The Natural History Society of Maryland,* Baltimore, Maryland, 1940.

PAIGE, S.—"The Origin of Turquois in the Burro Mountains, New Mexico." *Economic Geology,* Vol. 7, 1912, pp. 382-392.

PALACHE, C.—"A Topaz Deposit in Topsham, Maine." *American Journal of Science,* Vol. 27, Jan. 1934.

————"The Minerals of Franklin and Sterling Hill, Sussex County, New Jersey." *U.S. Geological Survey, Professional Paper No. 180, 1935.* Thorough treatise on these unique deposits.

PALACHE, C. & H. V. ELLSWORTH—"Zircon from North Burgess, Ontario." *American Mineralogist,* Vol. 13, No. 7, Jul. 1928, p. 384.

PALACHE, C. & S. C. DAVIDSON, and E. A. GORANSON—"The Hiddenite Deposit in Alexander County, North Carolina." *American Mineralogist,* Vol. 15, No. 8, Aug. 1930.

PALLISTER, H. D.—"Index to the Minerals and Rocks of Alabama." *Geological Survey of Alabama, Bulletin 65,* 1955.

PARSONS, A. L.—"The Utilization of the Semi-Precious and Ornamental Stones of Canada." *University of Toronto Studies, Geological Series, No. 36: Contributions to Canadian Mineralogy,* 1934.

————"Additional Semi-Precious and Ornamental Stones of Canada." *University of Toronto Studies, Geological Series, No. 41: Contributions to Canadian Mineralogy,* 1938.

PEACOCK, M. A.—"Topaz from Devil's Head, Colorado." *American Mineralogist,* Vol. 20, No. 5, May 1935.

PEARL, R. M.—"*Colorado Gem Trails.*" Sage Books, Inc., Golden, Colorado, 1951. General coverage of the state.

PENFIELD, S. L. & W. E. FORD—"On Stibiotantalite." *American Journal of Science,* Vol. 22, pp. 61-77, July, 1906. This entire article is devoted to a discussion of the Mesa Grande, California crystals.

PHALEN, W. C.—"A New Occurrence of Unakite." *Smithsonian Miscellaneous Collections; Quarterly Issue,* Vol. 45, 1904.

POGUE, J. E.—"The Turquois." *3rd Memoir, Vol. XII, National Academy of Sciences,* 1919. A detailed account of this gemstone in all aspects and easily the most complete and authoritative work on the subject in any language; extensive bibliography.

POINDEXTER, O. F., H. M. MARTIN & S. G. BERGQUIST—"Rocks and Minerals of Michigan." *Michigan Department of Conservation, Geological Survey Division, Publication 42* (Revised 1951), 1953.

Bibliography 617

PRATT, J. H.—"Mineralogical Notes on Cyanite, Zircon, and Anorthite from North Carolina." *American Journal of Science*, Vol. V, Feb. 1898.

————"Corundum and Its Occurrence and Distribution in the United States." *United States Geological Survey, Bulletin No. 269*, 1906. Details on many Appalachian deposits.

PRINCE, A. T.—"A Study of Canadian Sphene." *University of Toronto Studies, Geological Series, No. 41*, 1938.

RANSOME, F. L.—"The Turquois Copper-mining District, Arizona." *U.S. Geological Survey, Bulletin 530*, 1911, p. 134. Brief geologic description of turquois in Dragoon Mts., Cochise County, Arizona.

REINER, T. A.—"Agates of the Yellowstone River Valley, Montana." *Rocks & Minerals Magazine*, Vol. 16, No. 9, Sept. 1941.

RICHMOND, W. E. & F. A. GONYER—"On Pollucite." *American Mineralogist*, Vol. 23, No. 11, Nov. 1938.

ROBINSON, S.—"*A Catalogue of American Minerals and Their Localities.*" Boston, Mass., 1825. The earliest compendium of American gemstone information.

ROGERS, A. F.—"Minerals From the Pegmatite Veins of Rincon, San Diego County, California." *Columbia School of Mines Quarterly*, Vol. 31, No. 3, 1910. Describes a number of gemstones and the deposits in which they occur.

SATTERLEY, J.—"Mineral Occurrences in the Renfrew Area." *Ontario Dept. Mines*, Vol. LIII, Part III, 1944.

SCHAIRER, J. F.—"The Minerals of Connecticut." *State Geological and Natural History Survey, Bulletin No. 51*, 1931. General locality information.

SHALLER, W. T.—"Crystallized Turquois from Virginia." *U.S. Geological Survey, Bulletin 509*, 1912, pp. 42-47.

————"The Crystal Cavities of the New Jersey Zeolite Region." *U.S. Geological Survey, Bulletin 832*, 1932. An excellent, thorough discussion.

SCHLEGEL, D. M.—"Gem Stones of the United States." *U.S. Geological Survey, Bulletin 1042-G*, 1957. A very brief discussion of properties of gemstones plus a listing of localities.

SCHOONER, R.—"Ninety Minerals from one Connecticut Hill." *Rocks & Minerals Magazine*, Vol. 30, Nos. 7-8, Jul.-Aug., 1955. Minerals of the Strickland Quarry on Collins Hill, Portland, Conn.

SHAININ, V. E. & L. F. DELLWIG—"Pegmatites and Associated Rocks in the Newry Hill Area, Oxford County, Maine." *Maine Geological Survey*, Maine Development Commission, Augusta, 1955. Detailed maps and data on the Nevel and Dunton mines.

SHANNON, E. V.—"The Minerals of Idaho." *Smithsonian Institution, U.S. National Museum, Bulletin 131*, 1926. Excellent, detailed account.

SHAUB, B. M.—"A New Discovery of Topaz Crystals." *Rocks and Minerals Magazine*, Vol. 30, Nos. 5-6, May-June 1955. Topaz from New Hampshire.

————"Recent Discovery of Fine Gem Tourmalines in Maine." *Gems & Gemology*, Vol. 8, No. 5, Spring 1955.

SIMONDS, F. W.—"The Minerals and Mineral Localities of Texas." *University of*

Texas Mineral Survey Bulletin No. 5, Dec. 1902. An out-of-date but still useful listing of localities.

SINKANKAS, J.—"Largest American Gem Find in 42 Years." *Lapidary Journal*, Vol. 12, No. 3, August 1958. Personal experiences in the Himalaya Mine.

————"Recent Gem Mining at Ramona, San Diego County, California." *Gems & Gemology*, Vol. VIII, No. 12, Winter 1956-57.

————"Recent Gem Mining at Pala, San Diego County, California." *Gems & Gemology*, Vol. IX, No. 3, Fall 1957.

————, —" 'Green' Amethyst from Four Peaks, Arizona." *Gems and Gemology*, Vol. IX, No. 3, Fall 1957, pp. 88-95.

SMITH, M.—"The Rubies of Cowee Valley, North Carolina." *Rocks & Minerals Magazine*, Vol. 25, Nos. 9-10, Sept.-Oct., 1950. A recent account of a field trip to this old locality.

SPENCE, H. S.—"Feldspar." *Canada Department of Mines Publication*, 1932. Gem Feldspar localities are described.

STAATZ, M. H. & A. F. TRITES—"Geology of the Quartz Greek Pegmatite District, Gunnison County, Colorado." *U.S. Geological Survey, Professional Paper 265*, 1955. Gemstones from pegmatites briefly mentioned.

STERRETT, D. B.—"Mica Deposits of the United States." *United States Geological Survey, Bulletin No. 740*, 1923. Many gemstone localities described, especially in New England.

————" 'Old Plantation' Emerald Mine." *Rocks & Minerals*, Vol. 33, Nos. 7-8, July-August 1958. The Turner emerald mine in Cleveland Co., N.C. is thoroughly described; maps & photos.

STOLL, W. C.—"Mica and Beryl Pegmatites in Idaho and Montana. *U.S. Geological Survey, Professional Paper 229*, 1950. Gem beryl briefly mentioned.

STOSE, G. W.—"The Copper Deposits of South Mountain in Pennsylvania." *United States Geological Survey, Bulletin 430*, pp. 122-129, 1910. Describes occurrence of cuttable rhyolites.

STOUT, W. & R. A. SCHOENLAUB—"The Occurrence of Flint in Ohio." *Geological Survey of Ohio, Fourth Series, Bulletin 46*, 1945. Describes the cherts of Flint Ridge.

SWITZER, G.—"Granite Pegmatites of the Mt. Antero Region, Colorado." *American Mineralogist*, Vol. 24, Dec. 1939, pp. 791-809. Personal observations on gemstone deposits in this area.

TANTON, T. L.—"Fort William and Port Arthur, and Thunder Cape Map-areas, Thunder Bay District, Ontario." *Canada Department of Mines, Geological Survey, Memoir 167*, 1931. Describes geology and mineralogy of the silver mines in which amethyst occurs.

TOLSTED, L. L. & A. SWINFORD—"Kansas Rocks and Minerals." *State Geological Survey of Kansas*, 1952. Gemstone deposits briefly mentioned.

U.S. GEOLOGICAL SURVEY—"Mineral Resources of the United States." Precious stones chapters were published in the "Resources" every year as follows: 1883-1905, G. F. Kunz; 1906-1914, D. B. Sterrett; 1915-1918, W. T. Schaller; 1919-1921, B. H. Stoddard. After this year the precious stones chapters were dropped and did not reappear until 1932 when they were resumed in the Minerals Yearbook published by the U.S. Bureau of Mines. The early period of publication provides much valuable information on gemstones in the United States and has been consulted frequently in the preparation of the present work.

————"Bibliography of North American Geology." Published as *U.S. Geological Survey Bulletins* commencing with No. 746. The most recent is No. 1065 (1955). Many gemstone occurrences are referenced.

VERROW, H. J.—"Amethyst, Smoky Quartz, Topaz, in Northern New Hampshire," *Rocks and Minerals Magazine*, Vol. 20, No. 6, June 1945. Excellent locality information.

VONSEN, M.—"Borates of California." *Rocks & Minerals Magazine*, Vol. 20, Nos. 9-10, Sept.-Oct., 1951. Ulexite and colemanite localities.

WAITE, G. G.—"Notes on Canadian Gems and Ornamental Stones." *University of Toronto Studies, Geological Series No. 49, Contributions to Canadian Mineralogy*, 1945.

WALKER, T. L.—"Chemawinite or Canadian Amber." *University of Toronto Studies, Geological Series, No. 40, Contributions to Mineralogy*, 1936-1937.

WILLIAMSON, G. C.—"*The Book of Amber*." Ernest Benn, Ltd., London, England, 1932. An excellent and thorough treatise devoted entirely to amber; some American localities are mentioned.

WITTICH, E.—"Uber Edelsteinfunde auf der Halbinsel Nieder-Kalifornien." *Centrallblatt für Mineralogie, Geologie, und Päleontologie*, Nr. 15, Aug. 1, 1914. Describes gemstone deposits in Baja California.

WITTICH, E. & M. VILLALVA—"Berylo en diques de Pegmatita de la Baja California." *Soc. Geol. Mex. Acta d. 1. asamblea gener.* invierno 1912, Vol. 7. Mentions gemmy beryls in Baja California pegmatites.

WOODFORD, A. O.—"Crestmore Minerals." *California Division of Mines, Report XXXIX of the State Mineralogist*, July 1943. Deals with the large assemblage of contact-metamorphic minerals found in the Crestmore Quarry near Riverside, California.

WOODHOUSE, C. D.—"The Mono County Andalusite Mine." *Rock & Minerals Magazine*, Vol. 26, No. 9-10, Sept.-Oct., 1951.

ZIEGLER, V.—"The Minerals of the Black Hills." *South Dakota School of Mines, Bulletin No. 10*, Feb. 1914. Detailed account of minerals and localities.

ZODAC, P.—"Special Opal Number." *Rocks & Mineral Magazine*, Vol. 8, No. 1, Mar. 1933. An entire issue devoted to opal; excellent glossary of opal terms and extensive bibliography.

APPENDIX 2

Glossary

A compilation of special terms, names, and mineral species not explained or described elsewhere in this book. Divisions of geologic time are listed in chronological order in a table under GEOLOGIC TIME.

Accessory minerals. Those occurring in rocks in small quantities and not ordinarily considered a regular constituent of same.

Acid rocks. Igneous rocks containing over 65 per cent silica.

Acmite. A dark green or brown pyroxene mineral; sodium iron silicate.

Adit. A horizontal passage entering a mine.

Age (era). A great period of time in the geologic history of the earth marked by major physical changes or development of life.

Agua. Spanish for water.

Algonkian. A period of geologic time within the Precambrian (see GEOLOGIC TIME).

Alkali. Chemically, any substance having marked basic properties; commonly used in the earth sciences in connection with the presence of the "alkali metals," i.e., lithium, sodium, potassium, rubidium, and cesium.

Alluvial (alluvium). Pertaining to deposits such as sand, clay, and gravel, laid down through the action of running water.

Alluvial fan. The gently-rising fan-shaped deposit of alluvium commonly found at the mouth of a ravine or canyon where it empties upon a plain or into a valley.

Alteration. Any chemical or physical change in rocks or minerals after original formation and usually involving the production of new minerals or significant changes in the texture and composition of rocks.

Amphibole. The name applied to a group of silicate minerals whose chief rock-

620

making member is hornblende; rocks in which an amphibole is prominent may be called amphibole-gabbro, amphibole-granite, etc.

Amphibolite. A granular rock composed mostly of hornblende and plagioclase feldspar but also often containing quartz, epidote, or garnet.

Amygdule. A rounded or almond-shaped gas cavity in volcanic rock which later fills with mineral matter, often chalcedony. **Amygdaloidal:** containing amygdules.

Analcite. Hydrous sodium aluminum silicate commonly found in opaque white crystals in volcanic rocks associated with zeolites.

Andesite. A volcanic rock composed of andesine or oligoclase feldspar and one or more dark-colored minerals such as biotite mica, hornblende, or pyroxene.

Anhedral. Applied to minerals whose crystals are embedded wholly in other minerals and have no external crystal forms; e.g., the grains of quartz and feldspar in granite.

Anhydrite. Calcium sulfate; often found with gypsum to which it alters by taking on water of crystallization.

Anhydrous. Lacking water of crystallization.

Ankerite. Calcium magnesium iron carbonate; often associated with dolomite and similar in appearance.

Anorthosite. A gabbro or norite almost without pyroxene and consisting principally of plagioclase feldspar, especially labradorite.

Aplite. A sugary-textured white to gray granite containing silvery muscovite; common in pegmatites.

Apophyllite. Calcium potassium silicate with water; color white to pink with strong pearly luster on the face parallel to the cleavage plane; common in cavities in volcanic rocks.

Argillaceous. Containing clay either soft or hardened; applied to rocks derived from clay or containing clay.

Argillite. A sedimentary rock composed essentially of clay but not so compact as slate nor showing such strong parting; commonly harder and more compact than shale.

Arkose. Sandstone derived from decayed granite and therefore containing considerable feldspar in addition to quartz grains.

Arroyo. A steep-walled channel cut in loose surface material by an intermittently flowing stream; a common landscape feature in the Southwestern United States and Mexico.

Arsenopyrite. Iron sulfur arsenide; forms small sharply-pointed wedge-shaped crystal of gray color and metallic luster.

Ash. Uncemented volcanic cinders of small size.

Augite. Calcium magnesium silicate with iron and aluminum; the commonest rock-making pyroxene; generally black in color; forms short stubby crystals of glassy luster.

Augite-diorite. A diorite in which augite is a prominent constituent.

Badlands. A region almost without vegetation in which soft sediments have been carved into fantastic gullies and pinnacles; e.g., the Badlands of the Dakotas.

Bakerite. Hydrous calcium borosilicate; in compact masses resembling porcelain; from the borax deposits of California.

Bar. An accumulation of gravel in streams and rivers where the currents are less swift.

Basal cleavage. A cleavage plane corresponding in direction to a basal plane.

Basal plane. A plane lying parallel to the horizontal axes of a crystal.

Basalt. An extremely fine-grained dark volcanic rock composed mainly of pyroxene and plagioclase feldspar; often contains gas cavities filled with crystallized minerals; forms angular columns as a result of contraction during cooling as for example in the Palisades of the Hudson River, Devil's Tower in Wyoming, etc.

Basic rocks. Igneous rocks containing less than 55 per cent silica.

Batholith. A huge mass of plutonic rock of unknown depth believed to be connected to or part of the enormous masses which lie beneath all other rocks exposed on the surface of the earth.

Bed (bedding). Pertaining to the stratification or laying down of rocks in approximately parallel layers.

Bentonite. A rock consisting principally of a clay mineral such as montmorillonite.

Bertrandite. Hydrous beryllium silicate; colorless and transparent; often found in small crystals associated with other beryllium minerals from which it forms by alteration.

Biotite. The common black mica of igneous and metamorphic rocks.

Biotite-gneiss. A gneiss in which biotite is a prominent mineral.

Bipyramid. A double-ended pyramid as observed on crystals.

Black sand. A sand containing considerable quantities of heavy dark-colored minerals such as magnetite, ilmenite, chromite, etc.

Bolson. Spanish for a flat-floored valley surrounded by high terrain on all sides and draining to a central pan or *playa*.

Borax. Sodium borate containing water; white in color; common in the borax deposits of California.

Bornite. Copper iron sulfide; sometimes called *"peacock ore"* because of the beautifully colored iridescent tarnish.

Botryoidal. Descriptive of a surface covered with spherical bulges.

Breccia. A jumbled mass of broken angular rock or mineral fragments firmly cemented together.

Brilliant (brilliant cut). A style of faceting round or oval gems by covering the surface with a series of kite-shaped facets joined by triangular facets; the style of cut most commonly employed in faceting diamonds.

Brochantite. Basic sulfate of copper; color emerald-green; in small needle-like crystals in oxidized portions of copper ore bodies.

Bustamite. Grayish-red rhodonite containing calcium.

Butte. An isolated hill or mountain with steep sides.

Calcareous. Containing calcium carbonate or calcite.

Caledonite. A green sulfate of lead and copper.

Carat. A unit of weight for gems equivalent to 1/5 gram or 200 milligrams; one avoirdupois ounce contains 141.75 carats.

Cerro. Spanish for hill or mountain.

Chalcocite. Copper sulfide; lead-gray in color and metallic in luster; common in the copper ore bodies of Arizona.

Chalcopyrite. Sulfide of iron and copper; rich yellow in color with metallic luster; abundant in many metallic ore bodies.

Chalk. A porous earthy gray or white limestone composed of the skeletons of minute marine shellfish.

Chlorite. Silicate of aluminum with iron, magnesium, and water; predominantly dull dark green in color and mica-like in texture; often present as an alteration product in metamorphic rocks.

Chromite. Iron chromate; massive black to brownish black; submetallic luster; common in serpentines.

Cinder cone. The conical pile of loose material surrounding the vent of a volcano and thrown out by a series of minor explosions.

Cinnabar. The bright red sulfide of mercury and its most common ore.

Claim. A portion of land held under Federal and local laws for the purpose of exploiting the mineral wealth believed to lie beneath the surface; in the United States a lode claim measures 600 x 1500 feet maximum.

Clay. Earthy material of exceptionally fine grain derived from the weathering of aluminous rocks such as granite; plastic when wet and hard when dry.

Clay slate. A slate derived principally from clay and showing a dull luster on the parting planes.

Conglomerate. A sedimentary rock consisting of rounded pebbles cemented together; also called pudding stone.

Contact. The place where two kinds of rock come together.

Contact metamorphism. The alteration or change brought about in rocks in contact with or near an intruded mass of igneous rock.

Cookeite. Hydrous aluminum silicate; commonly forms small scaly crystals in rounded masses in pegmatite; silvery to creamy in color.

Cordillera. Spanish for a continuous mountain chain.

Core, pegmatite. The innermost rock mass found within a pegmatite body often consisting of a disk-shaped or bean-shaped mass of quartz.

Corrosion. The eating away of rocks and minerals by chemical agencies.

Cove. A small flat area entering a mountainous area; e.g., Magnet Cove, Arkansas.

Crandallite. Hydrous calcium aluminum phosphate forming compact masses in the variscite nodules of Utah.

Crater. The depression marking the vent of a volcano.

Crinoid. An ancient sea animal resembling a lily in general form; the stem is segmented and pieces are frequently found as fossils.

Cristobalite. Silica forming white octahedral crystals.

Cobbing. Breaking ore to separate the better pieces.

Country rock. A general term for the mass of rock surrounding veins, dikes, ore bodies, etc.

Cuesta. A sloping plain terminating in a steep ridge at one end where underlying rocks are exposed.

Cueva. Spanish for cave or grotto.

Cuprite. Dark red oxide of copper; common in copper ore bodies.

Cushion cut. A style of faceting gems in which the finished gem is roughly rectangular in outline but with gently outward curving sides and rounded corners.

Dahllite. A dark green carbonated calcium phosphate found in fibrous masses, a variety of staffelite.

Dehrnite. Hydrous phosphate of calcium and sodium; forms white crusts in variscite nodules.

Deltaite. Hydrous phosphate of calcium and aluminum found with variscite.

Dennisonite. Hydrous phosphate of calcium and aluminum; found as white crusts in variscite nodules.

Deposit (deposition). Referring to anything laid down as a deposit or ore; used generally and loosely for all manner of mineral concentrations.

Diabase. A basic dark igneous rock composed mainly of plagioclase feldspar and augite with minor magnetite and apatite.

Diatom. A microscopic marine plant enclosed in a silica skeleton; abundant remains are found in many types of sedimentary rocks.

Diffraction. Modification of light caused by passage along edges of opaque bodies or through narrow slits, or by reflection from surfaces covered with many fine ruled lines such as a *diffraction grating;* the light is often changed into spectral colors.

Dike. A wall-like intruded body of igneous rock often cutting through country rock without regard for layering; pegmatite bodies are often dikes.

Diorite. An igneous rock similar to granite and composed of hornblende and plagioclase feldspar with minor amounts of biotite and augite, or augite alone; quartz may be present in considerable amount in which case the rock is termed *quartz-diorite.*

Dip. The angle below the horizontal made by ore bodies or strata.

Disseminated ore. Ore containing numerous small particles of metallic minerals sprinkled throughout the rock.

Divide. The land crest marking the boundary between adjacent watersheds; in North America the Continental Divide separates the waters flowing into the Atlantic Ocean from those flowing into the Pacific.

Dolomite. A mineral similar in many respects to calcite but containing principally magnesium in place of calcium; carbonate of magnesium; a rock containing much dolomite is called by that name while ordinary limestone in which dolomite is present is often called magnesian limestone.

Dome. A large rounded mass of rock.

Drift. A general term for all kinds of debris deposited by glaciers or by the outflow of waters resulting from their melting; in mining the term refers to a horizontal tunnel which follows the vein or ore body.

Druse. A cavity in rock lined with crystals of the same minerals which are found in the rock itself; distinguished from geode or amygdule in which the filling is not related to the country rock.

Drusy. Covered with crystals, usually of uniform size.

Dunite. An igneous rock composed mainly of olivine and chromite.

Eclogite (glaucophane schist). A glaucophane schist containing some of the minerals of eclogite, i.e., light green pyroxene, actinolite, and garnet.

Eluvial. Formed by the rotting or disintegration of rock in its place of origin.

Emerald cut. A rectangular step-cut faceted gem with corners beveled and all surfaces covered by a series of rectangular facets or steps.

Englishite. Hydrous phosphate of calcium, aluminum, and potassium; occurs as thin colorless layers in variscite nodules.

Eosphorite. Hydrous manganese iron aluminum phosphate; rose pink in color and found as small prismatic crystals or massive in pegmatites.

Era. See AGE.

Escarpment. A continuous line of cliffs.

Estuary. A bay at the mouth of a river where the tide meets the river current.

Etch figure. Characteristic pit or depression formed on the surface of a crystal by the action of solvents.

Euhedral. Descriptive of crystals covered by well-developed faces.

Exfoliation. The splitting off of sheets of rock from larger masses by weathering or other causes; the remaining masses are often rounded.

Extrusives. Volcanic or igneous rocks which reach the surface.

Fault. A break in rock along which one side has been displaced by slip.

Fault breccia. Broken rock filling the zone of the fault.

Felsite. An igneous rock in which the grain size is extremely fine; used in connection with porphyries and quartz-porphyries.

Ferruginous. Containing iron.

Fiord (fjord). A narrow, steep-walled inlet to the sea with deep soundings close to shore.

Fissure. Extensive crack or break.

Fissure vein. A fissure filled with vein minerals.

Float. A general term applied to pieces of rock some distance detached from their outcrop source.

Flow. A single large congealed outpouring of lava.

Foliated. Leaf-like; applied to many thin parallel layers as in schists.

Formation. A related group of rocks; a set of strata formed during the same period of time under generally the same circumstances.

Fossils. The remains of plants and animals preserved in rocks.

Franciscan formation. Jurassic rocks characteristic of the Pacific coastal ranges

of California and composed of sandstones, cherts, serpentines, and glaucophane schists.

Francolite. A variety of apatite forming compact masses.

Franklinite. Iron zinc manganese oxide forming black octahedral crystals in the
zinc ore body of Franklin, New Jersey.

Friable. Easily broken; crumbly.

Fumarole. A hole or vent upon or near a volcano from which issues hot gases.

Gabbro. A dark granite-like igneous rock composed of plagioclase feldspar and
a pyroxene.

Galena. Lead sulfide; gray with metallic luster when freshly broken; cubic cleavage; the most common ore of lead.

Gangue. The ordinarily worthless minerals associated with the valuable metalliferous ores in a vein.

Geode. A hollow secretion or concretion lined with crystals and easily separated
from the enclosing rock.

Geologic time. See Table. Geological history according to U.S. Geological Survey usage, is divided into four great eras which are further divided into
periods (systems) and epochs (series). The arrangement places the earliest
or lowest rocks at the bottom of the table, and, proceeding upward, the
most recent at the top.

Geology. The science treating of the origin, history, and structure of the earth
as recorded in its rocks.

Glacier. A stream or sheet of ice formed from the accumulation of unmelting
snow.

Glass. A general term for glass-like igneous rocks such as obsidian.

Glaucophane. An amphibole; sodium iron aluminum silicate; a common rock-
forming mineral.

Glaucophane-schist. An amphibole schist in which glaucophane is abundant along
with some epidote, quartz, and mica.

Glauconite. Hydrous iron potassium silicate; the ingredient making fertilizer marls
valuable for that purpose.

Gneiss. A banded metamorphic rock; predominantly composed of quartz, mica,
and some dark mineral such as hornblende; all minerals are more or less
drawn out in streaks. Gneiss and schist are similar but gneiss is far poorer
in mica and therefore much stronger.

Goethite. Hydrous oxide of iron; black to brown in color; often forms fibrous
masses of shining black surface; the principal constituent of limonite.

Gordonite. Hydrous phosphate of magnesium and aluminum; colorless crystals
occur with variscite in nodules at the deposits in Utah.

Gossan. The rusty, limonite-rich capping of ore outcrops resulting from the
weathering of sulfide minerals containing iron.

Gouge. The layer of soft material often found along the wall of a vein.

Granite. A granular igneous rock containing principally quartz and feldspar plus
a light or dark mica, with or without minor amounts of other minerals.

MAJOR STRATIGRAPHIC AND TIME DIVISIONS IN USE BY THE U.S. GEOLOGICAL SURVEY

Era	System or Period		Series or Epoch	Estimated ages of time in millions of years
Cenozoic	Quaternary		Recent	0-1
			Pleistocene	
	Tertiary		Pliocene	1-10
			Miocene	10-25
			Oligocene	25-40
			Eocene	40-60
			Paleocene	
Mesozoic	Cretaceous		Upper Lower	60-125
	Jurassic		Upper Middle Lower	125-150
	Triassic		Upper Middle Lower	150-180
Paleozoic	Permian			180-205
	Carboniferous Systems	Pennsylvanian	Upper Middle Lower	205-255
		Mississippian	Upper Lower	
	Devonian		Upper Middle Lower	255-315
	Silurian		Upper Middle Lower	315-350
	Ordovician		Upper Middle Lower	350-430
	Cambrian		Upper Middle Lower	430-510
Precambrian				510-3000

Granodiorite. Igneous rocks intermediate between granites and quartz-diorites.

Granulite. A metamorphic rock consisting of even-sized interlocking granular minerals.

Graphite. The soft steel-gray to black flaky crystallized form of carbon.

Greenstone. An old and vague term for greenish metamorphosed basalts or metamorphosed sediments derived from basalt which owe their color to green chlorite.

Grenville limestone. A Precambrian formation of the Ottawa River region of Canada.

Gulch. A narrow mountain ravine or small canyon.

Hacienda. Mexican landed estate.

Halloysite. Claylike aluminum silicate resembling kaolinite; found in pegmatites, especially in or near pockets.

Hanging wall. The upper wall of country rock bordering the vein or dike; opposite to foot wall.

Hematite. Red iron oxide; the most important ore of iron; black when compact but leaves a red streak when rubbed on a porcelain plate; crystals often form scaly bright steel gray masses as in *specularite*.

Hemimorphic. In crystallography, having no transverse plane of symmetry and no center of symmetry; hemimorphic development is shown by decided differences in the forms of crystal faces noted at opposing ends; zincite and tourmaline are hemimorphic.

Herderite. A fluorine phosphate of beryllium and calcium; yellowish and greenish-white crystals have been found in some Maine pegmatites.

Horizon. A particular depth in a sedimentary layer or stratum at which fossils or minerals of similar character appear throughout the formation.

Hornfels. A dense jaspery rock produced by contact with an igneous intrusion.

Horse. A mass of country rock lying within a vein.

Hydrothermal. Pertaining to the action of hot water solutions in dissolving and depositing minerals within the earth's crust.

Hydrous. Containing chemically combined water.

Igneous rocks. Those formed by solidification from a molten state; subdivided into plutonic, extrusive, and intrusive rocks.

Ilmenite. Iron titanium oxide; gray-black in color; heavy; common in many metamorphic and granite-like rocks.

Incline. A shaftlike mine excavation which is not vertical.

Inclusion. A crystal or fragment of foreign mineral enclosed within a larger crystal; also small cavities filled with gas or liquid or both.

Indurated. Hardened by heat, or pressure, or both as *indurated* clay.

Interpenetrant twins. Two or more twin crystals which pass through each other.

Intrusive. An igneous rock which is squeezed into cracks or crevices, or between layers of rocks already in existence.

Isomorphous minerals. Minerals in which several elements can change places without radically changing the crystal structure or essential physical properties; the gradual change in properties occurs from one *end member* to the other and gives rise to intermediate species comprising a *series*.

Jarosite. Hydrous potassium iron sulfate; massive; brown to brownish-yellow in color.

Joaquinite. Titanium-silicate of calcium and iron; occurs as deep honey-yellow crystals of small size with benitoite.

Joint. A parting plane separating a once continuous mass of rock; joints tend to cross each other at approximately right angles and to divide the rock mass into blocks.

Kaolinite. Hydrated silicate of aluminum forming from the decomposition of feldspars and crystallizing in exceedingly small mica-like plates; the principal constituent of clays; *kaolin* is the name applied to a mixture of kaolinite and fine crushed quartz.

Keeweenawan series. Rocks of the Upper Precambrian period in Michigan.

Kernite. Hydrated sodium borate; colorless crystals and masses found in quantity in Kern County, California.

Kidney. A rounded mass of ore or massive gemstone material resembling a kidney in form.

Kimberlite. See PERIDOTITE.

Knob. A rounded isolated mass of rock of the size of a hill or mountain.

Laccolith. A mass of intrusive rock which has forced its way between layers of rock, forming a large bulge by buckling the overlying rock.

Laguna. Spanish for lagoon.

Lamellar. Composed of thin layers, plates, or scales, like the leaves of a book.

Latite. An extrusive rock intermediate between trachyte and andesite.

Laurentian. Lower Precambrian rocks of Eastern Canada.

Lava. The liquid outpouring of a volcano.

Leach. To dissolve minerals from ore or from porous rock.

Ledge. Used to designate a mineralized outcrop, or, in pegmatite districts, to designate an outcropping pegmatite.

Lehiite. Hydrous phosphate of calcium, aluminum, sodium, and potassium; found as white crusts in variscite nodules.

Lens. A body or ore or portion of a mineral deposit shaped like a lens, i.e., thick in the center and tapering to each side.

Lenticular. Shaped like a lentil bean or like a lens.

Level. A horizontal passage or drift in a mine; levels are numbered from below the adit in descending order.

Lewistonite. Hydrous phosphate of calcium, potassium, and sodium; in minute hexagonal prisms in variscite nodules.

Lime. Calcium oxide; applied generally to indicate the presence of calcium.

Limestone. A sedimentary rock composed mainly of calcium carbonate (calcite) but often rendered quite impure by the presence of clay, sand, etc.; when magnesium carbonate is present it may be called magnesian limestone.

Limonite. A general term applied to mixtures containing hydrous iron oxides of uncertain identity; brown to black in color; commonly resulting from the decomposition of iron pyrites and other sulfides containing iron.

Linarite. Basic sulfate of lead and copper; deep blue in color; rare.

Lindgrenite. Basic molybdate of copper.

Lithophysae. Hollow spherulites in rhyolite, obsidian, and similar glassy rocks.

Locate. To mark out the boundaries of a claim and to establish possession.

Lode. Same as vein.

Lollingite. Iron arsenide; grayish-white in color with metallic luster.

Loma. Spanish for a long and narrow flat-topped ridge or series of hills.

Luster. The characteristic reflection of light from minerals.

Magma. The deep-seated molten material from which igneous rocks form.

Magnesite. Magnesium carbonate; generally white and like calcite in essential respects though seldom clear.

Magnetite. Black oxide of iron; an important ore of iron; attracted to a magnet and sometimes magnetized as in *lodestone.*

Manganite. Black hydrous oxide of manganese; luster submetallic to dull in earthy types.

Marble. The metamorphosed form of limestone; generally granular and exhibiting large crystals showing rhombohedral cleavage; colors generally pale.

Marcasite. Iron sulfide; similar in appearance to iron pyrite but decomposing quickly in air to form white powdery iron sulfate.

Mariposa formation. Rocks of the Upper Jurassic of California.

Marl. Calcareous clay or loam often containing glauconite; formerly used as fertilizer.

Martite. Hematite in the form of crystals resembling magnetite.

Massive. Without definite external crystal form and in masses composed of small crystals.

Matrix. The groundmass of rock containing streaks of ore or massive minerals; the mass of mineral matter upon which crystals are perched.

Mesa. Spanish for tableland or a flat-topped elevation with steep sides, generally isolated.

Metamorphic rocks. Those altered in some important fashion through pressure, heat, or chemical activity, or any combination of these agencies.

Mica schist. A general term for schist in which mica is a conspicuous and abundant ingredient.

Millisite. Hydrous calcium sodium aluminum phosphate; forms chalcedony-like masses in variscite nodules.

Mineralogy. The science which treats of minerals including their outward forms, atomic structure, chemical composition, properties, and occurrence.

Mina. Spanish for mine.

Molybdenite. Sulfide of molybdenum forming scaly crystals very similar to graphite but pale gray in color with splendant metallic luster.

Monazite. Phosphate of the cerium metals; brown in color; resinous luster; very heavy.

Montgomeryite. Basic hydrated phosphate of calcium and aluminum; deep green minute crystals occur in Utah variscite nodules.

Montmorillonite. A hydrous aluminum silicate claylike mineral commonly found in pegmatites in or near pockets; inherently colorless (white) but often deep pink to pale red; at times firm and translucent when wet but crumbly and opaque when dry.

Monzonite. A granular igneous rock composed mostly of plagioclase and orthoclase feldspars plus hornblende, biotite, or augite; if some quartz is present it is called *quartz-monzonite.*

Moraine. The accumulation of debris finally deposited by a glacier along its margin.

Mother lode. The principal vein or lode.

Native. Occurring pure or uncombined as native gold, silver, etc.

Nepheline-syenite. An igneous rock abundant in Ontario and Quebec composed mainly of potassium and sodium feldspars, nepheline, pyroxenes, and amphiboles; zircon, sphene, and apatite are often important accessories.

Nephelite (nepheline). Sodium potassium aluminum silicate; pale in color; transparent to translucent; greasy luster.

Neptunite. A complex sodium-potassium, iron-manganese titanium silicate forming lustrous black prismatic crystals in association with benitoite.

Nontronite. Hydrous iron silicate; a greasy soft variety of chloropal.

Norite. Gabbro consisting of plagioclase feldspar and hypersthene.

Oölite. A variety of limestone composed of numerous small spherules like fish-eggs in form; the spherules may be calcareous, siliceous, or ferruginous.

Opencut. A deposit worked from the surface in a trench-like excavation.

Orbicular. Containing numerous orbs or spherules solidly encased.

Ore. A mineral of sufficient value in respect to quality and quantity to be mined with profit.

Ore body. The more or less continuous mass, distinct from country rock, in which the minerals of value occur.

Organic. Dealing with those compounds produced in plants and animals; referring to living creation.

Outcrop. That part of an ore body, stratum, or other mass of rock which appears on the surface.

Overburden. Worthless surface material covering a mineral deposit.

Overite. Hydrated calcium aluminum phosphate; found in colorless to pale green platy crystals or masses in the variscite nodules of Utah.

Oxidized zone. The upper part of an orebody which has been altered as a result of the action of surface waters carrying oxygen, carbon dioxide, etc.

Parting. The tendency of crystals to separate along certain planes which are not true cleavage planes.

Patented claim. A claim to which permanent rights have been secured by a conveyance or *patent*.

Pegmatite. A very coarse granite which is generally found in sheetlike masses intruded into other rocks or formed within granite itself; most pegmatites show well-defined zones or *units* within which occur characteristic assemblages of minerals.

Periclase. Magnesium oxide; colorless to white; generally in small crystals; rare.

Peridotite. A granite-like igneous rock composed mainly of olivine and pyroxene; in the variety *kimberlite,* biotite mica is also present while the rock is generally broken or brecciated.

Perlite. A glassy volcanic rock like obsidian but made light and friable by a multitude of spheroidal cracks; "Apache tears" are small obsidian nodules found within masses of perlite.

Perovskite. Calcium titanate; yellowish to reddish in color; luster adamantine.

Perthite (perthitic). Referring to the plaid-like structure of feldspars in which two feldspar species are intergrown; commonly observed in pegmatite feldspars.

Petrography. A division of geology dealing with the description and classification of rocks.

Petrographic microscope. A microscope specially fitted with optical and mechanical accessories for identifying and studying the properties of minerals in granular form or in thin sections of rock.

Petrology. A division of geology dealing with the natural history of rocks; includes petrography and the genesis of rocks.

Phlogopite. The brown magnesian mica.

Phyllite. A lustrous compact schistose rock derived from clay sediments by metamorphic processes.

Piedmont. The area lying at the base of mountains and generally sloping shallowly.

Pierre shales. Sedimentary rocks of the Great Plains Region of the United States belonging to the Cretaceous period.

Piezoelectricity. Electrical charges of opposite sign developed upon opposite sides of certain hemimorphic crystal sections when subjected to pressure; e.g., observed in quartz and tourmaline.

Pillow basalt. Basalt in which large rounded masses of "pillows" of firm rock are abundant; the spaces between the masses are filled with friable rock in which cavities containing crystals are often present; commonly forms when lava flows meet water.

Pica. Spanish for the exact summit of a mountain.

Picacho. Spanish for summit.

Pipe. A vertical cylindrical mass of kimberlite or other igneous rock extending to an unknown depth.

Placer. Spanish for an alluvial deposit containing gold; in United States mining law usage the term placer refers to any mineral deposit in which minerals do not occur in place.

Plateau. A flat-topped region of considerable elevation and extent.

Playa. Spanish for the central flat area or depression in a bolson (which see); the *dry lakes* of California are playas.

Plug. The solidified core of lava found in the neck of an extinct volcano.

Plutonic rocks. Those which have cooled some distance below the surface of the earth and generally show grain textures like granite.

Pocket. Generally a small body of ore; in pegmatites, the central openings lined with crystals including those of gem species.

Polarized light. Rays of light which have been caused to vibrate only in one plane.

Porphyry. Any igneous rock consisting of larger, readily distinguished grains or crystals, set in a finer grained groundmass; most porphyries are rhyolitic.

Prismatic. Like a prism in form, i.e., a narrow form whose sides are covered with rectangular planes joining in parallel edges.

Prospect. A superficial pit or working which tests for the presence of valuable minerals.

Pseudomorph. A crystal which bears the faces and angles of one mineral species but actually is another; also applied broadly to other misleading or deceptive substitutions such as petrified wood in which quartz, opal, etc., are pseudomorphs of wood.

Pumice. Lava which has been made so frothy it resembles solidified sea-foam; it is frequently so filled with gas bubbles that pieces float on water.

Punta. Spanish for point or headland.

Pyrolusite. Black earthy manganese dioxide; often found associated with rhodonite in which it forms the black streaks.

Pyrophyllite. A hydrous aluminum silicate; white, green, gray, etc., in color; foliated like talc which it otherwise resembles and similarly useful in commerce and industry.

Pyroxene. The group name for a number of silicate minerals which are abundant in igneous and metamorphic rocks; composition chiefly silicates of calcium and magnesium but also of iron, zinc, and manganese.

Pyroxenite. A granite-like rock whose chief mineral is a pyroxene and lacking both feldspar and olivine.

Quartzite. Conglomerate or sandstone composed principally of quartz grains or pebbles converted to a solid coherent rock by metamorphic action.

Quartz monzonite. A kind of granite in which soda-lime and potash feldspars occur in about equal quantity.

Red beds. Reddish sandstones and other sediments formed during the Late Pennsylvanian to Jurassic periods.

Replacement. The process by which one mineral takes the place of another, often without changing the physical form of the first.

Replacement ore body. A mass of ore formed by the dissolution of previous minerals and their replacement by others.

Resin. An organic substance solidifying from the sap of trees, especially the conifers; generally brittle; low in specific gravity; mostly some shade of yellow to reddish-yellow.

Rhyolite. Volcanic rocks containing small crystals of orthoclase and quartz plus biotite, hornblende, or a pyroxene; most are light in color.

Rhyolite-porphyry. A rhyolite in which some grains or crystals are visibly larger than others.

Riffles. Slats placed across the bottom of sluices to catch heavy minerals.

Rincon. Spanish for recess in a mountain or cliff such as would be formed by a river bend.

Rubble. Rough, irregular pieces of broken rock.

Sandstone. A sedimentary rock consisting of sand grains cemented together; in most instances, quartz is the predominant mineral.

Scolecite. Hydrous calcium aluminum silicate; one of the zeolites; typically forms crystalline masses of radiate structure exhibiting silky luster.

Schist. Foliated metamorphic rocks characterized by long, drawn-out streaks and containing much mica which causes it to be readily separated along the layers.

Sedimentary rocks. Layered rocks formed from the accumulation and solidification of mineral, animal, or vegetable matter; water, wind, and glaciers are the principal means by which the loose sediments are transported and deposited.

Sepiolite. A fluffy to porous hydrous magnesium aluminum silicate; a firm kind is known as *meerschaum* and is used in making pipes.

Sericite. A soft fibrous form of muscovite mica derived from the alteration of feldspar.

Shale. A sedimentary rock consisting of cemented mud or silt.

Shard. A jagged splinter of some brittle substance such as glass or porcelain.

Sheet. An extensive bed of eruptive rock intruded between layers of a pre-existing rock; a similar body of volcanic rock poured out upon the surface in a layer of more or less uniform thickness.

Shear zone. The zone in a rock mass along which shearing has occurred and which is filled with crushed and brecciated rock.

Shingle. Beach gravel composed of rounded pebbles of about the same size.

Siderite. Brown iron carbonate; crystallizes in rhombohedra showing cleavage planes similar to those observed in calcite.

Sierra. Spanish for saw and hence applied to a row of narrow jagged mountain crests.

Silica (silicified) (siliceous). Terms referring to the presence of silica or quartz.

Sill. A thin sheet of igneous rock intruded parallel to the bedding of other rocks and lying horizontal or nearly so.

Sillimanite-schist. A schist containing an appreciable amount of sillimanite (fibrolite).

Sink hole. A steep-walled crater-like depression found in limestone regions and formed by the collapse of a cavern roof.

Shaft. A mining excavation of narrow width and considerable depth sunk in a vertical direction.

Slate. A rock similar to shale but more highly compressed and easily split along the bedding planes; small scales of mica are often present and give slate a somewhat silvery luster.

Sluice (sluice box). A narrow wooden trough lined on the bottom by riffles and through which is washed gravel in order to extract heavy minerals.

Socovan. Spanish for tunnel or adit.

Spectrum. The rainbow hues seen when white light is separated into its component wave lengths; the colors of the spectrum in order are violet, blue, green, yellow, orange, red, and an infinite number of intermediate hues between the principal ones mentioned.

Spherulites. Rounded aggregates or rosettes of very fine needle-like crystals radiating from common centers; orbicular jaspers show spherulitic structure.

Splendant. Brilliantly reflective.

Spoil. Debris or waste material from a mine.

Stalactite. A tapered column of mineral matter hanging from the roof of a cavern and deposited by dripping water.

Stalagmite. The cavern formation opposite to a stalactite, in this case, arising from the floor instead of depending from the ceiling.

Steatite. Massive, impure talc; often found in large beds.

Stellate. Radiated in structure and forming star-like patterns.

Step cut. A style of faceting in which the surface of a gem is covered by rectangular facets or steps; the profile at the girdle of the gem is unimportant although step cut generally implies a rectangular or square outline.

Sterrettite. Hydrous aluminum phosphate; found as colorless crystals with wardite in variscite nodules.

Stibnite. Antimony sulfide; soft, steel-gray, metallic luster; forms narrow splendant striated prismatic crystals.

Stilbite. Hydrous silicate of aluminum, calcium, and sodium; a zeolite; crystals form characteristic rounded bundles resembling wheat sheaves.

Stock (stockwork). A mass of country rock invaded by many small veins forming a complicated network.

Stope. The place above or below a mine level where ore has been extracted in a series of steps following an inclined ore body.

Stratum. A layer of rock of similar character throughout.

Streak. The colored mark left behind when a mineral is rubbed upon an unglazed white porcelain tile.

Striation. A minute groove or channel, especially upon crystal faces.

Strike. The horizontal trace or direction of an outcrop.

Stringer. A narrow vein or veinlet, generally irregular in thickness and following an erratic course.

Spall. To break off slabs or pieces of rock from a larger mass.

Sulfide. A mineral resulting from the combination of sulfur with another element; most sulfides are metallic in luster, very heavy, and easily broken.

Syenite. A granular igneous rock consisting of sodium or potassium feldspar plus a dark iron manganese silicate mineral such as hornblende; when quartz is present it is called quartz-syenite.

Symmetry. The regular and balanced arrangement of features, forms, and properties of crystals with reference to the crystal axes.

Talc. Hydrous silicate of aluminum, magnesium, and iron; the softest mineral of all; greasy feel; much used for powders, crayons, table tops, etc.

Talus. The sloping heap of debris at the base of a cliff or other promontory.

Tarnish. The thin, colored, often iridescent, film noted on the surface of minerals resulting from their decomposition or alteration upon exposure to the atmosphere.

Termination of a crystal. The group of planes which completely enclose the end; a doubly-terminated crystal has both ends covered with faces and hence is ordinarily covered over its entire area with crystal faces.

Tonalite. Quartz-diorite containing hornblende and biotite as the principal iron-magnesium minerals (see DIORITE).

Topographic quadrangle. An approximately rectangular map upon which is shown a small portion of land with elevations indicated by a series of curving lines each passing through a specified altitude; the curvature and crowding together of the *contour lines*, as they are called, indicate the nature of the terrain.

Torbernite. Hydrous phosphate of uranium and copper; forms small square crystals of bright green color.

Trachyte. An igneous rock consisting mostly of orthoclase feldspar and biotite mica, or hornblende, or augite.

Trap cut. Same as STEP CUT.

Tridymite. Silicon dioxide; forms minute tabular crystals.

Trilobite. Ancient fossil crustaceans somewhat resembling modern "sow bugs" in appearance but much larger and found in abundance in rocks of the Paleozoic era.

Trinity formation. Sediments laid down during the Cretaceous period.

Triphylite. Phosphate of iron, manganese, and aluminum; greenish-gray to blue in color; common in some pegmatites.

Triplite. Iron manganese phosphate; brownish or black in color; resinous luster; found in pegmatites.

Tuff. Cemented volcanic ash.

Tundra. Arctic lands in which the soil is black and mucky and the subsoil often permanently frozen; vegetation consists of mosses, lichens, and numbers of dwarfed shrubs.

Ultrabasic rocks. Generally, those igneous rocks containing little or no feldspar or quartz and in which the silica content is not over 45 per cent; the principal mineral is usually an iron-magnesium silicate.

Vein. An irregular twisting mineral deposit of considerable length but thin in proportion to length and breadth; generally formed as a result of hydrothermal activity.

Vesicle (vesicular). Referring to small cavities in glassy igneous rocks formed through expansion of gases.

Veta madre. Spanish for mother lode.

Vitreous. Like glass either in respect to physical properties or in appearance.

Vug. A cavity in rock lined with crystals which are firmly fastened to the walls and related to the minerals found in the country rock; vugs are believed to be caused by shrinkage of the enclosing rock.

Volcano. A vent in the earth's crust through which issues molten rock, various gases, mud, and hot water.

Wardite. Hydrous phosphate of calcium and aluminum; light green in color and found commonly with variscite.

Wash. The loose surface debris found in the bottoms of canyons and intermittent streams; also the depression in which such debris occurs.

Woodhouseite. A basic hydrous sulfate-phosphate of calcium and aluminum; colorless to flesh-pink; found in the andalusite deposit on White Mountain, Mono County, California.

X-ray crystal analysis. The process of passing x-rays through crystals to determine the spacing of atoms and hence the nature of the crystal structure; the traces of the rays are recorded on photographic film and from their interpretation the desired information is obtained.

Zeolites. Soft, fragile minerals of prevailingly light coloration found commonly in cavities in lavas; they have little economic importance but artificial zeolites are used extensively in water softening.

Tabular Review of Gemstone Deposits

GEMSTONES are found in many geological situations but all occurrences can be conveniently classed either as *in place deposits* (embedded in the rocks of origin), or *alluvial deposits* (loose in soil and gravel). The formation of gemstones is closely connected with the formation of the three major classes of rocks which make up the Earth's crust. The oldest rocks of all are *igneous* rocks which solidified from the original molten matter of which the Earth was composed. Most of the Earth is now believed to be solid but in favored spots, molten matter still issues from volcanoes. Almost as soon as rocks began to form, they began to be attacked by weathering, by chemical action, by heat, by pressure, and by combinations of these forces, resulting in the formation of still other rocks belonging to the remaining two great classes: *metamorphic* and *sedimentary*. Metamorphic rocks result when a rock previously in existence is altered in some important fashion; it may be sheared and crushed, squeezed together under enormous pressure and subjected to high heat, or it may be chemically changed. Perhaps all of these take place at once; in any case, it frequently bears little resemblance to its original state when metamorphism ceases. Sedimentary rocks, on the other hand, form mostly from the simple solidification of sedimentary materials or alluvium. For example, cemented sand becomes sandstone, gravel changes into conglomerate, and mud becomes shale. However, these may also be subjected to metamorphic action, changing eventually into rocks which look nothing at all like the starting material. Although not taking place rapidly according to our sense of time, all of the changes described above are subtly altering the face of the Earth beneath our very feet.

TABLE I

IN PLACE DEPOSITS

ROCK CLASS	SUB-CLASS	ORIGIN	FEATURES	VARIETIES	GEMSTONES
IGNEOUS ROCKS	PLUTONIC ROCKS	Deep-seated rocks which cooled slowly.	Coarse-grained; generally light in color. PEGMATITES are a special feature, exhibiting very coarse grain and containing very many cavities in which are found many gemstones. Plutonic rocks often form huge mountain masses (batholiths).	GRANITE, QUARTZ MONZONITE, SYENITE, DIORITE, ANORTHOSITE, GABBRO, AMPHIBOLITE, PYROXENITE, PERIDOTITE, DUNITE, etc.	DIAMOND (in Kimberlite, a variety of PERIDOTITE), CORUNDUM, SODALITE, CANCRINITE, FELDSPAR, DIASPORE, ENSTATITE, HYPERSTHENE, ZIRCON; from pegmatites: QUARTZ, FELDSPAR, BERYL, TOPAZ, SPODUMENE, TOURMALINE, LEPIDOLITE, GARNET, APATITE, etc.
	EXTRUSIVE ROCKS	Rapidly cooled igneous rocks poured out upon the surface of the Earth through fissures or from volcanoes.	Very fine-grained; generally dark to very dark in color; some are light in color; often form thin surface flows as in Western United States; form sheets and volcano plugs; often filled with gas cavities.	RHYOLITE, BASALT, OBSIDIAN, PERLITE, LATITE, PUMICE, VOLCANIC TUFF & BRECCIA, TRACHYTE, ANDESITE, etc.	OPAL, OLIVINE, QUARTZ, OBSIDIAN, RHYOLITES, PECTOLITE, DATOLITE, PREHNITE, MORDENITE, NATROLITE, MESOLITE, THOMSONITE, CALCITE, GARNET, etc.
	INTRUSIVE ROCKS (HYPABYSSAL)	Igneous rocks squeezed through fissures into pre-existing rocks; cooled less rapidly than extrusive rocks.	Sometimes show coarse grain or types in which some crystals grow to large size (porphyries); generally dark in color; often contain gas cavities; form sills, sheets, dikes, and laccoliths.	DIABASE, PORPHYRY.	OPAL, QUARTZ, PREHNITE, CALCITE, and others from the group immediately above.
SEDIMENTARY ROCKS	MECHANICALLY DEPOSITED ROCKS	Formed by the simple consolidation of bedded loose material such as sand, clay, and gravel; derived from the disintegration of previously existing rocks.	Often sharply stratified; porous; generally friable or easily broken; layers mostly horizontal; frequently contain fossil plant remains; vary from very coarse-grained types to very fine-grained; composed chiefly of quartz and other silicate minerals; abundant.	SANDSTONE (principally grains of quartz), ARKOSE (considerable feldspar in addition to quartz), CONGLOMERATE (waterworn gravel), SHALE (clay, mud or silt), ARGILLITE (clay), LIMESTONE (calcite), etc.	QUARTZ, CATLINITE, ARGILLITE.
	CHEMICALLY DEPOSITED ROCKS	Formed by the deposition of minerals from solution as upon the bottom of lakes, seas, and oceans; also from cold and warm springs.	Less distinctly or often obscurely stratified; often compact, hard and strong; abundant.	LIMESTONE, CHALK, CHERT, TRAVERTINE, MARL, GYPSUM, ROCK SALT, IRON ORES, DOLOMITE.	QUARTZ, GYPSUM, CALCITE, ONYX, CALCITE, HOWLITE, ULEXITE, COLEMANITE, BARITE, CELESTITE, etc.
	ORGANIC ROCKS	Vegetable or animal matter, rotted or decayed, covered by other sedimentary formations.	Poorly to distinctly stratified; often so altered by pressure, heat, etc., that all traces of original structure are lost; abundant in places.	LIGNITE, COAL, OIL SHALES.	AMBER, JET, ANTHRACITE COAL, PYRITE.

ROCK CLASS	SUB-CLASS	ORIGIN	FEATURES	VARIETIES	GEMSTONES
METAMORPHIC ROCKS	ROCKS PRIMARILY ALTERED BY HEAT AND PRESSURE	Formed from previously existing rocks without addition or subtraction of constituents ("regionally" metamorphosed rocks).	Often show traces of original bedding or stratification if formed from sedimentary rocks; frequently streaked, banded, and folded; generally light in color; mica and garnet common; constituents often well crystallized; abundant.	GNEISS, MICA-, TALC-, CHLORITE-SCHISTS, QUARTZITE, SLATE, MARBLE.	JADEITE, NEPHRITE, RHODONITE, IDOCRASE, GARNET, SERPENTINE, IOLITE, ANDALUSITE, KYANITE, EPIDOTE, PIEDMONTITE, STAUROLITE, CONGLOMERATE.
	CONTACT ROCKS	Altered radically by nearness or contact with deep-seated molten igneous rocks.	Contain many new minerals resulting from interaction of vapors and liquids from igneous mass, often coarse-grained; fine and large crystals common; limited in extent.	MARBLE, HORNFELS, QUARTZITE.	RHODONITE, CASSITERITE, DIOPSIDE, SERPENTINE, WOLLASTONITE, LAPIS LAZULI, FIBROLITE, ZOISITE, CLINOZOISITE, GARNET, APATITE, SPHALERITE, TOPAZ.
	SOLUTION OR VEIN DEPOSITS	Formed by deposition of minerals in crevices, pores, and openings, by hot solutions under pressure.	Veins, stocks, and fillings common; adjacent rock often altered or permeated by introduced minerals; secondary solution deposits frequent; sulfide minerals abundant.	ORE BODIES & VEINS; REPLACEMENT ORE BODIES.	MALACHITE, AZURITE, TURQUOIS, VARISCITE, QUARTZ, ALGODONITE, DOMEYKITE, SPHALERITE, NICCOLITE, SMALTITE, COBALTITE, BREITHAUPTITE, ZINCITE, RHODOCHROSITE, WILLEMITE, FRIEDELITE, BENTOITE, CALCITE, FLUORITE, etc.

TABLE 2   ALLUVIAL GEMSTONE OCCURRENCES*

TYPE OF DEPOSIT	ORIGIN	FEATURES	GEMSTONES
STREAM, RIVER, and GLACIAL GRAVELS	From disintegrated rocks and rock fragments transported and tumbled by strong, turbulent waters.	Well-rounded pebbles; durable minerals are often found detached from matrix; quartz abundant; minerals and rocks often transported long distances.	DIAMOND, CORUNDUM, TOPAZ, QUARTZ both crystalline and crypto-crystalline varieties, CASSITERITE (wood tin), GARNET, NEPHRITE, JADEITE, IDOCRASE, RHODONITE.
RESIDUAL (eluvial)	Rotting and disintegration of rock in place.	Outcrop often littered with fragments of most resistant minerals such as quartz; soil filled with angular rock fragments; masses of altered minerals commonly cover portions of outcrop.	STAUROLITE, QUARTZ, BERYL, TOPAZ, NEPHRITE, JADEITE, RHODONITE, IDOCRASE, GARNET, ANDALUSITE.
DETRITAL	Breakage of rock by mechanical means, such as frost, collapse of cliffs, undercutting by water, etc.	Commonly form talus slopes and other areas of broken rock in mountainous regions; material generally transported only over very short distances.	Almost any reasonably durable species may be found in detrital material.

* Note: Although the term *alluvial* refers strictly to the transport of material by running water, it is here used to include disintegration and transport of rock by other weathering agencies.

APPENDIX 4

Notes on Collections and Collecting

To APPRECIATE the wonders of native gemstones, visits to public and private collections in museums, colleges, and universities are strongly encouraged. Nothing can take the place of seeing the actual rough material and the glittering gems prepared from them. Perhaps the outstanding collections in the world are housed in the U.S. National Museum in Washington, D.C., and in the American Museum of Natural History in New York City. Both institutions strive to emphasize native gems and as a consequence show a fine variety from the most important localities.

Public-spirited citizens of means have contributed collections amassed over a period of many years. J. Pierpont Morgan donated a magnificent and costly collection to the American Museum of Natural History while Colonel Washington A. Roebling left an equally important one to the U.S. National Museum. Morgan's collection was formed under the direction of George F. Kunz while the latter was employed as Vice President of the famous jewelry establishment of Tiffany's in New York City. This gentleman was an ardent promoter of American gems and perhaps did most as a single individual to arouse public interest in them. The splendid specimens in the Morgan Collection are testimony to his zeal and skill. Colonel Roebling, better known as the builder of the Brooklyn Bridge, became interested in minerals in mid-career and continued as an active and discriminating collector up to the time of his death. His exceptionally complete suite of specimens includes many cut and rough specimens from famous American localities, the most fabled being the gorgeously fiery black opal from Virgin Valley, Nevada which bears his name.

Excellent general collections are also to be found in the Chicago Natural History Museum and in the Cranbrook Institute of Science. The latter is a smaller museum of very high caliber located in Bloomfield Hills, Michigan. The famed gem-producing regions of New England are probably best represented in the Mineralogical Museum of Harvard University at Cambridge, Massachusetts and in Wesleyan University, Middletown, Connecticut. Additional fine New England material can be viewed at the Peabody Museum of Natural History, Yale University, New Haven, Connecticut. Magnificent suites of rough and cut gemstones from Southern California localities appear in the Warner Collection in the Geological Sciences Building of the California Institute of Technology at Pasadena. In San Francisco, another important collection from the same region as well as from other areas of the state can be seen in the museum of the California State Division of Mines in the Ferry Building.

Canadian gemstones are well represented in the collections of the Royal Ontario Museum of Geology and Mineralogy in Toronto, Ontario. Mexican gems and an exceptional suite of jade carvings of pre-Columbian age are on exhibit in the archaeological sciences section of the Museo Nacional in Mexico City. Many other museums contain important collections of American gemstones but space prevents discussing them here.

Aside from public collections, many fine specimens are owned by individuals who bring them out for display during county fairs and gem shows. The latter are staged with increasing frequency by the several hundred mineral and gem societies which have sprung up with the growth of amateur interest in gemstones. Taking place in key cities throughout the United States, each show strives to exhibit the best in the possession of its members. Heavy emphasis is placed upon regional minerals which members have collected themselves and no better view of local gemstone resources can be had anywhere.

The collecting of minerals and gemstones is an avocation which daily attracts increasing numbers of followers. Equipment needs are very modest, some old hands getting along year after year with nothing more than a mineral hammer, magnifying glass, and a sack for specimens. Techniques are discussed in a number of inexpensive books currently on the market, one of the best and most up-to-date being Dr. F. H. Pough's *Field Guide to Rocks and Minerals*. Many of the regional collecting guides listed in the Bibliography in Appendix 1, also contain hints and tips on collecting as well as specific directions to numerous localities. A subscription to any of the popular magazines listed in the Bibliography is also rewarding since all phases of the hobby are covered and many pages devoted to advertisements of equipment and supplies. In recent years, a number of concerns have begun catering specially to the needs of the amateur interested in gemstones by providing rough specimens and inexpensive examples of cut gems, and it is now possible to accumulate a modest collection of stones for a comparatively small outlay. In addition, an increasing number have taken up the fascinating and rewarding hobby of cutting and polishing personally-collected gemstones, becoming experts in the lapidary art and the associated art of setting finished gems in jewelry. The author's book on lapidary work, *Gem Cutting—A Lapidary's*

Manual, is the most modern and complete treatise available while jewelry making is similarly described in Greta Pack's *Jewelry Making for Beginning Craftsmen* and Wiener's *Hand Made Jewelry*.

Readers are expressly cautioned against collecting at any of the localities mentioned in this book unless prior permission has been obtained from property owners or owners of mineral rights. Embarrassment and possible prosecution can be avoided by local inquiry beforehand at collecting localities. In recent years, the increasing number of mineral, fossil, and gemstone collectors has led to property owners or owners of mineral rights permitting collecting after payment of modest fees. This scheme provides some recompense to owners for the inconvenience or damage inflicted upon property and at the same time, removes any shadow of doubt as to collecting rights. In many instances, such localities are advertised in the several magazines devoted to the earth science hobbies and reference to past issues may assist in planning pleasant and successful field trips. Although there are many square miles of Federally-owned land in the sparsely-populated regions of North America upon which prospecting and collecting may be legally engaged in, much land is held privately and deserves the same consideration as is given to any other form of private property. In respect to government lands the policy of the U.S. Government forbids removal of, or marring, defacing, destroying, or otherwise injuring in any manner any natural feature or object within the boundaries of any National Monument or National Park, including rocks and minerals. Similar regulations are in force in other countries.

Geographical and Locality Index

The same locality arrangement used in the text is used here also, that is, major political divisions such as states and provinces are listed in order from north to south with localities under smaller political divisions listed in the same way. For example, Greenland and Alaska will appear before Canada and the latter before the United States, while within each, localities will be listed beginning from the north and east and progressing to the south and west. By this method all localities reasonably close to each other will appear together in the index as well as in the text. Bodies of water in which shellfish may be found are not susceptible to this treatment and are therefore excluded. However, geographical distribution is indicated in the text for saltwater species on pages 577-588, *passim*, and for freshwater species on pages 589-592, *passim*, and more specifically by political divisions on pages 593-595, inclusive.

The arrangement key below will be useful in quickly finding areas of interest in this index.

ARRANGEMENT KEY

GREENLAND

ALASKA

CANADA:

>North: Yukon Territory, North West Territories, Labrador
>East: New Brunswick, Nova Scotia, Quebec, Ontario
>Central: Manitoba, Alberta
>West: British Columbia

UNITED STATES:

>Northeast: Maine, New Hampshire, Vermont, Massachusetts, Rhode Island, Connecticut
>East: New York, New Jersey, Pennsylvania, Maryland, West Virginia, Virginia, Kentucky, Tennessee
>Southeast: North Carolina, South Carolina, Georgia, Alabama, Florida, Mississippi, Louisiana, Arkansas

Central: Ohio, Indiana, Illinois, Michigan, Wisconsin, Minnesota, Iowa, Missouri, North Dakota, South Dakota, Nebraska, Kansas, Oklahoma, Texas

West: Montana, Wyoming, Colorado, New Mexico, Arizona, Utah, Idaho, Washington, Oregon, Nevada, California

MEXICO:

North: Sonora, Chihuahua, Coahuila, Tamaulipas

Central: San Luis Potosi, Zacatecas, Durango, Sinaloa, Nayarit, Jalisco, Guanajuato, Queretaro, Hidalgo, Puebla, Tlaxcala, Morelos, Mexico, Michoacan

South: Guerrero, Oaxaca, Veracruz, Chiapas

West: Baja California Norte, Baja California Sud

CENTRAL AMERICA:

Guatemala, Honduras, El Salvador, Panama

WEST INDIES:

Cuba, Jamaica, Dominican Republic, Puerto Rico, Anguilla, Antigua, Guadeloupe, Martinique

GREENLAND

Upernivik District, Tasiusuk Island, Nusak, Ikerarsuk Fjord, Ntivdlinguak, *garnet,* 277; Upernaviarssuak, *enstatite,* 435; Uiordlersuak Island, Upernivik Island, *iolite,* 474; Lango Island, *feldspar,* 135, 136, *garnet,* 277, 278, *iolite,* 474, Svartenhuk Peninsula: Taujat, *garnet,* 277. **Umanak District,** Ubekendt Island, Nugssuaq Peninsula, *quartz,* 316; Niaquornat: Kangeq, *scapolite,* 467; Qeqertarssuaq, *prehnite,* 516; Storo Island, *garnet,* 277, 278; Hare Island, *opal,* 108, *amber,* 597, 598. **Ritenbenk District,** Atanikerdluk, Arsaruk, Unartuarssuk, Ujaragsugssuak, *amber,* 598. **Godhavn District** (Disko Island), *amber,* 597, 598; Kagsiarik, Uperniviksnaes, Kiporkafik, Sermersok Valley, Kjod Island, *feldspar,* 135, 136; Per Dams Skib, Kuanersuit, *opal,* 108; Nangisat, *opal,* 108, *feldspar,* 135, 136; Stordalen, Marrak, Eguluit, etc., *quartz,* 317. **Christianshaab District,** Kakarsuit, *nephrite,* 240, 241; Akugdleq, *quartz,* 317. **Egedesminde District,** Maneetsok Island, Niakornak, Equalugssuit, Tinuktekasak, Sungausak Peninsula, *feldspar,* 136; Atanek Fjord: Simiutaluk Island, *garnet,* 278. **Holsteinsborg District,** Sondre Stromfjord: Bluie West Eight, *garnet,* 278, Sandhullet, Umanarsuk Island, *feldspar,* 136. **Godthaab District,** Godthaab Fjord: Kanajorssuit, *feldspar,* 136; Bjorne Island, *serpentine,* 543; Godthaab Peninsula: Vildmansnaes, Thor Halleson's Varde, Store Mallene, Qasigigianguit, *feldspar,* 136; Kuanebucht, *feldspar,* 136, *nephrite,* 241; Hjorte-

Nova Scotia

Pictou Co., Pictou, *jet,* 604. **Cumberland Co.,** Cape d'Or, Five Islands, Horse Shoe Cove, Swan Creek, *natrolite,* 522, Two Islands, *natrolite,* 522, *quartz,* 319, Clark Head, *prehnite,* 516, Partridge Island, Cape Sharp, *quartz,* 319. **Halifax Co.,** Pace's Lake, *quartz,* 319, Geizer's Hill, *andalusite,* 477. **Hants Co.,** Clifton, *prehnite,* 516, Windsor, Brookville, Wentworth, Newport Station, Noel, *howlite,* 563. **Kings Co.,** Cape Blomidon, *opal,* 108, *quartz,* 319, *natrolite,* 522, Cape Split, *opal,* 108, *quartz,* 319, Scotts Bay, Ross Creek, Long Island, Canada Creek, Harbourville, *quartz,* 319, Morden, *mordenite,* 521, Black Rock, *prehnite,* 516. **Annapolis Co.,** Paradise River, Bridgeton, Lawrencetown, Annapolis, Trout Cove, Granville, Chute Cove, *quartz,* 319, North Mt., Port George, *natrolite,* 522. **Lunenburg Co.,** Joe Bell Creek, Chester, Lake Ramsay, *quartz,* 320. **Digby Co.,** Digby Neck, St. Mary Bay, Sandy Cove, Mink Cove, Cape d'Or, Briar Island, Nichol's Mt., *quartz,* 320. **Shelburne Co.,** Kail's Point, Shelburne, *quartz,* 320, Jordan River, Sable River, *staurolite,* 484.

Quebec.

New Quebec Territory, Hamilton River, Ungava River, *quartz,* 318, Paint Hills Group (islands), *feldspar,* 138, Hudson Bay: Belanger's Island, *quartz,* 318. **Kamouraska Co.,** River Ouelle, *quartz,* 318. **Montmorency Co. No. 1,** Chateau Richer, *feldspar,* 138. **Megantic Co.,** Coleraine Twp., Black Lake: Megantic Mine, *serpentine,* 543, Southwark Asbestos Pit, *garnet,* 280, Little St, Francis Lake: Montreal Chrome Pit, *diamond,* 31, *idocrase,* 266, *serpentine,* 543. **Frontenac Co.,** Lake St. Francis, *andalusite,* 477. **Compton Co.,** Compton, Eaton, Emberton, Hampden, Marsden twps., *andalusite,* 477. **Sherbrooke Co.,** Sherbrooke, *quartz,* 318, Orford Twp., *diopside,* 462. **Stanstead Co.,** Stanstead, Hatley, Barbstone, *andalusite,* 477. **Brome Co.,** Brome, *sodalite,* 201. **Terrebonne Co.,** St. Jerome, St. Morin, *feldspar,* 138. **Argenteuil Co.,** Sixteen Island Lake: Laurel, *idocrase,* 266, 267, *diopside,* 462, Grenville Twp., *zircon,* 438, *scapolite,* 467, Chatham Twp., *tourmaline,* 175, Kilmar, *serpentine,* 543. **Papineau Co.,** Villeneuve Twp., West Portland Twp., *feldspar,* 138. **Hull Co.,** *quartz,* 318, Templeton Twp., *zircon,* 438, *sphene,* 454, King Edward Mine, Wallingford Mine, *scapolite,* 467. **Gatineau Co.,** Wakefield Twp., *garnet,* 279, 280, *serpentine,* 543, Leduc Quarry, *feldspar,* 138, Hull Twp., *garnet,* 279, 280, *feldspar,* 138, Nellie & Blanche Mine, Dacey Mine, *scapolite,* 467. **Pontiac Co.,** Litchfield Twp., Calumet Falls, *tourmaline,* 175.

Ontario

Tourmaline, 174. **Leeds Co.,** Black Rapids: Red Horse Lake, *quartz,* 320, North Crosby Twp., Westport, *sphene,* 454. **Lanark Co.,** Perth area, *zircon,* 437, Bathurst Twp., North Burgess Twp., *feldspar,* 138, North Burgess Twp., *diopside,* 462. **Renfrew Co.,** Sebastopol, Eganville, Grenville, Ross, Brudenell twps., *sphene,* 453, 454, Eganville, *scapolite,* 468, Sebastopol Twp., *zircon,* 437, *apatite,* 422, 423, Brudenell Twp., Lake Clear, *sodalite,* 201, *zircon,* 437, Lyndoch Twp., *beryl,* 68, *feldspar,* 139, *quartz,* 320, Raglan Twp., Craigmont, *corundum,* 48, *sodalite,* 201, Griffith Twp., Griffith Bridge: Old Spain Mine, *scapolite,* 468. **Frontenac Co.,** Bedford Twp., Richardson Quarry, *tremolite,* 465, Portland Twp., Burnham Mine, *feldspar,* 139. **Hastings Co.,** Hybla: MacDonald Mine, *feldspar,* 139, Burgess Twp., *corundum,* 47, Monteagle Twp., Woodcox Mine, *feldspar,* 139, Herschel Twp.,

UNITED STATES

MAINE

NEW HAMPSHIRE

VERMONT

MASSACHUSETTS

lusite, 477, Royalston, *beryl*, 73. **Franklin Co.**, Deerfield, *quartz*, 326, East Deerfield: Cheapside Quarry, *prehnite*, 517, Conway, *quartz*, 326. **Hampshire Co.**, Pelham, *apatite*, 424, Amherst area, *quartz*, 326, Goshen, Lithia, *beryl*, 73, *spodumene*, 155, Cummington Twp., *rhodonite*, 262, Chesterfield Twp., *staurolite*, 485. **Hampden Co.**, Westfield: Lane Quarry, *datolite*, 514, *prehnite*, 517, Chester, *diaspore*, 434. Nantucket Island, Martha's Vineyard: Gay Head, *amber*, 599.

RHODE ISLAND

Cumberland Twp., Diamond Hill, Calumet Hill, *quartz*, 326, Lincoln Twp., Dexter Quarry, Limerock area, *serpentine*, 544; Pawtuxet, *quartz*, 326, Bristol, Mt. Hope area, *quartz*, 326.

CONNECTICUT

Hartford Co., East Granby: Roncari Quarry, *datolite*, 514, Farmington area, *quartz*, 327. **Litchfield Co.**, Torringford, Woodbury, *quartz*, 327, New Milford Twp., New Milford:Roebling (Merryall) Mine, *beryl*, 74. **Litchfield Co.-Middlesex Co.**, *staurolite*, 485. **Middlesex Co.**, Middletown area, *beryl*, 73, 74, Portland Twp., Strickland Quarry, *beryl*, 74, *spodumene*, 155, *tourmaline*, 180, 181, *quartz*, 326, 327, *apatite*, 424, 425, Pelton Quarry, *quartz*, 326, 327, East Hampton Twp., Slocum Quarry, *beryl*, 74, Middletown Twp., Riverside Quarry, *beryl*, 74, Haddam Twp., Gillette Quarry, *tourmaline*, 181. **New Haven Co.**, Guilford Twp., Hungry Horse Hill, *iolite*, 475, Milford-West Haven, *quartz*, 327. **Fairfield Co.**, Trumbull Twp., Long Hill, *topaz*, 96.

NEW YORK

St. Lawrence Co., Massena, *diamond*, 41, DeKalb Twp., Richville: Reese Farm, *tourmaline*, 181, 182, Mitchell Farm, *diopside*, 462, 463, Gouverneur, *tourmaline*, 182, Gouverneur: Oswegatchie River, *serpentine*, 544, Hailesboro, *tourmaline*, 182, *apatite*, 425, Macomb, *fluorite*, 528, Fowler, *tremolite*, 466. **Jefferson Co.**, Muskalonge Lake, *fluorite*, 528, Pillar Point, *barite*, 490. **Lewis Co.**, Bonaparte Lake, *wollastonite*, 537, Natural Bridge, *serpentine*, 544. **Essex Co.**, Keeseville, Mineville, Opalescent River, *feldspar*, 139, 140, Newcomb, *feldspar*, 139, 140, *tourmaline*, 182, Olmstedville, *feldspar*, 140. **Warren Co.**, Horicon: Brant Lake, *tourmaline*, 182, North Creek area, *garnet*, 280. **Saratoga Co.**, Saratoga Springs, *chrysoberyl*, 408, Overlook, *quartz*, 327. **Herkimer Co.**, Middleville area, *quartz*, 327, 328. **Schoharie Co.**, Schoharie, Catskill, *quartz*, 328. **Dutchess Co.**, *serpentine*, 544. Putnam Co., Brewster: Tilly Foster Mine, *apatite*, 425, *sphene*, 454, 455, *chondrodite*, 469, 470. **Westchester Co.**, Bedford area, *quartz*, 328, Portchester, *serpentine*, 544. **Rockland Co.**, *serpentine*, 544. **New York Co.**, Borough of Richmond (Staten Island), *serpentine*, 544, Kreischerville, *amber*, 599. **Erie Co.**, Buffalo, *calcite*, 553.

NEW JERSEY

Sussex Co., Newton, Sparta, Franklin, *corundum*, 48, Franklin, *rhodonite*, 262, *idocrase*, 267, *axinite*, 415, *sphalerite*, 441, *zincite*, 445, *willemite*, 447-450, *friedelite*, 450, 451, *hodgkinsonite*, 451, 452, *serpentine*, 545, Ogdensburg, *rhodonite*, 262, *sphalerite*, 441, *zincite*, 445, *willemite*, 447-450, *friedelite*, 450, 451, *hodgkinsonite*, 451, 452. **Passaic Co.**, *quartz*, 328, *datolite*, 514, *natrolite*, 522, Great Notch, Paterson, etc., *opal*, 109, Paterson area, *prehnite*, 517, Packanack Lake, *pectolite*,

512. **Bergen Co.**, *quartz*, 328, *datolite*, 514, *natrolite*, 522. **Essex Co.**, *quartz*, 328, Upper Montclair, Short Hills, *prehnite*, 518. **Morris Co.**, *quartz*, 328, Lake Valhalla, *serpentine*, 544, 545, Dover, *opal*, 109, Alan Wood Mine, *feldspar*, 140, Millington, *prehnite*, 518. **Union Co.**, Summit, Plainfield, North Plainfield, *prehnite*, 518. **Somerset Co.**, *quartz*, 328, Somerville, *turquois*, 213, Bound Brook, Rocky Hill, Somerville, *prehnite*, 518. **Hunterdon Co.**, *quartz*, 328. **Mercer Co.**, *quartz*, 328, Princeton, Hopewell, *prehnite*, 518. **Burlington Co.**, Crosswicks Creek, Vincentown, *amber*, 600. **Gloucester Co.**, Mantua Creek, Oldmans Creek, *amber*, 600. **Salem Co.**, *amber*, 599.

PENNSYLVANIA

Northampton Co., Lower Saucon Twp., South Mt., *quartz*, 329, Easton: Chestnut Hill, Bushkill Creek, *serpentine*, 545. **Lehigh Co.**, Upper Milford Twp., Shimersville, *corundum*, 48, Vera Cruz, *quartz*, 329. **Bucks Co.**, *quartz*, 329, Southampton Twp., Vanartsdalen Quarry, *feldspar*, 140. **Montgomery Co.**, *quartz*, 329. **Delaware Co.**, numerous localities for: *corundum*, 48, *beryl*, 75, *feldspar*, 140, 141, *garnet*, 280, 281, *quartz*, 329, 330, *sphene*, 455, 456. **Chester Co.**, numerous localities for: *feldspar*, 140, *quartz*, 330, 331, *apatite*, 425, *diaspore*, 434, *serpentine*, 545. **Lancaster Co.**, Bart Twp., Paradise Twp., Fulton Twp.: Rock Springs, *quartz*, 331. **Schuylkill Co.**, Mahonoy City-Pottsville area, *pyrite*, 550. **Luzerne Co.**, Hazleton, W. Pittston, *pyrite*, 550, Wilkes Barre area, *anthracite*, 606. **York Co.**, York Haven, *quartz*, 331. **Cumberland Co.**, Carlisle, *quartz*, 331. **Adams Co.**, Hamiltonban Twp.-Washington Twp. area, copper rhyolite, 548, Buchanan Valley, Piney Mt., *piedmontite*, 481, 482. **Franklin Co.**, Morrison Cove, *quartz*, 331. **Westmoreland Co.**, Greensburg, *quartz*, 331.

MARYLAND

Cecil Co., Rock Springs: Line Pits, *serpentine*, 545, 546. **Baltimore Co.**, Raspeburg, *quartz*, 332. **Anne Arundel Co.**, Loper Hall, Fort Dorsey, *jet*, 604, Magothy River, Severn River, *amber*, 600. **Montgomery Co.**, Rockville Quarry, *idocrase*, 267, *diopside*, 463, 464. **Prince Georges Co.**, Beltsville, *quartz*, 331, 332.

WEST VIRGINIA

Monroe Co., Peterstown, *diamond*, 32. **Mercer Co.**, Willowton, *calcite*, 553.

VIRGINIA

Arlington Co., *quartz*, 332. **Fairfax Co.**, *quartz*, 332, Centreville Quarry, *prehnite*, 518. **Prince William Co.**, Minnieville, *quartz*. **Page Co.**, Fisher's Gap, Marksville, *unakite*, 499, Ida, *quartz*, 332. **Madison Co.**, Fisher's Gap, Rose River, *unakite*, 499. **Orange Co.**, Vaucluse Gold Mine, *diamond*, 32. **Louisa Co.**, Trevilians, *quartz*, 332, 333. **Goochland Co.**, Oliver: Mica Mine Farm, *feldspar*, 141, 142. **Powhatan Co.**, Flat Rock: Herbb Mine No. 2, *feldspar*, 144. **Amelia Co.**, Winterham: Morefield Mine, *topaz*, 96, 97, *feldspar*, 144, *phenakite*, 413, Richeson Mica Mine, *feldspar*, 142-144, Champion Mine, *feldspar*, 145, Rutherford Mines, *topaz*, 96, 97, *feldspar*, 142-144, *garnet*, 281, 282, *microlite*, 417, 418. **Henrico Co.**, Manchester, *diamond*, 32. **Prince Edward Co.**, Rice, *quartz*, 334. **Nelson Co.**, Lowesville, *quartz*, 333, Irish Creek, *feldspar*, 145. **Amherst Co.**, Sandidge, *quartz*, 334. **Rockbridge Co.**, Vesuvius area, *unakite*, 500. **Campbell Co.**, Lynch Station, *turquois*, 213, Brookneal, *quartz*, 334, 335. **Charlotte Co.**, Charlotte Court House, *quartz*, 334, 335. **Franklin Co.**, Patrick

486, 487. **Stearns Co.**, St. Cloud Twp., *granite*, 497. **Stevens Co.**, *quartz*, 346. **Swift Co.**, *quartz*, 346. **Pipestone Co.**, Pipestone National Monument, *catlinite*, 568.

IOWA

Dickinson Co., Lake Okaboji, *corundum*, 54. **Palo Alto Co.**, Emmetsburg, Graettinger, *quartz*, 347, 348. **Linn Co.**, *calcite*, 556. **Johnson Co.**, Coralville, Iowa City, *calcite*, 556. **Muscatine Co.**, Mississippi River gravels, *quartz*, 347, 348. **Henry Co.**, *quartz*, 347, 348. Des Moines River-Mississippi River junction area, Lowell: Geode State Park, *quartz*, 346, 347.

MISSOURI

Clark Co., Fox River, *quartz*, 348. **Lewis Co.**, Mississippi River, *quartz*, 348. **Benton Co.**, **Dade Co.**, *quartz*, 348.

NORTH DAKOTA

Williams Co., **McKenzie Co.**, Yellowstone River-Missouri River area, *quartz*, 348. **Billings Co.**, Medora badlands, *quartz*, 348. **Hettinger Co.**, Mott area, *quartz*, 348. **Stark Co.**, Dickinson, *quartz*, 348. **Grant Co.**, Wade: Cannonball River, *quartz*, 348. **Morton Co.**, Mandan, Bismark, *quartz*, 348.

SOUTH DAKOTA

Minnehaha Co., Sioux Falls, *quartz*, 348, *catlinite*, 568. **Campbell Co.**, **Corson Co.**, Mobridge-Grand River area, *opal*, 111. **Harding Co.**, Little Missouri River, *quartz*, 348. **Meade Co.**, Fox Ridge, Deadwood, *quartz*, 348, Wasta: Elk Creek, *barite*, 490. **Lawrence Co.**, Whitewood Creek, Spearfish Canyon, *quartz*, 349, Black Hills area, *gypsum*, 566, *amber*, 601. **Pennington Co.**, Black Hills area, Badlands National Monument, *quartz*, 349, Keystone area, *beryl*, 85, Helen Beryl Mine, *spodumene*, 159, Bob Ingersoll Mine, *tourmaline*, 182, Fairburn area, *quartz*, 349. **Custer Co.**, Fairburn area, Custer State Park, *quartz*, 349, Glendale, *apatite*, 425, Elephant Gulch, *garnet*, 284, Hells Canyon, Scott Rose Quartz Quarry, *quartz*, 350. **Washabaugh Co.**, Interior, *quartz*, 349. **Shannon Co.**, Red Shirt, *quartz*, 349. **Fall River Co.**, Minnekahta: Cycad National Monument, *quartz*, 350.

NEBRASKA

Douglas Co., Platte River, *quartz*, 351. **Nemaha Co.**, Johnson, *quartz*, 351. **Jefferson Co.**, Fairbury, Stelle, *quartz*, 351. **Cherry Co.**, Valentine, *opal*, 109. **Sioux Co.**, Orella, *quartz*, 351. **Morrill Co.**, Bayard, *quartz*, 351, Angora, Angora Hill, *opal*, 109. **Deuel Co.**, Chappell area, *quartz*, 351.

KANSAS

Jefferson Co., McLouth, *quartz*, 351. **Marshall Co.**, Big Blue River area, *quartz*, 351. **Riley Co.**, Stockdale, *garnet*, 284. **Cloud Co.**, Republican River, *quartz*, 351. **Ottawa Co.**, Ada, *quartz*, 351. **Ellsworth Co.**, Carneiro, Smoky Hill River, *amber*, 601. **Phillips Co.**, Norton Co., *quartz*, 351. **Rawlins Co.**, *opal*, 109. **Ellis Co.**, *opal*, 109. **Trego Co.**, **Gove Co.**, *quartz*, 351. **Logan Co.**, *quartz*, 351, *opal*, 109. **Wallace Co.**, *quartz*, 351, Wallace, *opal*, 109. **Ness Co.**, *opal*, 109. **Barber Co.**, Medicine Lodge River, *quartz*, 351. **Clark Co.**, Ashland: Mt. Cassino, *quartz*, 351.

OKLAHOMA

Woods Co., Alva area, *quartz*, 351. **Harper Co.**, Buffalo, *quartz*, 351, *gypsum*, 566. **Major Co.**, *gypsum*, 566. **Blaine Co.**, *gypsum*, 566. **Beckham Co.**, *quartz*, 352,

COLORADO

Sedgwick, Logan, Morgan counties, *quartz*, 363. Yuma Co., Republican River, *opal*, 110. Prowers Co., Lamar area, *quartz*, 363, 364. Las Animas Co., Trinchera Mesa, *jet*, 604, 605. Weld Co., Kalouse area, *quartz*, 363, Stoneham, *barite*, 490. *Petrified wood* area: Adams, Arapahoe, Elbert, Douglas counties, 363. Jefferson Co., Centennial Cone, *beryl*, 85, Bear Creek, *gypsum*, 566. Douglas Co., Perry Park, *gypsum*, 566, Larkspur, *quartz*, 364, Pine Creek area, *feldspar*, 148, Devil's Head, *topaz*, 100, *feldspar*, 148. Teller Co., Florissant area, *topaz*, 100, 101, *feldspar*, 146, 147, *phenakite*, 414, Crystal Park, Cameron Cone, Bear Creek Canyon, Stove Mt., *feldspar*, 147, 148, Cripple Creek, *turquois*, 215. El Paso Co., Peyton, *quartz*, 363, coal beds, *jet*, 605, Colorado Springs: Austin Bluffs, *quartz*, 364, Crystal Park area, Glen Cove, Stove Mt., *topaz*, 101, 102, St. Peter's Dome, *feldspar*, 148, *zircon*, 438, 439. Larimer Co., Owl Canyon, *gypsum*, 566, Red Feather Lakes area, *quartz*, 363, Rocky Mountain National Park area, Specimen Mt., *opal*, 111, *quartz*, 363, *obsidian*, 507. Boulder Co., *amber*, 601. Gilpin Co., Central City, *quartz*, 363. Grand Co., Middle Park, Willow Creek, Hot Sulphur Springs, Williams Fork, *quartz*, 363. Summit Co., Green Mt. area, *sphalerite*, 441. Clear Creek Co., Lawson-Dumont District, Trail Creek, Idaho Springs area, *quartz*, 363. Park Co., Alma area, *rhodochrosite*, 447, Guffey-Hartsel area, South Park, South Platte River, *quartz*, 364, Tarryall Mts., *topaz*, 101. Lake Co., Alicante, *rhodochrosite*, 447, Leadville area, *turquois*, 215. Chaffee Co., Nathrop: Ruby Mt., *topaz*, 102, *garnet*, 284, *obsidian*, 507, Mt. Princeton, Mt. Antero, White Mt., Carbonate Mt. area, *beryl*, 83, 84, Calumet City, *corundum*, 54. Fremont Co., Royal Gorge area, *tourmaline*, 183, Garden Park, Felch Creek, Curio Hill, Twelve-mile Park, *quartz*, 364, Texas Creek area, *beryl*, 85, *quartz*, 364. Gunnison Co., Italian Mt., *lapis lazuli*, 538, Quartz Creek District, *tourmaline*, 183. Saguache Co., Villa Grove, *turquois*, 215, La Garita Creek area, *quartz*, 365. Mineral Co., Creede District, *quartz*, 365, Willow Creek, *turquois*, 215, Wolf Creek Pass, Wagon Wheel Gap, *quartz*, 365, 366. Rio Grande Co., Twin Mts., Rio Grande River, Loma, *quartz*, 365. Conejos Co., Pinon Mt. area, *turquois*, 214, 215. Moffat Co. Dinosaur National Monument area, *quartz*, 366. Mesa Co., Fruita area, Pinon Mesa, *opal*, 110, *quartz*, 366, Dinosaur Ridge, *quartz*, 366, Glade Park, Colorado River Valley, *opal*, 110. Montezuma Co., Cortez, Ute Peak, McElmo Creek area, *quartz*, 366.

NEW MEXICO

Colfax Co., Raton area, *amber*, 601. Taos Co., Red River District, *fluorite*, 530, Pilar, Harding Mine, *muscovite*, 502, Glenwoody District, Picuris District, Pilar, *staurolite*, 487, Pilar, *zoisite*, 541. Rio Arriba Co., Las Tablas: Canary Bird Mine, *tourmaline*, 183, Petaca District, *fluorite*, 530, Sunnyside Mine, *beryl*, 85, Pedernal, La Madera Mt., *quartz*, 366, 367, Bromide District, *fluorite*, 530, Abiquiu, *feldspar*, 150. San Juan Co., San Juan River-Chaco River area, *quartz*, 367, Durango (Colorado)-Gallup coalfield, *amber*, 601. McKinley Co., Buell Park, Furry Mt. area, *garnet*, 291, *diopside*, 464, Gallup-Zuni area, Devil's Pass, Thoreau, *amber*, 601, San Mateo area, Zuni Mts., Navajo Indian Reservation, *quartz*, 367. Sandoval Co., Jemez Sulphur Springs area, *opal*, 110, Jemez District, *quartz*, 367, *feldspar*, 150, Nacimiento Mts., *quartz*, 367, Cochiti area, Calla Canyon, *opal*, 110, Rio Puerco area, *opal*, 110, *quartz*, 367, Rio Puerco coalfield, *amber*, 601, Placitas area, *calcite*, 566. Santa Fe Co., Cerillos area, *turquois*, 215, 216, *quartz*, 367. San

ARIZONA

chite, azurite, 535, 536. **Pima Co.,** Cortaro area, *quartz,* 376, Ajo, *shattuckite,* 536. **Yuma Co.,** Crystal Peak area, Cibola, Brenda, Muggins Mts., *quartz,* 375, 376.

UTAH

Box Elder Co., Promontory Point, *obsidian,* 507, Lucin, *variscite,* 232, 233. **Tooele Co.,** Grantsville, Low, *calcite,* 556, Drum Mt., *quartz,* 376, Tooele: Amatrice Mine, *variscite,* 233, 234. **Utah Co.,** Pelican Point, Lehi, *calcite,* 556, Fairfield: Clay Canyon, *variscite,* 231, 232. **Juab Co.,** Levan area, Jericho, *quartz,* 376, Thomas Mts. area, *topaz,* 102, 103. **Millard Co.,** Clear Lake, *feldspar,* 149, Coyote Springs, Fort Cove, White Mt., *obsidian,* 507. **Emory Co.,** San Rafael Swell, Woodside, *quartz,* 376. **Grand Co.,** Cisco area, Moab area, *quartz,* 376, Colorado River, *opal,* 116. **Wayne Co.,** Hanksville area, *quartz,* 376, Coaly Wash: Coaly Basin, *jet,* 605. **Beaver Co.,** Beaver: Blue Valley, *quartz,* 376, 377, Milford: Mineral Mts., *quartz,* 376, 377, *scheelite,* 460. **Garfield Co.,** Circle Cliffs area, *quartz,* 377, Hatch, Mammoth Creek, *calcite,* 556. **Iron Co.,** Newcastle, *quartz,* 377. **Washington Co.,** Central, Cedar Breaks, *quartz,* 377, St. George: Dixie Apex Mine, *malachite,* 536, Castle Cliff Station: Beaverdam Wash, *rhyolite,* 510.

IDAHO

Kootenai Co., Setters, *opal,* 111. **Benewah Co.,** Fernwood, Emerald Creek, *garnet,* 285, 286. **Shoshone Co.,** Bathtub Mt., Avery, *staurolite,* 487. **Latah Co.,** Whelan, *opal,* 111. **Clearwater Co.,** Headquarters area, *garnet,* 286. **Nez Perce Co.,** Lewiston area, *garnet,* 286, Silcott, *opal,* 112, Clearwater River, *fibrolite,* 539. **Idaho Co.,** Resort, *corundum,* 64, Salmon River area, Slate Creek, McKinsey Creek, *quartz,* 377, Warren District: Paddy Creek, *topaz,* 99. **Lemhi Co.,** Parker Mt. District, Leesburg, *quartz,* 377, Panther Creek, May, *opal,* 112. **Valley Co.,** Yellow Pine District, *opal,* 112. **Adams Co.,** Little Goose Creek Canyon: Rock Flat, Snake River, *diamond,* 42, 43, New Meadows, *topaz,* 99, Mesa, *opal,* 112. **Washington Co.,** Rock Flat, *corundum,* 64, Grouse Creek, Hog Creek, Weiser area, *quartz,* 377, Fourth of July Canyon, Weiser Cove, *opal,* 112. **Gem Co.,** Emmett, Black Canyon Dam, *opal,* 112. **Boise Co.,** Deadwood Gulch, *garnet,* 286, Centerville-Garden Valley, *beryl,* 85, Idaho City: Moore Creek, *opal,* 112. **Canyon Co.,** Nampa: Graveyard Point, *quartz,* 377. **Custer Co.,** Big Lost River, *quartz,* 377. **Fremont Co.,** Crystal Butte, Macks Butte, *feldspar,* 148. **Bingham Co.,** Firth, Willow Creek, *quartz,* 377. **Blaine Co.,** Big Lost River, Cole Creek, Little Wood River, *quartz,* 377. **Lincoln Co.,** Bliss: Clover Creek, *opal,* 113. **Bear Lake Co.,** Montpelier: Hummingbird Mine, *quartz,* 378. **Cassia Co.,** Almo, *topaz,* 99. **Twin Falls Co.,** *quartz,* 378. **Owhyee Co.,** Nampa: Squaw Creek Canyon, Enterprise, Sommer Camp, *opal,* 112, 113, DeLamar, Orofino, *quartz,* 377, Cliffs, *opal,* 112, 113, Castle Creek, *opal,* 112, 113.

WASHINGTON

Pend Oreille Co., Metaline Falls, Josephine Mine, *smithsonite,* 531. **Okanogan Co.,** Nespelem area, *quartz,* 378, Riverside: Tunk Creek, *corundum,* 64, *zoisite,* 541. **Chelan Co.,** Wenatchee: No. 1 Canyon, *calcite,* 551. **Douglas Co.,** Waterville, Quincy, *opal,* 115. **Grant Co.,** Trinidad, Moses Coulee, Grand Coulee, *opal,* 115, Moses Coulee, Quincy, Smyrna, Corfu, *quartz,* 378. **Franklin Co.,** Ringgold, *quartz,* 378. **Kittitas Co.,** Cle Elum area, Yakima River-Saddle Mts. area, *quartz,* 378, Saddle Mts. area, *opal,* 115. **Yakima Co.,** Horse Heaven Hills, Yakima Ridge,

dale, *opal*, 123, *obsidian*, 508, Montezuma Mt., Goldfield, *opal*, 123, *quartz*, 388. **Nye Co.**, Millers area, Belmont, Goldfield area, *turquois*, 222, 223, Bullfrog, Ivanhoe, *quartz*, 388, Beatty, *opal*, 123. **Lincoln Co.**, Atlanta, *quartz*, 388, 389, Sugarloaf Peak, *turquois*, 224. **Clark Co.**, Crescent Peak area, *turquois*, 224, White Basin, *ulexite*, 564.

CALIFORNIA

Del Norte Co., Crescent City, *quartz*, 389, Smith River, *diamond*, 42. **Siskiyou Co.**, Hornbrook, Jenny Creek, *quartz*, 389, Indian Creek-Happy Camp area, *nephrite*, 250, *idocrase*, 267-269, *garnet*, 287, *serpentine*, 547, Thompson Mt., *rhodonite*, 263, Berryvale, *calcite*, 557. **Modoc Co.**, *feldspar*, 148, 149, Goose Lake, Pine Creek-Fort Bidwell area, *quartz*, 389, Sugarloaf Mt.-Glass Mt. area, *obsidian*, 508. **Humboldt Co.**, Trinity River, *diamond*, 42. **Trinity Co.**, Trinity River, *diamond*, 42, *nephrite*, 250. **Plumas Co.**, Indian Valley: Peters Mine, Taylorsville, Genessee Valley, *rhodonite*, 263, Nelson Point, Sawpit Flat, Gopher Hill, etc., *diamond*, 42, Pulga, *idocrase*, 269, 270, Big Bar, *garnet*, 287, Yankee Hill, *axinite*, 415, Cherokee Flat, Oroville, Yankee Hill, Thompson's Flat, *diamond*, 42. **Mendocino Co.**, Mina, Eel River, Covelo: Williams Creek, *nephrite*, 250, *jadeite*, 256, Leech Lake, *jadeite*, 256. **Lake Co.**, Clear Lake area, Cole Creek, *obsidian*, 508, Middletown, *pectolite*, 512. **Colusa Co.**, Sulphur Creek, *calcite*, 557. **Yuba Co.**, Feather River, *axinite*, 415. **Nevada Co.**, French Corral, *diamond*, 42, Nevada City area, *opal*, 124. **Placer Co.**, Shady Creek, *quartz*, 389. **Eldorado Co.**, Georgetown, Traverse Creek, *idocrase*, 270, *garnet*, 287, Placerville area, etc., *diamond*, 42, *quartz*, 389, American River, *nephrite*, 250. **Alpine Co.**, Markleeville, Sonora Pass, *quartz*, 389. **Amador Co.**, Oleta, Volcano, *quartz*, 391, 392, Fiddletown, Plymouth, Volcano, Oleta, *diamond*, 42. **Napa Co.**, Knoxville, Lone Pine Chromite Mine, *opal*, 124, Manhattan Quicksilver Mine, *calcite*, 557. **Sonoma Co.**, Valley Ford, *jadeite*, 256, Healdsburg, *calcite*, 557, Calistoga area, *opal*, 124, Petaluma, Adobe Creek, *quartz*, 389, Mt. Kanaktai, *obsidian*, 508. **Marin Co.**, Vonsen Ranch, *nephrite*, 249, Sausalito, Marin Peninsula, San Francisco area, Point Bonita, Coyote Point, *quartz*, 390, 391. **Solano Co.**, Fairfield-Vacaville area, *calcite*, 557, 558. **Calaveras Co.**, Mokelumne Hill area, *quartz*, 392, 393. **Mono Co.**, Mono Lake, *feldspar*, 149, Mono Craters, *obsidian*, 509, White Mt., Champion Mine, *quartz*, 393, *lazulite*, 431, *augelite*, 459. **Mariposa Co.**, Moore's Flats, Hornitos, *andalusite*, 477. **Contra Costa Co.**, Berkeley Hills, *quartz*, 393. **San Mateo Co.**, Pescadore Beach, *quartz*, 391. **Santa Clara Co.**, Gilroy, Morgan Hill, New Almaden Mine, *quartz*, 391. **Madera Co.**, Ritter Range, *lazulite*, 431, Coarse Gold, Springerville, *axinite*, 415, 416, Chowchilla area, Daulton, *andalusite*, 477. **San Benito Co.**, Clear Creek area, *jadeite*, 255, 256, Hernandez, *benitoite*, 472. **Fresno Co.**, Watts Valley, *idocrase*, 270, 271, *garnet*, 287, Coalinga: Jacolito Canyon, *quartz*, 393. **Inyo Co.**, Bishop, *scheelite*, 461, Cerro Gordo District, *smithsonite*, 531, Death Valley area, *colemanite*, 488, *ulexite*, 564, Little Lake, *feldspar*, 149. **Tulare Co.**, Lemon Cove, *rhodonite*, 264, Selma, *garnet*, 287, Venice Hill, *quartz*, 393, 394, *serpentine*, 547, Exeter, Lindsay, *idocrase*, 271, Lindsay, *opal*, 124, *quartz*, 393, 394, Porterville, *nephrite*, 249, *quartz*, 393, 394, Plano, *quartz*, 393, 394, Coso Mts., *obsidian*, 508. **Monterey Co.**, Plaskett Point, Willow Creek, etc., *nephrite*, 247-249, Lime Kiln Creek, *rhodonite*, 264, Bradley: Stone Canyon, *quartz*, 393. **San Luis Obispo Co.**, Paso Robles, *jadeite*, 256, Coso, Salt Creek, *calcite*, 558. **Kern Co.**, Greenhorn Mts. tungsten mines area, *quartz*, 394, 395, *scheelite*, 460, 461, *epidote*, 482, Bakersfield:

MEXICO

Sonora

Chihuahua

Cerro Campuzano, *opal*, 125, Leon de los Aldamas District: Hacienda de Tlachiquera, *topaz*, 105.

QUERETARO

Toliman District: Hacienda La Esperanza, Hacienda La Jurada; Amelaco District: Mina La Purissima; Cadereyta District: Moconi, Hacienda Foentesuela; San Juan del Rio District: Hacienda Tesquisquiapan, Hacienda La Llave, Mina Carbonera, *opal*, 125-128; San Juan del Rio District, *obsidian*, 509.

HIDALGO

Zimapan District: *garnet*, 292, *opal*, 128; Zacaultipan, *obsidian*, 509; Huichapan District: Salitera Mine, Hacienda de Yextho, *quartz*, 402; Atotonilco District: Sierra de la Navajas, *obsidian*, 509, Cerro de las Figas, Barranca de Tepezala, *opal*, 128; Pachuca: Del Monte Mine, Cuesta de San Bernardo, etc., *quartz*, 402; Tulancingo District: Cerro del Nado, *topaz*, 105, Barranca Agua Dulce, *opal*, 128; Laguna Haso Chuhuahan, *garnet*, 292.

PUEBLA

Huachinango District: Naupan, Copila, *opal*, 129; Ciudad Puebla area, *calcite*, 561; Izucar de Matamoros District: Puebla San Miguel de Ayotla, Lomas del Calvario, *gypsum*, 566; San Juan de los Llanos, *obsidian*, 509.

TLAXCALA

Hidalgo District: Cerro Las Silicates, *opal*, 129, *quartz*, 402.

MORELOS

Morelos District: Puebla Ayala, *quartz*, 402, Xalostoc: Rancho San Juan, *garnet*, 292, 293, *wollastonite*, 537.

MEXICO

Mexico, D.F., *obsidian*, 509, Atzcapotzalco: Hacienda de Aspeita, *opal*, 129; Texcoco District: Chiautla, Puebla de San Lucas, *opal*, 129; Valle de Bravo District: Ixtapan del Oro, *andalusite*, 478.

MICHOACAN

Maravatio District: Tlapujahua, Espiritu Santo Mine, *quartz*, 402, Contepec, Hacienda San Isidro, Maravatio, Cerro Agustino, *opal*, 129, Zinapecuaro, *obsidian*, 509; Villa Madera, *garnet*, 292.

GUERRERO

Taxco area: Barranca de los Ocotes, *quartz*, 403; Hidalgo District: Huitzuco, *opal*, 129, *gypsum*, 566, San Nicolas de Oro, Coacoyula, *opal*, 129; Municipio Balsas; Alvarez District: Ollas de Chilapa; Amatillan: Sierra Madre del Sur, *quartz*, 403; Tabares District: Coyuca de Benitez, *topaz*, 105.

OAXACA

Tlaxiaco, *opal*, 129; Isthmus de Tehuantepec: Cuesta de Tlanjuapan, *amber*, 602.

ANGUILLA

Crows Bay, *amber*, 603.

ANTIGUA

Corbizon Point, Willoughby Bay, Belleview, Cassada Gardens, Wetherill's Bay, etc., *quartz*, 406.

GUADELOUPE

Ste. Anne, Savane de Salines, *quartz*, 406, *opal*, 130.

MARTINIQUE

Opal, 130, 131.

General Index

Gemstones accorded formal discussion in the text and principal references are indicated by **bold face** type. Shellfish names are indicated by *italics*. Specialized mineralogical, geological and mining terms are defined in the Glossary which also contains brief descriptions of non-gem or accessory minerals as well as definitions of a few Spanish terms commonly used in parts of North America.

Abalones: mentioned 573; classification of, 583, 584; Pacific species tabulated, 584; natural history of, 584, 585; enemies of, 584; fishing of, 584, 585; ornamental uses of shell, 585; pearls in, 585, 586; blister pearls, 585; value of pearls, 586

Achroite, 167

Actinolite, 464

Adamantine luster, 26

Adamantine spar, 43, 47

Adularescence: cause of, 23; direction of sheen related to crystal structure, 24

Adulteration: of turquois, 213, 220, 226; of staurolite, 483. *See also* Staining

Agate: defined, 303; varieties, 303, 304, 305

Aguila Azteca Opal, 126

Alabaster: confused with calcite, 550; gypsum variety, 565

Alasmodons, general form of, 589

Albite, 132, 133, 135; as impurity in jadeite, 259

Algodonite and domeykite, 439

Alluvial gemstone deposits: defined, 638; tabulated, 639-641

Almandine: mentioned, 272; **273**, 274; classification and composition of, 273; properties, 274; localities, 277-293, *passim*; star stones, 285, 286. *See also* Garnet Group

Amarillas, 426

Amatrice, 229

Amazonite, 132, 133

Amber: classed as gemstone, 4; **596-603**; general remarks, 596, 597; chemical and physical properties, 597, 599, 600; appearance of, 597; localities, 597-603

Amblygonite, **427**, 428

Amethyst: growth habit, 12; color zoning in, 12; described and illustrated, 297, 298; coloration of, 311, 312; crystallization of, 312; ripple fracture in, 312; mode of occurrence, 313

Amorphous minerals: described, 7; characteristic fracture in, 7; properties of, 7, 8; lack of cleavage planes in, 13; optical properties related to structure of, 16; absence of dichroism in, 22

Amphibolite: with red corundum, 53, 549

Andalusite (chiastolite): general, **475**, 476; peculiar patterns in, 476; localities, 477, 478

Andesine: 133, 135; sunstone variety, 149

Andradite: dispersion in, 20; classification and composition of, 273; varieties and properties, **276**, 277; localities, 277-293, *passim. See also* Garnet Group

Anodontas, 572, 589

Anorthite, 133, 135

Anthophyllite, Actinolite, Tremolite: general, 464, 465; localities, 465, 466

Anthracite Coal, **605**, 606

Apache tears, 503

Apatite: mentioned, 16; 420-426; general, 420, 421; localities, 422-426

Aquamarine, 64, 65

Aragonite, in nacre, 573

Argillite (Haida Slate): **569-571**; carving of, 570

Arkansas stone, 342

Arrows of Love, 301, 408

Asterism: explained, 22; in corundum, 43, 47; in garnet, 285, 286; in rose quartz, 298

Atomic arrangement in minerals, 6, 7, 8, 9, 10

Augelite, **458**, 459

Au Sable Granite, 140

Australites, 492

Aventurescence: explained, 22, 23; in feldspar, 134, 202; in quartz, 302; in willemite, 450

Avicula vinesi: general remarks, 577; distribution of in Gulf of California, 583; pearls yielded by, 583

Aviculidae: pearls provided by genera of, 572, 577; single Atlantic species, 577. *See also Avicula vinesi*.

Axes: crystal, 8-11, *passim*; optical, 17, 18

Axinite: general, 414, 415; localities, 415, 417

Aztec Sun God Opal, Aztec Eagle Opal, 126

Azules opal, 128

Azurite: color of, 20; 533. *See also* Malachite and Azurite

Azurmalachite, 533